The Human Record

SOURCES OF GLOBAL HISTORY

VOLUME II:

SINCE 1500

The Human Record

SOURCES OF GLOBAL HISTORY

VOLUME II:

SINCE 1500

SEVENTH EDITION

Alfred J. Andrea
Emeritus Professor of History, University of Vermont

James H. Overfield
Emeritus Professor of History, University of Vermont

WADSWORTH
CENGAGE Learning·

Australia · Brazil · Japan · Korea · Mexico · Singapore · Spain · United Kingdom · United States

WADSWORTH
CENGAGE Learning

The Human Record: Sources of Global History, Volume II: Since 1500, **Seventh Edition**
Alfred J. Andrea, James H. Overfield

Senior Publisher: Suzanne Jeans

Senior Sponsoring Editor: Nancy Blaine

Associate Editor: Adrienne Zicht

Editorial Assistant: Emma Goehring

Senior Marketing Manager: Katherine Bates

Marketing Coordinator: Lorreen Pelletier

Marketing Communications Manager: Caitlin Green

Senior Content Project Manager: Jane Lee

Art Director: Cate Barr

Senior Print Buyer: Mary Beth Hennebury

Senior Rights Acquisition Specialist: Katie Huha

Production Service: MPS Limited, a Macmillan Company

Senior Photo Manager: Jennifer Meyer Dare

Text Designer: Dare Porter

Cover Designer: Dare Porter

Cover Image (also on page iii): Giuseppe Castiglione, *Qianlong at Leisure on New Year's Eve* (1738), Palace Museum, Beijing 7. The Palace Museum.

Compositor: MPS Limited, a Macmillan Company

For product information and technology assistance, contact us at **Cengage Learning Customer & Sales Support, 1-800-354-9706**
For permission to use material from this text or product, submit all requests online at **www.cengage.com/permissions**. Further permissions questions can be emailed to **permissionrequest@cengage.com**.

Library of Congress Control Number: 2010937457

Student Edition:

ISBN-13: 978-0-495-91308-5

ISBN-10: 0-495-91308-1

Wadsworth
20 Channel Center Street
Boston, MA 02210
USA

Cengage Learning is a leading provider of customized learning solutions with office locations around the globe, including Singapore, the United Kingdom, Australia, Mexico, Brazil and Japan. Locate your local office at **international.cengage.com/region**

Cengage Learning products are represented in Canada by Nelson Education, Ltd.

For your course and learning solutions, visit **www.cengage.com**.

Purchase any of our products at your local college store or at our preferred online store **www.cengagebrain.com**.

Printed in the United States of America
3 4 5 6 15 14 13 12

CONTENTS

GEOGRAPHIC CONTENTS

Western Hemisphere

Latin America/Caribbean

TOPICAL CONTENTS

Religion

Western Expansion and Colonialism

PREFACE

The seventh edition of *The Human Record: Sources of Global History* follows the principles that have guided the book since its inception in 1990. Foremost is our commitment to the proposition that all students of history must meet the challenge of analyzing primary sources, thereby becoming active inquirers into the past. Working with primary source evidence enables students to see that historical scholarship is an intellectual process of drawing inferences and discovering patterns from clues yielded by the past, not of memorizing someone else's judgments. Furthermore, such analysis motivates students to learn by stimulating their curiosity and imagination, and it helps them develop into critical thinkers who are equipped to deal with the complex intellectual challenges of life.

Themes and Structure

We have compiled a source collection that traces the course of human history from the rise of the earliest civilizations to the present. Volume I follows the evolution of cultures that most significantly influenced the history of the world from around 3500 B.C.E. to 1500 C.E., with emphasis on the development of the major social, religious, intellectual, and political traditions of the societies that flourished in Eurasia and Africa. Although our focus in Volume I is on Afro-Eurasia, we do not neglect the Americas. Volume I concurrently develops the theme of the growing links and increasingly important exchanges among the world's cultures down to the dawn of full globalization. Volume II, which begins in the 1400s, picks up this theme of growing human interconnectedness by tracing the gradual establishment of Western global hegemony; simultaneous historical developments in other civilizations and societies around the world; the anti-Western, anticolonial movements of the twentieth century; and the emergence of the twenty-first century's integrated but still often bitterly divided world.

To address these themes in the depth and breadth they deserve, we have chosen primary sources that present an overview of global history in mosaic form. Each source serves two functions: It presents an intimate glimpse into some meaningful aspect of the human past and simultaneously contributes to the creation of a single large picture—an integrated history of the world. With this dual purpose in mind, we have tried to avoid isolated sources that provide a taste of some culture or age but, by their dissociation, shed no light on patterns of cultural creation, continuity, change, and interchange—the essential components of world history.

In selecting and arranging the various pieces of our mosaic, we have sought to create a balanced picture of human history that reflects many different perspectives and experiences. Believing that the study of history properly concerns every aspect of past human activity and thought, we have chosen sources that mirror the practices and concerns of as wide a variety of representative persons and groups as availability and space allow.

Our pursuit of historical balance has also led us into the arena of artifactual evidence. Although most historians center their research on documents, the discipline of history requires us to consider all of the clues surrendered by the past, and these include its artifacts. Moreover, we have discovered that students enjoy analyzing artifacts and remember vividly the insights they draw from them. For these reasons, we have included works of art and other artifacts that users of this book can and should analyze as historical sources.

New to This Edition

We have been gratified with the positive response by colleagues and especially students to the first six editions of *The Human Record*. Many have taken the trouble to write or otherwise contact us to express their satisfaction. No textbook is perfect, however, and these correspondents have been equally generous in sharing their perceptions of how we might improve our book and meet more fully the needs of its readers. Such suggestions, when combined with continuing advances in historical scholarship and our own deeper reflections on a variety of issues, have mandated periodic revisions. In the current revision, as was true in the previous six, our intent has been to make the book as interesting and useful as possible to students and instructors alike.

In this continuing (and never-ending) pursuit of trying to find the best and most useful documents and artifacts, we have made several significant changes. First, we have introduced a large number of new sources. Inasmuch as many of the sources consist of two or more discrete elements, any number that we offer as an exact count is subject to debate, but the most conservative estimate is that, together, the two volumes contain more than 75 new sources. Needless to say, in order to keep these volumes within manageable boundaries, we have had to excise almost a like number of "old" sources, many of which undoubtedly have their advocates, who will be disappointed at their excision from the present edition. Persons who disagree with our judgments as to what to cut and what to add should feel free to contact us (see "Feedback" below) and to argue their case. There will be an eighth edition.

Instructors who have used earlier editions of *The Human Record* will recognize immediately that we have added a large number of new artifactual sources, and unlike earlier editions, most are now in four-color reproduction, making it far easier for student and instructor alike to identify details and allowing us greater latitude in selecting images. We no longer need to reject an image because important elements would be lost in black and white.

Instructors who have read and used a variety of world history textbooks will also note that many of the artifactual sources that we selected for inclusion and analysis are unique to this work. In other words, many are the fruit of our own research and do not come from the usual cast of world history images. By their very inclusion they will expand the store of important images, illustrations, and sources available to colleagues and students alike. Each, however, was not chosen because we thought it offbeat or uncommon or were overcome with whimsy. It was selected because we deemed it telling and important to the story of world history.

Multiple Voices, a feature new to the sixth edition, received near-universal acclaim from the instructors who used these exercises in the classroom. We have retained this feature, while adding a few new Multiple Voices sections and revising several of the ones carried over from the previous edition. Whether new, revised, or recycled intact, a simple philosophy lies behind each Multiple Voices exercise. Two of the most important skills that every student of history must acquire and sharpen are an ability to identify, evaluate, and use evidence that reflects different perspectives and an ability to trace historical development over time. Together, the two volumes contain 14 Multiple Voices units, with each containing three to six sources and clearly set apart from other elements in the chapter. We believe that this enables instructors to use each unit as a coherent whole in the classroom and as a focal point for out-of-class essays. Beyond that, we are confident that each Multiple Voices unit will help students acquire and deepen habits of the mind that are necessary for not only their successful mastery of history but also, more important, their functioning in the world as educated individuals and citizens. These include, but are not limited to, a high degree of comfort with nuance and ambiguity; a sensitivity to the ways in which personality, time, place, culture, and other circumstances influence perspectives; an understanding that change and continuity are equally important elements in the dynamics of human history; a willingness to offer provisional answers to complex phenomena in which some or much of the desired evidence is not available; and an intellectual humility that allows one to modify and even radically change previous judgments once new evidence or insights become available.

Beyond helping to stimulate these skills and habits of the mind, we also have an obligation to reflect in our work the most up-to-date scholarly discoveries and controversies. With that in mind, we have revised many of our introductions and commentaries. In several cases we have explicitly corrected statements made in previous editions that can no longer be held as valid in the light of new research. More than one third of the pages dedicated to editorial commentary and notes have been rewritten.

Each volume also has a few new features unique to it, reflecting both new currents in scholarship and pedagogy and maybe even the perspectives of its author-editor (Andrea for Volume I and Overfield for Volume II).

The first six editions of Volume I extended the story to 1700; that volume now ends in 1500, reflecting the current trend to break world history at that point, leaving 1500 to the present for the second semester or, in rare cases, the following year. This has enabled us to reduce the volume's length by a chapter without sacrificing any substance. Indeed, we even cut out a second chapter by eliding two into one, again, we trust, without any substantial loss. The former Chapter 6, "New Developments in Three Ancient Religions," and Chapter 7, "Christianity," have been reformulated into a new Chapter 6, "Universal Religions of Salvation in an Uncertain World: 1–600 c.e." This reformulation helps instructors and students alike to perceive the widespread currents across much of Afro-Eurasia that provided fertile ground for such religions of salvation as the Hellenistic mystery religions, Mahayana Buddhism, and Christianity. It further allows them to see not only their striking similarities but also their profound differences. By reducing the volume's number of chapters from 13 to 11, and its sources from 97 to 89, a leaner Volume I lends itself to fuller use in the normal semester.

Whereas some things have been cut in Volume I, other things have been added. The most significant addition is a greater emphasis on the role of Central Asia and its peoples as a driving force in premodern world history. All too often, world history textbooks treat that vast expense of territory and cultures as a wasteland of steppe, desert, and mountain out of which various nomadic confederations erupt periodically but otherwise have little or no impact on world history. Indeed, some texts begin to concern themselves with Central Asia and its peoples only with the rise of the Mongols in the thirteenth century. Although the first six editions treated Central Asia more generously than that, it seemed to us that, because recent archaeological discoveries and advances in historical research have increasingly pointed to the centrality of Central Asia and its peoples in the long story of cultural contact and exchange across Eurasia, especially before 1500, Central Asia deserved a larger role in Volume I. For that reason, 25 of the sources, of which 14 are artifacts, deal in whole or in part with Central Asia and its impact on world history. There are many discoveries awaiting the student who explores and studies these sources.

Finally, a few words about several specific sources in Volume I that might well challenge users' views of the past. The *Compendium of Caraka* (Multiple Voices II) presents the theory and practice of Indian ayurvedic medicine. Source 30, a Bactrian ewer, which was placed as a tomb offering in a sixth-century c.e. grave along China's northwest frontier, presents several scenes relating to the Homeric story of the abduction of Helen. The recently translated *Chronicle of the Western Regions* (Multiple Voices III) contains a second-century c.e. account (from the Chinese perspective) of a Roman imperial embassy to China. Two paintings of the Virgin Mary suggest connections between Byzantine and Ethiopian iconographical traditions. Source 74, two effigies, one from the Moche culture of Peru and the other a product of the Adena culture of the Ohio Valley, offer some tantalizing hints of possible long-distance cultural influences in the Americas.

In Volume II the coverage of a number of key topics has been strengthened. In past editions, the topic of the impact of the Industrial Revolution on Europe's working class had mainly been covered by presenting excerpts from testimony taken by various British Parliamentary committees investigating conditions of child labor in the mills and coal mines in the 1830s and 1840s. Although an effort was made to include testimony from individuals from different backgrounds (mill owners, the children's parents, clergymen, schoolteachers), the lurid testimony of the children may have described conditions that were untypical. The coverage of this topic, therefore, has been expanded in Chapter 5 to include petitions from Yorkshire Cloth Workers (1786) and what amounts to a response by the cloth merchants of Leeds (1791). These sources also remind our readers that the Industrial Revolution in England began well before the 1800s. Then, in Chapter 8, our Multiple Voices selection "Working Class and Middle Class in Nineteenth-Century Europe" includes source material pertaining not just to England but also to France and Germany. Our coverage of Islam also has been expanded and given greater balance. In addition to sources from previous editions that focus on Sunni–Shia controversies, revival movements, jihad, and modern links between Islam and terrorism, we have included a section in Chapter 9 on Islamic Modernism, which introduces students to three prominent nineteenth-century Muslim intellectuals who advocated accommodation between Islam and Western science, secular education, constitutionalism, and greater rights for women. The new excerpt from the Peel Report (1937) on Palestine provides insights into the origins of the Arab–Israeli conflict. Finally, responding to suggestions from many of our readers, we have made an effort to expand our coverage of Africa. In this edition, in addition to ample coverage of the slave trade (and its demise), we have included in Chapter 3 a Multiple Voices selection, "Africa's Diversity Through Europeans' Eyes," in which our sources describe societies in four distinct regions: the Western Sudan, the Gulf of Guinea, Southeastern Africa, and the east coast. Coverage of Africa also has been expanded in Chapter 9, which now includes a sampling of treaties between Africans and European imperialists; an early exposé of the atrocities in King Leopold's Congo by an extraordinary African-American journalist, clergyman, and historian, George Washington Williams; and finally a defense of the Congo Free State by King Leopold II himself.

These are but some of many new sources that we hope will stimulate anew instructors who have used earlier editions and excite the imagination of their students. As for the many sources that are not new to this edition: some treasures are too valuable to leave behind.

Learning Aids

Source analysis can be a daunting challenge for any student. With this in mind, we have labored to make these sources as accessible as possible by providing the student-user with a variety of aids.

Each volume has a *Prologue*, in which we explain, initially in a theoretical manner and then concretely, how a historian interprets written and artifactual sources. Because the book's Multiple Voices units are probably its most challenging elements, the Prologue offers a sample Multiple Voices exercise followed by our explanation of what insights we gleaned from these four sources and how we arrived at them. After studying our step-by-step analysis of this Multiple Voices module, the student-reader should realize that source analysis is largely common sense and care to detail and is well within her or his ability.

Within the body of each volume, we offer *part, chapter, sub-chapter,* and *individual source introductions,* all to help the reader place each selection into a meaningful context and understand each source's significance. Because we consider *The Human Record* to be an interpretive overview of global history and therefore a survey of the major patterns of global history that stands on its own as a text, our introductions are significantly fuller than what one normally encounters in a book of sources.

Suggested *Questions for Analysis* precede each source; their purpose is to help the student make sense of each piece of evidence and wrest from it as much insight as possible. Ideally, and more often than not, the questions are presented in a three-tiered format designed to resemble the historian's approach to source analysis and to help students make historical comparisons on a global scale. The first several questions are usually quite specific and ask the reader to pick out important pieces of information. These initial questions require the student to address two issues: What does this document or artifact say, and what meaningful facts can I garner from it? Addressing concrete questions of this sort prepares the student researcher for the next, more significant, level of critical thinking and analysis: drawing inferences. Questions that demand inferential conclusions follow the fact-oriented questions. Finally, whenever possible, we offer a third tier of questions that challenge the student to compare the individual or society that produced a particular source with an individual, group, or culture encountered earlier in the volume. We believe such comparisons help students fix more firmly in their minds the distinguishing cultural characteristics of the various societies they encounter in their survey of world history. Beyond that, it underscores the fact that global history is, at least on one level, comparative history.

Another form of help we offer is to *gloss the sources,* explaining words and allusions that students cannot reasonably be expected to know. To facilitate reading and to encourage reference, the notes appear at the bottom of the page on which they are cited. A few documents also contain *interlinear notes* that serve as transitions or provide needed information.

Some instructors might use *The Human Record* as their sole textbook. Most, however, will use it as a supplement to a standard narrative textbook, and most of these will probably decide not to require their students to analyze every source. To assist instructors (and students) in selecting sources that best suit their interests and needs, we have prepared *two analytical tables of contents* for each volume. The first lists readings and artifacts by geographic and cultural area, the second by topic. The two tables suggest to professor and student alike the rich variety of material available within these pages, particularly for essays in comparative history.

In summary, our goal in crafting *The Human Record* has been to do our best to prepare the student-reader for success—*success* being defined as comfort with historical analysis, proficiency in critical thinking, learning to view history on a global scale, and a deepened awareness of the rich cultural varieties, as well as shared characteristics, of the human family.

Using The Human Record: Suggestions from the Editors

We have also not forgotten our colleagues. Specific suggestions for assignments and classroom activities appear in the online manual *Using* The Human Record: *Suggestions from the Editors,* which may be accessed through the textbook website at www.college.hmco.com/history/instructors. It is also available in print format. In it we explain why we have chosen the sources that appear in this book and what insights we believe students should be capable of drawing from them. We also describe classroom exercises for encouraging student thought and discussion on the various sources. The advice we present is the fruit of our own use of these sources in the classroom.

Feedback

As already suggested, we want to receive comments and suggestions from instructors and students who use this book. Comments on the Prologue and Volume I should be addressed to A. J. Andrea, whose e-mail address is aandrea@uvm.edu; comments on Volume II should be addressed to J. H. Overfield at James.Overfield@uvm.edu.

Acknowledgments

We are in debt to the many professionals who offered their expert advice and assistance during the various incarnations of *The Human Record.* Scholars and friends at The University of Vermont who generously shared their expertise with us over the years as we crafted these six editions include Abbas Alnasrawi, Doris Bergen, Holly-Lynn Busier, Ernesto Capello, Robert V. Daniels, Carolyn Elliott, Bogac Ergene, Erik Esselstrom, Shirley Gedeon, Erik Gilbert, William Haviland, Walter Hawthorn, Dennis Herron, Richard Horowitz, Abigail McGowan, Wolfgang Mieder, William Mierse, George Moyser, Francis Nicosia, Kristin M. Peterson-Ishaq, Abubaker Saad, Wolfe W. Schmokel, Peter Seybolt, John W. Seyller, Sean Stilwell, Mark Stoler, Marshall True, Diane Villemaire, Janet Whatley, and Denise Youngblood. Additionally, Ms. Tara Coram of the Arthur M. Sackler Gallery and Freer Gallery of Art of the Smithsonian Institution deserves special thanks for the assistance she rendered A. J. Andrea in his exploration of the Asian art holdings of the two museums. He also extends his appreciation to the Silkroad Foundation of Saratoga, California, and especially its executive director, Adela Lee. Participation in three of its summer seminars in China on the artifacts of the Silk Road enabled him to identify and study several of the sources that appear in Volume I. He also thanks Sun Yue, of Capital Normal University, Beijing, China, for translation assistance in our photo research efforts. Finally, he must single out an act of great collegiality: John E. Hill shared his translation of the *Chronicle of the Western Regions,* inclusion of which has added immeasurably to the value of Chapter 5 of Volume I. Professor Overfield gratefully acknowledges the help of Professor Timon Screech of the University of London School of Oriental and African Studies for his insights into Shiba Kōkan's *A Meeting of Japan, China and the West* in Chapter 7 of Volume II, and to James Cahill, Professor Emeritus of Art History at the University of California at Berkeley, for his help in locating Zhang Hong's landscape in Chapter 4 of that same volume.

We wish also to acknowledge the following instructors whose comments on the sixth edition helped guide our revision: Kim Brinck-Johnsen, Simmons College; Denise Davidson, Georgia State University; Michelle DuRoss, Siena College; Valerie Emanoil, Oakland Community College; James Fuller, University of Indianapolis; JaNae Haas, Utah Valley University; Randy Kidd, Bradley University; Marilynn Kokoszka, Oakland Community College; David Lindenfeld, Louisiana State University; Neal Palmer, Christian Brothers University; Amy Piccarreto, University of Memphis; Alexander Stecker, Utah Valley University; and Michael Vollbach, Oakland Community College.

Finally, our debt to our spouses is beyond payment, but the dedication to them of each edition reflects in some small way how deeply we appreciate their support and good-humored tolerance.

A. J. A. / J. H. O.

PROLOGUE

Primary Sources and How to Read Them

Imagine a course in chemistry in which you never set foot in a laboratory or a course on the history of jazz in which you never listen to a note of music. You would consider such courses deficient and would complain to your academic advisor or college dean about flawed teaching methods and wasted tuition. And you would be right. No one can understand chemistry without doing experiments; no one can understand music without listening to performances.

In much the same way, no one can understand history without reading and analyzing *primary sources*. Simply defined, *in most instances, primary sources are historical records produced at the same time the event or period that is being studied took place or soon thereafter.* They are distinct from *secondary sources*—books, articles, television documentaries, and even historical films produced well after the events they describe and analyze. Secondary sources—*histories* in the conventional sense of the term—organize the jumble of past events into understandable narratives. They provide interpretations, sometimes make comparisons, and almost always discuss motive and causation. When done well, they provide pleasure and insight. But such works, no matter how well done, are still *secondary* in that they are written well after the fact and derive their evidence and information from primary sources.

History is an ambitious discipline that deals with all aspects of past human activity and belief. This means that the primary sources historians use to recreate the past are equally wide-ranging and diverse. Most primary sources are written—government records, law codes, private correspondence, literary works, religious texts, merchants' account books, memoirs, and the list goes on. So important are written records to the study of history that some historians refer to societies and cultures with no system of writing as "prehistoric." This does not mean they lack a history; it means there is no way to construct a detailed narrative of their histories due to the lack of written records. Of course, even so-called prehistoric societies leave behind evidence of their experiences, creativity, and belief systems in their *oral traditions* and their *artifacts*.

Let us look first at oral traditions, which can include legends, religious rituals, proverbs, genealogies, and a variety of other forms of wisdom and knowledge. Simply put, they constitute a society's remembered past as passed down by word of mouth. The difficulty of working with such evidence is significant. You are aware of how stories change as they are transmitted from person to person. Imagine how difficult it is to use such stories as historical evidence. Yet, despite the challenge they offer, these sources cannot be overlooked.

Although the oral traditions of ancient societies were in many cases written down long after they were first articulated, they are often the only recorded evidence that we have of a far-distant society or event. So, the farther back in history we go, the more we see the inadequacy of the definition of primary sources that we offered above ("historical records produced at the same time the event or period that is being studied took place or soon thereafter"). The early chapters of Volume I contain quite a few primary sources based on oral traditions; in some cases, they were recorded many centuries after the events and people they deal with. We will inform you when this is the case and offer information and suggestions as to which questions you can validly ask of them to enable you to use them effectively.

Artifacts—anything, other than a document, that was crafted by hand or machine—can help us place oral traditions into a clearer context by producing tangible evidence that supports or calls into question this form of testimony. Artifacts can also tell us something about prehistoric societies whose oral traditions are lost to us. They also serve as primary sources for historians who study literate cultures. Written records, no matter how extensive and diverse, never allow us to draw a complete picture of the past, and we can fill at least some of those gaps by studying what human hands have fashioned. Everyday objects—such as fabrics, tools, kitchen implements, weapons, farm equipment, jewelry, pieces of furniture, and family photographs—provide windows into the ways that people lived. Grander cultural products—paintings, sculpture, buildings, musical compositions, and, more recently, film—are equally important because they also reflect the values, attitudes, and styles of living of their creators and those for whom they were created.

To be a historian is to work with primary sources in all their diverse forms. But to do so effectively is not easy. Each source provides only one glimpse of reality, and no single source by itself gives us the whole picture of past events and developments. Many sources are difficult to understand and can be interpreted only after the precise meaning of their words has been deciphered and their backgrounds thoroughly investigated. Many sources contain distortions and errors that can be discovered only by rigorous internal analysis and comparison with evidence from other sources. Only after all these source-related difficulties have been overcome can a historian hope to achieve a coherent and reasonably accurate understanding of the past.

To illustrate some of the challenges of working with primary sources, let us imagine a time in the future when a historian decides to write a history of your college class in connection with its fiftieth reunion. Since no one has written a book or article about your class, our historian has no secondary sources to consult and must rely entirely on primary sources. What primary sources might he or she use? The list is a long one: the school catalogue, class lists, academic transcripts, yearbooks, college rules and regulations, and similar official documents; lecture notes, syllabi, examinations, term papers, and textbooks; diaries and private letters; articles from the campus newspaper and programs for sporting events, concerts, and plays; posters and handbills; recollections written down or otherwise recorded by some of your classmates long after they graduated. With a bit of thought, you could add other items to the list, among them some artifacts, such as souvenirs sold in the campus store, and other unwritten sources, such as recordings of music popular at the time and photographs and videotapes of student life and activity.

Even with this imposing list of sources, our future historian will have only an incomplete record of the events that made up your class' experiences. Many of those moments—telephone conversations, meetings with professors, and gossip exchanged at the student union—never made it into any written record. Also consider the fact that all the sources available to our future historian will be fortunate survivors. They will represent only a small percentage of the material generated by you, your classmates, professors, and administrators over a two- or four-year period. Wastebaskets and recycling bins will have claimed much written material; the "delete" key, inevitable changes in computer technology, and old websites dumped as "obsolete" will make it impossible to retrieve some basic sources, such as your college's website, e-mail, and a vast amount of other online materials. It is also probable that it will be difficult to find information about certain groups within your class, such as part-time students, nontraditional students, and commuters. The past always has its so-called silent or near-silent groups of people. Of course, they were never truly silent, but often nobody was listening to them. It is the historian's task to find whatever evidence exists that gives them a voice, but often that evidence is tantalizingly slim.

For these reasons, the evidence available to our future historian will be fragmentary at best. This is always the case when doing historical research. The records of the past cannot be retained in their totality, not even records that pertain to the recent past.

How will our future historian use the many individual pieces of surviving documentary evidence about your class? As he or she reviews the list, it will quickly become apparent that no single primary source provides a complete or unbiased picture. Each source has its own perspective, value, and limitations. Imagine that the personal essays submitted by applicants for admission were a historian's only sources of information about the student body. On reading them, our researcher might draw the false conclusion that the school attracted only the most gifted, talented, interesting, and intellectually committed students imaginable.

Despite their flaws, however, essays composed by applicants for admission are still important pieces of historical evidence. They reflect the would-be students' perceptions of the school's cultural values and the types of people it hopes to attract, and usually the applicants are right on the mark because they have studied the college's or university's website and read the brochures prepared by its admissions office. Admissions materials and, to a degree, even the school's official catalogue (assuming a fifty-year-old online catalogue can be recovered) are forms of creative advertising, and both present an idealized picture of campus life. But such publications have value for the careful researcher because they reflect the values of the faculty and administrators who composed them. The catalogue also provides useful information regarding rules and regulations, courses, instructors, school organizations, and similar items. Such factual information, however, is the raw material of history, not history itself, and certainly it does not reflect anything close to the full historical reality of your class' collective experience.

What is true of the catalogue is equally true of the student newspaper and every other piece of evidence pertinent to your class. Each primary source is a part of a larger whole, but as we have already seen, we do not have all the pieces. Think of historical evidence in terms of a jigsaw puzzle. Many of the pieces are missing, but it is possible to put the remaining pieces together to form a fairly accurate and coherent picture. The picture that emerges will not be complete, but it is valid and useful, and from it, one can often make educated guesses as to what the missing pieces look like. The keys to putting together this historical puzzle are hard work and imagination. Each is absolutely necessary.

Examining Primary Sources

Hard work speaks for itself, but students are often unaware that historians also need imagination to reconstruct the past. After all, many students ask, doesn't history consist of irrefutable dates, names, and facts? Where does imagination enter into the process of learning these facts? Again, let us consider your class's history and its documentary sources. Many of those documents provide factual data—dates, names, grades, statistics. While these data are important, individually and collectively they have no historical meaning until they have been *interpreted*. Your college class is more than a collection of statistics and facts. It is a group of individuals who, despite their differences, shared and molded a collective experience. It was and is a community evolving within a particular time and place. Any valid or useful history must reach beyond dates, names, and facts and interpret the historical characteristics and role of your class. What were its values? How did it change and why? What impact did it have? These are some of the important questions a historian asks of the evidence.

To arrive at answers, the historian must examine every piece of relevant evidence in its full context and wring from that evidence as many *inferences* as possible. *An inference is a logical conclusion drawn from evidence,* and it is the heart and soul of historical inquiry. Facts are the raw materials of history, but inferences are its finished products.

Every American schoolchild learns at an early age that "in fourteen hundred and ninety-two, Columbus sailed the ocean blue." In subsequent history classes, he or she might learn other facts about the famous explorer: that he was born in Genoa in 1451; that he made three other transatlantic voyages in 1493, 1497, and 1503; that he died in Spain in 1506. Knowing these facts is of little value, however, unless it contributes to our understanding of the motives, causes, and significance of Columbus's voyages. Why did Columbus sail west? Why did Spain support such enterprises? Why were Europeans willing and able to exploit, as they did, the so-called New World? What were the short- and long-term consequences of the European presence in the Americas? Finding answers to questions such as these are the historian's ultimate goal, and these answers can be reached only by studying primary sources.

One noted historian, Robin Winks, wrote a book entitled *The Historian as Detective,* and the image is appropriate although inexact. Like a detective, the historian examines evidence to reconstruct events. Like a detective, the historian is interested in discovering "what happened, who did it, and why." Like a detective interrogating witnesses, *the historian also must carefully examine the testimony of sources.*

First and foremost, the historian must evaluate the *validity* of the source. Is it what it purports to be? Artful forgeries have misled many historians. Even authentic sources still can be misleading if the author lied or deliberately misrepresented reality. In addition, the historian can easily be led astray by not fully understanding the *perspective* reflected in the document. As is soon learned by any detective who has examined eyewitnesses to an event, even honest witnesses' accounts can differ widely. The detective has the opportunity to re-examine witnesses and offer them the opportunity to change their testimony in the light of new evidence and deeper reflection. The historian is not so fortunate. Even when the historian compares a piece of documentary evidence with other evidence in order to uncover its flaws, there is no way to cross-examine its author. Given this fact, the historian must understand as fully as possible the source's perspective. Thus, the historian must ask several key questions—all of which share the letter *W*:

- *What* kind of document is it?
- *Who* wrote it?
- For *whom* and *why*?
- *Where* was it composed and *when*?

What is important because understanding the nature of a source gives the historian an idea of what kind of information he or she can expect to find in it. Many sources simply do not address the questions a historian would like to ask of them, and knowing this can prevent a great deal of frustration. Your class's historian would be foolish to try to learn much about the academic quality of your school's courses from a study of the registrar's class lists and grade sheets; student and faculty class notes, copies of syllabi, examinations, student papers, and textbooks would be far more useful.

Who, for whom, and *why* are equally important questions. The official catalogue and publicity materials prepared by the admissions office undoubtedly address some issues pertaining to student social life. But should documents such as these— designed to attract potential students and to place the school in the best possible light—be read and accepted uncritically? Obviously not. They must be tested against student testimony discovered in such sources as private letters, memoirs, posters, the student newspaper, and the yearbook.

Where and *when* are also important questions to ask of any primary source. As a rule, distance from an event in space and time colors perceptions and can diminish the reliability of a source. Imagine that a classmate had celebrated the twenty-fifth class reunion by recording her or his memories and reflections. That document or video could be an insightful and valuable source of information for your class's historian. Conceivably this graduate would have had a perspective and information that he or she lacked a quarter of a century earlier. Just as conceivably, that person's memory of what college was like might have faded to the point where the recollections have little evidentiary value.

You and the Sources

This book will actively involve you in the work of historical inquiry by asking you to draw inferences based on your analysis of primary source evidence. This might prove difficult at first, but it is well within your capability.

You will analyze two types of evidence: documents and artifacts. Each source in *The Human Record* is authentic, so you do not have to worry about validating it. Editorial material in this book also supplies you with the information necessary to place each piece of evidence into its proper context and will suggest questions you legitimately can and should ask of each source.

It is important to keep in mind that historians approach each source with questions, even though they might be vaguely formulated. Like detectives, historians want to discover some particular truth or shed light on an issue. This requires asking specific questions of the witnesses or, in the historian's case, of the evidence. These questions should not be prejudgments. *One of the worst errors a historian can make is setting out to prove a point or to defend an ideological position.* Questions are essential, but they are starting points, nothing else. Therefore, as you approach a source, have your question or questions fixed in your mind, and constantly remind yourself as you work your way through a source what issue or issues you are investigating—but at the same time, keep an open mind. You are not an advocate or a debater. Your mission is to discover the truth, insofar as you can, by following the evidence and asking the right questions of it. Each source in this anthology is preceded by a number of suggested *Questions for Analysis.* You or your professor might want to ask other questions. Whatever the case, keep focused on your questions and issues, and take notes as you read a source. Never rely on unaided memory; it will almost inevitably lead you astray.

Above all else, you must be honest and thorough as you study a source. Read each explanatory footnote carefully to avoid misunderstanding a word or an allusion. Try to understand exactly what the source is saying and what its author's perspective is. Be careful not to wrench items, words, or ideas out of context, thereby distorting them. Be sure to read the entire source so that you understand as fully as possible what it says and does not say.

This is not as difficult as it sounds, but it does take concentration and work. And do not let the word "work" mislead you. True, primary source analysis demands attention to detail and some hard thought, but it is also rewarding. There is great satisfaction in developing a deeper and truer understanding of the past based on a careful exploration of the evidence. What is more, an ability to analyze and interpret evidence is a skill that will serve you well in whatever career you follow.

Analyzing Sample Sources

To illustrate how you should go about this task and what is expected of you, we will now take you through an exercise. One of the features of this source book is what we call "Multiple Voices." Each volume is divided into parts, and each part contains one or more Multiple Voices sections. Each Multiple Voices feature is a set of short source excerpts that illustrates one of three phenomena: (1) multiple, more-or-less contemporary perspectives on a common event or phenomenon; (2) multiple sources that illustrate how something changes over time; (3) multiple perspectives from different cultures regarding a common concern or issue. The sample exercise we have constructed for this Prologue is a Multiple Voices feature that illustrates the third phenomenon: multiple perspectives from different cultures regarding a common concern or issue. We have chosen three documents and an artifact that shed light on the importance and economic policies of the Indian port city of Calicut in the years preceding the entry on a large scale of Europeans into the Indian Ocean. We present this grouping of sources as it would appear in the book: first a bit of background; next a discussion of the individual sources; then suggested Questions for Analysis; and finally the sources themselves, with explanatory notes.

Everyone Meets in Calicut

BACKGROUND

On May 20, 1498, after almost eleven months of sailing, the Portuguese captain-major Vasco da Gama anchored his three ships a few miles from Kozhikode (known to the Arabs as Kalikut and later to the British as Calicut) on India's Malabar, or southwestern, Coast, thereby inaugurating Europe's entry into the markets of the Indian Ocean. At the time of da Gama's arrival, Calicut was the capital of the most important state in a region dotted with small powers. Despite lacking a good natural harbor, Calicut prospered as a center of trade for reasons suggested in the following sources. However, with the establishment of competitive Portuguese trading stations along the Malabar Coast and elsewhere in the Indian Ocean as a consequence of da Gama's initial contact with India and following da Gama's bombardment of the city in 1503, Calicut's fortunes rapidly declined, and its prominence ended.

THE SOURCES

We begin with an account of Calicut contained in the anonymous *Logbook (Roteiro) of the First Voyage of Vasco da Gama,* often referred to simply as the Roteiro. The journal, which is incomplete, was kept by an anonymous crew member aboard the *San Rafael.* Although the author's identity is unknown, what is certain is that the *Roteiro* is authentic.

The second source, Ibn Battuta's *Rihla,* or *A Gift to Those Who Contemplate the Wonders of Cities and the Marvels Encountered in Travel,* predates the *Roteiro* by a century and a half. Abu Abdallah Muhammad Ibn Battuta (1304–1368?) left his home in Tangier on the coast of Morocco in 1325 at the age of 21 to begin a 26-year journey throughout the Islamic World and beyond. When he returned to Morocco in 1349, he had logged about 73,000 miles of travel, including more than seven years spent as a *qadi,* or religious judge, in the Islamic sultanate of Delhi in northern India. In 1341, Sultan Muhammad Tughluq (r. 1325–1351) invited Ibn Battuta to travel to China as his ambassador. On his way to China, Ibn Battuta stopped at Calicut. In 1354, the traveler began to collaborate with a professional scribe, Ibn Juzayy, to fashion his many adventures into a *rihla,* or book of religious travels, one of the most popular forms of literature in the Islamic world. It took almost two years to complete his long and complex story. Some of that story was fabricated, as even contemporaries noticed, but most of the *rihla* has the ring of authenticity. The excerpt describes Calicut as seen in 1341 and remembered about 15 years later, and there is no good reason to doubt that this is an eyewitness account.

The third source, *The Overall Survey of the Ocean's Shores,* is Chinese. Its author, Ma Huan (ca. 1380–after 1451), accompanied the fourth (1413–1415), sixth (1421–1423), and seventh (1431–1433) expeditions of the great Ming fleets that the Yongle Emperor (r. 1402–1424) and his successor sent into the Indian Ocean under the command of Admiral Zheng He (1371–1433). The main purpose of the seven expeditions, which began in 1405 and ended in 1433, was to reassert Chinese hegemony in coastal lands touched by the Indian Ocean. Ma Huan, who was a Chinese Muslim, served as an Arabic translator on his first voyage and upon his return home transcribed his notes into book form. After sailing on two other expeditions, he amended his account accordingly and published a book in 1451 that encapsulated all three expeditions and described in detail the lands visited and actions taken by the fleets during those voyages. In this excerpt he describes Calicut, known to the Chinese as Guli.

The fourth source, an artifact, is a detail of the western portions of India and the adjoining Arabian Sea from the *Catalan World Atlas,* which was drawn in 1375 on the island of Majorca, probably by Abraham Cresques (1325–1387), a Jewish "master of maps of the world" who served the king of Aragon in northeastern Spain (Catalonia), which had seized Majorca from the Moors in 1229. Cresques's map was based on the best available literary and cartographic sources and reflected the facts and fictions regarding Afro-Eurasia (the vast connected landmass that constitutes Africa and Eurasia) that circulated in educated circles in late-fourteenth-century Western Europe. In the segment shown here, we see at the top the Three Magi on their way to visit the Christ Child. Below them is the sultan of Delhi, whose Muslim state dominated northern India; below him is the raja of Vijayanagara, who presided over the most powerful Hindu state in southern India. Between them are an elephant and its handler. In the Arabian Sea, at the bottom of the map are pearl divers, as described by Marco Polo. Above the pearl divers is a vessel with two men in conical hats.

QUESTIONS FOR ANALYSIS

1. According to the *Roteiro,* why was Calicut so important, and, by implication, why was it necessary for Portugal to gain direct access to it?

2. What does Ibn Battuta tell us about the roles of foreigners in Calicut, and specifically which foreigners?

3. From what the three documentary sources tell us, what factors contributed to Calicut's prosperity?

4. What does the *Catalan World Atlas* tell us about Western Europe's knowledge of the Malabar Coast and India in general by the late fourteenth century?

5. Overall, what can we say with certainty about Calicut prior to its rapid decline in the sixteenth century?

---

1 • Roteiro

From this country of Calicut . . . come the spices that are consumed in the East and the West, in Portugal, as in all other countries of the world, as also [are] precious stones of every description. The following spices are to be found in this city of Calicut, being its own produce: much ginger and pepper and cinnamon, although the last is not of so fine a quality as that brought from an island called Çillon [Ceylon],[1] which is eight days journey from Calicut. Calicut is the staple for all this cinnamon. Cloves are brought to this city from an island called Melqua (Melaka).[2] The Mecca vessels carry these spices from there to a city in Mecca[3] called Judeâ [Jeddah],[4] and from the said island to Judeâ is a voyage of 50 days sailing before the wind. . . . At Judeâ they discharge their cargoes, paying customs duties to the Grand Sultan.[5] The merchandise is then transshipped to smaller vessels, which carry it through the Red Sea to a place close to Santa Catarina of Mount Sinai,[6] called Tuuz [El Tûr][7] where customs dues are paid once more. From

that place the merchants carry the spices on the backs of camels . . . to Quayro [Cairo], a journey occupying ten days. At Quayro duties are paid again. On this road to Cairo they are frequently robbed by thieves. . . .

At Cairo the spices are embarked on the river Nile . . . and descending[8] that river for two days they reach a place called Roxette [Rosetta], where duties have to be paid once more. There they are placed on camels, and are conveyed in one day to a city called Alexandria, which is a sea-port.[9] This city is visited by the galleys of Venice and Genoa, in search of these spices, which yield the Grand Sultan [an annual] revenue of 600,000 cruzados.[10]

[1]The present-day island nation of Sri Lanka. At this time, Ceylon alone produced true cinnamon. The other cinnamon-like spice is cassia, which is made from the bark of a related tree that originated in China.
[2]The straits and city of Melaka (also known as Malacca) were not the source. Cloves came from the Southeast Asian islands known as the Moluccas (or Spice Islands), which today constitute the province of Maluku in the Republic of Indonesia.
[3]Actually Arabia, Mecca (or Makkah) being the inland holy city of Islam in the Arabian Peninsula. Today Mecca is located in Saudi Arabia.

[4]Jeddah (or Jidda) is the Arabian Peninsula's main port city on the Red Sea.
[5]The Mamluk dynasty of sultans that ruled Egypt from 1250 to 1517.
[6]Saint Catherine's Monastery—an ancient Christian monastery in Egypt that still exists.
[7]A port on Egypt's Sinai Peninsula.
[8]Sailing north.
[9]On the Mediterranean.
[10]A Portuguese gold coin that received its name from the crusader's cross emblazoned on it.

2 • Ibn Battuta, A Gift to Those Who Contemplate the Wonders of Cities and the Marvels Encountered in Travel

The sultan of Calicut is an infidel,[1] known as "the Samari."[2] . . . In this town too lives the famous ship-owner Mithqal,[3] who possesses vast wealth and many ships for his trade with India, China, Yemen, and Fars.[4] When we reached the city, the principal inhabitants and merchants and the sultan's representative came out to welcome us, with drums,

trumpets, bugles and standards on their ships. We entered the harbor in great pomp. . . . We stopped in the port of Calicut, in which there were at the time thirteen Chinese vessels, and disembarked. Every one of us was lodged in a house, and we stayed three months as the guests of the infidel, awaiting the season of the voyage to China.[5] On the Sea of China traveling is done in Chinese ships only. . . .

The Chinese vessels are of three kinds: large ships called *chunks* [junks], middle-sized ones called *zaws* [dhows], and small ones called *kakams*. The large

[1]A Hindu.
[2]In the local language, the title was *Samudri raja*, which means "Lord of the Sea." The Portuguese would corrupt this to "Zamorin."
[3]A strange name, very much like being called "Goldie" in English. A measure of weight throughout the Islamic world, a *mithqal* was 4.72 grams of gold. This might mean the man was a Muslim from across the Arabian Sea.

[4]Yemen is the southwestern tip of the Arabian Peninsula; Fars is the southern region of Iran along the Gulf of Oman.
[5]They awaited the lessening of the northeastern monsoon winds, which blow from late November to April. The period around 11 April was considered the best time to begin a voyage from the Malabar Coast to the Bay of Bengal, which lies east of India.

ships have from twelve down to three sails, which are made of bamboo rods plaited like mats. They are never lowered, but turned according to the direction of the wind. . . . A ship carries a complement of a thousand men, six hundred of whom are sailors and four hundred men-at-arms, including archers . . . and arbalists, who throw naptha.[6] . . . The vessel has four decks and contains rooms, cabins, and salons for merchants; a cabin has chambers and a lavatory, and can be locked by its occupant, who takes along with him slave girls and wives. Often a man will live in his cabin unknown to any of the others on board until they meet on reaching some town. The sailors have their children on board ship, and they cultivate green stuffs, vegetables, and ginger in wooden tanks. The owner's factor [agent-in-charge] on board ship is like a great amir.[7] When he goes on shore he is preceded by archers and Abyssinians[8] with javelins, swords, drums, trumpets, and bugles. On reaching the house where he stays, they stand their lances on both sides of the door, and continue thus during his stay. Some of the Chinese own large numbers of ships on which their factors are sent to foreign countries. There is

no people in the world wealthier than the Chinese. When the time came for the voyage to China, the sultan Samari made provision for us on one of the thirteen junks in the port of Calicut. The factor on the junk was called Sulayman of Safad,[9] in Syria. . . .

> Disaster strikes. Ibn Battuta's ship sinks in a storm in the harbor before he boards it, but it carries with it to the bottom all of his baggage, servants, and slaves.

Next morning we found the bodies of Sumbal and Zahir ad-Din,[10] and having prayed over them buried them. I saw the infidel, the sultan of Calicut . . . a fire lit before him on the beach; his police officers were beating the people to prevent them from plundering what the sea had cast up. In all the lands of Malabar, except in this one land alone, it is the custom that whenever a ship is wrecked all that is taken from it belongs to the treasury. At Calicut, however, it is retained by its owners, and for that reason Calicut has become a flourishing city and attracts large numbers of merchants.

---

[6]Crossbowmen who shoot missiles containing a mixture of fiery materials.

[7]Lord or commander.

[8]Persons from the Horn of Africa—present-day Ethiopia, Eritrea, Dhbouti, and Somalia—and maybe even farther south along the Swahili Coast.

[9]Zefat in present-day Israel.

[10]Envoys whom the sultan of Delhi had dispatched to accompany him.

---

3 • Ma Huan, The Overall Survey of the Ocean's Shores

The Country of Guli

The king of the country is a Nankun[1] man; he is a firm believer in the Buddhist religion and he venerates the elephant and the ox.[2] . . .

The king of the country and the people of the country all refrain from eating the flesh of the ox. The great chiefs are Muslim people; they all refrain from eating the flesh of the pig. Formerly there was a king who made a sworn compact with the Muslim people [who said to him], "You do not eat the ox; I do not eat the pig; we will reciprocally

---

[1]High caste—probably a member of the Kshatriya, or warrior-ruler, caste.

[2]Actually, he was a Hindu. His veneration of an ox (probably a bull) suggests he was a devotee of Shiva.

respect the taboo"; [and this compact] has been honored right down to the present day. . . .

The king has two great chiefs who administer the affairs of the country; both are Muslims.

The majority of the people in the country all profess the Muslim religion. There are twenty or thirty temples of worship,[3] and once in seven days they go to worship. . . .

If a [Chinese] treasure-ship goes there,[4] it is left entirely to the two men to superintend the buying and selling; the king sends a chief and a Zhedi Weinoji[5] to examine the account books in the official bureau; a broker comes and joins them; [and] a high officer who commands the ships discusses the choice of a certain date for fixing prices. When the day arrives, they first of all take the silk embroideries . . . and other such goods that have been brought there [by the ship], and discuss the price of them one by one; when [the price] has been fixed, they write out an agreement stating the amount of the price, [which] is retained by these persons.

The chief and the Zhedi, with his excellency the eunuch,[6] all join hands together, and the broker then says, "In such and such a moon, on such and such a day, we have all joined hands and sealed our agreement with a hand-clasp; whether [the price] be dear or cheap, we will never repudiate or change it."

After that, the Zhedi and the men of wealth then come bringing precious stones, pearls, corals, and other such things, so that they may be examined and the price discussed; [this] cannot be settled in a day; [if done] quickly, [it takes] one moon; [if done] slowly, two or three moons.

Once the money-price has been fixed after examination and discussion, if a pearl or other such article is purchased, the price that must be paid for it is calculated by the chief and the Weinoji who carried out the original transaction. As to the quantity of the hemp-silk or other such article that must be given in exchange for it, goods are exchanged according to [the price fixed by] the original hand-clasp—there is not the slightest deviation. . . .

The king uses gold of 60 percent to cast a coin for current use. . . . He also makes a coin of silver . . . for petty transactions. . . .

The people of the country also take the silk of the silk-worm, soften it by boiling, dye it all colors, and weave it into kerchiefs with decorative stripes at intervals . . . ; each length is sold for 100 gold coins.

As to pepper; the inhabitants of the mountainous countryside have established gardens, and it is extensively cultivated. When the period of the tenth moon arrives, the pepper ripens. It is collected, dried in the sun, and sold. Of course, big pepper-collectors come and collect it, and take it to the official storehouse to be stored; if there is a buyer, an official gives permission for the sale. The duty is collected according to the amount [of the purchase price] and is paid to the authorities. . . .

Foreign ships from every place come there; and the king of the country also sends a chief and a writer and others to watch the sales; thereupon they collect the duty and pay it to the authorities.

---

[3]The preceding sentence and the following reference to the weekly day of worship make it appear that these temples were mosques. It seems unlikely, however, that the majority of the population was Muslim and that Calicut had 20 or 30 mosques. More likely, it had several mosques and many Hindu temples. As a Muslim, Ma Huan might have thought, incorrectly, that Hindus, like Muslims, have a once-a-week day of communal prayer.

[4]The fleets commanded by Zheng He contained a significant number of treasure ships—large ships along the lines described by Ibn Battuta that carried Chinese trade goods and gifts, but which also were meant to carry back tribute, foreign trade goods, exotic items, and persons of importance invited (or compelled) to visit the imperial court at Nanjing. By extension, Ma Huan means any Chinese trading vessel.

[5]Probably his attempt to transliterate *Waligi Chitty*, or accountant.

[6]The reference is to Zheng He, a eunuch, who commanded the treasure ships that visited Calicut during these voyages, but more broadly it probably also refers to the commander of any Chinese ship.

4 • **The Catalan World Atlas**

Interpreting the Sources

These four pieces of evidence allow us to say quite a bit about Calicut before Europeans established a strong presence in the Indian Ocean. Let us begin with the two Western sources.

The *Catalan World Atlas* depicts what is unmistakably a Chinese vessel off the west coast of India. The plaited bamboo sails, which Ibn Battuta described, as well as the distinctive hats worn by the two men, make that identification easy. Clearly, Westerners realized as early as the fourteenth century that the Chinese were major players in the commerce of the Indian subcontinent. The West's knowledge of the great wealth of India, as well as its high degree of urbanization and its political fragmentation, is obvious from the portraits of the sultan of Delhi and the raja of Vijayanagara, as well as the symbols for the many cities dotting the coastline and interior. The pearl divers, elephant, and Three Magi only add to the overall picture of India's riches and wonders. The fact is that between roughly 1250 and 1350, a significant number of Europeans, especially missionaries and merchants, had traveled, largely by land, to China and India, and some of them, such as Marco Polo, had written widely circulated accounts of their experiences. Even if you did not know that, you can infer from this map segment alone that the fourteenth-century West was not totally ignorant of India's geography and dynamics, including the importance of Chinese merchants in the commerce of the Malabar Coast.

The *Roteiro* illustrates why the Portuguese desired direct overseas access to the rich markets of India and beyond. Given the numerous duties and profit margins placed on spices that made their way to Egypt and from there to Europe, the Portuguese realized that access to the markets of the Malabar Coast and beyond would enable them cut out many of the middle agents who profited greatly from this lucrative trade. At this point, there is no good reason for you to know that the overland trade routes between Europe and the "Indies" (a vague term that referred to India, China, and other distant lands in Asia and East Africa) had largely broken down after about 1350 (see Vol. I, Chapter 11) and that the closing down of those routes spurred Portugal and Spain to find alternate ways by sea. What you can easily infer from this source is that the Portuguese expected to make much more per year than the 600,000 *cruzados* that the sultan of Egypt enjoyed, once they had direct access to Calicut. As we learn from this anonymous author, not only was Calicut a major commercial emporium, it was also a center of spice and gemstone production.

The *Roteiro* makes clear how important Calicut was to the commerce of Arabia and Egypt, Venice, Genoa, and the Spice Islands; Ibn Battuta and Ma Huan show us how central Calicut was to the overseas trade of China and other segments of the Islamic world. Our Moroccan and Chinese eyewitnesses further depict Calicut as an international city, where Muslims served both Chinese shipowners and the Hindu ruler of Calicut as trusted, high-ranking officials in charge of commercial activities. Both authors also shed light on policies adopted by the rulers of Calicut to encourage commerce and friendly relations with neighboring and far-distant powers.

Ibn Battuta tells us how his diplomatic party was received with great ceremony and how the *Samudri raja* arranged for his transportation aboard a Chinese vessel. Even more revealing are his descriptions of the sizes and types of the Chinese ships that did business at Calicut; the high status and honor accorded the factors, or agents-in-charge, of these Chinese ships; and the manner in which the ruler of Calicut protected the goods of shipwrecked merchants. The size of their ships alone suggests that the Chinese invested heavily in their trade with Calicut, but they did so because they knew that they would be welcomed and treated fairly at the port city. And why not? The rulers of Calicut understood that the prosperity of their city depended on the satisfaction of visiting merchants.

Ma Huan provides additional detail in this regard. The rajas of Calicut maintained a policy of religious toleration, which, given how much they depended on Muslim officials and merchants, was the only logical policy to follow. And this was in an age when bitter wars were fought between the Muslim-dominated sultanate of Delhi and Hindu Vijayanagara. The rajas also provided for a well-run and honest marketplace by commissioning officials who were responsible for facilitating all commercial transactions and guaranteeing all contracts. Inasmuch as a tax on all sales was paid into the ruler's treasury, it was in his best interest to grease the wheels of trade and to guarantee that once a deal was struck, it was inviolate. The fact that the raja minted gold and silver coins suggests that these policies worked well.

Finally, Ma Huan supports and supplements evidence from the Roteiro regarding Calicut's industries. Pepper production, which was carefully regulated by the state in regard to collection, storage, and sale (although the trees were apparently cultivated in small family garden plots), was a major staple of Calicut's economy. Likewise, Calicut's silk industry produced expensive bolts of silk, and the region was also a major source for coral and gemstones, especially pearls. Despite its native silk production, however, Calicut was a center for trade in Chinese embroidered silk. Apparently the high quality of this product allowed it to compete favorably with Indian silk.

Well, as you can see, interpreting historical sources is not an arcane science or esoteric art. Yes, it is challenging, but it is a skill that you can master. Look at it this way: it is an exercise that mainly requires close attention and common sense. You must first read and study each source carefully and thoroughly. Then, using the evidence you have picked up from the documents and artifacts, answer the Questions for Analysis. It is that straightforward. If you work with us, trusting us to provide you with all of the necessary background information and clues that you need to make sense out of these sources, you will succeed.

One last word: Have fun doing it because you should find it enjoyable to meet the challenge of reconstructing the past through its human records.

PART ONE

An Era of Change and Increased Global Interaction: The Fifteenth Through Seventeenth Centuries

"CHANGE" is a word that can be used to describe each and every era in world history. Wars are won and lost; empires rise and fall; new ideas are discovered and old ones discarded. Only a few eras, however, can be considered true turning points. The two centuries from the 1400s to the 1600s, when changes occurred rapidly and affected every part of the globe, were just such an era.

What changes took place? In politics the 1400s saw the consolidation of authority by the Ming dynasty in China (1368–1644) and the establishment of new empires by the Ottoman Turks in Asia Minor and southeastern Europe; the Aztecs in Central Mexico; and the Incas in South America. More political changes took place in the 1500s and early 1600s, when the Songhai Empire in West Africa, the Safavid Empire in Persia, and the Mughal Empire in India emerged; the Tokugawa clan ended decades of civil war in Japan; and the princes of Muscovy established a unified Russian state. Europe remained politically divided among hundreds of large and small states, but here too important political changes took place, notably the winning of independence by the Netherlands from Spain, the establishment of Spanish control of Italy, religious war in France, and the strengthening of monarchical governments in Spain and England.

Significant religious developments also occurred. In Europe the Protestant challenge to Roman Catholicism brought with it sectarian conflict and religious wars. In India Nanak (1469–1539) drew on Hinduism and Islam to develop a unique religious perspective that became the basis for Sikhism, a religion that today commands the allegiance of millions. Also in India, Bhakti Hinduism, with its emphasis on divine love and devotion to a single god, gained new adherents. In the world of Islam, expansion continued in Africa and Southeast Asia, and Shiism, whose followers viewed Ali, Muhammad's son-in-law, and his heirs as the only legal successors to the Prophet, became the state religion in Persia.

Innovation also took place in other areas. In the realm of ideas, Europe experienced the climax of the Renaissance and the beginnings of the Scientific Revolution. In Asia, Confucian scholarship in China flourished, as did painting and poetry in India, Persia, and the Ottoman Empire. New technologies took root. In Europe printed books (which had appeared in China and Korea centuries earlier) proliferated after the development of printing by movable type by Gutenberg in the 1450s. Across Eurasia gunpowder weapons, first developed in China several centuries earlier, proliferated. International trade increased, and world population grew from approximately 350 million in 1400 to 550 million in 1600, despite catastrophic population losses in the Americas. Even the climate changed. Europe experienced cold, harsh weather in the early 1300s, followed by a century and a half of warming and then a return to colder temperatures in the late 1500s.

Although significant, these changes are not the reason the period from the fifteenth through seventeenth centuries is viewed as a major turning point in world history. The reason lies instead in the upsurge in human interaction and interconnectedness that took place. Although cross-cultural interaction had been a part of human history from its beginnings, the world in 1400 was far from being "one world." It consisted of many worlds—the worlds of China, India, the Middle East, sub-Saharan Africa, and Europe, and two worlds that no one in Africa-Eurasia knew existed, Oceania and the Americas. The people who lived in these "worlds" ate locally grown foods and wore clothes made of locally produced materials. They had distinctive religions and cultures. Outside military threats and political interference were rare or nonexistent, and as a result, their histories followed trajectories that rarely intersected.

By the middle of the seventeenth century, however, the world was quite different. The output of silver mines in Mexico and South America affected the price of silk in China; the growing taste of Europeans for sweets led to the enslavement of Africans on sugar plantations in Brazil and the West Indies; political disorder in China following the collapse of the Ming Dynasty stimulated the porcelain industry in the Netherlands and England; policies adopted by Japanese shoguns and Chinese emperors drew the attention of papal officials in Rome; wealthy Europeans kept warm by wearing coats and hats made from the furs of animals that had been trapped in North America or Siberia; millions of Native Americans died in disease epidemics caused by pathogens imported from Europe and Africa.

In explaining how and why the world became more integrated between the 1400s and 1600s, historians emphasize the role of Europe, specifically Europe's voyages of exploration that began in the early 1400s with the first Portuguese efforts to explore Africa's west coast. By the 1450s the Portuguese added another goal, to reach the Indian Ocean by sailing around the southern tip of Africa. The Portuguese captain Vasco da Gama accomplished this in 1498, 6 years after the Italian mariner in the service of Spain, Christopher Columbus, had discovered the Americas while seeking Asia. During the 1500s and 1600s Europe's worldwide expansion continued. The Portuguese pushed on from East Africa and India to the East Indies, China, and Japan. Spain extended its power in the Americas. The French, Dutch, English, Danes, and Swedes struck claims to lands in the Americas and the Caribbean, and the Dutch challenged the Portuguese in Asia.

The consequences of Europe's expansion were momentous. Millions of Native Americans died from Old World diseases. Survivors immediately or gradually lost their lands and independence, and many were converted to Christianity. The New World became a major grower of tobacco and sugar, and to meet demand, by the middle of the seventeenth century more than a million African slaves had been imported to the Americas to do the work. The world's money supply received a major infusion from American gold and silver, and this resulted in increased investment, international commercial growth, and widespread inflation. The opening of the Americas also had biological consequences. Horses, cattle, swine, and chickens as well as wheat, oats, barley, and fruit trees were introduced to the Americas, while American crops such as potatoes, tomatoes, peppers, and cassava came to be grown in Africa and Eurasia.

As important as it was, Europe's expansion must be kept in perspective. Other surges in global interaction had taken place earlier—for example, in the thirteenth century, when the Mongols conquered a vast Eurasian empire in which merchants, travelers, and ideas moved freely. Some historians would push the first example of global integration back even further, to the Muslim Abbasid Empire, which in its heyday included the Middle East, northern Africa, and the Iberian Peninsula in Europe.

It is also important to note that Europe's global expansion in the 1500s and 1600s did not mean that Europe had become the world's leading power. Europeans achieved dominance only in the Americas, the Philippines, and the Atlantic islands off Africa's west coast, where political disunity, epidemics, and the native people's unsophisticated technology gave them an advantage. In Asia and Africa, they conquered and held a few coastal cities such as Goa in India and Melaka on the Malay Peninsula, but otherwise they carried on commerce from widely separated trading posts, which they held at the pleasure of local rulers. Although Europe had become a new presence in world markets, its overall economic output was dwarfed by that of India and China. Europeans neither grew nor manufactured products that interested Asian buyers, meaning that they paid for their purchases in Asian markets with silver mined in the Americas. Without that silver, European's participation in world trade would have been negligible.

By the mid-seventeenth century, Europeans had changed the world in many ways. But it still was not Europe's world. This would be the case 250 years later, but only after the world had experienced a host of other far-reaching changes.

Chapter 1

Europe in an Age of Conflict and Expansion

FROM THE 1400s THROUGH THE MID-1600s, Europe changed in many ways. Religious uniformity under the Roman Catholic Church gave way to religious diversity as new Protestant churches rejected papal authority and Catholic doctrine. A political order characterized by local aristocratic power, decentralized authority, and weak monarchies was undermined by the emergence of increasingly centralized and fiercely competitive states. Armies grew in size, and battles were fought by soldiers with artillery and firearms in addition to longbows, pikes, and lances. Intellectuals lost interest in the theological and philosophical speculations of their thirteenth-century predecessors, and inspired by new interests in Greek and Roman antiquity, they broke new ground in science, philosophy, and political thought. Writers, artists, and architects developed new styles and themes, and explorers discovered new ocean routes to Africa, Asia, and the Americas.

Taken together, these changes mark the end of the Middle Ages, that long, formative period of European civilization that began with the fall of the Western Roman Empire in the fifth century C.E. These changes are generally viewed as indicators of progress and growth—an age of renaissance, or rebirth—after centuries of medieval stagnation. Such a view is problematic. Aside from belittling the impressive achievements of the Middle Ages, it ignores the many tensions, doubts, and conflicts that accompanied the political, economic, and cultural changes of the immediate post-medieval era.

In the areas of thought and religion, for example, the emergence of Protestantism may ultimately have led to an acceptance of religious diversity and toleration in most of Europe, but in the sixteenth and early seventeenth centuries, it was a cause of war, rebellion, and persecution. Tens of thousands of Europeans were exiled, imprisoned, or executed because of their beliefs, and millions died in the religious wars that stretched from the 1520s to the 1640s. Ideas proposed by Copernicus, Kepler, and Galileo provided the foundation for Europe's Scientific Revolution, and the discoveries of Renaissance humanists broadened Europe's intellectual perspectives by introducing scholars and the educated public to a wide range of previously unknown ancient philosophies. At the time, however, this proliferation of new and contending ideas led to the pessimistic view that humans could know little if anything with certainty. Nor did these scientists' and humanists' discoveries dispel the irrational fears and superstitions of the age. Witch hunts and witch trials claimed the lives of thousands of individuals who supposedly had pledged themselves to the Devil in return for supernatural powers.

The sixteenth century witnessed spectacular economic growth. But inflation caused hardship for landlords and peasants, and around 1600, plague, famine, and war slowed economic growth and caused a decline in Europe's overall standard of living. Political changes also increased tensions. Advocates of centralized monarchy contended with defenders of local autonomy, divine right absolutists faced believers in regicide, and kings battled parliaments. Wars were fought to gain or protect territory, to advance the cause of Catholicism or Protestantism, to settle dynastic claims, or to fulfill personal ambitions. The Thirty Years' War (1618–1648) involved every major European state and caused suffering unmatched in Europe until the wars of the twentieth century.

Expansionist Europe was not a stable, cohesive, and self-confident society. The Europeans, in their efforts to reach Asia by sailing west, luckily discovered the Americas, where the inhabitants were easily subdued after millions of them died from imported diseases. Elsewhere, the Europeans' aggressiveness, single-mindedness, and weaponry enabled them to expand their commercial activities and establish a measure of political power on the fringes of Africa and Asia. But these accomplishments, rightly deemed significant by historians, gave scant comfort to the majority of Europeans, who faced a troubled present and anticipated the future with as much foreboding as hope.

European Expansion: Goals and Motives

The Europeans' explorations, discoveries, and expansion from the fifteenth through the seventeenth centuries had ramifications for people across Eurasia, in much of Africa, and especially in the Americas. A story with elements of bravery, idealism, greed, and cruelty, and an event that brought wealth and power to some but suffering and death to many others, Europe's expansion has been intensively studied and debated from the time it began to the present day. Nonetheless, its meaning and significance are frequently misunderstood.

One misconception about the Age of Expansion is that during the early modern period "expansion and discovery" were unique European accomplishments. In truth, states in other regions also were expanding, and some were expanding into what for them was "unknown territory." The Ottoman Empire grew to incorporate northern Africa, the Arabian Peninsula, and Southeastern Europe. Between 1405 and 1433, China's emperors sponsored a series of maritime expeditions designed to establish a Chinese presence in the Indian Ocean basin. Commanded by Admiral Zheng He, Chinese fleets consisting of 200 ships or more reached the west coast of India, the Arabian Peninsula, and the east coast of Africa. Beginning in the 1500s, Russia began to expand to the east, not halting until by the eighteenth century the Russians had conquered Siberia, reached the Pacific Ocean, and staked claims to Alaska and parts of the North American west coast. The expansion of the Mughals in India, the Aztecs in central Mexico, and the Incas in South America could be added to the list of expansionist states in the early modern era.

Another misconception is that Europe's expansion was somehow the result of Europeans' superiority over the rest of the world's peoples. The Europeans, it is argued, took the lead in overseas exploration because they had better ships, a more sophisticated economy, better organized states, more freedom, and more effective weapons than anyone else in the world. Some would go further to suggest it was the unique adventurous spirit of the Europeans that made the difference. Of all these arguments and assertions, only one holds up under scrutiny: European gunpowder weapons did give them an advantage when faced with resistance from the people they encountered. But this is the only area in which Europe's "superiority" caused or made possible its expansion.

Instead, the causes of Europe's expansion are best understood if the issue is broken down into three questions. First, what developments in ship construction, navigational skills, and geographical knowledge enabled Europeans to sail across the world's oceans? Advances in ship design (ships outfitted with pintle and gudgeon rudders and a combination of triangular and square sails) and improved navigation techniques (better maps and instruments such as the compass, quadrant, astrolabe, and hourglass) are important parts of the story. Second, what advantages did Europeans have in their early encounters with the peoples of Asia, Africa, and the Western Hemisphere? European firearms were important, but other factors, which varied from region to region, also played key roles. In the Americas, susceptibility of the native populations to Old World diseases weakened resistance to the Europeans, as did political and religious divisions in Asia. A third question pertains to motive. What did the Europeans hope to accomplish? The sources in this section provide some of the answers.

The Portuguese Imperial Venture

1 • AFONSO D'ALBUQUERQUE, SPEECH TO MEN OF THE PORTUGUESE FLEET BEFORE THE SECOND ATTACK ON MELAKA (AUGUST 11, 1511)

The exploits of four men dominate the history of early Portuguese exploration: Prince Henry the Navigator (1394–1460), who sponsored the first Portuguese voyages down Africa's west coast; Bartholomeu Dias (1451–1500), who in 1488 first sailed around the tip of Africa; Vasco da Gama (1460–1524), who in 1498 reached India by sailing around Africa; and finally, Afonso d'Albuquerque (1453–1515), who turned these discoveries into a Portuguese commercial empire stretching from Africa to Japan.

Known as the "Caesar of the East," Albuquerque was born in 1453 to aristocratic parents, and served as an officer in the Portuguese army in northern Africa, Castile, and southern Italy before making his first voyage to India in 1503. On his return, he convinced King Manuel I of the feasibility of a plan to monopolize Indian Ocean trade by establishing Portuguese control of the narrow sea passages leading to the Indian Ocean. This meant control of fortified trading posts on Africa's coasts; the island of Socotra (at the entrance to the Red Sea); Hormuz (at the entrance to the Persian Gulf); and Goa (on India's Malabar Coast). Farther east it meant establishing small trading enclaves in the East Indies; taking control of Melaka (also Malacca), the prosperous trading city on the Malay Peninsula; and ultimately opening commercial contacts with China and Japan.

Following a failed Portuguese effort to take Melaka in 1509, Albuquerque returned in 1511 with a fleet of 14 ships and approximately 1,100 men. After the first Portuguese attack on the strongly defended city in late July failed, he delivered the following speech to his officers before a second attack on August 11. His words are recorded in a detailed history of Albuquerque's exploits written by his son, Braz de Albuquerque, sometime after Afonso's death in 1515 and published in 1576 as *Commentarios do Grande Afonso D'albquerque*. In the speech, d'Albuquerque reminds the Portuguese of what is at stake, and in doing so, provides insights into the motives behind the Portuguese imperial enterprise.

QUESTIONS FOR ANALYSIS

1. What appear to be the reasons for the hesitancy of some of Albuquerque's officers and men to support another attack on Melaka?
2. What does Albuquerque believe to be the overall religious importance of the Portuguese effort to take Melaka?
3. What does Albuquerque believe to be the overall economic significance of taking control of Melaka?
4. Why is Albuquerque confident that the Portuguese effort will succeed?

When the great Afonso de Albuquerque had completed all the necessary preparations for renewing the attack on the city, he heard that some of the captains were saying that it was not in the king's interest to keep Malacca or to build a fortress there. When he learnt this, he summoned them to his ship, together with all the noblemen and officers of his fleet, and addressed them thus:

"Gentlemen, you will recall that, when it was agreed that we should attack this city, it was also decided that we should build a fortress here, because we all considered it necessary.

Accordingly, once the city had been taken, I had no intention of abandoning it, and it was only because you advised me to that I called off the attack and withdrew. Now that I am ready, as you see, to go back again and capture the city, I find that you have changed your opinion. . . . Since I have to give my own account of these matters and justify my actions to our lord, King Manuel, I do not wish to be the only one to take the blame for them. There are many reasons I could give you why we should take the city and build a fortress there to keep control of it. However, I will now only put to you two for not going back on what you have agreed.

The first of these is the great service we shall render to Our Lord by throwing the Moslems out of this country and preventing the fire of the Mohammedan sect from spreading any further. I hope in Our Lord[1] that, as a result of our doing this, the Moslems may be driven out of India[2] altogether, because most, if not all, of them live from the trade of this country and so have become powerful and rich and the owners of great treasures. I believe that the king of Malacca [Sultan Mahmud Shah] will not attempt to negotiate terms with us in order to safeguard his position. He has once already suffered defeat and experienced our strength and now, after sixteen days have passed, is no longer able to hope that any help will come to him from outside. I also believe that Our Lord will close his mind and harden his heart, because he wants this business of Malacca to be brought to a conclusion so as to open the route through the Straits [of Melaka] to us. The king of Portugal has often commanded me to go to the Straits, because it seemed to His Highness that this was the best place to intercept the trade which the Moslems of Cairo and of Mecca and Jiddah[3] carry on in these parts. So it was to do Our Lord's service that we were brought here; by taking Malacca, we would close the Straits so that never again would the Moslems be able to bring their spices by this route.

The other reason I put to you is the great service that we shall do to King Manuel by taking this city. It is the source of all the spices and drugs that the Moslems ship from here each year to the Straits, without our being able to stop them. If we cut them off from their traditional market, there will be no port or other place in the region as convenient as this that they can use. Since we gained control of the Malabar [southwest Indian] pepper trade, Cairo has not received any except what the Moslems have been able to take from this region. Forty of fifty [ships] sail every year from here bound for Mecca, laden with all kinds of spices. They cannot be prevented without great expense and large fleets constantly patrolling the Gulf of Cape Comorin.[4]

Source: T. F. Earle and John Villiers, trans. and eds., *Albuquerque Caesar of the East* (Warminster, England: Aris & Phillips, 1990), pp. 79–82. Reprinted by permission of Oxbow Books.

[1] "Our Lord" refers to Jesus Christ, not "our lord," the king of Portugal.

[2] A term used for the general region of South and Southeast Asia.

[3] Jiddah (also Jeddah) is the major port city on the Arabian side of the Red Sea. Mecca, where Muhammad received his revelations, was a caravan center and the destination of Muslim pilgrims from around the world. It was some 50 miles inland from Jiddah.

[4] The Gulf of Cape Comorin is off the southernmost tip of India.

Malabar pepper, of which they might have some expectations, because the king of Calicut is their ally, is in our control under the eyes of the [Portuguese] governor of India, and the Moslems cannot take so much from there as they suppose. I am very sure that, if this Malacca trade is taken out of their hands, Cairo and Mecca will be completely lost and no spices will go to the Venetians except those that they go to Portugal to buy.

If it seems to you that Malacca, being a great city with a large population, will be difficult to hold, you need have no misgivings on that score. Once the city has been taken, all the rest of the kingdom is so small that the king would have no source of reinforcements. If you fear that the capture of the city will entail great expense and that then there will be nowhere where our men and ships can be re-equipped, I trust in God's mercy that, once we have gained mastery of Malacca with a fine fortress, and provided that the Portuguese crown appoints someone who knows well how to govern it and to make it grow rich, all its expenses will be met from local taxes. Once the merchants who frequent Malacca and are accustomed to live under the tyranny of the Malays have had a taste of our justice and honesty, our plain-dealing and clemency and see the decrees of King Manuel, our lord,

in which he commands that all their vassals in these parts be well treated, I am convinced that they will come and settle here and build . . . their houses. All the things I am proposing to you are summed up in this one key point, which is that we build a fortress in this city of Malacca and hold it, that this country be governed by the Portuguese and that King Manuel be recognized as its rightful king. I therefore beg you as a favour to consider well the enterprise you have in hand and not to let it be lost."

When Afonso de Albuquerque had finished his discourse, as I have recorded it, the members of his council put forward varying opinions, some for and some against him. The result of their discussion was that the majority repeated their conviction that is was in the king's service to take the city of Malacca, to expel the Moslems, and to build a fortress there.

Afonso de Albuquerque . . . , took the side of the majority and decided to attack Malacca and secure his position there. He decided to leave all the questions which had been raised on the other side in the hands of Our Lord Jesus Christ, because he would dispose everything according to his will. He ordered the secretary to draw up an agreement, which he and all the captains, noblemen and knights who were present signed.

1492: What Columbus and His Patrons Hoped to Gain

2 • FERDINAND OF ARAGON AND ISABELLA OF CASTILE, AGREEMENTS WITH COLUMBUS, APRIL 17 AND APRIL 30, 1492

Among the many factors that contributed to Europe's expansion in the early modern period, perhaps none was more important than simple human ambition. There is no better example of this truth than Christopher Columbus, the Genoese mariner credited with the discovery of the New World. The best available evidence suggests that Columbus was born in 1451 into a weaver's family and went to sea as a teenager. As a young sailor, he gained experience with voyages as far north as Ireland, as far south as Mina on the Gulf of Guinea, and as far west as the Azores, an island grouping some 800 miles west of Portugal. Having taught himself to read, he studied geographical texts, maps, and even biblical passages that provided him with a set of assumptions concerning the circumference of the earth, the size of Europe, and the distance of Japan from the Asian mainland. Although inaccurate, these assumptions convinced him it would be possible to reach Asia by sailing west into the Atlantic. In 1484, Columbus sought support for an exploratory voyage from King John (João) II of Portugal (r. 1481–1495), but the king was convinced that sailing around Africa was the more promising route to Asia, and refused.

Undeterred, in 1486 Columbus gained an audience with the Spanish monarchs Ferdinand and Isabella, who on hearing Columbus's proposal gave him a small stipend and appointed a commission of "learned men and mariners" to examine his plan. For 5 years, he followed the Spanish court from city to city, awaiting a final decision. Negotiations broke down in early 1492, when the monarchs balked at Columbus's demands. With Columbus preparing to take his ideas to the king of France, a last-minute appeal to Isabella resulted in an agreement. In two capitulations (in this sense, simply a set of terms for an agreement, not an "act of surrender") issued by Ferdinand and Isabella in April 1492, Columbus was promised a large share of any economic benefits that might accrue from his voyage and extensive authority over any lands he might discover. The monarchs also stood to benefit. Preparations could now begin for Columbus's historic voyage, which departed the Spanish port of Palos on August 3, 1492.

Columbus never realized his dreams of wealth and power. After his discoveries failed to produce either the gold or rich commercial opportunities he had promised, he lost favor at court, and from 1495 onward, the agreements of 1492 were simply ignored by the monarchs. Columbus made his fourth and last voyage across the Atlantic in 1502, 4 years before he died in Valladolid, Spain, still pressing his claims with the crown and still convinced he had reached Asia.

QUESTIONS FOR ANALYSIS

1. What assumptions underlie Columbus's and the monarchs' statements concerning the authority they expect to exercise in the lands Columbus discovers?
2. What kinds of authority will Columbus exercise over the lands he discovers? What role will be played by the monarchs?
3. What kind of material benefits do Columbus and the monarchs expect to gain from Columbus's discoveries? How will these gains be divided?
4. How do the stated and implied goals of Columbus's enterprise compare with the motives of Albuquerque in the conquest of Melaka?

Agreement of April 17, 1492

The things supplicated and which your Highnesses give and declare to Christopher Columbus

in some satisfaction . . . for the voyage which now, with the aid of God, he is about to make therein, in the service of your Highnesses, are as follows:

Source: J. B. Thatcher, *Christopher Columbus, His Life and Work* (New York and London: Putnam's Sons, 1903), vol. 2, pp. 442–451.

Firstly, that your Highnesses as Lords that are of the said oceans, make from this time the said Don [Lord] Christopher Columbus your Admiral in all those islands and mainlands which by his hand and industry shall be discovered or acquired in the said oceans, during his life, and after his death, his heirs and successors, from one to another perpetually, with all the pre-eminences and prerogatives belonging to the said office. . .

Likewise, that your Highnesses make the said Don Christopher your Viceroy and Governor General in all the said islands and mainlands and islands which as has been said, he may discover or acquire in the said seas; and that for the government of each one and of any one of them, he may make selection of three persons for each office, and that your Highnesses may choose and select the one who shall be most serviceable to you, and thus the lands which our Lord shall permit him to discover and acquire will be better governed, in the service of your Highnesses. . .

Item, that all and whatever merchandise, whether it be pearls, precious stones, gold, silver, spices, and other things whatsoever, and merchandise of whatever kind, name, and manner it may be, which may be bought, bartered, discovered, acquired, or obtained within the limits of the said Admiralty, your Highnesses grant henceforth to the said Don Christopher, and will that he may have and take for himself, the tenth part of all of them, deducting all the expenses which may be incurred therein; so that of what shall remain free and clear, he may have and take the tenth part for himself, and do with it as he wills, the other nine parts remaining for your Highnesses. . . .

Item, that in all the vessels which may be equipped for the said traffic and negotiation each time and whenever and as often as they may be equipped, the said Admiral Don Christopher Columbus may, if be wishes, contribute and pay the eighth part of all that may be expended in the equipment. And also that he may have and take of the profit, the eighth part of all which may result from such equipment. . . .

These are executed and despatched with the responses of your Highnesses at the end of each article in the town of Santa Fe de la Vega de Granada, on the seventeenth day of April in the year of the nativity of our Savior Jesus Christ one thousand four hundred and ninety-two.

Agreement of April 30, 1492

Forasmuch as you, Christopher Columbus, are going by our command, with some of our ships and with our subjects, to discover and acquire certain islands and mainland in the ocean, and it is hoped that, by the help of God, some of the said islands and mainland in the said ocean will be discovered and acquired by your pains and industry; and therefore it is a just and reasonable thing that since you incur the said danger for our service you should be rewarded for it . . . it is our will and pleasure that you, the said Christopher Columbus, after you have discovered and acquired the said islands and mainland in the said ocean, or any of them whatsoever, shall be our Admiral of the said islands and mainland and Viceroy and Governor therein, and shall be empowered from that time forward to call and entitle yourself Don Christopher Columbus, and that your sons and successors in the said office and charge may likewise entitle and call themselves Don, and Admiral and Viceroy and Governor thereof; and that you may have power to use and exercise the said office of Admiral, together with the said office of Viceroy and Governor of the said islands and mainland . . . and to hear and determine all the suits and causes civil and criminal appertaining to the said office of Admiralty, Viceroy, and Governor according as you shall find by law, . . . and may have power to punish and chastise delinquents, and exercise the said offices . . . in all that concerns and appertains to the said offices . . . and that you shall have and levy the fees and salaries annexed, belonging and appertaining to the said offices and to each of them, according as our High Admiral in the Admiralty of our kingdoms levies and is accustomed to levy them.

Why England Should Sponsor Colonies

3 • RICHARD HAKLUYT, A DISCOURSE ON WESTERN PLANTING

Although King Henry VII and a group of Bristol merchants had dispatched the Italian mariner Giovanni Caboto (in English, John Cabot) to North America in 1497 to search for what came to be known as the Northwest Passage to Asia, no further exploration under English auspices took place until the reign of Elizabeth I (r. 1558–1603). England's renewed efforts were not auspicious. Backed by a group of investors who formed the Company of Cathay (China), Martin Frobisher made three voyages to North America between 1576 and 1578 in search of gold and the Northwest Passage, but found neither. Five years later, an effort promoted by Sir Humphrey Gilbert to colonize North America ended in tragedy when the expedition was lost at sea while sailing south from Newfoundland. These setbacks failed to discourage a small group of merchants, mariners, and courtiers who continued to devise plans for colonization and promote them at Elizabeth's court.

Included in this group was Richard Hakluyt (1552–1616), the son of a London merchant who was orphaned at the age of 5 and raised by a cousin, a lawyer. Through contacts with his cousin's friends and business associates, the young man developed an interest in trade and exploration. Although he studied Greek and Latin at Oxford University, his passion was geography, which he learned from books, maps, and reports from mariners, merchants, and explorers. Ordained a priest in the Church of England, Hakluyt still had time to write books on exploration and lobby Queen Elizabeth and her officials on behalf of various proposals to colonize North America.

In 1584, he wrote a lengthy memorandum to the queen in support of a proposal by Sir Walter Raleigh to colonize Norumbega, or the east coast of North America. Elizabeth granted Raleigh a charter but declined to support the expedition financially, and thin funding was one of several reasons why the Roanoke Colony failed. Hakluyt and others continued to lobby on behalf of their ideas, however, and during the reign of James I (r. 1603–1625) the chartering of the Virginia Company and Plymouth Company marked the true beginnings of the English colonization of North America.

The following excerpt is the concluding summary to Hakluyt's 1584 memorandum to Elizabeth.

QUESTIONS FOR ANALYSIS

1. According to Hakluyt, what economic advantages might England expect from colonizing Norumbega?
2. According to Hakluyt, how will colonization strengthen England and weaken its rivals?
3. According to Hakluyt, how will colonization help solve England's domestic problems?
4. How important is religion in Hakluyt's thinking about colonization?
5. How much concrete knowledge of the Americas does Hakluyt seem to have?

A brief collection of certain reasons to induce her Majesty and the state to take in hand the western voyage and the planting there.

1. The soil yields and may be made to yield all the several commodities of Europe. . . .

2. The passage thither and home is neither too long nor too short, but easy, and to be made twice in the year.

3. The passage cuts not near the trade of any prince, nor near any of their countries or territories, and is a safe passage, and not easy to be annoyed [interfered with] by prince or potentate whatsoever.

4. The passage is to be performed at all times of the year, and in that respect passes our trades in the Levant Seas within the Straits of Gibraltar, and the trades in the seas within the King of Denmark's Strait,[1] and the trades to the ports of Norway and of Russia, etc. . . .

5. And where England now for certain hundred years last passed, by the peculiar [distinctive] commodity of wool, and of later years, by clothing of the same, has raised itself from meaner state to greater wealth and much higher honor, might, and power than before, to the equaling of the princes of the same to the greatest potentates of this part of the world; it comes now so to pass that by the great endeavor of the increase of the trade of wool in Spain and in the West Indies, now daily more and more multiplying, that the wool of England, and the cloth made of the same, will become base [inferior], and every day more base than [the] other; which, prudently weighed, it behooves this realm, if it mean not to return to former old means and baseness, but to stand in present and late former honor, glory, and force, and not negligently and sleepingly to slide into beggary, to foresee and to plant at Norumbega or some like place, were it not for anything else but for the hope of the sale of our wool. . . .

6. This enterprise may stay the Spanish king from flowing over all the face of that waste [wild and uninhabited] firmament of America, if we seed and plant there in time. . . . And England possessing the purposed [proposed] place of planting, her Majesty may, by the benefit of the seat, having won good and royal havens, have plenty of excellent trees for masts, of goodly timber to build ships and to make great navies, of pitch, tar, hemp, and all things incident for a navy royal, and that for no price, and without money or request. How easy a matter may it be to this realm, swarming at this day with valiant youths, rusting [degenerating] and hurtful by lack of employment, and having good makers of cable and of all sorts of cordage,[2] and the best and most cunning shipwrights of the world, to be lords of all those seas, and to spoil Philip's Indian navy,[3] and to deprive him of yearly passage of his treasure to Europe, and consequently to abate the pride of Spain and of the supporter of the great Anti-christ of Rome,[4] and to pull him down in equality to his neighbor princes, and consequently to cut off the common mischiefs that come to all Europe by the peculiar abundance of his Indian treasure, and this without difficulty.

Source: Richard Hakluyt, "A Discourse on Western Planting," in Charles Deane and Leonard Woods, *Documentary History of the State of Maine* (Collections of the Maine Historical Society, 2nd series, vol. 2, 1877).

[1]The Levant Sea refers to the area of the eastern Mediterranean; the "seas within the King of Denmark's Strait" refers to the Baltic Sea.

[2]Ropes used in rigging sailing ships.

[3]Phillip II, king of Spain from 1556 to 1598; his "Indian navy" refers to Spanish ships carrying gold, silver, and other commodities between Europe and America.

[4]The pope.

7. This voyage, albeit it may be accomplished by bark or smallest pinnace[5] . . . yet for the distance, for burden[6] and gain in trade, the merchant will not for profit's sake use it but by ships of great burden; so as this realm shall have by that means ships of great burden and of great strength for the defense of this realm. . . .

9. The great mass of wealth of the realm embarked in the merchants' ships, carried out in this new course, shall not lightly, in so far distant a course from the coast of Europe, be driven by winds and tempests into ports of any foreign princes, as the Spanish ships of late years have been into our ports of the West countries, etc. . . .

10. No foreign commodity that comes into England comes without payment of custom once, twice, or thrice, before it comes into the realm, and so all foreign commodities become dearer to the subjects of this realm; and by this course to Norumbega foreign princes' customs are avoided; and the foreign commodities cheaply purchased, they become cheap to the subjects of England, to the common benefit of the people, and to the saving of great treasure in the realm; whereas now the realm becomes poor by the purchasing of foreign commodities in so great a mass at so excessive prices.

11. At the first traffic [trade] with the people of those parts, the subjects of this realm for many years shall change many cheap commodities of these parts for things of high value there not esteemed; and this to the great enriching of the realm, if common use fail not.

12. By the great plenty of those regions the merchants and their factors [agents] shall lie there cheap, buy and repair their ships

cheap, and shall return at pleasure without stay or restraint of foreign prince; whereas upon stays and restraints the merchant raiseth his charge in sale over of his ware. . . .

13. By making of ships and by preparing of things for the same, by making of cables and cordage, by planting of vines and olive trees, and by making of wine and oil, by husbandry, and by thousands of things there to be done, infinite numbers of the English nation may be set on work, to the unburdening of the realm with many that now live chargeable to the state at home.

14. If the sea coast serve for making of salt, and the inland for wine, oils, oranges, lemons, figs, &c., and for making of iron, all which with much more is hoped, without sword drawn, we shall cut the comb[7] of the French, of the Spanish, of the Portuguese, and of enemies, and of doubtful friends, to the abating of their wealth and force, and to the greater saving of the wealth of the realm.

15. The substances serving, we may out of those parts receive the mass of wrought wares that now we receive out of France, Flanders, Germany, &c.; and so we may daunt [subdue] the pride of some enemies of this realm, or at the least in part purchase those wares, that now we buy dearly of the French and Flemish, better cheap; and in the end, for the part that this realm was wont to receive, drive them out of trade to idleness for the setting of our people on work.

16. We shall by planting there enlarge the glory of the gospel, and from England plant sincere religion, and provide a safe and a sure place to receive people from all parts of the world that are forced to flee for the truth of God's word.

---

[5]Barks and pinnaces are small sailing ships.
[6]Capacity of ships for carrying cargo.

[7]Comb refers to the red crest of a rooster. To "cut one's comb" is to humble or humiliate someone.

17. If frontier wars there chance to arise, and if thereupon we shall fortify, it will occasion the training up of our youth in the discipline of war, and make a number fit for the service of the wars and for the defence of our people there and at home.

18. The Spaniards govern in the Indies with all pride and tyranny; and like as when people of contrary nature at sea enter into galleys, where men are tied as slaves, all yell and cry with one voice, *Liberta, liberta,* as desirous of liberty and freedom, so no doubt whensoever the Queen of England, a prince of such clemency, shall seat upon that firmament of America, and shall be reported throughout all that tract to use the natural people there with all humanity, courtesy, and freedom, they will yield themselves to her government, and revolt clean from the Spaniard. . . .

19. The present short [insufficient] trades cause the mariner to be cast off, and often to be idle, and so by poverty to fall to piracy. But this course to Norumbega being longer, and a continuance of the employment of the mariner, doth keep the mariner from idleness and from necessity; and so it cuts off the principal actions of piracy, and the rather because no rich prey for them to take comes directly in their course or anything near their course.

20. Many men of excellent wits and of diverse singular gifts, overthrown by suretyship [indebtedness] or by some folly of youth, that are not able to live in England, may there be raised again, and do their country good service; and many needful uses there may (to great purpose) require the saving of great numbers, that for trifles may otherwise be devoured by the gallows.

21. Many soldiers, in the end of the wars, that might be hurtful to this realm, may there be unladen, to the common profit and quiet of this realm, and to our foreign benefit there, as they may be employed.

22. The fry[8] of the wandering beggars of England, that grow up idly, and hurtful and burdenous to this realm, may there be unladen, better bred up, and may people waste countries to the home and foreign benefit, and to their own more happy state. . . .

---

[8] A "swarm" or crowd of insignificant persons.

Religious Controversy in the Reformation Era

During the High Middle Ages, "the Age of Faith," the devotion accorded the Catholic Church resulted in part from the clergy's moral example and leadership and in part from the Church's promise that its doctrines and practices, if followed, ensured eternal salvation. During the fourteenth and fifteenth centuries, however, the Church was rocked by schism, scandal, deficits, political challenges, and uninspired and corrupt leadership. Anger over such abuses intensified, and many Europeans began to question the Church's ability to deliver the salvation they fervently sought. These doubts go far in explaining the success of the Protestant revolt, sparked in 1517 when a German friar, Martin Luther, challenged Catholic teachings, especially the doctrine that people could atone for their sins by purchasing indulgences. By 1650, Protestants dominated northern Germany, Scandinavia, England, Scotland, the Netherlands, and major Swiss cities and were a significant minority in France and parts of central Europe.

No area of European life was unaffected by the Protestant Reformation. In the religious sphere, new Protestant churches proliferated, and Catholic reforms revitalized an institution that had lost its spiritual focus and vitality. Education expanded because of the Protestants' emphasis on Bible reading by the laity and the needs of churches for educated leadership. Literacy among women increased as a result of Protestant educational efforts, and according to some historians, a more positive view of women resulted from the Protestant affirmation of clerical marriage. Conversely, Protestant women made no appreciable legal or economic gains and were just as likely as their Catholic sisters to be victimized by witch hunts and witch trials. The religious struggles of the Reformation era also affected politics. With religious passions exacerbating dynastic rivalries and internal conflicts, Europe endured a century of religious wars, including both civil wars and wars between states.

Most importantly, the Reformation era contributed to Europe's ongoing secularization. In the short run, the Protestant and Catholic reformations intensified religious feeling and thrust religion into the forefront of European life. In the long run, however, the proliferation of competing faiths divided and weakened Europe's churches, and the long years of religious intolerance and war discredited religion in the eyes of many. The gradual acceptance of religious diversity within individual states and Europe as a whole was a sign of growing secularism. Paradoxically, the very intensity of the era's religious passions ultimately weakened the role of religion in European life and thought.

A Protestant View of Christianity

4 • MARTIN LUTHER, TABLE TALK

The Protestant Reformation had many voices, but its first prophet was Martin Luther (1483–1546), whose Ninety-Five Theses of 1517 sparked the momentous anti-Catholic rebellion. Born into the family of a German miner and educated at the University of Erfurt, Luther was preparing for a career as a lawyer when suddenly, in 1505, he changed course and became an Augustinian friar. Luther's decision followed a terrifying experience in a thunderstorm but at a deeper level resulted from his dissatisfaction over his relationship with God and doubts about his salvation. He hoped that life as a friar would shield him from the world's temptations and allow him to win God's favor by devoting himself to prayer, study, and the sacraments. His spiritual doubts remained, however. Intensely conscious of his inadequacies and failings, he was convinced he could never earn his salvation or live up to the high standards of selflessness, charity, and purity prescribed by Jesus' teachings and the Catholic Church. He despaired of ever satisfying an angry, judging God and was terrorized by the prospect of eternal damnation.

During the 1510s, however, while teaching theology at the University of Wittenberg, Luther found spiritual peace through his reflections on the Scriptures. He concluded that weak, sinful human beings were incapable of earning their salvation by leading blameless lives and performing the pious acts enjoined by the Catholic Church. Rather, he came to view salvation as an unmerited divine gift, resulting from God-implanted faith in Jesus, especially in the redemptive power of his death and resurrection. This doctrine of "justification by faith alone" inspired the Ninety-Five Theses, in which Luther attacked Catholic teaching, especially the doctrine of indulgences, which taught that people could atone for their sins and ensure their own and their loved ones' salvation by contributing money to the Church. Within 5 years after posting the theses, Luther was the recognized leader of a religious movement—Protestantism—that broke with the Catholic Church not only over the theology of salvation but also over a host of other issues concerning Christianity and the Christian life.

As Protestantism spread to other parts of Europe, Luther remained in Wittenberg as a pastor and professor and wrote hundreds of sermons, books, and treatises in defense of his beliefs. He and his wife, Katharina, a former nun, made their home in the Augustinian convent where Luther had lived as a friar. Here they raised a family and entertained scores of visitors with whom Luther discussed the issues of the day. From 1522 to 1546, some of these guests recorded Luther's most notable sayings as they remembered them, and from their journals we have what is known as Luther's *Tischreden* or *Table Talk*.

QUESTIONS FOR ANALYSIS

1. According to Luther, what role should the Bible play in a Christian's life? In his view, how does the Roman Catholic Church obscure the Bible's meaning and message?
2. What does Luther mean by "good works"? Why does he believe that the Roman Catholic Church distorts the role of good works in a Christian's life?
3. What role does faith play in a Christian's life, according to Luther? Why is he convinced that faith is superior to external acts of devotion?
4. What are Luther's criticisms of the pope and other high officials of the Catholic Church?
5. Why does Luther single out monks and members of religious orders for special criticism? What are their shortcomings?

Salvation and Damnation

Because as the everlasting, merciful God, through his Word[1] and Sacraments,[2] talks and deals with us, all other creatures excluded, not of temporal things which pertain to this vanishing life . . .

but as to where we shall go when we depart from here, and gives unto us his Son for a Savior, delivering us from sin and death, and purchasing for us everlasting righteousness, life, and salvation, therefore it is most certain, that we do not

---

Source: From *The Reformation Writings of Martin Luther*, vol. 1, *The Basis of the Protestant Reformation*, translated and edited by Bertram Lee Woolf (London: Lutterworth Press, 1953). Reprinted with permission of Lutterworth Press.

[1]The *Word* is God's message, especially as revealed through Jesus' life.

[2]Sacraments are sacred rites that are outward visible signs of an inward spiritual grace to which the promise of Christ is attached. Of the seven Catholic sacraments, Luther retained two, baptism and the Eucharist.

die away like the beasts that have no understanding; but so many of us . . . shall through him be raised again to life everlasting at the last day, and the ungodly to everlasting destruction.

Faith versus Good Works

He that goes from the gospel to the law,[3] thinking to be saved by good works,[4] falls as uneasily as he who falls from the true service of God to idolatry; for, without Christ, all is idolatry and fictitious imaginings of God, whether of the Turkish Quran, of the pope's decrees, or Moses' laws; if a man think thereby to be justified and saved before God, he is undone.

• • •

The gospel preaches nothing of the merit of works; he that says the gospel requires works for salvation, I say, flat and plain, is a liar.

Nothing that is properly good proceeds out of the works of the law, unless grace be present; for what we are forced to do, goes not from the heart, nor is acceptable.

• • •

A Capuchin[5] says: wear a grey coat and a hood, a rope round thy body, and sandals on thy feet. A Cordelier says: put on a black hood; an ordinary papist says: do this or that work, hear mass, pray, fast, give alms, etc. But a true Christian says: I am justified and saved only by faith in Christ, without any works or merits of my own; compare these together, and judge which is the true righteousness.

• • •

I have often been resolved to live uprightly, and to lead a true godly life, and to set everything aside that would hinder this, but it was far from being put in execution; even as it was with Peter,[6] when he swore he would lay down his life for Christ.

• • •

I will not lie or dissemble before my God, but will freely confess, I am not able to effect that good which I intend, but await the happy hour when God shall be pleased to meet me with his grace.

• • •

A Christian's worshiping is not the external, hypocritical mask that our friars wear, when they chastise their bodies, torment and make themselves faint, with ostentatious fasting, watching, singing, wearing hair shirts, scourging themselves, etc. Such worshiping God does not desire.

The Bible

Great is the strength of the divine Word. In the epistle to the Hebrews,[7] it is called "a two-edged sword." But we have neglected and scorned the pure and clear Word, and have drunk not of the fresh and cool spring; we are gone from the clear fountain to the foul puddle, and drunk its filthy water; that is, we have diligently read old writers and teachers, who went about with speculative reasonings, like the monks and friars.

• • •

The ungodly papists prefer the authority of the church far above God's Word; a blasphemy

---

[3]By *law* Luther meant religious rules and regulations; he believed that futile human efforts to live strictly according to the dictates of the law undermined true faith.

[4]All the ceremonies and pious activities such as pilgrimages, relic veneration, and attendance at Mass that the Catholic Church promoted as vehicles of God's grace and eternal salvation.

[5]The Capuchins and Cordeliers were both branches of the Franciscan religious order noted for their austerity and strict poverty. A distinctive feature of the Capuchins' dress was their peaked hood, or *capuche*.

[6]One of Jesus' 12 apostles. Following Jesus' arrest by Roman soldiers before his crucifixion, Peter three times denied any relationship with Jesus, despite having vowed shortly before to lay down his life for his teacher. Eventually, Peter died a martyr in Rome.

[7]Paul's Letter to the Hebrews, a part of the Christian Bible, or New Testament.

abominable and not to be endured; void of all shame and piety, they spit in God's face. Truly, God's patience is exceeding great, in that they are not destroyed; but so it always has been.

The Papacy and the Monastic Orders

How does it happen that the popes pretend that they form the Church, when, all the while, they are bitter enemies of the Church, and have no knowledge, certainly no comprehension, of the holy gospel? Pope, cardinals, bishops, not a soul of them has read the Bible; it is a book unknown to them. They are a pack of guzzling, gluttonous wretches, rich, wallowing in wealth and laziness, resting secure in their power, and never, for a moment, thinking of accomplishing God's will.

• • •

Kings and princes coin money only out of metals, but the pope coins money out of everything— indulgences, ceremonies, dispensations, pardons; all fish come to his net. . . .

• • •

A gentleman being at the point of death, a monk from the next convent came to see what he could pick up, and said to the gentleman: Sir, will you give so and so to our monastery? The dying man, unable to speak, replied by a nod of the head, whereupon the monk, turning to the gentleman's son, said: You see, your father makes us this bequest. The son said to the father: Sir, is it your pleasure that I kick this monk down the stairs? The dying man nodded as before, and the son immediately drove the monk out of doors.

• • •

The papists took the invocation of saints from the pagans, who divided God into numberless images and idols, and ordained to each its particular office ansd work. . . .

The invocation of saints is a most abominable blindness and heresy; yet the papists will not give it up. The pope's greatest profit arises from the dead; for the calling on dead saints brings him infinite sums of money and riches, far more than he gets from the living. . . .

• • •

In Italy, the monasteries are very wealthy. There are but three or four monks to each; the surplus of their revenues goes to the pope and his cardinals.

• • •

The fasting of the friars is more easy to them than our eating to us. For one day of fasting there are three of feasting. Every friar for his supper has two quarts of beer, a quart of wine, and spice-cakes, or bread prepared with spice and salt, the better to relish their drink. Thus go on these poor fasting brethren; getting so pale and wan, they are like the fiery angels.

• • •

In Popedom they make priests, not to preach and teach God's Word, but only to celebrate mass, and to roam about with the sacrament. For, when a bishop ordains a man, he says: Take the power to celebrate mass, and to offer it for the living and the dead. But we ordain priests according to the command of Christ and St. Paul, namely, to preach the pure gospel and God's Word. The papists in their ordinations make no mention of preaching and teaching God's Word, therefore their consecrating and ordaining is false and wrong, for all worshiping which is not ordained of God, or erected by God's Word and command, is worthless, yea, mere idolatry.

The Reform of the Church

The pope and his crew can in no way endure the idea of reformation; the mere word creates more alarm at Rome than thunderbolts from heaven or the day of judgment. A cardinal said the other day: Let them eat, and drink, and do what they will; but as to reforming us, we think that is a vain idea; we will not endure it. Neither will we Protestants be satisfied, though they administer the sacrament in both kinds, and permit priests to marry;[8] we will also have the doctrine of the faith pure and unfalsified, and the righteousness that justifies and saves before God, and which expels and drives away all idolatry and false-worshiping; with these gone and banished, the foundation on which Popedom is built also falls.

* * *

The chief cause that I fell out with the pope was this: the pope boasted that he was the head of the church, and condemned all that would not be under his power and authority. . . . Further, he took upon him power, rule, and authority over the Christian church, and over the Holy Scriptures, the Word of God; no man must presume to expound the Scriptures, but only he, and according to his ridiculous conceits; this was not to be endured. They who, against God's word, boast of the church's authority, are mere idiots.

---

[8]Two of the many changes that Protestants demanded were allowing all Christians to receive the sacrament of the Eucharist in the forms of bread and wine (in medieval Roman Catholic practice, only the priest drank the Eucharistic wine) and allowing priests to marry. The principle behind both changes was Luther's teaching that all Christians are in a sense priests—that is, responsible for their own religious faith.

Art as Protestant Propaganda

5 • LUCAS CRANACH THE YOUNGER, TWO KINDS OF PREACHING: EVANGELICAL AND PAPAL

Some 70 years before Luther posted his Ninety-five Theses, another German, Johannes Gutenberg (ca. 1395–1468), perfected a method of printing books through movable metal type. Printing shops soon were established in Europe's major towns and cities, and by the middle of the sixteenth century hundreds of thousands of books and pamphlets had been published.

Many of these publications played key roles in the era's religious struggles. The Ninety-Five Theses, intended by Luther to spark academic debate at the University of Wittenberg, brought him instant prominence when they were translated into German and made available in inexpensive printed editions. Subsequently, Protestants, much more than Catholics, used the printed page to promote their ideas in Latin treatises for learned audiences and, more tellingly, in German books and pamphlets for the general population. Illustrations in the form of woodcuts were included in many of these works to make Protestant teachings accessible even to the illiterate.

One of the most famous of these illustrations is *Two Kinds of Preaching: Evangelical and Papal,* the work of a lifelong resident of Wittenberg and a close friend of Luther's, Lucas Cranach the Younger (1515–1586). Produced in 1547, it was distributed as a broadsheet—a single large printed sheet sold for a few small coins.

We have reproduced the woodcut on two pages, but in its original form it is undivided. The preacher facing left is Luther. Before him rests an open Bible, and on his side of the pulpit are words from the New Testament Book of Acts: "All prophets attest to this, that there is no other name in heaven than that of Christ." Above Luther is a dove, representing the Holy Spirit, the third person of the Holy Trinity, whose major functions are illumination, solace, and sanctification. Luther is pointing

Lucas Cranach the Younger, Two Kinds of Preaching: Evangelical

Lucas Cranach the Younger, Two Kinds of Preaching: Papal

to three figures: the Paschal Lamb (a symbol of the risen Christ), the crucified Christ, and God the Father, who holds an orb symbolizing his dominion over creation. The crucified Christ directs the following words to God the Father: "Holy Father, save them. I have sacrificed myself for them with my wounds." Directly below is written, "If we sin, we have an advocate before God, so let us turn in consolation to this means of grace." In the center and lower left corner, the two Lutheran sacraments, baptism and the Eucharist, are depicted. It is noteworthy that in celebrating the Eucharist, the Lutheran pastor offers to laypeople both the communion wafer, representing Christ's body, and also wine, representing Christ's blood, as opposed to the Catholic practice of restricting the drinking of the wine to the priest. Above the communion table and to the left of the crucified Christ are the words uttered by Christ at the Last Supper according to Matthew 26: "Drink of it, all of you."

The right side of the woodcut is a Lutheran perspective on how Roman Catholicism has perverted Christianity. The preaching friar receives inspiration from an imp-like demon that pumps air into his ear with a bellows. The words above him claim that the practices going on about him are theologically sound and offer an easy path to salvation. His audience consists mainly of clergy, with only a handful of laypeople. In the upper right corner, God rains down thunderbolts while Francis of Assisi, the founder of the Franciscan order and a revered medieval saint, attempts in vain to intercede on behalf of wayward humanity. The rest of the scene ridicules various Catholic practices. They include, in the lower right corner, the sale of indulgences by the pope, who holds a sign reading: "Because the coin rings, the soul to heaven springs." The sign on the money bag reads: "This is shame and vice, squeezed from your donations." Directly behind the pope is a priest celebrating a private Mass and an altar being consecrated by a birdlike demon. In the background is a dying man having his hair clipped in the style of a monk and having a monk's cowl, or hood, placed on his head, steps that supposedly would ensure his salvation. The attending nun sprinkles the man with holy water and holds a banner reading: "The cowl, the tonsure, and the water aid you." To the right of this scene, a bishop consecrates a bell. In the far background, two pilgrims approach a small chapel, around which marches a procession honoring the saint depicted on the banner. To Lutherans, all these practices represent misguided rituals that replace faith with meaningless "works."

QUESTIONS FOR ANALYSIS

1. What differences do you see in the makeup of the crowds surrounding the pulpits on the two sides of the picture? What point is Cranach trying to make?
2. What views of the Bible are presented in the woodcuts?
3. Examine the attire of the clergy crowded around the pulpit in the right half of the woodcut. What point is Cranach attempting to make?
4. The woodcuts depict the Catholic Church as full of abuses. What are these abuses, and how are they illustrated?
5. How many specific points made by Luther in his *Table Talk* can you find illustrated in the Cranach woodcut?

Marriage and Families in Early Modern Europe

The assumption that general progress marked Europe's transition from the Middle Ages to the Renaissance and early modern era is contradicted by the experiences of many European women. Although medieval women were far from having equality with men, they enjoyed more freedom and higher status than in antiquity and the post-medieval period. Aristocratic women in the Middle Ages often managed their families' estates while their husbands were on military campaigns and some owned land themselves. Urban women joined guilds, were apprenticed to learn craft skills, and in some cities monopolized whole professions, such as leatherworking, brewing, weaving, and cloth finishing. Religious women were admired for their charity and piety, and many achieved distinction as models of spirituality.

During the fourteenth and fifteenth centuries, however, women's economic and social prospects declined, and continued to do so in the early modern period. Urban guilds excluded women from membership, and municipal councils barred women from work as physicians and apothecaries. For more urban women, work meant domestic service, spinning, shopkeeping, or some other poorly paid, low-status job. In the countryside, women's work remained essential to the peasant household's economic survival. Women tended gardens, raised poultry, helped with planting and harvesting, cooked, preserved food, and cared for children and the elderly.

In the early modern period, everyone agreed that irrespective of her social status, a woman's primary purpose was to marry and have children. Large families, especially ones with more sons than daughters, were viewed as economic necessities by rich and poor alike. Peasants relied on children as workers, while aristocrats and businessmen considered children necessities for the continuation of the family line and the preservation of family wealth and property. Moralists and religious leaders agreed that matrimony offered men and women the best opportunity for fulfillment and happiness and was the foundation for a sound, God-fearing society.

Many writers praised marriage so fervently because they were convinced it was being threatened. In Renaissance Italy, upper-class parents deplored the reluctance of their sons to marry. In northern Europe, the age of first marriage steadily rose, and the proportion of unmarried individuals grew. Estimates of the number of single women during the 1500s and early 1600s range from 20 to 40 percent, equally divided between widows and spinsters. For those who married, writers and preachers give the impression that more and more husbands and wives were unhappy. Although moralists affirmed that a strong marriage depended on mutual affection and clearly defined spousal responsibilities and rights, custom deprived young women of a meaningful say in the choice of a spouse, and laws clearly made wives subservient to husbands. The endless stream of commentaries on unhappy marriages, abusive husbands, and disobedient wives suggest that harmonious marriages were far from universal.

The written sources in this section, one representing Renaissance Italy and the other sixteenth-century Germany, along with a painting by the Flemish master Jan van Eyck, provide insight into the institution of marriage and in more general terms women's place in society.

Upper-Class Marriage in Renaissance Florence

6 • LEON BATTISTA ALBERTI, ON THE FAMILY

More so than any other city, Florence was the heart and soul of the Italian Renaissance. Its painters, sculptors, and architects produced works of great beauty, and its humanist scholars inspired a new appreciation and understanding of Greek and Roman antiquity. None of this would have been possible without a relatively small number of elite Florentine families who made fortunes in business and, under the guidance and control of the Medici family, made up the city's political oligarchy. These families, along with patronage provided by the Catholic Church, provided the money to support humanist scholarship, the work of painters and sculptors, and the construction and remodeling of countless buildings.

Some members of the Florentine elite were artists and scholars in their own right. Such was the case with Leon Battista Alberti (1404–1472), viewed by many as a personification of the ideal "Renaissance man." The illegitimate son of one of Florence's wealthiest merchants, Alberti studied at the universities of Padua and Bologna before becoming a papal official in Rome. He wrote books on mathematics, ancient literature, painting, and architecture and designed churches and private residences in Florence and other Italian cities. He also wrote the book *On the Family* (1443), a dialogue among Alberti men that supposedly took place in 1421 at the funeral of Alberti's father. Written in Italian and translated into the major European languages, Alberti's work expresses views of marriage and children common among wealthy and privileged Europeans of his era.

In the first section of the following excerpt Lionardo, a man in his late twenties or thirties, discusses marriage and the choice of wives; in the second section, an older gentleman, Gionnozzo, recalls the steps he took as a new husband to train his wife.

QUESTIONS FOR ANALYSIS

1. According to the speaker Lionardo, what discourages young men from marrying?
2. What is the main purpose of marriage, according to the characters in the dialogue?
3. In arranging marriages, how much input did the future wife and husband have? Who else influenced the final choice of a mate?
4. According to Lionardo, what considerations should affect the choice of a future wife? What qualities of a future wife are most important?
5. What did Gionnozzo hope to accomplish when he showed his new bride around the house, especially his private apartment?
6. What views of women underlie Alberti's description of marriage?

Arranging a Marriage

LIONARDO: Most times, the young do not appreciate the welfare of the family. Perhaps it seems to them that by bowing to matrimony they will lose much of their freedom in life. Perhaps they are overcome at times and caught in the clutches of a woman they love, as the comic poets are pleased to portray them. Perhaps the young find it most annoying having to maintain themselves, and therefore think that providing for a wife and children in addition to themselves is an overwhelming and hateful burden and are afraid they cannot properly take care of the needs which keep pace with the family's growth. Because of this, they consider the marriage bed too bothersome and avoid their duty honestly to enlarge the family. For these reasons, we must convince the young to marry by using reason, persuasion, rewards, and all other arguments so that the family may not be reduced to few members, . . . but grow in glory and the number of its young. . . .

• • •

Once the young men have been persuaded through the efforts and advice of all the elders of the family, the mothers and other old relatives and friends, who know the customs and behavior of almost all the girls of the city from the time they were born, must select all the well-born and properly-raised girls and propose their names to the youth who is to be married. The latter will choose the one he prefers, and the elders must not reject her as a daughter-in-law, unless she brings with her the breath of scandal or blame. . . . He should, however, follow the example of a good family-head who, when buying something, insists on examining the property many times before signing any contract. . . . One who wishes to marry must be even more diligent. My advice to him is

to show forethought and, over a period of time and in various ways, learn what kind of woman his intended bride is, for he will be her husband and companion for the rest of his life. In his mind he must have two reasons for marrying: the first is to beget children, the other, to have a faithful and steadfast companion throughout his life. We must, therefore, seek a woman suited to childbearing and pleasant enough to be our constant companion.

For this reason, then, they say that in a wife we must seek beauty, family, and wealth. . . . The first prerequisite of beauty in a woman is good habits. It is possible for a foolish, ignorant, slovenly, and drunken woman to have a beautiful body, but no one will deem her to be a beautiful wife. . . . As for physical beauty, we should not only take pleasure in comeliness, charm, and elegance, but should try to have in our house a wife well built for bearing children and strong of body to insure that they will be born strong and robust. An ancient proverb states: "As you want your children, so choose their mother." . . . Physicians say that a wife should not be thin, but neither should she be burdened with fat, for the fat are very weak, have many obstructions, and are slow in conceiving. . . . They believe that a woman who is tall but full in all her limbs is very useful for begetting many children. They always prefer one of girlish age for many reasons, such as ease in conforming with her husband's wishes and others which we do not have to discuss here. Girls are pure because of their age, simple through inexperience, modest by nature and without malice. They are eager to learn their husbands' habits and desires and acquiesce without any reluctance. Thus we must follow all the precepts mentioned, for they are most useful for recognizing and choosing a prolific wife. To this we may add that it is a good sign for the girl to

---

Source: From *Delia Famiglia,* Guido Guarino, trans. and ed., 1971, pp. 120–124, 216–219. Reprinted by permission of Bucknell University Press.

have many brothers, for you may then hope that she will be like her mother.

Thus we have finished speaking of beauty. Next comes the bride's family. . . . I believe first of all we must examine with care the life and ways of all those who will become our relatives. Many marriages have been the cause of great misfortunes to families because they became related with quarrelsome, contentious, proud, and hateful men, as we hear and read every day. . . .

Therefore, to conclude this part of my argument . . . let one try to find new relatives who are not of vulgar blood, little wealth, or humble profession. In other things let them be modest and not too far above you so that their greatness will not cast a shadow on your honor and dignity and will not disturb your family's peace and tranquility. . . . Nor do I want these relatives to be inferior to you, for if it is an expense to aid the fallen relatives I mentioned above, these others will keep you in slavery. Let them, therefore, be your equals, modest, noble, and of honorable profession, as we have said.

Next comes the dowry,[1] which I believe should be modest, sure, and given at once rather than large, doubtful, and to be given in the future. . . . Let them not be too large, for the larger they are, the greater is the delay in receiving payment, the chance of litigation, and the reluctance to pay. In addition, in the case of a large dowry you will be much more inclined to undergo great expense in order to collect it. . . . Having discussed how a wife is to be chosen and how she is to be received, we must now learn how she is to be treated at home.

Instructions for a New Wife

LIONARDO [Addressing Giannozzo]: You can be glad you had a most virtuous wife, perhaps more virtuous than others. I do not know where you could find another woman as industrious and prudent in managing the family as your wife was.

GIANNOZZO: She certainly was an excellent mother by nature and upbringing, but even more through my instruction. . . .

LIONARDO: How did you go about it?

GIANNOZZO: I shall tell you. When after a few days my wife began to feel at ease in my house and did not miss her mother and family so much, I took her by the hand and showed her the whole house. I showed her that upstairs was the place for storing grain and down in the cellar that for wine and firewood. I showed her where the tableware was and everything else in the house, so that she saw where everything was kept and knew its use. Then we returned to my room, and there, after closing the door, I showed her our valuables, silver, tapestries, clothes, and jewels, and pointed out their proper storage places.

I kept only the ledgers and business papers, my ancestors' as well as mine, locked so that my wife could not read them or even see them then or at any time since. . . . I never allowed my wife to enter my study either alone or in my company, and I ordered her to turn over to me at once any papers of mine she should ever find. . . .

No matter how trifling a secret I had, I never shared it with my wife or with any other woman. I disapprove of those husbands who consult their wives and do not know how to keep any secret to themselves. They are mad to seek good advice and wisdom in women, and even more so if they think a wife can guard a secret with greater jealousy and silence than her husband. O foolish husbands, is there ever a time when you chat with a woman without being reminded that women can do anything but keep silent? For this

---

[1]The dowry is the payment in money, goods, or land made by the bride's family to the groom. During the marriage the dowry was controlled by the husband, but if the husband predeceased the wife, it returned to the wife under most circumstances. The amount of the dowry depended on the wealth of the families involved. The increasing size of dowries in Italy in the 1400s became a hardship for families with several daughters. Daughters whose families could not raise a suitable dowry typically joined a religious order and entered a convent.

reason, then, I always took care that none of my secrets should ever become known to women. . . .

LIONARDO: What an excellent warning! And you are no less prudent than fortunate if your wife was never able to draw out any of your secrets.

GIANNOZZO: She never did, my dear Lionardo, and I shall tell you why. First of all, she was very modest, and so never cared to know more than she should. Then, I never spoke to her about anything but household matters, habits, and our children. Of these subjects I spoke to her often and at length so that she might learn what to do. . . . As for the household goods, I deemed it proper . . . to entrust them to my wife's care, but not entirely, for I often wanted to know and see where the least thing was kept and how safe it was. After my wife had seen and understood where everything was to be kept,

I said to her: "My dear wife, you must take no less care than myself of those things which will be useful and convenient to you and to me both while we preserve them in good condition. . . . You have seen our possessions, which, thank God, are such that we can well be satisfied. If we know how to take care of them, they will be useful to you, to me, and to our children. Therefore, my dear wife, it is your duty as well as mine to be diligent and take care of them."

LIONARDO: What did your wife answer?

GIANNOZZO: She answered that she had learned to obey her father and mother, and that they had instructed her to obey me always. She was ready, therefore, to do whatever I commanded. And I said to her: "Well then, my dear wife, one who knows how to obey her father and mother will soon learn to satisfy her husband." . . .

A Fifteenth-Century Wedding (?)

7 • JAN VAN EYCK, ARNOLFINI PORTRAIT

Portraits—pictorial representations of individuals—are usually thought of as paintings, but they also can be photographs, sculptures, drawings, medallions, coins, or engravings. They can depict their subjects sitting, standing, involved in an activity, or as part of a group. Portraits can be as large as the 60-foot colossal busts of the four American presidents sculpted into Mount Rushmore in South Dakota, or as tiny as photographs encased in lockets and worn as jewelry. They can be as priceless as the *Mona Lisa* or as ordinary as the image of Lincoln on a U.S. penny. Not all cultures value portraiture. Africa, for example, has a rich tradition of mask-making, but its masks do not portray chieftains or kings, but rather deities, ancestral spirits, mythological beings, the dead, animal spirits, and other beings and forces believed to have power over humanity. In Jewish and Islamic cultures, portraiture smacks of idolatry and hence is rare. However, in other cultures such as Europe and China, where portraiture was valued, it can offer valuable insights into the past.

More so than most sources, portraits need to be "read" with care. Although portraiture is associated with the idea of "likeness," and to its detractors is little more than the mechanical duplication of a person's features, in fact each portrait is the result of a long series of decisions made by the artist, the subject (who in most cases "sits" for the portrait), and the patron (who in many cases is also the subject). How will the subject be posed and in what setting? What will be the subject's facial expression? What will he or she be wearing? What props and other human figures will be included? Answers to these questions are based on yet other considerations: What is the portrait's intended audience, and what message is it meant to convey about the subject's physical characteristics, values, social status, and personality? Such questions are not always easy to answer, but they should be kept in mind as this and other portraits in *The Human Record* are analyzed.

The Flemish artist Jan van Eyck's *Arnolfini Portrait* or *Arnolfini Marriage* is one of the most admired, enigmatic, and analyzed portraits in the history of European art. Van Eyck, who was born in the town of Maaseik in present-day Belgium some time between 1370 and 1390, was living in the thriving Flemish city of Bruges as court painter of Duke Philip the Good of Burgundy when he completed the painting some time during or after 1434. Although there is little scholarly agreement about many of the details of the painting, a few things can be said with certainty: for example, its setting is Bruges and it takes place during the summer, because a cherry tree can be seen blossoming through the window. It is agreed that despite appearances, the woman is not pregnant; she is simply gathering the folds of her gown in front of her. It also is agreed that the man is a member of a wealthy Italian business family, the Arnolfini, which represented the interests of an even wealthier Italian business family, the Medici, in Bruges. For many years, it was thought that the subject of the painting is the betrothal or marriage ceremony of Giovanni di Arrigo Arnolfini and Giovanna Cenami, the daughter of another wealthy Italian merchant, in a Flemish bedchamber. Recent scholarship has revealed, however, that this marriage actually took place in 1447, six years after van Eyck's death. The male figure is now thought to be an older cousin, Giovanni di Nicolao Arnolfini, whose first wife, Constanza Trenta, died in 1433. This was one year before the event depicted in the painting took place. We know this because of the message inscribed on the wall next to the bed, which states, "Johannes van Eyck was here, 1434." This new identification has given rise to theories that the painting depicts Giovanni's second wedding to an unknown, but possibly Flemish woman, or that the painting is a memorial portrait to his first wife showing one dead and one living person. Most commentators believe the painting depicts a marriage ceremony, but some believe it is simply a portrait of a married couple; one art historian argues that what we see is a business agreement by which Giovanni di Nicolao agrees to give his wife control of his business interests while he is away from Bruges.

Barring the discovery of some new document that will shed light on the particulars of the painting, debates on the painting among scholars will undoubtedly continue. Why is there only one candle burning in the candelabra (on the side closer to the male figure)? What is the meaning of the convex mirror, which is surrounded by images of Christ's crucifixion and resurrection? Why can we see two figures reflected in the mirror, and who are they? Almost everyone believes one of them is van Eyck, but if so, why is he not shown painting the scene?

Meanwhile, non-experts can admire the painting for its beauty and gain insights from it about male–female relationships and fifteenth-century upper-class matrimony.

Van Eyck, Arnolfini Portrait

QUESTIONS FOR ANALYSIS

1. Note the placement of the two figures, with the woman next to the bed and the man by the window. What may be the significance of this?
2. Note how and where each of the two figures is looking, and how they are holding and gesturing with their hands.
3. How does the painting illustrate the wealth of Arnolfini and his bride?
4. The top of the far bedpost has an image of St. Margaret, the patron saint of pregnancy and childbirth. What other features of the painting emphasize the same theme?
5. On the sides of the mirror hang a brush or small broom and rosary beads (used in Catholic devotions to count certain prayers). What may these refer to?
6. What may be the significance of the small dog and the clogs, which the man has taken off?
7. Overall, how does the message of the painting compare with the views of marriage expressed by Alberti?

A Sixteenth-Century Commentary on Marriage

8 • ERHARD SCHÖN AND HANS SACHS, NO MORE PRECIOUS TREASURE IS ON THE EARTH THAN A GENTLE WIFE WHO LONGS FOR HONOR

Many Europeans were introduced to the new technology of printing not through books but through broadsheets. Printed on a single sheet and usually consisting of a woodcut illustration and a brief text, these inexpensive publications were meant for a mass audience. As seen earlier in this chapter, such broadsheets served as instruments of propaganda during the Reformation era. They also offered satire, social commentary, moral instruction, and news about murders, witchcraft trials, astronomical portents, monsters, strange births, and countless other matters.

The following broadsheet is a collaboration between Erhard Schön (ca. 1491–1550), a Nuremberg artist who produced hundreds of woodcuts for books and broadsheets, and Hans Sachs (1494–1576), a prolific Nuremberg poet who provided the text. It is referred to by several titles, including *The Husband Who Does Not Rule* and *No More Precious Treasure Is on the Earth Than a Gentle Wife Who Longs for Honor*, which is a translation of the German words at the top of the woodcut. It appeared in 1533. The woodcut shows, from left to right, a husband (pulling a cart that carries a laundry tub), the wife, a young man, his sweetheart, an old woman wearing a fool's cap, and finally an old man. In Hans Sachs' accompanying text, these six characters state their opinions about marriage.

QUESTIONS FOR ANALYSIS

1. What qualities of his wife does the husband in Schön's woodcut most bitterly complain about?
2. What is the significance of the britches, purse, and sword that the wife holds in Schön's print?

Erhard Schön, No More Precious Treasure Is on the Earth Than a Gentle Wife Who Longs for Honor

3. According to the words ascribed to the wife, how does she justify her actions and behavior? How do her justifications compare to the expectations about marriage set forth by the young girl?
4. Compare and contrast the arguments for and against marriage presented by the old man and the female fool in Sachs' accompanying poem. To what extent do the comments of the old man confirm the fears about marriage expressed by the young man?

No More Precious Treasure

The Wretched Idol (the Husband)
Oh woe, oh woe to me, wretched fool,
With what difficulty I pull this cart
To which point marriage has brought me.
I wish I had never thought of it!
A shrewish scold has come into my house
and has taken my sword, pants and purse.
Night and day I have no peace
And no good word from her.
My fidelity does not please her;

My words provoke hostility from her.
Thus is the fate of many a man
Who has, knows and can do nothing,
And yet in time must have a wife.

The Wife Speaks
Hey, beloved mate, but is this really true?
Be quiet! Or I will pull you by the hair.
If you want a nice and gentle wife
Who will always be subservient to you
Then stay at home in your own house

Source: Courtesy of Schlossmuseum Gotha, Gotha, Germany.

And stop your carousing.
Naked I go running around to peddle things,
Suffering from hunger and quaffing water.
It's difficult for a nice young wife
To maintain her wifely honor.
If you won't work to support me,
Then you have to wash, spin and pull the cart
And must let your back be bared.

The Journeyman

What do you say about this, young lady?
Would you like to be like her
And yourself hold sword, pants, purse and
    authority?
With words that bite, rasp and cut?
That I should and would never suffer.
Should I fight and brawl with you,
Then perhaps I would end up
Pulling a cart like this poor man,
Who has lost all joy and pleasure.
Should I waste my life of freedom
With spinning, washing, cooking and carting?
I would rather swear off from taking up
    marriage.

The Girl

Boy, believe me on my honor.
I don't wish for such power.
If you want to fight over rank,
Then you will be the man in all things.
What a wife deserves,
To love, to experience hardship together and
    honor,
I will demand nothing besides this.
You should have no doubt about it.
I will devote my life to serving you

And love you in constant friendship.
And you won't be scolded by a single word.

The Woman Fool

Watch yourself, young man.
I, a poor fool speak the truth.
Much good is said about marriage
But it means more correctly "Woe."
You must suffer 'til you die
Much anxiety, uncertainty, worry and want.
From this no married person is spared.
Now when you see a pretty girl,
She will gladly do what you want
For a bottle of wine.
Afterwards you can let her go
And take on another.
A wife you have forever.

The Wise Man

Young man I will teach you better.
Do not listen to this woman fool.
Beware of the tricks of whores,
Who are always there to deceive you.
Take a young lady into marriage.
God will guide your lives.
Stay with her in love and pain
And always be patient.
If you experience aggravation,
Consider it to be God's will.
Provide for your wife by the sweat of your
    brow,
As God commands in the Book of Genesis.
Patience and suffering make a door
Through which we arrive at that place
Where the angels have their home.

An Expanding Intellectual Universe

Between the fifteenth and seventeenth centuries European intellectuals and artists rejected the heritage of their medieval past. That they did so does not diminish the achievements of the High Middle Ages (ca. 1000–1300 C.E.), an era for which the term "dark ages" could not be more inaccurate. These were centuries that saw the emergence of national literatures, technological innovation, the establishment of Europe's first universities, profound discussions of law, religion, and philosophy, and wondrous artistic and architectural achievements. The stained glass windows and soaring spires of Europe's Gothic churches still inspire awe and admiration.

Nonetheless, there were limitations to the medieval intellectual vision. Intellectuals were convinced that everything worth knowing already had been discovered by ancient authorities or revealed in holy writ. This meant, for example, that scientific inquiry in the Middle Ages was a matter of poring over the works of the ancient Greek philosopher Aristotle and trying to understand the exact meaning of his words. Science, or, as it was then called, "natural philosophy," was something that took place in one's study or a library, not a laboratory, and rarely generated new ideas. Innovation and originality also were discouraged by the strong religious atmosphere of the age. As brilliant as Aristotle and other ancient philosophers might have been, in the eyes of the Roman Catholic Church and its theologians, nothing they wrote matched the authority of the Bible, the very word of God. Since any thinker who proposed an idea that challenged Christian orthodoxy risked scorn, reprimand, and possible punishment, such thinkers were rare.

Between 1400 and the early 1600s, every one of these medieval assumptions faced serious challenge. We have already seen how the Protestant Reformation rejected the Roman Catholic Church's claims that it was the final arbiter of all intellectual and political disputes and provided Christians with one true path to salvation. The secularism of the Italian Renaissance, new scientific theories, surprising geographical discoveries, and more intense interactions with Africans, Asians, and Native Americans all changed the intellectual landscape. As revered authorities and ancient assumptions were challenged, intellectuals' reactions ranged from dogmatism to skepticism to bewilderment to optimism. No serious thinker, however, was immune from the unsettling new ideas and events that characterized the age.

Renaissance Humanism and the Recovery of Greco-Roman Thought

9 • LETTER OF CENCIO DE' RUSTICI TO FRANCESCO DE' FIANA AND LETTER OF LEONARDO BRUNI TO POGGIO BRACCIOLINI

The first step in Europe's intellectual transformation took place during the Italian Renaissance, a movement centered in Venice, Milan, Rome, and especially Florence from the late fourteenth to the early sixteenth century. That this step was taken in Italy is not surprising. Ever since the eleventh century, when Genoese and Venetian merchants began trading in the eastern Mediterranean, Italy was Europe's most cosmopolitan region. It also was wealthier and more urbanized than northern Europe and had governments in which participation by urban merchants and even artisans was common.

In this distinctive setting, authors, scholars, churchmen, and wealthy patrons began to develop new enthusiasm for the writings of Greek and Roman antiquity. This was the beginning of Renaissance humanism, a term that has little in common with the modern sense of humanism as an aggressively secular, or even antireligious, point of view. Instead the term "humanist," as it was used in the Renaissance, was based on the Latin phrase *studia humanitatis,* which refers to disciplines other than theology and the law—ethics, poetry, history, rhetoric, grammar, and certain branches of philosophy. The humanists were convinced that the study of such subjects, when based on the models of antiquity, was a source of wisdom and moral inspiration, capable of transforming individuals and rejuvenating family life, politics, and social relationships. During the fifteenth century the study of the Latin language, Roman literature, and Roman history became the basis of education, and interest in antiquity broadened to include Greece in addition to Rome. By the late 1400s knowledge of Greek and Roman classics had become the hallmark of a learned person, and Greek and Roman antiquity inspired everything from painting and architecture to the writing of history.

Aside from its influence on education, art, and architecture, Renaissance humanists broadened Europe's intellectual horizons by recovering, editing, and making available literally hundreds of ancient writings that had been lost through neglect and lack of interest. This work of recovering lost texts became the passion of a dozen or so fifteenth-century humanists whose discoveries resulted from contacts with Greek scholars from the Byzantine Empire and searches in centuries-old European monastic libraries.

The following section consists of excerpts from two letters written in connection with a major discovery of ancient manuscripts in the Abbey of St. Gall in Switzerland by three humanist churchmen while attending the Council of Constance. Both letters were written in Latin in 1416 or 1417. The first was sent from Cencio de' Rustici (ca. 1390–1445), an official in the papal chancery with a knowledge of Greek, to his fellow churchman and mentor Francesco de' Fiana; the second was written by Leonardo Bruni (1370–1444), one of the leading early humanists, to Poggio Bracciolini, another prominent humanist and the movement's most tireless searcher for lost manuscripts. In the letters, all their names have been Latinized.

QUESTIONS FOR ANALYSIS

1. What generalizations can be made about the subject matter of the works that were discovered? What does this reveal about the interests of the humanists?
2. Cincius bitterly complains about the lack of respect shown for ancient writings, buildings, and works of art. Whom does he blame for this neglect?
3. The letter writers are both convinced that discoveries such as these were of monumental importance. Why?

Cincius Romanus to his most learned teacher Franciscus de Fiana

In Germany there are many monasteries with libraries full of Latin books. This aroused the hope in me that some of the works of Cicero, Varro, Livy,[1] and other great men of learning, which seem to have completely vanished, might come to light, if a careful search were instituted. A few days ago, Poggius and Bartholomeus Montepolitianus and I, attracted by the fame of the library, went by agreement to the town of St. Gall. As soon as we went into the library, we found *Jason's Argonauticon,* written by C. Valerius Flaccus[2] in verse that is both splendid and dignified and not far removed from poetic majesty. Then we found some discussions in prose of a number of Cicero's orations which make clearly comprehensible many legal practices and many modern equivalents of ancient institutions. We also found one book, a small volume but remarkable in the greatness of the eloquence and wisdom: Lactantius[3] *On Men of Both Sorts,* which plainly contradicts the statements of those who claim that the state of mankind is lower than that of beasts and more hopeless. Among other books we found Vitruvius *On Architecture* and Priscianus the grammarian's comments on some of the poems of Vergil.[4] . . . When we carefully inspected the nearby tower of the church of St. Gall in which countless books were kept like captives and the library neglected and infested with dust, worms, soot, and all the things associated with the destruction of books, we all burst into tears, thinking that this was the way in which the Latin language had lost its greatest glory and distinction. Truly, if this library could speak for itself, it would cry loudly: "You men who love the Latin tongue, let me not be utterly destroyed by this woeful neglect. Snatch me from this prison in whose gloom even the bright light of the books within cannot be seen." There were in that monastery an abbot and monks totally devoid of any knowledge of literature. What barbarous hostility to the Latin tongue! What damned dregs of humanity!

But why do I hate a tribe of barbarians for this kind of indifference to literature when the Romans,[5] the parents of the Latin tongue, have inflicted a greater wound and heaped greater abuse on our native language, the prince over all the others? I call to mind innumerable libraries of Latin and Greek books in ruins in Rome which were carefully built by our ancestors. . . .

These libraries were destroyed partly through ignorance, partly through neglect, and partly so that the divine face of Veronica[6] might be painted. Anyway, I think that the perpetrators of this loathsome crime and those who did not stop them ought to suffer the severest punishment. Indeed if the laws say that he who has killed a man deserves capital punishment, what penalty and what suffering shall we require for those who deprive the public of culture, of the

Source: Phyllis Walter Goodhart Gordan, *Two Renaissance Book Hunters* (New York: Columbia University Press, 1974), pp. 187–192. Reprinted by permission of Columbia University Press.

[1] Cicero (106–64 B.C.E.) was a Roman statesman and philosopher, famous for his eloquence; Marcus Terentius Varro (116 B.C.E.–27 B.C.E) was a prolific writer on many topics; Livy (Titus Livius, 59 B.C.E.–17 C.E.) was a historian.

[2] Valerius Flaccus (d. CA. 90 C.E.) was a poet whose epic *The Argonautica* retold the legend of Jason and the Golden Fleece.

[3] Lactantius (ca. 240–ca. 320) was an early Christian writer admired by the humanists because of the clarity and elegance of his Latin writing.

[4] Vitruvius (c. 80–70 B.C.E.–Ca. 15 B.C.E.) was an architect who wrote *De Architectura libri decem* (Ten Books on Architecture); Priscianus, who lived around 500 B.C.E., was a Latin grammarian.

[5] In this case the reference is to Romans in recent history, not antiquity.

[6] According to tradition, St. Veronica offered her veil to Jesus so he could wipe his face while bearing his cross on the way to Calvary. When he returned it to her, it had Jesus' image on it. A relic of the blessed veil exists at St. Peter's in Rome.

liberal arts and actually of all nourishment of the human mind, without which men can hardly live at all or live like beasts? . . . Every day you see citizens . . . demolishing the Amphitheater or the Hippodrome or the Colosseum or statues or walls made with marvelous skill and marvelous stone and showing that old and almost divine power and dignity. . . . But if anyone asks these men why they are led to destroy marble statues, they answer that they abominate the images of false gods. Oh voice of savages, who flee from one error to another! For it is not contrary to our religion if we contemplate a statue of Venus or of Hercules made with the greatest of skill and admire the almost divine art of the ancient sculptors. . . . So these priests of our religion, since they could not appreciate the excellence and beauty of the City and could accomplish nothing, strove for this kind of ruin and destruction. Let us pursue such inhuman, such savage stupidity with curses. And you, my teacher, gifted as you are in both poetry and prose, write something against these destroyers of our illustrious monuments. If you do so, you will assure yourself henceforth immortal glory and them perpetual shame. Farewell.

Leonardus Brunus to Poggius

If you are well, good; so am I. At our friend Nicolaus'[7] house I read the letter which you wrote about your last trip and your discovery of some books. I think there is cause for rejoicing not only about them but also about your apparent confident expectation of finding others. Surely this will be your glory, that by your efforts and diligence you are restoring to our age the writings of great men that were already lost and gone. And this will be a joy not only to us but to our descendants, that is, to our successors in our studies. For your deeds will not be passed over in silence or be wiped from memory, but the story will persist that what was regarded as gone beyond recall was recovered through your industry and restored to us. . . . And so I would urge you and beg you insistently not to give up this glorious endeavor but to rise up and persevere. It will be our concern here that lack of money does not interfere with you, and you must realize that there is a great deal more profit in this discovery of yours than you seem to think. For Quintilian,[8] who used to be mangled and in pieces, will recover all his parts through you. I have seen the headings of the chapters; he is whole, while we used to have only the middle section and that incomplete. Oh wondrous treasure! Oh unexpected joy! Shall I see you, Marcus Fabius [Quintilian], whole and undamaged, and how much will you mean to me now? For I loved you even when you were cruelly deprived of your mouth, of your mouth and both your hands, when you were "spoil'd of your nose and shorten'd of your ears"; still I loved you for your grace. Please, Poggius, satisfy this deep desire of mine as quickly as possible, so that if kindness means anything I may see him before I die.

---

[7]Niccolo Niccoli (1364–1437) was a Florentine book collector who spent his fortune on the purchase of books and manuscripts.

[8]Quintilian (ca. 35–ca. 100) was the author of books on rhetoric, oratory, and education.

Renaissance Culture and Art

10 • RAPHAEL, SCHOOL OF ATHENS

During the lifetime of the painter Raphael (1483–1520), the Renaissance in Italy was at its peak. Classical studies dominated Italian schools and universities; countless ancient manuscripts had been recovered; knowledge of ancient Greek and the study of ancient philosophers other than Aristotle were now common. In art, sculptors and architects drew on classical models to create a distinctive Renaissance style and painters used their mastery of perspective and anatomy to produce works of supreme beauty and power.

Raphael (Raffaello Sanzio or Santi), a contemporary of artists Leonardo da Vinci and Michelangelo and the political thinker Niccolo Machiavelli, was born in the central Italian city of Urbino, an important center of humanist culture. There, under the direction of his father, a painter, he received his early training as an artist. After further training in Perugia and Florence, he gained a reputation in the early 1500s for his portraits and beautiful religious paintings. In 1508, he received a commission from Pope Julius II to paint the walls of a room (later known as the *Stanza della Segnatura*—"room of the signature") in the Vatican apartments used by the pope as a library and study. The result was four magnificent frescoes (wall paintings in which the paint is applied to plaster) depicting individuals from antiquity and the more recent past connected with the study of philosophy, theology, poetry, and the law. The most famous of the four, which deals with philosophy and came to be known as *The School of Athens,* is shown here.

The figures are placed in an architectural background reflecting the influence of ancient Roman architecture. It is thought that Raphael was inspired by the plans drawn up for the renovation of St. Peter's basilica by Donato Bramante (1444–1514), whose designs included many features of ancient Roman buildings. Above the figures are classically inspired statues of the Apollo, the god of poetry, on the left, and Athena, the goddess of wisdom, on the right. Although Raphael provided no hints about the specific identities of all the figures in the painting, quite a few can be identified with confidence. The central figures are Plato, holding his work *Timaeus* and gesturing upward to the realm of ideas or "Platonic forms," and Aristotle, holding a copy of his *Ethics* and gesturing toward the earth, where things can be known through the senses. Below them are the old man Diogenes, the Cynic who lived in a tub and wandered about Athens "looking for an honest man," and Heraclitus, who taught that change was the key to understanding the universe. On the left side is a group gathered around Socrates, who is making points to a group of avid listeners; below the Socrates group is another group gathered around a figure writing in a book who is thought to represent the mathematician/philosopher Pythagoras. On the right side, at the lower corner is the mathematician Euclid, who is drawing on a slate, and behind him are Ptolemy, the astronomer, who is holding a globe of the universe, and a figure who is thought to be Zoroaster, the ancient Persian prophet and philosopher connected during the Renaissance to astrology. There is no consensus about the identification of any of the other figures, although the solitary figure on the right is thought by some to be Plotinus, an important interpreter of Plato. Interestingly, several of the figures are portraits of Raphael's contemporaries. Plato, for example, is modeled after Leonardo da Vinci; Heraclitus has the features of Michelangelo; Euclid is painted as Bramante. Raphael also includes a likeness of himself: he is the young man standing to the right of Ptolemy and Zoroaster, along with an older man thought to represent his teacher, Perugino.

Raphael, School of Athens

QUESTIONS FOR ANALYSIS

1. Aside from the philosophers represented, what aspects of the painting show the influence of Renaissance classicism?
2. How are the various figures interacting with one another? How would you characterize the conversations they are having with one another? What might you conclude about the painter's intent in presenting the figures in this way?
3. What might be the reasons for portraying contemporaries in the painting?

Science and the Claims of Religion

11 • GALILEO GALILEI, LETTER TO THE GRAND DUCHESS CHRISTINA

Science, or natural philosophy as it was known at the time, was nothing new for Europeans in the 1500s and 1600s. Many medieval and Renaissance scholars had sought to understand the natural world, but their need to make science conform to Catholic doctrine discouraged speculation, and their reliance on past authorities hampered new discoveries. The first major break from ancient Greek science was made by the Polish astronomer Nicolaus Copernicus, who, in *On the Revolutions of the Heavenly Spheres,* rejected the theories of the ancient authorities Aristotle and Ptolemy and argued that the sun, not the Earth, was the center of the universe. Although they originally met with skepticism and religious opposition, Copernicus's theories inspired the work of Tycho Brahe (1546–1601), whose observations provided astronomers with a body of accurate and comprehensive astronomical data, and Johannes Kepler (1571–1630), who proved that planets moved in elliptical orbits rather than perfect circles. It was only with the work of Galileo Galilei (1564–1642), however, that helocentrism gained general acceptance among Europe's scientists.

Galileo, an Italian physicist, mathematician, and astronomer, was the greatest European scientist in the early 1600s. In the field of mechanics, he developed the theory of inertia and described the laws that dictate the movement of falling bodies. In astronomy, he pioneered the use of the telescope and defended the theory of a sun-centered universe. His public support of Copernicus disturbed Catholic theologians, who were convinced it undermined correct belief and the authority of the Church. The Church officially condemned Copernican theory in 1616 and forced Galileo to renounce many of his ideas in 1632. Galileo's works continued to be read, however, and despite his condemnation, his writings contributed to the acceptance of Copernican theory and the new methodology of science.

In the following selection, Galileo, a devout Catholic, defends his approach to science in a published letter addressed to Christina, the grand duchess of Tuscany, in 1615.

QUESTIONS FOR ANALYSIS

1. According to Galileo, what are his enemies' motives? Why in his view do they use religious arguments against him?
2. According to Galileo, why is it dangerous to apply passages of Scripture to science?
3. To Galileo, how does nature differ from the Bible as a source of truth?
4. In Galileo's view, what is the proper relationship between science and religion?

Some years ago, as Your Serene Highness well knows, I discovered in the heavens many things that had not been seen before our own age. The novelty of these things, as well as some consequences which followed from them in contradiction to the physical notions commonly held among academic philosophers, stirred up against me no small number of professors—as if I had placed these things in the sky with my own hands in order to upset nature and overturn the sciences. They seemed to forget that the increase of known truths stimulates the investigation, establishment, and growth of the arts; not their diminution or destruction.

Showing a greater fondness for their own opinions than for truth, they sought to deny and disprove the new things which, if they had cared to look for themselves, their own senses would have demonstrated to them. To this end they hurled various charges and published numerous writings filled with vain arguments, and they made the grave mistake of sprinkling these with passages taken from places in the Bible which they had failed to understand properly, and which were ill suited to their purposes.

Persisting in their original resolve to destroy me and everything mine by any means they can think of, these men are aware of my views in astronomy and philosophy. They know that as to the arrangement of the parts of the universe, I hold the sun to be situated motionless in the center of the revolution of the celestial orbs while the Earth rotates on its axis and revolves about the sun. They know also that I support this position not only by refuting the arguments of Ptolemy[1] and Aristotle, but by producing many counter-arguments; in particular, some which relate to physical effects whose causes can perhaps be assigned in no other way. In addition there are astronomical arguments derived from many things in my new celestial discoveries that plainly confute the Ptolemaic system while admirably agreeing with and confirming the contrary hypothesis. Possibly because they are disturbed by the known truth of other propositions of mine which differ from those commonly held, and therefore mistrusting their defense so long as they confine themselves to the field of philosophy, these men have resolved to fabricate a shield for their fallacies out of the mantle of pretended religion and the authority of the Bible. These they apply, with little judgment, to the refutation of arguments that they do not understand and have not even listened to.

First they have endeavored to spread the opinion that such propositions in general are contrary to the Bible and are consequently damnable and

---

Source: From *Discoveries and Opinions of Galileo* by Galileo Galilei, translated by Stillman Drake. Copyright © 1957 by Stillman Drake. Used by permission of Doubleday, a division of Random House, Inc.

[1]Ptolemy (ca. 100–170 C.E.), who spent most of his life in Alexandria, Egypt, was the Greek astronomer who propounded key aspects of the geocentric planetary system that prevailed in Europe until the time of Copernicus.

heretical. . . . Next, becoming bolder, . . . they began scattering rumors among the people that before long this doctrine would be condemned by the supreme authority.[2] They know, too, that official condemnation would not only suppress the two propositions which I have mentioned, but would render damnable all other astronomical and physical statements and observations that have any necessary relation or connection with these. . . .

To this end they make a shield of their hypocritical zeal for religion. They go about invoking the Bible, which they would have minister to their deceitful purposes. Contrary to the sense of the Bible and the intention of the holy Fathers, if I am not mistaken, they would extend such authorities until even in purely physical matters—where faith is not involved—they would have us altogether abandon reason and the evidence of our senses in favor of some biblical passage, though under the surface meaning of its words this passage may contain a different sense. . . .

The reason produced for condemning the opinion that the Earth moves and the sun stands still is that in many places in the Bible one may read that the sun moves and the earth stands still. Since the Bible cannot err, it follows as a necessary consequence that anyone takes an erroneous and heretical position who maintains that the sun is inherently motionless and the earth movable.

With regard to this argument, I think in the first place that it is very pious to say and prudent to affirm that the holy Bible can never speak untruth—whenever its true meaning is understood. But I believe nobody will deny that it is often very abstruse, and may say things which are quite different from what its bare words signify. Hence in expounding the Bible if one were always to confine oneself to the unadorned grammatical meaning, one might fall into error. Not only contradictions and propositions far from true might thus be made to appear in the Bible, but even grave heresies and follies. Thus it would be necessary to assign to God feet, hands, and eyes, as well as corporeal and human affections, such as anger, repentance, hatred, and sometimes even the forgetting of things past and ignorance of those to come. . . .

This being granted, I think that in discussions of physical problems we ought to begin not from the authority of scriptural passages but from sense-experiences and necessary demonstrations; for the holy Bible and the phenomena of nature proceed alike from the divine Word, the former as the dictate of the Holy Ghost[3] and the latter as the observant executrix of God's commands. It is necessary for the Bible, in order to be accommodated to the understanding of every man, to speak many things which appear to differ from the absolute truth so far as the bare meaning of the words is concerned. But Nature, on the other hand, is inexorable and immutable; she never transgresses the laws imposed upon her, or cares a whit whether her abstruse reasons and methods of operation are understandable to men. For that reason it appears that nothing physical which sense-experience sets before our eyes, or which necessary demonstrations prove to us, ought to be called in question (much less condemned) upon the testimony of biblical passages which may have some different meaning beneath their words. For the Bible is not chained in every expression to conditions as strict as those which govern all physical effects; nor is God any less excellently revealed in Nature's actions than in the sacred statements of the Bible.

---

[2] The pope.
[3] The Holy Ghost (or Holy Spirit) is the third divine person of the Trinity (God the Father, God the Son, God the Holy Ghost), who sanctifies and inspires humankind. Christians believe the authors of the Bible wrote under the sacred and infallible inspiration of the Holy Ghost.

Chapter 2

The Islamic Heartland and India

FOLLOWING YEARS OF upheaval three large empires emerged in South and Southwest Asia between the middle of the fifteenth and the early sixteenth centuries. The first empire to take shape was that of the Ottoman Turks, a semi-nomadic people who, after migrating to Anatolia from Persia and Central Asia in the 1100s, embarked on successful conquests in Anatolia and surrounding regions. In 1453, they conquered the last remnant of the Byzantine Empire by capturing the imperial city, Constantinople, and, as Istanbul, made it the seat of their government. After further conquests, by the mid-1500s, the Ottomans ruled an empire that included Anatolia, Egypt, Syria, and lands in North Africa, the western coast of the Arabian Peninsula, and southeastern Europe. Meanwhile, in the early sixteenth century, on the Ottoman Empire's eastern flank, Ismail Safavi created the Safavid Empire in Persia, which was distinguished by its rulers' fervent devotion to Shia Islam. Finally, during the 1500s, the Mughal Empire emerged in India as a result of the exploits of Babur (1483–1530), a military adventurer from Central Asia who conquered northwest India, and those of his grandson, Akbar (1542–1605), who extended and consolidated Mughal authority on the subcontinent.

The three empires were similar in several respects. Each was established through military conquest, each was governed by all-powerful Islamic rulers, and each was a formidable military power. In each, the arts and literature flourished. Each at first rested on a strong economic foundation, and each experienced an erosion of that foundation by inflation, high taxation, and changes in the world economy.

Differences among the empires also existed. In the sphere of religion, the Shiism of the Safavid Empire was a source of ongoing tension with the Ottoman Empire, whose leaders and Muslim subjects were largely Sunni. The Mughal emperors also were Sunnis, although the religious eclecticism of rulers such as Akbar (r. 1556–1605) and their policy of religious toleration troubled the orthodox. In contrast to Safavid Persia, which had relatively few non-Muslims, the Ottoman Empire included large numbers of Jewish and especially Christian subjects, while the subjects of the Mughal emperors were predominantly Hindu.

The three empires also had different experiences with Europeans. The Ottomans and Europeans were archrivals, each representing to the other a despised religion and, moreover, a threat to their territory. European and Ottoman fleets clashed in the Mediterranean, and their armies fought in southeastern and central Europe. Nonetheless, European merchants continued to trade and even reside in Ottoman cities, and European powers such as France forged military alliances with the Ottoman sultan when it suited their purposes.

Relations between Europeans and Safavid Persia, on the other hand, were generally more cordial, mainly because they shared a common enemy in the Ottomans. Although Shah Abbas I (r. 1587–1629) resented Portuguese incursions in the Persian Gulf, he drew on the expertise of European military advisors and sent missions to Europe in 1599 and 1608 to discuss joint military action against the Ottomans.

In India, the Portuguese quickly capitalized on Vasco da Gama's voyage around Africa to Calicut in 1498. They undercut Arab merchants' dominance of the spice trade on the west Indian coast and established a base of operations in Goa, which they forcibly annexed from the local Muslim ruler. The Dutch, English, and French, however, became involved in India only in the 1600s. Akbar was intrigued by Christianity, and his successor Jahangir was impressed by European art, but overall, emperors and local rulers were indifferent to the small number of Europeans who came to their shores.

During the seventeenth century, all three Islamic empires began to deteriorate. By the middle of the eighteenth century, the Safavids had been overthrown, and the Mughal Empire was in ruins. The Ottoman Empire was still a formidable power, but it was entering a period in its history marked by military defeats, territorial losses, and weakened central authority.

Rulers and Their Challenges in the Ottoman and Mughal Empires

Many extraordinary rulers put their stamp on the early histories of the Ottoman, Safavid, and Mughal Empires. Early Ottoman expansion resulted from the conquests of three men—Mehmet II (r. 1451–1481), who directed the successful siege of Constantinople in 1453; Selim I (r. 1512–1520), who conquered Egypt, Syria, Palestine, and parts of southern and western Arabia; and Suleiman I (r. 1520–1566), who added Hungary, the Mediterranean island of Rhodes, and some Persian territory to Ottoman domains. The Safavid Empire was forged by the charismatic Ismail Safavi, whose original power base was Azerbaijan in northern Persia. Believed by his followers to be a descendant of Muhammad's son-in-law, Ali, he defeated his rivals and in 1501 assumed the title Shah (Emperor) Ismail I. The founding of the Mughal Empire was the work of two men. Babur (1483–1531), a military adventurer of Mongol-Turkish ancestry invaded northern India in 1526 and defeated the Lodis, the Delhi sultanate's last dynasty; his grandson Akbar (1542–1605) defeated rival Pashtun and Indian armies and ensured the empire's survival.

Individual rulers also contributed to the cultural achievements of all three empires. Akbar patronized painters, poets, historians, and religious thinkers. Under his free-spending successors, Jahangir (r. 1605–1627) and Shah Jahan (r. 1627–1658), Mughal culture reached new heights. Shah Abbas I (r. 1587–1629) transformed the Safavid capital, Isfahan, through the construction of mosques, formal gardens, palaces, royal tombs, and public squares. Similarly, early Ottoman sultans left their marks on Islamic culture by sponsoring ambitious building programs and the work of scholars, poets, and artists.

The sources in this section provide insights into the personalities and policies of two of the most renowned Islamic rulers of the sixteenth and seventeenth centuries—Suleiman I and Jahangir. They provide an opportunity to analyze their styles of leadership and the strengths and weaknesses of their regimes.

A European Diplomat's Impressions of Suleiman I

12 • OGIER GHISELIN DE BUSBECQ, TURKISH LETTERS

Suleiman I, known to Europeans as Suleiman the Magnificent, is remembered mainly for his military exploits, but his accomplishments go beyond the battlefield. He patronized history and literature, oversaw the codification of Ottoman law, and contributed to the architectural grandeur of Istanbul, the seat of Ottoman government. He was one of the outstanding rulers of the age.

The following observations of Suleiman and Ottoman society were recorded by Ogier Ghiselin de Busbecq (1522–1590), a Flemish nobleman who spent most of his life in the service of the Hapsburg dynasty, in particular Ferdinand I, who was the archduke of Austria, king of Hungary and Bohemia, and, from 1558 to 1564, Holy Roman Emperor. In 1555, Ferdinand sent Busbecq to Istanbul to represent his interests in an ongoing dispute with Suleiman over the division of the Kingdom of Hungary, which had broken apart after the Ottoman victory at the Battle of Mohács in 1526. After 6 years of discussions, the two sides agreed on a compromise by which Austria controlled the western third of Hungary and portions of today's

Croatia, while the Ottomans held central Hungary and were allowed to collect tribute from semi-independent Transylvania.

During his 6 years in Ottoman lands, Busbecq recorded his observations and impressions, which he sent in the form of four long letters to his friend Nicholas Michault, a Hapsburg official in a position to communicate Busbecq's views to Ferdinand and his advisors. All four letters were published in Paris in 1589 and in many subsequent editions.

The following excerpt begins with a description of Busbecq's first meeting with Suleiman I in 1555 and goes on to discuss Ottoman military power. It concludes with a retelling of the events surrounding the assassination in 1553 of Suleiman's oldest son and most likely successor, Mustafa. It is an example of the conflict and intrigue surrounding issues of succession in the Ottoman state, in which one of the sons of the sultan would succeed his father, but not necessarily the eldest. As Busbecq explains, Mustafa's interests clashed with the ambitions of Roxelana, Suleiman's Russian-Ukrainian concubine and later wife, who bore him two sons and a daughter. To ensure that her son Selim would become sultan after Suleiman's death, she convinced her aging husband that Mustafa was plotting against him and had to be killed.

QUESTIONS FOR ANALYSIS

1. What does Busbecq's first meeting with Suleiman reveal about the sultan's attitudes toward Europeans? What further insights into his attitudes are provided later in the excerpt?
2. What does Busbecq see as the main difference between Ottoman and European attitudes toward social privilege and inherited status? How, in his view, do these attitudes affect Ottoman government?
3. What insights does Busbecq provide about the Ottoman military?
4. What does the episode of Mustafa's assassination reveal about the power and influence of Roxelana? About Ottoman attitudes toward the imperial succession? About Suleiman's character?
5. What advantages and disadvantages were there in the Ottoman practice of not making the eldest son the automatic heir of the reigning sultan?
6. Shortly after Suleiman's reign, some observers sensed that the Ottoman Empire was beginning to decline. What in Busbecq's account points to future problems?

First Impressions

On our arrival . . . we were taken to call on Achmet Pasha (the chief Vizier) and the other pashas[1]—for the Sultan himself was not then in the town—and commenced our negotiations with them touching the business entrusted to us by King Ferdinand. The pashas . . . told us that the whole matter depended on the Sultan's pleasure. On his arrival we were admitted to an audience; but the manner and spirit in which he . . . listened to our address,

Source: Ogier Ghiselin de Busbecq, *The Life and Letters of Ogier Ghiselin de Busbecq* (London: Kegan Paul, 1881), pp. 113–120 (passim), 153–155, 218–220, 254.

[1]*Pasha* was an honorary title for a high-ranking military or government official; the *grand vizier* was the sultan's chief advisor and head of the Ottoman administration.

our arguments, and our message was by no means favorable. . . .

On entering we were separately conducted into the royal presence by the chamberlains, who grasped our arms. . . . After having gone through a pretense of kissing his [Suleiman's] hand, we were conducted backwards to the wall opposite his seat, care being taken that we should never turn our backs on him. The Sultan then listened to what I had to say; but the language I used was not at all to his taste, for the demands of his Majesty[2] breathed a spirit of independence and dignity, which was by no means acceptable to one who deemed that his wish was law; and so he made no answer beyond saying in an impatient way, "Giusel, giusel," i.e., well, well. After this we were dismissed to our quarters.

The Sultan's hall was crowded with people, among whom were several officers of high rank. Besides these there were all the troopers of the Imperial guard, and a large force of Janissaries, but there was not in all that great assembly a single man who owed his position to anything save his valor and his merit. No distinction is attached to birth among the Turks; the respect to be paid to a man is measured by the position he holds in the public service. There is no fighting for precedence; a man's place is marked out by the duties he discharges. . . . It is by merit that men rise in the service, a system which ensures that posts should only be assigned to the competent. . . . Those who receive the highest offices from the Sultan are for the most part the sons of shepherds or herdsmen, and so far from being ashamed of their parentage, they actually glory in it, and consider it a matter of boasting that they owe nothing to the accident of birth; for they do not believe that high qualities are either natural or hereditary, nor do they think

that they can be handed down from father to son, but that they are partly the gift of God, and partly the result of good training, great industry, and unwearied zeal. . . . Among the Turks, therefore, honors, high posts, and judgeships are the rewards of great ability and good service.[3]

Ottoman Military Strength

Against us stands Suleiman, that foe whom his own and his ancestors' exploits have made so terrible; he tramples the soil of Hungary with 200,000 horses, he is at the very gates of Austria, threatens the rest of Germany, and brings in his train all the nations that extend from our borders to those of Persia. The army he leads is equipped with the wealth of many kingdoms. Of the three regions, into which the world is divided,[4] there is not one that does not contribute its share towards our destruction. . . .

• • •

The Turkish monarch going to war takes with him over 40,000 camels and nearly as many baggage mules, of which a great part, when he is invading Persia, are loaded with rice and other kinds of grain. These mules and camels also serve to carry tents and armor, and likewise tools and munitions for the campaign. The territories, which bear the name of Persia, . . . are less fertile than our country, and even such crops as they bear are laid waste by the inhabitants in time of invasion in hopes of starving out the enemy, so that it is very dangerous for an army to invade Persia if it is not furnished with abundant supplies. . . .

• • •

After dinner I practice the Turkish bow, in the use of which weapon people here are marvelously

---

[2]Archduke Ferdinand, Busbecq's employer.
[3]Busbecq fails to mention that all the officials he observed were the sultan's slaves recruited through the *devshirme*, or "child contribution" system. Young boys were taken from non-Muslim families and converted to Islam. The brightest were educated in foreign languages, the law, and administrative procedures, after which they took jobs in the sultan's "Inner Service" and could rise to the level of pasha. The less gifted were given jobs in the military and made up the core of the famous Ottoman janissary corps.
[4]Asia, Europe, and Africa.

expert. From the eighth, or even the seventh, year of their age they begin to shoot at a mark, and practice archery ten or twelve years. This constant exercise strengthens the muscles of their arms, and gives them such skill that they can hit the smallest marks with their arrows. . . . So sure is their aim that in battle they can hit a man in the eye or in any other exposed part they choose.

• • •

No nation in the world has shown greater readiness than the Turks to avail themselves of the useful inventions of foreigners, as is proved by their employment of cannons and mortars, and many other things invented by Christians. . . . The Turks are much afraid of carbines and pistols, such as are used on horseback. The same, I hear, is the case with the Persians, on which account someone advised Rustem,[5] when he was setting out with the Sultan on a campaign against them, to raise from his household servants a troop of 200 horsemen and arm them with firearms, as they would cause much alarm . . . in the ranks of the enemy. Rustem, in accordance with this advice, raised a troop of dragoons,[6] furnished them with firearms, and had them drilled. But they had not completed half the journey when their guns began to get out of order. Every day some essential part of their weapons was lost or broken, and it was not often that armorers could be found capable of repairing them. So, a large part of the firearms having been rendered unserviceable, the men took a dislike to the weapon; and this prejudice was increased by the dirt which its use entailed, the Turks being a very cleanly people; for the dragoons had their hands and clothes begrimed with gunpowder, and moreover presented such a sorry appearance, with their ugly boxes and pouches hanging about them, that their comrades laughed at them and called

them apothecaries. So, . . . they gathered around Rustem and showing him their broken and useless firearms, asked what advantage he hoped to gain from them when they met the enemy, and demanded that he should relieve them of them, and give them their old arms again. Rustem, after considering their request carefully, thought there was no reason for refusing to comply with it, and so they got permission to resume their bows and arrows.

Problems of the Succession

Suleiman had a son by a concubine who came from the Crimea. . . . His name was Mustafa, and at the time of which I am speaking he was young, vigorous, and of high repute as a soldier. But Suleiman had also several other children, by a Russian woman.[7] . . . To the latter he was so much attached that he placed her in the position of wife. . . .

Mustafa's high qualities and matured years marked him out to the soldiers who loved him, and the people who supported him, as the successor of his father, who was now in the decline of life. On the other hand, his step-mother [Roxelana], by throwing the claim of a lawful wife onto the balance, was doing her utmost to counterbalance his personal merits and his rights as eldest son, with a view to obtaining the throne for her own children. In this intrigue, she received the advice and assistance of Rustem, whose fortunes were inseparably linked with hers by his marriage with a daughter she had had by Suleiman. . . .

Inasmuch as Rustem was chief Vizier, . . . he had no difficulty . . . in influencing his master's mind. The Turks, accordingly, are convinced that it was by the calumnies of Rustem and the spells of Roxelana, who was in ill repute as a practitioner of sorcery, that the Sultan was so estranged from his son as to entertain the design of getting rid of him. A few believe

---

[5]Rustem, the grand vizier, also was Suleiman's son-in-law. He married the daughter of Suleiman and Roxelana.

[6]Heavily armed mounted troops.
[7]A reference to Roxelana.

that Mustafa, being aware of the plans, . . . decided to anticipate them, and thus engaged in designs against his father's throne and person. The sons of Turkish Sultans are in the most wretched position in the world, for, as soon as one of them succeeds his father, the rest are doomed to certain death. The Turk can endure no rival to the throne, and, indeed, the conduct of the Janissaries renders it impossible for the new Sultan to spare his brothers; for if one of them survives, the Janissaries are forever asking generous favors. If these are refused, the cry is heard, "Long live the brother!" "God preserve the brother!"—a tolerably broad hint that they intend to place him on the throne. So that the Turkish Sultans are compelled to celebrate their succession by staining their hands with the blood of their nearest relatives. . . .

Being at war with Shah Tahmasp, Shah of the Persians, he [Suleiman] had sent Rustem against him as a commander-in-chief of his armies. Just as he was about to enter Persian territory, Rustem suddenly halted, and hurried off dispatches to Suleiman, informing him that affairs were in a very critical state; that treason was rife; . . . that the soldiers had been tampered with, and cared for no one but Mustafa; . . . and he must come at once if he wished to preserve his throne. Suleiman was seriously alarmed by these dispatches. He immediately hurried to the army, sent a letter to summon Mustafa to his presence, inviting him to clear himself of those crimes of which he was suspected. . . .

There was great uneasiness among the soldiers, when Mustafa arrived. . . . He was brought to his father's tent, and there everything betokened peace. . . . But there were in the tent certain mutes—. . . strong and sturdy fellows, who had been appointed as his executioners. As soon as he entered the inner tent, they threw themselves upon him, and endeavored to put the fatal noose around his neck. Mustafa, being a man of considerable strength, made a stout defense and fought—

there being no doubt that if he escaped . . . and threw himself among the Janissaries, the news of this outrage on their beloved prince would cause such pity and indignation, that they would not only protect him, but also proclaim him Sultan. Suleiman felt how critical the matter was, being only separated by the linen hangings of his tent from the stage on which this tragedy was being enacted. When he found that there was an unexpected delay in the execution of his scheme, he thrust out his head from the chamber of his tent, and glared on the mutes with fierce and threatening eyes; at the same time, with signs full of hideous meaning, he sternly rebuked their slackness. Hereon the mutes, gaining fresh strength from the terror he inspired, threw Mustafa down, got the bowstring round his neck, and strangled him. Shortly afterwards they laid his body on a rug in front of the tent, that the Janissaries might see the man they had desired as their Sultan. . . .

Meanwhile, Roxelana, not content with removing Mustafa from her path, . . . did not consider that she and her children were free from danger, so long as his offspring survived. Some pretext, however, she thought necessary, in order to furnish a reason for the murder, but this was not hard to find. Information was brought to Suleiman that, whenever his grandson appeared in public, the boys of Ghemlik[8]—where he was being educated—shouted out, "God save the Prince, and may he long survive his father;" and that the meaning of these cries was to point him out as his grandsire's future successor, and his father's avenger. Moreover, he was bidden to remember that the Janissaries would be sure to support the son of Mustafa, so that the father's death had in no way secured the peace of the throne and realm. . .

Suleiman was easily convinced by these arguments to sign the death-warrant of his grandson. He commissioned Ibrahim Pasha to go to the Ghemlik with all speed, and put the innocent child to death.[9]

---

[8]A town in northwest Turkey.

[9]The assassination was carried out by a eunuch hired by Ibrahim Pasha, who had succeeded Rustem as grand vizier.

A Self-Portrait of Jahangir

13 • JAHANGIR, MEMOIRS

Jahangir, Mughal emperor from 1605 to 1627, modestly increased the size of the empire through conquest, snuffed out half a dozen rebellions, and generally continued the policies of his illustrious father, Akbar. His lands provided him the wealth to indulge his tastes for formal gardens, entertaining, ceremony, sports, literature, and finely crafted books. In addition to subsidizing the work of hundreds of painters and writers, Jahangir himself contributed to the literature of his age by writing a memoir. Intended to glorify himself and instruct his heirs, it covered the first 13 years of his reign, before his addiction to alcohol and opium sapped his energy and effectiveness.

QUESTIONS FOR ANALYSIS

1. Other than to glorify the person of the emperor, what political purposes might have been served by Jahangir's elaborate coronation ceremony?
2. What do the "twelve special regulations" issued at the beginning of Jahangir's reign reveal about his priorities as emperor?
3. How does Jahangir view his Hindu subjects? What are his reasons for allowing them to practice their religion?
4. What does the episode of the Afghan bandits reveal about Jahangir's view of the emperor's responsibilities?
5. What similarities and differences do you see in the authority and leadership style of Suleiman I (source 13), Abbas I (source 14), and Jahangir?

Jahangir's Coronation

On the eighth of the latter month of Jammaudy, of the year of the Hegira one thousand and fourteen,[1] in the metropolis of Agra, and in the forenoon of the day, being then at the age of thirty-eight, I became Emperor, and under the most felicitous auspices, took my seat on the throne of my wishes. . . . Hence I assumed the titles of Jahangir Padshah, and Jahangir Shah: the world-subduing emperor; the world-subduing king.

I ordained that the following legend should be stamped on the coinage of the empire: "Stricken at Agra by that . . . safeguard of the world; the sovereign splendor of the faith, Jahangir son of the imperial Akbar."

On this occasion I made use of the throne prepared by my father, and enriched at an expense without parallel, for the celebration of the festival of the new year. . . . In the fabrication of the throne a sum not far short of ten krours of ashrefies[2] was expended in jewels alone. . . .

Source: David Price, trans. *Memoirs of the Emperor Jahangir Written by Himself* (London: Oriental Translation Society, 1928), pp. 8–12, 13–20, 33–36, 51–53, 65–66.

[1]October 10, 1605. Jahangir uses the Muslim calendar, dated from the *hijra*, Muhammad's flight from Mecca to Medina in 1622.

[2]A *krour* is a measurement of weight, and an *ashrefy* is a unit of money. Although it is impossible to determine the exact value of ten "krours of ashrefies," it is an enormous sum.

Having thus seated myself on the throne of my expectation and wishes, I caused also the imperial crown, which my father had caused to be made after the manner of that which was worn by the great kings of Persia, to be brought before me, and then, in the presence of the whole assembled Emirs,[3] having placed it on my brows, as an omen auspicious to the stability and happiness of my reign, kept it there for the space of a full . . . hour. On each of the twelve points of this crown was a single diamond . . . the whole purchased by my father with the resources of his own government, not from anything accruing to him by inheritance from his predecessors. At the point in the center of the top part of the crown was a single pearl . . . and on different parts of the same were set altogether two hundred rubies. . . .

For forty days and forty nights I caused the . . . great imperial state drum to strike up, without ceasing, the strains of joy and triumph; and . . . around my throne, the ground was spread by my directions with the most costly brocades and gold embroidered carpets. Censers[4] of gold and silver were disposed in different directions for the purpose of burning fragrant drugs, and nearly three thousand camphorated wax lights, . . . in branches of gold and silver perfumed with ambergris, illuminated the scene from night till morning. Numbers of blooming youth, . . . clad in dresses of the most costly materials, woven in silk and gold, with . . . amulets sparkling with the lustre of the diamond, the emerald, the sapphire, and the ruby, awaited my commands, rank after rank, and in attitude most respectful. And finally, the Emirs of the empire . . . stood round in brilliant array, also waiting for the commands of their sovereign. . . .

The Emperor's Decrees

The very first ordinance that issued from me . . . related to the chain of justice, one end of which I caused to be fastened to the battlements of the royal tower of the castle of Agra, and the other to a stone post near the bed of the river Jumnah; to the end that whenever those charged with administering the courts were slack in dispensing justice to the downtrodden, he who had suffered injustice by applying his hand to the chain would find himself in the way of obtaining speedy redress.[5] . . .

I issued twelve special regulations to be implemented and observed in all the realm.

1. I canceled the tamgha, the mirabari,[6] and all other imposts the jagirdars[7] of every province and district had imposed for their own profit.

2. I ordered that when a district lay wasted by thieves and highway bandits or was destitute of inhabitants, that towns should be built, . . . and every effort made to protect the subjects from injury. I directed the jagirdars in such deserted places to erect mosques and caravansaries, or places for the accommodation of travelers, in order to render the district once more an inhabited country, and that men might again be able to travel back and forth safely. . . .

3. Merchants travelling through the country were not to have their bales or packs opened without their consent.

4. When a person shall die and leave children, whether he is an infidel[8] or Muslim, no man was to interfere a pin's point in his property; but when he has no children or direct and unquestionable heirs his inheritance is to be spent on approved expenditures such as construction of mosques and caravansaries, repair of bridges, and the creation of water-tanks and wells.

5. No person was permitted either to make or to sell wine or any other intoxicating liquor. I undertook to institute this regulation,

---

[3]High government officials.

[4]A container for burning incense.

[5]Presumably pulling the chain would be the first step in bringing the perceived injustice to the emperor's attention.

[6]The *tamgha* and *mirabari* were both customs duties.

[7]A *jagir* was a grant of land by the emperor that entitled the holder to the income from the land. The income was to be used mainly to maintain troops. A *jagirdar* was the holder of a jagir.

[8]A Hindu.

although it is sufficiently well known that I myself have the strongest inclination for wine, in which from the age of sixteen I have liberally indulged. . . .

6. No official was permitted to take up his abode in the house of any subject of my realm. On the contrary, when individuals serving in the state armies come to any town, and can rent a place to live, it would be commendable; otherwise they were to pitch their tents outside the town. . . .

7. No person was to suffer, for any offence, the cutting off of a nose or ear. For theft, the offender was to be scourged with thorns, or deterred from further transgressions by an oath on the Quran.[9]

8. I decreed that superintendents of royal lands and jagirdars were prohibited from seizing the lands of their subjects or cultivating the lands themselves for their own benefit. . . . On the contrary, his attention was to be wholly and exclusively devoted to the cultivation and improvement of the district allotted to him.

9. The tax collectors of royal lands and jagirdars may not intermarry with the people of the districts in which they reside without my permission.[10]

10. Governors in all the large cities were directed to establish infirmaries and hospitals with physicians appointed to treat the sick. Expenses are to be covered by income from royal lands.

11. During the month of my birth there could be no slaughter of animals in my realm. . . . In every week also, on Thursday, that being the day of my accession, and Sunday, my father's birthday, . . . and also because it is the day attributed to the sun and the day on which the creation of the world was begun. . . .

12. I issued a decree confirming the dignitaries and jagirs of my father's government in all that they had enjoyed while he was living; and where I found sufficient merit, I conferred an advance of rank. . . .

Policy Toward the Hindus

I am here led to relate that at the city of Banaras[11] a temple had been erected [in which] . . . the principal idol . . . had on its head a tiara or cap, enriched with jewels. . . . [Also] placed in this temple, moreover, as the associates and ministering servants of the principal idol, [were] four other images of solid gold, each crowned with a tiara, in like manner enriched with precious stones. It was the belief of these non-believers that a dead Hindu, provided when alive he had been a worshiper, when laid before this idol would be restored to life. As I could not possibly give credit to such a pretense, I employed a confidential person to ascertain the truth; and, as I justly supposed, the whole was detected to be an impudent fraud. . . .

On this subject I must however acknowledge, that having on one occasion asked my father [Akbar] the reason why he had forbidden anyone to prevent or interfere with the building of these haunts of idolatry, his reply was in the following terms: "My dear child," said he, "I find myself a powerful monarch, the shadow of God upon earth. I have seen that he bestows the blessing of his gracious providence upon all his creatures without distinction. . . . With all of the human race, with all of God's creatures, I am at peace: why then should I permit myself, under any consideration, to be the cause of molestation or aggression to any one? Besides, are not five parts in six . . . either Hindus or aliens to the faith; and were I to be governed by motives of the kind suggested in your inquiry,

---

[9]Islam's sacred book.

[10]This was to prevent any tax collector or jagirdar from gaining a vested interest in the fortunes of a particular region or family.

[11]A city on the Ganges River.

what alternative can I have but to put them all to death! I have thought it therefore my wisest plan to let these men alone. Neither is it to be forgotten, that the class of whom we are speaking . . . are usefully engaged, either in the pursuits of science or the arts, or of improvements for the benefit of mankind, and have in numerous instances arrived at the highest distinctions in the state, there being, indeed, to be found in this city men of every description, and of every religion on the face of the earth." . . .

• • •

In the practice of being burnt on the funeral pyre of their husbands[12] as sometimes exhibited among the widows of the Hindus, I had previously directed that no woman who was the mother of children should be thus made a sacrifice, however willing to die; and I now further ordained, that in no case was the practice to be permitted, when compulsion was in the slightest degree employed, whatever might be the opinions of the people. In other respects they were in no way to be molested in the duties of their religion, nor exposed to oppression or violence in any manner whatever. . . .

The Duties of the Emperor

. . . It had been made known to me that the roads about Kandahar[13] were grievously infested by the Afghans, who by their vexatious exactions rendered the communications in that quarter extremely unsafe for travelers of every description. . . .

Lushker Khan . . . was despatched by my orders toward Kabul for the purpose of clearing the roads in that direction, which had been rendered unsafe by the outrages of licentious

bandits. It so happened that when this commander had nearly reached the point for which he was destined he found opposed to him a body of mountaineers . . . , who had assembled to the number of forty thousand, horse and foot and musketeers, had shut up the approaches against him, and prevented his further advance. . . . A conflict began, which continued . . . from dawn of day until nearly sunset. The enemy were however finally defeated, with the loss of seventeen thousand killed, a number taken prisoners, and a still greater proportion escaping to their hiding-places among the mountains. The prisoners were conducted to my presence yoked together, with the heads of the seventeen thousand slain in the battle suspended from their necks. After some deliberation as to the destiny of these captives, I resolved that their lives should be spared, and that they should be employed in bringing forage for my elephants.

. . . The shedding of so much human blood must ever be extremely painful; but until some other resource is discovered, it is unavoidable. Unhappily the functions of government cannot be carried on without severity, and occasional extinction of human life: for without something of the kind, some species of coercion and chastisement, the world would soon exhibit the horrible spectacle of mankind, like wild beasts, worrying each other to death with no other motive than rapacity and revenge. God is witness that there is no repose for crowned heads. There is no pain or anxiety equal to that which attends the possession of sovereign power, for to the possessor there is not in this world a moment's rest. . . .

---

[12]A woman who burned herself in this way was known as *sati* (Sanskrit for "virtuous woman"). The word *sati* also is used to describe the burning itself.

[13]A city in Afghanistan.

Religion, Society, and Culture in South and Southwest Asia

Although many religions—Hinduism, Buddhism, Zoroastrianism, Judaism, Islam, and Christianity—originated in South and Southwest Asia, by the sixteenth century, two faiths dominated the region. One was Islam, ascendant everywhere except India, and the other was Hinduism, India's ancient religion that endured despite centuries of competition from Buddhism, Jainism, and Islam.

At first glance, one is struck by the differences between Islam and Hinduism. Islam is distinguished by uncompromising monotheism; the centrality of a single holy book, the Quran; and its origin in the prophecies of a single human being, Muhammad. In contrast, Hinduism is characterized by its pantheon of thousands of gods, its slow and continuous evolution, and its lack of a single creed or holy book. Yet on a deeper level, the two religions are similar. Both reject any separation between the religious and secular spheres. Islam and Hinduism not only guide each believer's spiritual development but also define the believer's roles as a parent, spouse, subject, and worker. Secularism is a foreign concept in both religions.

Islam is based on the prophecies and doctrines revealed by Allah (Arabic for God) to Muhammad (ca. 570–632 C.E.) and later recorded in the Quran. *Islam* in Arabic means "submission," and a Muslim is one who submits to God's will. Islam's basic creed is the statement that every follower must say daily: "There is no God but God, and Muhammad is the Prophet of God." All Muslims are expected to accept the Quran as the word of God, perform works of charity, fast during the month of Ramadan, say daily prayers, and, if possible, make a pilgrimage to Mecca, the city where Muhammad received Allah's revelation. Islam teaches that at death each person will be judged by Allah, with the faithful rewarded by Heaven and the unbelievers damned to Hell.

Hinduism has no single creed, set of rituals, or holy book. It is a religion of thousands of deities, although all are believed to be manifestations of the Divine Essence or Absolute Reality, called Brahman. In addition, some Hindus follow the "path of devotion," or *bhakti,* in which they focus their faith on devotion to a single god such as Vishnu or his incarnation, Krishna. Hindus believe many paths lead to enlightenment, and Hinduism thus encompasses a wide range of beliefs and rituals.

All Hindus are part of the caste system, a religiously sanctioned order of social relationships that goes back to the beginnings of Indian civilization between 1500 and 1000 B.C.E. A person's caste, into which he or she is born, determines the individual's social and legal status, restricts marriage partners to other caste members, limits the individual to certain professions, and, in effect, minimizes contacts with members of other castes. Hindus use two different words for caste: *varna* (color) and *jati* (birth). *Varna* refers only to the four most ancient and fundamental social-religious divisions: *Brahmins* (priests and teachers), *Kshatriyas* (warriors, nobles, and rulers), *Vaisyas* (landowners, merchants, and artisans), and *Sudras* (peasants and laborers). At the bottom of the Hindu hierarchy are the untouchables, who are relegated to despised tasks such as gathering manure, sweeping streets, and butchering animals. *Jati* refers to the many subdivisions of the four major varna groups; by the 1600s, these local hereditary occupational groups numbered around 3,000.

The caste system is related to the doctrine of the transmigration of souls, or reincarnation. This is the belief that each individual soul, or *atman*, a fragment of the Universal Soul, or Brahman, strives through successive births to reunite with Brahman and win release from the chains of material existence and the cycle of death and rebirth. Reincarnation is based on one's *karma*, the fruit of one's actions, which is decided by how well or poorly a person has conformed to *dharma*, the duty to be performed by members of each jati and varna. If a person fulfills his or her dharma, in the next incarnation he or she will move up the cosmic ladder, closer to ultimate reunion with the One.

Sunni–Shia Conflict in the Early Sixteenth Century

14 • SULTAN SELIM I, LETTER TO SHAH ISMAIL OF PERSIA

The following letter, written by the Ottoman sultan Selim I (r. 1512–1520) to the founder of the Persian Safavid Empire, Ismail I (r. 1501–1524), illustrates the ongoing bitterness between Shia and Sunni Muslims. Selim, who in the Ottoman tradition was a Sunni, was deeply disturbed by the emergence of a Shia state in Persia under Ismail. Ismail, believed by his followers to have descended from Ali, Muhammad's son-in-law, had many supporters among the Turks of eastern Anatolia and had aided Selim's brother and rival, Ahmed, in the succession conflict following Sultan Bayezid's death in 1512. When Ismail invaded eastern Ottoman territory in 1513, war seemed inevitable. Nonetheless, Selim wrote this letter to Ismail in early 1514 offering him an opportunity to escape defeat by embracing Sunni Islam and abandoning his conquests. Ismail did neither, and later in 1514, Selim's armies defeated Ismail's forces at the Battle of Chaldiran. Despite this loss, Ismail remained in power and affirmed his commitment to Shiism. Chaldiran was only the first act in a long rivalry between the two empires.

QUESTIONS FOR ANALYSIS

1. Even though Selim's letter is designed to malign Shiism, not define Islam, it contains many references to essential Muslim beliefs. Which ones can you find?
2. What does Selim's letter reveal about the differences between Sunnis and Shias?
3. How does Selim perceive himself within the Islamic world?
4. Selim must have realized that the deeply religious Ismail was unlikely to abandon Shiism. Why might he have written the letter, despite the likelihood that its appeal would fall on deaf ears?

The Supreme Being who is at once the sovereign arbiter of the destinies of men and the source of all light and knowledge, declares in the holy book[1] that the true faith is that of the Muslims, and that whoever professes another religion, far from being hearkened to and saved, will on the contrary be cast out among the rejected on the great day of the Last Judgment; He says further . . . that he who abandons the good way will be condemned to hell-fire and eternal torments. Place yourself, O Prince, among the true believers, those who walk in the path of salvation, and who turn aside with care from vice and infidelity. . . .

I, sovereign chief of the Ottomans, master of the heroes of the age; . . . I, the exterminator of idolators, destroyer of the enemies of the true faith, the terror of the tyrants and pharaohs of the age; I, before whom proud and unjust kings have humbled themselves, and whose hand breaks the strongest scepters. . . . I address myself graciously to you, Emir Ismail, . . . in order to make known to you that the works emanating from the Almighty are not the fragile products of caprice or folly, but make up an infinity of mysteries impenetrable to the human mind. . . . Man . . . attains this divine knowledge only in our religion and by observing the precepts of the prince of prophets [Muhammad] . . . ; it is then only by practicing the true religion that man will prosper in this world and merit eternal life in the other. As to you, Emir Ismail, such a recompense will not be your lot; because you have denied the sanctity of the divine laws; . . . have deserted the path of salvation and the sacred commandments; . . . have impaired the purity of the dogmas of Islam; . . . have dishonored, soiled, and destroyed the altars of the Lord,

usurped the scepter of the East by unlawful and tyrannical means; . . . have raised yourself by odious devices to a place shining with splendor and magnificence; . . . have opened to Muslims the gates of tyranny and oppression; . . . have joined iniquity, perjury, and blasphemy to your sectarian impiety; . . . have raised the standard of irreligion and heresy; . . . have dared to throw off the control of Muslim laws and to permit lust and rape, the massacre of the most virtuous and respectable men, the destruction of pulpits and temples, the profanation of tombs, the ill-treatment of the *ulama,* the doctors and emirs[2] descended from the Prophet, the repudiation of the Quran, the cursing of the legitimate Caliphs.[3] Now as the first duty of a Muslim and above all of a pious prince is to obey the commandment, "O, you faithful who believe, be the executors of the decrees of God!" the *ulama* and our doctors have pronounced sentence of death against you, . . . and have imposed on every Muslim the sacred obligation to arm in defense of religion and destroy heresy and impiety in your person and that of all your partisans.

Animated by the spirit of this *fatwa,*[4] conforming to the Quran, the code of divine laws, and wishing on one side to strengthen Islam, on the other to liberate the lands and peoples who writhe under your yoke, we have resolved to lay aside our imperial robes in order to put on the shield and coat of mail [armor], to raise our ever victorious banner, to assemble our invincible armies, to take up the gauntlet of the avenger, to march with our soldiers, whose sword strikes mortal blows, and whose point will pierce the enemy. . . . In pursuit of this noble resolution, we have entered upon the campaign, and guided by the hand of

---

Source: John J. Saunders, ed., *The Muslim World on the Eve of Europe's Expansion* (Englewood Cliffs, NJ: Prentice Hall, 1966), pp. 41–43. Reprinted by permission.

[1]The Quran.

[2]Shias originally broke away from mainstream Islam over disagreements concerning the early caliphate. They believe that Ali, Muhammad's cousin and son-in-law (the fourth

caliph), should have been the first. As a result, the Shias believe that the first three caliphs (all legitimate according to the Sunnis) are illegitimate.

[3]*Ulama* (or *ulema*) refers to the community of religious teachers and interpreters of Muslim law; *doctors* here means teachers; *emirs* were military commanders and princes.

[4]A religious decree or opinion.

the Almighty, we hope soon to strike down your tyrannous arm, blow away the clouds of glory and grandeur which trouble your head and cause your fatal blindness, release from your despotism your trembling subjects, smother you in the end in the very mass of flames which your infernal *jinn*[5] raises everywhere along your passage. . . . However, anxious to conform to the spirit of the law of the Prophet, we come, before commencing war, to set out before you the words of the Quran, in place of the sword, and to exhort you to embrace the true faith; this is why we address this letter to you. . . .

We urge you to look into yourself, to renounce your errors, and to march towards the good with a firm and courageous step; we ask further that you give up possession of the territory violently seized from our state and to which you have only illegitimate pretensions, that you deliver it back into the hands of our lieutenants and officers; and if you value your safety and repose, this should be done without delay.

But if, to your misfortune, you persist in your past conduct, puffed up with the idea of your power and your foolish bravado, you wish to pursue the course of your iniquities, you will see in a few days your plains covered with our tents and inundated with our battalions. Then prodigies of valor will be done, and we shall see the decrees of the Almighty, Who is the God of Armies, and sovereign judge of the actions of men, accomplished. For the rest, victory to him who follows the path of salvation!

---

[5]Supernatural spirit.

Women and Islamic Law in the Ottoman Empire

15 • KHAYR AL-DIN RAMLI, LEGAL OPINIONS

Many of Muhammad's teachings were favorable to women. He taught the spiritual equality between men and women, and his treatment of his own wives and daughters exemplifies his teachings about the moral and ethical dimensions of marriage. Women were among his earliest and most important followers. As Islam evolved, however, women's status declined. Women, especially from the upper classes, were secluded in their homes and expected to wear clothes covering their bodies and faces in public. Their role in religious affairs virtually disappeared, and vocational and educational opportunities declined. Some Islamic scholars came to believe that Heaven itself was closed to females.

As the following legal opinions show, however, women in the Ottoman Empire were not without legal rights during the seventeenth century. The empire had a complex and sophisticated court system staffed by *qadi* (judges), whose job was to interpret Islamic law (Sharia) and apply it to specific cases. In making decisions, they drew on their knowledge of the Quran and Hadith (traditions connected with Muhammad's life and teachings), legal precedent, and textbooks and commentaries on Islamic law. They also took into account *fatwas*, legal opinions provided by learned men known as *muftis*. Such opinions could be solicited by judges or by an individual involved in a court case. A fatwa was not a binding legal judgment but rather one scholar's opinion that would be included in the record of the trial and might affect the judge's decision. In some provincial courts, however, the standing of a mufti might be so high that his fatwa would override a decision of the court.

The following fatwas were written by Khayr al-Din Ramli (1585–1671), who, after advanced studies in Cairo, returned to his native city of Ramla in Palestine, where he supported himself through farming, income from property, and teaching Islamic law. His fame, however, was based on his work as a mufti. By the 1650s, his reputation throughout Syria and Palestine was such that no judge would go against one of his opinions. The following examples all pertain to women's position in society. The judgments take male dominance for granted but also accord legal rights and protections to women.

Many of the decisions involve marriage, a state into which every adult Muslim was expected to enter. Most marriages were arranged by legal guardians (usually fathers or grandfathers), often when the future wife and husband were still children. On reaching a marriageable age, the young people had no choice but to acquiesce to their guardians' wishes and accept the planned marriage. For marriages arranged between adults, however, individuals had the right to reject the proposed match. Similarly, if a marriage was arranged by someone other than a father or grandfather for a minor, then on reaching adulthood the person could refuse.

Islamic law affirmed that no social good was served by continuing defective or unhappy marriages. Hence, divorce was permissible and fairly common. A husband could divorce his wife by saying before her and a witness, "I divorce you, I divorce you, I divorce you." This meant that the woman was irrevocably and finally divorced ("thrice-divorced") and could remarry if she wished. For a specified time or until the divorced wife remarried, the former husband was required to support her. A woman could also demand a divorce by demonstrating in court that her husband had failed to fulfill his financial or sexual obligations. Or alternatively, she could convince her husband to annul the marriage by offering him financial concessions. For example, she might return some or all of the dowry payment she had received or release the husband from support obligations after the annulment.

Many of the cases on which Khayr al-Din Ramli commented centered on relations between unmarried men and women, child custody, crimes against women, and sexuality. Together they provide many insights into male–female relations in seventeenth-century Syria-Palestine.

QUESTIONS FOR ANALYSIS

1. In making arrangements for marriage, how much legal authority is exercised by the following: the future husband and wife; fathers and grandfathers; male relatives of the future husband and wife?
2. What do the divorce cases reveal about the obligations of husbands to their wives?
3. What rights does a married woman have against an abusive husband?
4. How did Khayr al-Din Ramli view rapists and abductors of women? What penalties are prescribed for perpetrators of such crimes?
5. In one case a widow is appointed by her dying husband to be guardian of their children. What does this reveal about inheritance practices?

6. Taking all the cases together, what do they tell about women's legal standing in seventeenth-century Syria-Palestine? What situations and legal opinions underscore women's legal inferiority to men? What situations and decisions accord women legal rights in their dealings with men?

Arranging Marriages

QUESTION: There is a minor girl whose brother married her off, and she came of age and chose annulment in her "coming-of-age" choice. Her husband claimed that her brother had acted as the agent of her father and she does not have a choice. She then claimed that [her brother] married her off during [her father's] brief absence on a journey. If the husband provides evidence for his claim, is her choice canceled or not? If he does not have evidence, and wants her oath on that, must she swear an oath?

ANSWER: Yes, if the husband proves his claim, then her choice is canceled. . . . Only the father's and grandfather's marriage arrangements cannot be canceled . . . [and] if the marriage was arranged by way of a proxy for her father, then she has no choice. If the marriage was arranged as a result of [the brother's] guardianship, then she has a choice.

• • •

QUESTION: A virgin in her legal majority and of sound mind was abducted by her brother and married off to an unsuitable man. Does her father have the right to annul the marriage contract on the basis of the [husband's] unsuitability?

ANSWER: Yes, if the father asks for that, then the judge should separate the spouses whether or not the marriage was consummated, so long as she has not borne children, and is not pregnant, and did not receive the dower[1] before the marriage. . . . This is the case if her brother has married her off with her consent. But if she was given in marriage without her consent, she can reject [the marriage], and there is no need for the father [to ask for] separation [and raise] opposition, for he is not [in this case] a commissioned agent. [But] if she authorizes him to represent her, then he has the right to request from the judge an annulment of the marriage and a separation, and the judge should separate them. . . .

Divorce and Annulment

QUESTION: There is a poor woman whose husband is absent in a remote region and he left her without support or a legal provider, and she has suffered proven harm from that. She has made a claim against him for that [support], but the absent one is very poor. The resources [intended] for her support were left in his house and in his shop, but they are not sufficient for her to withstand her poverty. She therefore asked the Shafi'i[2] judge to annul the marriage, and he ordered her to bring proof. Two just men testified in conformity with what she had claimed, and so the judge annulled the marriage. . . . Then, following her waiting period, she married another man. Then the first husband returned and wanted to nullify the judgment. Can that be done for him, when it was all necessary and had ample justification?

ANSWER: When the harm is demonstrated and the evidence for that is witnessed, the annulment of the absent [one's marriage] is sound. . . . It is not for the Hanafi[3] or others to nullify this. . . .

• • •

Source: From Judith E. Tucker, *In The House of the Law Gender and Islamic Law in Ottoman Syria and Palestine*, 1988, pp. 26, 47, 68, 69, 78, 83, and 165. Reprinted with permission of The University of California Press.

[1]In contrast to practice in Europe, dowry payments were paid by the husband to the wife.

[2]One of the four schools of Sunni Muslim jurisprudence; it tended to be more favorable to women seeking divorce.

[3]Another school of Sunni Muslim jurisprudence, less favorable to women seeking divorce.

QUESTION: There is a poor man who married a virgin in her legal majority, but he did not pay her stipulated dower expeditiously, nor did he provide support, nor did he clothe her. This caused her great harm. Must he follow one of God's two commands: "Either you maintain her well or you release her with kindness?" And if the judge annuls the marriage, is it on account of the severe harm being done to her?

ANSWER: Yes, the husband should do one of the two things, according to God's command: "maintain her well or release her with kindness." . . . You cannot sustain [indefinitely] such needs through borrowing, and it appears that she does not have anyone to lend her money, and the husband has no actual wealth. . . .

• • •

QUESTION: A man consummated his marriage with his virgin legally major wife, and then claimed that he found her deflowered. He was asked, "How was that?" And he said, "I had intercourse with her several times and I found her deflowered." What is the legal judgment on that?

ANSWER: The judgment is that all of the dower is required, and it is fully and entirely incumbent on him. Her testimony on her own virginity [is sufficient] to remove the shame. And if he accuses her without [evidence], he is punished and his testimony is not accepted, as is her right. If he defamed her with a charge of adultery, he must now make a sworn allegation of adultery if she so requests, [and take the consequences].[4] Such is the case, and God knows best.

Violence Against Women

QUESTION: A man approached a woman, a virgin in her legal majority who was married to someone else,[5] abducted her in the month of Ramadan, and took her to a village near her own village. He brought her to the shaykh[6] of the village, who welcomed him and gave him hospitality and protection. There the man consummated the "marriage," saying "between us there are relations." Such is the way of the peasants. . . . What is the punishment for him and the man who helped him? . . . Should Muslim rulers halt these practices of the peasants . . . even by combat and killing?[7]

ANSWER: The punishment of the abductor and his accomplice for this grave crime is severe beating and long imprisonment, and even worse punishment until they show remorse. It is conceivable that the punishment could be execution because of the severity of this act of disobedience to God. This practice— and one fears for the people of the region if it spreads and they do not halt it—will be punished by God. The one who commits this act, and those who remain silent about it, are like one who punches a hole in a ship, [an act] that will drown all the passengers. . . .

• • •

QUESTION: There is a *muhsan*[8] criminal who kidnapped a virgin and took her virginity. She fled from him to her family and now her seducer wants to take her away by force. Should he be prevented, and what is required of him?

ANSWER: Yes, he should be prevented [from taking] her. If he claimed *shubha*[9] [judicial doubt], there is no *hadd* punishment but he must [pay] a fair dower. If he did not claim *shubha*, and admission and testimony prove [his actions], the specified *hadd* punishment[10] is required: if he is *muhsan*, then he is stoned; if not, he is flogged. In the event the *hadd* penalty is canceled, a dower is required.

---

[4]In order to prove adultery, an accuser had to present four witnesses to testify that it occurred. A failure to prove such an accusation carried severe legal penalties.
[5]The marriage had been legally contracted but not consummated.
[6]In this context, the village leader, often a man with some religious training and standing.

[7]In other words, by sending in troops to enforce the law.
[8]A legally married person.
[9]An issue about which legal authorities disagree.
[10]A *hadd* punishment is one prescribed by Islamic law.

QUESTION: There is an evil man who harms his wife, hits her without right and rebukes her without cause. He swore many times to divorce her until she proved that a thrice divorce [a final and irrevocable divorce] had taken effect.

ANSWER: He is forbidden to do that, and he is rebuked and enjoined from her. If she has proved that a thrice divorce has taken place, it is permissible for her to kill him, according to many of the *'ulama'* [jurists] if he is not prevented [from approaching her] except by killing.

A Muslim's Description of Hindu Beliefs and Practices

16 • ABUL FAZL, AKBARNAMA

As Akbar, Mughal ruler from 1556 to 1605, expanded and strengthened his empire, at his side was Abul Fazl, his close friend and advisor from 1579 until his assassination in 1602. Abul Fazl is best known as the author of the *Akbarnama,* a laudatory history of Akbar's reign full of information about the emperor's personality and exploits. At the time of Abul Fazl's assassination, instigated by Akbar's son and future emperor Jahangir, his history had covered only the first 46 years of Akbar's life, but that was enough to ensure his work's standing as one of the masterpieces of Mughal literature.

The *Akbarnama* is more than a chronicle of Akbar's life; it also contains numerous descriptions of Indian society, such as the following passage on Hinduism. Abul Fazl, who shared Akbar's tolerant religious views, was interested in presenting Hinduism favorably to his Islamic readers, many of whom were uncomfortable with Akbar's tolerant polices toward his Hindu subjects. Equally disturbing was his interest in Christianity, Jainism, and Zoroastrianism, all of which helped inspire his new religious cult, *Din-i Ilahi,* or Divine Faith. In the *Akbarnama,* Abul Fazl sought to lessen the concerns of orthodox Muslims that Hindus were guilty of the two greatest sins—idolatry (the worship of idols) and polytheism (a belief in many gods). He also explained the religious basis of the Hindu caste system, whose rigid hierarchies were far removed from the Muslim belief in the equality of all believers before Allah.

QUESTIONS FOR ANALYSIS

1. How does Abul Fazl counter the charge that Hindus are polytheists? Do you find his arguments convincing? Why or why not?
2. How does Abul Fazl address the charge that Hindus are idol worshipers?
3. In what ways do caste and karma provide Hindus with a moral understanding of the universe?
4. What do the dharmas of the castes reveal about Hindu social values?
5. Where do women fit into the structure of the ladder of reincarnation? What does this suggest about their status in Hindu society?
6. On the basis of Abul Fazl's account, what conclusions can you reach about the ways Hindus perceive and relate to Divine Reality?

They [Hindus] one and all believe in the unity of God, and as to the reverence they pay to images of stone and wood and the like, which simpletons regard as idolatry, it is not so. The writer of these words has exhaustively discussed the subject with many enlightened and upright men, and it became evident that these images . . . are fashioned as aids to fix the mind and keep the thoughts from wandering, while the worship of God alone is required as indispensable. In all their ceremonial observances and usage . . . they regard the pure essence of the Supreme Being as transcending the idea of power in operation.

Brahma . . . they hold to be the Creator; Vishnu, the Nourisher and Preserver; and Rudra,[1] called also Mahadeva, the Destroyer. Some maintain that God who is without equal, manifested himself under these three divine forms, without thereby sullying the garment of His inviolate sanctity, as the Nazarenes [Christians] hold of the Messiah.[2] Others assert that these were human creatures exalted to these dignities through perfectness of worship, probity of thought and righteousness of deed. The godliness and self-discipline of this people is such as is rarely to be found in other lands.

They hold that the world had a beginning, and some are of opinion that it will have an end. . . . They allow of no existence external to God. The world is a delusive appearance, and as a man in sleep sees fanciful shapes, and is affected by a thousand joys and sorrows, so are its seeming realities. . . .

Brahman is the Supreme Being; and is essential existence and wisdom and also bliss. . . . Since according to their belief, the Supreme Deity can assume an elemental form . . . they first make various idols of gold and other substances to represent this ideal and gradually withdrawing the mind from this material worship, they become meditatively absorbed in the ocean of His mysterious Being. . . .

They believe that the Supreme Being in the wisdom of His counsel assumes an elementary form of a special character[3] for the good of the creation, and many of the wisest of the Hindus accept this doctrine. . . .

Caste

The Hindu philosophers reckon four states of auspiciousness which they term *varna*. 1. *Brahmin*. 2. *Kshatriya*. 3. *Vaisya*. 4. *Sudra*. Other than these are termed *Mlechchha*.[4] At the creation of the world the first of these classes was produced from the mouth of Brahma . . . ; the second, from his arms; the third, from his thigh and the fourth from his feet; the fifth from the cow *Kamadhenu*, the name of Mlechchha being employed to designate them.

The *Brahmins* have six recognized duties. 1. The study of the Vedas[5] and other sciences. 2. The instruction of others (in the sacred texts). 3. The performance of the *Jag*, that is oblation [a religious offering] of money and kind to the Devatas.[6] 4. Inciting others to the same. 5. Giving presents. 6. Receiving presents.

Source: Abul Fazl, *The Ain-l-Akan*, ed. and trans. by H. S. Jarrett (Calcutta, India: Baptist Mission Press, 1868–1894), vol. 3, pp. 8, 114–119, 159–160, 225–232, 279, 284, 285–286, 291–292.
[1]Also known as Shiva.
[2]Abul Fazl is making two comparisons. First he compares this Hindu trinity to the Christian Trinity (three divine and full separate persons in one God); then he points out the similarities in Christian and Hindu beliefs in incarnation, whereby God or a god becomes embodied in an earthly form. His Muslim readers would have known basic Christian beliefs.
[3]That is, the Hindu Supreme Being assumes various bodies known as *avataras*.
[4]The "untouchables" or outcasts of Hindu society.
[5]The four collections of ancient poetry that are sacred texts among Hindus.
[6]Hindu deities.

Of these six the *Kshatriya* must perform three. 1. Perusing the holy texts. 2. The performance of the Jag. 3. Giving presents. Further they must, 1. Minister to Brahmins. 2. Control the administration of worldly government and receive the reward thereof. 3. Protect religion. 4. Exact fines for delinquency and observe adequate measure therein. 5. Punish in proportion to the offense. 6. Amass wealth and duly expend it. 7. Supervise the management of elephants, horses, and cattle and the functions of ministerial subordinates. 8. Levy war on due occasion. 9. Never ask for alms. 10. Favor the meritorious and the like.

The *Vaisya* also must perform the same three duties of the Brahmin, and in addition must occupy himself in: 1. Service. 2. Agriculture. 3. Trade. 4. The care of cattle. 5. The carrying of loads. . . .

The Sudra is incapable of any other privilege than to serve these three castes, wear their cast-off garments and eat their leavings. He may be a painter, goldsmith, blacksmith, carpenter, and trade in salt, honey, milk, butter-milk, clarified butter and grain.

Those of the fifth class are reckoned as beyond the pale of religion, like infidels, Jews, and the like.[7]

By the intermarriages of these, sixteen other classes are formed. The son of Brahmin parents is acknowledged as a Brahmin. If the mother be a Kshatriya (the father being a Brahmin), the progeny is called *Murdhavasikta*. If the mother be a Vaisya, the son is named *Ambastha,* and if a Sudra girl, *Nishada*. If the father and mother are both Kshatriya, the progeny is Kshatriya. If the mother be a Brahmin (and the father a Kshatriya), the son is called *Suta*. If the mother be a Vaisya, the son is *Mahisya*. If the mother be a Sudra, the progeny is *Ugra*. If both parents be Vaisya, the progeny is *Vaisya*. If the mother be a Brahmin (which

is illicit), the progeny is *Vaideha* but if she be a Kshatriya, which also is regarded as improper, he is *Magadha*. From the Vaisya by a Sudra mother is produced a *Karana*. When both parents are Sudra, the progeny is *Sudra*. If the mother be a Brahmin, the progeny is *Chandala*. If she be a Kshatriya, it is called *Chatta*. From a Sudra by a Vaisya girl is produced the *Ayogava*.

In the same way still further ramifications are formed, each with different customs and modes of worship and each with infinite distinctions of habitation, profession, and rank of ancestry that defy computation. . . .

Karma

. . . This is a system of knowledge of an amazing and extraordinary character, in which the learned concur without dissenting opinion. It reveals the particular class of actions performed in a former birth which have occasioned the events that befall men in this present life, and prescribes the special expiation of each sin, one by one. It is of four kinds.

The first kind discloses the particular action which has brought a man into existence in one of the five classes into which mankind is divided, and the action which occasions the assumption of a male or female form. A *Kshatriya* who lives continently, will, in his next birth, be born a *Brahmin*. A *Vaisya* who hazards his transient life to protect a Brahmin, will become a *Kshatriya*. A *Sudra* who lends money without interest and does not defile his tongue by demanding repayment, will be born a *Vaisya*. A *Mlechchha* who serves a *Brahmin* and eats food from his house till his death, will become a *Sudra*. A *Brahmin* who undertakes the profession of a *Kshatriya* will become a *Kshatriya,* and thus a *Kshatriya* will become a *Vaisya,* and a *Vaisya* a *Sudra,* and a *Sudra* a *Mlechchha*. Whosoever

---

[7]Abul Fazl is drawing an analogy for his Muslim readers. Just as Muslims consider all nonbelievers to be outside the community of God, so Hindus regard the Mlechchha as outside their community.

accepts in alms . . . the bed on which a man has died[8] . . . will, in the next birth, from a man become a woman. Any woman or *Mlechchha,* who in the temple . . . sees the form of *Narayana,*[9] and worships him with certain incantations, will in the next birth, if a woman, become a man, and if a *Mlechchha,* a *Brahmin.* . . .

The second kind shows the strange effects of actions on health of body and in the production of manifold diseases.

Madness is the punishment of disobedience to father and mother. . . .

Pain in the eyes arises from having looked upon another's wife. . . .

Dumbness is the consequence of killing a sister. . . .

Colic results from having eaten with an impious person or a liar. . . .

Consumption is the punishment of killing a *Brahmin.* . . .

The third kind indicates the class for actions which have caused sterility and names suitable remedies. . . .

A woman who does not menstruate, in a former existence . . . roughly drove away the children of her neighbors who had come as usual to play at her house. . . .

A woman who gives birth to only daughters is thus punished for having contemptuously regarded her husband from pride. . . .

A woman who has given birth to a son that dies and to a daughter that lives, has, in her former existence, taken animal life. Some say that she had killed goats. . . .

The fourth kind treats of riches and poverty, and the like. Whoever distributes alms at auspicious times, as during eclipses of the moon and sun, will become rich and bountiful (in his next existence). Whoso at these times, visits any place of pilgrimage . . . and there dies, will possess great wealth, but will be avaricious and of a surly disposition. Whosoever when hungry and with food before him, hears the supplication of a poor man and bestows it all upon him, will be rich. . . .

---

[8]An "unclean" object.

[9]The personification of solar and cosmic energy underlying creation.

Paintings from the Mughal Court

17 • *LORD KRISHNA LIFTS MOUNT GOVARDHAN* AND *ABU AL-HASAN, JAHANGIR'S DREAM*

Mughal emperors were ardent book-lovers for whom a large and impressive library was a sign of political and dynastic power. Their workshops produced histories, memoirs, legends, and poetry. Many projects involved hundreds of artists and craftsmen—paper-makers, leather workers (for the books' covers), gilders (experts in making gold overlays), painters, and scribes. The painters were strongly influenced by Persian miniaturists, and in fact, many of them were Persian by birth and training. Their pictures, small enough to fit on a page of a large book, were characterized by bright colors, crowded scenes, and rich detail. During Jahangir's reign, painting was influenced by European techniques and subject matter, largely as a result of the paintings given to the emperor by Sir Thomas Roe, a representative of the English East India Company who arrived at the Mughal court in 1615.

The first painting in this section, *Lord Krishna Lifts Mount Govardhan,* is an illustration by an unknown artist that was included in a Persian translation from Sanskrit of the Hindu work *Harivamsa,* commissioned by Emperor Akbar in 1585. The *Harivamsa* chronicles the deeds of Krishna, an incarnation of Vishnu, who was worshiped as the Supreme God by many Hindus who were devotees of the Bhakti ("way of devotion") movement. This movement, which originated in southern India and gradually spread north between the fourteenth and seventeenth centuries, downplayed ritual, caste distinctions, and theological subtleties in favor of overwhelming love and worship of a single Supreme God. Akbar, with his liberal and tolerant religious views, assigned the work of translating the *Harivamsa* to Abdul Qadir Badaoni (b. 1540), a court scholar known for his intense devotion to Islam.

The painting depicts a story connected with Krishna (normally depicted as blue or black—there are many theories why this is the case) in which he convinces farmers in the Gokul region to end their rituals and sacrifices to Indra, the god of clouds and rainfall. When the angry Indra responds by unleashing torrential rains on the farmers, Krishna protects them by raising Mount Govardhan and holding it over them as a huge umbrella for seven days and seven nights. The humbled Indra then descends from the heavens and becomes a follower of Krishna.

The second painting, *Jahangir's Dream,* is the work of Abu al-Hasan (1589–c. 1630), who was born in Herat (in the northwest region of present-day Afghanistan) and spent his whole artistic career in service to Jahangir. It is part of an album of paintings commissioned by Jahangir and is thought to have been painted between 1618 and 1622. This was a time when tensions were growing with the shah of Persia Abbas I over the city of Kandahar, in present-day Afghanistan. During the dispute, Jahangir had a dream in which Abbas "appeared to him in a bright light and made him happy." In Abu al-Hasan's rendition of the dream, the painter shows Abbas (on the left) and Jahangir standing on a lion and a lamb, which in turn are lying on a terrestrial globe. The caption states that they are bathed in the "Light of Religion" provided by two angel-borne spheres representing the sun and the moon.

QUESTIONS FOR ANALYSIS

1. Review what Jahangir had to say in his memoirs (source 13) about the religious policies of his father Akbar, especially his tolerance of Hinduism. How might the commissioning of the translation of the *Harivamsa* (a work that focuses on Krishna, who many Hindus believed to be the one Supreme God) have fit in with these policies?
2. Why might Akbar have chosen the religiously conservative Badaoni to translate the work?
3. How has the artist tried to represent a cross-section of India's people? How are the people in the crowd reacting to the miracle they are observing?
4. What does the painting convey about Krishna's qualities and powers?
5. How does *Jahangir's Dream* convey the superiority of Jahangir over Abbas?
6. What does the placement of the animals in *Jahangir's Dream* suggest about the hoped-for outcome of the dispute over Kandahar?
7. How does this pictorial representation of Jahangir compare to what Jahangir wrote about himself in his memoir (source 15)?

Lord Krishna Lifts Mount Govardhan

Jahangir's Dream

Chapter 3

Africa and the Americas

O F ALL THE WORLD'S REGIONS, Africa and the Americas experienced the most profound effects of European expansion between the fifteenth and seventeenth centuries. On both sides of the Atlantic, the arrival of Europeans resulted in demographic changes, efforts to spread Christianity, political disruption, new patterns of trade, and the introduction of new weapons and new species of plants and animals. But the magnitude of Europe's impact on the two regions varied greatly—Africa was significantly affected, but the Americas were transformed.

The European presence in Africa primarily meant trade—trade in which Europeans exchanged iron, hardware, textiles, and other goods for pepper, gold, ivory, and, above all, human beings. European involvement in the slave trade began in 1441, when a Portuguese raiding party captured twelve Africans on a small coastal island and sold them into slavery in Portugal. After the plantation system of agriculture was established on São Tomé, Cape Verde, and other South Atlantic islands and later spread to the West Indies and the Americas, the demand for slaves grew from fewer than 1,000 a year in the fifteenth century, to 7,500 a year in the mid-seventeenth century, to more than 50,000 a year in the eighteenth and early nineteenth centuries. The slave trade, however, did not translate into European political dominance or permanent European settlements in Africa. Except for the Dutch farmers who began to migrate to South Africa in 1652, Europeans in Africa stayed on the coast, completed their business, and then departed. Missionary efforts were limited, and Portuguese dominance in Angola, in southwest Africa, is the only example of anything that approximated a European colony. As a result, Africans kept control of their political lives and experienced few changes in their distinctive cultures and religions until the late nineteenth century, when a new wave of European expansion occurred.

In the Americas, however, the Europeans' arrival had immediate and catastrophic consequences. By the mid-1600s, Portugal ruled Brazil; Spain controlled major Caribbean islands, Mexico, Central America, and most of South America; Britain, France, and the Netherlands ruled territories in the West Indies, North America's Atlantic coastal regions, and the St. Lawrence River basin; Sweden and Denmark also had small territorial claims. In the 200 years following Columbus's discoveries, throughout the Western Hemisphere, wealth was plundered, political structures were destroyed, millions of Native Americans were killed by Old World diseases, and traditional patterns of life and belief disappeared or managed only a tenuous survival.

Of the many factors that explain the differences in the African and the American experiences, two stand out. First, unlike the Americas, where more than half a dozen European states from Portugal to Sweden competed for trade and territory, in Africa only Portugal was involved. Portugal led the way in African exploration and trade and by the end of the fifteenth century had established commercial contacts and trading posts that discouraged European competitors. Only in the seventeenth century did merchants from other states show an interest in the African slave trade. Second, all Europeans were convinced that in comparison to other parts of the world, Africa offered few economic rewards other than gold and the slave trade. Furthermore, Portugal's merchants and politicians concluded in the sixteenth century that their money and energy would better be spent on Asian trade and Brazilian development than on Africa. Neither they nor any other Europeans were willing to make the economic and military commitments necessary to support European settlement or establish their political authority.

Europeans faced a far different situation in the Americas. They soon discovered that the region contained easily exploitable sources of wealth such as gold, silver, and furs and was capable of growing profitable crops such as tobacco and sugar. All these things were more or less theirs for the taking, not only in the thinly populated regions of North America and eastern and southern South America but also in the more populous regions of Mexico, Peru, and the Caribbean.

The Europeans' guns, steel swords, and horses certainly gave them an initial advantage over the American Indians. The relative ease of the European conquest, however, owed more to germs than superior technology. Under normal circumstances several hundred Spaniards fighting for Hernán Cortés in Mexico in the early 1500s, even with their firearms and Native American allies, would have been no match for many thousands of Aztec warriors with arrows, clubs, lances, and spears. In the midst of fighting, however, the Aztecs were struck by a debilitating epidemic of smallpox, a disease introduced by the Spaniards. It was a sorely weakened and demoralized Aztec Empire that succumbed to the Spaniards and their allies in 1521.

All American Indians, not just the Aztecs, had to contend with the bacteria, viruses, and parasites Europeans and Africans carried in their bodies from across the Atlantic. Because of their long isolation, they lacked immunity to imported diseases such as diphtheria, measles, chickenpox, whooping cough, yellow fever, influenza, dysentery, and smallpox. Thus, the arrival of outsiders had devastating consequences. On the island of Hispaniola, where Columbus established the first Spanish settlement in the New World, the Tainos numbered between 300,000 and 400,000 in 1492 but had virtually disappeared 50 years later. In Mexico, within 50 years after the arrival of the Spaniards, the region's population had fallen by 90 percent, and in this case millions, not tens of thousands, were victimized.

Such human devastation not only made it relatively easy for the Europeans to conquer or displace the Native Americans but also led to the enslavement of Africans in the New World. The massive die-offs created labor shortages that Europeans overcame by importing enslaved Africans. Before the transatlantic slave trade ended, as many as 11 million Africans had been sold into slavery in the Americas, and millions more died in slave raids and in the holds of slave ships crossing the Atlantic. These Africans, too, were indirect victims of the bacteria, viruses, and parasites brought to the New World in the early years of European expansion.

Multiple Voices I

Africa's Diversity Through Visitors' Eyes

BACKGROUND

Writing Africa's early history is an especially difficult and daunting task. Because traditional non-Muslim and non-Christian African societies left no written records, historians have relied on oral traditions, rare travelers' accounts, and insights from the work of linguists, archeologists, anthropologists, and art historians. They have been able to reconstruct the broad outlines of Africa's early political and cultural development, but with many gaps and few details. The amount of available source material increases dramatically with the arrival in the fifteenth century of Europeans, who produced a trove of letters, diaries, memoirs, books, and business records pertaining to Africa. The utility of such records is limited by the cultural and religious biases of the Europeans who produced them and by the fact that Europeans rarely traveled beyond Africa's coasts. Nonetheless, if used with care, the observations and commentaries of Europeans can provide much useful information to reconstruct Africa's past.

Three of the four selections in this section were written by Europeans and one was written by a person who was born in Europe but moved to Africa at an early age. Describing societies in different parts of Africa, together they provide a small sample of Africa's rich political, religious, and social diversity in the sixteenth and seventeenth centuries.

THE SOURCES

The author of our first source, Leo Africanus, was a man with several names. Born in 1494 as Al-Hassan ibn-Muhammad al Wazzan al-Fasi into a Muslim family in Granada, the last Muslim foothold in Spain, he was raised in Fez (in present-day Morocco) and entered the service of the sultan of Fez after studying Islamic law. His diplomatic and commercial missions for the sultan involved travel across North Africa and as far as the Arabian Peninsula, Istanbul, and the eastern Mediterranean. He became Giovanni Leone around 1520, when after having been captured by Spanish privateers, he was taken to Rome, and on becoming a Christian was given his new name by no less a figure than Pope Leo X. He remained in Italy for several years and came to be known as Leo Africanus (Leo the African) after the book he completed in 1526, *The History and Description of Africa,* was translated and published in a Latin version. Sometime after 1530, he returned to Tunis, where he died around 1554.

In the excerpts from his *History and Description of Africa,* Leo describes several places he visited in the Western Sudan, a belt of dry grassland running from the Atlantic Ocean to the region of present-day eastern Nigeria. When Leo visited the region in the 1510s, its strongest state was the Songhai Empire, in which the most important cities were Gao, the capital, and Timbuktu, which was ruled by a governor in the name of the emperor. Songhai's rise came at the expense of the Mali Empire, which had dominated the region since the thirteenth century. To the east of Songhai was the kingdom of Bornu, which had recently displaced Kanem as the most powerful state in this particular area.

Our second excerpt is a description of the Kingdom of Benin, on Africa's Guinea Coast, taken from a Dutch work, *An Accurate Description of the Regions of Africa* (1668). Its author, Olfert Dapper (ca. 1635–1689), published a number of books describing parts of the world in which the Dutch carried on trade, all without his leaving the Netherlands. The section of his book on Benin is based on a number of published and unpublished accounts of Benin written by Dutch merchants and may also include information derived from interviews with travelers

1 • Leo Africanus, History and Description of Africa

The Kingdom of Mali

In this kingdom there is a large and ample village containing more than six thousand families, and named Mali, which is also the name of the whole kingdom. . . . The region itself yields great abundance of wheat, meat and cotton. Here are many craftsmen and merchants in all places: and yet the king honorably entertains all strangers. The inhabitants are rich and have plenty of merchandise. Here is a great number of temples, clergymen, and teachers, who read their lectures in the mosques because they have no colleges at all. . . .

The City of Timbuktu

All its houses are . . . cottages, built of mud and covered with thatch. However, there is a most stately mosque to be seen, whose walls are made of stone and lime, and a princely palace also constructed by the highly skilled craftsmen of Granada.[1] Here there are many shops of artisans and merchants, especially of those who weave linen and cotton, and here Barbary[2] merchants bring European cloth. The inhabitants, and especially resident aliens are exceedingly rich, since the present king[3] married both of his daughters to rich merchants. Here are many wells, containing sweet water. Whenever the Niger River overflows, they carry the water into town by means of sluices. This region yields great quantities of grain, cattle, milk, and butter, but salt is very scarce here, for it is brought here by land from Taghaza,[4] which is five hundred miles away. . . .

The rich king of Timbuktu . . . keeps a magnificent and well-furnished court. When he travels anywhere, he rides upon a camel, which is led by some of his noblemen. He does so likewise when going to war; and all his soldiers ride upon horses. Whoever wishes to speak to this king must first of all fall down before his feet and then taking up earth must sprinkle it on his own head and shoulders. . . . [The king] always has under arms 3,000 horsemen and a great number of foot soldiers who shoot poisoned arrows. They often skirmish with those who refuse to pay tribute and whomever they capture they sell as slaves to the merchants of Timbuktu. . . . Their best horses are brought out of North Africa. . . .

Here are great numbers of religious teachers, judges, scholars and other learned persons, who are bountifully maintained at the king's expense. Here too are brought various manuscripts or written books from Barbary, which are sold for more money than any other merchandise.

The coin of Timbuktu is gold, without any stamp or inscription, but in matters of small value they use certain shells from the kingdom of Persia.[5] . . .

The inhabitants are gentle and cheerful and spend a great part of the night in singing and dancing throughout the city streets. They keep large numbers of male and female slaves . . .

Source: Robert Brown, ed., *The History and Description of Africa* (London: The Hakluyt Society, 1896), vol. 3, pp. 823–827, 832–834.

[1] Granada was the last Muslim emirate to fall to Spain in 1492. Until then the merchants, builders, and scholars of Granada had numerous interactions with the Muslim states of the Western Sudan.

[2] The northern region of Africa from the Atlantic to the Egyptian border.

[3] The "king" of Timbuktu was a vassal of the Songhai emperor.

[4] Founded in the tenth century, Taghaza was an important salt-mining center located in the northernmost region of present-day Mali. It was destroyed by Moroccan invaders in 1591.

[5] The reference is to cowry shells, harvested in the tropic waters of the Indian Ocean and widely used as currency in Africa.

The Town and Kingdom of Gao

Here are very rich merchants and to here journey continually large numbers of Negroes who purchase cloth from Barbary and Europe. . . . Here also is a certain place where slaves are sold, especially upon those days when merchants assemble. . . .

The king of this region has a certain private palace in which he keeps a large number of concubines and slaves, who are watched by eunuchs. To guard his person he maintains a sufficient troop of horsemen and foot soldiers. Between the first gate of the palace and the inner part, there is a walled enclosure wherein the king personally decides all of his subjects' controversies. Although the king is most diligent in this regard and conducts all business in these matters, he has in his company counsellors and such other officers as his secretaries, treasurers, stewards and auditors.

It is a wonder to see the quality of merchandise that is daily brought here and how costly and sumptuous everything is. Horses purchased in Europe for ten ducats[6] are sold here for forty and sometimes fifty ducats apiece. There is not European cloth so coarse as to sell for less than four ducats an ell.[7] If it is anywhere near fine quality, they will give fifteen ducats for an ell, and an ell of the scarlet of Venice or of Turkish cloth is here worth thirty ducats. A sword is here valued at three or four crowns,[8] and likewise are spears, bridles and similar commodities, and spices are all sold at a high rate. . . .

The rest of this kingdom contains nothing but villages and hamlets inhabited by herdsmen and shepherds, who in winter cover their bodies with the skins of animals, but in summer they go naked, save for their private parts. . . . They are an ignorant and rude people, and you will scarcely find one learned person in the square of a hundred miles. They are continually burdened by heavy taxes; to the point that they scarcely have anything left on which to live.

The Kingdom of Borno

They have a most powerful prince. . . . He has in readiness as many as three thousand horsemen and a huge number of foot soldiers; for all his, subjects are so serviceable and obedient to him, that whenever he commands them, they will arm themselves and will follow him wherever he leads them. They pay him no tribute except tithes on their grain; neither does the king have any revenues to support his state except the spoils he gets from his enemies by frequent invasions and assaults. He is in a state of perpetual hostility with a certain people who live beyond the desert . . . who in times past marching with a huge army of footsoldiers over the said desert, devastated a great part of the Kingdom of Borno. Whereupon the king sent for the merchants of Barbary and ordered them to bring him a great store of horses: for in this country they exchange horses for slaves, and sometimes give fifteen or twenty slaves for a horse. And by this means there were a great many horses bought. . . .

---

[6] An Italian coin.

[7] A measurement of length, approximately 45 inches.

[8] A gold coin, worth substantially more than a ducat.

2 • Olfert Dapper, An Accurate Description of the Regions of Africa

Commercial dealings between foreigners and inhabitants take place up the river Benin in the town of Gotton, which the Hollanders reach in long boats and yachts. Such trade cannot take place without the King's permission. The King chooses certain overseers and merchants, and they alone are allowed to approach the Europeans, whom they call 'Whites.' . . .

Whenever a ship with its cargo has anchored on this coast a messenger is sent to inform the King, and he calls two or three overseers, accompanied by twenty or thirty . . . merchants, who are commanded to go and trade. They go forthwith and travel posthaste overland to Gotton, commandeering on their way as many canoes and oarsmen as they require, even when the owners need them for themselves. If the owners complain they remind them of the King and . . . and command them to be silent in future . . . When they arrive in Gotton . . . they choose the best houses and dwellings and, without asking the owners' leave, use them to house all their goods. . . . Also the owner is often obliged to cook for them on the first day without getting anything for his pains.

Whenever these overseers come for the first visit to the warehouses they are magnificently dressed, wearing jasper necklaces; and kneeling, they bring greetings from their king, from his mother, and from the greatest overseers, in whose names they bring gifts of food, and with much ceremony they then inquire about the state of the country and the wars against their [the Hollanders'] enemies and similar things. Afterwards there is drinking and leave-taking, without there having been any mention of trade. On the following days they return with requests to see the newly-arrived merchandise [and a price is fixed.]

The wares which the Hollanders and other Europeans acquire in exchange for goods from our lands are cotton cloths, . . . jasper stones, slaves (none but women, because they are not willing to have men leave the country) leopardskins, pepper and . . . a kind of blue coral which is got out of the ground by diving, because it grows, like a species of coral, treelike upon stony ground in the water. Our people buy this to sell to the Negroes of the Gold Coast because the women wear them in their hair for the decoration.

. . . In exchange for these things the Hollanders give the Negroes, among the wares of our land, the following: gold and silver brocade; red cloth; . . . white cloth with a red stripe at one end; all kinds of fine cotton; linen; orange, lemon and green beads; red velvet; brass bracelets . . . ; small lavender and violet beads; coarse flannel; fine coral; . . . fabrics, starched and flowered; red glass earrings; iron bars; gilded mirrors; crystal beads; East Indian cowries, which are used by them instead of money.

The larger cloths, particularly the striped ones, our people sell again on the Gold Coast, where they are greatly in demand; but the plain blue ones are traded most in the region of Gabon and Angola.

• • •

The weapons of these people are shields, spears, bows, assegais,[1] and poisoned arrows. . . .

In battle they maintain good order and discipline because nobody may yield a step even if he has death before his eyes.

There are three chief Ministers of State in Great Benin, appointed by the King to govern the realm, called 'Fiadors' by the Portuguese, who are the most senior in the land next to the King (because above them there is nobody closer to the King apart from the Field-marshal [high military commander] and the King's mother), each of whom has authority over one quarter, or ward, of the city, and they derive large profits from this. In the same manner every town is governed by a certain number of nobles . . . who are responsible for trying all cases not involving corporal

Source: From Thomas Hodgkin, *Nigerian Perspectives* (London: Oxford University Press, 1975), pp. 164–168. Reprinted by permission of Oxford University Press.

[1]Wooden spears with iron tips.

punishment and for condemning the accused man to certain punishments according to the extent of his misdeeds. But cases involving corporal punishment are referred to Great Benin where the high court is and are tried there because the court sits every day. Yet often the judges are bought over with bribes of cowries without the King's knowledge.

The King comes out of his court only once a year on an established feast-day and appears before the populace on horseback, beautifully adorned with all kinds of royal decorations and in the company of three or four hundred noblemen, either on foot or on horseback, with many players before and behind acting out all kinds of merriment. . . . He does not ride far, but turns after a small distance and heads again for the court. Then the King has certain tame leopards, which he keeps for his amusement, paraded on chains. Also many dwarfs and deaf-mutes, in whom he takes his pleasure, make an appearance. On this holiday ten, twelve or thirteen slaves are killed by strangling or decapitation in the King's honor, because they believe that these slaves, after they have been dead a little while, enter another land where they return to life and live more pleasantly. . . .

3 • Damião de Góis, *Chronicle of King Manuel the Fortunate*

The king . . . is a great lord, because according to report his dominions are more than eight hundred leagues[1] in circumference, besides the lands of several kings and lords who obey him and pay him a tribute of gold, the love of which had already been imparted to them many years before this time by the Moors [Muslims] who lived among them. . . .

All this kingdom . . . is most abundant in provisions, fruits, and cattle; and there are such great herds of wild elephants there that not a year passes in which the number killed by those who hunt them does not amount to four or five thousand, by which means a large quantity of ivory is sent to India. The land abounds in gold, which is found in great quantity in mines, rivers, and marshy ground; some of the mines are situated in the kingdom of Batua, the king of which is a vassal of the king. . . .

The inhabitants of the country are black with woolly hair, and are commonly called Kaffirs.[2] They do not make or worship idols, but believe in one God, the creator of all things, whom they adore and to whom they pray. . . . They have certain feast days in their religion, among others the day on which their king was born. No crime is punished among them with such rigor as is witchcraft: all sorcerers being executed by law, not one receiving pardon. . . .

This king keeps great state, and is served on bended knees with reverence. When he drinks, coughs, or sighs, every person in the house wishes him well in a loud voice, and the same thing is done by those outside the house, the word being passed from mouth to mouth all round the town, so that it is known that the king has drunk, or coughed, or sighed. In this kingdom there are no doors to the houses, with the exception of those of the lords and principal persons, to whom this privilege is granted by the king. They say that houses are built with doors for fear of thieves and malefactors, from whom it is the king's duty to protect his people and above all the poor. The houses are all built of wattles[3] plastered with clay.

The said king uses two insignia, one being a small hoe with an ivory point, which he always wears in his belt to show his subjects that they should cultivate and profit by the land . . . ; the other consists of two assagais [spears], showing that with one the king administers justice and with the other defends his

Source: George McCall Theal, *Records of South-Eastern Africa* (Cape Town: C. Struik Ltd., for the government of the Cape Colony, 1899), pp. 127–131.

[1]A measure of length, anywhere from three to five miles.
[2]Based on the Arab word *kafir*, meaning black, kaffir was used to refer to the Bantu-speaking peoples of southeast Africa and more generally to non-Muslim black Africans. Today in South Africa it is a derogatory term used by some whites for all blacks.
[3]Poles interwoven with small branches or reeds.

people. He constantly keeps at his court all the sons of the kings and lords who are his vassals, the former that they may have filial affection for him, and the latter that their fathers may not rise against him with the lands which they hold from him. Whether in time of peace or war he always maintains a large standing army, of which the commander-in-chief is called Zono, to keep the land in a state of peace and to prevent the lords and kings who are subject to him from rising in rebellion.

Every year he sends a number of his chief courtiers through all his kingdoms and dominions to light new fires, which is done in the following manner. Each of these courtiers on reaching the houses of the kings and lords of the cities and towns commands all the fires in the place to be put out in the king's name, and after they are extinguished they all come in sign of obedience and take fire from him, and any one who does not do so is looked upon as a traitor and rebel, and the king commands him to be punished as such. If the offender is a powerful person, or represents a powerful town, the king sends the captain Zono against him, who is always present in the camp to attend to these matters.

---

4 • Duarte Barbosa, *Account of the Countries Bordering on the Indian Ocean and Their Inhabitants*

Kilwa

Going along the coast, . . . there is an island hard by the mainland which is called Kilwa, in which is a Moorish town with many fair houses of stone and mortar, with many windows after our fashion, very well arranged in streets, with many flat roofs. The doors are of wood, well carved, with excellent joinery. . . . It has a Moorish king over it. From this place they trade with Sofala, from which they bring back gold, and from here they spread all over Arabia. . . . On the moors there are some fair and some black, they are finely clad in many rich garments of gold and silk and cotton, and the women as well; also with much gold and silver in chains and bracelets, which they wear on their legs and arms; and many jeweled earrings in their ears. . . .

Mombasa

Further on, an advance along the coast toward India, there is an island hard by the mainland, on which is a town called Mombasa. It is a very fair place, with lofty stone and mortar houses, well aligned in streets after the fashions of Kilwa. The wood is well-fitted with excellent joiner's work. It has its own king, himself a Moor. . . . This is a place of great trade, and has a good harbor, in which are always moored craft of many kinds and also great ships, both of those which come from Sofala and those which go there, and others which come from the great kingdom of Cambay and from Malindi; others which sail to the islands of Zanzibar. . . .

The men are oft-times at war . . . but at peace with those of the mainland, and they carry on trade with them, obtaining great amounts of honey, wax, and ivory.

Mafia, Zanzibar, and Pemba

Between this island of San Lorenzo and the continent, not very far from it, are three islands, which are called one Mafia, another Zanzibar, and the other Pemba; these are inhabited by Moors; they are very fertile islands, with plenty of provisions, rice, millet, and flesh, and abundant oranges, lemons, and citrons. All the mountains are full of them; they produce many sugar canes, but do not know how to make sugar. These islands have their kings. The inhabitants trade with the mainland with their provisions and fruits; they have small vessels, very loosely and badly made, without decks, and with a single mast; all their planks are sewn together with cords of

Source: Mansel Longworth Dames, ed., *The Book of Duarte Barbosa* (London: Hakluyt Society, 1918), pp. 6–8, 17, 18, 20–22, 26–28, 31, 39–42.

reed or matting, and the sails are of palm mats. They are very feeble people, with very few and despicable weapons. In these islands they live in great luxury and abudance. . . . Their wives adorn themselves with many jewels of gold from Sofala, and silver, in chains, earrings, bracelets, and ankle rings, and are dressed in silk stuffs: and they have many mosques. . . .

Mogodishu

PROCEEDING coastwise towards the Red Sea there is a very great Moorish town called Mogodishu; it has a king over it; the place has much trade in diverse kinds, by reason whereof many ships come hither from the great kingdom of Cambay, bringing great plenty of cloths of many sorts, and diverse other wares, also spices. And they carry away much gold, ivory, wax and many other things, whereby they make exceeding great profits in their dealings. . . .

They speak Arabic. The men are for the most part brown and black, but a few are fair. They have but few weapons, yet they use poisons on their arrows to defend themselves against their enemies.

Kingdom of Prester John[1]

. . . This kingdom is very large and peopled with many cities, towns, and villages, with many inhabitants, and it has many kings subject to it and tributary kings. And in their country there are many who live in the fields and mountains, like Bedouins: they are black men; very well made: they have many horses, and make use of them, and are good riders, and there are great sportsmen and hunters amongst them. These people are Christians of the doctrine of the blessed Saint Bartholomew.[2] . . . Many of them are deficient in our true faith, because the country is very large, and whilst in the principal city of Babel Melech,[3] where Prester John resides, they may be Christians, in many other distant parts they live in error and without being taught; so that they are only Christians in name. . . .

In this city [Babel Melech] a great feast takes place in the month of August, for which so many kings and nobles come together, and so many people that they are innumerable: and they take an image out of a church, which is believed to be that of Our Lady, or that of St. Bartholomew, which image is of gold and of the size of a man; its eyes are of very large and beautiful rubies of great value, and the whole of it is adorned with many precious stones of much value, and placing it in a great carriage of gold, they carry it in procession with very great veneration and ceremony, and Prester John goes in front of this carriage . . . in another gold carriage very richly dressed in cloth of gold with much jewellery. And they begin to go out thus in the morning, and go in procession through all the city with much music of all sorts of instruments, until the evening, when they go home, And so many people throng to this procession, that in order to arrive at the carriage of the image many die of being squeezed and suffocated; and those who die in this way are held as saints and martyrs; and many old men and old women go with a good will to die in this manner.

---

[1]Prester John ("Priest John") is a name commonly used by the Portuguese for the king of Ethiopia in the sixteenth century. This usage was based on their assumption that they had finally made contact with the Christian king in the east long thought by Europeans to be a potential ally in their conflict with Islam.

[2]According to tradition, St. Bartholomew, one of Jesus' twelve disciples, introduced Christianity to Ethiopia in the first century C.E.

[3]Babel Melech is a Portuguese version of the Arabic term *Bab-el-Malik*, the "king's court." Duarte may be referring to Axum, the historic capital of the ancient kingdom of Axum. If so, he has misrepresented its importance. Although a significant religious center and the place where kings often held their coronation rituals, it was not a "capital city" in any sense. The royal court, consisting of thousands of nobles, soldiers, and retainers, moved from place to place every three or four months after exhausting food supplies in the surrounding region.

Africans and the Portuguese

When the Portuguese began sending ships into the Atlantic to explore Africa's offshore islands and west coast in the early 1400s, their goals were shaped by their limited and often inaccurate perceptions of Africa. They knew about Madeira and the Canary Islands, which French, Spanish, and Genoese mariners had visited in the late 1300s and perhaps even earlier. They knew that the North African coast was a Muslim stronghold, that beyond the coast lay a vast desert, and that south of the desert was a region rich in gold and pepper. Many also were convinced that in eastern Africa there existed a potential ally in the struggle against Islam—a Christian kingdom ruled by Prester John, whose existence had intrigued Europeans since the twelfth century. Based on this meager information and legend, the Portuguese gambled that their voyages down the African coast would enable them to bypass Muslim traders in North Africa and give them direct access to Africa's gold and pepper. They also dreamed of making contact with the mighty kingdom of Prester John and joining him in a new crusade against their common Muslim enemy.

In time, the Portuguese expanded their knowledge of Africa, and as they did, some of their original goals were abandoned and new ones emerged. They did find a Christian kingdom in eastern Africa; it was not the realm of Prester John, but the kingdom of Ethiopia, a weak state vulnerable to attack by its Muslim neighbors. No Portuguese–Ethiopian alliance would tip the military balance in favor of Christians. On Africa's west coast, the Portuguese discovered economic opportunities beyond trading for gold, pepper, and ivory. Beginning in the 1400s, purchasing or capturing slaves in Africa and transporting and reselling them throughout the Atlantic world became a major Portuguese enterprise.

In 1498, the Portuguese made an even more important discovery: that by sailing around the Cape of Good Hope, they could reach the rich markets of India, Southeast Asia, China, and Japan by an all-ocean route. This transformed Portuguese thinking about Africa. Having direct access to the luxury goods and spices of Asia generated opportunities for profits that trade in African goods could never match. As a result, from the sixteenth century onward, the Portuguese came to view Africa mainly as a source of slaves for the New World and a place to sail around in order to reach Asia.

Africa in the age of European discovery assumed a more prominent role in the world economy, but at great cost—the enslavement of millions of Africans. The growth of slavery in the New World, and the slave trade that made it possible, gave birth to the myth of the Africans' moral and intellectual inferiority, used by defenders of slavery to justify a cruel and vicious institution. Thus, the Europeans' involvement in Africa resulted in no massive epidemics, no toppling of empires, and no wholesale religious changes as it did in the Americas. It was, however, no less traumatic and tragic.

Political Breakdown in the Kingdom of Kongo

18 • NZINGA MBEMBA (AFONSO I), LETTERS TO THE KING OF PORTUGAL

The largest state in central West Africa around 1500 was the Kingdom of Kongo, stretching along the estuary of the Congo River in territory that lies within present-day Angola and the Democratic Republic of Congo. In 1483, the Portuguese navigator Diogo Cão made contact with Kongo and several years later visited its inland capital. When he sailed home, he was accompanied by Kongo emissaries whom King Nzinga a Kuwu dispatched to Lisbon to learn European ways. They returned in 1491, along with Portuguese priests, artisans, and soldiers, who brought with them European goods, including a printing press. In the same year, the king and his son, Nzinga Mbemba, were baptized as Catholics.

Around 1506, Nzinga Mbemba, who took the name Afonso after his baptism, succeeded his father and ruled until about 1543. Afonso promoted European culture by proclaiming Christianity the state religion (a step that affected few of his subjects), imitating the etiquette of Portuguese royalty, and using Portuguese in state business. His son Henrique was educated in Portugal and returned to serve as sub-Saharan Africa's first black Roman Catholic bishop. European firearms, horses, and cattle were introduced, and Afonso dreamed of achieving a powerful and prosperous state with European help. By the time of his death, however, his kingdom verged on disintegration, in no small measure because of the Portuguese. As many later African rulers were to discover, the introduction of European products and customs caused dissension and social instability. Worse, Portuguese involvement in the slave trade undermined Afonso's authority and made his subjects restive. In 1526, Afonso wrote the following letters to King João III (r. 1521–1528), urging him to control his subjects. They are two of twenty-four letters Afonso and his Portuguese-educated, native secretaries dispatched to the kings of Portugal on a variety of issues. If the Portuguese kings ever responded to Afonso's letters, the documentation has been lost.

QUESTIONS FOR ANALYSIS

1. According to Afonso, what were the detrimental effects of the Portuguese presence in his kingdom?
2. What do the letters reveal about the workings of the slave trade in the kingdom? Who participated in it?
3. What do the letters reveal about Afonso's attitude toward slavery? Does he oppose the practice as such or only certain aspects of it?
4. What steps had Afonso taken to deal with the problems caused by the Portuguese? What do the letters suggest about the effectiveness of these steps?
5. How would you characterize Afonso's attitude toward the power and authority of the king of Portugal? Does he consider himself inferior to the Portuguese king or his equal?
6. How would you characterize King Afonso's conception of the ideal relationship between the Portuguese and his kingdom?

Sir, Your Highness should know how our Kingdom is being lost in so many ways that it is convenient to provide for the necessary remedy, since this is caused by the excessive freedom given by your agents and officials to the men and merchants who are allowed to come to this Kingdom to set up shops with goods and many things which have been prohibited by us, and which they spread throughout our Kingdoms and Domains in such an abundance that many of our vassals, whom we had in obedience, do not comply because they have the things in greater abundance than we ourselves; and it was with these things that we had them content and subjected under our vassalage and jurisdiction, so it is doing a great harm not only to the service of God, but the security and peace of our Kingdoms and State as well.

And we cannot reckon how great the damage is, since the mentioned merchants are taking every day our natives, sons of the land and the sons of our noblemen and vassals and our relatives, because the thieves and men of bad conscience grab them wishing to have the things and wares of this Kingdom which they are ambitious of; they grab them and get them to be sold; and so great, Sir, is the corruption and licentiousness that our country is being completely depopulated, and Your Highness should not agree with this nor accept it as in your service. And to avoid it we need from those [your] Kingdoms no more than some priests and a few people to teach in schools, and no other goods except wine and flour for the holy sacrament. That is why we beg of Your Highness to help and assist us in this matter, commanding your factors that they should not send here either merchants or wares, because it is *our will that in these Kingdoms there should not be any trade of slaves nor outlet for them.* Concerning what is referred [to] above, again we beg of Your Highness to agree with it, since otherwise we cannot remedy such an obvious damage. Pray Our Lord in His mercy to have Your Highness under His guard and let you do forever the things of His service. I kiss your hands many times.

At our town of Kongo, written on the sixth day of July, João Teixeira did it in 1526. The King. Dom Afonso.

• • •

Moreover, Sir, in our Kingdoms there is another great inconvenience which is of little service to God, and this is that many of our people, keenly desirous as they are of the wares and things of your Kingdoms, which are brought here by your people, and in order to satisfy their voracious appetite, seize many of our people, freed and exempt men, and very often it happens that they kidnap even noblemen and the sons of noblemen, and our relatives, and take them to be sold to the white men who are in our Kingdoms; and for this purpose they have concealed them; and others are brought during the night so that they might not be recognized.

And as soon as they are taken by the white men they are immediately ironed and branded with fire, and when they are carried to be embarked [on ships], if they are caught by our guards' men the whites allege that they have bought them but they cannot say from whom, so that it is our duty to do justice and to restore to the freemen their freedom, but it cannot be done if your subjects feel offended, as they claim to be.

And to avoid such a great evil we passed a law so that any white man living in our Kingdoms and wanting to purchase goods in any way should first inform three of our noblemen and officials of our court whom we rely upon in this matter, . . . who

Source: Basil Davidson, trans., *The African Past* (London: Curtis Brown, Ltd., 1964).

should investigate if the mentioned goods are captives or free men, and if cleared by them there will be no further doubt nor embargo [an act prohibiting the departure of a trading vessel] for them to be taken and embarked. But if the white men do not comply with it they will lose the aforementioned goods. And if we do them this favor and concession it is for the part Your Highness has in it, since we know that it is in your service too that these goods are taken from our Kingdom, otherwise we should not consent to this. . . .

• • •

Sir, Your Highness has been kind enough to write to us saying that we should ask in our letters for anything we need, and that we shall be provided with everything, and as the peace and the health of our Kingdom depend on us, and as there are among us old folks and people who have lived for many days, it happens that we have continuously many and different diseases which put us very often in such a weakness that we reach almost the last extreme; and the same happens to our children, relatives and natives owing to the lack in this country of physicians and surgeons who might know how to cure properly such diseases. And as we have got neither dispensaries nor drugs which might help us in this forlornness, many of those

who had been already confirmed and instructed in the holy faith of Our Lord Jesus Christ perish and die; and the rest of the people in their majority cure themselves with herbs and . . . and other ancient methods, so that they put all their faith in the mentioned herbs and ceremonies if they live, and believe that they are saved if they die; and this is not much in the service of God.

And to avoid such a great error and inconvenience, since it is from God in the first place and then from your Kingdoms and from Your Highness that all the good and drugs and medicines have come to save us, we beg of you to be agreeable and kind enough to send us two physicians and two apothecaries and one surgeon, so that they may come with their drugstores and all the necessary things to stay in our kingdoms, because we are in extreme need of them all and each of them. We shall do them all good and shall benefit them by all means, since they are sent by Your Highness, whom we thank for your work in their coming. We beg of Your Highness as a great favor to do this for us, because besides being good in itself it is in the service of God as we have said above.

(Extracts from letter of King Afonso to the King of Portugal dated Oct. 18, 1526. By hand of Dom João Teixeira.)

Sixteenth-Century Benin Art and the Portuguese

19 • A BENIN-PORTUGUESE SALTCELLAR AND A BENIN WALL PLAQUE

Over many centuries, sub-Saharan Africans have produced some of the world's most impressive artworks, especially sculpture. Since at least 500 B.C.E., sculptors used clay, wood, ivory, and bronze to create masks, animal figures, ceremonial weapons, images of rulers, and religious objects that were of central importance to African society, politics, and religion. In some regions, bronze casting and ivory carving were royal monopolies carried on by highly trained professionals.

Such was the case in Benin, a kingdom described by Olfert Dapper in Multiple Voices I, source 2. The kingdom took shape in the 1200s and 1300s when a number of agricultural villages accepted the authority of an *oba*, or divine king, who ruled with a hierarchy of chiefs from the capital, Benin City. When the Portuguese arrived in 1485, Benin was a formidable military and commercial power and a center of state-sponsored artistic activity. Ivory carvers and bronze casters were organized into hereditary guilds and resided in their own neighborhoods in Benin City. They produced bronze heads, animal and human figures, pendants, plaques, musical instruments, drinking vessels, and armlets that were sold in trade or used for ceremonial purposes.

The arrival of the Portuguese affected Benin's art in two ways. First, Portuguese merchants, unable to establish Benin as a major source of slaves, turned to other commodities, including artworks, as objects of trade. Benin ivory carvers received commissions from Portuguese merchants to produce condiment sets, utensils, and hunting horns for sale in Europe. Second, the Portuguese stimulated the production of artworks for use in Benin itself by purchasing African goods with copper, the major component of the alloys used by Benin artists to create plaques and many of their sculptures.

The two sculptures in this section provide an opportunity to appreciate the skills of Benin artists and to gains insights into Benin attitudes toward their rulers and Europeans. The ivory saltcellar was crafted in the sixteenth or early seventeenth century. It depicts two Portuguese officials (only one of which is visible in our photograph), flanked by two assistants. Above them is a Portuguese ship, with a man peering out of a crow's nest.

The second work is a sixteenth-century bronze plaque, approximately 18 inches high, designed to be hung on a wall in the oba's palace in Benin City. (One can see the holes on the top and bottom of the plaque where it was attached.) The central figure is the oba, shown holding a spear and shield. On each of his sides are represented three subordinate chiefs. The one on the left is holding a C-shaped iron bar, used as currency in trade; the figure next to him is holding a ceremonial sword; the figure on the far right is playing a flute-like musical instrument. The two figures in the background, on each side of the oba's head, represent the Portuguese. In one hand, each figure holds a rectangular object, perhaps a glass mirror, and in the other hand what appears to be a goblet. Most experts believe these objects represent items the Portuguese traded for Benin goods.

QUESTIONS FOR ANALYSIS

1. In the saltcellar, notice what hangs around the standing figure's neck, what he holds in his hands, and his facial expression. What is the sculptor trying to communicate about this figure?
2. Why might this image of the Portuguese official have appealed to the European purchasers for which the carving was intended?
3. In the bronze plaque, what distinguishes the oba from the other figures? What details illustrate the oba's power and perhaps his divinity?
4. How does the representation of the oba compare to the description of his power in Dapper's *An Accurate Description of the Regions of Africa* (Multiple Voices I, source 2)?
5. What might you infer from these works about Portuguese–Benin relations and attitudes of the Benin people toward the Portuguese?

A Benin-Portuguese Saltcellar

A Benin Wall Plaque

Military Conflict in Southeast Africa

20 • JOÃO DOS SANTOS, EASTERN ETHIOPIA

An example of the African response to the Portuguese presence is provided by the military campaigns in southeast Africa launched in the late sixteenth century by the people known as the Zimba. The Portuguese used the term *Zimba* to describe any and all marauders from north of the Zambezi River, but the "Zimba" described in this source were in fact warriors of the Mang'aja tribe, whose attacks on the Portuguese and other African peoples to their east were ordered by their *lundu*, or chief, in the late 1580s in response to disruption of their traditional trade. During the sixteenth century, the market for Mang'aja ivory was ruined when the gold-obsessed Portuguese took over the coastal cities with which the Mang'aja had traded. The Zimba's military campaigns were intended to force the reopening of these markets. The Portuguese efforts to suppress the Zimba's attacks failed. The Mang'aja continued their attacks until the early 1600s, but they never succeeded in re-establishing the traditional market for their ivory.

The following excerpt is from *Eastern Ethiopia* by João dos Santos, about whom little is known except that he was a Catholic clergyman who traveled along the east African coast and resided for a time in Sofala during the late sixteenth century. He uses the term *eastern Ethiopia* to include all of Africa's east coast from the Cape of Good Hope to the Red Sea.

QUESTIONS FOR ANALYSIS

1. According to dos Santos's account, why do the Portuguese decide to resist the Zimba?
2. What seems to have been the Zimba's attitude toward the Portuguese?
3. How would you characterize the attitude of the African allies of the Portuguese toward the Zimba? How dedicated were the allies to the Portuguese themselves?
4. How great an advantage did Portuguese firearms give them over their enemy?
5. What tactics of the Zimba were most effective in the conflict with the Portuguese and their allies? What purposes did cannibalism play in the Zimba's overall strategy?
6. What hints does dos Santos's account provide about the motives of the Zimba's military campaign?

Opposite the fort of Sena, on the other side of the river, live some Kaffirs,[1] lords of those lands, good neighbors and friends of the Portuguese, and always most loyal to them. It so happened at the time I was there that the Zimba Kaffirs, . . . who eat human flesh, invaded this territory and made war upon one of these friendly Kaffirs, and by force of arms took from him the kraal[2] in which he resided and a great part of his land, besides which they killed and ate a number of his people. The Kaffir, seeing himself thus routed and his power destroyed, proceeded to Sena[3] to lay his trouble before the captain, who was then André de Santiago, and to beg for assistance in driving out . . . the enemy who had taken possession of it. The captain, upon hearing his pitiful request, determined to assist him, both because he was very friendly to us and because he did not wish to have so near to Sena a neighbor as wicked as the Zimba.

Therefore, having made all necessary preparations for this war, he set out, taking with him a great number of the Portuguese of Sena with their guns and two pieces of heavy cannon from the fort. On arriving at the place where the Zimba were, they found them within a strong double palisade of wood, with its ramparts and loopholes for arrows, surrounded by a very deep and wide trench, within which the enemy were most defiant. André de Santiago, seeing that the enterprise was much more formidable than he had anticipated and that he had brought with him but few men to attack so strong an enemy and his fortress,

fixed his camp on the bank of a rivulet which ran by the place, and sent a message to the captain of Tete, Pedro Fernandes de Chaves, to come to his assistance with the Portuguese of Tete and as many Kaffir vassals of his fort as he could bring.

Pedro Fernandes de Chaves . . . assembled more than a hundred men with their guns, Portuguese and half-castes,[4] and the eleven vassal chiefs. They all crossed to the other side of the river and proceeded by land until they were near the place where the Zimba had fortified themselves. These had information of their approach, and greatly feared their arrival. For this reason they sent out spies secretly upon the road, that when they approached they might see them, and report concerning the men who were coming. And learning from these spies that the Portuguese were in front of the Kaffirs in palanquins[5] and hammocks and not disposed in order of battle, they sallied out of their fortress by night secretly, without being heard by André de Santiago, and proceeded to conceal themselves in a dense thicket at about half a league's[6] distance, through which the men of Tete would have to pass. When they were thus stationed the Portuguese came up nearly half a league in advance of the Kaffirs of their company, quite unsuspicious of what might befall them in the thicket. Just as they were entering it the Zimba fell upon them suddenly with such violence that in a short time they were all killed, not one surviving, and when they were dead the Zimba cut off their legs and arms, which they carried away

---

Source: George McCall Theal, ed. and trans., *Records of South-Eastern Africa* (London: F. W. Clowes for the Government of the Cape Colony, 1898), vol. 7, pp. 293–300.

[1]Based on the Arab word *kafir*, meaning "black," Kaffir was used to refer to the Bantu-speaking peoples of southeastern Africa and more generally to non-Muslim black Africans. Today in South Africa it is a derogatory term used by some whites for all blacks.

[2]Based on the Portuguese word *curral*, an enclosed pen for cattle, kraal refers to the enclosed area surrounding a royal residence.

[3]Sena and Tete were towns on the Zambezi River where the Portuguese had established trading posts.

[4]People of mixed Portuguese and African ancestry.

[5]Covered litters or couches that were mounted on long horizontal poles so they could be carried about.

[6]A measure of the distance a man or horse could walk in an hour. In Spain and Portugal, a league was approximately three miles.

on their backs with all the baggage and arms they had brought with them, after which they returned secretly to their fortress. When the chiefs reached the thicket and found all the Portuguese and their captain dead, they immediately turned back from the place and retreated to Tete. . . .

At the time that preparations for this war were being made there was a friar of St. Dominic preaching at Tete, named Nicolau do Rosario. . . . In the ambush he was severely wounded, and seizing him yet alive the Zimba carried him away with them to put him to death more cruelly afterwards, which they did upon arriving at their fortress, where they bound him hand and foot to a tree and killed him with their arrows in the most cruel manner. This they did to him rather than to others because he was a priest and head of the Christians, as they called him, laying all the blame for the war upon him and saying that Christians did nothing without the leave and counsel of their [priests]. . . .

After the Zimba had put Father Nicolau to death . . . on the night that followed they celebrated their victory and success, playing upon many cornets and drums, and the next day at dawn they all sallied out of their fortress, the chief clothed in the chasuble[7] that the father had brought with him to say mass, carrying the golden chalice in his left hand and an assagai[8] in his right, all the other Zimba carrying on their backs the limbs of the Portuguese, with the head of the captain of Tete on the point of a long lance, and beating a drum they had taken from him. In this manner, with loud shouts and cries they came within sight of André de Santiago and all the Portuguese who were with him, and showed them all these things. . . .

André de Santiago . . . was greatly shocked, as also were all the other Portuguese, at this most horrible and pitiful spectacle, for which reason they decided to retreat as soon as night came on. In carrying this decision into execution they were

in so great a hurry to reach the other side of the river that they were heard by the Zimba, who sallied out of their fortress and falling upon them with great violence killed many of them on the bank of the river. Among the slain was André de Santiago, who died as the valiant man he was. . . .

Great sorrow was felt at the death of Father Nicolau, whom all looked upon as a saint, and for all the Portuguese who lost their lives in this most disastrous war, both because some of them were married and left wives and children at these rivers, and because the Zimba were . . . more insolent than before, and were within fortifications close to Sena, where . . . they might in the future do much damage to the Portuguese who passed up and down these rivers with their merchandise. For these reasons Dom Pedro de Sousa, captain of Mozambique, determined to chastise these Zimba, conquer them, and drive them from the vicinity of Sena. . . .

After obtaining information of the condition of the Zimba, he commanded all the necessary preparations to be made for this war, and assembled nearly two hundred Portuguese and fifteen hundred Kaffirs, with whom he crossed to the other side of the Zambesi and proceeded by land to the fortress of the Zimba, where he formed a camp at the same place that André de Santiago had formed his. Then he commanded that the various pieces of artillery which he had taken with him for the purpose should be fired against the wall of the fortress, but this had no effect upon it, as it was made of large wood, strengthened within by a strong and wide rampart which the Zimba had constructed with the earth from the trench.

Dom Pedro, seeing that his artillery had no effect upon the enemy's wall, determined to enter the fortress and take it by assault, and for this purpose he commanded part of the trench to be filled up, which was done with great difficulty and

---

[7]One of the vestments worn by a Catholic priest while celebrating Mass.

[8]A spear.

danger to our men, as the Zimba from the top of the wall wounded and killed some of them with arrows. When this part of the trench was filled up, a number of men crossed over with axes in their hands to the foot of the palisade, which they began to cut down, but the Zimba from the top of the wall poured so great a quantity of boiling fat and water upon them that nearly all were scalded and badly wounded, especially the naked Kaffirs, so that no one dared go near the palisade, because they were afraid of the boiling fat and through fear of certain iron hooks similar to long harpoons, which the Zimba thrust through the loopholes in the wall and with which they wounded and caught hold of all who came near and pulled from within with such force that they drew them to the apertures, where they wounded them mortally. For this reason the captain commanded all the men to be recalled to the camp to rest . . .

The following day the captain commanded a quantity of wood and branches of trees to be collected, with which huge wicker-work frames were made, as high as and higher than the enemy's palisade, and he commanded them to be placed in front of the wall and filled with earth that the soldiers might fight on them with their guns, and the Zimba would not dare to appear on the wall or be able to pour boiling fat upon the men cutting down the palisade. When this stratagem of war was almost in readiness, another peaceful or cowardly device was planned. . . . The war had lasted two

months, for which reason the residents of these rivers, who were there rather by force than of their own free will, being away from their homes and trade, which is their profession, and not war, pretended to have received letters from their wives in Sena relating the danger they were in from a rebel Kaffir who they said was coming with a number of men to rob Sena, knowing that the Portuguese were absent, for which reason they ought immediately to return home. This false information was spread through the camp, and the residents of Sena went to the captain and begged him to abandon the siege of the Zimba and attend to what was of greater importance, as otherwise they would be compelled to return to their homes and leave him.

Dom Pedro, seeing their determination and believing the information said to be given in the letters to be true, abandoned the siege and commanded the men to pass by night to the other side of the river and return to Sena, but this retreat could not be effected with such secrecy as to be unknown to the Zimba, who sallied out of their fortress with great cries, fell upon the camp, killed some men who were still there, and seized the greater part of the baggage and artillery, that had not been taken away.

With this defeat and disappointment the captain returned to Sena, and thence to Mozambique, without accomplishing what he desired; and the Zimba's position was improved and he became more insolent than before. . . .

Encounters in the Americas

Beginning perhaps as early as 40,000 B.C.E., peoples from Asia began crossing the land bridge between northeast Siberia and present-day Alaska and gradually populated the Americas. Then after 10,000 B.C.E., as the Ice Age ended and the oceans rose, this link between Eurasia and the Americas was submerged under the Bering Sea, and the peoples of the Americas were cut off from the rest of the world. This isolation ended after 1492, when Europeans and Africans, along with their animals, plants, and pathogens, arrived in the wake of Columbus's voyages to the New World.

First on Caribbean islands, then in Mexico and Peru, and ultimately throughout the Americas, Native Americans faced the decision to resist or cooperate with the new European arrivals. Cooperation usually meant trade, in which they exchanged dyes, foodstuffs, and furs for hardware, firearms, and alcoholic beverages. Cooperation also took the form of military alliances. In Mexico, for example, thousands of warriors fought on Cortés's side against their hated enemy, the Aztecs, while in North America the Hurons allied with the French and the Iroquois allied with the Dutch and later the English in a long series of wars.

Many Native Americans also chose to resist, however, and did so well into the nineteenth century. In Mexico and Peru, such resistance meant military defeat with Cortés's conquest of the Aztec Empire between 1519 and 1521 and Pizarro's overthrow of the Inca Empire between 1531 and 1533. In North America, Indian raids inflicted considerable casualties and damage on early European settlements in New England, the middle colonies, and the Chesapeake region. But the colonists' reprisals were equally bloody and destructive, and in the Pequot War (1637) in Connecticut and the Algonquin-Dutch wars (1643–1645) in present-day New York and New Jersey, the Indians were routed and massacred. The long-term outcome of their resistance was never in doubt. The Europeans' single-mindedness and weaponry, when combined with the toll of epidemics from Old World diseases, made their victory inevitable.

The Battle for Tenochtitlan

21 • BERNARDINO DE SAHAGÚN, GENERAL HISTORY OF THE THINGS OF NEW SPAIN

Bernardino de Sahagún (ca. 1499–1590), a member of the Franciscan religious order, was one of the earliest Spanish missionaries in Mexico, arriving in 1529. He soon developed a keen interest in the culture of the peoples of Mexico, for whom he had deep affection and respect. Having mastered the Nahuatl language, spoken by the Aztecs and other central Mexican peoples, around 1545 he began to collect oral and pictorial information about Mexican culture. The result was his *General History of the Things of New Spain,* a major source of information about Mexican culture at the time of the conquest. Many Spaniards considered Sahagún's work dangerous because they feared his efforts to preserve the memory of native culture threatened their plans to exploit and Christianize the Indians. As a result, in 1578, his writings were confiscated by royal decree and sent back to Spain, where they gathered dust in an archive until they were rediscovered and published in the nineteenth century.

The following selection comes from the twelfth book of the *General History.* Based on interviews with Aztecs who had lived through the conquest some 25 years earlier, Book Twelve recounts the conquest of Mexico from the time Cortés arrived on the Mexican coast in April 1519 until the days following the Aztecs' capitulation in August 1521. Although the exact role of Sahagún and his Indian assistants in composing and organizing Book Twelve has been hotly debated by scholars, most agree that it accurately portrays Aztec views and perceptions of the events that unfolded between 1519 and 1521.

The following excerpt picks up the story in November 1519. By then, the Spaniards had allied with the Tlaxcalans, the Aztecs' bitter enemies, and were leaving Cholula, a city that the Spaniards and their allies had sacked and looted because of its leaders' lack of cooperation. They were on their way to Tenochtitlan, the splendid Aztec capital on Lake Texcoco for an anticipated meeting with Emperor Moctezuma.

QUESTIONS FOR ANALYSIS

1. What does the source reveal about the motives of the Spaniards and their Indian allies for their attack on the Aztecs?
2. What was Moctezuma's strategy for dealing with the Spaniards? Why did it fail?
3. Aside from their firearms, what other military advantages did the Spaniards have over their opponents?
4. On several occasions, the Aztecs routed the Spaniards. What explains these Aztec victories?
5. How did the Aztec view of war differ from that of the Spaniards?
6. What does the source reveal about Aztec religious beliefs and values?
7. What similarities and differences do you see between the Aztec-Spanish conflict and the armed clashes between the Zimba and the Portuguese (see source 20)?

And after the dying in Cholula, the Spaniards set off on their way to Mexico,[1] coming gathered and bunched, raising dust. . . .

Thereupon Moteuccoma[2] named and sent noblemen and a great many other agents of his . . . to go meet [Cortés] . . . at Quauhtechcac. They gave [the Spaniards] golden banners of precious feathers, and golden necklaces.

And when they had given the things to them, they seemed to smile, to rejoice and to be very happy. Like monkeys they grabbed the gold. It was as though their hearts were put to rest, brightened, freshened. For gold was what they greatly thirsted for; they were gluttonous for it, starved for it, piggishly wanting it. They came lifting up the golden banners, waving them from side to side, showing them to each other. They seemed to babble; what they said to each other was in a babbling tongue. . . .

Another group of messengers—rainmakers, witches, and priests—had also gone out for an encounter, but nowhere were they able to do anything or to get sight of [the Spaniards]; they did not hit their target, they did not find the people they were looking for, they were not sufficient. . . .

> Cortés and his entourage continue their march.

Then they set out in this direction, about to enter Mexico here. Then they all dressed and equipped

Source: The selections here from Book Twelve are translated from the Nahuatl by James Lockhart and appear in the book he edited, *We People Here: Nahuatl Accounts of the Conquest of Mexico*, University of California Press, 1993. Reprinted with permission of the author.

[1]Throughout this source, *Mexico* refers to the region around Tenochtitlan, the capital of the Aztec empire, and *Mexica* refers the people who lived there.
[2]One of several spellings of the Aztec emperor's name, including Moctezuma and Montezuma.

themselves for war. They girded themselves, tying their battle gear tightly on themselves and then on their horses. Then they arranged themselves in rows, files, ranks.

Four horsemen came ahead going first, staying ahead, leading. . . .

Also the dogs, their dogs, came ahead, sniffing at things and constantly panting.

By himself came marching ahead, all alone, the one who bore the standard on his shoulder. He came waving it about, making it spin, tossing it here and there. . . .

Following him came those with iron swords. Their iron swords came bare and gleaming. On their shoulders they bore their shields, of wood or leather.

The second contingent and file were horses carrying people, each with his cotton cuirass,[3] his leather shield, his iron lance, and his iron sword hanging down from the horse's neck. They came with bells on, jingling or rattling. The horses, the deer,[4] neighed, there was much neighing, and they would sweat a great deal; water seemed to fall from them. And their flecks of foam splatted on the ground, like soapsuds splatting. . . .

The third file were those with iron crossbows, the crossbowmen. Their quivers went hanging at their sides, passed under their armpits, well filled, packed with arrows, with iron bolts. . . .

The fourth file were likewise horsemen; their outfits were the same as has been said.

The fifth group were those with harquebuses,[5] the harquebusiers, shouldering their harquebuses; some held them [level]. And when they went into the great palace, the residence of the ruler, they repeatedly shot off their harquebuses. They exploded, sputtered, discharged, thundered,

disgorged. Smoke spread, it grew dark with smoke, everyplace filled with smoke. The fetid smell made people dizzy and faint.

Then all those from the various altepetl[6] on the other side of the mountains, the Tlaxcalans, the people of Tliliuhquitepec, of Huexotzinco, came following behind. They came outfitted for war with their cotton upper armor, shields, and bows, their quivers full and packed with feathered arrows, some barbed, some blunted, some with obsidian[7] points. They went crouching, hitting their mouths with their hands yelling, singing, . . . whistling, shaking their heads.

Some bore burdens and provisions on their backs; some used tump[8] lines for their forehead, some bands around their chests, some carrying frames, some board cages, some deep baskets. Some made bundles, perhaps putting the bundles on their backs. Some dragged the large cannons, which went resting on wooden wheels, making a clamor as they came.

> Cortés and his army entered Tenochtitlan in November 1519 and were amicably received by Moctezuma (Moteuccoma), who was nonetheless taken captive by the Spaniards. Cortés's army was allowed to remain in a palace compound, but tensions grew the following spring. Pedro de Alvarado, in command while Cortés left to deal with a threat to his authority from the governor of Cuba, became concerned for the Spaniards' safety as the Aztecs prepared to celebrate the annual festival in honor of the god Huitzilopochtli.

---

[3]A piece of armor covering the body from neck to waist.
[4]Having never seen horses, some Aztecs thought they were large deer.
[5]A heavy matchlock gun that was portable but capable of being fired only with a support.

[6]The Nahuatl term for any sovereign state, especially for the local ethnic states of central Mexico.
[7]A volcanic glass, generally black.
[8]A strap or sling passed around the chest or forehead to help support a pack being carried on a person's back.

And when it had dawned and was already the day of his[9] festivity, very early in the morning those who had made vows to him unveiled his face. Forming a single row before him they offered him incense; each in his place laid down before him offerings of food for fasting and rolled amaranth dough. And it was as though all the youthful warriors had gathered together and had hit on the idea of holding and observing the festivity in order to show the Spaniards something, to make them marvel and instruct them. . . .

When things were already going on, when the festivity was being observed and there was dancing and singing, with voices raised in song, the singing was like the noise of waves breaking against the rocks.

When it was time, when the moment had come for the Spaniards to do the killing, they came out equipped for battle. They came and closed off each of the places where people went in and out. . . . Then they surrounded those who were dancing, going among the cylindrical drums. They struck a drummer's arms; both of his hands were severed. Then they struck his neck; his head landed far away. Then they stabbed everyone with iron lances and struck them with iron swords. They struck some in the belly, and then their entrails came spilling out. They split open the heads of some, they really cut their skulls to pieces, their skulls were cut up into little bits. And if someone still tried to run it was useless; he just dragged his intestines along. There was a stench as if of sulfur. Those who tried to escape could go nowhere. When anyone tried to go out, at the entryways they struck and stabbed him.

And when it became known what was happening, everyone cried out, "Mexica warriors, come running, get outfitted with devices, shields, and arrows, hurry, come running, the warriors are dying; they have died, perished, been annihilated, O Mexica warriors!" Thereupon there were war cries, shouting, and beating of hands against lips. The warriors quickly came outfitted, bunched together, carrying arrows and shields. Then the fighting began; they shot at them with barbed darts, spears, and tridents, and they hurled darts with broad obsidian points at them.

> The fighting drove the Spaniards and their allies back to the palace enclave. Without a reliable supply of food and water; in July 1520 Cortés, who had returned with his power intact, led his followers on a desperate nocturnal escape from the city, but they were discovered and suffered heavy losses. They retreated to the other side of the lake, and the Aztecs believed the Spanish threat had passed.

Before the Spanish appeared to us, first an epidemic broke out, a sickness of pustules.[10] . . . Large bumps spread on people; some were entirely covered. They spread everywhere, on the face, the head, the chest, etc. The disease brought great desolation; a great many died of it. They could no longer walk about, but lay in their dwellings and sleeping places, no longer able to move or stir. They were unable to change position, to stretch out on their sides or face down, or raise their heads. And when they made a motion, they called out loudly. The pustules that covered people caused great desolation; very many people died of them, and many just starved to death; starvation reigned, and no one took care of others any longer.

On some people, the pustules appeared only far apart, and they did not suffer greatly, nor did

---

[9] A reference to the god Huitzilopochtli. An image of the god, made from amaranth seed flour and the blood of recently sacrificed victims, played a central role in the festival.

[10] The disease was smallpox.

many of them die of it. But many people's faces were spoiled by it, their faces and noses were made rough. Some lost an eye or were blinded.

This disease of pustules lasted a full sixty days; after sixty days it abated and ended. When people were convalescing and reviving, the pustules disease began to move in the direction of the Chalco.[11] And many were disabled or paralyzed by it, but they were not disabled forever. . . . The Mexica warriors were greatly weakened by it.

And when things were in this state, the Spaniards came, moving toward us from Tetzcoco. . . .

> Having resupplied his Spanish/Tlaxcalan army and having constructed a dozen cannon-carrying brigantines for use on the lake, Cortés resumed his offensive late in 1520. In April 1521 he reached Tenochtitlan and placed the city under a blockade.

The Tlatelolca fought in Coquipan, in war boats. And in Xoloco the Spaniards came to a place where there was a wall in the middle of the road, blocking it. They fired the big guns at it. At the first shot it did not give way, but the second time it began to crumble. The third time, at last parts of it fell to the ground, and the fourth time finally the wall went to the ground once and for all. . . .

Once they got two of their boats into the canal at Xocotitlan. When they had beached them, then they went looking into the house sites of the people of Xocotitlan. But Tzilacatzin and some other warriors who saw the Spaniards immediately came out to face them; they came running after them, throwing stones at them, and they scattered the Spaniards into the water. . . .

When they got to Tlilhuacan, the warriors crouched far down and hid themselves, hugging the ground, waiting for the war cry, when there

would be shouting and cries of encouragement. When the cry went up, "O Mexica, up and at them!" the Tlappanecatl Ecatzin, a warrior of Otomi[12] rank, faced the Spaniards and threw himself at them, saying, "O Tlatelolca warriors, up and at them, who are these barbarians? Come running!" Then he went and threw a Spaniard down, knocking him to the ground; the one he threw down was the one who came first, who came leading them. And when he had thrown him down, he dragged the Spaniard off.

And at this point they let loose with all the warriors who had been crouching there; they came out and chased the Spaniards in the passageways, and when the Spaniards saw it the Mexica seemed to be intoxicated. The captives were taken. Many Tlaxcalans, and people of Acolhuacan, Chalco, Xochimilco, etc., were captured. A great abundance were captured and killed. . . .

Then they took the captives to Yacacolco, hurrying them along, going along herding their captives together. Some went weeping, some singing, some went shouting while hitting their hands against their mouths. When they got them to Yacacolco, they lined them all up. Each one went to the altar platform where the sacrifice was performed. The Spaniards went first, going in the lead; the people of the different altepetl just followed, coming last. And when the sacrifice was over, they strung the Spaniards' heads on poles on skull racks; they also strung up the horses' heads. They placed them below, and the Spaniards' heads were above them, strung up facing east. . . .

> Despite this victory the Aztecs could not overcome the problems of shortages of food, water, and warriors. In mid-July 1521 the Spaniards and their allies resumed their assault, and in early August the Aztecs

---

[11]A city on the southeast corner of Lake Texcoco.

[12]Ehte warriors bound by oath never to retreat.

decided to send into battle a quetzal-owl warrior; whose success or failure, it was believed, would reveal if the gods wished the Aztecs to continue fighting.

And all the common people suffered greatly. There was famine; many died of hunger. They no longer drank good, pure water, but the water they drank was salty. Many people died of it, and because of it many got dysentery and died. Everything was eaten: lizards, swallows, maize, straw, grass that grows on salt flats. And they chewed at wood, glue flowers, plaster, leather, and deerskin, which they roasted, baked, and toasted so that they could eat them, and they ground up medicinal herbs and adobe bricks. There had never been the like of such suffering. The siege was frightening, and great numbers died of hunger. . . .

And . . . the ruler Quauhtemoctzin[13] and the warriors Coyohuehuetzin, Temilotzin, Topantemoctzin, the Mixcoatlailotlac Ahuelitoctzin, Tlacotzin, and Petlauhtzin took a great warrior named Tlapaltecatl Opochtzin . . . and outfitted him, dressing him in a quetzal-owl costume. . . . When they put it on him he looked very frightening and splendid. . . . They gave him the darts of the devil,[14] darts of wooden rods with flint tips. And the reason they did this was that it was as

though the fate of the rulers of the Mexica were being determined.

When our enemies saw him, it was as though a mountain had fallen. Every one of the Spaniards was frightened; he intimidated them, they seemed to respect him a great deal. Then the quetzal-owl climbed up on the roof. But when some of our enemies had taken a good look at him they rose and turned him back, pursuing him. Then the quetzal-owl turned them again and pursued them. Then he snatched up the precious feathers and gold and dropped down off the roof. He did not die, and our enemies did not carry him off. Also three of our enemies were captured. At that the war stopped for good. There was silence, nothing more happened. Then our enemies went away. It was silent and nothing more happened until it got dark.

And the next day nothing more happened at all, no one made a sound. The common people just lay collapsed. The Spaniards did nothing more either, but lay still, looking at the people. Nothing was going on, they just lay still. . . .

> Two weeks passed before the Aztecs capitulated on August 13, 1521.

---

[13]Quauhtemoctzin was now the Aztec emperor.

[14]Darts sacred to Huitzlopochtli.

Conflict in New Netherland

22 • DAVID PIETERZEN DEVRIES, VOYAGES FROM HOLLAND TO AMERICA

As a result of the efforts of Henry Hudson, who in 1609 explored present-day New York Harbor and the Hudson River, the Dutch claimed New Netherland, an area that included Long Island, eastern New York, and parts of New Jersey and Connecticut. To encourage colonization, the Dutch West India Company granted wealthy colonists large tracts of land, known as patroonships, with the understanding that each patroon would settle at least 50 tenants on the land within four years. At first, relations with the Native Americans (mostly members of the Lenape, or

Delaware tribe) in the area were generally cordial, but they deteriorated after the arrival of Willem Kieft as director-general of New Netherland in 1638. He sought to tax the Indians to pay for the construction of a fort and attempted to force them off their land to create new patroonships, even though few of them had attracted the minimum number of tenants. In 1643 Kieft ordered the massacre described by David DeVries in the following excerpt from his *Voyages from Holland to America*. Born in Rochelle, France, in 1592 or 1593, DeVries was a mariner before emigrating to New Netherland and becoming a patroon in in the late 1630s. In the wake of the 1643 massacre, two years of fighting, known as Kieft's War, ensued. During the war a disillusioned DeVries returned to the Netherlands, where he died around 1662.

QUESTIONS FOR ANALYSIS

1. Why does DeVries oppose the director-general's plan to attack the Indians?
2. What does this suggest about DeVries's attitude toward the Native Americans?
3. How did the Indians react immediately after the massacre?
4. What does the Indians' behavior suggest about their early relations with the Dutch?
5. What were the long-term results of the massacre?

The 24th of February, sitting at a table with the Governor, he [Governor Kieft] began to state his intentions, that he had a mind to *wipe the mouths* of the savages; that he had been dining at the house of Jan Claesen Damen, where Maryn Adriaensen and Jan Claesen Damen, together with Jacob Planck, had presented a petition to him to begin this work. I answered him that they were not wise to request this; that such work could not be done without the approbation of the Twelve Men;[1] that it could not take place without my assent, who was one of the Twelve Men; that moreover I was the first patroon, and no one else hitherto had risked there so many thousands, and also his person . . . ; and that he should consider what profit he could derive from this business, as he well knew that on account of trifling with the Indians we had lost our colony in the South River at Swanendael,[2]

with thirty-two men, who were murdered in the year 1630; and that in the year 1640, the cause of my people being murdered on Staten Island was a difficulty which he had brought on with the Raritan Indians, where his soldiers had for some trifling thing killed some savages. . . . But it appeared that my speaking was of no avail. He had, with his co-murderers, determined to commit the murder, deeming it a Roman deed,[3] and to do it without warning the inhabitants in the open lands [so] that each one might take care of himself against the retaliation of the savages, for he could not kill all the Indians. When I had expressed all these things in full, sitting at the table, and the meal was over, he told me he wished me to go to the large hall, which he had been lately adding to his house. Coming to it, there stood all his soldiers ready to cross the river to Pavonia[4] to commit the

---

Source: From David Pieterzen DeVries, *Voyages from Holland to America* (New York: Billin and Brothers, 1853), pp. 114–117.

[1]A group of 12 men formed by Governor Kieft to advise him on Dutch–Indian relations.

[2]A Dutch colony in present-day Delaware.

[3]A glorious deed in the manner of the ancient Romans.

[4]The Dutch settlement on the west bank of the North River (Hudson River) that would become today's Hudson County, New Jersey.

murder. Then spoke I again to Governor Willem Kieft: "Let this work alone; you wish to break the mouths of the Indians, but you will also murder our own nation, for there are none of the settlers in the open country who are aware of it. My own dwelling, my people, cattle, corn, and tobacco will be lost." He answered me, assuring me that there would be no danger; that some soldiers should go to my house to protect it. But that was not done. So was this business begun between the 25th and 26th of February in the year 1643. I remained that night at the Governor's, sitting up. I went and sat by the kitchen fire, when about midnight I heard a great shrieking, and I ran to the ramparts of the fort, and looked over to Pavonia. Saw nothing but firing, and heard the shrieks of the savages murdered in their sleep. I returned again to the house by the fire. Having sat there awhile, there came an Indian with his squaw, whom I knew well, and who lived about an hour's walk from my house, and told me that they had fled in a small skiff, which they had taken from the shore at Pavonia; that the Indians from Fort Orange had surprised them; and that they had come to conceal themselves in the fort. I told them that they must go away immediately; that this was no time for them to come to the fort to conceal themselves; that they who had killed their people at Pavonia were not Indians, but the Swannekens, as they call the Dutch, had done it. They then asked me how they should get out of the fort. I took them to the door, and there was no sentry there, and so they betook themselves to the woods. When it was day the soldiers returned to the fort, having massacred or murdered eighty Indians, and considering they had done a deed of Roman valor, in murdering so many in their sleep; where infants were torn from their mothers' breasts, and hacked to pieces in the presence of the parents, and the

pieces thrown into the fire and in the water, and other sucklings, being bound to small boards, were cut, stuck, and pierced, and miserably massacred in a manner to move a heart of stone. Some were thrown into the river, and when the fathers and mothers endeavored to save them, the soldiers would not let them come on land but made both parents and children drown—children from five to six years of age, and also some old and decrepit persons. Those who fled from this onslaught, and concealed themselves in the neighboring sedge [marsh grass], and when it was morning, came out to beg a piece of bread, and to be permitted to warm themselves, were murdered in cold blood and tossed into the fire or the water. Some came to our people in the country with their hands, some with their legs cut off, and some holding their entrails in their arms, and others had such horrible cuts and gashes, that worse than they were could never happen. And these poor simple creatures, as also many of our own people, did not know any better than that they had been attacked by a party of other Indians—the Maquas. After this exploit, the soldiers were rewarded for their services, and Director Kieft thanked them by taking them by the hand and congratulating them. At another place, on the same night, on Coder's Hook near Corler's plantation, forty Indians were in the same manner attacked in their sleep, and massacred there in the same manner. Did the Duke of Alva[5] in the Netherlands ever do anything more cruel? This is indeed a disgrace to our nation, who have so generous a governor in our Fatherland as the Prince of Orange,[6] who has always endeavored in his wars to spill as little blood as possible. As soon as the savages understood that the Swannekens had so treated them, all the men whom they could surprise on the farmlands, they killed; but we have never heard that they have ever permitted

---

[5]Spanish general in the service of Philip II of Spain responsible for carrying out harsh anti-Protestant measures in the Netherlands in the 1560s.

[6]Frederick Henry, *stadholder*, or elected executive and military commander of the Netherlands.

women or children to be killed. They burned all the houses, farms, barns, grain, haystacks, and destroyed everything they could get hold of. So there was an open destructive war begun. They also burnt my farm, cattle, corn, barn, tobacco-house, and all the tobacco. My people saved themselves in the house where I alone lived, which was made with embrasures, through which they defended themselves. Whilst my people were in alarm the savage whom I had aided to escape from the fort in the night came there, and told the other Indians that I was a good chief, that I had helped him out of the fort, and that the killing of the Indians took place contrary to my wish. Then they all cried out together to my people that they would not shoot them; that if they had not destroyed my cattle they would not do it, nor burn my house; that they would let my little brewery stand, though they wished to get the copper kettle, in order to make darts for their arrows; but hearing now that it had been done contrary to my wish, they all went away, and left my house unbesieged. When now the Indians had destroyed so many farms and men in revenge for their people, I went to Governor Willem Kieft, and asked him if it was not as I had said it would be, that he would only effect the spilling of Christian blood. Who would now compensate us for our losses? But he gave me no answer. He said he wondered that no Indians came to the fort. I told him that I did not wonder at it; "why should the Indians come here where you have so treated them?"

Land and Labor in Spanish America

Throughout its existence, Spain's empire in the Americas was based on the exploitation of Native Americans. Such exploitation began in the 1490s when Columbus sought to establish a settlement on Hispaniola, an island he discovered in 1492. The first Spanish settlers were determined to enrich themselves, and this spelled disaster for the island's Tainos, who were robbed of their food and forced to work as slaves in the Spaniards' homes, fields, and mines as slaves. In 1497, Columbus attempted to curb the rapaciousness of his countrymen by allocating groups of Tainos to individual Spaniards, who could demand tribute and labor from these Indians and these Indians alone. Abuses continued, however, and in 1512, the Crown issued the Laws of Burgos, which sought to regulate the treatment of Indians by requiring reasonable labor expectations, adequate food and housing, and restrictions on punishments. The laws were unenforceable, and by the mid-1500s were irrelevant. By then, slaves from Africa were doing the Spaniards' work on Hispaniola. The Tainos, who numbered between 300,000 and 400,000 in 1492, had virtually disappeared as a result of agricultural disruption, excessive labor, and epidemics.

Elsewhere in Spanish America the economic realities were no different from those in Hispaniola. Without cheap labor and tribute from the Indians, none of the Spaniards' objectives—income for the Crown, profit for individual Spaniards, and winning souls to Christ—could be attained. Although this rarely meant enslavement, Indians could be assigned to an individual Spaniard, or *encomendero,* who could demand tribute and labor from the Indians assigned to him in return for providing protection and religious instruction. Indians also could be required to pay tribute to the state or be subjected to state-controlled labor drafts (*repartimiento*). Some Indians also were forced to accept pittance wages for their work in the open market.

Reliance on native labor was hotly debated by Spanish settlers, clergy, and royal officials. Through what mechanisms should the Indians be compelled to work for the Spaniards? What kind of work could they reasonably be asked to do? What responsibilities did Spaniards have to protect Indians from mistreatment and abuse? Most fundamentally, how was it possible to reconcile the Spaniards' need to compel Indians to work for them with their responsibility to convert them to Christianity, civilize them, and treat them as human beings? The Spaniards never found satisfactory answers to these questions, even after 300 years of colonial rule.

Indian Labor and Tribute in Mexico

23 • ALONSO DE ZORITA, THE BRIEF AND SUMMARY RELATION OF THE LORDS OF NEW SPAIN

As the Spanish Empire expanded from the Caribbean islands to Mexico and Central and South America, the debate over Spain's Indian policy continued unabated. Despite the reservations of royal officials and the failure of the system on Hispaniola, Cortés, the conqueror of the Aztecs, established a version of the *encomienda* system in Mexico when he assigned the rights to Indian tribute and labor to his soldiers. With little legislative guidance or judicial oversight, abuses were inevitable. In response, pro-Indian reformers, many drawn from Catholic religious orders, sought the suppression of the encomiendas and the end of all forms of Indian servitude. They were opposed by the encomenderos, some Spanish officials, and a number of churchmen who defended their rights to Indian labor and tribute.

In the 1520s and 1530s, the royal government pursued a middle course, allowing the encomienda system to continue but trying to regulate it to protect the Indians. Then in 1542, the Crown issued the New Laws, a comprehensive legal code for Spanish America that addressed Indian issues in 23 of its 54 articles. It prohibited the future enslavement of Indians, ordered the release of slaves if owners could not provide documentary proof of ownership, established further regulations for tribute, and ordered that all encomienda agreements were to lapse after the deaths of current holders. The New Laws set off a storm of protest from encomenderos, and the Crown had no choice but to cancel some of its provisions, including the abolition of the encomiendas themselves. Thus, the encomienda system survived until the eighteenth century, but legislation continued to whittle away at the encomenderos' privileges, gradually transferring the assessment and collection of Indian tribute to royal officials.

To enforce these and other laws pertaining to life in the Americas, the Crown established a system of courts that ranged from small regional courts to *audiencias*, which served as supreme courts in their administrative districts. Staffed by royal appointees who served both as judges and as advisors to regional administrators, audiencias were probably the most important single civil institution in the Spanish American colonies.

In the midst of the debate over the New Laws, a young Spanish lawyer, Alonso de Zorita (1512–1585), arrived in the New World to serve as *odior,* or judge, in the Audiencia of Santo Domingo on the island of Hispaniola. This graduate of the University of Salamanca spent the next 20 years as judge in Spanish America, with postings in Guatemala, the region of present-day Colombia, and Mexico City. He was known as a defender of Indian rights and an adversary of the encomenderos, whose campaign against him probably caused his reassignment from Guatemala to Mexico City in 1556. After retiring to Spain in 1566, he wrote several lengthy works, including *The Brief and Summary Relation of the Lords of New Spain.* Begun during his tenure in Mexico as a report requested by the Crown on Indian conditions, the manuscript probably was completed around 1570 and sent to members of the Council of the Indies, the supreme governing council of Spain's empire. Although several laws issued in the late 1500s resemble suggestions made by Zorita in his report, a direct influence cannot be proved.

Because Zorita was an advocate of Indian rights, it is legitimate to raise the question of the book's objectivity and accuracy. The scholarly consensus is that he presented an overly idyllic picture of preconquest Mexico but that his portrayal of the Indians' plight under the Spaniards, although written with intense feeling, is not distorted. Certainly evidence of the practices he describes can be found in court records and the works of many contemporaries.

QUESTIONS FOR ANALYSIS

1. Based on Zorita's account, enumerate the ways in which Spaniards depended on the Indians to generate wealth for private individuals and colonial administrators.
2. What evidence does Zorita provide of the royal government's efforts to protect the Indians from abuse and excessive exploitation?
3. According to Zorita, why did such efforts fail?
4. According to Zorita, why did Indian efforts to redress grievances also fail?
5. According to Zorita, what was the effect of Spanish policies on Indian family life and, more generally, on Indian society?
6. How does Zorita characterize the encomenderos?
7. How did the requirement that Indians pay their tribute in silver money cause hardship for the Indians?

Indian Labor

It is said that the Indians are being worked to death cultivating fields for their caciques and principales,[1] and enriching these lords, but those who say this are very mistaken. . . .

Others say that drunkenness is the cause of their dying out, because many do die of it, and they kill one another when they are drunk. But this conclusion too is erroneous, for the same condition exists in other places where the people are not dying out. . . .

Neither drunkenness nor their well-organized communal labor is killing them off. The cause is their labor on Spanish public works and their personal service to the Spaniards, which they fulfill in a manner contrary to their own ways and tempo of work. . . .

Their numbers have . . . been diminished by their enslavement for work in the mines and in the personal service of the Spaniards. . . . The Spaniards pressed the Indian lords to bring in all the slaves, and such was the Indians' fear that to satisfy the Spaniards they brought their own vassals and even their own children when they had no others to offer. Much the same thing happens today in the provision of Indians for the Spaniards' service, and in the enslavement of Indians on the pretext that they had risen in rebellion, contrary to Your Majesty's orders.

They have been reduced by the thousands by their toil in the gold and silver mines; and on the journey to the mines 80 or 100 leagues[2] away they were loaded with heavy burdens to which they were not accustomed. They died in the mines or along the road, of hunger and cold or extreme heat, and from carrying enormous loads of implements for the mines or other extremely heavy things; for the Spaniards, not satisfied with taking them so far away to work, must load them down on the way. . . .

The Spaniards still compel the Indians to go to the mines on the pretext that they are being sent to construct buildings there and are going voluntarily; these Spaniards claim that Your Majesty does not prohibit such labor, but only forbids work in the mines. In actual fact the Indians never go voluntarily, for they are forced to go under the repartimiento system by order of the Audiencia, contrary to Your Majesty's orders. . . .

The Spaniards also loaded them down with their household furnishings, beds, chairs, tables, and all the other appointments for their household and kitchen service. Thus weighted down, women and boys as well as children, they trudged over field and mountain, and returned to their homes half dead, or died on the way. . . .

The Indians have also been laid low by the labor of making sheep, cattle, and pig farms, of fencing these farms, of putting up farm buildings, and by their labor on roads, bridges, watercourses, stone walls, and sugar mills. For this labor, in which they were occupied for many days and weeks, they were taken away from their homes, their accustomed tempo of work and mode of life were disrupted. . . .

Now they are paid, but so little that they cannot buy enough to eat, for they are still used for such labor with permission from the Audiencias. . . .

Source: From "Life and Labor in Ancient Mexico," *The Brief and Summary Relation of the Lords of New Spain*, Benjamin Keen, ed. and trans., Rutgers University Press, 1963, pp. 203, 204, 207–212 (passim), 219, 220, 223, 237–240 (passim). Reprinted with permission of Patricia Keen and Gail Keen.

[1]*Caciques* (pronounced kah´-si-kays) was originally an Arawak word borrowed by the Spaniards to designate Native American chiefs; *principales* (pronounced prin-si-pah´-lays) refers to descendants of the Aztec warrior aristocracy and certain community officials. Neither term does justice to the complexities of pre- and postconquest Mesoamerican society.

[2]A measure of distance used in Spain and Spanish America. It was roughly the distance a man or horse could walk in an hour, approximately three miles.

Yet another multitude has been killed off and continues to be killed off by being taken as carriers on conquests and expeditions, and still others to serve the soldiers. They were taken from their homes by force and separated from their women and children and kin, and few if any returned, for they perished in the conquests or along the roads, or died on their return home. . . .

I could mention other things that are causing the extinction of these wretched people, but the great increase in the number of farms owned by Spaniards is in itself a sufficient cause. Ten, fifteen, and twenty years ago there were fewer farms, and there were many more Indians. The Indians were forced to work on them and suffered hardships therefrom, but since they were many and the farms few, it was not so noticeable. Now the Spanish farms are many and large and the Indians very few, and they must clear, cultivate, and weed as well as harvest and store the crops, so that all this labor now falls on the few that remain. . . .

. . . The wishes of Your Majesty and his Royal Council are well known and are made very plain in the laws that are issued every day in favor of the poor Indians and for their increase and preservation. But these laws are obeyed and not enforced,[3] wherefore there is no end to the destruction of the Indians, nor does anyone care what Your Majesty decrees. . . .

Indeed, the more laws and decrees are sent, the worse is the condition of the Indians by reason of the false and sophistical interpretation that the Spanish officials give these laws, twisting their meaning to suit their own purposes. It seems to me that the saying of a certain philosopher well applies to this case: Where there is a plenty of doctors and medicines, there is a plenty of ill health. Just so, where there are many laws and judges, there is much injustice.

Indian Tribute

The first assessment was made by the Bishop of Mexico, who came with the title of Protector of the Indians.[4] . . . There were great frauds connected with this assessment, because many caciques and principales, fearing their encomenderos or wishing to please them, declared that the Indians could pay the amounts they were paying. Under pressure from their encomenderos, these caciques even overstated the amounts the Indians were paying, so that if some reduction were made, the assessment would remain what it had been.

As a result of failure to solve the problem once and for all, the Indians constantly clamor for relief from their heavy burdens. The Audiencia has sometimes lowered the assessments, sometimes raised them. In recent years the frauds and tricks practiced by the Spaniards have led to the increase or even doubling of the assessments, thus returning them to their former level or slightly below. This is the cause of the constant comings and goings of the Indians to and from the Audiencia, in which they waste their money and even lose their lives, but never obtain justice. . . .

The Indians, being generally a people of great simplicity, do not know how to demand their rights and so bear their woes in silence. If some of them . . . do complain in the name of all, this leads to another evil, namely, that the Indians squander their lives and money in suits, and all the while continue to pay tribute according to the first count. In the end they never obtain justice, for they drop the suit because they have run out of money or the encomenderos have bribed their leaders; or their leaders may have died; or they may be unable to prove that some of their people have fled or died, or that there was an error in the count. . . .

---

[3]A reference to the Spanish phrase *Obedezco pero no cumplo*, a formula employed by Spanish officials when a royal order was inconvenient or unenforceable.

[4]Juan de Zumarrago (1468–1548), a Spanish Franciscan.

Your Majesty has also ordered that assessments should be made, not on the basis of reports concerning the capacity to pay of the towns, but on the basis of personal observation and study of the character and capacities of each town, the fertility of its soil, and the like, in order that a just assessment may be made and each Indian may be made to understand precisely what he owes and is obliged to give, so much and no more. Your Majesty has also decreed that the Indians . . . should give only those things that are found in their native lands and regions and that they can easily obtain, namely, the produce of their fields or the products of their crafts. . . . Your Majesty has also ordered that the Indians must not be made to pay up to the limits of their capacity, that they should be allowed to get richer and not poorer, that they should be left with enough to take care of their needs, cure their ills, and marry off their children, and that they should enjoy rest and repose, with due regard for their preservation, increase, and religious instruction. . . .

. . . Many penalties, including loss of encomiendas, are prescribed for violation of these orders, but all of them together have not secured compliance. . . .

Throughout the Indies the natives are dying out and declining in number, though some assert that this is not so. Since the Indians are so heavily burdened with tribute payments that they cannot support themselves and their wives and children, they often leave them (although they loved them dearly), and abandon their wretched little homes and their fields. They depart for some other region and wander about from place to place or flee to the woods, where jaguars or other beasts eat them. Some Indians have hanged themselves . . .

As I said before, the Indians have little stamina. As a result, an Indian's planting is so small that his harvest will barely cover his needs for the year, for he cannot cultivate an area larger than the little plot that he and his wife and children (if he has them) can work. From this harvest half a fanega[5] of maize is taken for tribute. This amount is taken in good and bad years alike . . . . One might think they would not miss half a fanega, but it is a great deal to them because of their small harvest. Maize is their staff of life, the source of their food and clothing, and if they do not grow it themselves, they have no means of obtaining it. Consequently, if the crop fails, they suffer from famine and eat herbs, roots, and fruit that rot their guts. . . .

To ask the Indians for tribute in reales[6] is also a great injury to them. Unless an Indian lives in a town not far from a Spanish town, or on a main traveled road, or raises cacao[7] or cotton, or makes cotton cloth, or raises fruit, he does not receive money. There are regions where the Indians have never seen a real in all their lives, and do not even know what a real is. In order to earn money, therefore, they must quit their towns and homes, leaving their wives and children without means of support, and go 30, 40, and even more leagues to climates different from their own, where they sometimes lose their lives. Sometimes in their despair they prefer not to return home, or perhaps one will take to living with another woman and lead a depraved life, leaving all the burdens of supporting his family to his poor wife.

If an Indian cannot pay the money tribute because he lacks the means, or does not know where to go to earn reales, he goes to jail and his time at forced labor is sold to some Spaniard to cover the tribute and jailer's costs. He must toil for two, three, or four months or even longer, according to what he owes and what he is paid for his work, because he has no property that can be seized and sold by the authorities. . . .

---

[5]A dry measure of approximately 1.5 bushels.
[6]A *real* was one eighth of a *peso*. In 1537 King Charles I of Spain set the weight of a peso at just under 27.47 grams, slightly less than an ounce. In comparison, an American penny weighs 2.5 grams.

[7]The bean from the cacao plant is used to make cocoa and chocolate. The cacao bean was a form of currency before the conquest.

The "Mountain of Silver" and the Mita System

24 • ANTONIO VAZQUEZ DE ESPINOSA, COMPENDIUM AND DESCRIPTION OF THE WEST INDIES

In 1545, an Indian herder lost his footing on a mountain in the eastern range of the Andes while chasing a llama. To keep from falling, he grabbed a bush, which he uprooted to reveal a rich vein of silver. This is one story of how the world learned of the silver mine at Potosí, in present-day Bolivia. Located two miles above sea level in a cold, desolate region, Potosí became the site of the Western Hemisphere's first mining boomtown. By 1600, it had a population of 150,000 (more than half of whom were Indians), making it the largest, wildest, gaudiest city in the New World. With one-fifth of its silver going to the Spanish crown, Potosí had a major impact on the European Wars of Religion, in that it bankrolled Spanish military campaigns against the Protestants, and on world trade, since its silver was used by Europeans to purchase goods throughout Asia.

The backbone of the Potosí operation was a system of government-controlled draft labor known as the *repartimiento,* which also was practiced in Mexico and other parts of Spanish America. In Peru, it was referred to as the *mita* (Quechua for "time" or "distribution"), a term used by the Incas for their preconquest system of required state labor. In the repartimiento system, native communities were required to supply a portion of their population at fixed intervals for assignment to particular tasks. In theory, required work was distributed evenly throughout each community, and an individual might go months or even years without being called for labor service.

The following description of the mita system is provided by Antonio Vazquez de Espinosa (d. 1630), a Spanish Carmelite friar who abandoned an academic career to perform priestly work in the Americas. During his retirement in the 1620s, he wrote several books on Spanish America, the best known of which is his *Compendium and Description of the West Indies,* which contains his observations of conditions in Mexico and Spanish South America. In this excerpt, he describes mercury mining at Huancavelica and the "mountain of silver" at Potosí.

QUESTIONS FOR ANALYSIS

1. What was the range of annual wages for each laborer at Huancavelica? How do their wages compare with the annual salary of the royal hospital chaplain? How does the sum of the workers' annual wages compare with the cost of tallow candles at Potosí? Compare the wages of the mita workers at Potosí with the wages paid those Native Americans who freely hired themselves out. What do you conclude from all these figures?
2. What were the major hazards connected with the extraction and production of mercury and silver?

3. What evidence does this source provide of Spanish concern for the welfare of the Indian workers? What evidence of indifference does it provide? Where does the weight of the evidence seem to lie?
4. What does the document tell us about the impact of the mita system on native society?
5. What similarities and differences do you see between the Mexican repartimiento described by Zorita (source 25) and the mita described by Vazquez?

Huancavelica

. . . It contains 400 Spanish residents, as well as many temporary shops of dealers in merchandise and groceries, heads of trading houses, and transients, for the town has a lively commerce. It has a parish church . . . a Dominican convent, and a Royal Hospital under the Brethren of San Juan de Dios for the care of the sick, especially Indians on the range; it has a chaplain with a salary of 800 pesos[1] contributed by His Majesty; he is curate of the parish of San Sebastian de Indios, for the Indians who have come to work in the mines and who have settled down there. . . .

Every two months His Majesty sends by the regular courier from Lima[2] 60,000 pesos to pay for the mita of the Indians, for the crews are changed every two months, so that merely for the Indian mita payment . . . 360,000 pesos are sent from Lima every year, not to speak of much besides, which all crosses . . . that cold and desolate mountain country which . . . has nothing on it but llama ranches.

Up on the range there are 3,000 or 4,000 Indians working in the mine; it is colder up there than in the town, since it is higher. The mine where the mercury is located is a large layer which they keep following downward. When I was in that town [in 1616] I went up on the range and down into the mine, which at that time was considerably more than 130 stades[3] deep. The ore was very rich black flint, and the excavation so extensive that it held more than 3,000 Indians working away hard with picks and hammers, breaking up that flint ore; and when they have filled their little sacks, the poor fellows, loaded down with ore, climb up those ladders or rigging, some like masts and others like cables, and so trying and distressing that a man empty-handed can hardly get up them. . . . Nor is that the greatest evil and difficulty; that is due to thievish and undisciplined superintendents. As that great vein of ore keeps going down deeper and they follow its rich trail, in order to make sure that no section of that ore shall drop on top of them, they keep leaving supports or pillars of the ore itself, even if of the richest quality, and they necessarily help to sustain and insure each section with less risk. This being so, there are men so heartless that for the sake of stealing a little rich ore, they go down out of hours and deprive the innocent Indians of this protection by hollowing into these pillars to steal the rich ore in them, and then a great section is apt to fall in and kill all the Indians, and sometimes the unscrupulous and grasping superintendents themselves . . . and much of this is kept quiet so that it shall not come to the notice of the manager and cause the punishment of the accomplices. . . .

. . . On the other side of the town there are structures where they grind up the mercury ore and then put it in jars with . . . many little holes . . . and a channel for it to drip into and pass into the

Source: Excerpt from Antonio Vazquez de Espinosa, *Description of the Indies,* c. 1620, trans. by Charles Upson Clark, Smithsonian Institution Press, 1968.

[1] See source 23, note 6.
[2] The capital city of the Viceroyalty of Peru, one of the major administrative units of Spanish America.
[3] A measure of length, approximately 200 feet.

jar or place where it is to fall. Then they roast the ore with a straw fire. . . . Under the onset of this fire it melts and the mercury goes up in vapor or exhalation until, passing through the holes in the first mold, it hits the body of the second, and there it coagulates, rests, and comes to stop where they have provided lodging for it; but if it does not strike any solid body while it is hot, it rises as vapor until it cools and coagulates and starts falling downward again. Those who carry out the reduction of this ore have to be very careful and test cautiously; they must wait till the jars are cold before uncovering them for otherwise they may easily get mercury poisoning and if they do, they are of no further use; their teeth fall out, and some die.

Potosí

According to His Majesty's warrant, the mine owners on this massive range have a right to the mita of 13,300 Indians in the working and exploitation of the mines. . . . It is the duty of the Corregidor[4] of Potosí to have them rounded up and to see that they come in from all the provinces between Cuzco over the whole of El Collao and as far as the frontiers of Tarija and Tomina;[5] this Potosí Corregidor has power and authority over all the Corregidors in those provinces mentioned; for if they do not fill the Indian mita allotment assigned each of them in accordance with the capacity of their provinces as indicated to them, he can send them, and does, salaried inspectors to report upon it, and when the remissness is great or remarkable, he can suspend them, notifying the Viceroy[6] of the fact.

These Indians are sent out every year under a captain whom they choose in each village or tribe, for him to take them and oversee them for the year each has to serve; every year they have a new election, for as some go out, others come in. This works out very badly, with great losses and gaps in the quotas of Indians, the villages being depopulated; and this gives rise to great extortions and abuses on the part of the inspectors toward the poor Indians, ruining them and thus depriving the . . . chief Indians of their property and carrying them off in chains because they do not fill out the mita assignment, which they cannot do, for the reason given and for others which I do not bring forward.

These 13,300 are divided up every 4 months into 3 mitas, each consisting of 4,433 Indians, to work in the mines on the range and in the 120 smelters in the Potosí and Tarapaya areas; it is a good league [about three miles] between the two. These mita Indians earn each day, or there is paid each one for his labor, 4 reals.[7] Besides these there are others not under obligation, who . . . hire themselves out voluntarily: these each get from 12 to 16 reals, and some up to 24, according to their reputation of wielding the pick and knowing how to get the ore out. These . . . will be over 4,000 in number. They and the mita Indians go up every Monday morning to the locality of Guayna Potosí which is at the foot of the range; the Corregidor arrives with all the provincial captains or chiefs who have charge of the Indians assigned them, and he there checks off and reports to each mine and smelter owner the number of Indians assigned him for his mine or smelter; that keeps him busy till 1 p.m., by which time the Indians are already turned over to these mine and smelter owners.

After each has eaten his ration, they climb up the hill, each to his mine, and go in, staying there from that hour until Saturday evening without coming out of the mine; their wives bring them food, but they stay constantly underground, excavating and carrying out the ore from which they get the silver. They all have tallow candles, lighted day and night; that is the light they work with, for as they are underground, they have need of it all the time. The mere cost of these candles used

---

[4]A Spanish official with military and executive functions.
[5]The region consisted of approximately 139 villages.

[6]The official who governs a province in the name of the king.
[7]A *real* is one-eighth of a *peso*.

in the mines on this range will amount every year to more than 300,000 pesos, even though tallow is cheap in that country, being abundant; but this is a very great expense, and it is almost incredible, how much is spent for candles in the operation of breaking down and getting out the ore.

These Indians have different functions in the handling of the silver ore; some break it up with bar or pick, and dig down in, following the vein in the mine; others bring it up; others up above keep separating the good and the poor in piles; others are occupied in taking it down from the range to the mills on herds of llamas; every day they bring up more than 8,000 of these native beasts of burden for this task. These teamsters who carry the metal do not belong to the mita, but are mingados—hired.

So huge is the wealth which has been taken out of this range since the year 1545, when it was discovered, up to the present year of 1628, which makes 83 years that they have been working and reducing its ores, that merely from the registered mines, as appears from an examination of most of the accounts in the royal records, 326,000,000 assay[8] pesos have been taken out. At the beginning when the ore was richer and easier to get out, for then there were no mita Indians and no

mercury process, in the 40 years between 1545 and 1585, they took out 111,000,000 of assay silver. From the year 1585 up to 1628, 43 years, although the mines are harder to work, for they are deeper down, with the assistance of 13,300 Indians whom His Majesty has granted to the mine owners on that range, and of other hired Indians, who come there freely and voluntarily to work at day's wages, and with the great advantage of the mercury process, in which none of the ore or the silver is wasted, and with the better knowledge of the technique which the miners now have, they have taken out 215,000,000 assay pesos. That, plus the 111 extracted in the 40 years previous to 1585, makes 326,000,000 assay pesos, not counting the great amount of silver secretly taken from these mines . . . and to other countries outside Spain; and to the Philippines and China, which is beyond all reckoning. . . .

Over and above that, such great treasure and riches have come from the Indies in gold and silver from all the other mines in New Spain and Peru, Honduras, the New Kingdom of Granada, Chile, New Galicia, New Vizcaya,[9] and other quarters since the discovery of the Indies, that they exceed 1,800 millions.

---

[8]Measured so the silver content met official standards.

[9]New Galicia and New Vizcaya were regions and administrative jurisdictions located in north-central and northwestern Mexico.

Chapter 4

Continuity and Change in East and Southeast Asia

IMPORTANT CHANGES TOOK PLACE in East and Southeast Asia in the early modern era: Islam continued to make converts in Southeast Asia and western China; a new dynasty, the Tokugawa, stabilized Japan after decades of civil war; the Chinese Ming Dynasty declined precipitously in the late 1500s and was overthrown in 1644; and European merchants and missionaries appeared in ever greater numbers. All these changes, however, took place in a region that in most respects remained what it had been for more than a millennium. For the societies of East and Southeast Asia, continuity rather than change was the hallmark of the early modern era.

One constant was the primacy of China. In terms of size, wealth, population, technology, trade, military might, and cultural influence, China, as it had for centuries, overshadowed the smaller states and nomadic societies that surrounded it. With some justification, the Chinese considered China the "central kingdom" and viewed all other peoples as their inferiors. On China's periphery were three neighboring states—Japan, Korea, and Vietnam—that were politically independent, and in certain ways culturally distinct, but whose religious practices, formal thought, writing systems, and political institutions all reflected long centuries of Chinese influence. In Southeast Asia, an area of small kingdoms and city-states rather than large territorial states, Chinese influence was less pervasive. Hinduism, Buddhism, and Islam had many adherents as a result of longstanding commercial and cultural contacts with India and Arabia. Nonetheless, China was the most important market for Southeast Asian merchants, and a number of Southeast Asian rulers paid tribute to the Chinese emperor as a token of their loyalty and subservience. The sparsely populated arid regions to the west and north of China lacked large cities and centralized states. They were populated by Uighurs, Turks, Khitans, Jurchens, Manchus, and Mongols, who supported themselves through pastoralism and limited agriculture. Their raids were a constant threat to China and sometimes developed into full-blown invasions. No less than four Chinese dynasties—the Liao, Jin, Yuan, and Qing—originated among these so-called barbarian peoples on China's northern and western flanks.

Another constant was East and Southeast Asia's important role in the world economy. Southeast Asia was a commercial crossroads linking Chinese and Japanese markets with those of India, Southwest Asia, Europe, and Africa. It also was a source of cotton, rice, fish, forest products, copper, lead, and other items that were exchanged for Indian textiles and Chinese silks, ceramics, medicines, paper, and tea. More important, Southeast Asia grew pepper, nutmeg, cloves, and mace, spices that were coveted throughout the Afro-Eurasian world. When Europeans began seeking ocean routes to Asia in the fifteenth century, their primary goal was direct access to the spice markets of Southeast Asia.

China, however, was the region's economic powerhouse. Its population in 1500 was between 100 and 125 million, well above Europe's estimated 80 million. Its two largest cities, Beijing and Nanjing, with populations around 700,000 each, were slightly smaller than Istanbul, the world's most populous city, but were almost six times larger than Paris, Europe's largest city. Much Chinese economic activity was devoted to supplying this vast domestic market, but China also played a major role in international trade. China's main exports were luxurious silk textiles and ceramics, the quality of which was recognized throughout Eurasia and Africa. Although the Chinese imported spices from Southeast Asia and cotton textiles from India, they were interested in few other foreign products. Thus, foreign merchants had no choice but to pay for their goods with gold and silver, meaning that year after year, China had a favorable balance of trade.

Until the sixteenth century, contact between these Asian societies and Europe had been limited. Although trade between the two regions had existed for centuries, the goods exchanged had always been carried by Arab, Indian, or Central Asian intermediaries. The number of European travelers to China increased in the thirteenth century, when the Mongol Empire made travel across Eurasia less dangerous and arduous. But with the breakup of the Mongol Empire in the mid-fourteenth century and the antipathy toward foreigners shown by Ming Dynasty rulers, European contact with China was reduced to a trickle.

Then in the early 1500s, the Portuguese arrived in the region seeking trade and converts to Christianity. The Spanish, Dutch, and English soon followed, and in time these and other Westerners would have an immense impact on the region. In the sixteenth and seventeenth centuries, however, the Europeans' arrival had little immediate significance. The exception was Southeast Asia, where the Portuguese captured the port city of Melaka in 1511, and the Spaniards gradually subjugated the Philippines beginning in the 1560s. Even in Southeast Asia, however, the Portuguese failed to dominate the region's spice trade, and European Catholic missionaries made few converts except in the Philippines and briefly in Japan.

Elsewhere, the Europeans' arrival was a relatively minor event. In Japan the most significant development was its political recovery after decades of civil war. In 1603, the Tokugawa clan and its followers seized power and installed Tokugawa Ieyasu as *shogun*, or military ruler. Tokugawa rulers expelled European missionaries, suppressed Christianity, and limited trade with Europe to one Dutch ship a year. In China, emperors permitted the Portuguese to trade at a single port, Macao, and allowed a small number of Jesuit missionaries to reside at the imperial court in Beijing. Here they impressed the Chinese elite with their mechanical clocks and astronomical knowledge but had little effect on Chinese politics or culture.

Confucianism in China and Japan

No philosopher has influenced the values and behavior of more human beings than the Chinese thinker Kong Fuzi (ca. 551–479 B.C.E.), known in the West by his Latinized name Confucius. Like other thinkers of his day, Confucius, a scholar intent on a career in public service, was distressed by the political fragmentation and turbulence plaguing China during the Eastern Zhou Era (771–256 B.C.E.). Only after failing to achieve a position as a ruler's trusted advisor did he turn to teaching. He proved to be a gifted teacher, one who is reputed to have had more than 3,000 students.

Confucius taught that China's troubles were rooted in the failure of its people and leaders to understand and act according to the rules of proper conduct. Proper conduct meant actions conforming to the standards of an idealized past, when China was structured along lines paralleling those of a harmonious family. He taught that just as fathers, wives, sons, and daughters have specific roles and obligations within families, individuals, depending on their age, gender, marital status, ancestry, and social standing, have specific roles and obligations in society. Subjects owed rulers obedience, and rulers were expected to be models of virtue and benevolence. Children owed parents love and reverence, and parents, especially fathers, were expected to be kind and just. Children learned from parents, and subjects from rulers. Confucius also taught that whatever one's status, one must live according to the principles of *jen,* which means humaneness, benevolence, and love, and *li,* a term that encompasses the concepts of ceremony, propriety, and good manners. Because the wisdom and practices of ancient sages were central to his teaching, Confucius taught that one could achieve virtue by studying the literature, history, and rituals of the past. Education in traditional values and behavior was the path to sagehood, the quality of knowing what is proper and good and acting accordingly.

Although Confucius's philosophy competed with many other schools of thought in his own day, during the era of the Han Dynasty (206 B.C.E.–220 C.E.), it became the official program of studies for anyone seeking an office in the imperial administration. Mastery of the writings ascribed to Confucius became the path to success on the civil service examinations by which China chose its officials. Although the examination system was abolished by China's Mongol rulers during the Yuan Era (1264–1368), it was revived under the Ming (1368–1644) and continued in use until 1905. For almost 2,000 years, China was administered by a literary elite devoted to Confucianism.

Confucianism's influence was not limited to China. Although it had to compete with Buddhism and other indigenous religions, Confucianism deeply affected the thought, politics, and everyday life of Korea, Vietnam, and Japan.

"Doing Good" in Seventeenth-Century China

25 • MERITORIOUS DEEDS AT NO COST

During the sixteenth and seventeenth centuries, interpreters of Confucianism drew mainly on the work of scholars from the Song Era (960–1279 C.E.). Known as Neo-Confucianists, these scholars had brought new energy and rigor to Confucian scholarship after several centuries of stagnation and declining influence. The greatest Neo-Confucianist was Zhu Xi (1130–1200), who presided over a huge project of historical research and wrote detailed commentaries on most of the Confucian Classics. His commentaries came to be viewed as the orthodox version of Confucianism and the official interpretation for evaluating performance on the civil service examinations during the Ming and Qing eras.

Confucian scholarship in the 1500s and 1600s, however, was more than a rehashing and refining of Neo-Confucian formulas. Supported by the emperor and high officials, Ming scholars completed vast research projects on history, medicine, ethics, and literature. In reinterpreting Confucianism, they sought to apply the Sage's wisdom to their own society—one experiencing population growth, commercialization, urbanization, and ultimately dynastic decline and foreign conquest. Many endeavored to make Confucianism less elitist and more "popular."

Traditional Confucianism had taught that the erudition and virtue necessary for sagehood were theoretically attainable by anyone, but that in reality, they could be achieved only by small numbers of privileged males who had the wealth and leisure for years of study and self-cultivation. Women, artisans, peasants, and even merchants were capable of understanding and internalizing some Confucian principles by observing the behavior of their superiors, but serious scholarship and true morality were beyond them. In the early 1500s, such ideas were challenged by the scholar-official Wang Yangming (1472–1529), who taught that everyone, regardless of station, was capable of achieving sagehood. He was convinced that a healthy Chinese polity depended on teaching sound moral principles to all classes of people.

Wang's ideas were well received in a China where urbanization, increased literacy, and growing wealth were creating a burgeoning demand for books, many of which brought Confucian ideas to the broad reading public. These included summaries of the Confucian Classics, editions of the Classics themselves, manuals to prepare candidates for the civil service examinations, and "morality books." Morality books, which first appeared in the Song and Yuan eras, discussed proper behavior not only for the learned elite but also for common people. With titles such as *A Record of the Practice of Good Deeds* and *Establishing One's Own Destiny*, morality books taught that good deeds would be rewarded by worldly success, robust health, many sons, and a long life.

Among the most popular morality books was the anonymous *Meritorious Deeds at No Cost*, which appeared in the mid-seventeenth century. Unlike other such books, which recommended costly good deeds such as paying for family rituals connected with marriage, coming of age, funerals, and ancestral rites, it discussed laudable acts that required little or no money. It lists actions considered good for "people in general" but mainly concentrates on good deeds appropriate to specific groups, ranging from local gentry and scholars to soldiers and household servants. Its prescriptions provide insights into both Confucian values and contemporary Chinese views of class, family, and gender.

Meritorious Deeds at No Cost begins with the "local gentry," individuals who have the rank and status of government officials but who reside at home and may not have any specific political responsibilities. The next group is "scholars," which refers to individuals at various stages of preparing for the civil service examinations. As educated individuals and potential officials, their status placed them below the gentry but above the common people. The recommended meritorious deeds for this group reveal that many "scholars" were also teachers.

QUESTIONS FOR ANALYSIS

1. In what ways do the responsibilities of the various groups differ from one another? In what ways do they reflect certain underlying assumptions about what makes a good society?
2. According to this document, what should be the attitude of the upper classes (gentry and scholars) to those below them? Conversely, how should peasants, merchants, and artisans view their superiors?
3. What views of women and sexuality are stated or implied in this treatise?
4. What views of money and moneymaking are stated or implied in this treatise?

5. According to this treatise, what specific kinds of behaviors and attitudes are components of filial piety?
6. Taking the document as a whole, what conclusions can be drawn about the ultimate purpose or highest good the author hopes to achieve through the various kinds of behaviors he describes?

Local Gentry

Rectify your own conduct and transform the common people. . . .

If people have suffered a grave injustice, expose and correct it.

Settle disputes among your neighbors fairly.

When villagers commit misdeeds, admonish them boldly and persuade them to desist. . . .

Be tolerant of the mistakes of others.

Be willing to listen to that which is displeasing to your ears.

Do not make remarks about women's sexiness.

Do not harbor resentment when you are censured. . . .

Hold up for public admiration women who are faithful to their husbands and children who are obedient to their parents. . . .

Prevent plotting and intrigue. . . .

Prevent the younger members of your family from oppressing others by taking advantage of your position. . . .

Do not be arrogant, because of your own power and wealth, toward relatives who are poor or of low status. . . .

Do not ignore your own relatives and treat others as if they were your kin.

Influence other families to cherish good deeds. . . .

Do not disport yourself with lewd friends. . . .

Instruct your children, grandchildren, and nephews to be humane and compassionate toward all and to avoid anger and self-indulgence.

Do not deceive or oppress younger brothers or cousins.

Encourage others to read and study without minding the difficulties.

Urge others to esteem charity and disdain personal gain. . . .

Persuade others to settle lawsuits through conciliation.

Try to settle complaints and grievances among others. . . .

Curb the strong and protect the weak.

Show respect to the aged and compassion for the poor.

Do not keep too many concubines.

Scholars

Be loyal to the emperor and filial to your parents.

Honor your elder brothers and be faithful to your friends. . . .

Instruct the common people in the virtues of loyalty and filial piety. . . .

Be wholehearted in inspiring your students to study. . . .

Try to improve your speech and behavior.

Teach your students also to be mindful of their speech and behavior. . . .

Be patient in educating the younger members of poor families. . . .

Do not write or post notices which defame other people. . . .

Source: From Self and Society & Ming Thought, by William Theodore de Bary, pp. 352–361. Copyright © 1970 Columbia University Press. Reprinted with permission of the publisher.

Do not encourage the spread of immoral and lewd novels [by writing, reprinting, expanding, etc.]. . . .

Do not attack or vilify commoners; do not oppress ignorant villagers. . . .

Do not ridicule other people's handwriting. . . .

Make others desist from unfiliality toward their parents or unkindness toward relatives and friends.

Educate the ignorant to show respect to their ancestors and live in harmony with their families. . . .

Peasants

Do not miss the proper time for farm work. . . .

Do not obstruct or cut off paths. Fill up holes that might give trouble to passersby . . .

Do not damage crops in your neighbors' fields by leaving animals to roam at large, relying on your landlord's power and influence to protect you.

Do not encroach [on others' property] beyond the boundaries of your own fields and watercourses, thinking to ingratiate yourself with your landlord. . . .

In plowing, do not infringe on graves or make them hard to find. . . .

Do not damage the crops in neighboring fields out of envy because they are so flourishing. . . .

Do not become lazy and cease being conscientious because you think your landlord does not provide enough food and wine or fails to pay you enough.

Fill up holes in graves.

Take good care of others' carts and tools. . . .

Keep carts and cattle from trampling down others' crops.

Craftsmen

. . . Whenever you make something, try to make it strong and durable.

Do not be resentful toward your master if he fails to provide enough food and drink. . . .

Do not reveal and spread abroad the secrets of your master's house.

Do not make crude imitations.

Finish your work without delay.

In your trade with others, do not practice deceit through forgery.

Do not mix damaged articles with good.

Do not break or damage finished goods.

Do not recklessly indulge in licentiousness. . . .

Do not steal the materials of others.

Do not use the materials of others carelessly. . . .

Merchants

Do not deceive ignorant villagers when fixing the price of goods.

Do not raise the price of fuel and rice too high.

When the poor buy rice, do not give them short measure. . . .

When sick people have urgent need of something, do not raise the price unreasonably.

Do not deceitfully serve unclean dishes or leftover food to customers who are unaware of the fact.

Do not dispossess or deprive others of their business by devious means.

Do not envy the prosperity of others' business and speak ill of them wherever you go. . . .

Treat the young and the aged on the same terms as the able-bodied.

When people come in the middle of the night with an urgent need to buy something, do not refuse them on the ground that it is too cold. . . .

Give fair value when you exchange silver for copper coins. Especially when changing money for the poor, be generous to them.

When a debtor owes you a small sum but is short of money, have mercy and forget about the difference. Do not bring him to bankruptcy and hatred by refusing to come to terms.

When the poor want to buy such things as mosquito nets, clothing, and quilts, have pity on them and reduce the price. Do not refuse to come to terms.

People in General

Do not show anger or worry in your parents' sight.

Accept meekly the reproaches and anger of your parents.

Persuade your parents to correct their mistakes and return to the right path.

Do not divulge your parents' faults to others.

Do not let your parents do heavy work.

Do not be disgusted with your parents' behavior when they are old and sick.

Do not yell at your parents or give them angry looks.

Love your brothers. . . .

If you are poor, do not entertain thoughts of harming the rich.

If you are rich, do not deceive and cheat the poor. . . .

Do not speak of others' humble ancestry.

Do not talk about the private [women's] quarters of others. [Commentary: When others bring up such things, if they are of the younger generation, reprimand them with straight talk, and if they are older or of the same generation as you, change the subject.] . . .

Respect women's chastity. . . .

Do not stir up your mind with lewd and wanton thoughts.

Do not besmirch others' honor or chastity.

Do not intimidate others to satisfy your own ambition.

Do not assert your own superiority by bringing humiliation upon others. . . .

Do not dwell on others' faults while dilating [expounding at length] on your own virtues.

Try to promote friendly relations among neighbors and relatives. . . .

When you hear someone speaking about the failings of others, make him stop.

When you hear a man praising the goodness of others, help him to do so. . . .

When you see a man about to go whoring or gambling, try to dissuade him. . . .

Do not deceive cripples, fools, old men, the young, or the sick. . . .

Make peace between husbands and wives who are about to separate. . . .

Help the blind and disabled to pass over dangerous bridges and roads. . . .

Cut down thorns by the roadside to keep them from tearing people's clothes. . . .

Put stones in muddy places [to make them passable].

Lay wooden boards where the road is broken off.

At night, light a lamp for others. . . .

Do not listen to your wife or concubines if they should encourage you to neglect or abandon your parents. . . .

Do not humiliate or ridicule the aged, the young, or the crippled. . . .

Do not be impudent toward your superiors. . . .

Do not sell faithful dogs to dog butchers. . . .

Even if you see that the good sometimes suffer bad fortune and you yourself experience poverty, do not let it discourage you from doing good.

Even if you see bad men prosper, do not lose faith in ultimate recompense.[1] . . .

In all undertakings, think of others.

---

[1] Reward for one's good deeds.

Teaching the Young in Tokugawa Japan

26 • KAIBARA AND TOKEN EKIKEN, COMMON SENSE TEACHINGS FOR JAPANESE CHILDREN AND GREATER LEARNING FOR WOMEN

Although Chinese Neo-Confucianism had been brought to Japan by Zen Buddhist monks in the fourteenth and fifteenth centuries, it had little influence on Japan's aristocratic ruling class until the Tokugawa Era, when the new regime actively supported it. Tokugawa rulers were attracted to Confucianism because it emphasized the need for social hierarchy and obedience to the ruler of a centralized state. Hayashi Razan (1583–1657), a leading Confucian scholar, was an advisor to Tokugawa Ieyasu, and the school founded by the Hayashi family at Edo in 1630 became the nation's center of Confucian scholarship. Many provincial lords founded similar academies in their domains, and the education that samurai received in these schools and from private tutors helped transform Japan's warrior aristocracy into a literate bureaucratic ruling class committed to Confucian values.

Among the Confucian scholars of the early Tokugawa Era, few matched the literary output and popularity of Kaibara Ekiken (1630–1714). After studying in Kyoto and Edo, he served the Kuroda lords of the Fukuoka domain in southwestern Japan as physician, tutor, and scholar-in-residence. He wrote more than 100 works on medicine, botany, philosophy, and education.

This selection draws on material from two of Ekiken's works. The first part is excerpted from his *Common Sense Teachings for Japanese Children*, a manual for tutors in aristocratic households. The second part is taken from *Greater Learning for Women*, a discussion of moral precepts for girls. It is thought that this treatise was written in collaboration with Token, Ekiken's wife.

QUESTIONS FOR ANALYSIS

1. According to *Common Sense Teachings for Japanese Children*, what moral qualities should be inculcated in students?
2. What attitudes toward the lower classes are expressed in these two treatises?
3. How do the goals and purposes of education differ for Japanese boys and girls? How are they similar?
4. What do these treatises say about Japanese marriage customs and family life?
5. What is there in these treatises that would have furthered the Tokugawa shoguns' ambition to provide Japan with stable and peaceful government (see Multiple Voices II)?

Common Sense Teachings for Japanese Children

In January when children reach the age of six, teach them numbers one through ten, and the names given to designate 100, 1,000, 10,000 and 100,000,000. Let them know the four directions, East, West, North and South. Assess their native intelligence and differentiate between quick and slow learners. Teach them Japanese pronunciation from the age of six or seven, and let them learn how to write. . . . From this time on, teach them to respect their elders, and let them know the distinctions between the upper and lower classes and between the young and old. Let them learn to use the correct expressions.

When the children reach the age of seven, do not let the boys and girls sit together, nor must you allow them to dine together. . . .

For the eighth year. This is the age when the ancients began studying the book *Little Learning.*[1] Beginning at this time, teach the youngsters etiquette befitting their age, and caution them not to commit an act of impoliteness. Among those which must be taught are: daily deportment, the manners set for appearing before one's senior and withdrawing from his presence, how to speak or respond to one's senior or guest, how to place a serving tray or replace it for one's senior, how to present a wine cup and pour rice wine and to serve side dishes to accompany it, and how to serve tea. Children must also learn how to behave while taking their meals.

Children must be taught by those who are close to them the virtues of filial piety and obedience. To serve the parents well is called filial piety, and to serve one's seniors well is called obedience. The one who lives close to the children and who is able to

teach must instruct the children in the early years of their life that the first obligation of a human being is to revere the parents and serve them well. Then comes the next lesson which includes respect for one's seniors, listening to their commands and not holding them in contempt. One's seniors include elder brothers, elder sisters, uncles, aunts, and cousins who are older and worthy of respect. . . . As the children grow older, teach them to love their younger brothers and to be compassionate to the employees and servants. Teach them also the respect due the teachers and the behavior codes governing friends. The etiquette governing each movement toward important guests—such as standing, sitting, advancing forward, and retiring from their presence—and the language to be employed must be taught. Teach them how to pay respect to others according to the social positions held by them. Gradually the ways of filial piety and obedience, loyalty and trustworthiness, right deportment and decorum, and sense of shame must be inculcated in the children's minds and they must know how to implement them. Caution them not to desire the possessions of others, or to stoop below one's dignity in consuming excessive amounts of food and drink. . . .

Once reaching the age of eight, children must follow and never lead their elders when entering a gate, sitting, or eating and drinking. From this time on they must be taught how to become humble and yield to others. Do not permit the children to behave as they please. It is important to caution them against "doing their own things."

At the age of ten, let the children be placed under the guidance of a teacher, and tell them about the general meaning of the five constant virtues and let them understand the way of the

Source: David J. Lu, *Japan: A Documentary History* (New York: M. E. Sharpe, 1997), pp. 258–261. Translation copyright © 1997 by David J. Lu. Reprinted with permission of M. E. Sharpe, Inc.

[1]The *Little Learning* was written in 1187 by the Song scholar Liu Zucheng. A book for children, it contains rules of behavior and excerpts from the Classics and other works.

five human relationships.[2] Let them read books by the Sage [Confucius] and the wise men of old and cultivate the desire for learning. . . . When not engaged in reading, teach them the literary and military arts. . . .

Fifteen is the age when the ancients began the study of the *Great Learning*.[3] From this time on, concentrate on the learning of a sense of justice and duty. The students must also learn to cultivate their personalities and investigate the way of governing people. . . .

Those who are born in the high-ranking families have the heavy obligations of becoming leaders of the people, of having people entrusted to their care, and of governing them. Therefore, without fail, a teacher must be selected for them when they are still young. They must be taught how to read and be informed of the ways of old, of cultivating their personalities, and of the way of governing people. If they do not learn the way of governing people, they may injure the many people who are entrusted to their care by the Way of Heaven. That will be a serious disaster. . . .

Greater Learning for Women

Seeing that it is a girl's destiny, on reaching womanhood, to go to a new home, and live in submission to her father-in-law, it is even more incumbent upon her than it is on a boy to receive with all reverence her parents' instructions. Should her parents, through their tenderness, allow her to grow up self-willed, she will infallibly show herself capricious in her husband's house, and thus alienate his affection; while, if her father-in-law be a man of correct principles, the girl will find the yoke of these principles intolerable. She will hate and decry her father-in-law, and the end of those domestic dissensions will be her dismissal

from her husband's house and the covering of herself with ignominy. Her parents, forgetting the faulty education they gave her, may indeed lay all the blame on the father-in-law. But they will be in error; for the whole disaster should rightly be attributed to the faulty education the girl received from her parents.

● ● ●

More precious in a woman is a virtuous heart than a face of beauty. . . . The only qualities that befit a woman are gentle obedience, chastity, mercy, and quietness.

● ● ●

From her earliest youth a girl should observe the line of demarcation separating women from men. The customs of antiquity did not allow men and women to sit in the same apartment, to keep their wearing apparel in the same place, to bathe in the same place, or to transmit to each other anything directly from hand to hand. A woman . . . must observe a certain distance in her relations even with her husband and with her brothers. In our days the women of lower classes, ignoring all rules of this nature, behave disorderly; they contaminate their reputations, bring down reproach upon the head of their parents and brothers, and spend their whole lives in an unprofitable manner. Is not this truly lamentable?

● ● ●

It is the chief duty of a girl living in the parental house to practice filial piety towards her father and mother. But after marriage her duty is to honor her father-in-law and mother-in-law, to honor them beyond her father and mother, to love and reverence them with all ardor, and to tend them with practice of every filial piety. . . . Even if your

---

[2]The *five virtues* are human-heartedness, righteousness, propriety, wisdom, and good faith. The *five relationships* are ruler–subject, father–son, husband–wife, older brother–younger brother, and friend–friend.

[3]The *Great Learning* consists of a short main text thought to have been written by Confucius and nine chapters of commentary written by Confucius's disciple, Zengzi.

father-in-law and mother-in-law are inclined to hate and vilify you, do not be angry with them, and murmur not. If you carry piety towards them to its utmost limits, and minister to them in all sincerity, it cannot be but that they will end by becoming friendly to you.

• • •

The great lifelong duty of a woman is obedience. . . . When the husband issues his instructions, the wife must never disobey them. In a doubtful case, she should inquire of her husband and obediently follow his commands. . . .

Should her husband be roused at any time to anger, she must obey him with fear and trembling, and not set herself up against him in anger and forwardness. A woman should look upon her husband as if he were Heaven itself, and never weary of thinking how she may yield to her husband and thus escape celestial castigation.

• • •

Her treatment of her servant girls will require circumspection. Those low-born girls have had no proper education; they are stupid, obstinate, and vulgar in their speech. . . . Again, in her dealings with those lowly people, a woman will find many things to disapprove of. But if she be always reproving and scolding, and spend her time in hustle and anger, her household will be in a continual state of disturbance. When there is real wrongdoing, she should occasionally notice it, and point out the path of amendment, while lesser faults should be quietly endured without anger. . . .

Merchants in a Confucian World

27 • WANG DAOKUN, BIOGRAPHIES OF ZHU JIEFU AND GENTLEMAN WANG

The Confucian tradition considered merchants as necessary evils at best. Farmers were the backbone of a healthy society, but merchants, according to many Confucians, were unproductive, uncultured, and preoccupied with profit rather than the good of society. Their travels kept them away from the ancestral hearth and prevented them from performing their duties to parents and ancestral spirits. Until 775 C.E., merchants were not permitted to take the civil service examinations, and their business activities were closely regulated by frequently unsympathetic government officials. Despite merchants' low status, commerce flourished in most periods of Chinese history, and during the Ming Era, in which the population grew and trade expanded, the merchant's calling gradually came to be viewed more favorably. More sons and daughters of merchants married into the families of officials and great landowners, and more sons of merchants became government officials after passing the civil service examinations. Some Confucian thinkers praised commerce as necessary for the well-being of society, and others even proposed that successful merchants were equal to or just slightly below officials and gentry in terms of status. Such views remained in the minority, however, and throughout the Ming Era, suspicion of merchants and doubts about their calling remained strong among intellectuals and commoners alike.

Wang Daokun (1525–1593) exemplifies this ambivalence about merchants in both his life and writings. He combined a merchant's background with a Confucian education and a career in the imperial bureaucracy. His father and grandfather had been salt merchants, but the gifted Wang passed the civil service examinations while in his twenties and entered government service. Having served as governor of several provinces and as an army official, in 1575 he resigned to care for his aged parents and to write books on a variety of topics, including card playing, drinking games, and ancestral rites. He also wrote a series of biographies of Ming Era merchants, many of whom combined business success with Confucian morality. Wang's sketches provide many insights into Confucian ethics and the business climate of late Ming China.

QUESTIONS FOR ANALYSIS

1. According to Wang, what are the virtues of Zhu Jiefu and Gentleman Wang? To what extent do the two merchants represent different virtues?
2. What is the point about the incident involving Gentleman Wang and Magistrate Xu?
3. What do these biographies reveal about Chinese attitudes toward the elderly? Toward political authority? Toward wealth? Toward women?
4. What do these biographies reveal about the government's attitudes and policies in regard to merchants? What episodes illustrate these attitudes?
5. Do the author's sympathies lie with the merchants or the government officials in their dealings with one another?

The Biography of Zhu Jiefu

Zhu Jiefu . . . started as a Confucian scholar [whose] father Hsing . . . was a salt merchant who lived away from home at Wulin. Hsing had taken Shaoji of Wulin as his concubine[1] but she was barren. Later, when he returned home for his father-in-law's birthday, his primary wife became pregnant and gave birth to Zhu Jiefu. . . . Shaoji . . . did not treat him as her son. Jiefu, however, served her respectfully and worked diligently in school. At the age of fourteen, he officially registered Wulin as his native place and was designated an official student of that place.[2] Shortly thereafter, his father died at Wulin. His concubine took the money and hid it with some of her mother's relatives and would not return to her husband's hometown.

Jiefu wept day and night, saying, "However unworthy I may be, my late father was blameless." Finally the concubine arranged for the funeral and burial. . . . Thus, everything was done properly.

After the funeral, Jiefu was short of funds. Since for generations his family had been in commerce, he decided not to suffer just to preserve his scholar's cap.[3] Therefore he handed in his resignation to the academic officials and devoted himself to the salt business. He thoroughly studied the laws on salt merchandising and was always able to talk about the strengths and weaknesses of the law. . . . Therefore, all the other salt merchants respected him as their leader.

During the Jiaqing period [1522–1567], salt affairs were handled by the Central Law Officer,[4]

Source: Reprinted with the permission of The Free Press, a Division of Simon & Schuster Adult Publishing Group. From *Chinese Civilization and Society* by Patricia Buckley Ebrey, pp. 157–160. Copyright © 1981 by The Free Press. All rights reserved.

[1]It was common for men to have concubines, in some cases several of them, in addition to their wives. Laws did not prohibit children of concubines from inheriting their father's property.

[2]This meant that Zhu Jiefu was being groomed to take the civil service examinations.

[3]A specially designed hat given to young boys in the hope they would do well on the civil service examinations.

[4]An imperial official,

who increased the taxes suddenly, causing great inconvenience for the merchants. They gathered in Jiefu's house and asked him to serve as their negotiator. Jiefu entered the office and stated the advantages and disadvantages of the new law eloquently in thousands of words. Leaning against his couch, the Central Law Officer listened to Jiefu's argument and finally adopted his suggestion.

At that time, the merchants suffered greatly from two scoundrels who often took them to court in the hopes of getting bribes from them. During tense moments at trials, the merchants usually turned to Jiefu as their spokesman. Being lofty and righteous, he always disclosed the scoundrels' crimes and condemned them. The merchants thus esteemed Jiefu for his virtue and wanted to give him a hundred taels[5] of gold as a birthday present. But he protested: "Even if my acts have not been at the lofty level of a knight-errant, I did not do them for the sake of money." Thus, the merchants respected him even more and no longer talked about giving him money.

When there was a dispute among the merchants which the officials could not resolve, Jiefu could always mediate it immediately. Even when one group would go to his house and demand his compliance with their views, he would still be able to settle the dispute by indirect and gentle persuasion. . . . Yet, after settling a dispute, Jiefu would always step aside and never take credit himself.

The populace in Tunxi city where Jiefu lived was militant and litigious. When he returned home for his father's funeral, slanderous rumors were spread about him, but Jiefu humbled himself and never tried to get back at the instigators. Later, when he grew rich rapidly, people became even more critical. Jiefu merely behaved with even greater deference. When the ancestral shrine fell into disrepair, Jiefu on his own sent workmen to repair it. When members of his lineage started

talking about it, he had the workmen work during the day and consulted with his relatives in the evening. Finally the whole lineage got together and shared the task with him. . . .

Jiefu finally discontinued his salt business and ordered his son to pursue a different career. By that time he was already planning to retire to his hometown. Then in 1568 a Central Law Officer who was appointed to inspect the salt business started to encourage secret informants. Soon Jiefu was arrested, an enemy having laid a trap for him. However, the official could not find any evidence against him. But then Ho, whose son Jiefu had once scolded, came forward to testify. Consequently, Jiefu was found guilty. When the litigation against him was completed, he was sentenced to be a frontier guard at Dinghai. . . .

When Jiefu received his sentence to enter the army, he controlled his feelings and immediately complied. His son, fearing his father would acquire a bad name, suggested that he send a petition to the Emperor. Jiefu merely sighed and said, "Your father must have offended Heaven. The truth is that the Central Law Officer is a representative of his Heavenly Majesty, not that your father is falsely charged."

. . . [Before he died] he advised his son, Zhengmin: "Your father's name has been recorded in the official labor records. Now he is about to die as a prisoner. Never let your father's example stop you from behaving righteously. Remember this." Then, at the age of sixty-five, he died.

The Biography of Gentleman Wang

. . . At first, Mr. Wang's capital was no greater than the average person's. Later, as he grew more prosperous every day, the number of his associates also steadily increased. . . .

Mr. Wang set up the following guidelines for his associates: do not let anyone who lives

---

[5]A tael was a coin weighing approximately one and a half ounces.

in another county control the banking; when lending money, never harass law-abiding people unnecessarily or give them less than they need; charge low interest on loans; do not aim at high profit and do not ask for daily interest. These principles led customers to throng to him, even ones from neighboring towns and provinces. Within a short time, Mr. Wang accumulated great wealth; in fact, of all the rich people in that area he became the richest.

Mr. Wang liked to help people and to give assistance to the poor. If anyone among his kinsmen could not afford a funeral for his parents, Mr. Wang would always buy some land and build a tomb for him. As soon as he heard someone could not make ends meet, he would buy land to rent to him. . . .

During the Jiaqing period there was a serious drought, and the Prefect[6] proposed opening the granary. Considering the hardship this would cause the people, Mr. Wang sent a written report to the Prefect, as follows:

> This proposal will cause starving people to travel here from hundreds of li[7] away to wait for the distribution. Even if there are no delays on route, they may die before they get here. Yet if we make them stay home and wait for a pint of food, it will be like abandoning them to die in the gutters. I suggest that we exchange the grain for money and distribute it around the area. All the wealthy people ought to donate some money to help the poor. I myself will start with a donation of a hundred taels of gold.

The Prefect accepted his suggestion and everyone said that this was much more convenient. Then Mr. Wang also prepared some food to feed people in his own county and caused similar actions to be taken throughout the whole of Shanghai. Thus most people in this area survived. . . .

Whenever there was a dispute, Mr. Wang could always resolve it immediately, even if it was quite serious. When Magistrate Xu was in charge of Shanghai, he imprisoned someone named Zhu, who died in jail. The victim's father then presented a petition to the Emperor which worried the Magistrate. The officials, elders, and local leaders were willing to offer the father a thousand taels of gold on the Magistrate's behalf, but on discussing it, they decided only Mr. Wang could settle the matter, and indeed he persuaded the father to accept the terms. Then the Magistrate was transferred to another position. Upon learning this fact, the officials, elders, and local leaders all quickly dispersed. Mr. Wang sighed and said, "It isn't easy to collect a thousand taels of gold but I will not break the promise made to the Magistrate in trouble." He then paid the thousand taels of gold and the Magistrate was out of his difficulties. Even when Magistrate Xu was dismissed soon thereafter, Mr. Wang did not voice any concern, and after two years Xu returned the thousand taels of gold to him. . . .

When Mr. Wang is at home he is always in high spirits. . . . In his later years he has become particularly fond of chess, often staying up all night until he either wins or loses a game. The youths say that Mr. Wang is no ordinary person, that he must have received instruction from Heaven.

Now Mr. Wang is almost one hundred years old. He has at least thirty sons and grandsons living at home with him. It is said, "One who seeks perfection will attain it." This describes Mr. Wang perfectly.

---

[6] An imperial official.

[7] A measure of distance, approximately one-third of a mile.

Humanity and Nature in Chinese Painting

28 • ZHANG HONG, *LANDSCAPE OF SHIXIE HILL* AND SHENG MAOYE, *SCHOLARS GAZING AT A WATERFALL*

Chinese painters over the centuries have produced portraits, religious works, pictures of animals and plants, and palace scenes, but their greatest contribution to the world's art has been the landscape. Landscapes began to attract the interest of Chinese painters and connoisseurs during the Tang Dynasty (618–907 C.E.), and by the eleventh and twelfth centuries, artists had developed a distinctly Chinese approach to the genre. From then until the twentieth century, the painting of landscapes on silk or paper with ink and muted watercolor shading inspired China's greatest painters and attracted countless collectors and patrons.

The Chinese devotion to landscape painting was closely tied to the views of nature in Daoism and Confucianism, both of which saw the natural world as a metaphor for the moral and metaphysical order underlying the universe. Thus, despite the many different schools and styles of landscape painting, all Chinese landscape painters sought to capture the inner quality, or vital spirit (*qi*), of nature rather than simply to reproduce what the eye perceives. By communicating this inner quality, artists enabled viewers to see how the ever-changing phenomena of the visible landscape—wind, rain, mountains, rivers, lakes, trees, storms, mist, and snow—reveal higher realities and capture certain moods. Landscape painting had a strong appeal for many Confucian scholar-officials, who were the main patrons for landscape painters, and in many instances were accomplished amateur painters themselves. For them, being close to nature or being able to contemplate a painting of nature provided spiritual freedom from the distractions of urban life and the pressures of their administrative duties.

Ming Era landscape painting was characterized by many different schools and individual styles. Some drew inspiration from the masters of the Song Era, while others sought to recapture the stylistic qualities of Yuan Era (1279–1368) painters. Different artists depicted nature's vital spirit as tranquil, powerful, charming, wild, forbidding, lonely, or cold. Each artist had a distinctive style of brushwork and color.

Because of this diversity of styles, the two paintings included here cannot be considered "typical" Ming landscapes, but they do capture some of the general characteristics of landscape painting of the period. Both are large wall scrolls, and both were produced by painters from the city of Suzhou, an important commercial hub and cultural center in the Yangzi Delta region. The first is Zhang Hong's *Landscape of Shixie Hill,* a painting in ink and light colors approximately five feet high and two feet wide. Although Zhang was one of the outstanding painters of the age, little is known about him other than that he was born in 1557, lived most of his life in Suzhou, and probably died in 1652. The inscription on the upper-right corner of

Zharg Hung Landscape at Shixie Hill

Shang Maoye Scholars Gazing at a WaterFall

the painting reads, "In the summer of 1613, I traveled to Shixie with my revered older brother Chunyu and painted this for him." One must look closely to see the human beings in the painting. A group of travelers is gathering at the bridge as the bottom of the painting, perhaps planning a walk up the mountain. Mountains, which were close to heaven and were believed to be the home of the "eight immortals" of Chinese folklore, were a common subject for Chinese landscape painters. Farther upstream, one finds four gentlemen-scholars gazing at a waterfall, while a Buddhist monk and his servant approach them with tea. Their two servants stand by, looking away.

The second painting is *Scholars Gazing at a Waterfall* by Sheng Maoye. Painted on silk in 1630, it is slightly longer and approximately a foot wider than Zhang's painting. Sheng's works are dated from 1594 to 1634, but the dates of his birth and death are unknown. Shang also lived in Suzhou and, like many late Ming painters, included in his works lines of poetry, usually drawn from famous poets of the Tang Era. In this painting, the poetic inscription reads, "Pines and rocks lean fittingly for their age/Wisteria vines do not count the years." It is taken from a poem by an early Tang Era poet, Wang Po (ca. 750–ca. 776). As in Zhang's painting, the learned scholars contemplate the rushing torrent, while their servants look away.

QUESTIONS FOR ANALYSIS

1. How would you characterize the "inner spirit" of nature each artist seeks to communicate? How are the two artists' visions similar and different?
2. How are the human beings in each picture interacting with nature?
3. What message does each painting communicate about humanity's relationship to the natural world? Consider both the actions of the human beings in each painting as well as the man-made structures in Zhang's painting.
4. Both paintings show scholars contemplating a waterfall, a scene depicted in literally hundreds of Chinese landscape paintings. Why would the contemplation of a waterfall be particularly meaningful?
5. In each painting, the scholars' servants are not paying attention to the waterfall. What message does this communicate?

Political Decline in China and Political Recovery in Japan

Eighteenth-century China and Japan were models of well-governed, prosperous states. This had seemed highly unlikely a century and a half earlier, when political problems plagued both societies: Japan, in the midst of a decades-long civil war, was on the brink of disintegration; China, meanwhile, was suffering from the erratic rule of a declining Ming Dynasty.

The incessant civil strife of sixteenth-century Japan was rooted in long-standing tensions inherent in Japan's feudal society. In the 1300s, power began to shift away from the shogun, a military commander who ruled in the name of the emperor, to local military families who controlled districts and provinces. With a weakened central government, wars and feuds became endemic among the *daimyo*, the emerging provincial lords, who enlisted *samurai*, lesser members of the nobility, and commoners to fight in their armies. Warfare intensified between the mid-fifteenth and early seventeenth centuries, a period sometimes called the Warring States Era.

This ruinous feudal anarchy ended as a result of the efforts of three strong military leaders bent on unifying Japan. Oda Nobunaga (1534–1582) brought approximately half of Japan under his rule before a traitorous vassal assassinated him. His successor, Toyotomi Hideyoshi (1536–1598), a commoner who had risen through the ranks to become Nobunaga's ablest general, continued the work of consolidation. It was completed by Tokugawa Ieyasu (1542–1616), who conquered his rivals after Hideyoshi's death and declared himself shogun in 1603. Ieyasu and his successors stabilized Japan by imposing a sociopolitical order that lasted until 1867.

China's political problems had multiple causes, ranging from foreign military threats and fluctuations in the value of silver to a series of poor harvests after the weather turned cold and wet around 1600. Just as these problems were mounting, the quality and effectiveness of Ming rulers plummeted, especially during the long reign of the Wanli Emperor (r. 1572–1620). Disgusted with his bickering and quarrelsome advisors, Wanli withdrew from politics, ceased meeting with high officials, and failed to fill vacancies in the administration. Paralyzed by feuding between court eunuchs and Confucian officials, the central government drifted as China's problems worsened. Factional strife, oppressive taxation, corruption, unchecked banditry, and famine led to rebellion, the dynasty's collapse, and foreign conquest. In 1644, a rebel leader, Li Zicheng (1605–1645), captured Beijing, and in despair the last Ming emperor hanged himself. Within months, however, Li was driven from the city by the Manchus, northern invaders from the Amur River region. In the following decades, the Manchus extended their authority over all of China; established China's last dynasty, the Qing; and breathed new life into the imperial system.

Symptoms of Ming Decline

29 • YANG LIAN, MEMORIAL TO EMPEROR MING XIZONG CONCERNING EUNUCH WEI ZHONGXIAN

In the late sixteenth century, the formidable task of governing China became even harder. Mongol military pressure grew in the north, pirate raids increased on coastal cities, and in the 1590s the Japanese invaded China's client state, Korea. Peasant discontent boiled over into peasant rebellion as rural misery deepened in the face of poor harvests, worsening banditry, rising taxes, and currency fluctuations. From the 1580s onward, however, emperors ignored or were distracted from dealing with these new challenges. They paid a price for their indifference: rebellion overwhelmed the government and brought about the fall of the Ming in 1644.

The following selection, a memorial (memorandum) directed to the Xizong emperor by a high official, Yang Lian, highlights another problem of late Ming government, the rising power of court eunuchs. Eunuchs, castrated males responsible for of managing the day-to-day business of the palace, assumed a greater importance in government when the Wanli Emperor secluded himself and refused to communicate with his officials except through eunuch intermediaries. Eunuch influence was opposed by Confucian officials, especially those who supported the Donglin Society, a group of scholar-officials and former officeholders connected with the Donglin Academy at Wuxi on the lower Yangzi River.

Conflict between court eunuchs and scholar-officials came to a head in the 1620s, when the eunuch Wei Zhongxian rose to power during the reign of Emperor Xizong from 1621 to 1627. Backed by spies and eunuch supporters in the palace, Wei, a former butler for the emperor's mother and a friend of the emperor's former wet nurse, purged his enemies, levied new taxes, and flouted rules and procedures.

In 1624, Yang Lian, a supporter of the Donglin movement, took the bold step of denouncing Wei in a memorandum to the emperor. He was fulfilling his duties as a member of the Board of Censors, a branch of the administration that served as the "eyes and ears" of the emperor by investigating officials' conduct and hearing subjects' complaints. The emperor ignored the memorandum, however, and in 1625, on Wei's orders, Yang was accused of treason, tortured, and executed. Wei fell from power in 1627 when the new emperor Chongzhen (r. 1627–1644) exiled him to Anhui province; there, Wei hanged himself rather than face an official inquiry. But the Ming government had suffered another wound.

QUESTIONS FOR ANALYSIS

1. According to Yang, what motivated him to write this memorandum to the emperor?
2. This excerpt specifically lists only a few of Wei's 24 alleged "crimes." Based on your reading of the entire excerpt, what other "crimes" might have been on the list?
3. What is it about Wei's actions that violated Yang's Confucian sensibilities?
4. What does the memorandum reveal about the basis of Wei's authority and political strength?
5. What does the memorandum tell us about the qualities of Emperor Ming Xizong?

A treacherous eunuch has taken advantage of his position to act as emperor. He has seized control and disrupted the government, deceived the ruler, and flouted the law. He recognizes no higher authority, turns his back on the favors the emperor has conferred on him, and interferes with the inherited institutions. I beg Your Majesty to order an investigation so that the dynasty can be saved.

When Emperor Hongwu[1] first established the laws and institutions, eunuchs were not allowed to interfere in any affairs outside the palace; even within it they did nothing more than clean up. Anyone who violated these rules was punished without chance of amnesty, so the eunuchs prudently were cautious and obedient. The succeeding emperors never changed these laws. . . .

How would anyone have expected that, with a wise ruler like Your Majesty on the throne, there would be a chief eunuch like Wei Zhongxian, a man totally uninhibited, who destroys court

---

[1]The first Ming emperor, who ruled from 1368 to 1398.

precedents, ignores the ruler to pursue his selfish ends, corrupts good people, ruins the emperor's reputation . . . and brews unimaginable disasters? The entire court has been intimidated. No one dares denounce him by name. My responsibility really is painful. . . . If today out of fear I also do not speak out, I will be abandoning my determination to be loyal and my responsibility to serve the state. I would also be turning my back on your kindness in bringing me back to office after retirement. . . .

I shall list for Your Majesty Zhongxian's twenty-four most heinous crimes. Zhongxian was originally an ordinary, unreliable sort. He had himself castrated in middle age in order to enter the palace. He is illiterate. . . . Your Majesty was impressed by his minor acts of service and plucked him out of obscurity to confer honors on him. . . .

Our dynastic institutions require that rescripts[2] be delegated to the grand secretaries. This not only allows for calm deliberation and protects from interference, but it assures that someone takes the responsibility seriously. Since Zhongxian usurped power, he issues the imperial edicts. If he accurately conveys your orders, it is bad enough. If he falsifies them, who can argue with him? . . . It is possible for a scrap of paper in the middle of the night to kill a person without Your Majesty or the grand secretaries knowing anything of it. The harm this causes is huge. The grand secretaries are so depressed that they ask to quit. . . .

One of your concubines, of virtuous and pure character, had gained your favor. Zhongxian was afraid she would expose his illegal behavior, so conspired with his cronies. They said she had a sudden illness to cover up his murdering her. Thus Your Majesty is not able to protect the concubines you favor. . . .

During the forty years that your father the former emperor was heir apparent, Wang An[3] was unique in worrying about all the dangers he faced, protecting him from harm, never giving in to intimidation or temptation. Didn't he deserve some of the credit for your father's getting to the throne? When he died and Your Majesty succeeded, Wang An protected you, so he cannot be called disloyal. Even if he had committed some offense, Your Majesty should have explained what he had done wrong publicly for all to see. Instead Zhongxian, because of his personal hatreds, forged an imperial order and had him killed in Nanhai park. His head and body were separated, his flesh given to the dogs and pigs. This not only revealed his enmity toward Wang An, but his enmity toward all the former emperor's old servants, even his old dogs and horses. It showed him to be without the slightest fear. From that time on, which of the eunuchs was willing to be loyal or principled? I do not know how many thousands or hundreds of the rest of the eunuchs, important and unimportant alike, were slaughtered or driven away for no crime. . . .

Doesn't Your Majesty remember the time when Zhongxian, against all rules, rode his horse in the palace grounds? Those who are favored too much become arrogant; those who receive too many favors grow resentful. I heard that this spring when he rode a horse in front of Your Majesty, you shot and killed the horse, but forgave Zhongxian. Despite your generosity, Zhongxian did not beg to die for his offense, but rather acted more arrogantly in Your Majesty's presence and spoke resentfully of Your Majesty when away. . . . In the past traitors and bandits have struggled to wreak havoc and take over. This is in fact what Your Majesty now faces. . . . Even if Zhongxian were cut into mincemeat, it would not atone for his sins. . . .

---

[2]Official decrees and edicts.
[3]The eunuch Wang An was a supporter of the Donglin party and a bitter opponent of Wei Zhongxian. He was killed on Wei's orders in 1621.

. . . Zhongxian . . . kills or replaces any eunuch he fears will expose his treachery. Thus those close at hand are terrified and keep silent. He expels or imprisons any of the officials he fears will expose his villainy, so the officials also all look the other way and keep silent. There are even ignorant spineless fellows eager to get rich and powerful who attach themselves to him or hang around his gate. They praise whatever he likes and criticize whatever he hates, doing whatever is needed. . . .

As a consequence, everyone in the palace recognizes the existence of Zhongxian but not of Your Majesty; everyone in the capital recognizes the existence of Zhongxian but not of Your Majesty. Even the major and minor officials and workers, by turning toward the sources of power, unconsciously show that they do not recognize the existence of Your Majesty, only of Zhongxian. Whenever they see that some matter needs urgent attention or an appointment needs to be made, they always say, "It must be discussed with the eunuch." . . . All matters, large and small, in both the palace and the government offices, are decided by Zhongxian alone. . . .

I beg Your Majesty to take courage and thunder forth. Take Zhongxian to the ancestral temple in fetters. Assemble the military and civil officials of all ranks and have the judicial officials interrogate him. Check all the precedents from previous reigns on eunuchs having contacts with the outside, usurping imperial authority, breaking dynastic laws, disrupting court business, alienating the people, and violating the trust of the ruler. Sentence him in a way that will please the gods and satisfy public indignation. . . .

If all this is done and yet Heaven does not show its pleasure, the people do not rejoice, and there is not a new era of peace within the country and at its borders, then I ask that you behead me as an offering to Zhongxian. I am well aware that once my words become known, Zhongxian's clique will detest me, but I am not afraid. . . . My lifetime goal has been to serve loyally. I would not regret having to die as a way of paying back the extraordinary favors I have received during two reigns. I hope Your Majesty recognizes my passion and takes prompt action.

Multiple Voices II

The Reunification of Japan Under Hideyoshi and the Tokugawa Clan

BACKGROUND

In the last three decades of the nineteenth century, Japan abolished its ancient class system, introduced modern industry, reformed its educational system, and created a new national army outfitted with the best modern equipment and by doing so, transformed itself in into a major world power. Japan experienced an equally rapid transformation 300 years earlier, between 1570 and the opening years of the 1600s. In 1570, Japan, although theoretically under the control of the Ashikaga shoguns, had no central government. Warfare among its powerful aristocratic families, which had begun in the mid-1400s, showed no signs of ending. Portuguese traders and missionaries had arrived in 1543, and already by 1570 tens of thousands of Japanese had accepted Christianity. Rural rebellion, brought on by new and higher taxes, was a growing problem.

And yet, in a remarkably short time—by the early seventeenth century—the Warring States Era had ended and order had been restored: Japan had been reunified, the foreigners had been expelled, Christianity had been outlawed, and rural violence had abated. Japan had entered what proved to be a 300-year period of tranquility under Tokugawa rule. Japan's reunification resulted from the military prowess of Oda Nobunaga, Toyotomi Hideyoshi, and Tokugawa Ieyasu, but the country's long-term pacification resulted from more than battlefield victories. Such stability was achieved by the rigorous enforcement of new policies that provided a strong foundation for a disciplined and stable Japan. The sources that follow—edicts issued by Hideyoshi and the early Tokugawa shoguns—provide insight into the range and substance of these new policies.

THE SOURCES

The Edicts on Christianity were issued in 1587 by Toyotomi Hideyoshi, who by then was well on his way to bringing all of Japan under his control. To understand his motives for making these pronouncements, it is necessary to briefly review the religious dynamics of Japan in the late 1580s. By 1587, Christianity had made impressive progress. In less than four decades after the first Portuguese Jesuits arrived, they had converted a number of daimyo from Kyushu, the southernmost and westernmost of Japan's four major islands, and these daimyo in turn used various forms of coercion to convince their subjects to become Christians. The Jesuit fathers also had won the support of Oda Nobunaga, who had unified much of Japan before his death in 1582; for a time, they also had the support of his successor, Hideyoshi. Both rulers were interested in things European and, more importantly, viewed Christianity as a counterweight to certain Buddhist sects that had established independent political bases or were connected with popular rebellion. These included the Honganji branch of Jodo Shinshu (True Pure Land Sect) Buddhism, which had a large following across central Japan and maintained imposing fortified temples in key cities. It increased its authority by fanning violent uprisings of *ikko ikki*, loosely structured "leagues of one mind" made up mostly of commoners who banded together to fight against taxes or for (or against) other causes. It gained control of Kaga province in 1488 and was connected with insurrection and antitax movements in the 1500s. By 1587, only a few months after he had invaded Kyushu, Hideyoshi had concluded that Christianity also was a serious political threat.

The Sword Collection Edict (1588) and the Edict on Change of Status (1591), both issued by Hideyoshi, were designed to end the blurring of social distinctions that had occurred during the decades of fighting. Of particular concern were the large number of commoners who had left farming for careers as soldiers and the smaller number of samurai and lesser nobles who had illegally changed masters or abandoned their military obligations.

The Laws Governing Military Households (1615), proclaimed by Tokugawa Ieyasu (who continued to rule Japan until his death in 1616, despite having named his son Hidetada shogun in 1605 to avoid a succession dispute), spelled out rules for members of Japan's aristocratic (daimyo) families. Their feuds had been largely responsible for Japan's civil wars.

The final edict, known as the Closed Country Edict, was issued by Tokugawa Iemitsu in 1635 to the two commissioners of Nagasaki, the city on the island of Kyushu that was the major port of entry for European traders. It addressed issues relating to trade and foreign relations and also clarified the status of Japanese Christians, who had been the subject of brutal but only sporadic persecution since Hideyoshi issued his anti-Christian edicts in 1587.

QUESTIONS FOR ANALYSIS

1. What reasons does Hideyoshi provide to justify his move against Christianity in 1587? How are his views of Christianity shaped by his experience with Japan's Buddhist sects?
2. How are the Sword Collection Edict and the Edict on Change of Status related? What are their implications for the structuring of Japanese society?
3. In what ways does the edict on military households ensure the shogun's control of the daimyo?
4. Even though Tokugawa policies limited the independence of the daimyo, the daimyo retained certain political powers. How many such powers can be identified in the Laws Governing Military Households?
5. According to the Closed Country Edict, what is the greater threat to Japan: Christianity or trade with foreigners?
6. Did the Closed Country Edict really close Japan?
7. Based on the presented documents, what conclusions can be drawn about the political and social philosophies behind the efforts of Hideyoshi and the Tokugawa to bring order to Japan? What signs of Confucian teachings are discernable?

1 • Edicts on Christianity

Notice

1. The matter of [becoming] a sectarian of the Bateren[1] shall be the free choice of the individual concerned.

2. That enfeoffed recipients[2] of provinces, districts, and estates should force peasants registered in [Buddhist] temples . . . against their will into the ranks of the Bateren sectarians is unreasonable beyond words and is outrageous. . . .

Source: Excerpted from George Ellison, *Deus Destroyed: The Image of Christianity in Early Modern Japan* (Cambridge: Harvard University Council on East Studies, 1988), pp. 115–118. Copyright © The President and Fellows of Harvard College, 1973. Reprinted with permission of the Harvard University Asian Center.

[1]Japanese approximation of the word "padre"; used to designate Catholic priests.
[2]Those invested by a higher authority with territory and, with it, various rights and duties connected with that territory; sometimes translated as "vassals."

4. Persons holding above 200 *cho* of land or can expect 2 or 3 thousand *kan* of rice harvest each year,[3] may become [followers of the] Bateren upon obtaining official permission, acceding to the pleasure of the lord of the *Tenka*.[4] . . .

6. The Bateren sectarians . . . are even more given to deceits . . . than the Ikkō Sect. The Ikkō Sect established temple precincts[5] in the provinces and districts and did not pay the yearly dues to their enfeoffed recipients [local lords]. Moreover, they made the entire Province of Kaga into [Ikkō] sectarians, chased out . . . the lord of the province, delivered the stipends over to [monks] of the Ikkō Sect . . . That this was harmful to the *Tenka* is the undisguisable truth. . . .

7. That daimyo . . . should force their retainers into the ranks of the Bateren sectarians is even more undesirable by far than the Honganji[6] sectarians' establishment of temple precincts, and is bound to be of great harm to the *Tenka*. These individuals . . . shall be subject to punishment.

8. Bateren sectarians by their free choice, [insofar as they] are of the lower classes, shall be unmolested. . . .

10. The sale of Japanese to China, South Barbary,[7] and Korea is outrageous[8]. . .

11. Trade and slaughter of cattle and horses for use as food shall also be considered criminal.[9]

The above items shall rest under strict prohibition. Any transgressor shall immediately be put to severe punishment.

Ordained

1. Japan is the Land of the Gods. Diffusion here from Christian Country of a pernicious doctrine is most undesirable.

2. To approach the people of our provinces and districts and, making them into [Christian] sectarians, cause them to destroy the shrines of the gods and the temples of the Buddhas is a thing unheard of in previous ages. . . . But to corrupt and stir up the lower classes is outrageous.

3. It is the judgment [of the lord of the *Tenka*] that since the Bateren by means of their clever doctrine amass parishioners as they please, the aforementioned violation of the Buddhist Law in these Precincts . . . has resulted. That being outrageous, the Bateren can hardly be allowed to remain on Japanese soil. Within twenty days they must make their preparations and return to their country. . . .

4. The purpose of the Black Ships[10] is trade, and that is a different matter. As years and months pass, trade may be carried on in all sorts of articles . . .

---

[3]One *cho* equals approximately 2.9 acres; one *kan* equals approximately 8.25 pounds. Clearly, this provision refers to wealthy landowners—members of the aristocracy.

[4]A reference to Hideyoshi; *tenka* means the "whole realm."

[5]Refers to villages or regions under political control of Buddhist monks connected with a temple or monastery.

[6]Honganji refers to a militant faction within the Jodo Shinshu (True Pure Land Sect) of Japanese Buddhism. The term also refers to the various temples controlled by the faction. The Ishiama Honganji in Osaka was controlled by the movement's most fanatical disciples, the Ikko-ikki, and was burned to the ground by Nobunaga after a siege.

[7]Europeans were called "Southern Barbarians," so South Barbary may refer to Europe itself, but it more likely refers to the parts of South Asia where the Portuguese had established a presence.

[8]There is evidence that European merchants for a time did purchase small numbers of Japanese and sell them into slavery to Asian trading partners. When confronted by Hideyoshi on this matter, the Jesuits denied any involvement and claimed they had no influence on the practices of European merchants.

[9]The Japanese, who considered the slaughter of animals as work suitable for the lowest groups in their social hierarchy, viewed the eating of useful animals such as horses and cattle as a sign of barbarism. The Japanese diet consisted almost exclusively of rice, vegetables, and seafood.

[10]The term used by the Japanese for the ships of the Europeans.

2 • Edict on the Collection of Swords (1588)

1. The farmers of all provinces are strictly forbidden to have in their possession any swords, bows, spears, firearms or other types of weapons. If unnecessary implements of war are kept, the collection of annual rent may become more difficult, and without provocation uprisings can be fomented. Therefore those who perpetrate improper acts against samurai who receive a grant of land must be brought to trial and punished. . . .

2. The swords and short swords collected in the above manner will not be wasted. They will be used as nails and bolts in the construction of the Great Image of Buddha. In this way, the farmers will benefit not only in this life but also in the lives to come.

3. If farmers possess only agricultural implements and devote themselves exclusively to cultivating the fields, they and their descendants will prosper. This compassionate concern for the well-being of the farmers is the reason for issuance of this edict, and such a concern is the foundation for the peace and security of the country and the joy and happiness of all the people. . . .

Source: From *Japan: A Documentary History*, ed. and trans., David J. Lu (Armonk, NY: M. E. Sharpe, 1997), p. 191.

3 • Edict on Change of Status (1591)

1. If there should be living among you men who were in military service including those who served Hideyoshi, higher ranking warriors of the *daimyo* [samurai], those who took their orders from samurai, lowest ranking warriors, and those who performed miscellaneous chores for samurai—who have assumed the identity of a townsman or farmer . . . they must be expelled. . . . If anyone as described is kept concealed, the entire town or village shall be held responsible and punished accordingly.

2. If any farmer abandons his wet and dry fields and engages in trade or offers himself for hire for wages, not only is he to be punished, but also his fellow villagers. If there is anyone who neither serves in the military nor cultivates land, it is the responsibility of the deputies and other local officials to investigate and expel him. If they do not take action, those local officials shall be stripped of their posts on account of negligence. If a townsman is disguised as a farmer, and that fact is concealed, that county or town shall be regarded as committing a culpable offense.

3. No employment shall be given to a military retainer—be he a samurai, or *komono*, the lowest rank of warrior—who has left his former master without permission. In employing a retainer, you must investigate thoroughly his background, and insist on having a guarantor. If the above already has a master and that fact is discovered, he shall be arrested for not following this provision, and shall be returned to his former master. If this regulation is violated, and the offender is willfully set free, then three persons shall be beheaded in place of the one, and their heads sent to the offender's original master. . . .

Source: From *Japan: A Documentary History*, ed. and trans., David J. Lu (Armonk, NY: M. E. Sharpe, 1997). Translation

4 • Laws Governing Military Households (1615)

1. The study of literature and the practice of the military arts, archery and horsemanship, must be cultivated diligently. . . .

From of old the rule has been to practice "the arts of peace on the left hand, and the arts of war on the right"; both must be mastered. . . .

2. Drinking parties and wanton revelry should be avoided. . . .

3. Offenders against the law should not be harbored or hidden in any domain.

Law is the basis of social order. . . . Those who break the law deserve heavy punishment.

4. Great lords [daimyo], the lesser lords, and officials should immediately expel from their domains any among their retainers or henchmen who have been charged with treason or murder.

Wild and wicked men may become weapons for overturning the state and destroying the people. How can they be allowed to go free?

5. Henceforth no outsider, none but the inhabitants of a particular domain, shall be permitted to reside in that domain. . . .

6. Whenever it is intended to make repairs on a castle of one of the feudal domains, the [shogunate] should be notified. The construction of any new castles is to be halted and stringently prohibited. . . .

7. Immediate report should be made of innovations which are being planned or of factional conspiracies being formed in neighboring domains. . . .

8. Do not enter into marriage privately [i.e., without notifying the shogunate]. . . . To form an alliance by marriage is the root of treason.

9. Visits of the daimyo to the capital are to be in accordance with regulations.[1]

. . . Daimyo should not be accompanied by a large number of soldiers. Twenty horsemen shall be the maximum escort for daimyo with an income of from one million to two hundred thousand *koku* of rice.[2] For those with an income of one hundred thousand koku or less, the escort should be proportionate to their income. . . .

10. Restrictions on the type and quality of dress to be worn should not be transgressed.

Lord and vassal, superior and inferior, should observe what is proper to their station in life . . .

11. Persons without rank shall not ride in palanquins.[3]

From [times] of old there have been certain families entitled to ride in palanquins without special permission and others who have received such permission. Recently, however, even the ordinary retainers and henchmen of some families have taken to riding about in palanquins, which is truly the worst sort of presumption. Henceforth permission shall be granted only to the lords of the various domains, their close relatives and ranking officials, medical men and astrologers, those over sixty years of age, and those ill or infirm. . . .

12. The samurai of the various domains shall lead a frugal and simple life.

When the rich make a display of their wealth, the poor are humiliated and envious. Nothing engenders corruption so much as this, and therefore it must be strictly curbed.

13. The lords of the domains should select officials with a capacity for public administration.

Good government depends on getting the right men. Due attention should be given to their merits and faults; rewards and punishments must be properly meted out. If a domain has able men, it flourishes; if it lacks able men it is doomed to perish. This is the clear admonition of the wise men of old.

Source: From *Japan: A Documentary History*, ed. and trans. David J. Lu (Armonk, NY: M. E. Sharpe, 1997), p. 191. Translation copyright © 1997 by David J. Lu. Reprinted with permission of M. E. Sharpe, Inc.

[1] This refers to the policy of requiring daimyo to reside every other year in Edo, the seat of shogunal government.
[2] One *koku* equals five bushels.
[3] Enclosed carriages borne on the shoulders of carriers by means of poles.

5 • Closed Country Edict (1635)

1. Japanese ships are strictly forbidden to leave for foreign countries.

2. No Japanese is permitted to go abroad. If there is anyone who attempts to do so secretly, he must be executed. The ship so involved must be impounded and its owner arrested, and the matter must be reported to the higher authority.

3. If any Japanese returns from overseas after residing there, he must be put to death.

4. If there is any place where the teaching of the [Catholic] priests is practiced, the two of you[1] must order a thorough investigation.

5. Any informer revealing the whereabouts of the followers of the priests must be rewarded accordingly. If anyone reveals the whereabouts of a high ranking priest, he must be given one hundred pieces of silver. For those of lower ranks, . . . the reward must be set accordingly. . . .

7. If there are any Southern Barbarians [Europeans] who propagate the teachings of the priests, or otherwise commit crimes, they may be incarcerated in the prison. . . .

8. All incoming ships must be carefully searched for the followers of the priests.

9. No single trading city shall be permitted to purchase all the merchandise brought by foreign ships. . . .

12. After settling the price, all white yarns [raw silk] brought by foreign ships shall be allocated to the five trading cities[2] and other quarters as stipulated.

13. After settling the price of white yarns, other merchandise [brought by foreign ships] may be traded freely between the [licensed] dealers. . . .

14. The date of departure homeward of foreign ships shall not be later than the twentieth day of the ninth month. Any ships arriving in Japan later than usual shall depart within fifty days of their arrival. . . .

Source: From *Japan: A Documentary History*, ed. and trans. David J. Lu (Armonk, NY: M. E. Sharpe, 1997), p. 191. Translation copyright © 1997 by David J. Lu. Reprinted with permission of M. E. Sharpe, Inc.

[1]Refers to the two commissioners of Nagasaki, to whom the edict is addressed.
[2]The cities of Kyoto, Edo, Osaka, Sakai, and Nagasaki.

PART TWO

A World in Transition, from the Mid-Seventeenth Century to the Early Nineteenth Century

ETWEEN 1633 and 1639, the Japanese shogun, Tokugawa Hitetada, in an effort to solidify his authority and further stabilize Japan, outlawed Christianity, expelled Spanish and Portuguese missionaries, and severely restricted trade with the English, Portuguese, Spanish, and Dutch. The Portuguese decided to test the shogun's resolve in 1640 by sending a trading ship to Japan. In response, the shogun ordered the execution of the captain and 60 members of the crew, leaving alive 13 sailors to sail the ship back to Macao, the Portuguese enclave in China, to tell what had happened. The Europeans withdrew from Japan, except the Dutch, who were permitted to send one ship a year to Japan under strict conditions dictated by the government. Two hundred years later, another Asian state, China, sought to impose controls on trade with Europeans: in 1838, the emperor banned the sale of opium by the British, and in 1839, his official Lin Zexu forced British merchants to hand over 20,000 chests of opium and had it dissolved and flushed into the sea. This time, the European response was quite different. The British declared war on China and dispatched 16 warships, 4 armed steamers, 28 transports, and 4,000 troops to China. After their victory, they forced China to accept the humiliating Treaty of Nanjing, which ceded Hong Kong to the British, opened five ports to foreign trade, and required the Chinese to pay the British $21 million.

The starkly different outcomes of these two episodes show how much the world had changed between the seventeenth and early nineteenth centuries. In the early 1600s, the states of Western Europe, still fighting among themselves over religion, were in no position to challenge the great imperial states of Asia. Their armies were too small, their finances too precarious, and the distances too great to even consider such an undertaking. Economically, by the early 1600s, Europeans had expanded their role in world trade, but when they built warehouses and wharves on the coasts of India, China, Southeast Asia, and Africa, they did so at the pleasure of local rulers and with the understanding they would follow rules set down by those same rulers. When they purchased Asian goods, they paid exclusively with silver, because they produced no manufactured or agricultural products that interested sophisticated Asian buyers.

By the early 1800s, Europe and Europe's role in the world had both changed significantly. By then, intellectuals had lost interest in the religious issues that had drawn the attention of thinkers in the Medieval, Renaissance, and Reformation eras, and had formulated views of society, politics, and human nature that were increasingly secular and scientific. In politics, revolutions in Europe and its offshoots in the Americas had challenged royal authority, aristocratic privilege, and state-controlled churches and had introduced concepts of popular sovereignty, constitutionalism, legal equality, nationalism, and freedom. Rising populations, urbanization, commercial expansion, and greater productivity in agriculture and manufacturing all contributed to impressive economic growth. Most importantly, beginning in the 1760s, mechanization of the English textile industry, new techniques of iron smelting, and the development of the steam engine heralded the beginning of the Industrial Revolution, which would give the Europeans productive capacities unimagined in human history.

While Europe drew strength from these changes, Asian empires had grown weaker by 1800. The Safavid Empire no longer existed, and in an India now dominated by the British, the Mughal Empire had shrunk to a small piece of territory around the imperial capital. Both empires had fallen victim to declining revenues, religious tensions, provincial rebellions, and attacks by powerful coalitions of tribal warriors from Central

Asia. The Ottoman Empire had a lengthening list of problems: budgetary shortfalls, the *de facto* breakaway of provinces on the empire's periphery, stagnating trade, bureaucratic corruption, inflation, higher taxes, peasant violence, and religiously inspired rebellion in Arabia. Not surprisingly, it was no longer the formidable military and economic power that had awed and worried Europeans in the 1500s.

In East Asia, decline came later. During the first part of Qianlong's long reign (r. 1736–1799), China's population continued to grow, commerce expanded, and the empire doubled in size as a result of conquests in the west. In the late 1700s, however, China faced a series of crises. Military campaigns in Burma and Vietnam went poorly; rural misery bred discontent as China's expanding population drove up rents and created land shortages; the bureaucracy, which had failed to grow to keep pace with the size of China's population and territory, was hard pressed to carry out its functions effectively. The problems of Japan, still largely isolated from the outside world, seemed less severe, but even here, land shortages, population growth, urbanization, and commercialization were beginning to strain the social order.

By the early 1800s, world relationships had undergone a historic shift in favor of a small group of states on the far western tip of Eurasia, a region that for millennia had played a negligible role in history's major events. By the early 1800s, however, these states had exported their languages, culture, and ideas to two continents in the Western Hemisphere, gained political control of much of island Southeast Asia and parts of India, and established commercial ascendancy on the world's oceans. They had become the source of ground-breaking innovations in government, economics, technology, and science. They were on the verge of establishing unprecedented dominance over the world.

Chapter 5

Europe and the Americas in an Age of Science, Economic Growth, and Revolution

O N OCTOBER 24, 1648, the work of hundreds of diplomats and dozens of heads of state ended when signatures were affixed to the last agreements that collectively make up the Treaty of Westphalia, named after the northwest German territory where negotiations had taken place for the previous six years. With this treaty, one of Europe's most devastating and demoralizing wars, the Thirty Years' War, came to an end. In no small measure because of this war's horrors and destructiveness, it was the last of the religious wars that had plagued Europe since the early 1500s. After more than a century of attempting to exterminate each other with armies, the executioner's axe, and instruments of the torture chamber, Protestants and Catholics accepted the permanence of Europe's religious divisions.

Religion was not the only area in which tensions eased in the second half of the seventeenth century. Conflicts between centralizing monarchs and independent-minded nobles and provinces ended in most European states with the triumph of absolutism—a form of government in which monarchs claimed the exclusive right to make and enforce laws. In a handful of states, notably the Netherlands and England, wealthy landowners and merchants were able to strengthen representative assemblies and limit royal authority. In these states too, however, many conflicts over fundamental constitutional issues were resolved in the late 1600s.

A resolution of uncertainties also took place in the realm of ideas. The work of Isaac Newton (1642–1727) settled perplexing scientific issues that had emerged in the sixteenth century when Nicolaus Copernicus and others revealed the flaws of ancient Greek science but sought in vain for a coherent, all-encompassing model to replace it. Newton's theory of universal gravitation provided such a model. It enabled scientists to understand a host of natural phenomena, including the Earth's tides, the acceleration of falling bodies, and lunar and planetary movement. In the 1700s, the acceptance of Newton's theories along with advances in mathematics and other branches of science inspired the secularism and confidence in human reason of Europe's Age of Enlightenment.

Europe in the eighteenth century was more civil, orderly, and tranquil than it had been in hundreds of years. Wars were fought, but none matched the devastation of the wars of religion. Steady economic growth—fueled by trade with the Americas, modest inflation, and greater agricultural productivity—increased per capita wealth within Europe's expanding population. Peasant revolts and urban violence declined, and old class antagonisms seemed to have abated.

The Atlantic community's outward tranquility, however, was deceptive. A host of issues increasingly divided the governments of Spain, Brazil, and Great Britain from colonists across the Atlantic, many of whom now considered themselves more American than European. The result was a series of revolts between the 1770s and 1810s that led to the establishment of more than a dozen new independent states in the Americas.

Discontent also was growing in Europe. Peasants faced land shortages and higher rents as a result of rural population growth. Artisans were pinched by decades of gradual inflation. Many merchants, manufacturers, lawyers, and other members of the middle class prospered, but they resented the nobles' privileges and their rulers' ineffectiveness. The intellectual atmosphere of the Age of Enlightenment, with its belief in reason and progress, heightened political expectations, as did events in North America, where the thirteen colonies threw off British rule and established the United States of America, a new type of state based on constitutionalism and popular sovereignty. The meeting of France's representative assembly, the Estates General, in May 1789 was the first step toward a revolution that reverberated throughout the world.

In England another revolution, an economic revolution, also was under way by century's end. The adoption of new spinning and weaving devices driven by water power and steam was transforming the textile industry, while new methods of smelting and casting brought fundamental changes to iron production. By the early nineteenth century, as domestic industry gave way to factory production, output soared, urban populations swelled, and work was redefined. Collectively known as the Industrial Revolution, these economic changes reshaped the human condition to a degree even greater than the political revolution in France.

An Age of Monarchy—Absolute and Limited

In many history books, the era of European history from the mid-1600s to the end of the eighteenth century is known as the Age of Absolutism, a term that accurately describes the political systems of France, Spain, Portugal, Sweden, Denmark, Austria, Hungary, Prussia, Russia, and many small principalities in Germany and Italy. In these states, monarchs were absolute in the dictionary sense of "having no restriction, exception, or qualification." Representative assemblies no longer met to offer advice or approve taxes; great nobles no longer maintained private armies; church leaders became royal appointees; and monarchs were free to use their subjects' money to fight wars and build palaces. These monarchs ruled by divine right, meaning that God had chosen them to rule, and, as a corollary, that opposition to such rulers was an affront to the Divinity. Louis XIV, who built Europe's most extravagant royal palace at Versailles and plunged France into years of warfare, captured the spirit of absolutism when he told his minister of finance Colbert, "After I have heard your arguments and those of your colleagues, and having given my opinion on all your claims, I do not wish to hear further talk about it. . . . [After] a decision I give you I wish no word of reply."[1] More famously and simply, he is said to have proclaimed, *"L'état, c'est moi"* ("I am the state").

Like every historical label, however, the term "age of absolutism" has its weaknesses. Among the more than 300 large and small sovereign states in Europe, a few were republics, in which at least part of the population exercised political authority without benefit of a king. They included Venice and Genoa, a number of German city-states, and one major economic and political power, the United Provinces of the Netherlands. In a few other states, monarchs reigned, but with nominal authority. Of these, the most prominent was England, which, after a century of political

---

[1]C. B. Cole, *Colbert and a Century of French Mercantilism* (1939), vol. 1, p. 290.

turmoil, forged a government in which royal power was limited by an elected assembly, the Parliament. As had been true for hundreds of years, European politics in the early modern era was marked by pluralism and diversity.

A Classic Statement of Absolutist Principles

30 • JACQUES-BÉNIGNE BOSSUET, POLITICS DERIVED FROM THE WORDS OF HOLY SCRIPTURE

Living through decades of civil war, regicide, religious conflict, and rebellion, European intellectuals in the sixteenth and seventeenth centuries sought to understand the underlying causes of Europe's political turmoil and theorized about what form of government might best be able to bring this turmoil to an end. Most believed that Europe's political salvation lay in strong, centralized monarchy, a type of government they defended from a number of theoretical perspectives. Some drew an analogy between the state and well-run families: just as a father exercised unquestioned authority over his spouse, children, and servants, so a king should have unquestioned authority over his subjects. Others, most notably Thomas Hobbes in *Leviathan* (1660), based their pro-absolutist arguments on purely rational principles. Most, however, relied on religious arguments.

Among the writers who defended absolutism on religious grounds, none was so widely cited as Jacques-Bénigne Bossuet, a French churchman. Born into a family of prominent lawyers in Dijon in 1627, Bossuet entered the priesthood and became one of the great preachers of his day. After moving to Paris in 1659, he frequently was asked to preach before the royal family, and in 1670 Louis XIV chose him to tutor his son and heir to the throne. As part of his duties, in 1678 Bossuet composed a treatise on the authority and duties of kings, which later was published under the title *Politics Derived from the Words of Holy Scripture*. After his duties as royal tutor ended in 1681, he was appointed bishop of Meaux and became embroiled in a number of controversies with Protestants, Jesuits, and Catholic freethinkers who questioned the reality of miracles and the literal truth of the Bible. He died in 1704.

QUESTIONS FOR ANALYSIS

1. According to Bossuet, in what ways are kings "divine"?
2. How does he prove his assertion concerning the divinity of kings?
3. In terms of monarchs' relationship with their subjects, what are the implications of kings' divine nature?
4. According to Bossuet, what are the purposes of government?
5. Bossuet asserts that royal authority is "absolute," but not "arbitrary." What does he mean by this distinction?
6. According to Bossuet, what is the appropriate response on the part of royal subjects when their king would seem to act against justice and the true faith?

On the Nature and Properties of Royal Authority

God establishes kings as his ministers, and reigns through them over the peoples. We have already seen that all power comes from God. The Prince, adds Saint Paul,[1] "is a minister of God to you for good. But if you do that which is evil, be afraid; for he bears not the sword in vain: for he is a minister of God, an avenger for wrath to him that does evil" [Romans 13:4]. So princes act as ministers of God and his lieutenants on earth. It is through them that He rules His empire. This is why we have seen that the royal throne is not the throne of a man, but the throne of God Himself. . . . He governs all peoples, and gives kings to all. . . .

It appears from all this that the person of the king is sacred, and that it is a sacrilege to attack him. God has His prophets anoint them with a sacred unction,[2] as He has His pontiffs and His altars anointed. But, even without the external application of this unction, their charge renders them sacred, as being the representatives of the divine majesty, delegated by His providence to the execution of His designs. . . .

Saint Paul, after having said that the prince is the minister of God, concludes thus: "Wherefore you need to be in subjection, not only because of the wrath, but also for conscience's sake" [Romans 13:5]. . . . And again, "servants, obey in all things your temporal masters and whatever you do, do it heartily as to the Lord, and not as unto men." If the apostle speaks thus of servitude, which is an unnatural condition; what should we think of legitimate subjection to princes and to the

magistrates who are the protectors of public liberty? This is why Saint Peter[3] says, "submit yourselves to every ordinance of man for the Lord's sake: whether it be to the king as supreme, or unto governors, as unto them that are sent by him for the punishment of evildoers and for the praise of them that do well" [1 Peter 2:13]. And, even if they did not carry out their duty, we must respect in them their charge and their ministry. . . . The service of God and the respect for kings are one; and Saint Peter puts these two duties together: "Fear God; honor the king" [1 Peter 2:17]. . . .

The kings must respect their own power and use it only to the public good. Their power coming from above, as we have said, they must not believe that it belongs to them to be used as they please; but they must use it with fear and restraint, as a thing which comes from God and for which God will call them to account. Kings should therefore tremble when using the power that God has given them, and think how horrible is the sacrilege of misusing a power which comes from God.

The Royal Authority Is Paternal, and Its Inherent Character Is Goodness

We have seen that kings take the place of God, who is the true father of all mankind. We have also seen that the first idea of power arrived at by men is that of paternal power; and that kings have been made on the model of fathers. Also, everybody agrees that the obedience which is due to the public power is to be found in the Ten Commandments, in the commandment which obliges men to honor their parents. From all this,

---

Source: From Bossuet, *Politique tirée des paroles de l'Ecriture sainte* in *Oeuvres choisies de Bossuet,* 5 vols. (Paris: Hachette, 1897–1901), vol. 2, trans. by James H. Overfield.

[1] Paul (ca. 10–67 C.E.) was, along with Peter (see footnote 3), an early convert to Christianity and missionary. Fourteen letters attributed to him are included in the Christian New Testament.

[2] Ointment used in a consecration ceremony.

[3] One of Jesus' twelve apostles and along with Paul an important early missionary. Two letters attributed to him, thought to have been written while he served as the first bishop of Rome, are included in the Christian New Testament.

it follows that the title of king is the title of a father, and that goodness is the most natural characteristic of kings. . . .

The Royal Authority Is Absolute

In order to render this idea odious and unbearable, many pretend to confuse absolute government with arbitrary government. But there are no two more dissimilar things. . . . The prince need render no account to anyone for the orders he gives. "I counsel you to keep the king's commandment and that in regard to the oath of God. Be not hasty to go out of his sight: . . . for he does whatsoever pleases him. Where the word of a king is, there is power; and who may say unto him, What are you doing?" [Ecclesiastes 8:2] Without this absolute authority the king can do no good, nor punish evil; his power must be such that no one can hope to escape it. . . .

Men must therefore obey princes as they obey justice itself, without which there can be no order or purpose in things. They are Gods, and share in a fashion the divine independence. . . .

The Royal Authority Must Be Invincible

If there is in a State any authority which can stand in the path of public power and hinder it in its exercise, no one is safe. . . .

If the prince himself, who is the judge of judges, fears powerful men, what stability could there be in the State? It is therefore necessary that authority should be invincible, and that nothing should be able to breach the rampart behind which the public peace and private weal are safe.

Of Majesty

Majesty is the reflection of the greatness of God in the prince. God is infinite, God is all. The prince, as a prince, is not regarded as a private individual: he is a public figure, the whole State rests in him; the will of the whole people is comprehended in his. Just as all perfection and all virtue are concentrated in God, so all the power of private individuals is concentrated in the person of the prince. What greatness, that one man should carry so much! The power of God makes itself felt in an instant from one end of the world to the other: the royal power acts in the same way throughout the whole kingdom. It keeps the whole kingdom in being, as God keeps the whole world. If God were to withdraw His hand, the world would fall back into nothingness: if authority ceased in the kingdom, everything would be confusion. . . .

Now, put together all the great and august things that we have said. . . . See a great people united in one person: see this sacred, paternal, and absolute power: see the secret purpose which governs the whole body of the State comprehended in one head: you see the image of God in the kings; and you get an idea of royal majesty. . . . God is holiness itself, goodness itself, power itself, reason itself. The majesty of God is in these things. The majesty of the prince is in the image of these things. This majesty is so great that its source cannot be in the prince; it is borrowed from God who gives it to him for the good of the peoples, for whom it is salutary that they should be held in by a superior power. . . .

Therefore, use your power boldly, oh, kings! For it is divine and salutary to mankind; but use it with humility. You are endowed with it from outside. Fundamentally, it leaves you weak; it leaves you mortal; it leaves you sinners; and burdens you with greater responsibility towards God.

On the Obedience Due to the Prince

The subjects owe unlimited obedience to the prince. If the prince is not punctually obeyed, the public order is overthrown and there is no more unity, and consequently no more cooperation or peace in a State. . . .

Open godlessness, and even persecution, do not absolve the subjects from the obedience they owe to princes. The character of royalty is holy and sacred, even in infidel princes; and we have seen that Isaiah[4] calls Cyrus "the anointed of the Lord." Nebuchadnezzar[5] was godless, and proud to the point of wanting to equal God and put to death those who refused him a sacrilegious worship; and nevertheless Daniel addresses him thus: "You are the king of kings: and the God of Heavens has given you the kingdom and the power and the empire and the glory" [Daniel 2:37]. . . .

The subjects may oppose to the violence of princes only respectful remonstrances, without murmurs or rebellion, and prayers for their conversion.

If God does not hearken to the prayers of His faithful; if in order to try and chasten His children He permits their persecution to grow worse, they must then remember that Jesus Christ has "sent them as lambs in the midst of wolves." [Luke 10:3] Here is a truly holy doctrine, truly worthy of Jesus Christ and of His disciples.

On the Duties of the Prince

The purpose of government is the welfare and conservation of the State. . . .

The good constitution of the body of the State consists in two things: religion and justice. These are the internal and constitutive principles of States. By the one we render to God what is owed to Him, and by the other we render to men that which they deserve . . . He is the protector of the public peace which is based upon religion; and he must maintain his throne, of which, as we have seen, religion is the foundation. Those who will not allow the prince to act strictly in religious matters, because religion should be free, make an impious error. Otherwise, one would have to tolerate in all the subjects and in all the country idolatry, Mohammedanism, Judaism, any false religions; blasphemy, even atheism, and the greatest crimes would be the least punished.

[4]A Hebrew prophet to whom is attributed the Book of Isaiah, part of the Hebrew Scriptures and the Christian Old Testament. In the Book of Isaiah he discusses Cyrus the Great (r. 550–529 B.C.E.), founder of the first Persian Empire. After conquering Babylon, Cyrus freed the Jews from captivity and allowed them to return to Palestine.

[5]Ruler of Babylon from 605 to 562 B.C.E. One of his advisors, Daniel, is the main character in the Book of Daniel, part of the Hebrew Scriptures and the Christian Old Testament, written in the Maccabean period (167–63 B.C.E.).

Peter the Great's Blueprint for Russia
31 • PETER THE GREAT, EDICTS AND DECREES

The growth of strong central government in Russia, halted during two centuries of Mongol domination and impeded by decades of turmoil and foreign invasion following the death of Ivan IV in 1584, resumed during the reigns of Alexis (r. 1645–1676) and his son Peter the Great (r. 1682–1725). Alexis streamlined the central bureaucracy, extended his control over church affairs, issued a new law code (which imposed serfdom on all Russian peasants), and generally ignored advisory bodies such as the Council of State and Assembly of the Land. Alexis also initiated reforms of the Russian military and founded state-sponsored factories for the manufacture of weapons, glass, brick, textiles, and agricultural tools.

Despite Alexis's accomplishments, when his son Peter became tsar, Russia still lagged behind the nations of Western Europe. Russia lacked the economic base and government institutions to match the size, weaponry, and training of its rivals' armies. Peter learned this bitter truth in November 1700 at the Battle of Narva, the first major battle in the Great Northern War, when a Swedish army of just over 8,000 routed a poorly trained and equipped Russian army four times its size. Peter responded with characteristic energy. Already enamored of western European technology, military drill, shipbuilding, fashion, and government as a result of boyhood contacts with European visitors to Moscow and his travels through Europe in 1697 and 1698, Peter threw himself into a campaign to transform Russia along European lines. Issuing no fewer than 3,000 decrees in the next 25 years on everything from the structure of government to male shaving habits, Peter became the first ruler who sought to transform his state and subjects through a process that came to be known as Westernization.

QUESTIONS FOR ANALYSIS

1. What do these decrees reveal about Peter the Great's motives for his reforms?
2. What can be learned from these decrees about Russian social relationships and the state of the Russian economy?
3. Why do you think Peter believed it was necessary for Russians to change their dress, shaving habits, and calendar?
4. What evidence do these edicts provide about opposition or indifference to Peter's reforms on the part of his subjects?
5. What do these edicts reveal about Peter's views of the state and its relationship to his subjects?
6. What groups within Russia might have been most likely to oppose Peter's reforms? Why?

Learning from Europe

Decree on the New Calendar (1699)

It is known to His Majesty that not only many European Christian lands, but also Slavic nations which are in total accord with our Eastern Orthodox Church . . . agree to count their years from the eighth day after the birth of Christ, that is from the first day of January, and not from the creation of the world,[1] because of the many difficulties and discrepancies of this reckoning. It is now the year 1699 from the birth of Christ, and from the first of January will begin both the new year 1700 and a new century; and so His Majesty has ordered . . . that from now on time will be reckoned in government offices and dates be noted on documents and property deeds, starting from the first of January 1700.

Source: Marte Blinoff, *Life and Thought in Old Russia* (University Park: Pennsylvania State University Press, 1961), pp. 49–50; Eugene Schuyler, *Peter the Great*, vol. 2, pp. 176–177; L. Jay Oliva, *Peter the Great* (Englewood Cliffs, NJ: Prentice-Hall, 1970), p. 50; George Vernadsky et al., *A Source Book for Russian History from Early Times to 1917*, vol. 2 (New Haven and London: Yale University Press, 1972), pp. 347, 329, 357.

[1]Before January 1, 1700, the Russian calendar started from the date of the creation of the world, which was reckoned at 5508 B.C.E. The year began on September 1.

And to celebrate this good undertaking and the new century . . . in the sovereign city of Moscow . . . let the reputable citizens arrange decorations of pine, fir, and juniper trees and boughs along the busiest main streets and by the houses of eminent church and lay persons of rank. . . . Poorer persons should place at least one shrub or bough on their gates or on their house. . . . Also, . . . as a sign of rejoicing, wishes for the new year and century will be exchanged, and the following will be organized: when fireworks are lit and guns fired on the great Red Square, let the boyars,[2] the Lords of the Palace, of the Chamber, and the Council, and the eminent personages of Court, Army, and Merchant ranks, each in his own grounds, fire three times from small guns, if they have any, or from muskets and other small arms, and shoot some rockets into the air.

Decree on the Invitation of Foreigners (1702)

Since our accession to the throne all our efforts and intentions have tended to govern this realm in such a way that all of our subjects should, through our care for the general good, become more and more prosperous. For this end we have always tried to maintain internal order, to defend the state against invasion, and in every possible way to improve and to extend trade. With this purpose we have been compelled to make some necessary and salutary changes in the administration, in order that our subjects might more easily gain a knowledge of matters of which they were before ignorant, and become more skillful in their commercial relations. We have therefore given orders, made dispositions, and founded institutions indispensable for increasing our trade with foreigners, and shall do the same in the future. Nevertheless we fear

that matters are not in such a good condition as we desire, and that our subjects cannot in perfect quietness enjoy the fruits of our labors, and we have therefore considered still other means to protect our frontier from the invasion of the enemy, and to preserve the rights and privileges of our State, and the general peace of all Christians. . . .

To attain these worthy aims, we have endeavored to improve our military forces, which are the protection of our State, so that our troops may consist of well-drilled men, maintained in perfect order and discipline. In order to obtain greater improvement in this respect, and to encourage foreigners, who are able to assist us in this way, as well as artisans profitable to the State, to come in numbers to our country, we have issued this manifesto, and have ordered printed copies of it to be sent throughout Europe. . . . And as in our residence of Moscow, the free exercise of religion of all other sects, although not agreeing with our church, is already allowed, so shall this be hereby confirmed anew in such maner that we, . . . shall exercise no compulsion over the consciences of men, and shall gladly allow every Christian to care for his own salvation at his own risk.

An Instruction to Russian Students Abroad Studying Navigation (1714)

1. Learn how to draw plans and charts and how to use the compass and other naval indicators.

2. Learn how to navigate a vessel in battle as well as in a simple maneuver, and learn how to use all appropriate tools and instruments; namely, sails, ropes, and oars, and the like matters, on row boats and other vessels.

3. Discover . . . how to put ships to sea during a naval battle. . . . Obtain from foreign naval officers written statements, bearing their signatures

---

[2]Members of the hereditary nobility.

and seals, of how adequately you are prepared for naval duties.

4. If, upon his return, anyone wishes to receive from the Tsar greater favors, he should learn, in addition to the above enumerated instructions, how to construct those vessels [aboard] which he would like to demonstrate his skills.

5. Upon his return to Moscow, every foreign-trained Russian should bring with him at his own expense, for which he will later be reimbursed, at least two experienced masters of naval science. They the returnees will be assigned soldiers, one soldier per returnee, to teach them what they have learned abroad. . . .

Creating a New Russian

Decree on Western Dress (1701)

Western dress shall be worn by all the boyars, members of our councils and of our court . . . gentry of Moscow, secretaries . . . provincial gentry, gosti,[3] government officials, streltsy,[4] members of the guilds . . . citizens of Moscow of all ranks, and residents of provincial cities . . . excepting the clergy and peasant tillers of the soil. The upper dress shall be of French or Saxon cut, and the lower dress . . . —waistcoat, trousers, boots, shoes, and hats—shall be of the German type. They shall also ride German saddles. Likewise the womenfolk of all ranks, including the priests', deacons', and church attendants' wives, the wives of the dragoons, the soldiers, and the streltsy, and their children, shall wear Western dresses, hats, jackets, and underwear— undervests and petticoats—and shoes. From now on no one of the above-mentioned is to wear Russian dress . . . , sheepskin coats, or Russian peasant coats, trousers, boots, and shoes. It is also forbidden to ride Russian saddles. . . .

Decree on Shaving (1705)

Henceforth, in accordance with this, His Majesty's decree, all court attendants . . . provincial service men, government officials of all ranks, military men, all the gosti, members of the wholesale merchants' guild, and members of the guilds purveying for our household must shave their beards and moustaches. But, if it happens that some of them do not wish to shave their beards and moustaches, let a yearly tax be collected from such persons; from court attendants. . . . As for the peasants, let a toll of two half-copecks[5] per beard be collected at the town gates each time they enter or leave a town; and do not let the peasants pass the town gates, into or out of town, without paying this toll.

Military and Economic Reforms

Decree on Promotion to Officer's Rank (1714)

Since there are many who promote to officer rank their relatives and friends—young men who do not know the fundamentals of soldiering, not having served in the lower ranks—and since even those who serve do so for a few weeks or months only, as a formality; therefore . . . henceforth there shall be no promotion of men of noble extraction or of any others who have not first served as privates in the Guards. This decree does not apply to soldiers of lowly origin who, after long service in the ranks, have received their commissions through honest service or to those who are promoted on the basis of merit, now or in the future. . . .

Statute for the College of Manufactures[6] (1723)

His Imperial Majesty is diligently striving to establish and develop in the Russian Empire such

---

[3]Merchants who often served the tsar in some capacity.
[4]Members of the imperial guard in Moscow.
[5]One-twentieth of a ruble, the basic unit of Russian currency.

[6]One of several administrative boards created by Peter in 1717 modeled on Swedish practice.

manufacturing plants and factories as are found in other states, for the general welfare and prosperity of his subjects. He [therefore] most graciously charges the College of Manufactures to exert itself in devising the means to introduce, with the least expense, and to spread in the Russian Empire these and other ingenious arts, and especially those for which materials can be found within the empire. . . .

His Imperial Majesty gives permission to everyone, without distinction of rank or condition, to open factories wherever he may find suitable. . . .

Factory owners must be closely supervised, in order that they have at their plants good and experienced [foreign] master craftsmen, who are able to train Russians in such a way that these, in turn, may themselves become masters, so that their produce may bring glory to the Russian manufactures. . . .

By the former decrees of His Majesty commercial people were forbidden to buy villages [i.e., to

own serfs], the reason being that they were not engaged in any other activity beneficial for the state save commerce; but since it is now clear to all that many of them have started to found manufacturing establishments and build plants, . . . which tend to increase the welfare of the state . . . therefore permission is granted both to the gentry and to men of commerce to acquire villages for these factories without hindrance. . . .

In order to stimulate voluntary immigration of various craftsmen from other countries into the Russian Empire, and to encourage them to establish factories and manufacturing plants freely and at their own expense, the College of Manufactures must send appropriate announcements to the Russian envoys accredited at foreign courts. The envoys should then, in an appropriate way, bring these announcements to the attention of men of various professions, urge them to come to settle in Russia, and help them to move.

The Foundations of Parliamentary Supremacy in England

32 • ENGLISH BILL OF RIGHTS

The English Bill of Rights, accepted in 1689, kept England on a path that set it apart from the absolutist governments then taking hold in most of continental Europe. It also ended a clash between the Crown and Parliament that had convulsed English politics for almost a century. Ever since the reigns of James I (r. 1603–1625) and his son Charles I (r. 1625–1649), the landowners, merchants, and lawyers who dominated the House of Commons had fought the monarchy over religion, economic policies, foreign relations, and political issues that all centered on the fundamental question of Parliament's place in England's government. An impasse over new taxes led to civil war between parliamentarians and royalists in 1642. After a triumphant Parliament ordered the execution of Charles I in 1649, a faction of Puritans led by Oliver Cromwell seized power and imposed strict Protestant beliefs on the country for the next eleven years. The Puritans' grip on England loosened after the death of Cromwell in 1658 and was lost altogether when a newly elected Parliament restored the Stuarts in 1660.

Charles II (r. 1660–1685) and his brother James II (r. 1685–1688), however, alienated their subjects through pro-French and pro-Catholic policies and a disregard for Parliament. James II was a professed Catholic, and when a male heir was born in 1688, this raised the possibility of a long line of English Catholic kings. Many of his predominantly Protestant subjects found this unacceptable, and the result was the Glorious Revolution of 1688–1689. In a change that resembled a coup d'état more than a revolution, Parliament offered the crown to James's Protestant daughter Mary and her husband, William of Orange of Holland. After James mounted only token resistance and then fled the country, his son-in-law and daughter became King William III and Queen Mary II after signing the Bill of Rights, presented to them by Parliament in 1689. By doing so, they accepted parliamentary limitations on royal authority that became a permanent part of England's constitution.

QUESTIONS FOR ANALYSIS

1. What abuses of royal power seem to have most disturbed the authors of the English Bill of Rights?
2. Were the authors of the Bill of Rights most concerned with political, economic, or religious issues?
3. What role does the Bill of Rights envision for the English Crown?
4. When the Bill of Rights speaks of "rights," to whose rights does it refer?
5. In what ways might the common people of England benefit from the Bill of Rights?
6. If given the opportunity, how might Bossuet (source 30) have criticized the premises of the English Bill of Rights?

Whereas the late King James the Second, by the assistance of diverse evil counselors, judges and ministers employed by him, did endeavor to subvert and extirpate the Protestant religion and the laws and liberties of this kingdom;

By assuming and exercising a power of dispensing with and suspending of laws and the execution of laws without consent of Parliament;

By committing and prosecuting diverse worthy prelates for humbly petitioning to be excused from concurring to the said assumed power;

By issuing and causing to be executed a commission under the great seal for erecting a court called the Court of Commissioners for Ecclesiastical Causes;[1]

By levying money for and to the use of the Crown by pretense of prerogative for other time and in other manner than the same was granted by Parliament;

By raising and keeping a standing army within this kingdom in time of peace without consent of Parliament, and quartering soldiers contrary to law;

By causing several good subjects being Protestants to be disarmed at the same time when papists were both armed and employed contrary to law;

By violating the freedom of election of members to serve in Parliament; . . .

And whereas of late years partial corrupt and unqualified persons have been returned and served on juries in trials, and particularly diverse jurors in trials for high treason . . .

And excessive bail hath been required of persons committed in criminal cases to elude the benefit of the laws made for the liberty of the subjects;

Source: The Statutes: Revised Edition (London: Eyre and Spottiswoode, 1871), vol. I, pp. 10–12.

[1]A royal court established to try religious cases.

And excessive fines have been imposed;

And illegal and cruel punishments inflicted; . . .

All which are utterly and directly contrary to the known laws and statutes and freedom of this realm;

And thereupon the said Lords Spiritual and Temporal and Commons,[2] pursuant to their respective letters and elections, being now assembled . . . , taking into their most serious consideration the best means for attaining the ends aforesaid, do in the first place (as their ancestors in like case have usually done) for the vindicating and asserting their ancient rights and liberties declare;

That the pretended power of suspending of laws or the execution of laws by regal authority without consent of Parliament is illegal;

That the pretended power of dispensing with laws or the execution of laws by regal authority, as it hath been assumed and exercised of late, is illegal;

That the commission for erecting the late Court of Commissioners for Ecclesiastical Causes, and all other commissions and courts of like nature, are illegal and pernicious;

That levying money for or to the use of the Crown by pretense of prerogative, without grant of Parliament, for longer time, or in other manner than the same is or shall be granted, is illegal;

That it is the right of the Subjects to petition the king, and all commitments and prosecutions for such petitioning are illegal;

That the raising or keeping a standing army within the kingdom in time of peace, unless it be with consent of Parliament, is against law;

That the subjects which are Protestants may have arms for their defense suitable to their conditions and as allowed by law;

That election of members of Parliament ought to be free;

That the freedom of speech and debates or proceedings in Parliament ought not to be impeached or questioned in any court or place out of Parliament;

That excessive bail ought not to be required, nor excessive fines imposed nor cruel and unusual punishments inflicted; . . .

That all grants and promises of fines and forfeitures of particular persons before conviction are illegal and void;

And that for redress of all grievances, and for the amending, strengthening and preserving of the laws, Parliaments ought to be held frequently. . . .

[2]The Lords Spiritual were the prelates of the Anglican Church who sat in the House of Lords, the Lords Temporal were titled peers who sat in the House of Lords, and Commons refers to the House of Commons, to which nontitled Englishmen were elected.

An Age of Science and Enlightenment

Although secularism had been a growing force in European intellectual life since the Italian Renaissance of the fourteenth and fifteenth centuries, only in the eighteenth century—the Age of Enlightenment—did it eclipse religion as the dominant influence on thought and culture. Catholic and Protestant churches still had millions of followers, and new religious movements such as English Methodism were signs of continuing religious vitality. Nonetheless, intellectuals of the eighteenth century largely ignored religion, artists painted fewer religious scenes, and rulers gave little thought to religion in making political and diplomatic decisions.

The main inspiration for the secularism of the eighteenth century was the Scientific Revolution, especially the work of Isaac Newton (1642–1727). When Newton revealed the physical laws that determined the movement of bodies throughout the universe, and did so without relying on religious authority or ancient texts, he demonstrated to eighteenth-century intellectuals the full power of human reason. These intellectuals, known as *philosophes* (French for philosophers), came from every corner of Europe and disagreed on many issues, but all were convinced that reason could be applied to social, political, and economic problems with results as spectacular as those achieved by Newton and other seventeenth-century scientists. Specifically, reason could expose the weaknesses, flaws, and injustices carried over from Europe's "unenlightened" past. The philosophes, therefore, were social and political critics who scrutinized and frequently condemned their era's legal codes, schools, churches, government policies, wars, sexual mores, class privileges, and much else.

The Enlightenment was not, however, purely negative. The philosophes rejected passive acceptance of the status quo and proclaimed that human beings through reason could plan and achieve a better future. They disagreed about what that future would be like, but none doubted that improvement of the human condition was not just possible but inevitable, if only reason were given freedom to inquire, question, plan, and inspire.

Two Images of Seventeenth-Century Science

33 • SÉBASTIEN LE CLERC, THE ROYAL ACADEMY AND ITS PROTECTORS AND A DISSECTION AT THE JARDIN DES PLANTES

Many contributors to Europe's scientific revolution were solitary scholars who had few contacts with others who shared their interests. By the late 1600s, however, leading scientists were all members of one of several scientific societies that supported and publicized their work and provided opportunities for exchanging ideas. The four most prestigious academies were the Academy of Experiment, founded in 1657 in Florence by Prince Leopold de Medici; the Royal Society of London, licensed but not financially supported by Charles II in 1660; the French Royal Academy of Sciences, founded in 1661 and supported by Louis XIV; and the Berlin Academy of Sciences, created in 1700 under the auspices of Elector Frederick III of Brandenburg-Prussia. Although these academies varied in terms of their size, organization, and activities, they all contributed to Europe's ongoing scientific development.

Many Europeans were introduced to the ideals and goals of the French Royal Academy of Sciences through the engravings of Sébastien Le Clerc (1637–1714), an artist with a lifelong interest in science. As the engraver for many of the Academy's books, he set a new standard for accurate scientific illustration. Among his works was a series of engravings depicting the activities of the academicians themselves. These engravings appeared in several of the Academy's publications, with individual copies made for the king, interested courtiers, and collectors. Two of them are reproduced here.

The first, *The Royal Academy and Its Protectors* (1671), centers on Louis XIV, with two aristocrats, the Prince of Condé and the Duke of Orléans, to his right and Jean-Baptiste Colbert, the French controller general of finances, to his left. They are surrounded by members of the Academy and their scientific instruments. Seen through the window are a formal garden and the Royal Observatory, which is under construction. At the center of the second engraving, entitled *A Dissection at the Jardin des Plantes* (1671), two academicians are dissecting a fox, with their observations being recorded by the individual seated at their right. In the foreground, an Academy member points to a printed book, in which the observations made during the dissection will be published, and behind the table stands Le Clerc himself, pointing to a page of his scientific engravings. On the far left, two figures are making observations with a magnifying glass and a microscope, while on the right stand Colbert and another courtier.

Neither engraving is realistic. Louis XIV made his first visit to the Academy in 1681, ten years after *The Royal Academy and its Protectors* was engraved. And none of the Academy's rooms would have afforded a window view of the Royal Observatory. Furthermore, the room where dissections were carried out was notoriously rank, probably closer in appearance and smell to a butcher shop than the genteel scene portrayed by Le Clerc. The artist's goal, however, was not to depict the day-to-day reality of the Academy's activities but rather to communicate an idealized vision of the methods and purposes of science.

QUESTIONS FOR ANALYSIS

1. How many different pieces of scientific equipment can you identify in the engravings? What do the equipment and other paraphernalia reveal about the scientific interests and methodology of the academicians?
2. What is the significance of the picture toward which Colbert is pointing? What might be the significance of the map on the floor?
3. What point is Le Clerc trying to make about the Academy in the following details from the engraving of the dissection room: the two figures at the window, the figure pointing to the book, and the artist pointing to the page of engravings?
4. Note the formal gardens that can be seen through the windows in both engravings. What attitude toward nature is expressed in gardens such as these?
5. How does this view of nature differ from that expressed in the two Ming Era landscape paintings in Chapter 4 (source 28)?

Sébastien Le Clerc, The Royal Academy and Its Protectors.

Sébastien Le Clerc, A Dissection at the Jardin des Plantes

A Plea for Religious Understanding and Tolerance

34 • VOLTAIRE, TREATISE ON TOLERATION

Francois-Marie Arouet (1694–1778), better known by his pen name, Voltaire, combined wit, literary elegance, and a passionate social conscience in a long literary career that epitomizes the values and spirit of the Age of Enlightenment. Born into a well-to-do Parisian bourgeois family, Voltaire published his first work, the tragic drama *Oedipus,* in 1717. In the next 61 years, he wrote thousands of poems, histories, satires, novels, short stories, essays, and reviews. The European reading public avidly bought his works, making him one of the first authors to make a fortune through the sale of his writings.

Although Voltaire's output and popularity ensured his influence on the Enlightenment at many different levels, one particular contribution stands out: his devotion to the principles of religious toleration and freedom of thought. Voltaire was convinced that the intolerance of organized religions, not just Christianity, had caused much of the world's suffering and conflict. He was angered that even in the "enlightened" eighteenth century, Protestant–Catholic enmity resulted in episodes such as the torture and execution of Jean Calas, a French Protestant convicted unjustly of murdering his son, supposedly after learning of the son's intent to become a Catholic. Voltaire's devotion to religious toleration is revealed in the following selection, taken from his *Treatise on Toleration,* written in 1763 in response to the execution of Calas.

QUESTIONS FOR ANALYSIS

1. Does Voltaire believe that intolerance is a special trait of Christianity, or does he think that it characterizes other organized religions as well?

2. What point is Voltaire trying to make in his reference to the various dialects of the Italian language?
3. What does Voltaire suggest as the essence of a truly religious person?
4. What attitude toward humankind does Voltaire express in the "Prayer to God"?
5. What does the excerpt tell us about Voltaire's views of the nature of God?

Of Universal Tolerance

No great art or studied eloquence is needed to prove that Christians should tolerate one another. I go even further and declare that we must look upon all men as our brothers. But the Turk, my brother? the Chinese, the Jew, the Siamese? Yes, of course; are we not all the children of one father and creatures of the same God?

But these people despise us; they call us idolaters! Then I'll tell them they are quite wrong. I think I could at least shock the proud obstinacy of an imam[1] if I said to them something like this:

This little globe, nothing more than a point, rolls in space like so many other globes; we are lost in this immensity. Man, some five feet tall, is surely a very small part of the universe. One of these imperceptible beings says to some of his neighbors in Arabia or Africa: "Listen to me, for the God of all these worlds has enlightened me: there are nine hundred million little ants like us on the earth, but only my anthill is beloved of God; He will hold all others in horror through all eternity; only mine will be blessed, the others will be eternally wretched."

At that, they would cut me short and ask what fool made that stupid remark. I would be obliged to reply, "You yourselves." Then I would try to mollify them; but that would not be easy.

I would speak now to the Christians and dare say, for example, to a Dominican Inquisitor,[2] "My brother, you know that every province in Italy has its dialect, and people in Venice and Bergamo speak differently from those in Florence. The Academy della Crusca[3] has standardized the language; its dictionary is an inescapable authority, and Buonmattei's[4] grammar is an absolute and infallible guide; but do you believe that the head of the Academy and in his absence, Buonmattei, would have been able in all good conscience to cut out the tongues of all those from Venice and Bergamo who persisted in using their own dialect?"

The Inquisitor replies: "There is a great difference; here it's a question of your salvation. It's for your own good the Director of the Inquisition orders that you be seized on the testimony of a single person, no matter how infamous or criminal he may be; that you have no lawyer to defend you; that the very name of your accuser be unknown to you; that the Inquisitor promise you grace and then condemn you; that you undergo five different degrees of torture and then be whipped or sent to the galleys, or ceremoniously burned at the stake. . . ."

I would take the liberty of replying: "My brother, perhaps you are right: I am convinced that you wish me well, but couldn't I be saved without all that?"

Source: From *Les Philosophes* ed. and trans. by Norman L. Torrey. Copyright © 1960 by Norman L. Torrey. Used by permission of G. P. Putnam's Sons, a division of Penguin Group (USA) Inc.

[1]In this context, a recognized Islamic religious leader or teacher.

[2]A Catholic official responsible for uncovering and punishing erroneous belief, or heresy.
[3]The Florentine Academy of Letters, founded in 1582.
[4]A seventeenth-century Italian grammarian.

To be sure, these horrible absurdities do not soil the face of the earth everyday, but they are frequent enough, and a whole volume could easily be written about them much longer than the Gospels which condemn them. Not only is it very cruel to persecute in this brief existence of ours those who differ from us in opinion, but I am afraid it is being bold indeed to pronounce their eternal damnation. It hardly seems fitting for us atoms of the moment, for that is all we are, to presume to know in advance the decrees of our own Creator. . . .

Oh, sectarians of a merciful God, if you had a cruel heart, if, while adoring Him whose only law consists in the words: "Love God and thy neighbor as thyself (Luke X, 27)," you had overloaded this pure and holy law with sophisms and incomprehensible disputations; if you had lighted the torch of discord either over a new word or a single letter of the alphabet; if you had made eternal punishment the penalty for the omission of a few words or ceremonies which other nations could not know about, I would say to you, as I wept in compassion for mankind: "Transport yourselves with me to the day when all men will be judged and when God will do unto each man according to his works."

"I see all the dead of all centuries, past and present, appear before His presence. Are you quite sure that our Creator and Father will say to the wise and virtuous Confucius, to Solon the law-giver, to Pythagoras, Zaleucus, Socrates, and Plato, to the divine Antoninus, good Trajan, and Titus, the flowering of mankind, to Epictetus and so many other model men:[5] "Go, you monsters; go and suffer punishment, limitless in time and intensity, eternal as I am eternal. And you, my beloved, Jean Chatel, Ravaillac, Damiens, Cartouche, etc.,[6] who died according to the prescribed formulas,

share forever at my right hand my empire and my felicity."

You draw back in horror from these words, and since they escaped me, I have no more to say.

Prayer to God

I no longer address myself to men, but to thee, God of all beings, all worlds, and all ages. If indeed it is allowable for feeble creatures, lost in immensity and imperceptible to the rest of the universe, to dare ask anything of Thee who hast given all things, whose decrees are as immutable as they are eternal, deign to look with compassion upon the failings inherent in our nature, and grant that these failings lead us not into calamity.

Thou didst not give us hearts that we should hate each other or hands that we should cut each other's throats. Grant that we may help each other bear the burden of our painful and brief lives; that the slight difference in the clothing with which we cover our puny bodies, in our inadequate tongues, in all our ridiculous customs, in all our imperfect laws, in all our insensate opinions, in all our stations in life so disproportionate in our eyes but so equal in Thy sight, that all these little variations that differentiate the atoms called *man,* may not be the signals for hatred and persecution. . . .

May all men remember that they are brothers; may they hold in horror tyranny that is exercised over souls, just as they hold in execration the brigandage that snatches away by force the fruits of labor and peaceful industry. If the scourge of war is inevitable, let us not hate each other, let us not tear each other apart in the lap of peace; but let us use the brief moment of our existence in blessing in a thousand different tongues, from Siam to California, Thy goodness which has bestowed this moment upon us.

---

[5]These were moralists, enlightened political leaders, and philosophers who had either lived before Christianity or had never become Christians.

[6]Five notorious criminals from Voltaire's day.

An Affirmation of Human Progress

35 • MARQUIS DE CONDORCET, SKETCH OF THE PROGRESS OF THE HUMAN MIND

Throughout history, most human beings have valued tradition and resisted change. Reform of governments and religious institutions was deemed possible, but it typically did not mean going forward to something new, but going back to recapture a lost "golden age." Thinkers who studied the past and contemplated the future concluded that the human condition had always been more or less the same, or that history ran in cycles, or that it was the story of gradual decline from a lost golden age. Only in the West in the eighteenth and nineteenth centuries did intellectuals and much of the general populace come to believe that the past was a burden and that human beings could and would bring about changes that were beneficial, not destructive. In a word, people began to believe in progress.

This belief in progress began in the eighteenth century, when many thinkers became convinced that well-intentioned human beings could employ reason to erase at least some of the cruelties, superstitions, and prejudices that had diminished the human condition in the past. By the end of the century, some went further and developed a theory of progress that saw humanity ascending from ignorance and darkness to a utopian future. The most famous prophet of progress was the Marquis de Condorcet (1743–1794), a mathematician, philosopher, and educational reformer. He supported the French Revolution but, like many moderates, fell afoul of the radical Jacobins and was forced into hiding in July 1793. It was then that he wrote his *Sketch of the Progress of the Human Mind*, which traces human progress in ten stages from the dawn of history to the French Revolution and beyond. Having completed his work in March 1794, he emerged from hiding, was arrested immediately, and was found dead the next morning of unknown causes.

The following excerpts come from "The Ninth Epoch," in which he discusses developments from the mid-seventeenth century to the beginning of the French Revolution, and "The Tenth Epoch," in which he describes the future.

QUESTIONS FOR ANALYSIS

1. What factors, according to Condorcet, have impeded progress in the past?
2. According to Condorcet, scientific achievement was the outstanding feature of humanity's "ninth stage." In what ways did science in this era change human thinking and affect human society?
3. Condorcet is not proud of the Europeans' record in dealing with the peoples of Asia, Africa, and the Americas. What groups does he blame for the Europeans' unenlightened behavior in these regions?
4. Why is Condorcet confident that Europeans will modify their behavior in Asia and Africa? What will be the result? Does Condorcet show any interest in preserving the customs and beliefs of Asians and Africans?
5. According to Condorcet, what caused the oppression of women in the past? Why does he reject such oppression, and what positive results in his view will result from ending it?

Ninth Epoch

From Descartes to the Formation of the French Republic

Until now we have demonstrated the progress of philosophy only in those men who have cultivated, deepened, and perfected it: it now remains to reveal what have been its effects on general opinion, and how reason . . . learned how to preserve itself from the errors into which respect for authority and the imagination have often dragged it: at the same time it destroyed within the general mass of people the prejudices that have afflicted and corrupted the human race for so long a time.

Humanity was finally permitted to boldly proclaim the long ignored right to submit every opinion to reason, that is, to utilize the only instrument given to us for grasping and recognizing the truth. Each human learned with a sort of pride that nature had never destined him to believe the word of others. The superstitions of antiquity and the abasement of reason before the madness of supernatural religion disappeared from society just as they had disappeared from philosophy. . . .

If we were to limit ourselves to showing the benefits derived from the immediate applications of the sciences, or in their applications to man-made devices for the well-being of individuals and the prosperity of nations, we would be making known only a slim part of their benefits. The most important, perhaps, is having destroyed prejudices and re-established human intelligence, which until then had been forced to bend down to false instructions instilled in it by absurd beliefs passed on to the children of each generation by the terrors of superstition and the fear of tyranny. . . .

Tenth Epoch

The Future Progress of the Human Mind

Our hopes for the future of the human species may be reduced to three important points: the destruction of inequality among nations; the progress of equality within nations themselves; and finally, the real improvement of humanity. Should not all the nations of the world approach one day the state of civilization reached by the most enlightened peoples such as the French and the Anglo-Americans? Will not the slavery of nations subjected to kings, the barbarity of African tribes, and the ignorance of savages gradually disappear? Are there on the globe countries whose very nature has condemned them never to enjoy liberty and never exercise their reason?

Can it be doubted that either wisdom or the senseless feuds of the European nations themselves, working with the slow but certain effects of progress in their colonies, will not soon produce the independence of the new world; and that then the European population, spreading rapidly across that immense land, must either civilize or make disappear the savage peoples that now inhabit these vast continents?

If one runs through the history of our undertakings and establishments in Africa and Asia, you will see our commercial monopolies, our treacheries, our bloodthirsty contempt for people of a different color and belief; the insolence of our usurpations; the extravagant missionary activities and intrigues of our priests which destroy their feelings of respect and benevolence that the superiority of our enlightenment and the advantages of our commerce had first obtained. But the moment is approaching, without any doubt, when ceasing to present ourselves to these peoples as tyrants or corrupters, we will become

Source: *Esquisse d'un tableau historique des progrès de l'esprit humain* (Paris: Firmin Didot Frères, 1847), pp. 186–187, 223–225, 229–231, 237–244, 250–251, 255–256, 263–266, 272–276, trans. by James Overfield.

instruments of their improvement and their noble liberators. . . .

> Slavery will be abolished, free trade established on the world's oceans, and European political authority in Asia and Africa ended.

Then the Europeans, limiting themselves to free trade, too knowledgeable of their own rights to show contempt for the rights of others, will respect this independence that until now they have violated with such audacity. Then their settlements, instead of being filled with government favorites . . . who hasten by pillaging and dishonesty to amass fortunes so they can return to Europe to buy honors and titles, will be populated by hard-working men, seeking in these happy climates the affluence that eluded them in their homeland. . . . These settlements of robbers will become colonies of citizens who will plant in Africa and Asia the principles and the example of European liberty, enlightenment, and reason. In place of clergy who carry to these people nothing but the most shameful superstitions and who disgust them and menace them with a new form of domination, one will see men taking their place who are devoted to spreading among the nations useful truths about their happiness, and explaining to them both the concept of their own interest and of their rights. . . .

Thus the day will come when the sun will shine only on free men born knowing no other master but their reason; where tyrants and their slaves, priests and their ignorant, hypocritical writings will exist only in the history books and theaters; where we will only be occupied with mourning their victims and their dupes; when we will maintain an active vigilance by remembering their horrors; when we will learn to recognize and stifle by the force of reason the first seeds of superstition and tyranny, if ever they, dare to appear! . . .

> Condorcet explains how education and scientific knowledge will be made available to all.

If we consider the human creations based on scientific theories, we shall see that their progress can have no limits; that the procedures in constructing them can be improved and simplified just like those of scientific procedures; that new tools, machines, and looms will add every day to the capabilities and skill of humans; they will improve and perfect the precision of their products while decreasing the amount of time and labor needed to produce them. Then the obstacles in the path of this progress will disappear, accidents will be foreseen and prevented, the unhealthful conditions that are due either to the work itself or the climate will be eliminated.

A smaller piece of land will be able to produce commodities of greater usefulness and value than before; greater benefits will be obtained with less waste; the production of the same industrial product will result in less destruction of raw materials and greater durability. We will be able to choose for each type of soil the production of goods that will satisfy the greatest number of wants and with the least amount of labor and expenditure. Thus without any sacrifice, the means of achieving conservation and limiting waste will follow the progress of the art of producing various goods, preparing them, and making them into finished products. Thus . . . each individual will work less but more productively and will be able to better satisfy his needs. . . .

Among the advances of the human mind we should reckon as most important for the general welfare is the complete destruction of those prejudices that have established an inequality of rights between the sexes, an inequality damaging even to the party it favors. One will look in vain for reasons to justify it on the basis of differences in physical make up, the strength of intellect, and moral sensibility. This inequality has no other root cause than the abuse of force, and it is to no purpose to try to excuse it through sophistical arguments. We will show how the abolition of practices condoned by this prejudice will increase the well-being of families and encourage domestic virtues, the prime foundation of all others; how it will favor the progress of education, and especially make it truly universal, partly because it will be extended to both sexes more equitably, and partly because it cannot be truly universal even for males without the cooperation of mothers in families. . . .

The most enlightened people, having seized for themselves the right to control their life and treasure, will slowly come to perceive war as the deadliest plague and the most monstrous of crimes. . . . They will understand that they cannot become conquerors without losing their liberty; that perpetual alliances are the only way to preserve independence; and that they should seek their security, not power. . . .

We may conclude then that the perfectibility of humanity is indefinite. However, until now, we have imagined humanity with the same natural abilities and physical make-up as at the present. How great will our certitude be, and how limitless our hopes, if one were to believe that these natural abilities themselves, this physical make-up, are also capable of improvement? This is the last question we shall consider. . . .

No one can doubt that progress in preventive medicine, the use of healthier food and housing, a way of living that increases strength through exercise without destroying it through excess, and finally, the destruction of the two most persistent causes of deterioration, poverty and excessive wealth, will lengthen for human beings the average life span and assure more good health and a stronger constitution. Clearly, improvements in medical practices . . . , will cause transmittable and contagious diseases to disappear as well as diseases caused by climate, nourishment, and certain vocations. . . . Would it be absurd then to imagine . . . that we will arrive at a time when death will be nothing more than the result of extraordinary accidents or of the gradual destruction of vital forces, and that as a result, the interval between birth and the time of that destruction will no longer have a fixed term? . . .

Finally, can we not also extend the same hopes to the intellectual and moral faculties? . . . Is it not also probable that education, while perfecting these qualities, will also influence, modify, and improve that bodily nature itself? Analogy, analysis of the development of human faculties, and even certain facts seem to prove the reality of such conjectures, which extend even further the limits of our hopes. . . .

How much does this picture of the human species, freed of all chains, released from the empire of blind fate and the enemies of progress, and marching with a firm and sure pace on the path of truth, virtue, and honor, present the philosopher with a scene that consoles him for the errors, crimes, and injustices that still defile the earth and often victimize him? In contemplation of this scene he receives the reward for his efforts on behalf of the advance of reason and the defense of liberty. . . . Such contemplation is a place of refuge where the memories of his persecutors cannot follow him, where living with the thought of humans established in their natural rights and dignity, he forgets the way greed, fear, and envy have tormented and corrupted them. It is there he truly exists with his fellow humans in an Elysium[1] which his reason has created and which his love of humanity adorns with the purest pleasures.

---

[1]In Greek mythology, Elysium, also known as the Elysian Fields on the Isles of the Blessed, was the dwelling place after death of virtuous mortals or those given immortality by divine favor.

Stirrings of Economic Change

Unlike political revolutions, which tend to start suddenly and unfold quickly, revolutions in thought and economic life proceed in small steps and may take many decades to develop fully. This was true of Europe's scientific revolution, which reached a climax with the work of Isaac Newton in the 1680s but began a century and a half earlier when Copernicus and other astronomers first raised questions about the structure of the universe. It is equally true of the Industrial Revolution. Although industrialization occurred mainly in the nineteenth century, its roots go back to the 1700s, when much of the capital for industrialization was raised, much of the infrastructure for industrialization was built, and many of the financial institutions on which businessmen rely—banks and stock markets, for example—developed significantly. In addition, important technological breakthroughs occurred, and new ways of thinking about economic growth and policy were developed. The two selections in this section focus on these last two topics—technology and ideas.

Our first selection is from *An Inquiry into the Nature and Causes of the Wealth of Nations*, published in 1776 by the Scottish writer Adam Smith. The work was groundbreaking firstly because of its new approach to the study of economics. Before Smith, many philosophers, religious writers, and moralists had speculated about specific economic issues such as the causes of inflation; others had discussed the ethical and religious implications of the profit motive, the accumulation of wealth, and the lending of money for interest. In contrast, in *The Wealth of Nations,* Smith systematically analyzed wages, labor, trade, population, rents, and money supply and discussed the implications of his analysis for economic practice and policy. The work's importance also lies in its advocacy of free markets as an engine for economic growth and rising prosperity. Smith attacked guilds for their efforts to stifle competition; internal tariffs for raising the price of food and other commodities; and especially mercantilism for strangling economic growth.

Mercantilism refers to the economic assumptions and policies adopted by many European governments in the seventeenth century to strengthen the state by regulating commerce, manufacturing, and agriculture. A main goal of the mercantilists was to increase the nation's gold and silver supply by exporting more than it imported. To achieve this favorable balance of trade, governments subsidized industries that produced exportable goods, protected native industries from foreign competition through tariffs, and instituted policies that favored their own countries' merchants over foreign competitors. Governments viewed colonies as sources of raw materials and markets for their nation's own manufactures. Smith, in contrast, favored free trade among nations and economic freedom for individuals, making the paradoxical argument that by encouraging individuals to pursue their self-interest, society as a whole benefited through economic growth. Thus, he is viewed as one of the first prophets of capitalism, whose values and assumptions provided the ideological foundation for nineteenth-century industrialization.

Our second selection focuses on the benefits and costs of technological innovation in the early stages of the Industrial Revolution. The invention of the steam engine and the development of new methods for smelting iron, both of which occurred in the 1700s, were key events in the origins of the Industrial Revolution, but inventions relating to the textile industry affected the greatest number of human beings. A labor-intensive, multistep process, the manufacture of finished textiles from raw wool and cotton employed more English people than any economic pursuit other than agriculture. In the eighteenth century, mechanization made many textile workers' jobs superfluous. Notable breakthroughs were John Kay's flying shuttle (1733), which speeded up weaving; Richard Arkwright's water frame (1769), which used water power to spin fine, strong yarns between rollers; James Hargreave's spinning jenny (1770), which enabled one person to spin eight, then sixteen, and finally over one hundred threads of yarn at once; a number of carding and scribbling machines (1750s through 1770s) to prepare raw wool for spinning; Samuel Compton's spinning mule (1779), which combined features of the water frame and jenny; and Edmund Cartwright's power loom (1785), which could be driven by water power or steam engines. Such innovations lowered costs and increased production, but took away jobs for tens of thousands of men, women, and children.

Capitalism's Prophet

36 • ADAM SMITH, THE WEALTH OF NATIONS

Born in 1723 in a Scottish fishing village and educated at the universities of Glasgow and Oxford, Adam Smith taught logic and moral philosophy at the University of Glasgow between 1751 and 1763, served for a time as the private tutor for the son of a Scottish aristocrat, and from 1778 until his death in 1790 served as commissioner of the customs of Scotland. He was an eccentric but likable individual who felt most comfortable in the company of his books and in conversations with other intellectuals. Never having married, he lived his whole life in the house of his mother, who lived to be 90. In 1764 he made his one trip to Europe, where he met Voltaire and other prominent figures of the French Enlightenment. His conversations with the economic thinkers Anne-Robert-Jacques Turgot (1727–1781) and François Quesnay (1694–1774) influenced his views on the sources of national wealth and free trade, topics he examined fully in *The Wealth of Nations*, published in 1776.

QUESTIONS FOR ANALYSIS

1. Smith denies that a nation's wealth consists of the amount of gold and silver it controls. What arguments does he present to defend his position, and what are their implications for trade policy?
2. Smith proposes that each individual, by pursuing his or her own self-interest, promotes the general welfare of society. What examples of this paradox does he provide?

3. What implications does this paradox have for government policy?
4. What groups in society would you expect to be most enthusiastic about Smith's ideas? Why? What groups might be expected to oppose them?

Self-Interest and the Free Market

This division of labor,[1] from which so many advantages are derived, is not originally the effect of any human wisdom, which foresees and intends that general opulence to which it gives occasion. It is the necessary, though very slow and gradual consequence of a certain propensity in human nature which has in view no such extensive utility; the propensity to truck,[2] barter, and exchange one thing for another.

. . . It is common to all men, and to be found in no other race of animals, which seem to know neither this nor any other species of contracts. . . . Nobody ever saw a dog make a fair and deliberate exchange of one bone for another with another dog. Nobody ever saw one animal by its gestures and natural cries signify to another, this is mine, that yours; I am willing to give this for that. . . . In almost every other race of animals each individual, which it is grown up to maturity, is entirely independent, and in its natural state has occasion for the assistance of no other living creature. But man has almost constant occasion for the help of his brethren, and it is in vain for him to expect it from their benevolence only. He will be more likely to prevail if he can interest their self-love in his favor, and show them that it is for their own advantage to do for him what he requires of them. Whoever offers to another a bargain of any kind, proposes to do this. Give me that which I want, and you shall have this which you want, is the meaning of every such offer; and it is in this manner that we obtain from one another the far greater part of those good offices which we stand in need of. It is not from the benevolence of the butcher, the brewer, or the baker, that we expect our dinner, but from their regard to their own interest. We address ourselves, not to their humanity but to their self-love, and never talk to them of our own necessities but of their advantages. . . .

Prices and the Free Market

. . . It is the interest of all those who employ their land, labor, or stock,[3] in bringing any commodity to market, that the quantity never should exceed the effectual demand; and it is the interest of all other people that it never should fall short of that demand.

If at any time it exceeds the effectual demand, some of the component parts of its price must be paid below their natural rate. If it is rent,[4] the interest of the landlords will immediately prompt them to withdraw a part of their land; and if it is wages or profit, the interest of the laborers in the one case, and of their employers in the other, will prompt them to withdraw a part of their labor or stock from this employment. The quantity brought to market will soon be no more than sufficient to supply the effectual demand. All the different parts of its price will rise to their natural rate, and the whole price to its natural price.

If, on the contrary, the quantity brought to market should at any time fall short of the effectual

Source: Adam Smith, *An Inquiry into the Nature and Causes of the Wealth of Nations* (Hartford, CT: Cooke and Hale, 1818), vol. 7, pp. 10–12, 40, 43, 299–304, 316, 317, 319, 330, 331.

[1]This section follows Smith's discussion of the *division of labor.* He uses this term in reference to economic specialization, both in terms of different professions and in terms of the separate tasks carried out by different individuals in the process of manufacturing or preparing commodities for the market.

[2]A synonym for barter.

[3]Money or capital invested or available for investment or trading.

[4]In this sense, the cost of land; payments made by tenants to their landlord.

demand, some of the component parts of its price must rise above their natural rate. If it is rent, the interest of all other landlords will naturally prompt them to prepare more land for the raising of this commodity; if it is wages or profit, the interest of all other laborers and dealers will soon prompt them to employ more labor and stock in preparing and bringing it to market. The quantity brought thither will soon be sufficient to supply the effectual demand. All the different parts of its price will soon sink to their natural rate, and the whole price to its natural price. . . .

The monopolists, by keeping the market constantly under-stocked, by never fully supplying the effectual demand, sell their commodities much above the natural price, and raise their emoluments,[5] whether they consist in wages or profit, greatly above their natural rate.

The price of monopoly is upon every occasion the highest which can be got. The natural price, or the price of free competition, on the contrary, is the lowest which can be taken, not upon every occasion, indeed, but for any considerable time together. The one is upon every occasion the highest which can be squeezed out of the buyers, or which, it is supposed, they will consent to give: The other is the lowest which the sellers can commonly afford to take, and at the same time continue their business.

The exclusive privileges of corporations, statutes of apprenticeship,[6] and all those laws which restrain . . . the competition to a smaller number than might otherwise go into them, have the same tendency, though in a less degree. They are a sort of enlarged monopolies, and may frequently, for ages together and in whole classes.

Mercantalist Fallacies

. . . A rich country, in the same manner as a rich man, is supposed to be a country abounding in money; and to heap up gold and silver in any country is supposed to be the readiest way to enrich it. . . .

In consequence of these popular notions, all the different nations of Europe have studied, though to little purpose, every possible means of accumulating gold and silver in their respective countries. Spain and Portugal, the proprietors of the principal mines which supply Europe with those metals, have either prohibited their exportation under the severest penalties, or subjected it to a considerable duty. The like prohibition seems anciently to have [been] made a part of the policy of most other European nations. When those countries became commercial, the merchants found this prohibition, upon many occasions, extremely inconvenient. . . .

They represented [stated forcefully], first, that the exportation of gold and silver in order to purchase foreign goods, did not always diminish the quantity of those metals in the kingdom. . . .

They represented, secondly, that this prohibition could not hinder the exportation of gold and silver, which, on account of the smallness of their bulk in proportion to their value, could easily be smuggled abroad. . . .

Those arguments . . . were solid. . . . But they were sophistical in supposing, that either to preserve or to augment the quantity of those metals required more the attention of government, than to preserve or to augment the quantity of any other useful commodities, which the freedom of trade, without any such attention, never fails to supply in the proper quantity. . . .

A country that has no mines of its own must undoubtedly draw its gold and silver from foreign countries, in the same manner as one that has no vineyards of its own must draw its wines. It does not seem necessary, however, that the attention of government should be more turned towards the one than towards the other object. A country that

---

[5]The returns from employment, usually in the form of compensation.

[6]Laws that restricted the number of individuals who could receive training in trades through apprenticeship.

has wherewithal to buy wine, will always get the wine which it has occasion for; and a country that has wherewithal to buy gold and silver, will never be in want of those metals. They are to be bought for a certain price like all other commodities, and as they are the price of all other commodities, so all other commodities are the price of those metals. We trust with perfect security that the freedom of trade, without any attention of government, will always supply us with the wine which we have occasion for: and we may trust with equal security that it will always supply us with all the gold and silver which we can afford to purchase or to employ, either in circulating our commodities, or in other uses.

• • •

By restraining, either by high duties, or by absolute prohibitions, the importation of such goods from foreign countries as can be produced at home, the monopoly of the home market is more or less secured to the domestic industry employed in producing them. . . . But whether it tends either to increase the general industry of the society, or to give it the most advantageous direction, is not, perhaps, altogether so evident. . . .

Every individual is continually exerting himself to find out the most advantageous employment for whatever capital he can command. It is his own advantage, indeed, and not that of the society, which he has in view. But the study of his own advantage, naturally, or rather necessarily, leads him to prefer that employment which is most advantageous to the society.

First, every individual endeavors to employ his capital as near home as he can, and consequently as much as he can in the support of domestic industry, provided always that he can thereby obtain the ordinary, or not a great deal less than the ordinary, profits of stock.

Secondly, every individual who employs his capital in the support of domestic industry, necessarily endeavors so to direct that industry, that its produce may be of the greatest possible value. . . .

As every individual, therefore, endeavors . . . both to employ his capital in the support of domestic industry, and so to direct that industry that its produce may be of the greatest value, every individual necessarily labors to render the annual revenue of the society as great as he can. He generally, indeed, neither intends to promote the public interest, nor knows how much he is promoting it. By preferring the support of domestic to that of foreign industry, he intends only his own security; and by directing that industry in such a manner as its produce may be of the greatest value, he intends only his own gain, and he is in this, as in many other cases, led by an invisible hand to promote an end which was no part of his intention. . . . By pursuing his own interest he frequently promotes that of the society more effectually than when he really intends to promote it. . . .

To give the monopoly of the home market to the produce of domestic industry, in any particular art or manufacture, is in some measure to direct private people in what manner they ought to employ their capital, and must, in almost all cases, be either a useless or a hurtful regulation. If the produce of domestic [industry] can be brought there as cheap as that of foreign industry, the regulation is evidently useless. If it cannot, it must generally be hurtful. It is the maxim of every prudent master of a family, never to attempt to make at home what it will cost him more to make than to buy. . . .

What is prudence in the conduct of every private family, can scarce be folly in that of a great kingdom. If a foreign country can supply us with a commodity cheaper than we ourselves can make it, better buy it of them with some part of the produce of our own industry, employed in a way in which we have some advantage. . . .

To expect, indeed, that the freedom of trade should ever be entirely restored in Great Britain, is as absurd as to expect that an Oceana or Utopia should ever be established in it. Not only the prejudices of the public, but what is much more unconquerable, the private interests of many individuals, irresistibly oppose it. . . .

The undertaker of a great manufacture, who, by the home markets being suddenly laid open to the competition of foreigners, should be obliged to abandon his trade, would no doubt suffer very considerably. That part of his capital which had usually been employed in purchasing materials and in paying his workmen might, without much difficulty perhaps, find another employment. But that part of it which was fixed in workhouses, and in the instruments of trade, could scarce be disposed of without considerable loss. The equitable regard, therefore, to his interest requires that changes of this kind should never be introduced suddenly, but slowly, gradually, and after a very long warning.

The Costs and Benefits of Machines

37 • PETITION OF THE YORKSHIRE CLOTH WORKERS (1786) AND PROCLAMATION OF THE LEEDS CLOTH MERCHANTS (1791)

Beginning in the 1500s, the manufacture of woolen cloth was England's major source of exports and non-agricultural employment. It remained so until the eighteenth century, when the growth of the cotton industry and the diversification of the nation's economy diluted its importance. Nonetheless, in the mid-1700s, anywhere from 800,000 to 1.5 million English people were employed in turning raw wool into usable textiles. In the western counties of Somerset, Wiltshire, and Gloucestershire, cloth was produced by the "putting out" system, in which a gentleman clothier typically purchased and dyed the wool himself and then "put out" the rest of the work to a series of rural households in each of which a specific task was performed: carding and scribbling (preparing the wool for spinning); spinning the wool into yarn; weaving the yarn into fabric; fulling (softening and tightening the weave by soaking, heating, and pounding the cloth); and finally finishing (the process of singeing, brushing, or shearing the fabric to achieve the desired degree of softness and smoothness). After finishing, the clothier who had moved along the process from household to household would have a product to sell.

In Yorkshire, another important center for wool manufacturing in the north, a different system emerged. Here, the work was carried on by "master manufacturers," who purchased small quantities of wool, usually on a weekly basis, and then in their own houses or outbuildings, assisted by their wives, children, and anywhere from two to a dozen journeymen, carded, spun, and wove the cloth. After weaving, the cloth was taken to a fulling mill for finishing, and then sold at a cloth hall in a nearby town or city. In both regions, wool manufacturing was a rural industry, carried on in households that also were involved in farming. The technology was simple—hand carders, scribbling frames, spinning wheels, and hand looms. Fulling mills depended on water or horse power, but otherwise the energy was supplied by the craftspersons themselves.

The introduction of machinery was a challenge to the lives of textile workers throughout England. In Yorkshire and the Western counties, the first flying shuttle was introduced in the 1760s and the first spinning jennies and scribbling mills in the 1770s, with power looms coming later, in the 1790s. Although such devices were not at first introduced in great numbers, they were met with strong resistance. In 1776, a crowd in Shepton Market attacked a building in which spinning jennies had been installed, smashed the machines, and then entered one of the owners' homes, where they destroyed his furniture and drank two casks of his beer. Troops were called out and one rioter was killed. Machine smashing peaked in 1811 and 1812, when "Luddites," followers of legendary "King Ludd," rampaged through textile-producing regions burning homes and smashing machines. The authorities answered in kind, and in the 1810s, violence directed against the new machines finally abated.

The authors of our first excerpt were not ready for violence. Instead, they published an open letter "signed on behalf of thousands" to the owners of scribbling mills around Leeds, the largest city in the Yorkshire region. It was published in two newspapers, the *Leeds Mercury* and the *Leeds Intelligencer*, in 1786. The second excerpt is from a proclamation issued as a broadsheet five years later by the "cloth merchants of Leeds."

QUESTIONS FOR ANALYSIS

1. According to the authors of the workers' proclamation, how will the introduction of machines affect their opportunities for employment?
2. In their view, what will be the broader implications of mechanization?
3. According to the workers, why should the owners of machinery agree to end the use of the new technology?
4. According to the Leeds cloth merchants, what would result if the use of machinery was curtailed? Conversely, what benefits will result from its continued use?

Petition of Yorkshine Cloth Workers, 1786

TO the Merchants, Clothiers and all such as wish well to the Staple [Textile] Manufactory of this Nation.

The Humble ADDRESS and PETITION of Thousands, who labour in the Cloth Manufactory.

SHEWETH, That the Scribbling-Machines have thrown thousands of your petitioners out of employ, whereby they are brought into great distress, and are not able to procure a maintenance for their families, and deprived them of the opportunity of bringing up their children to labour: We have therefore to request, that prejudice and self-interest may be laid aside, and that you may pay that attention to the following facts. . . .

The number of Scribbling-Machines extending about seventeen miles south-west of LEEDS, exeed all belief, being no less than *one hundred and seventy!* and as each machine will do as much work in twelve hours, as ten men can in that time do by hand, and they working night-and day, one machine will do as much work in one day as would otherwise employ twenty men . . . and as it may be supposed the number of machines in all the other quarters together, nearly equal those in the South-West, full four thousand men are left to shift for a living how they can, and must of course fall to the Parish.[1] If not timely relieved. Allowing one boy to be bound apprentice from each family out of work, eight thousand hands are deprived of the opportunity of getting a livelihood.

Leeds Woollen Industry, 1780–1820 (Leeds: Publications of the Thoresby Society, vol. 32, 1931).

[1]To accept poor relief.

Source: Cloth workers' petition: *Leeds Mercury*, June 13, 1786, and Cloth Merchants' Proclamation: Broadsheet originally printed in 1791. Taken from W. B. Crump, The

We therefore hope, that the feelings of humanity will lead those who have it in their power to prevent the use of those machines, to give every discouragement they can to what has a tendency so prejudicial to their fellow-creatures.

This is not all, the injury to the Cloth is great, in so much that in Frizing [part of the finishing process], instead of leaving a nap[2] upon the Cloth, the wool is drawn but, and the Cloth is left thread-bare.

Many more evils we could enumerate, but we would hope, that the sensible part of mankind, who are not biased by interest, must see the dreadful tendancy of their continuance; a depopulation must be the consequence; trade being then lost, the landed interest [large landowners] will have no other satisfaction but that of being *last devoured.*

How are those men, thus thrown out of employ to provide for their families—and what are they to put their children apprentice to, that the rising generation may have something to keep them at work, in order that they may not be like vagabonds strolling about in idleness? Some say, Begin and learn some other business—Suppose we do; who will maintain our families, whilst we undertake the arduous task; and when we have learned it, how do we know we shall be any better for all our pains; for by the time we have served our second apprenticeship, another machine may arise, which may take away that business also. . . .

But what are our children to do; are they to be brought up in idleness? Indeed as things are, it is no wonder to hear of so many executions; for our parts, though we may be thought illiterate men, our conceptions are, that bringing children up to industry, and keeping them employed, is the way to keep them from falling into those times, which an idle habit naturally leads to.

These things impartially considered will we hope, be strong advocates in our favour, and we conceive that men of sense, religion and humanity, will be satisfied of the reasonableness, as well as necessity of this address, and that their own feelings will urge them to espouse the cause of us and our families—

Proclamation of the Leeds Cloth Merchants (1791)

The Cloth Merchants of Leeds

BEING informed that various Kinds of MACHINERY, for the better and more expeditious DRESSING OF WOOLLEN-CLOTH, have been lately invented, that many such Machines are already made and set to work in different Parts of this County, and that great Numbers more are contracted for, . . . [the cloth merchants] thought it necessary to meet together on the Eighteenth of October, to take into their most serious Consideration what Steps were needful to be taken, to prevent the Merchants and Cloth-Dressers in other Parts, from diminishing the Staple Trade of this Town, by the Enjoyment of superior Implements in their Business.

At a time when the People, engaged in every other Manufacture in the Kingdom, are exerting themselves to bring their Work to Market at reduced Prices, which can alone be effected by the Aid of Machinery, it certainly is not necessary that the Cloth Merchants of Leeds, who depend chiefly on a Foreign Demand, where they have for Competitors the Manufacturers of other Nations, whose Taxes are few, and whose manual Labour is only Half the Price it bears here, should have Occasion to defend a Conduct, which has for its Aim the Advantage of the Kingdom in general, and of the Cloth Trade in particular; yet anxious to prevent Misrepresentations, which have usually attended the Introduction of the most useful Machines, they wish to remind the Inhabitants of this Town, of the Advantages derived to every flourishing Manufacture from the Application of Machinery; they instance [to cite as an example] that of Cotton

---

[2]The raised surface of a piece of cloth.

in particular, which in its internal and foreign Demand is nearly alike to our own, and has in a few Years by the Means of Machinery advanced to its present Importance, and is still increasing.

If then by the Use of Machines, the Manufacture of Cotton, an Article which we import, and are supplied with from other Countries, and which can every where be procured on equal Terms, has met with such amazing Success, may not greater Advantages be reasonably expected from cultivating to the utmost the Manufacture of Wool, the Produce of our own Island, an Article in Demand in all Countries, and almost the universal Cloathing of Mankind?

In the Manufacture of Woollens, the Scribbling Mill, the Spinning Frame, and the Flying Shuttle, have reduced manual Labour nearly One-third, and each of them at its first Introduction carried an Alarm to the Work People, yet each has contributed to advance the Wages and to increase the Trade, so that if an Attempt was now made to deprive us of the Use of them, there is no Doubt, but every Person engaged in the Business, would exert himself to defend them.

From these Premises, we the undersigned Merchants, think it a Duty we owe to ourselves, to the Town of Leeds, and to the Nation at large, to declare that we will protect and support the free Use of the proposed Improvements in Cloth-Dressing, by every legal Means in our Power; and if after all, contrary to our Expectations, the Introduction of Machinery should for a Time occasion a Scarcity of Work in the Cloth Dressing Trade, we have unanimously agreed to give a Preference to such Workmen as are now settled Inhabitants of this Parish, and who give no Opposition to the present Scheme.

Appleby & Sawyer
Bernard Bischoff & Sons
[and 59 other names]

The Era of the French Revolution and Napoleon

Political revolutions involve more than changing leaders or replacing one ruling faction with another. Revolutions bring about fundamental changes in the political order itself, often resulting in the transfer of power from one social group to another. Moreover, they affect more than just politics: revolutions reshape legal systems, education, religious life, economic practices, and social relationships. Because revolutions occur in societies already undergoing intellectual, economic, and social transformations, it is not surprising that history's first revolutions took place in Western Europe and the Americas in the seventeenth through nineteenth centuries, when economic change undermined old social hierarchies and the emergence of new secular values weakened the foundations of divine right monarchies and privileged churches.

The events that unfolded in France between 1789 and 1799 were not the Western world's first political revolutions. The clash in England between royalists and parliamentarians in the 1640s and 1650s, the overthrow of James II in 1688–1689, and the successful rebellion of the thirteen American colonies against British rule—respectively the Puritan, Glorious, and American revolutions—all occurred earlier.

No previous revolution, however, came close to matching the impact and importance of the revolution in France. More social groups participated, and it inspired more people around the globe. More importantly, the French Revolution went beyond the principles of constitutionalism and representative government. It championed the democratic idea that every person, irrespective of social standing, should have a voice in government and that all people should be treated equally before the law. It also aroused the first nationalist movements in Europe and inspired disaffected groups throughout the world to seek political and social change through revolution.

The French Revolution began because of a problem that has plagued rulers since the beginning of organized government—King Louis XVI (r. 1774–1792) and his ministers could not balance the government's budget. Having exhausted every other solution, the king, in 1789 agreed to convene a meeting of the Estates General, France's representative assembly, which had last met in 1614. He hoped it would solve the government's fiscal plight by approving new taxes, while the nobility sensed it would be an opportunity to strengthen their role in government. For both the king and nobility, the calling of the Estates General had unexpected results: the nobility lost its privileges, and the king lost power and, ultimately, his life when in 1793 a revolutionary assembly judged him a traitor and ordered his execution.

Neither Louis nor the nobles had comprehended the depth of the French people's disgust with royal absolutism and aristocratic privilege. Nor had they sensed the degree to which the Enlightenment and the English and American revolutions had committed the people to fundamental change. Having convened in May 1789, the Estates General transformed itself into a National Assembly, and within months, it replaced the laws and institutions of the Old Regime with a new political order based on constitutionalism, equality, and natural rights.

The Principles of the French Revolution

38 • DECLARATION OF THE RIGHTS OF MAN AND OF THE CITIZEN

The Estates General convened at Versailles on May 5, 1789. After six weeks of wrangling over voting procedures, in mid-June, representatives of the Third Estate (commoners), along with a handful of clergy and nobles, broke away to form a National Assembly and pledged to continue meeting until they wrote a constitution for France. On June 27, the king gave his grudging approval to the new assembly and ordered all representatives of the clergy and nobility to join its deliberations. The revolution was under way.

Among the National Assembly's most notable achievements was the approval of the Declaration of the Rights of Man and of the Citizen on August 26, 1789. Drawing on the principles of English constitutionalism, the American Revolution, and the Enlightenment, this document summarizes the original political and social goals of the French Revolution.

QUESTIONS FOR ANALYSIS

1. In what ways does the Declaration limit the power of the Crown and the authority of government?
2. According to the Declaration, what rights and responsibilities does citizenship entail?
3. What does the Declaration state about the origin and purpose of law?
4. How does the concept of rights in the Declaration differ from the concept of rights in the English Bill of Rights (source 32)?

The representatives of the people of France, empowered to act as a national assembly, taking into consideration that ignorance, oblivion, or scorn of the rights of man are the only cause of public misery and the corruption of government, have resolved to state in a solemn declaration the natural, inalienable, and sacred rights of man, so that this declaration, continually offered to all the members of society, may forever recall them to their rights and duties; so that the actions of the legislative and executive power, able to be compared at every instant to the goal of any political institution, may be more respected; so that the demands of the citizens, from now on based on straightforward and incontestable principles, will revolve around the maintenance of the constitution and the happiness of everyone.

Consequently, the National Assembly recognizes and declares, in the presence and under the auspices of the Supreme Being, the following rights of man and citizen:

Article 1. Men are born and remain free and equal in rights; social distinctions can be established only for the common benefit.

2. The goal of every political association is the conservation of the natural and indefeasible rights of man; these rights are liberty, property, security, and resistance to oppression.

3. The source of all sovereignty is located essentially in the nation; no body, no individual can exercise authority which does not emanate from it expressly.

4. Liberty consists in being able to do anything that does not harm another. Thus the exercise of the natural rights of each man has no limits except those which assure to other members of society the enjoyment of these same rights; these limits can be determined only by law.

5. The law has the right to prohibit only those actions harmful to society. All that is not prohibited by the law cannot be hindered, and no one can be forced to do what it does not order.

6. The law is the expression of the general will; all citizens have the right to concur personally or through their representatives in its formation; it must be the same for everyone, whether it protects or punishes. All citizens, being equal in its eyes, are equally admissible to all honors, offices, and public employments, according to their abilities and without any distinction other than those of their virtues and talents.

7. No man can be accused, arrested, or detained except in instances determined by the law, and according to the practices which it has prescribed. Those who solicit, draw up, carry out, or have carried out arbitrary orders must be punished; but any citizen summoned or seized by virtue of the law must obey instantly; he renders himself guilty by resisting.

Source: "Declaration of the Rights of Man and of the Citizen," in Buchez and Roux, *Histoire parlementaire de la Révolution française* (Paris: Librarie Pauhn, 1834), vol. 11, pp. 404–406.

8. The law must establish only penalties that are strictly and plainly necessary, and no one can be punished except in virtue of a law established and published prior to the offense and legally applied.

9. Every man being presumed innocent until he has been declared guilty, if it is judged indispensable to arrest him, all harshness that is not necessary for making secure his person must be severely limited by the law.

10. No one may be disturbed because of his opinions, even religious, provided that their public manifestation does not disturb the public order established by law.

11. The free communication of thoughts and opinions is one of the most precious rights of man: every citizen can therefore freely speak, write, and print, except he is answerable for abuses of this liberty in instances determined by the law.

12. The guaranteeing of the rights of man and citizen requires a public force; this force is therefore instituted for the advantage of everyone, and not for the private use of those to whom it is entrusted.

13. For the maintenance of the public force, and for the expenses of administration, a tax supported in common is indispensable; it must be apportioned among all citizens on grounds of their capacities to pay.

14. All citizens have the right to determine for themselves or through their representatives the need for taxation of the public, to consent to it freely, to investigate its use, and to determine its rate, basis, collection, and duration.

15. Society has the right to demand an accountability from every public agent of his management.

16. Any society in which guarantees of rights are not assured nor the separation of powers determined has no constitution.

17. Property being an inviolable and sacred right, no one may be deprived of it except when public necessity, legally determined, requires it, and on condition of a just and predetermined compensation.

Nationalism and Revolution in France

39 • DECREE FOR PROCLAIMING THE LIBERTY AND SOVEREIGNTY OF ALL PEOPLES; PROPOSAL FOR THE LEVÉE EN MASSE; REPORT OF THE COMMITTEE OF PUBLIC SAFETY ON DRAFTING POETS AND CITIZENS FOR THE CAUSE OF REVOLUTION; REPORT OF THE COMMITTEE OF PUBLIC SAFETY ON REVOLUTIONARY EDUCATION

Nationalism combines dedication to the interests, purposes, and well-being of one's nation-state and a sense of belonging to a larger national community that shares common values, traditions, and purposes. This powerful ideology emerged only in the 1790s, during the first years of the French Revolution, when the French people transformed themselves from subjects to citizens by abolishing monarchy and establishing a regime based on equality and popular sovereignty. For millions of French, *la patrie,* or the fatherland, became more than their ancestral territory: it was their spiritual homeland and a beacon of liberty and equality for which citizens were willing to sacrifice and soldiers were prepared to die.

When war broke out in April 1792 between France and antirevolutionary Austria and Prussia, previously apathetic Frenchmen eagerly volunteered to serve in the army, especially after the enemy pushed across the French frontier and threatened Paris. The French repulsed the Austro-Prussian threat and, in the fall of 1792, pushed into German territory to the east and the Austrian Netherlands to the north. At that point, the newly elected National Convention, having voted the execution of Louis XVI in September, turned the war into an ideological crusade by pledging aid to all peoples "who wish to recover their liberty." In its Decree for Proclaiming the Liberty and Sovereignty of All Peoples of December 15, 1792 (first excerpt), the Convention ordered its generals to implement the full program of the revolution in conquered territories.

In 1793, however, disaster again threatened. With new enemies, including Britain, Holland, and Spain, and reversals on every front, the Committee of Public Safety, the twelve-man committee that had taken over the executive functions of government, took action. In August, it proposed a decree (second excerpt) that ordered a program of national mobilization. Approved by the Convention on August 23, the *levée en masse* permanently requisitioned all French people to protect the *patrie* and its revolution by aiding the military effort. Despite some resistance, the *levée* resulted in an army of 1,169,000 within a year; although only about 800,000 troops were trained and equipped for battle, this still was the largest army Europe had ever seen. The army was unique in other ways. The fighting men were largely citizen-soldiers committed to their cause and country, not indifferent mercenaries or unwilling recruits; officers won their commissions on merit, not through purchase or privilege.

Throughout the fighting, the Committee of Public Safety made efforts to maintain the nation's fervor by ordering schools to instill patriotism in their students and by sponsoring patriotic clubs, festivals, ceremonies, music, theatrical productions, and monuments. The third excerpt describes a plan to enlist France's poets on behalf of the revolution. The fourth and last excerpt describes a plan to found a School of Mars (the Roman god of war), a special school to train elite sixteen- and seventeen-year-old boys for service to the revolution.

QUESTIONS FOR ANALYSIS

1. How do these various decrees and proposals characterize France and its mission?
2. According to these documents, what principles does the French Revolution represent?
3. How do these documents represent France's prerevolutionary government and France's foreign enemies?
4. What does the French fatherland (*patrie*) provide for its citizens? What does it expect in return?
5. Do these edicts and proposals represent what you understand to be "propaganda"? Why or why not?

Decree for Proclaiming the Liberty and Sovereignty of All Peoples (December 15, 1792)

The National Convention, . . . faithful to the principles of the sovereignty of the people . . . and wishing to determine the rules to be followed by generals of the armies of the Republic in the countries where they shall carry its arms, decrees:

In the countries which are or shall be occupied by the armies of the Republic, the generals shall proclaim at once, in the name of the French nation, the sovereignty of the people, the suppression of all the established authorities and of the existing imposts and taxes, the abolition of the tithe, of feudalism, of seigniorial rights, . . . of real and personal servitude, of the privileges of hunting and fishing, of *corvées,* of the nobility, and generally of all privileges.[1] . . .

The French nation declares that it will treat as enemies the people who, refusing liberty and equality, or renouncing them, may wish to preserve, recall, or deal with the prince and the privileged estates;[2] it promises . . . not to subscribe to any treaty, and not to lay down its arms until after the establishment of the sovereignty and independence of the people whose territory the troops of the Republic have entered upon and who shall have adopted the principles of equality, and established a free and popular government.

Proposal for the Levée En Masse (August 23, 1793)

Let us state a great truth: liberty has become the creditor of all citizens. Some owe it their labor, others their wealth, some their counsel, others the strength of their arms; all owe it the blood which flows in their veins. Thus all the French, men and women alike, people of all ages, are summoned by the *Patrie* to defend liberty. All physical and moral faculties, all political and economic means, belong to it by right. . . . Let everyone take up his post; let everyone behave as he should in this national and military outpouring that the ending of the campaign demands of us, and all will soon be proud that they had worked together to save the *Patrie.* . . .

Young men will fight, young men are called to conquer. Married men will forge arms, transport military baggage and guns and will prepare food supplies. Women, who finally are to take their rightful place in the revolution and follow their true destiny, will forget their everyday tasks: their delicate hands will work at making clothes for soldiers; they will make tents and they will extend their tender care to shelters where the defenders of the *Patrie* will receive the help that their wounds require. Children will make lint of old cloth. It is for them that we fight: children, . . . destined to gather all the fruits of the revolution, will raise their pure hands toward the skies. And old men, performing their missions again, as

---

Source: (1) From Leo Gershoy, ed., *The Era of the French Revolution 1789–1799,* Van Nostrand, 1957, pp. 152, 156, 157, 161, 162, and 163. Reprinted with permission of Krieger Publishing Company. (2) Translated from original text: Rapport et décrêt, du 23 août, l'an II de la République, sur la requisition civique des jeunes citoyens pour la defense de la Patrie (Paris: 1793). (3) Translated from original text in F. A. Aulard, *Recueil des actes du Comite de salut public, avec la correspondance officielle des representants en mission et le registre du Conseil executif provisoire* (Paris: Imprimerie nationale, 1889–1951) XIII, 546. (4) Translated from *Rapport fait*

à la Convention nationale . . . dans la séance de du 13 prairial (Paris: 1794).

[1] In other words, generals were charged with imposing on conquered territories what already had been accomplished by the National Assembly in 1789—the abolition of "feudalism." This meant the end of the privileges of noble and ecclesiastical landowners, including a variety of payments and unpaid labor (*corvée service*) owed by peasants to their lords and certain other privileges, such as exclusive hunting and fishing rights on the estate.

[2] The privileged estates are the clergy and the nobility.

in the past, will be guided to the public squares of cities where they will inspire the courage of young warriors and preach the doctrines of hate for kings and the unity of the Republic.

Report of the Committee of Public Safety on Drafting Poets and Citizens for the Cause of Revolution (May 16, 1794)

The Committee of Public Safety summons poets to celebrate the principal events of the French Revolution, to compose hymns and poems and republican dramas, to make known the heroic deeds of the soldiers of liberty, the courage and loyalty of republicans, and the victories gained by French arms. It also summons citizens who cultivate literature to preserve for posterity the most noteworthy facts and great epochs in the rebirth of the French people, to give to history that firm and stern character which befits the annals of a great people engaged in winning the liberty which all the tyrants of Europe are attacking. It bids them to . . . inject republican morality into works intended for public instruction, while the Committee will be preparing for the Convention a type of national award to be decreed for their labors, and the date and form of the competition.

Report of the Committee of Public Safety on Revolutionary Education (June 1, 1794)

What is involved here is the procedure that must be followed quickly to rear truly republican defenders of the *Patrie* and to revolutionize the youth as we have revolutionized the armies. . . .

. . . The young man of sixteen, seventeen, or seventeen and a half, is best prepared to receive a republican education. Nature's work is accomplished. At that moment the *Patrie* asks each citizen: What will you do for me? What means will

you employ to defend my unity and my laws, my territory and my independence?

The Convention gives its reply to the *Patrie* today, a School of Mars is going to open its doors. Three thousand young citizens, the strongest, the most intelligent and the most commendable in conduct, are going to attend this new establishment. Three thousand children of honorable parents are going to devote themselves to shared tasks, to fashion themselves for military service. They will come from the heart of the new generation . . . to dedicate their nightly toil and their blood to their country. . . .

Love for the *Patrie,* this pure and generous sentiment which knows no sacrifice that it cannot make . . . ; love for the *Patrie* which was only a myth in the monarchies and which has filled the annals of the Republic with heroism and virtue, will become the ruling passion of the pupils of the School of Mars. . . .

In founding this outstanding revolutionary establishment, the National Convention ought thus to address the families of . . . the young citizens whom it calls to the School of Mars: "Citizens, for too long has ignorance dwelt in the countryside and the workshops; for too long fanaticism and tyranny have prevailed over the convictions of young citizens to enslave them or arrest their development. It is not for slaves or mercenaries to nurture free men; the *Patrie* itself today assumes this important function, which it will never relinquish to prejudice, deviousness, and aristocracy. Loyalty to your own families must end when the great family calls you. The Republic leaves to parents the guidance of your first years, but as soon as your intelligence develops, it loudly proclaims the right it has over you. You are born for the Republic and not to be the pride of family despotism or its victims. It takes you at that happy age when your ardent feelings are directed to virtue and respond naturally to enthusiasm for the good of and love of the *Patrie.*"

Images of the Emperor: Napoleon

40 • JACQUES-LOUIS DAVID, NAPOLEON CROSSING THE ALPS AND NAPOLEON IN HIS STUDY

Napoleon Bonaparte, who between 1799 and 1815 ruled France as first consul, first consul for life, and finally as emperor, is a prime example of how the French Revolution provided opportunities for men of talent and ambition. Born into the minor nobility of Corsica shortly after the island's annexation by France, his military schooling in France and his formidable intelligence would have done him little good in France's pre-1789 army, where birth, wealth, and connections determined promotions. But when many aristocratic, antirevolutionary officers left France in the early 1790s, Bonaparte became a general while still in his twenties and, after two brilliant campaigns in Italy against the Austrians and an extraordinary invasion of Egypt, a national hero.

In the late 1790s, France needed heroes. Under the control of the five-man executive board known as the Directory, the government had sought to maintain a moderate republican regime after Jacobin rule had collapsed in 1794. Unloved by committed democrats and monarchists alike, the Directory was plagued by inflation, corruption, and military setbacks. In 1799, Napoleon and a small group of politicians engineered a *coup d'état* that replaced the Directory with a regime known as the Consulate. Napoleon began as first consul, but in 1804, at age 35, he became emperor.

Napoleon promoted himself as a supporter and savior of the revolution, but few historians agree with his self-assessment. Although in sympathy with the principles of legal equality and religious freedom, he subverted representative government and respected individual liberties only when it suited his purposes. His government eliminated free speech, not just by censoring newspapers, plays, art, classroom instruction, and books, but also by using all of them as instruments of propaganda.

Napoleon's use of art as a means of self-promotion took several forms. He generously supported the art museum established at the Louvre, a royal palace that had in the 1790s been turned into a public museum for the display of royal and confiscated émigré art. He allocated money to upgrade the museum and filled it with works taken from collections in the Vatican, Florence, and Egypt to remind viewers of his conquests. In 1803, the museum at the Louvre was named the Musée Napoléon, by which time it was a venue for the display of many paintings that centered on the emperor. Most of them were paid for with government funds and commissioned by Napoleon himself; even for those commissioned by private individuals, Napoleon had a say about their content. The paintings included many portrayals of his battlefield victories, but since Napoleon wanted to be known as more than a great general, many of them depicted him in other roles—as the defender of the revolution, the sage statesman, the champion of science and progress, the enlightened lawgiver, and the man of destiny ordained to introduce a new European order based on reason.

The two paintings we have included are both by Jacques-Louis David (1748–1825), the most prominent painter of his age and an ardent supporter of the Revolution. As a member of the Convention, he voted for the execution of King Louis XVI (causing his royalist wife to divorce him) and organized dozens of revolutionary ceremonies and festivals inspired by his close friend, Robespierre. Imprisoned after the fall of Robespierre, he was released in 1797 (with the help of his ex-wife, whom he remarried) and gained the notice of Napoleon, whom David came to admire. After Napoleon became first consul, David accepted a commission from King Charles IV of Spain, who was interested in currying Napoleon's favor, to commemorate the crossing of the Alps by Napoleon's army into Italy in 1800 and his subsequent victory over Austria at Marengo. After consulting with Napoleon, David produced his *Napoleon Crossing the Alps,* which so impressed Napoleon that he ordered four other versions, which differ mainly in the color of the general's horse and cape. The painting commissioned by Charles is shown here.

Although leading an army of 60,000 through the snow and mud of the Alps in May was an impressive achievement, David embellished it further. As Napoleon's soldiers trudge by in the background, the first consul is shown on a rearing horse (not the mule he actually rode) and dressed in tights and a flowing cape (not the mud-spattered coat he wore). On stones below the horse's front legs are inscribed the names of Hannibal (247–183 B.C.E.), the Carthaginian general who famously led an army replete with elephants through the Saint Bernard Pass to attack Rome in the Second Punic War, and Charlemagne, who as king of the Franks also led an army through the pass in 773 C.E. when he attacked the Lombards.

The second painting, *The Emperor Napoleon in His Study at the Tuileries* (1812), shows Napoleon rising from his desk after a long night of work to leave his office and review his troops. Napoleon is dressed in a military uniform and, as is suggested by the maps on his desk, has been giving some thought to military campaigns. But as can be seen by the words on the paper on top of the pile, he also has been working on the Civil Code, the mammoth codification of French law that was one of his regime's lasting achievements. David's painting is deceptive in that most of the work on the Civil Code was done by a panel of experts Napoleon appointed. Another notable detail is the copy on the floor of Plutarch's *Lives,* biographical sketches of ancient Greek statesmen written in the first century C.E. The medallion he is wearing is the medallion of the Legion of Honor, an organization founded by Napoleon to honor outstanding military achievement and other service to the state. Although Napoleon did not pose for the painting, after he saw it, Napoleon told the painter, "You have understood me well, my dear David."

QUESTIONS FOR ANALYSIS

1. In the painting of Napoleon crossing the Alps, why did the artist include the soldiers in the background and the stones with the names of Hannibal and Charlemagne?
2. What is significant about the bearing of the horse, the posture of Napoleon, his gestures, his gaze, and his dress? What impressions of Napoleon is David trying to communicate through these details?

3. In David's painting of Napoleon in his study, what clues does the artist provide to show that Napoleon has been working through the night?
4. Why did he include the book by Plutarch, the sword, the maps, and the papers scattered across the desk?
5. What significance do you find in the glimpse of the library shown on the far left?

Napoleon Crossing the Alps

Napoleon in His Study

Anticolonialism and Revolution in the Americas

Despite the many contrasts between the British colonies of North America and the Portuguese/Spanish colonies of Mexico and Central and South America, all of them won their independence between the 1770s and the 1830s. Although the independence movements in North and Latin America unfolded differently, throughout the Americas, the revolutionaries shared similar grievances and ideals. Grievances included mercantilist restrictions on trade, high taxes, and a lack of self-government; the ideals were inspired by English constitutionalism, the Enlightenment, and, in the case of Latin America, the revolutions in North America and France.

Although rooted in similar causes, the revolutions had different results. In the thirteen colonies, opponents of British rule coalesced in a unified movement under the Continental Congress and George Washington, and after independence, this unity was preserved in the U.S. Constitution. In Latin America, where struggles for independence were waged on a regional basis, the end of Spanish and Portuguese authority resulted in more than a dozen independent states. In North America, federal and state governments drew on the principles of English constitutionalism to guarantee basic freedoms and extend political rights to a majority of adult white males. In Latin America, with its traditions of Spanish/Portuguese absolutism and aristocratic privilege, wealthy landowners controlled the new states and excluded the peasant masses from politics. Social and economic relationships also differed markedly in the postcolonial era. Although the new U.S. government preserved slavery and continued to restrict women's legal and political rights, property holding was widespread. A fluid class structure and economic expansion meant that not only the political elite but also the common people would benefit from independence. In Latin America, however, continuation of the colonial class structure meant that the economic and social chasm between the mass of propertyless Indian peasants and the tiny elite of white property owners remained intact. In this respect, the independence movement in Latin America ended colonialism but lacked important features of a true revolution.

"Simple Facts, Plain Arguments, and Common Sense"

41 • THOMAS PAINE, COMMON SENSE

After years of growing tensions over taxes, British imperial policy, the power of colonial legislatures, and a host of other issues, in April 1775, the American Revolution began with a clash between British regulars and American militiamen at the Battles of Lexington and Concord. In May, the Green Mountain Boys under Ethan Allen took Fort Ticonderoga on Lake Champlain, and in June, the British defeated colonial troops in the Battle of Bunker Hill outside of Boston at the cost of more than a thousand casualties.

Despite these events, in the summer and fall of 1775, most Americans still supported compromise and reconciliation with Great Britain. They were convinced that evil ministers, not the king, were responsible for British policy and hoped that views of conciliatory British politicians would prevail. Then in January 1776, there appeared in Philadelphia a 35-page pamphlet titled *Common Sense* by Thomas Paine (1737–1809), a bankrupt onetime corset-maker, sailor, tobacconist, and minor customs official who had migrated to Pennsylvania from England only 14 months earlier to escape debtor's prison. It was the most brilliant political pamphlet written during the American Revolution, and perhaps ever in the English language.

In three months, *Common Sense* sold more than 100,000 copies, one for every eight or ten adults in the colonies. It "burst from the press," wrote Benjamin Rush, a Pennsylvania physician and signer of the Declaration of Independence, "with an effect which has rarely been produced in any age or country." Written with passion and vivid imagery, Paine's pamphlet brought into focus American reservations about England and expressed American aspirations to create a newer, freer, more open society as an independent nation. It accelerated the move toward the events of July 2, 1776, when the delegates to the Second Continental Congress created the United States of America, and of July 4, when they signed the Declaration of Independence.

During the Revolutionary War, Paine fought in Washington's army and composed pamphlets to bolster American spirits. In the late 1780s, he returned to England but in 1792 fled to France after his public support of the French Revolution led to an indictment for sedition. Chosen as a delegate to the French National Convention (although he knew no French), Paine was later imprisoned for 10 months during the Reign of Terror, and on his release, he resided with James Monroe, the American ambassador to France. While in France, he attacked Christianity in his pamphlet *The Age of Reason*, whose notoriety was such that on his return to the United States in 1802 he was vilified as an atheist. Impoverished and disgraced, he died in New York City in 1809.

QUESTIONS FOR ANALYSIS

1. What are Paine's views of the origins and defects of monarchy as a form of government and hereditary succession as a principle of government?
2. What are his views of King George III?
3. What characteristics does Paine ascribe to Great Britain in general and the British government in particular? How might his background explain his negative views?
4. How does Paine counter the arguments of Americans who still sought reconciliation with Great Britain?
5. Despite Paine's rejection of the British government, do his ideas in *Common Sense* owe a debt to the principles of the English Bill of Rights (source 32)?
6. What is there about the pamphlet's language, tone, and arguments that might explain its enormous popularity?

Of Monarchy and Hereditary Succession

Government by kings was first introduced into the world by the heathens, from whom the children of Israel copied the custom. It was the most prosperous invention the Devil ever set on foot for the promotion of idolatry. The heathens paid

Source: Thomas Paine, *The Political Writings of Thomas Paine* (New York: Solomon King, 1830), vol. 1, pp. 21, 22, 25, 28, 29, 31, 33–35, 40–47.

divine honors to their deceased kings, and the Christian world has improved on the plan by doing the same to their living ones.[1] How impious is the title of sacred Majesty applied to a worm, who in the midst of his splendor is crumbling into dust! . . .

To the evil of monarchy we have added that of hereditary succession; and as the first is a degradation and lessening of ourselves, so the second, claimed as a matter of rights, is an insult and imposition on posterity. For all men being originally equals, no *one* by *birth* could have a right to set up his own family in perpetual preference to all others forever, and though himself might deserve *some* decent degree of honors of his contemporaries, yet his descendants might be far too unworthy to inherit them. . . .

Secondly, as no man at first could possess any other public honors than were bestowed upon him, so the givers of those honors could have no power to give away the right of posterity, and though they might say "we choose you for our head," they could not without manifest injustice to their children say "that your children and your children's children shall reign over our's forever." Because such an unwise, unjust, unnatural compact might perhaps, in the next succession put them under the government of a rogue or a fool. . . .

The most plausible plea which hath ever been offered in favor of hereditary succession is that it preserves a nation from civil wars; and were this true, it would be weighty; whereas, it is the most barefaced falsity ever imposed upon mankind. The whole history of England disowns the fact. Thirty kings and two minors have reigned in that distracted kingdom since the conquest,[2] in which time there have been . . . no less than eight civil wars and nineteen rebellions. Wherefore instead of making for peace, it makes against it, and destroys the very foundation it seems to stand upon. . . .

Thoughts on the Present State of American Affairs

In the following pages I offer nothing more than simple facts, plain arguments, and common sense; and have no other preliminaries to settle with the reader, than that he will divest himself of prejudice and prepossession, and suffer his reason and his feelings to determine for themselves; that he will put on . . . the true character of a man, and generously enlarge his views beyond the present day.

Volumes have been written on the subject of the struggle between England and America. Men of all ranks have embarked in the controversy, from different motives, and with various designs; but all have been ineffectual, and the period of debate is closed. Arms as the last resource decide the contest; the appeal was the choice of the king, and the continent has accepted the challenge. . . .

The sun never shined on a cause of greater worth. 'Tis not the affair of a city, a county, a province, or a kingdom; but of a continent—of at least one-eighth part of the habitable globe. 'Tis not the concern of a day, a year, or an age; posterity are virtually involved in the contest, and will be more or less affected even to the end of time by the proceedings now. Now is the seedtime of continental union, faith, and honor. . . .

I have heard it asserted by some, that as America has flourished under her former connection with Great Britain, the same connection is necessary towards her future happiness. . . . Nothing can be more fallacious than this kind of argument. We may as well assert that because a child has thrived upon milk, that it is never to have meat, or that the first twenty years of our lives is to become a precedent for the next twenty. But even this is admitting more than is true; for I answer roundly that America would have flourished as much, and

---

[1]The reference is to the theory of divine right monarchy, which asserted that kings were God's lieutenants to rule his subjects and were even in some limited sense divine figures themselves. See source 30.

[2]A reference to the conquest of England in 1066 by the Duke of Normandy, who reigned as King William I until his death in 1087.

probably much more, had no European power taken any notice of her. The commerce by which she hath enriched herself are the necessaries of life, and will always have a market while eating is the custom of Europe.

But she has protected us, say some. That she hath engrossed[3] us is true, and defended the continent at our expense as well as her own is admitted; and she would have defended Turkey from the same motive, viz., for the sake of trade and dominion. . . .

We have boasted the protection of Great Britain without considering that her motive was *interest,* not *attachment;* and that she did not protect us from *our enemies* on *our account,* but from her enemies on her own account, from those who had no quarrel with us on any *other account,* and who will always be our enemies on the *same account.* . . .

As I have always considered the independency of this continent an event which sooner or later must arrive, so from the late rapid progress of the continent to maturity, the event cannot be far off. . . . No man was a warmer wisher for a reconciliation than myself, before the fatal nineteenth of April, 1775 [the battles of Lexington and Concord], but the moment the event of that day was made known, I rejected the hardened, sullen-tempered Pharaoh of England[4] forever; and disdain the wretch, that with the pretended title of FATHER OF HIS PEOPLE can unfeelingly hear of their slaughter, and composedly sleep with their blood upon his soul.

But admitting that matters were now made up, what would be the event? I answer, the ruin of the continent. And that for several reasons.

First. The powers of governing still remaining in the hands of the king, he will have a negative [veto] over the whole legislation of this continent. And as he hath shown himself such an inveterate enemy to liberty, and discovered such a thirst for arbitrary power, is he, or is he not, a proper person to say to these colonies, *You shall make no laws but what I please!* . . .

Secondly. That as even the best terms which we can expect to obtain can amount to no more than a temporary expedient, or a kind of government by guardianship, which can last no longer than till the colonies come of age, so the general face and state of things in the interim will be unsettled and unpromising. Emigrants of property will not choose to come to a country whose form of government hangs but by a thread, and who is every day tottering on the brink of commotion and disturbance; and numbers of the present inhabitants would lay hold of the interval to dispose of their effects, and quit the continent. . . .

If there is any true cause of fear respecting independence, it is because no plan is yet laid down. Men do not see their way out. Wherefore, as an opening into that business I offer the following hints; at the same time modestly affirming that I have no other opinion of them myself than that they may be the means of giving rise to something better. . . .

Let the assemblies be annual, with a president only. The representation more equal, their business wholly domestic, and subject to the authority of a continental congress.

Let each colony be divided into six, eight, or ten, convenient districts, each district to send a proper number of delegates to congress, so that each colony send at least thirty. The whole number in congress will be at least 390. Each congress to sit and to choose a president by the following method. When the delegates are met, let a colony be taken from the whole thirteen colonies by lot, after which let the congress choose (by ballot) a president from out of the delegates of that province. In the next congress, let a colony be taken by lot from twelve only, omitting that colony from which the

---

[3]To occupy with troops.

[4]A reference to King George III.

president was taken in the former congress, and so proceeding on till the whole thirteen shall have had their proper rotation. And in order that nothing may pass into a law but what is satisfactorily just, not less than three fifths of the congress to be called a majority. He that will promote discord, under a government so equally formed as this, would have joined Lucifer in his revolt. . . . But where, say some, is the king of America? I'll tell you, friend, he reigns above, and doth not make havoc of mankind like the Royal Brute of Great Britain. Yet that we may not appear to be defective even in earthly honors, let a day be solemnly set apart for proclaiming the charter; let it be brought forth placed on the divine law, the Word of God; let a crown be placed thereon, by which the world may know, that so far as we approve of monarchy, that in America THE LAW IS KING. For as in absolute governments the king is law, so in free countries the law *ought* to BE king, and there ought to be no other. But lest any ill use should afterwards arise, let the crown at the conclusion of the ceremony be demolished, and scattered among the people whose right it is. . . .

Bolívar's Dreams for Latin America

42 • SÍMON BOLÍVAR, THE JAMAICA LETTER

Símon Bolívar, the most renowned leader of the Latin American independence movement, was born to a wealthy Venezuelan landowning family in 1783. Orphaned at an early age, he was educated by a private tutor who inspired in his pupil an enthusiasm for the principles of the Enlightenment and republicanism. After spending three years in Europe, Bolívar returned in 1803 to Venezuela, where the death of his new bride plunged him into grief and caused his return to France and Italy. In 1805, in Rome, he took a vow to dedicate his life to the liberation of his native land from Spain. On his return, he became a leading member of the republican-minded group in Caracas that in 1808 began to agitate for independence and in 1810 deposed the colonial governor and created the Republic of Venezuela. Until his death in 1830, Bolívar dedicated himself to the independence movement as a publicist, diplomat, and statesman. His greatest contribution was as the general who led the armies that defeated the Spaniards and liberated the northern regions of South America.

The so-called Jamaica Letter was written in 1815 during a self-imposed exile in Jamaica. It was addressed to "an English gentleman," probably the island's governor, the Duke of Manchester. The Venezuelan Republic had collapsed in May as a result of a viciously fought Spanish counteroffensive, divisions among the revolutionaries, and opposition from many Indians, blacks, and mulattos, who viewed the Creole landowners, not the Spaniards, as their oppressors. The letter was written in response to a request from the Englishman for Bolívar's thoughts about the background and prospects of the liberation movement.

QUESTIONS FOR ANALYSIS

1. Why does Bolívar believe that Spain's efforts to hold on to its American territories are doomed?

2. According to Bolívar, what Spanish policies made Spanish rule odious to him and other revolutionaries?
3. In Bolívar's view, what complicates the task of predicting Spanish America's political future?
4. Does Bolívar's letter reveal concern for the economic and social condition of South America's nonwhite population? What are some of the implications of Bolívar's attitudes?
5. Based on your reading of Bolívar, what guesses can you make about the reasons that the new nations of South America found it difficult to achieve stable republican governments?

. . . Success will crown our efforts, because the destiny of America has been irrevocably decided; the tie that bound her to Spain has been severed. . . . That which formerly bound them now divides them. The hatred that the Peninsula[1] inspired in us is greater than the ocean between us. It would be easier to have the two continents meet than to reconcile the spirits of the two countries. The habit of obedience; a community of interest, of understanding, of religion; mutual goodwill; a tender regard for the birthplace and good name of our forefathers; in short, all that gave rise to our hopes, came to us from Spain. As a result there was born a principle of affinity that seemed eternal. . . . At present the contrary attitude persists: we are threatened with the fear of death, dishonor, and every harm; there is nothing we have not suffered at the hands of that unnatural stepmother—Spain. . . . We have already seen the light, and it is not our desire to be thrust back into darkness. . . .

The role of the inhabitants of the American hemisphere has for centuries been purely passive. Politically they were non-existent. We are still in a position lower than slavery, and therefore it is more difficult for us to rise to the enjoyment of freedom. . . . States are slaves because of either the nature or the misuse of their constitutions; a people is therefore enslaved when the government, by its nature or its vices, infringes on and usurps the rights of the citizen or subject. Applying these

principles, we find that America was denied not only its freedom but even an active and effective tyranny. Under absolutism there are no recognized limits to the exercise of governmental powers. The will of the great sultan, khan, bey, and other despotic rulers is the supreme law, carried out more or less arbitrarily by the lesser pashas, khans, and satraps of Turkey and Persia, who have an organized system of oppression in which inferiors participate according to the authority vested in them. To them is entrusted the administration of civil, military, political, religious, and tax matters. But, after all is said and done, the rulers of Isfahan are Persians; the viziers of the Grand Turk are Turks; and the sultans of Tartary are Tartars. . . .

How different is our situation! We have been harassed by a conduct which has not only deprived us of our rights but has kept us in a sort of permanent infancy with regard to public affairs. If we could at least have managed our domestic affairs and our internal administration, we could have acquainted ourselves with the processes and mechanics of public affairs. . . .

Americans today, and perhaps to a greater extent than ever before, who live within the Spanish system occupy a position in society no better than that of serfs destined for labor. . . . Yet even this status is surrounded with galling restrictions, such as being forbidden to grow European crops, or to store products which are royal monopolies, or

---

Source: From Simón Bolívar, *Selected Writings,* ed. Harold A. Bierck, Jr., trans. by Lewis Bertrand (New York: Colonial Press, 1951), pp. 103–122.

[1]Refers to the Iberian Peninsula, consisting of Spain and Portugal.

to establish factories of a type the Peninsula itself does not possess. To this add the exclusive trading privileges, even in articles of prime necessity, and the barriers between American provinces, designed to prevent all exchange of trade, traffic, and understanding. In short, do you wish to know what our future held?—simply the cultivation of the fields of indigo, grain, coffee, sugar cane, cacao, and cotton; cattle raising on the broad plains; hunting wild game in the jungles; digging in the earth to mine its gold—but even these limitations could never satisfy the greed of Spain.

So negative was our existence that I can find nothing comparable in any other civilized society. . . .

As I have just explained, we were cut off and, as it were, removed from the world in relation to the science of government and administration of the state. We were never viceroys or governors, save in the rarest of instances; seldom archbishops and bishops; diplomats never; as military men, only subordinates; as nobles, without royal privileges. In brief, we were neither magistrates nor financiers and seldom merchants—all in flagrant contradiction to our institutions. . . .

It is harder, Montesquieu[2] has written, to release a nation from servitude than to enslave a free nation. This truth is proven by the annals of all times, which reveal that most free nations have been put under the yoke, but very few enslaved nations have recovered their liberty. Despite the convictions of history, South Americans have made efforts to obtain liberal, even perfect, institutions, doubtless out of that instinct to aspire to the greatest possible happiness, which, common to all men, is bound to follow in civil societies founded on the principles of justice, liberty, and equality. But are we capable of maintaining in proper balance the difficult charge of a republic? Is it conceivable that a newly emancipated people can soar to the

heights of liberty, and, unlike Icarus, neither have its wings melt nor fall into an abyss? Such a marvel is inconceivable and without precedent. There is no reasonable probability to bolster our hopes.

More than anyone, I desire to see America fashioned into the greatest nation in the world, greatest not so much by virtue of her area and wealth as by her freedom and glory. Although I seek perfection for the government of my country, I cannot persuade myself that the New World can, at the moment, be organized as a great republic. Since it is impossible, I dare not desire it; yet much less do I desire to have all America a monarchy because this plan is not only impracticable but also impossible. Wrongs now existing could not be righted, and our emancipation would be fruitless. The American states need the care of paternal governments to heal the sores and wounds of despotism and war. . . .

From the foregoing, we can draw these conclusions: The American provinces are fighting for their freedom, and they will ultimately succeed. Some provinces as a matter of course will form federal and some central republics; the larger areas will inevitably establish monarchies, some of which will fare so badly that they will disintegrate in either present or future revolutions. To consolidate a great monarchy will be no easy task, but it will be utterly impossible to consolidate a great republic. . . .

When success is not assured, when the state is weak, and when results are distantly seen, all men hesitate; opinion is divided, passions rage, and the enemy fans these passions in order to win an easy victory because of them. As soon as we are strong and under the guidance of a liberal nation which will lend us her protection, we will achieve accord in cultivating the virtues and talents that lead to glory. Then will we march majestically toward that great prosperity for which South America is destined. . . .

---

[2]Montesquieu (1689–1755) was a French philosopher, historian, and jurist best known for his *Spirit of the Laws* (1755) and his theory that the powers of government—executive, legislative, and judicial—must be separated to ensure individual freedom.

Chapter 6

Africa, Southwest Asia, and India in the Seventeenth and Eighteenth Centuries

AROUND 1600, SOUTHWEST ASIA and India, regions dominated by the large and powerful Ottoman, Safavid, and Mughal empires, would seem to have had little in common with Africa, a continent divided into hundreds of kingdoms, confederations, chiefdoms, city-states, and regions with no formal states. In comparison to Africa, India and Southwest Asia had more people, more cities, and more commercial and cultural contacts with Europe and East Asia. Moreover, India and Southwest Asia were dominated by two major faiths, Islam and Hinduism, while Africa had many religions: Islam in the Mediterranean north, the Sudan, and on the east coast; Christianity in Ethiopia; and numerous varieties of native religions throughout the continent.

Despite these differences, the histories of these regions in the seventeenth and eighteenth centuries were similar in several respects. All three areas, for example, experienced political instability, which in some cases led to the collapse of once-formidable states. The Safavid Empire collapsed in the 1730s, and the Mughal Empire had been reduced to impotence and irrelevance by the mid-1700s. The Ottoman Empire survived, but with shrunken borders, a demoralized populace, and an army that was a shadow of the force that had marched from victory to victory in the fifteenth and sixteenth centuries. In west Africa, the Songhai

Empire fell apart after a defeat by invading Moroccans in 1591, and in the southeast, the Kingdom of Mutapa, following years of Portuguese penetration, was overrun by the Changamire Kingdom in the 1680s. Other African states experienced civil war, invasion, or gradual decline. These included Ethiopia, in east Africa; Benin, on the Gulf of Guinea; and Kanem-Bornu, in the central Sudan. Political decline in Africa was not universal: Dahomey, the Asante Confederation, and Oyo all emerged as formidable powers, and hundreds of chieftainships maintained their traditional lines of authority. Overall, however, African political life became less stable and more subject to conflict in the 1600s and 1700s.

Increased interaction with Europe is another common thread in the histories of the three regions. In South and Southwest Asia, with strong European demand for these regions' agricultural products, textiles, and a host of other products, trade expanded, especially between Europe and India. In India, however, interaction with Europeans went beyond commerce. Beginning in the 1750s, officials of the British East India Company took advantage of the Mughal Empire's disintegration to establish the Company's authority over Bengal in the northeast and other regions of the subcontinent. In Africa, increased interaction with Europe meant the establishment of the first permanent European settlement with the arrival of Dutch farmers in southern Africa in 1652. It also meant a substantial expansion of the slave trade on Africa's west and east coasts, with just over 6 million African slaves transported to the Americas in the 1700s, and smaller numbers to the Middle East, India, and French-controlled islands in the Indian Ocean. This spectacular growth in the slave trade underlined Africa's vulnerability in an age of growing global interaction.

The African Slave Trade and Its Critics

Slavery has been practiced throughout history in every corner of the globe. It has existed in small farming villages in China and great imperial cities such as ancient Rome; it has been practiced by pastoral nomads, plantation owners, small farmers, emperors, city-dwellers, and modern totalitarian dictators. Slavery is mentioned in ancient Sumerian law codes from the fourth millennium B.C.E. and is still the lot of millions of human beings today despite its official condemnation by the world's governments.

In recent history, slavery has uniquely affected the people of Africa, who became a source of unpaid labor in many parts of the world, especially the Americas. The transatlantic slave trade began in the fifteenth century under the Portuguese, who at first shipped Africans to Portugal to serve as domestics and then to the Canary Islands, the Madeiras, and São Tomé to work on sugar plantations. By 1500, Portuguese merchants were exporting approximately 500 slaves each year. That number grew in the mid-1500s, when the plantation system was established in Brazil and subsequently spread to Spanish America, the West Indies, and British North America. In the 1700s, when Great Britain became the leading purveyor of slaves, the transatlantic slave trade peaked, with more than 6 million slaves transported to the Americas and the Caribbean.

Almost every aspect of African slavery is the subject of debate among historians. Did the enslavement of Africans result from racism, or were Africans enslaved because they were available and convenient to the market across the Atlantic? Did the loss of millions of individuals to slavery have serious or minimal demographic consequences for Africa? Was the political instability of Africa linked to the slave trade or to other factors? To what extent did reliance on selling slaves to Europeans impede Africa's economic development? Did European governments abolish the slave trade because of humanitarianism or hard-headed economic calculation?

One thing is certain. For the millions of Africans who were captured, shackled, wrenched from their families, branded, sold, packed into the holds of ships, sold once more, and put to work in American mines and fields, enslavement meant pain, debasement, and fear. For them, slavery was an unmitigated disaster.

The Path to Enslavement in America

43 • OLAUDAH EQUIANO, THE INTERESTING NARRATIVE OF OLAUDAH EQUIANO WRITTEN BY HIMSELF

In 1789, no fewer than 100 abolitionist books and pamphlets were published in England, but none had more readers than the autobiography of the former slave Olaudah Equiano. In his memoir, Equiano relates that he was born in 1745 in Iboland, an area east of the Niger River delta that today is part of Nigeria. He also describes how he was captured and sold into slavery when he was about eleven years old and, having survived the harrowing Atlantic crossing, served three masters, including an officer in the British navy; an English sea captain who took him to the West Indian island of Montserrat; and finally, Robert King, a Quaker merchant from Philadelphia.

In many ways, Equiano's experiences as a slave were exceptional. He never served as a plantation worker, and he learned to read and write while owned by his first master. He made numerous trips back and forth across the Atlantic and, in the process, learned skills relating to navigation, bookkeeping, and commerce. Having purchased his freedom from his last owner in 1766, he took up residence in England, where he supported himself as a barber, servant, and crew member on voyages to the Mediterranean and around the Atlantic. In the 1770s, he joined the English abolitionist movement. As a result of the contacts he made with the movement's leaders, in the late 1780s he was given a government post with the responsibility of arranging the transfer of food and other provisions to Sierra Leone, a newly founded colony that abolitionists hoped would serve as an African homeland for freed slaves. Dismissed after a year, Equiano turned to writing his autobiography, which was published with the financial support of leading abolitionists. Heavily promoted by Equiano on lecture tours, his book went through eight editions in the 1790s. It is generally acknowledged that his autobiography strengthened the abolitionist cause and helped bring about the act of Parliament in 1807 that abolished the British slave trade.

How factual is Equiano's narrative? Historians must raise such a question about any historical source, especially autobiographies, whose authors cannot be expected to be totally objective when writing about themselves or totally accurate in recalling childhood events. Equiano's memoirs, furthermore, were written with a specific purpose: to discredit slavery and garner support for the abolitionist cause. One scholar, Vincent Carretta of the University of Maryland, has suggested that Equiano fabricated the account of his kidnapping and his voyage across the Atlantic on a slave ship. A baptismal certificate and a Royal Navy document, he argues, show that Equiano was actually born in South Carolina.

Scholars who consider Carretta's evidence inconclusive continue to believe that the memoir is generally accurate. Certainly, a comparison of Equiano's description of his slave experience with what we know from other sources suggests that his work is free of exaggeration and distortion. This includes the following excerpt, in which he describes his harsh introduction to slavery.

QUESTIONS FOR ANALYSIS

1. On the basis of Equiano's account, what is the role of Africans in the slave trade?
2. What does Equiano's account reveal about the effect of slavery and the slave trade on African society?
3. What were the characteristics of slavery that Equiano encountered in Africa?
4. Once the slaves were on board the slave ship, what experiences contributed to their despair and demoralization, according to Equiano?
5. What factors might have contributed to the brutal treatment of the slaves by the ship's crew?

Taken Captive

Generally when the grown people in the neighborhood were gone far in the fields to labor, the children assembled together in some of the neighbors' premises to play, and commonly some of us used to get up a tree to look out for any assailant or kidnapper that might come upon us, for they sometimes took those opportunities of our parents' absence to attack and carry off as many as they could seize. . . . One day, when all our people were gone out to their work as usual and only I and my

Source: Paul Edwards, ed. and trans., *Equiano's Travels* (Oxford: Heinemann Educational Books, 1967), pp. 25–42.

Reprinted by permission of Pearson Education UK.

dear sister were left to mind the house, two men and a woman got over our walls, and in a moment seized us both, and without giving us time to cry out or make resistance they stopped our mouths and ran off with us into the nearest wood. . . .

For a long time we had kept to the woods, but at last we came into a road which I believed I knew. I had now some hopes of being delivered, for we had advanced but a little way before I discovered some people at a distance, on which I began to cry out for their assistance: but my cries had no other effect than to make them tie me faster and stop my mouth, and then they put me into a large sack. They also stopped my sister's mouth and tied her hands, and in this manner we proceeded till we were out of the sight of these people. When we went to rest the following night they offered us some victuals, but we refused it, and the only comfort we had was in being in one another's arms all that night and bathing each other with our tears. But alas! we were soon deprived of even the small comfort of weeping together. The next day proved a day of greater sorrow than I had yet experienced, for my sister and I were then separated while we lay clasped in each other's arms. It was in vain that we besought them not to part us; she was torn from me and immediately carried away, while I was left in a state of distraction not to be described. I cried and grieved continually, and for several days I did not eat anything but what they forced into my mouth. At length, after many days' traveling, during which I had often changed masters, I got into the hands of a chieftain in a very pleasant country. This man had two wives and some children, and they all used me extremely well and did all they could to comfort me, particularly the first wife, who was something like my mother. . . . This first master of mine, as I may call him, was a smith, and my principal employment was working his bellows, which were the same kind as I had seen in my vicinity. . . . I believe it was gold he worked, for it was of a lovely bright yellow color and was worn by the women

on their wrists and ankles. I was there I suppose about a month, and they at last used to trust me some little distance from the house. This liberty I used in embracing every opportunity to inquire the way to my own home: and I also sometimes, for the same purpose, went with the maidens in the cool of the evenings to bring pitchers of water from the springs for the use of the house.

> Equiano escapes, but terrified of being alone in the forest at night returns to his household.

Soon after this my master's only daughter and child by his first wife sickened and died, which affected him so much that for some time he was almost frantic, and really would have killed himself had he not been watched and prevented. However, in a small time afterwards he recovered and I was again sold. I was now carried to the left of the sun's rising, through many different countries and a number of large woods. The people I was sold to used to carry me very often when I was tired either on their shoulders or on their backs. I saw many convenient well-built sheds along the roads at proper distances, to accommodate the merchants and travelers who lay in those buildings along with their wives, who often accompany them; and they always go well armed.

> Equiano encounters his sister, but again they are quickly separated.

I did not long remain after my sister [departed]. I was again sold and carried through a number of places till, after traveling a considerable time, I came to a town called Tinmah in the most beautiful country I had yet seen in Africa. . . . I was sold here . . . by a merchant who lived and brought me there. I had been about two or three days at his house when a wealthy widow, a neighbor of his, came there one evening, and brought with her an only son, a young gentleman about my own age and size. Here they saw me; and, having taken a fancy to me, I was bought of the merchant, and went home with them. . . . The next day I was washed and perfumed, and when meal-time came I was led into the presence of my mistress, and ate and drank before her with her son. This filled me with astonishment; and I could scarce help expressing my surprise that the young gentleman should suffer me, who was bound, to eat with him who was free. . . . There were likewise slaves daily to attend us, while my young master and I with other boys sported with our darts and bows and arrows, as I had been used to do at home. In this resemblance to my former happy state I passed about two months; and I now began to think I was to be adopted into the family . . . and to forget by degrees my misfortunes, when all at once the delusion vanished; for without the least previous knowledge, one morning early, while my dear master and companion was still asleep, I was wakened out of my reverie to fresh sorrow, and hurried away. . . .

At last I came to the banks of a large river, which was covered with canoes in which the people appeared to live with their household utensils and provisions of all kinds. I was beyond measure astonished at this, as I had never before seen any water larger than a pond or a rivulet: and my surprise was mingled with no small fear when I was put into one of these canoes and we began to paddle and move along the river. . . Thus I continued to travel, sometimes by land, sometimes by water, through different countries and various nations, till at the end of six or seven months after I had been kidnapped I arrived at the sea coast.

The Slave Ship

The first object which saluted my eyes when I arrived on the coast was the sea, and a slave ship which was then riding at anchor and waiting for its cargo. These filled me with astonishment, which was soon converted into terror when I was carried on board. I was immediately handled and tossed up to see if I were sound by some of the crew, and I was now persuaded that I had gotten into a world of bad spirits and that they were going to kill me. Their complexions too differing so much from ours, their long hair and the language they spoke (which was very different from any I had ever heard) united to confirm me in this belief. Indeed such were the horrors of my views and fears at the moment that, if ten thousand worlds had been my own, I would have freely parted with them all to have exchanged my condition with that of the meanest slave in my own country. When I looked round the ship too and saw a large furnace or copper boiling and a multitude of black people of every description chained together, every one of their countenances expressing dejection and sorrow, I no longer doubted of my fate; and quite overpowered with horror and anguish, I fell motionless on the deck and fainted. When I recovered a little I found some black people about me, who I believed were some of those who had brought me on board and had been receiving their pay; they talked to me in order to cheer me, but all in vain. . . .

I was soon put down under the decks, and there I received such a salutation in my nostrils as I had never experienced in my life: so that with the loathsomeness of the stench and crying together, I became so sick and low that I was not able to eat, nor had I the least desire to taste anything. I now wished for the last friend, death, to relieve me; but soon, to my grief, two of the white men offered me eatables, and on my refusing to eat, one of them held me fast by the hands and laid me across I think the windlass, and tied my feet while the other flogged me severely. I had never experienced anything of this kind before, and although, not being used to the water, I naturally feared that element the first time I saw it, yet nevertheless could I have got over the nettings I would have jumped over the side, but I could not; and besides, the crew used to watch us very closely who were not chained down to the decks, lest we should leap into the water: and I have seen some of these poor African prisoners most severely cut for attempting to do so, and hourly whipped for not eating. This indeed was often the case with myself. In a little time after, amongst the poor chained men I found some of my own nation, which in a small degree gave ease to my mind. I inquired of these what was to be done with us; they gave me to understand we were to be carried to these white people's country to work for them. I then was a little revived, and thought if it were no worse than working, my situation was not so desperate: but still I feared I should be put to death, the white people looked and acted, as I thought, in so savage a manner; for I had never seen among my people such instances of brutal cruelty, and this not only shown towards us blacks but also to some of the whites themselves. One white man in particular I saw, when we were permitted to be on deck, flogged so unmercifully with a large rope near the foremast that he died in consequence of it; and they tossed him over the side as they would have done a brute. . . .

At last, when the ship we were in had got in all her cargo, they made ready with many fearful noises, and we were all put under deck so that we could not see how they managed the vessel. But this disappointment was the last of my sorrow. The stench of the hold while we were on the coast was so intolerably loathsome that it was dangerous to remain there for any time, and some of us had been permitted to stay on the deck for the fresh air; but now that the whole ship's cargo were confined together it became absolutely pestilential. The closeness of the place and the heat of the climate, added to the number in the ship, which was so crowded that each had scarcely room to turn himself, almost suffocated us. This produced copious perspirations, so that the air soon became unfit for respiration from a variety of loathsome smells, and brought on a sickness among the slaves, of

which many died. . . . This wretched situation was again aggravated by the galling of the chains, now become insupportable, and the filth of the necessary tubs [latrines], into which the children often fell and were almost suffocated. The shrieks of the women and the groans of the dying rendered the whole a scene of horror almost inconceivable. Happily perhaps for myself I was soon reduced so low here that it was thought necessary to keep me almost always on deck, and from my extreme youth I was not put in fetters. . . .

One day, when we had a smooth sea and moderate wind, two of my wearied countrymen who were chained together (I was near them at the time), preferring death to such a life of misery, somehow made through the nettings and jumped into the sea: immediately another quite dejected fellow, who on account of his illness was suffered to be out of irons, also followed their example; and I believe many more would very soon have done the same if they had not been prevented by the ship's crew, who were instantly alarmed. Those of us that were the most active were in a moment put down under the deck, and there was such a noise and confusion amongst the people of the ship as I never heard before, to stop her [the ship] and get the boat out to go after the slaves. However two of the wretches were drowned, but they got the other and afterwards flogged him unmercifully for thus attempting to prefer death to slavery.

At last we came in sight of the island of Barbados, at which the whites on board gave a great shout and made many signs of joy to us. We did not know what to think of this, but as the vessel drew nearer we plainly saw the harbor and other ships of different kinds and sizes, and we soon anchored amongst them off Bridgetown. Many merchants and planters now came on board, though it was in the evening. They put us in separate parcels and examined us attentively. They also made us jump, and pointed to the land, signifying we were to go there. . . .

We were not many days in the merchant's custody before we were sold after their usual manner, which is this: On a signal given, (as the beat of a drum) the buyers rush at once into the yard where the slaves are confined, and make choice of that parcel they like best. The noise and clamor with which this is attended and the eagerness visible in the countenances of the buyers serve not a little to increase the apprehensions of the terrified Africans, who may well be supposed to consider them as the ministers of that destruction to which they think themselves devoted. In this manner, without scruple, are relations and friends separated, most of them never to see each other again. I remember in the vessel in which I was brought over, in the men's apartment there were several brothers who, in the sale, were sold in different lots; and it was very moving on this occasion to see and hear their cries at parting. O, ye nominal Christians! might not an African ask you, learned you this from your God who says unto you, Do unto all men as you would men should do unto you?

Multiple Voices III:

Ending the Slave Trade: European and African Perspectives

BACKGROUND

In 1453, in his *Chronicle of the Discovery and Conquest of Guinea*, the Portuguese author Gomes Eannes de Azurara became one of the first Europeans to record his thoughts and feelings about the deportation and sale of African slaves by Europeans. Eannes acknowledged that he was deeply saddened by the sight of African slaves disembarking from a ship in the Portuguese port city of Lagos. He deplored their "wretched state" and was reduced to tears by the sobs of families that soon would be broken apart and sold to different owners. His remorse was fleeting, however. He took comfort in the fact that in Portugal these slaves would be converted to Christianity, treated well, and given an opportunity to overcome their "bestial sloth."

For the next three centuries, many Europeans depended on such rationalizations to dull their unease about the slave trade. Others defended it as an economic necessity. Most ignored it. As a result, the slave trade steadily grew, until in the eighteenth century, just over 6 million Africans were transported across the Atlantic as slaves. At century's end, however, the institution of slavery was on the defensive. In the 1790s, French revolutionaries outlawed slavery throughout France's empire, and slaves and former slaves in the French colony of Saint Domingue rose up in a rebellion that led to the funding of an independent Haiti in 1804. Three years later, the United States and Great Britain both outlawed the slave trade. Great Britain's decision turned the world's leading slave-trading nation into its leading opponent.

What explains the sudden rise in abolitionist sentiment? Some Europeans turned against slavery out of religious conviction. Many early abolitionists were Quakers, members of the Religious Society of Friends, a small English religious organization with a tradition of egalitarianism and pacifism. They wrote many of the first antislavery treatises and were prime movers in the founding of the first abolitionist societies, including the Pennsylvania Society for Promoting the Abolition of Slavery in 1784 and, in England, the Society for the Abolition of the Slave Trade in 1787. Others were tied with Methodism, an eighteenth-century offshoot of the Church of England with a broad popular following and a commitment to personal rebirth and social reform. John Wesley (1703–1791), Methodism's founder along with his brother Charles (1707–1788), denounced slavery for brutalizing the slave and threatening the salvation of slave owners and traders. Abolitionist sentiment also was encouraged by the intellectual atmosphere fostered by the Enlightenment, with its emphasis on freedom, natural rights, and progress. Finally, the campaign against slavery was strengthened by the American and French revolutions, movements dedicated to furthering the rights of man—even though many of their leaders were slaveholders.

Abolitionists were opposed by slave traders, planters, and some politicians, who marshaled a variety of religious, economic, and political arguments to support their cause. Ending the slave trade also was opposed by many Africans who depended on the capture and sale of slaves as a source of wealth and power. Slavery's defenders failed, however. When Brazil outlawed slavery in 1888, slavery and the slave trade in the Atlantic world had come to an end. By then, however, untold damage had been done, and slavery's racist legacy remained.

THE SOURCES

The excerpts that follow represent arguments for and against the slave trade made between 1774 and 1820. The first excerpt is from the pamphlet "Thoughts Upon Slavery," written by the charismatic Methodist leader John Wesley in 1774. With much material borrowed from *Some Historical Accounts of Guinea,* published in 1771 by the American Quaker Anthony Benezet, Wesley's widely read treatise reveals the moral earnestness and emotional fervor of evangelical Protestant abolitionists. The second excerpt is from the *Address to the National Assembly in Favor of the Abolition of the Slave Trade,* a pamphlet published in 1790 by the Society of the Friends of Blacks, a French antislavery organization founded in 1788. Its anonymous author draws on moral principles derived from the Enlightenment and the early stages of the French Revolution to oppose slavery.

The views of those who favored the continuation of the slave trade are represented by two sources. The first is taken from a memorandum prepared in 1797 by W. S. van Ryneveld, a director of the Dutch East India Company, at the request of the British government. The British had seized the Dutch settlement at the Cape of Good Hope in southern Africa in 1795 to prevent it from coming under the control of France, and then after briefly returning it to the Dutch, took definitive control in 1806. In 1797, the British sought van Ryneveld's views on a variety of issues, including the feasibility of eliminating slavery from the colony, whose farmers had depended on slave labor imported from East Africa and Madagascar since the 1600s.

Van Ryneveld, a South African slave owner himself, strongly opposed ending slavery for practical reasons. Following his advice, before the abolition of the slave trade in 1807, the British allowed the import of another 3,500 slaves to the Cape before 1807. Between 1808 and 1816, they also brought in another 2,100 Africans who had been "rescued" by the British navy from outlawed slave ships but then were forced to enter into fourteen-year "apprenticeships" with South African employers.

The final source contains the words of Osei Bonsu, the king of Asante, as recorded by Joseph Dupuis, a British envoy sent to the Asante capital city of Kumasi in 1820 to discuss Asante–British commerce. Beginning in the 1680s, Asante had become a powerful state on the Guinea Coast, with much of its income derived from the sale of prisoners of war, criminals, and other social outcasts to European slavers. Clearly, Osei Bonsu was unhappy when he learned that the British had decided to end the slave trade.

QUESTIONS FOR ANALYSIS

1. Consider the arguments of slavery's detractors, Wesley and the author representing the Society of the Friends of Blacks. On what do they agree and disagree? What are their reasons for opposing the slave trade and slavery? What can be inferred about the intended audience for their writings? How do they try to appeal to that audience?
2. Obviously van Ryneveld and Osei Bonsu both oppose the arguments of Wesley and the French abolitionists. On what other matters do this African king and this wealthy European agree and disagree?
3. On the basis of these four excerpts, what conclusions can you draw about the reasons that the abolitionists, not the defenders of slavery, were successful in attaining their goals?

---

1 • John Wesley, Thoughts Upon Slavery

> After describing the cruelties of slavery, Wesley makes an appeal directly to the sea captains, merchants, and planters who profit from slavery.

And, first, to the captains. . . . Most of *you* know, the country of *Guinea* . . . how populous, how fruitful, how pleasant it was a few years ago. You know the people were not stupid, not wanting in sense, considering the few means of improvement they enjoyed. Neither did you find them savage, fierce, cruel, treacherous, or unkind to strangers. On the contrary, they were in most parts a sensible and ingenious people. They were kind and friendly, courteous and obliging, and remarkably fair and just in their dealings. Such are the men whom you . . . tear away from this lovely country; part by stealth, part by force, part made captives in those wars, which you raise or foment on purpose. You have seen them torn away, children from

Source: John Wesley, *Thoughts Upon Slavery*, in *The Works of John Wesley*, Thomas Jackson, ed., 14 vols., 3rd ed., (London: Wesleyan Methodist Book Room, 1872), vol. XI, pp. 59–79.

their parents, parents from their children: Husbands from their wives, wives from their beloved husbands, brethren and sisters from each other. You have dragged them who had never done you any wrong, perhaps in chains, from their native shore. You have forced them into your ships like a herd of swine, them who had souls immortal as your own. . . . You have carried the survivors into the vilest slavery, never to end but with life. . . .

May I speak plainly to you? I must. Love constrains me: Love to *you,* as well as to those you are concerned with. Is there a GOD? You know there is. Is He a just GOD? Then there must be a state of retribution: A state wherein the just GOD will reward every man according to his works. Then what reward will he render to you? O think betimes! Before you drop into eternity! Think now, *He shall have judgment without mercy, that showed no mercy.*

Are you a man? Then you should have a *human* heart. But have you indeed? What is your heart made of? Is there no such principle as compassion there? Do you *never feel* another's pain? . . . When you saw the flowing eyes, the heaving breasts, the bleeding sides and tortured limbs of your fellow-creatures, [were] you a stone, or a brute? Did you look upon them with the eyes of a tiger? When you squeezed the agonizing creatures down in the ship, or when you threw their poor mangled remains into the sea, had you no relenting? Did not one tear drop from your eye, one sigh escape from your breast? Do you feel no relenting now? If you do not, you must go on, till the measure of your iniquities is full. Then will the great GOD deal with *you,* as you have dealt with *them,* and require all their blood at your hands. And at that day it shall be more tolerable for *Sodom* and *Gomorrah*[1] than for you! But if your heart does relent, though in a small degree, know it is a call from the GOD of love. . . . Today resolve, GOD being your helper, to escape for your life.—Regard not money! All that a man hath will he give for his life? Whatever you lose, lose not your soul: nothing can countervail that loss. Immediately quit the horrid trade: At all events, be an honest man.

This equally concerns every merchant, who is engaged in the slave-trade. . . . O let his resolution be yours! Have no more any part in this detestable business. Instantly leave it to those unfeeling wretches, "Who laugh at human nature and compassion!" Be *you* a man! Not a wolf, a devourer of the human species! Be merciful, that you may obtain mercy!

And this equally concerns every gentleman that has an estate in our *American* plantations. . . . Instantly, at any price, were it the half of your goods, deliver thyself from blood-guiltiness! Thy hands, thy bed, thy furniture, thy house, thy lands are at present stained with blood. Surely it is enough; accumulate no more guilt; spill no more blood of the innocent! Do not hire another to shed blood: Do not pay him for doing it! Whether you are a Christian or no, show yourself a man; be not more savage than a lion or a bear!

O thou GOD of love, thou who art loving to every man . . . have compassion upon these outcasts of men, who are trodden down as dung upon the earth! Arise and help these that have no helper, whose blood is spilt upon the ground like water! . . . O burst thou all their chains in sunder; more especially the chains of their sins: Thou, Saviour of all, make them free, that they may be free indeed!

---

[1]According to the Book of Genesis, Sodom and Gomorrah were two cities destroyed by God for their sins.

2 • Society of the Friends of Blacks, Address to the National Assembly in Favor of the Abolition of the Slave Trade

The immediate emancipation of the blacks would not only be a fatal operation for the colonies; it would even be a deadly gift for the blacks, in the state of abjection and incompetence to which cupidity has reduced them. It would be to abandon to themselves and without assistance children in the cradle or mutilated and impotent beings.

It is therefore not yet time to demand that liberty; we ask only that one cease butchering thousands of blacks regularly every year in order to take hundreds of captives; we ask that one henceforth cease the prostitution, the profaning of the French name, used to authorize these thefts, these atrocious murders; we demand in a word the abolition of the slave trade. . . .

In regard to the colonists, we will demonstrate to you that if they need to recruit blacks in Africa to sustain the population of the colonies at the same level, it is because they wear out the blacks with work, whippings, and starvation; that, if they treated them with kindness and as good fathers of families, these blacks would multiply and that this population, always growing, would increase cultivation and prosperity. . . .

If some motive might on the contrary push them [the blacks] to insurrection, might it not be the indifference of the National Assembly about their lot? Might it not be the insistence on weighing them down with chains, when one consecrates everywhere this eternal axiom: *that all men are born free and equal in rights*. . . .

It is worthy of the first free Assembly of France to consecrate the principle of philanthropy which makes of humankind only one single family, to declare that it is horrified by this annual carnage which takes place on the coasts of Africa, that it has the intention of abolishing it one day, of mitigating the slavery that is the result, of looking for and preparing, from this moment, the means.

The humanity, justice, and magnanimity that have guided you [members of the National Assembly] in the reform of the most profoundly rooted abuses gives hope to the Society of the Friends of Blacks that you will receive with benevolence its demand in favor of that numerous portion of humankind, so cruelly oppressed for centuries. . . .

. . . You have engraved on an immortal monument[1] that all men are born and remain free and equal in rights; you have restored to the French people these rights that despotism had for so long despoiled; . . . you have broken the chains of feudalism that still degraded a good number of our fellow citizens; you have announced the destruction of all the stigmatizing distinctions that religious or political prejudices introduced into the great family of humankind. . . .

We are not asking you to restore to French blacks those political rights which alone, nevertheless, attest to and maintain the dignity of man; we are not even asking for their liberty. No; slander, bought no doubt with the greed of the shipowners, ascribes that scheme to us and spreads it everywhere; they want to stir up everyone against us, provoke the planters and their numerous creditors, who take alarm even at gradual emancipation. They want to alarm all the French, to whom they depict the prosperity of the colonies as inseparable from the slave trade and the perpetuity of slavery.

No, never has such an idea entered into our minds. . . .

Source: Lynn Hunt, ed., *The French Revolution and Human Rights* (Boston: Bedford/St Martin's, 1999), pp. 107, 108. Reproduced with permission.

[1]Declaration of the Rights of Man and of the Citizen (see source 38).

3 • W. S. van Ryneveld, Response to Governor Macartney's Questionnaire

We know very well, that here, both within and without the Colony, no sufficient number of white people can be obtained to perform in culture [cultivation] the labour of the slaves; and, on the other hand, experience shows us every day that the procreation of slaves, in proportion to number, is very trifling, and even not worth mentioning; and that, moreover, a very considerable number of slaves is lost by continual disorders, especially by bile and putrid fevers, to which they are very subject.

The political state of this Colony, I think, is actually of that nature that, however injurious slavery of itself may be to the morals and industry of the inhabitants, still the keeping of slaves has now become, as it is styled, a necessary evil; and, at least, a sudden interdiction to the importation of slaves would occasion a general injury, as long as such a number of hands as is requisite for the culture cannot be obtained from another part, at a rate that may be thought proportionate to the produce arising from the lands. . . .

I perfectly acknowledge . . . that if there were no slaves at the Cape the peasants would then be more industrious and useful to the State, and that the facility of procuring slaves renders the inhabitants of this country lazy, haughty and brutal.

Every kind of vice and a perfect corruption of morals is owing to that. But how to help it? If slavery had been interdicted at the first settling of this Colony, then the inhabitants would doubtless have become more industrious and useful to each other. . . .

Yet, the business is done. Slavery exists and is now even indispensable. It is absolutely necessary because there are no other hands to till this extensive country, and therefore it will be the work, not of years, but as it were of centuries to remove by attentive and proper regulation this evil established with the first settling of the Colony. Should the slaves be now declared free, that would immediately render both the country and these poor creatures themselves miserable; not only all tillage would then be at an end, but also the number of freemen, instead of their being (as now) useful members of, would then really become a charge to, society. And should the importation of slaves be interdicted, on a sudden [at once], without any means being provided towards supplying other hands for the tillage, then the Colony would thereby be caused to languish . . . and especially the culture of grain would thereby be reduced to decay.

Source: W. S. van Ryneveld, Response to Governor Macartney's Questionnaire, November 29, 1797, reprinted in Andre Du Toit and Hermann Giliomee, eds., *Afrikaner Political Thought* (Berkeley: University of California Press, 1983), pp. 46–49.

4 • Joseph Dupuis, Summary of a Conversation with Osei Bonsu, King of Asante

"Now," said the king, after a pause, "I have another palaver [long discussion], and you must help me to talk it. A long time ago the great king [of England] liked plenty of trade, more than now; then many ships came, and they bought ivory, gold, and slaves; but now he will not let the ships come as before, and the people buy gold and ivory only. This is what I have in my head, so now tell me truly, like a friend, why does the king do so? . . . I only want to hear what you think as a friend: this is not like the other palavers." I [Dupuis] was confessedly at a loss for an argument that might pass as a satisfactory reason. . . . The king did not deem it plausible, that this obnoxious traffic should have been abolished from motives of humanity alone; neither would he admit that it lessened the number either of domestic or foreign wars.

Source: Joseph Dupuis, *Journal of a Residence in Ashantee, Comprising Notes and Researches Relative to the Gold Coast, and the Interior of Western Africa* (London: Henry Colburn, 1824), pp. 162–164.

Taking up one of my observations, he remarked, "the white men who go to council with your master, and pray to the great God for him, do not understand my country, or they would not say the slave trade was bad. But if they think it bad now, why did they think it good before. . . . If the great king would like to restore this trade, it would be good for the white men and for me too, because Asante is a country for war, and the people are strong; so if you talk that palaver for me properly, in the white country, if you go there, I will give you plenty of gold, and I will make you richer than all the white men.

. . . "And when he [the king of England] sees what is true, he will surely restore that trade. I cannot make war to catch slaves in the bush, like a thief. My ancestors never did so. But if I fight a king, and kill him when he is insolent, then certainly I must have his gold, and his slaves, and the people are mine too. Do not the white kings act like this? Because I hear the old men say, that before I conquered Fante[1]. . . white men came in

great ships, and fought and killed many people; and then they took the gold and slaves to the white country: and sometimes they fought together. That is all the same as these black countries. . . . When I fought Gyaman,[2] I did not make war for slaves, but because Dinkera [the king] sent me an arrogant message and killed my people, and refused to pay me gold as his father did. Then . . . like my ancestors, I killed Dinkera, and took his gold, and brought more than 20,000 slaves to Kumasi. Some of these people being bad men, I washed my stool[3] in their blood. . . . But then some were good people, and these I sold or gave to my captains: many, moreover, died, because this country does not grow too much corn . . . and what can I do? Unless I kill or sell them, they will grow strong and kill my people. Now you must tell my master [the king of England] that these slaves can work for him, and if he wants 10,000 he can have them. And if he wants fine handsome girls and women to give his captains, I can send him great numbers."

---

[1]The Fante arrived on the Guinea Coast sometime after 1600 and established a number of small states before being conquered by Asante in the 1760s.

[2]A rival state to the northwest of Asante.
[3]A reference to the "Golden Stool," a symbol of Asante royal power.

Political Change in the Ottoman and Mughal Empires

Empires are forged through military conquest, and most disintegrate and disappear as a result of military defeat. So it was for the Muslim empires of South and Southwest Asia. The Safavid Empire of Persia came to an abrupt end in 1722, when Afghan warriors took the capital city of Isfahan and the Safavids fled to the hills, leaving the region open to Ottoman invasion, decades of anarchy, and the establishment of the weak Qajar Dynasty in the 1790s. In India, the Mughal Empire, for all intents and purposes, ceased to exist after the warlord Nadir Shah—who had seized power in Persia—invaded India in 1739 and sacked Delhi, the Mughal capital. The Ottoman Empire outlasted the other Islamic empires, but in the end, it too disappeared in the wake of military defeat, in this case in World War I.

In each of these empires, decay had set in long before military defeat led to their demise. All of them faced deteriorating financial situations once their expansion ended. Large armies were still needed to defend borders and maintain authority over newly conquered peoples, many of whom resented their new rulers and resisted integration into a new state. Rulers themselves added to the financial strain by spending lavishly on court life, the arts, and building projects. While expanding, the empires could meet such costs by confiscating the wealth of newly conquered peoples and adding these new subjects to the tax rolls. After expansion ended, however, expenses could be met only by raising taxes, running deficits, and selling offices and titles. Such expedients simply put off the day of fiscal reckoning. Another solution was to undertake new conquests. This was the strategy of Mughal emperor Aurangzeb (r. 1658–1707), whose armies conquered new territories in southern and northwest India, but at the cost of rebellion, constant warfare, religious conflict, and financial collapse.

The Ottoman, Safavid, and Mughal empires all were plagued by succession struggles and deteriorating leadership. The Ottoman and Safavid practice of raising the rulers' sons as indulged prisoners in the palace to prevent rebellions contributed to a long series of uninformed, inexperienced, and often debauched sultans and shahs. Leadership of the Mughal Empire also deteriorated after the death of Aurangzeb, although it would have taken a leader with extraordinary qualities to have revived Mughal fortunes in the early 1700s.

An Insider's View of Ottoman Decline

44 • MEHMED PASHA, THE BOOK OF COUNSEL FOR VIZIERS AND GOVERNORS

Along with battlefield defeats, fiscal crises, internal turmoil, and palace intrigues, another sign of Ottoman decline in the seventeenth and eighteenth centuries was the appearance of numerous plans for reviving the empire's fortunes. Among the most candid and insightful works of this type was *The Book of Counsel for Viziers and Governors*, written in the early eighteenth century by an Ottoman treasury official, Mehmed Pasha. Although little is known about Mehmed Pasha's early life, it is likely that he was born into the family of a petty merchant in Istanbul in the 1650s. While in his teens, he was apprenticed to an official in the Ottoman treasury department, in which he worked for the rest of his career. His service was rewarded in 1702, when he was named chief *defterdar*, or treasurer, of the empire. Over the next fifteen years, Mehmed Pasha lost and regained this office no fewer than seven times as different factions became ascendant in the sultan's administration. In 1717, however, he was executed on order of the sultan after he was blamed for the loss of a fortress in the Balkans.

It is unknown when exactly Mehmed Pasha wrote *The Book of Counsel for Viziers and Governors*, but internal evidence suggests it was around 1703 or 1704. It is a book written by a man who had firsthand knowledge of the failings of the Ottoman state and was deeply disturbed by what he knew.

QUESTIONS FOR ANALYSIS

1. Mehmed Pasha cites several examples of how the sultan's subjects suffer as a result of government policies and practices. What examples does he cite, and what are their causes?
2. What, according to the author, are the reasons for the government's financial problems? What solutions does he propose?
3. How does Mehmed Pasha's description of the Ottoman military and government differ from the observations made by Ogier Ghiselin de Busbecq in the sixteenth century (source 12)?
4. What do Mehmed Pasha's comments reveal about the economic situation in the Ottoman Empire around 1700?
5. Little was done to implement the changes suggested by Mehmed Pasha and other Ottoman reformers. What do you think made it so difficult to achieve meaningful reforms?

The Results of Bribery

It is essential to guard against giving an office through bribery to the unfit and to tyrannical oppressors. For giving office to such as these because of bribes means giving permission to plunder the property of the subjects. . . . In addition to what is given as a bribe, he must make a profit for himself and his followers. . . . If it becomes necessary to give a position because of bribes, in this way its holder has permission from the government for every sort of oppression. Stretching out the hand of violence and tyranny against the poor subjects along his route of travel[1] and spreading fear among the poor, he destroys the wretched peasants and ruins the cultivated lands. As the fields and villages become empty of husbandmen, day by day weakness comes to land and property, which remain destitute of profits, revenues, harvest, and benefit. In addition to the fact that it causes a decline in the productivity of the subjects and in the revenues of the Treasury, through neglect of the employment of tilling and lack of the work of agriculture, there is the greatest probability . . . that it will cause scarcity, dearth, mishaps and calamities.

Financial Issues

The business of the Treasury is among the most important and essential affairs of the Exalted Government. The man who is chief treasurer needs to know and understand . . . the Treasury employees who for their own advantage are the cause of ruin and destruction to the government service in obtaining tax farms.[2] He must know how they behave in getting money from the Treasury through "invalid receipts"[3] and in other cases, and he must understand what are their tricks and wiles. . . . Every one of them is waiting and watching in the corner of opportunity, taking care to cause certain matters outside the regular procedure to appear correct. . . . In case the chief treasurer is not informed about such persons, they cause the wasting of the public wealth through various frauds, and of disordering affairs. . . .

Source: From Walter L. Wright, *The Book of Counsel for Viziers and Governors.* Princeton University Press, 1935, pp. 88–89, 95, 96, 102–106, 111, 112, and 126.

[1]Officials traveling on government business were entitled to horses, food, and lodging from the people of the districts they visited.

[2]Tax farms were purchased by private individuals who in return for paying the government a lump sum received the right to collect taxes owed the government.

[3]Forged documents showing that a person had paid his taxes.

Those who are chief treasurers should be extremely circumspect in behavior, upright and devout, devoid of avarice and spite. . . . They . . . should strive to increase the income of the Treasury and to diminish expenditures. But the reduction of expenditures cannot come about through the care and industry of the chief treasurer alone. These must be supplemented by the Sovereign and personal help of his imperial majesty the sultan, who is the refuge of the universe, and by the good management of his excellency the grand vizier.[4] . . .

Certain tax concessions, instead of being farmed out, should be committed to the charge of trustworthy and upright persons on government account.[5]

Let the janissary corps[6] not be increased. Let them be well disciplined, few but elite, and all present in time of need. In this connection also it is fitting to be extremely careful and to be attentive in keeping their rolls in proper order and in having the soldiers actually present. The late Lutfi Pasha, who was formerly grand vizier, has written: "Fifteen thousand soldiers are a great many soldiers. It is a heroic deed to pay the wages year by year of fifteen thousand men with no decrease." But under the present conditions the soldiers and pensioned veterans . . . who get pay and rations have exceeded all limits.

In order that the income and expenditure of the Treasury may be known and the totals inspected, the rolls of the bureaus must be investigated and the numbers known. There are on a war footing 53,200 janissary infantry, consisting of janissaries of the imperial court and pensioned veterans, including those who are in the fortresses protecting the ever-victorious frontier. There are 17,133 cavalrymen of the sipahis, silahdars,[7] and four other regiments of cavalry. The armorers of the imperial court and artillerymen and artillery drivers and bostanjis[8] of the bodyguard . . . and the aghas[9] of the imperial stirrup and mtiteferriqas[10] and sergeants and gatemen and those who belong to the imperial stables and the flourishing kitchens and to the dockyard and to the *peikan*[11] and to other units, making up 17,716 persons, the total of all these amounts to 96,727 persons.

The expense for meat and value of the winter allowance[12] together with the yearly pay of the janissaries of the lofty court and armorers and artillerymen and artillery drivers in the fortresses on the ever-victorious frontier exceeds a total of ten thousand purses of aspers.[13] And in addition to these, the local troops in the fortresses on the ever-victorious frontier number seventy thousand persons and certain veterans pensioned from the income of the custom house and tax farms, together with those who have the duty of saying prayers amount to twenty-three thousand five hundred. Their yearly pay amounts to five thousand nine hundred and ten purses. Those who are on the government galleys total six thousand persons and their yearly pay eight hundred purses. Accordingly, the total of those who receive pay and have duties is 196,227 and their yearly pay amounts to 16,710 purses.[14]

---

[4]A *vizier* was a government minister. The *grand vizier* was chief minister.

[5]In other words, tax farming should be abandoned and taxes collected directly by the government.

[6]Infantry fighters in the Ottoman army, originally recruited from the sultan's Christian subjects, who were converted to Islam and given over to military training. Their effectiveness had severely declined by the eighteenth century.

[7]*Sipahis* and *silahdars* were cavalry troops supported by land grants from the sultan.

[8]Imperial guards responsible for protecting the imperial palace and its grounds.

[9]Commanders.

[10]Mounted bodyguards who accompanied diplomats on missions.

[11]An elite bodyguard numbering thirty to forty men who wore distinctive gilded helmets.

[12]Payments over and above the troops' regular salaries.

[13]A *purse* was a unit of money made up of approximately 420 *piasters*; one piaster equaled 120 *aspers*.

[14]A sum that exceeded the estimated annual income of the government.

In addition to these salaries there are incomes of the illustrious princes and princesses and the grand vizier and the yearly allowance of the Tatar princes[15] and of the commanders of the sea and the expenditures of the imperial kitchens and stables, of the flourishing dockyards, of the prefect of the capital, of the chief butcher, of the agha of Istanbul, of the chief biscuit maker, of the cannon factory, some expenditures of mtiteferriqas, and in addition to these, chance expenditures which do not come to mind. . . . For this reason the income does not cover the expenditure, and of necessity the farmed taxes, and other taxes such as the capitation tax,[16] have each fallen a year or two in arrears.

The State of the Military

The troops on the frontiers are actually too numerous on their rolls and in the summaries given, although it is certain that in their appointed places each battalion is deficient, some being perhaps half lacking and others even more, nevertheless they let the salaries be sent from here for all. As for the extra money which they get, they have agreed to divide it among themselves. Care and thought and trustworthiness and uprightness in the officers is needed for the separation and distinguishing of those who are present and those who are absent. . . .

Everyone knows that there are very many people outside the corps who pretend they are janissaries. Especially in recent times, because of the long continuance of campaigns which have taken place against the Magyars[17] and in various other regions, outsiders have joined and mixed themselves among this janissary corps more than among all the others. Becoming mingled with all sorts of people, the janissaries have broken down their fixed regulations. In the towns and villages situated on the coasts of Anatolia and in many regions of Rumelia[18] likewise, many of the subject population, in order to free their necks from the obligations which are incumbent upon them, have changed their dress.[19] Because of their pretensions of being janissaries and because of aid from the commanders of the latter,[20] the civilians cannot be separated from the janissaries. There is no distinction between this sort of men and the faithful guardians of the frontier, veterans who have undergone fatigue and hard usage on campaigns, who have perhaps been several times wounded and injured, who have suffered cuts and bruises for the welfare of faith and state, who have pillowed their heads on stones and lain down to sleep upon the ground. . . .

When either the glorious commander-in-chief or the generals go on campaign, their true purpose should be the animating of religion and the execution of the words of the Prophet. . . . Let them not be unjust or oppressive to any one, but just and equitable, and let them seek to win affection and praises. . . .

For when soldiers are charged with a campaign, they join in bands and agree together to consider one of themselves as chief. Practicing brigandage, they are not satisfied with free fodder for their horses and food for their own bellies from the villages they meet. They covet the horse-cloth and rags of the peasants, and if they can get their

[15]Chieftains on the borders of the empire who were allies of the Ottomans.
[16]A tax on individuals; a head tax.
[17]The term *Magyar,* meaning Hungarian, often was used to refer to any of the Ottomans' Christian enemies in southeastern Europe.
[18]An area north of Greece, including the regions of Albania, Macedonia, and Thrace.
[19]The people have purchased and wear the uniforms of the janissaries and claim to be members of the corps to avoid paying taxes.
[20]The commanders have accepted bribes to enter their names on the corps' roles.

hands on the granaries they become joyful, filling their sacks with barley and oats for provisions and fodder. While they behave in this way . . . the sighs and groans of mankind attain the heavens and it is certain that they will be accursed. . . .

Economic Regulations

It is essential at all times for every ruler to keep track of the small things relating to the general condition of the people. He must set the proper market prices. Everything must be sold at the price it is worth. For in case the sultan and the viziers say: "The fixing of market prices, though part of the public business, is insignificant," and are not diligent about it, the city judge alone cannot carry it out. . . . Under such circumstances everyone buys and sells as he pleases.

Through senseless avarice the venom of vipers is added to lawful goods. The most contemptible of the people, useless both for the services of the sultan and for warfare, become possessors of all the wealth . . . while the great men of the people who deserve respect, becoming poor and powerless, pursue the road of bankruptcy. Then, when it comes about that both horsemen and footmen who go on campaign must sell all their property,[21] it is troublesome and difficult to determine all at once how to restrain those men who have them by the throat and how to change their demeanor and diminish their arrogance. . . . The fruiterers and merchants put a double price on provisions and supplies and reap a harvest of profits. They rob the people. . . .

---

[21]Many soldiers paid for their own military equipment and provisions before a campaign. They hoped to recoup their expenses through plunder.

European Designs on India

45 • JOSEPH FRANÇOIS DUPLEIX, MEMORANDUM TO THE DIRECTORS OF THE FRENCH EAST INDIA COMPANY; ROBERT CLIVE, LETTER TO WILLIAM PITT THE ELDER

As the Mughal Empire disintegrated in the eighteenth century, Indian–European relations underwent a dramatic change. Until then (with a few exceptions, such as the Portuguese colony at Goa), European merchants had stayed out of Indian politics and were content to trade from coastal cities, where, with the approval of the emperor and local rulers, they built wharves, warehouses, and offices. As Mughal authority deteriorated, however, agents of the British East India Company, founded in 1600, and the French East India Company, founded in 1664, sought to improve their financial situation by entering into agreements with local princes. By mid-century, they were laying plans for actual territorial conquest.

A Frenchman, Joseph François Dupleix (1697–1763), and an Englishman, Robert Clive (1725–1774), were the two principal advocates of greater European involvement in India. Dupleix, the son of a merchant, was sent by his father on a voyage to India in 1715 to divert him from a career in science to one in commerce. The elder Dupleix's strategy was successful. After amassing a fortune in Indian trade, in 1742, his son was appointed governor-general of the French East India Company's interests in India. He was convinced that the French could gain a decisive advantage over their British rivals by gaining political control over Indian territories and using local tax revenues to increase profits and pay the costs of fighting the British. In 1749, in return for intervening in a local struggle, France gained control of territories in and around the southeast coastal city of Pondicherry. In the next four years, the French extended their influence in southern India through diplomacy and conquest. Worried about expenses and conflict with the British, the directors of the French East India Company opposed such ventures, and to overcome their doubts, Dupleix sent them the following memorandum in 1753. His efforts failed, however, and in 1754, he was recalled in disgrace when he defied the directors' orders to abandon his policies.

The dismissal of Dupleix, who died in obscurity and poverty in 1763, provided an opening for his rival, Robert Clive. The son of an English landowner and politician, Clive entered the service of the East India Company at age eighteen and sailed to India after an unspectacular career as a student. Commissioned in the company army four years later, he distinguished himself in the defeat of the French and their Indian allies at the Battle of Arcot in 1751. Six years later, he led British forces to another important victory at the Battle of Plassey. With financial support from Indian bankers and merchants, they defeated the forces of Siraj-ud-Daula, the *nawab,* or governor, of the large northeastern state of Bengal, who had earned the enmity of the company for his harassment of English traders and his attack on the fortified English trading town of Calcutta (present-day Kolkata). In the wake of their victory, the British placed in power their own puppet nawab Mir Jafar, who in return for the promise of British support in his quarrels with neighboring princes was happy to grant the British the rights to collect taxes in a few districts around Calcutta, and to mint their own coin. Clive and the directors of the East India Company were confident that the issue of British trade in Bengal had been settled.

This was hardly the case, however. Less than three years later, having realized that the costs of maintaining their (increasingly unreliable) ally Mir Jafar were higher than expected, Clive began to formulate a plan to bring Bengal under direct British control. He outlined his ambitions in the excerpt from a letter he wrote on January 7, 1759, to William Pitt the Elder (1708–1778), later Earl of Chatham, who since 1757, as secretary of state, had been the minister responsible for directing the fight against France in the Seven Years' War (1756–1763).

QUESTIONS FOR ANALYSIS

1. According to Dupleix, what are the anticipated benefits from the extension of French political authority in India?
2. According to Clive, what benefits will accrue to Great Britain once it establishes its authority in India? How do his views resemble and differ from those of Dupleix?

3. Why are Dupleix and Clive convinced that the Europeans will encounter little difficulty in establishing their political authority in India?
4. What does Clive's letter reveal about the state of the Mughal Empire in the mid-1700s?
5. What does Clive's letter reveal about his attitudes toward the Indians and their rulers?

Memorandum to the Directors of the French East India Company (1753)

All the Company's commerce in India is shared with the English, the Dutch, the Portuguese and the Danes. . . . This division of trade, or rather this rivalry, has served to raise considerably the price of merchandise here and has contributed quite a little toward cheapening the quality—two unfortunate circumstances which, of course, further reduce the price and profits in Europe. . . . Our Company can hope for no monopoly in the Indian trade. We shall always share whatever we deal in with other countries. We can, therefore, hope for no other profits than those being made at present. We should even anticipate that instead of increasing, they are likely to decline and that very soon. . . . The only possible way of making profits on inferior merchandise would be to have a large and regular revenue; then the losses could be offset by our income. Those of our rivals who did not have such a resource would be obliged to give up this branch of commerce, or else restrict themselves to their national market. . . .

I pass now to the second truth, which is that every commercial company should avoid the exportation of bullion [gold and silver] from the kingdom. It is a maxim long established that the more the specie [coined money] circulates in a state, the more flourishing is the state's condition, and the more the state can be helped and sustained by it. It is, then, good policy to seek every means of preventing its exportation. But it is very hard, not to say impossible, to trade in China and India without exporting specie. . . . Since it is obviously impossible to keep all our specie in France, we should neglect nothing to reduce to a minimum its exportation to India, whence it will never flow back to Europe. Our manufactures . . . can diminish such exportation, but not to the extent we desire; we need something else, and this can only be found in a fixed, constant, and abundant local revenue. . . .

Let us suppose that the Company is obliged yearly to send twelve millions to India. Wool, cloth, and other exported manufactures amount to two millions, so there remains ten millions to be sent in specie, a large sum and one exported only too frequently. It could be reduced by at least half, and might even entirely cease, if the local revenue amounted to ten millions. . . .

. . . This work would have been already accomplished, if I had been better supported, not only here but in my native land, which has looked upon the benefits I have acquired for it with too great indifference. . . . I shall content myself by saying that, in spite of all the obstacles, I have succeeded in procuring for my nation a revenue of at least five millions. My intention was to raise it to ten millions, and I would have succeeded. . . . Yes, I can truly say that if what [military support] has arrived this year had been drawn from France's regular troops, all the fighting would now be over and the Company would be enjoying more than ten millions in revenue.

Source: (1) Joseph Francois Dupleix, "Memorandum to the Directors of the French East India Company," from Virginia Thompson, *Dupleix and His Letters* (New York: Baillou, 1933), pp. 801–202. (2) Robert Clive in a letter to William Pitt, in John Malcolm, *The Life of Robert, Lord Clive* (London: John Murray, 1836), vol. 2, pp. 119–125.

Letter to William Pitt the Elder (1759)

The great revolution that has been effected here by the success of the English arms, and the vast advantages gained to the Company . . . have, I observe, in some measure, engaged the public attention; but much more may yet in time be done, if the Company will exert themselves in the manner the importance of their present possessions and future prospects deserves. I have represented to them in the strongest terms the expediency of sending out and keeping up constantly such a force as will enable them to embrace the first opportunity of further aggrandizing themselves; and I dare pronounce, from a thorough knowledge of this country's government, and of the genius of the people, acquired by two years' application and experience, that such an opportunity will soon offer. The reigning Subah,[1] whom the victory at Plassey invested with the sovereignty of these provinces, still, it is true, retains his attachment to us, and probably, while he has no other support, will continue to do so; but Muslims are so little influenced by gratitude, that should he ever think it his interest to break with us, the obligations he owes us would prove no restraint. . . . Moreover, he is advanced in years; and his son is so cruel, worthless a young fellow, and so apparently an enemy to the English, that it will be almost unsafe trusting him with the succession. So small a body as two thousand Europeans will secure us against any apprehensions from either the one or the other; and, in case of their daring to be troublesome, enable the Company to take the sovereignty upon themselves.

There will be the less difficulty in bringing about such an event, as the natives themselves have no attachment whatever to particular princes; and as, under the present Government, they have no security for their lives or properties, they would rejoice in so happy an exchange as that of a mild for a despotic Government: and there is little room to doubt our easily obtaining the Mughal's [Mughal emperor's] grant in confirmation thereof, provided we agreed to pay him the stipulated allotment out of the revenues, viz. fifty lacs[2] annually. . . .

But so large a sovereignty may possibly be an object too extensive for a mercantile Company; and it is to be feared they are not of themselves able, without the nation's assistance, to maintain so wide a dominion. I have therefore presumed, Sir, to represent this matter to you, and submit it to your consideration, whether the execution of a design, that may hereafter be still carried to greater lengths, be worthy of the Government's taking it into hand. . . . Now I leave you to judge, whether an income yearly of upwards of two millions sterling, with the possession of three provinces [Bengal, Bihar, and Orissa] abounding in the most valuable productions of nature and of art, be an object deserving the public attention; and whether it be worth the nation's while to take the proper measures to secure such an acquisition—an acquisition which, under the management of so able and disinterested a minister, would prove a source of immense wealth to the kingdom, and might in time be appropriated in part as a fund towards diminishing the heavy load of debt under which we at present labor. Add to these advantages the influence we shall thereby acquire over the several European nations engaged in the commerce here, which these could no longer carry on but through our indulgence, and under such limitations as we should think fit to prescribe. It is well worthy of consideration, that this project may be brought about without draining the mother country, as has been too much the case with our possessions in America. A small force from home will be sufficient, as we always make sure of any number we please of black [Indian] troops, who, being both much better paid and treated by us than by the country powers, will very readily enter into our service. . . .

---

[1] A synonym for nawab, governor of an Indian province. This specific reference is to Mir Jafar, the British puppet installed in power after the Battle of Plassey.

[2] Synonymous with *lakh*, meaning 100,000. Clive states that the British will pay 5 million rupees (in British currency approximately 260,000 pounds) per year to the emperor

The Expansion of British Power in India

Territory under British control

Before 1770
1770–1800
1800–1830
1830–1860
Princely states

AFGHANISTAN

PERSIA (IRAN)

CHINA

TIBET

NEPAL

BHUTAN

KASHMIR

PUNJAB
Lahore • • Amritsar

SINDH

Karachi •

RAJPUTANA
Jaipur •

AJMER

Ahmadabad •

Surat •

SINDH

Delhi •
• Agra

OUDH
Lucknow •
• Benares

BIHAR

CHOTA-NAGPUR

BENGAL
Dakha •
Calcutta (Kolkata) •

MANIPUR

BURMA (MYANMAR)

Irrawaddy R.

SIAM (THAILAND)

NAGPUR

BERAR

HYDERABAD

Pune •

Bombay (Mumbai) •

Goa (Portugal) •

MYSORE
Bangalore •

Calicut •

Madras (Chennai) •
Pondicherry (France) •
Karikal •

CEYLON (SRI LANKA)
• Kandy
Colombo •

Arabian Sea

Bay of Bengal

Andaman Islands

Nicobar Islands

Indus R.

Ganges R.

Brahmaputra R.

Tropic of Cancer

400 Km.
400 Mi.
200
200
0
0

The Continuing Vitality of Islam

The resurgence of Islam in the late twentieth century, characterized by political militancy, intensification of personal devotion, and a drive to create societies based on Islamic law and teaching, has precedents that go far back in Islamic history. Time and again, the religion has been revitalized and renewed by movements inspired by visionaries, mystics, and scholars who have exhorted believers to purify doctrine and ritual and rededicate their lives to God. The eighteenth century was such a period of Islamic revitalization, despite the demoralizing political and military failures of the major Muslim empires. Islam continued to make converts in Southeast Asia and Africa and spread into areas such as eastern Bengal through migration. In addition, movements of reform and renewal took root in many parts of the Islamic world, including the religion's historic center in Arabia and its outermost fringes in Southeast Asia and West Africa.

Although eighteenth-century Muslim reform movements varied greatly, most were led by legal or Quranic scholars or devotees of Sufism, the mystical movement within Islam that emphasizes personal experience and closeness to God through devotion. Many reformers traveled widely and drew inspiration from experiences in religious centers such as Baghdad, Cairo, Mecca, and Medina. Some called for a purification of Muslim practices and a return to Islam's fundamentals as revealed in the Quran and the teachings and deeds of Muhammad. Many were convinced that Islam had been tainted by accommodating itself to local religious customs and beliefs. Some urged Muslims to seek social justice, while others preached a message of puritanical rigor and personal regeneration. A few called on their followers to take up the sword against unbelievers and heretics.

Eighteenth-century Islamic reform movements were not anti-Western, but they did affect later interactions between the West and the Islamic world. In the early history of Islam, many Muslim intellectuals and religious leaders considered certain Western and Islamic views compatible, and they had integrated aspects of Western thought, especially ancient Greek philosophy, into Islamic learning. The message of many eighteenth-century reformers, however, was that Islam was sufficient unto itself. Islam should be more exclusivist, more centered on its own writings and traditions, and more suspicious of outside ideas and practices. Such views were one of many factors that shaped relations between the Muslim and Western worlds in the modern era.

A Call to Recapture Islam's Purity

46 • ABDULLAH WAHHAB, THE HISTORY AND DOCTRINES OF THE WAHHABIS

Wahhabism, the dominant form of Islam in Saudi Arabia and Qatar and a growing influence in many parts of the Islamic world, traces its origins to Muhammad Ibn Abd al-Wahhab, whose teachings gave rise to a movement whose followers called themselves *Muwahhidun,* or "those who advocate oneness," because they rejected any belief or practice that even slightly detracted from the exclusive worship of God. Muhammad Ibn Abd al-Wahhab (1703–1792) was a native of Nejd, a region in the east-central part of the Arabian Peninsula, who as a student and teacher visited Mecca, Medina, Basra, Damascus, and Baghdad. After he returned to Arabia, Wahhab, influenced by the thought of the thirteenth century theologian Ibn Tamiyya and the teachings of the Hanbali School of jurisprudence, began to denounce what he viewed as the Arabs' religious failings. These included magical rituals, faith in holy men, worship of saints and their tombs, and veneration of supposedly sacred wells and trees. He also rejected Sufi mysticism, Shiism, and rationalist attempts to understand God's nature and purposes.

A key development in the history of the movement was the alliance forged in 1744 between Ibn Abd al-Wahhab and Muhammad Ibn Saud, who, as leader of the Saudi clan, sought to extend his authority throughout Arabia. The clan leader provided protection for Wahhab, who, in turn, supported the clan's claim to political authority. Although he therefore approved the Saudi's military campaigns, he never was willing to endorse them as jihads, or holy wars.

This changed after his death in 1792. In 1802, his followers captured Karbala in present-day Iraq and destroyed the tomb of the revered Shia Imam Husayn. One year later, they captured the holy city of Mecca, the immediate aftermath of which is described in the following selection. It is the work of the founder's grandson, Abdullah Wahhab, who participated in the conquest of Mecca and was executed when an army sent by the Ottoman sultan took the city in 1813. Abdullah Wahhab wrote this piece to answer critics and to clarify the beliefs of the Muwahhidun.

QUESTIONS FOR ANALYSIS

1. In the Wahhabi view, what are the most serious threats to the purity of Islam?
2. How did the Wahhabis attempt to change Mecca after they captured it? What do their acts reveal about their beliefs and purposes?
3. The Wahhabis have been characterized as puritanical and intolerant. Is such a view justified on the basis of this document?
4. The Wahhabis strongly opposed Shiism and the use of logic as a means of discovering religious truth. Why? (See the introduction to source 14 for a discussion of Shiism.)
5. How do the Wahhabis perceive their role in the history of Islam?

. . . Now I was engaged in the holy war, carried on by those who truly believe in the Unity of God, when God, praised be He, graciously permitted us to enter Mecca, the holy, the exalted, at midday, on the 6th day of the week on the 8th of the month Muharram, 1218, Hijri [April 1803]. Before this, Saud,[1] our leader in the holy war, whom the Lord protect, had summoned the nobles, the divines, and the common people of Mecca; for indeed the leaders of the pilgrims and the rulers of Mecca had

Source: J. O'Kinealy, "Translation of an Arabic Pamphlet on the History and Doctrines of the Wahhabis, Written by 'Abdullah, Grandson of 'Abdul Wahhab, the Founder of the Wahhabis," *Journal of the Asiatic Society of Bengal,* vol. 43 (1874), pp. 68–82.

[1]Saud ibn Abdul Aziz ibn Muhammad al Saud, head of the house of Saud from 1803 to 1814.

resolved on battle, and had risen up against us in the holy place, to exclude us from the house of God. But when the army of the true believers advanced, the Lord filled their hearts with terror, and they fled hither and thither. Then our commander gave protection to everyone within the holy place, while we, with shaven heads and hair cut short,[2] entered with safety, crying "Labbayka,"[3] without fear of any created being, and only of the Lord God. Now, though we were more numerous, better armed and disciplined than the people of Mecca, yet we did not cut down their trees, neither did we hunt,[4] nor shed any blood except the blood of victims, and of those four-footed beasts which the Lord has made lawful by his commands.

When our pilgrimage was over, we gathered the people together . . . , and our leader, whom the Lord saves, explained to the divines what we required of the people, . . . namely, a pure belief in the Unity of God Almighty. He pointed out to them that there was no dispute between us and them except on two points, and that one of these was a sincere belief in the unity of God, and a knowledge of the different kinds of prayer of which *dua*[5] was one. He added that to show the significance of *shirk*,[6] the prophet (may he be blessed!) had put people to death on account of it; that he had continued to call upon them to believe in the Unity of God for some time after he became inspired, and that he had abandoned shirk before the Lord had declared to him the remaining four pillars[7] of Islam. . . .

. . . They then acknowledged our belief, and there was not one among them who doubted or hesitated to believe that that for which we condemned men to death, was the truth pure and unsullied. And they swore a binding oath, although we had not asked them, that their hearts had been opened and their doubts removed, and that they were convinced whoever said, "Oh prophet of God!" or "Oh Ibn 'Abbas!" or "Oh 'Abdul Qadir!"[8] or called on any other created being, thus entreating him to turn away evil or grant what is good (where the power belongs to God alone), such as recovery from sickness, or victory over enemies, or protection from temptation, etc.; he is a *Mushrik*,[9] guilty of the most heinous form of shirk, his blood shall be shed and property confiscated. Nor is it any excuse that he believes the effective first cause in the movements of the universe is God, and only supplicates those mortals . . . to intercede for him or bring him nearer the presence of God, so that he may obtain what he requires from Him through them or through their intercession. Again, the tombs which had been erected over the remains of the pious, had become in these times as it were idols where the people went to pray for what they required; they humbled themselves before them, and called upon those lying in them, in their distress, just as did those who were in darkness before the coming of Muhammad.

When this was over, we razed all the large tombs in the city which the people generally worshipped and believed in, and by which they hoped to obtain benefits or ward off evil, so that there did not remain an idol to be adored in that pure city, for which God be praised. Then the taxes and customs we abolished, all the different kinds of instruments for using tobacco we destroyed, and

---

[2]A custom during the pilgrimage to Mecca.

[3]The loud cry uttered as Muslims begin their pilgrimage activities in Mecca.

[4]Not cutting down a defeated enemy's trees or hunting the enemy's animals was considered an act of mercy.

[5]A personal prayer uttered by a Muslim.

[6]*Shirk* is the opposite of surrender to God and the acceptance and recognition of His reality. It may mean atheism, paganism, or polytheism. According to Muslim doctrine, it is the root of all sin.

[7]The first pillar of Islam is the creed, which affirms "There is no god but God, and Muhammad is the messenger of God." The other four pillars are daily prayer, almsgiving, fasting during the month of Ramadan, and pilgrimage, at least once in every Muslim's life if possible, to Mecca, the city of Muhammad's birth and revelation.

[8]Calling out in prayer the name of Muhammad or these early caliphs in the Abbasid line detracted from the majesty of God.

[9]A person guilty of shirk.

tobacco itself we proclaimed forbidden.[10] Next we burned the dwellings of those selling *hashish*, and living in open wickedness, and issued a proclamation, directing the people to constantly exercise themselves in prayer. They were not to pray in separate groups according to the different Imams;[11] but all were directed to arrange themselves at each time of prayer behind any Imam who is a follower of any of the four Imams (may the Lord be pleased with them!). For in this way the Lord would be worshiped by as it were one voice, the faithful of all sects would become friendly disposed towards each other, and all dissensions would cease. . . .

We believe that good and evil proceed from God, the exalted; that nothing happens in His kingdom, but what He commands. . . . We believe that the faithful will see Him in the end, but we do not know under what form, as it was beyond our comprehension. And in the same way we follow Imam Ahmad Ibn Hanbal in matters of detail; but we do not reject anyone who follows any of the four Imams, as do the Shias, the Zaidiyyahs, and the Imamiyyahs,[12] &c. Nor do we admit them in any way to act openly according to their vicious creeds; on the contrary, we compelled them to follow one of the four Imams. We do not claim to exercise our reason in all matters of religion, and of our faith, save that we follow our judgment where a point is clearly demonstrated to us in either the Quran or the Sunnah.[13] . . . We do not command the destruction of any writings except such as tend to cast people into infidelity to injure their faith, such as those on Logic, which have been prohibited by all Divines. But we are not very exacting with regard to books or documents of this nature, if they

appear to assist our opponents, we destroy them. . . . We do not consider it proper to make Arabs prisoners of war, nor have we done so, neither do we fight with other nations. Finally, we do not consider it lawful to kill women or children. . . .

We do not deny miraculous powers to the saints, but on the contrary allow them. They are under the guidance of the Lord, so long as they continue to follow the way pointed out in the laws and obey the prescribed rules. But whether alive or dead, they must not be made the object of any form of worship. . . .

We prohibit those forms of Bidah[14] that affect religion or pious works. Thus drinking coffee, reciting poetry, praising kings, do not affect religion or pious works and are not prohibited. . . .

All games are lawful. Our prophet allowed play in his mosque. So it is lawful to chide and punish persons in various ways; to train them in the use of different weapons; or to use anything which tends to encourage warriors in battle, such as a war-drum. But it must not be accompanied with musical instruments. These are forbidden, and indeed the difference between them and a war drum is clear. . . .

Whoever is desirous of knowing our belief, let him come to us at al Diriyya,[15] and he will see what will gladden his heart, and his eyes will be pleased in reading the compilations on the different kinds of knowledge. . . . He will see God praised in a pleasing manner; the assistance He gives in establishing the true faith; the kindness, which He exerts among the weak and feeble, between inhabitants and travelers. . . . He is our Agent, our Master, our Deliverer. May peace and the blessing of God be upon our prince Muhammad and on his family and his companions!

---

[10] The Wahhabis saw no Quranic basis for the use of tobacco; its use is still rare in present-day Saudi Arabia.

[11] The author uses the term *imam* to refer to the founders of the four major schools of Sunni Muslim jurisprudence: Abu Hanifa (d. 767), founder of the Hanafite school; Malik ibn Anas (d. 795), founder of the Malikite school; al-Shafi (d. 820), founder of the Shafiite school; and Ahmad ibn Hanbal (d. 855), founder of the Hanbali school. The

Wahhabis were Hanbalis, but did not reject the authority of the other schools.

[12] Zaidiyyahs and Imamiyyahs were Shia sects.

[13] The body of traditional social and legal thought and practice that represent the proper observance of Islam.

[14] Erroneous or improper customs that grew after the third generation of Muslims died out.

[15] The Wahhabi capital, some fifteen miles northeast of Riyadh.

Jihad in the Western Sudan

47 • USMAN DAN FODIO, SELECTIONS FROM HIS WRITINGS

Although merchants and teachers from North Africa and Arabia had introduced Islam to Africa's western and central Sudan (the region south of the Saharan and Libyan deserts) as early as the tenth century, by 1800, Islam was not truly dominant in these regions. It was largely a religion of the cities, where resident Muslim traders had established Islamic communities, built mosques, introduced Arabic, and made converts. Many converts, however, continued non-Muslim religious rites and festivals, and in rural areas, peasants and herders remained animists. Rulers became Muslims in name, but often less for religious reasons than to ingratiate themselves with the merchant community and to attract Islamic scholars to their service as advisors, interpreters, and scribes. Most rulers tolerated their subjects' pagan practices, and many participated in such practices themselves.

This changed as a result of a series of jihads, or holy wars, which swept across the Sudan in the eighteenth and nineteenth centuries. Dedicated Muslims took up arms against nonbelievers and, after seizing power, imposed a strict form of Islam on their new subjects. In a matter of decades, these movements redrew the region's political and religious map.

The first major jihad of the era, known as the Sokoto Jihad, took place in Hausaland in the early nineteenth century under the leadership of Usman dan Fodio (1754–1817). Hausaland, an area that straddles the Niger River and today makes up the northern part of Nigeria, had been settled by Hausa speakers in the tenth century but also had substantial numbers of Fulani, pastoralists who had begun to migrate into the area in the 1500s. After the Songhai Empire's collapse around 1600, it was divided into approximately a dozen principalities.

Usman dan Fodio, a member of a Fulani clan with a tradition of Islamic scholarship and teaching, was a member of the *Qadiriyya,* a Sufi brotherhood dating from the twelfth century. Beginning in the 1770s, he began to travel and preach in Hausaland, denouncing corrupt Islamic practices and the rulers who tolerated them. His calls for religious and political renewal won him followers among the Fulani, who considered themselves oppressed by their rulers, and some Hausa farmers, who were feeling the effects of drought and land shortages. In 1804, when the Sultan of Gobir denounced Usman and prepared to attack his followers, Usman called on his supporters to take up arms and begin a jihad against Hausaland's rulers. By the late 1810s, Usman controlled Hausaland and established the Kingdom of Sokoto. After his retirement from public life, Usman's son and brother extended the campaign to the south and east of the kingdom. The era of Sudanese jihads had begun in earnest.

Usman wrote nearly 100 treatises on politics, religion, marriage customs, and education. Brief excerpts from four of them are included here. Together they provide a sampling of his thoughts on religion, government, and society.

QUESTIONS FOR ANALYSIS

1. What policies and values of the Hausa sultans does Usman criticize? Why?
2. How do the religious failings of the Hausa princes prevent them from being just and equitable rulers?
3. What groups in Hausa society would have been most likely to respond positively to Usman's criticisms of the sultans?
4. What is Usman's message concerning the treatment of Muslim women? Is it a message of equality with men?

The Faults of the Hausa Rulers[1]

And one of the ways of their government is the building of their sovereignty upon three things: the people's persons, their honor, and their possessions; and whomsoever they wish to kill or exile or violate his honor or devour his wealth they do so in pursuit of their lusts, without any right in the *Sharia*.[2] . . . One of the ways of their government is their intentionally eating whatever food they wish, whether it is religiously permitted or forbidden, and wearing whatever clothes they wish, whether religiously permitted or forbidden, and drinking what beverages they wish, whether religiously permitted or forbidden, and riding whatever riding beasts they wish, whether religiously permitted or forbidden, and taking what women they wish without marriage contract, and living in decorated palaces, whether religiously permitted or forbidden, and spreading soft carpets as they wish, whether religiously permitted or forbidden.

. . . One of the ways of their government is to place many women in their houses, until the number of women of some of them amounts to one thousand or more. . . . One of the ways of their government is to delay in the paying of a debt, and this is injustice. One of the ways of their government is what the superintendent of the market takes from all the parties to a sale, and the meat which he takes on each market day from the butchers, . . . and one of the ways of their government is the cotton and other things which they take in the course of the markets. . . . One of the ways of their government is the taking of people's beasts of burden without their permission to carry the sultan's food to him.

. . . One of the ways of their government which is also well known is that whoever dies in their country, they take his property, and they call it "inheritance," and they know that it is without doubt injustice.[3] One of the ways of their government is to impose tax on merchants, and other travellers. One of the ways of their government, which is also well known, is that one may not pass by their farms, nor cross them without suffering bad treatment from their slaves. One of the ways of their government, which is also well known, is that if the people's animals go among their animals, they do not come out again unless they give

Source: Usman dan Fodio, "The Book of Differences," from M. Hiskett, "Kitab al-farq: A Work on the Habe Kingdoms Attributed to Uth-mann dan Fodio," in *Bulletin of the School of Oriental and African Studies*, vol. 23 (1960); "Concerning the Government of Our Country," from *Tanbih al-ikhwan*, translation in Thomas Hodgkin, *Nigerian Perspectives* (Oxford: Oxford University Press, 1975), pp. 244, 245; "Light of Intellectuals," from *Nur al-albab*, in Hodgkin, pp. 254–255; "Dispatch to the Folk of the Sudan," from A. D. H. Bivar, "The Whatiqat ah al-Sudan: A Manifesto of the Fulani Jihad," in *The Journal of African History*, vol. 2 (1961).

[1]An excerpt from *Kitab al-farq*, "The Book of Differences between the Government of Muslims and Unbelievers," probably written around 1806.
[2]*Sharia*, literally "path" in Arabic, is the word for Islamic law.
[3]A grievance of foreign Muslim merchants who might die while residing in a Hausa city.

a proportion of them, and if the sultan's animals stray, and are found spoiling the cultivated land and other things, they are not driven off. . . .

One of the ways of their government, which is also well known, is that if you have an adversary in law and he precedes you to them, and gives them some money, then your word will not be accepted by them, even though they know for a certainty of your truthfulness, unless you give them more than your adversary gave. One of the ways of their government is to shut the door in the face of the needy. . . . Therefore do not follow their way in their government, and do not imitate them. . . .

Royal Religion[4]

It is well known that in our time Islam in these countries mentioned above is widespread among people other than the sultans. As for the sultans, they are undoubtedly unbelievers, even though they may profess the religion of Islam, because they practice polytheistic rituals and turn people away from the path of God and raise the flag of worldly kingdom above the banner of Islam. . . .

The government of a country is the government of its king without question. If the king is a Muslim, his land is Muslim; if he is an Unbeliever, his land is a land of Unbelievers. . . . There is no dispute that the sultans of these countries venerate certain places, certain trees, and certain rocks and offer sacrifice to them. This constitutes unbelief according to the consensus of opinion.

I say this on the basis of the common practice known about them, but I do not deny the existence of some Muslims here and there among them. Those however are rare and there is no place for what is rare in legal decisions.

The Treatment of Women and Slaves[5]

Most of our educated men leave their wives, their daughters, and the slaves morally abandoned, like beasts, without teaching them what God prescribes should be taught them, and without instructing them in the articles of the Law which concern them. Thus, they leave them ignorant of the rules regarding ablutions,[6] prayer, fasting, business dealings, and other duties which they have to fulfil, and which God commands that they should be taught.

Men treat these beings like household implements which become broken after long use and which are then thrown out on the dung-heap. This is an abominable crime! Alas! How can they thus shut up their wives, their daughters, and their slaves in the darkness of ignorance? . . .

Muslim women—Do not listen to the speech of those who are misguided and who sow the seed of error in the heart of another; they deceive you when they stress obedience to your husbands without telling you of obedience to God and to his Messenger [Muhammad] (May God show him bounty and grant him salvation), and when they say that the woman finds her happiness in obedience to her husband.

They seek only their own satisfaction, and that is why they impose upon you tasks which the Law of God and that of his Prophet have never especially assigned to you. Such are— the preparation of food-stuffs, the washing of clothes, and other duties which they like to impose upon you, while they neglect to teach you what God and the Prophet have prescribed for you.

Yes, the woman owes submission to her husband, publicly as well as in intimacy, even if he

---

[4]From *Tanbih al-Ikhwan* . . . "Concerning the Government of Our Country . . ." written around 1811.

[5]From *Nur al-albab,* "Light of the Intellects."
[6]Washing one's body as part of a religious rite.

is one of the humble people of the world, and to disobey him is a crime, at least so long as he does not command what God condemns; in that case she must refuse, since it is wrong of a human creature to disobey the Creator.

The Call to Holy War[7]

That to make war upon the heathen king who does not say "There is no God but Allah" on account of the custom of his town, and who makes no profession of Islam, is obligatory by assent,[8] and that to take the government from him is obligatory by assent.

And that to make war upon the king who is an apostate, and who has abandoned the religion of Islam for the religion of heathendom is obligatory by assent, and that to take the government from him is obligatory by assent; And that to make war against the king who is an apostate—who has not abandoned the religion of Islam as far as the profession of it is concerned, but who mingles the observances of Islam with the observances of heathendom, like the kings of Hausaland for the most part—is also obligatory by assent, and that to take the government from him is obligatory by assent. . . .

And to enslave the freeborn among the Muslims is unlawful by assent, whether they reside in the territory of Islam, or in enemy territory. . . .

---

[7]From *Wathiqat ahl al-Sudan wa man sha' Allah mm al-ikbwan,* "Dispatch to the Folk of the Sudan and to Whom so Allah Wills Among the Brethren," probably written in 1804 or 1805.

[8]"By assent" refers to the consensus of the Muslim community.

Chapter 7

Change and Continuity in East Asia

FOR THE OTTOMAN, SAFAVID, AND MUGHAL empires, the seventeenth and eighteenth centuries were times of military decline and growing political weakness after an era of strength and expansion. In East Asia, this pattern was reversed. For Japan, the sixteenth century was an era of civil war and social discord, made worse by the arrival of Europeans, who introduced firearms and converted tens of thousands of Japanese to Christianity. China entered a period of dynastic decline at the end of the sixteenth century, just when the empire was facing pressing new financial and diplomatic problems. Factionalism paralyzed the central administration, and peasant violence escalated in response to rising taxes, higher rents, natural catastrophes, and government corruption. The paved the way for the invasion of China by the Manchus, a seminomadic people who poured into China from their homeland to the northeast and established a new dynasty, the Qing, in 1644.

During the seventeenth century, however, conflicts and tensions abated in both China and Japan. In Japan, recovery began much earlier, in 1603, when the Tokugawa clan took power and ended the decades-long civil war, while in China, it began soon after the Manchus established their authority. Although China and Japan did not lack problems in the seventeenth and eighteenth centuries, compared to what had occurred earlier and what would follow, these were years of orderly government and social harmony.

These also were years in which European pressures on the region eased. The Qing continued to limit European merchants' activities to Macao and Guangzhou, and beginning in the early 1700s, they curtailed European missionary activity. They also checked Russian expansion in the Amur Valley. In 1689, they negotiated the Treaty of Nerchinsk, by which the Russians agreed to abandon their trading posts in Manchuria in return for modest commercial privileges in Beijing. In Japan, the Tokugawa shoguns, in the first half of the seventeenth century, expelled all foreigners, outlawed Christianity, and limited trade with Europeans to one Dutch ship a year. In the East Indies, the Dutch, after forcing out the Portuguese and establishing a political base in Java, were content after the mid-1600s to protect rather than extend their gains. Spain's involvement in the region never went beyond the Philippines.

By the end of the 1700s, however, signs of change were evident. In Japan, economic expansion, urbanization, and years of political stability created new tensions by enriching merchants and undermining the function and financial base of the military aristocracy. In China, continuing population growth caused hardship among peasants by driving up the cost of land; moreover, around 1800, budgetary shortfalls, higher taxes, abuses of the civil service examination system, court favoritism, and neglect of roads, bridges, and dikes were signs of impending dynastic decline.

In addition, European pressures in the region were building. In the 1780s, the English began to settle Australia and New Zealand. French missionaries increased their activities in Vietnam. In 1800, the Dutch government stripped the bankrupt Dutch East India Company of its administrative responsibilities in the East Indies and tightened its grip on agriculture and trade. From their base in India, British merchants opened a new chapter in the history of trade with China after finding a product that millions of Chinese deeply craved. The product—grown and processed in India, packed into 133-pound chests, shipped to Guangzhou, and purchased for silver by Chinese traders who sold it to millions of addicts—was opium. A new era of upheaval was about to begin.

China's Revival Under the Qing

On taking power, the Manchus made it clear that they were the rulers and the Chinese their subjects. They ordered courtiers and officials to abandon the loose-fitting robes of the Ming for the high-collared tight jackets favored by the Manchus. They also required all males to shave their foreheads and braid their hair in back in a style favored by the Manchus. In other ways, however, the Manchus themselves adapted to Chinese culture. They embraced the Chinese principle of centralized monarchy, learned Chinese, and supported Confucian scholarship. They reinstated the civil service examinations, which had been neglected during the last decades of Ming rule. Although Manchus were disproportionately represented in the bureaucracy,

Chinese were allocated half of all important offices, and gradually Chinese scholar-officials began to support and serve the new dynasty.

From 1661 through 1799, China had but three emperors: Kangxi (r. 1661–1722), Yongzhen (r. 1722–1736), and Qianlong (r. 1736–1796), who abdicated in 1796 to avoid exceeding the long reign of his grandfather Kangxi, but who actually ruled until 1799. Their reigns were among the most impressive in all of Chinese history. China reached its greatest size as a result of military campaigns in central Asia. Agriculture flourished, trade expanded, and China's population grew (how much and how fast it grew is a matter of ongoing scholarly debate). China's cultural vitality was no less remarkable. Painting and scholarship flourished, and the era's literary output included what many consider China's greatest novel, *The Dream of the Red Chamber* by Cao Xueqin.

Toward the end of Qianlong's reign, however, problems emerged. Rural poverty worsened, military effectiveness declined, and factionalism and favoritism at the imperial court resurfaced. Nonetheless, it was neither far-fetched nor fanciful when France's leading eighteenth-century writer, Voltaire, described China as a model of moral and ethical government and praised Qianlong as the ideal philosopher-king.

Emperor Kangxi Views His World

48 • KANGXI, SELF-PORTRAIT

In 1661, a seven-year-old boy became the second Qing emperor. He took as his reign name Kangxi, and during his long reign, which lasted until 1722, he crushed the last vestiges of Ming resistance, fortified China's borders, revitalized the civil service examination system, won the support of China's scholar-officials, eased tensions between ethnic Chinese and their Manchu conquerors, and brought vigor and direction to the government. A generous supporter of writers, artists, poets, scholars, and craftsmen, Kangxi himself was a scholar and writer of distinction. He studied Confucianism, Latin, music, mathematics, and science and left behind a rich store of writings, including poems, essays, aphorisms, and letters.

In 1974, the historian Jonathan Spence drew on these writings and statements to produce a self-portrait of the emperor. In the following excerpts, the emperor expresses his views on justice, government administration, and Europeans, with whom China's relations worsened during his reign.

Much of the friction between Kangxi and Europeans centered on religion. Since the 1500s, priests belonging to the Society of Jesus, a Catholic religious order, had sought to win converts by impressing the Chinese elite with their knowledge of astronomy and mathematics and their skills as cartographers, artists, and architects. The Jesuits at first had been welcomed at the imperial court in Beijing, where they wore Chinese garb, learned Chinese, and paid homage to the emperor. They also managed to convert some 200 court officials, who in keeping with a policy initiated by the founder of the Jesuit mission in China, Matteo Ricci, were permitted to continue traditional ceremonies in honor of deceased ancestors and offer public homage to Confucius. Kangxi had an avid interest in Western learning, and in 1692, he granted the Jesuits permission to preach outside Beijing. By the early eighteenth century, as many as 300,000 Chinese had converted to Christianity.

In the early 1700s, however, the Catholic missionary effort in China experienced a fatal schism. Members of the Franciscan and Dominican religious orders, fresh from their successes in the Philippines, attacked the Jesuit position on Confucian rites and won over Pope Clement XI to their point of view. In 1706, the pope decreed that Confucian ceremonies were religious, not civil, rites and henceforth would be prohibited for Chinese Catholics. When Kangxi responded by prohibiting Christian preaching, the Qing assault on Christianity was under way. Under Kangxi's successors, the Jesuits lost their privileged position at Beijing, and the main source of contact between the imperial court and the intellectual world of the West virtually disappeared.

QUESTIONS FOR ANALYSIS

1. What does Kangxi's treatment of delinquent and dishonest government officials reveal about his philosophy of government?
2. How do Confucian values affect Kangxi's decisions about whether to be lenient to men accused of killing their wives?
3. What are Kangxi's views of the civil service examination system? What ideas does he have for improving it?
4. What role do eunuchs play in Kangxi's administration? How does this compare with the situation during the late Ming Era (source 29)?
5. According to Kangxi, what are the strengths and limitations of Western science and mathematics?
6. According to Kangxi, what specific issues were involved in the dispute over Chinese rites?
7. What other characteristics and actions of the missionaries led to Kangxi's decision to ban further Christian preaching?

An Emperor's Responsibilities

Giving life to people and killing people—those are the powers that the emperor has. He knows that administrative errors in government bureaus can be rectified, but that a criminal who has been executed cannot be brought back to life any more than a chopped string can be joined together again. He knows, too, that sometimes people have to be persuaded into morality by the example of an execution. . . .

Hu Jianzheng was a subdirector of the Court of Sacrificial Worship whose family terrorized their native area in Jiangsu, seizing people's lands and wives and daughters, and murdering people after falsely accusing them of being thieves. . . . I ordered . . . that he be executed with his family and in his native place, so that all the local gentry might learn how I regarded such behavior. Corporal Yambu was sentenced to death for gross corruption in the shipyards. I not only agreed

Source: From *Emperor of China* by Jonathan D. Spence. Copyright © 1974 by Jonathan D. Spence. Used by permission of Alfred A. Knopf, a division of Random House, Inc.

to the penalty but . . . ordered that all shipyard personnel from generals down to private soldiers kneel down in full armor and listen to my warning that execution would be their fate as well unless they ended their evil ways. . . .

Of all the things that I find distasteful, none is more so than giving a final verdict on the death sentences that are sent to me for ratification. . . .

Each year we went through the lists, sparing sixteen out of sixty-three at one session, eighteen out of fifty-seven at another, thirty-three out of eighty-three at another. For example, it was clear to me that the three cases of husbands killing wives that came up . . . were all quite different. The husband who hit his wife with an ax because she nagged at him for drinking, and then murdered her after another domestic quarrel . . . how could any extenuating circumstances be found? But Baoer, who killed his wife for swearing at his parents; and Meng, whose wife failed to serve him properly and used foul language so that he killed her—they could have their sentences reduced. . . .

Eunuchs and Bureaucrats

You have to define and reward people in accordance with their status in life. If too much grace is shown to inferiors they become lazy and uppity and will be sure to stir up trouble—and if you neglect them they will abuse you behind your back. That was why I insisted on such strictness when the eunuch Jian Wenzai beat a commoner to death, saying strangulation was not enough. For eunuchs are basically Yin[1] in nature. They are quite different from ordinary people; when weak with age they babble like babies. In my court I never let them get involved with government—even the few . . . with whom I might chatter or exchange

family jokes were never allowed to discuss politics. I only have about four hundred, as opposed to the immense numbers there were in the Ming, and I keep them working at menial jobs; I ignore their frowns and smiles and make sure that they stay poor. Whereas in the later Ming Dynasty, besides being so extravagant and reckless, they obtained the power to write endorsements on the emperors' memorials, for the emperors were unable to read the one- or two-thousand-character memorials that flowed in; and the eunuchs in turn passed the memorials on to *their* subordinates to handle.

• • •

There are too many men who claim to be pure scholars and yet are stupid and arrogant; we'd be better off with less talk of moral principle and more practice of it. . . .

This is one of the worst habits of the great officials, that if they are not recommending their teachers or their friends for high office then they recommend their relations. This evil practice used to be restricted to the Chinese: they've always formed cliques and then used their recommendations to advance the other members of the clique. Now the practice has spread to the Chinese Bannermen[2] . . . and even the Manchus, who used to be so loyal, recommend men from their own Banners, knowing them to have a foul reputation, and will refuse to help the Chinese. . . .

In 1694 I noted that we were losing talent because of the ways the exams were being conducted: even in the military exams most of the successful candidates were from Zhejiang and Jiangnan, while there was only one from Henan and one from Shanxi.[3] The successful ones had often done no more than memorize old examination answer books, whereas the best *should* be

---

[1]In East Asian thought, Yin and Yang were the two complementary principles or forces that make up all aspects of life. Yin is conceived of as Earth, female, dark, passive, and absorbing.

[2]The banner system was the basis for Qing military organization, in which fighting men were grouped into divisions identified by different colored banners.

[3]Zhejiang and Jiangnan were southeast coastal regions of China, Henan and Shanxi were north-central provinces.

selected on the basis of riding and archery. Yet it is always the strong men from the western provinces who are eager to serve in the army, while not only are troops from Zhejiang and Jiangnan among the weakest, they also pass on their posts to their relatives who are also weak.

Even among the examiners there are those who are corrupt, those who do not understand basic works, those who ask detailed questions about practical matters of which they know nothing, those who insist entirely on memorization of the *Classics* and refuse to prescribe essays, those who put candidates from their own geographical area at the top of the list, or those who make false claims about their abilities to select the impoverished and deserving. . . . Other candidates hire people to sit [take] the exams for them, or else pretend to be from a province that has a more liberal quota than their own. . . . . As to the other problems, one can overcome some of them by holding the exams under rigorous armed supervision and then reading the exam papers oneself.

Dealing with Europeans

The rare can become common, as with the lions and other animals that foreign ambassadors like to give us and my children are now accustomed to. . . .

Western skills are a case in point: in the late Ming Dynasty, when the Westerners first brought the gnomon [sundial], the Chinese thought it a rare treasure until they understood its use. And when the Emperor Shunzhi got a small chiming clock in 1653, he kept it always near him; but now we have learned to balance the springs and to adjust the chimes and finally to make the whole clock, so that my children can have ten chiming clocks each to play with, if they want them. Similarly, we learned in a short time to make glassware that is superior to that made in the West, and our lacquer would be better than theirs, too,

were it not that their wet sea climate gives a better sheen than the dry and dusty Chinese climate ever could. . . .

I realized, too, that Western mathematics has its uses. . . . I ordered the Jesuits . . . to study Manchu also, and to compose treatises in that language on Western arithmetic and the geometry of Euclid.[4] In the early 1690's I often worked several hours a day with them. With Verbiest[5] I had examined each stage of the forging of cannons, and made him build a water fountain that operated in conjunction with an organ, and erect a windmill in the court; with the new group . . . I worked on clocks and mechanics. Pereira taught me to play the tune, "*P'u-yen-chou*" on the harpsichord and the structure of the eight-note scale, Pedrini taught my sons musical theory, and Gherardini painted portraits at the Court. I also learned to calculate the weight and volume of spheres, cubes, and cones, and to measure distances and the angle of river banks. On inspection tours later I used these Western methods to show my officials how to make more accurate calculations when planning their river works. . . . I showed them how to calculate circumferences and assess the area of a plot of land, even if its borders were as jagged as dogs' teeth, drawing diagrams for them on the ground with an arrow; and calculated the flow of river water through a lock gate by multiplying the volume that flowed in a few seconds to get a figure for the whole day. . . .

But I was careful not to refer to these Westerners as "Great Officials." . . . For even though some of the Western methods are different from our own, and may even be an improvement, there is little about them that is new. The principles of mathematics all derive from the *Book of Changes*[6] and the Western methods are Chinese in origin: this algebra—"A-erh-chu-pa-erh"—springs from

---

[4]The ancient Greek mathematician who lived around 300 B.C.E. and laid the foundation for the study of geometry.
[5]Verbiest, Pereira, Pedrini, and Gherardini were all Jesuit priests.

[6]One of the Classics, the *Book of Changes* was a work of divination that relied on the analysis of trigrams and hexagrams.

an Eastern word.[7] And though it was indeed the Westerners who showed us something our ancient calendar experts did not know—namely how to calculate the angle of the northern pole—this but shows the truth what Zhu Xi[8] arrived at through his investigation of things: the earth is like the yolk within an *egg*.

• • •

On the question of the Chinese Rites that might be practiced by the Western missionaries, de Tournon[9] would not speak, though I sent messages to him repeatedly. I had agreed with the formulation the Beijing fathers had drawn up in 1700: that Confucius was honored by the Chinese as a master, but his name was not invoked in prayer for the purpose of gaining happiness, rank, or wealth; that worship of ancestors was an expression of love and filial remembrance, not intended to bring protection to the worshiper; and that there was no idea when an ancestral tablet was erected, that the soul of the ancestor dwelt in that tablet. . . .

If de Tournon didn't reply, the Catholic Bishop Maigrot[10] did, . . . telling me that Heaven is a material thing and should not be worshiped, and that one should invoke only the name "Lord of Heaven" to show the proper reverence. Maigrot wasn't merely ignorant of Chinese literature, he couldn't even recognize the simplest Chinese characters; yet he chose to discuss the falsity of the Chinese moral system. . . .

Even little animals mourn their dead mothers for many days; these Westerners who want to treat their dead with indifference are not even equal to animals. How could they be compared with Chinese? We venerate Confucius because of his doctrines of respect for virtue, his system of education, his inculcation of love for superiors and ancestors. Westerners venerate their own saints because of their actions. They paint pictures of men with wings and say, "These represent heavenly spirits, swift as if they had wings, though in reality there are no men with wings." I do not find it appropriate to dispute this doctrine, yet with superficial knowledge Maigrot discussed Chinese sanctity. . . .

• • •

Since I discovered on the Southern Tour of 1703 that there were missionaries wandering at will over China, I had grown cautious and determined to control them more tightly: to bunch them in the larger cities and in groups that included men from several different countries, to catalogue their names and residences, and to permit no new establishments without my express permission. . . . I made all missionaries who wanted to stay on in China sign a certificate, stating that they would remain here for life and follow Ricci on the Rites. Forty or fifty who refused were exiled to Guangzhou; de Tournon was sent to Macao,[11] his secretary, Appiani, we kept in prison in Beijing.

Despite these sterner restrictions, the Westerners continued to cause me anxiety. Our ships were being sold overseas; reports came of iron-wood for keel blocks being shipped out of Guangdong; Luzon and Batavia[12] became havens for Chinese outlaws; and the Dutch were strong in the Southern Seas. I ordered a general inquiry among residents of Beijing who had once lived on the coast, and called a conference of the coastal governors-general. "I fear that some time in the future China is going to get into difficulties with these various Western countries," I said. "That is my prediction."

---

[7]*Algebra* is derived from the Arabic word *Al-jabr*. Kangxi is correct in stating that China had a long tradition of achievement in algebra, geometry, and trigonometry dating back at least as far as the Han Dynasty (206 B.C.E.–220 C.E.).

[8]Zhu Xi (1130–1200 C.E.), a famous commentator on Confucius.

[9]Charles de Tournon (1668–1710) was a papal envoy sent to Asia to oversee Catholic missions. His demand that Chinese Christians abandon traditional rites was deeply offensive to Kangxi. The emperor ordered him to prison, where he died in 1710.

[10]Charles Maigrot (1652–1730) was the apostolic vicar to China.

[11]Macao was the trading settlement near Guangzhou where Western merchants were permitted to do business.

[12]Luzon was the major island of the Spanish-ruled Philippines. Batavia (present-day Jakarta) was headquarters for the Dutch East India Company on Java.

Painting and Imperial Power Under Qianlong

49 • QIANLONG AT LEISURE ON NEW YEARS EVE; TAKING A STAG WITH A MIGHTY ARROW; QIANLONG IN HIS STUDY; TEN THOUSAND ENVOYS COME TO PAY TRIBUTE

Although many Chinese emperors were patrons and connoisseurs of painting, the fourth Qing emperor, Qianlong (r. 1736–1796), stands out for his devotion to this particular form of artistic expression. An accomplished calligrapher and a respectable painter himself, he expanded the painting studios set up by Kangxi and made major purchases of paintings from private collectors to enrich the imperial collection. At its peak, the imperial studios supported the work of 160 painters from all parts of the empire and several from Europe. The artists produced thousands of paintings and works of calligraphy that went into the emperor's private collection and were displayed on different occasions within the palace grounds in Beijing and at other sites where the emperor spent parts of the year. A frequent visitor to these studios, Qianlong suggested themes for paintings, monitored his painters' efforts, and often had his own comments or poems printed on completed works. Most of the paintings produced by the imperial artists featured Qianlong—on his throne, on horseback, in hunting scenes, on tour, with his family, or at his desk. Most of them had a political message.

Unlike Ming rulers, who had tended to view China as a Confucian state in which all subjects were expected to adhere to the same universal principles, early Qing rulers, including Qianlong, considered the empire to be a confederation of several distinct ethnic groups whose cultures deserved to be respected and whose allegiance needed to be won. These groups included not only Manchus and ethnic Chinese, but also Mongols, Tibetans, and Turkish-speaking Uighurs of Xinxiang. As universal ruler of all these peoples, Qianlong promoted Confucian scholarship; took steps to preserve Manchu culture; learned to speak Mongolian, Uighur, Tibetan, and Tangut; took a Muslim woman from a prominent Uighur family as a concubine and allowed her to continue to practice Islam; and built a replica of a famous Tibetan Buddhist temple on the grounds of his summer palace.

Many of the paintings produced in the imperial studios also were designed to promote this idea of empire. For his Buddhist subjects in Tibet and newly conquered western lands, for example, he was portrayed in several paintings as the incarnation of a Buddhist saint surrounded by figures representing Buddhist deities, saints, and teachers. For members of his own ethnic group, as well as his Mongol, Tibetan, and Uighur subjects—all nomadic peoples from the steppe—he was depicted as a warrior, skilled horseman, or fearless hunter. For his Chinese subjects, he was depicted as a supporter of the Confucian values of scholarship, filial piety, and traditional court ceremony.

Of the many paintings of Qianlong and his activities, we have chosen four for consideration. All of them are scrolls painted on silk that could easily be rolled up and stored when not being displayed. The first, *Qianlong at Leisure on New Year's Eve,* is the work of Giuseppe Castiglione (1688–1766), who went to China in 1715 as a Jesuit missionary and stayed on as a court painter until his death. In this painting, completed around 1738, Castiglione depicts Qianlong in a happy family scene dressed in traditional Chinese garb. Behind him stand two concubines, while on his lap and at his side are his three sons. The other six boys are thought to be nephews of the emperor. The event is a celebration of New Year's Eve, the culmination of a fifteen-day period in which the Chinese bid farewell to the old year and welcome the new. It is a time for family reunions, thanksgiving, and honoring the memory of ancestors. Outside the pavilion, one nephew is bringing in fruit, a frequent New Year's gift; another is distributing dried sesame stalks, which, as symbols of the old year, are either trampled on or burned; and a third is lighting firecrackers to welcome the new year. Aside from Qianlong himself, depicted as a dutiful father, the most important figure in the painting is his eldest son, shown holding a halberd. In written Chinese, the halberd is represented by the same character as "good fortune"; the musical stone attached to it has the same character as "felicity"; and the two fish below the musical stone have the same character as "plentifulness."

The next painting, also attributed to Castiglione, is entitled *Taking a Stag with a Mighty Arrow.* Completed around 1760, it shows Qianlong wearing a loosely fitted Manchu-style robe for ease in mounting a horse. The pouches at his side are in the style favored by northeastern tribal hunters. Already having released one arrow (resulting in a perfect heart shot, just behind the stag's front leg), he reaches back for another being offered by a young woman. Although there is disagreement about the identification of the woman, it is probably Princess Hexaio, Qianlong's tenth daughter. Manchu women, unlike their Chinese counterparts, were encouraged to ride, learn archery, and hunt, and Hexaio was famous for her skill in all such undertakings.

The third painting, *Qianlong in His Study,* is attributed to Castiglione in collaboration with Jin Tingbaiao and was completed around 1767. Qianlong is depicted in the garb of a Confucian scholar with a distinctive wispy beard often connected with sagehood. He is sitting at his desk contemplating a poem he is about to write, with his window open to the outside world of nature. On his desk are the basic Chinese writing tools—rice paper, writing brush, ink stick, and ink stone. Thus, he shows himself as a ruler interested in endeavors dear to the hearts of his Confucian officials—literature, calligraphy, and scholarship.

The final painting, *Ten Thousand Envoys Come to Pay Tribute,* is a large 10-foot-by-4-foot painting depicting the arrival of tribute missions from nearby Asian states and Europe. The work of anonymous court painters, it is an idealized picture of a practice that goes far back in Asian history. Smaller states on China's periphery

Giuseppe Castiglione, Qianlong at Leisure on New Year's Eve

Giuseppe Castiglione, Taking a Stag with a Mighty Arrow

Guiseppe Castiglione and Jin Tingbaiao, Qianlong in His Study

were expected annually or every two or three years to send gift-bearing emissaries to Beijing, where they would acknowledge China's cultural and political superiority and pay homage to the emperor. In return, the emperor gave them presents, promised their states continued protection, and granted their merchants permission to trade. This painting shows emissaries from a dozen states gathering just inside the courtyard of the Forbidden City, from which point they will proceed through the Gate of Supreme Harmony to the site of their audience with the emperor, the Hall of Supreme Harmony. To the right of the Hall of Supreme Harmony, court eunuchs prepare the emperor's presents for the visitors. The detail from the paint-ing shown on page 234 focuses on the arriving foreigners. In the foreground, the scene is dominated by the two elephants led in by the emissaries from Siam. On the other side of the fence, the Koreans lead, followed by representatives of the Sultanate of Brunei, "Pacific Islanders," and various Europeans.

Ten Thousand Envoys Come to Pay Tribute

The Palace Museum, Beijing

QUESTIONS FOR ANALYSIS

1. In regard to the three paintings that focus specifically on Qianlong, what impression does each painting convey, and what characteristics of Qianlong does each one communicate?
2. In *Qianlong at Leisure on New Year's Eve,* what is significant about the painting's setting and the placement and interaction of the various figures? What does the painting reveal about the Chinese conception of the ideal family?
3. In the hunting scene, why does the artist include a woman? What does it reveal about how Manchus and the Chinese had differing views of women and the family?
4. What does *Ten Thousand Envoys Come to Pay Tribute* reveal about China's views of foreigners and the place of China in the world? In what ways are the arrangements depicted in the painting meant to impress the foreign emissaries? How do the actions of the foreigners and their placement in the painting show their subservience to the emperor?
5. What is your judgment about the effectiveness of each of the works in communicating its message?
6. What do these paintings reveal about the usefulness of paintings such as these as sources for the historian?

Negotiating with the Qianlong Emperor

50 • EMPEROR QIANLONG, EDICT ON TRADE WITH GREAT BRITAIN

Chinese restrictions on Western commerce in the eighteenth century increasingly frustrated the British. According to the government's Guangzhou System, agents of the British East India Company and other European merchants could do business in the environs of only one city, Guangzhou, and only during the trading season, which ran from October to March. Subject to Chinese laws, they were barred from entering Guangzhou, learning Chinese, and being accompanied by their wives. Furthermore, they were required to deal only with a small number of merchant companies that formed a merchants' guild, the Cohong, which had a monopoly on trading with Westerners. Any grievance or dispute had to be referred to these merchants, who would pass it on to the *hoppo,* a government-appointed official who oversaw Guangzhou trade. The hoppo might make a decision himself, forward the grievance to Beijing, or simply ignore it. Efforts by the East India Company to have the system modified got nowhere. When the company sent James Flint to China in 1759 to negotiate trade issues with the emperor, the unfortunate envoy was imprisoned for three years on charges of learning Chinese, sailing to unapproved ports, and improperly addressing the emperor.

By the 1780s, with demand for Chinese tea soaring, at the urging of Sir Henry Dundas, a member of the government's Board of Control, which oversaw the political activities of the Company, the government decided to dispatch another embassy to China to resolve various trade issues. This time, it would be led by a representative of the king, not a company official. The first such embassy, under the command of Lieutenant Colonel Charles Cathcart, never reached China: Cathcart died en route and the British ships returned home. Undeterred, Dundas appointed the experienced diplomat Lord George Macartney to head a second mission.

Macartney sailed for China in September 1792 with an entourage of scientists, servants, artists, guards, and translators on a man-of-war accompanied by two support ships. The support ships were loaded with 600 boxes of gifts for the 82-year-old emperor and his officials, designed to show the sophistication and quality of British manufacturing and instrument making. The British reached Beijing in June 1793. After reaching a compromise on the issue of whether Macartney could kneel and bow before the emperor rather than prostrate himself in the ritual known as the kowtow, Macartney made his requests to the emperor and his high officials. Shortly thereafter, Qianlong rejected each and every British proposal in an edict to King George III. Macartney's mission had failed, and Sino-British relations continued to deteriorate until the Opium War (1839–1842) settled the two nations' many disputes through force rather than diplomacy.

QUESTIONS FOR ANALYSIS

1. What views of China's place in the world are revealed in Qianlong's letter?
2. What does the letter reveal about Qianlong's views of foreigners in general and the British in particular?
3. What are the emperor's stated reasons for rejecting any expansion of trade with Great Britain?
4. What unstated reasons might also have influenced his decision?

You, O King, from afar have yearned after the blessings of our civilization, and in your eagerness to come into touch with our converting influence have sent an Embassy across the sea bearing a memorial [memorandum]. I have already taken note of your respectful spirit of submission, have treated your mission with extreme favor and loaded it with gifts, besides issuing a mandate to you, O King, and honoring you with the bestowal of valuable presents. Thus has my indulgence been manifested.

Yesterday your Ambassador petitioned my Ministers to memorialize me regarding your trade with China, but his proposal is not consistent with our dynastic usage and cannot be entertained. Hitherto, all European nations, including your own country's barbarian merchants, have carried on their trade with our Celestial Empire at Guangzhou. Such has been the procedure for many years, although our Celestial Empire possesses all things in prolific abundance and lacks no product within its own borders. There was therefore no need to import the manufactures of outside barbarians in exchange for our own produce. But as the tea, silk, and porcelain which the Celestial Empire produces are absolute necessities to European nations and to yourselves, we have permitted, as a signal mark of favor, that *hong*[1] should be established at Guangzhou, so that your wants might be supplied and your country thus participate in our beneficence. But your Ambassador has now put forward new requests which completely fail to recognize the Throne's principle to "treat strangers from afar with indulgence," and to exercise a pacifying control over barbarian tribes the world over. Moreover, our dynasty, ruling over

Source: Emperor Qianlong, "Edict on Trade with Great Britain," in J. O. P. Brand, *Annals and Memoirs of the Court of Peking* (Boston: Houghton Mifflin, 1914), pp. 325–331.

[1]Approximately ten Chinese merchant guilds that alone were licensed to trade with Westerners.

the myriad races of the globe, extends the same benevolence towards all. Your England is not the only nation trading at Guangzhou. If other nations, following your bad example, wrongfully importune my ear with further impossible requests, how will it be possible for me to treat them with easy indulgence? Nevertheless, I do not forget the lonely remoteness of your island, cut off from the world by intervening wastes of sea, nor do I overlook your excusable ignorance of the usages of our Celestial Empire. I have consequently commanded my Ministers to enlighten your Ambassador on the subject, and have ordered the departure of the mission. But I have doubts that after your Envoy's return he may fail to acquaint you with my view in detail or that he may be lacking in lucidity, so that I shall now proceed . . . to issue my mandate on each question separately. In this way you will, I trust, comprehend my meaning. . . .

Your request for a small island near Zhoushan,[2] where your merchants may reside and goods be warehoused, arises from your desire to develop trade. As there are neither *hongs* nor interpreters in or near Zhoushan, where none of your ships has ever called, such an island would be utterly useless for your purposes. Every inch of the territory of our Empire is marked on the map and the strictest vigilance is exercised over it all: even tiny islets and far-lying sand-banks are clearly defined as part of the provinces to which they belong. Consider, moreover, that England is not the only barbarian land which wishes to establish . . . trade with our Empire: supposing that other nations were all to imitate your evil example and beseech me to present them each and all with a site for trading purposes, how could I possibly comply? This also is a flagrant infringement of the usage of my Empire and cannot possibly be entertained.

The next request, for a small site in the vicinity of Guangzhou city, where your barbarian merchants may lodge or, alternatively, that there be no longer any restrictions over their movements at Macao[3] has arisen from the following causes. Hitherto, the barbarian merchants of Europe have had a definite locality assigned to them at Macao for residence and trade, and have been forbidden to encroach an inch beyond the limits assigned to that locality. . . . If these restrictions were withdrawn, friction would inevitably occur between the Chinese and your barbarian subjects, and the results would militate against the benevolent regard that I feel towards you. From every point of view, therefore, it is best that the regulations now in force should continue unchanged. . . .

Regarding your nation's worship of the Lord of Heaven, it is the same religion as that of other European nations. Ever since the beginning of history, sage Emperors and wise rulers have bestowed on China a moral system and inculcated a code, which from time immemorial has been religiously observed by the myriads of my subjects [Confucianism]. There has been no hankering after heterodox doctrines. Even the European officials [missionaries] in my capital are forbidden to hold intercourse with Chinese subjects; they are restricted within the limits of their appointed residences, and may not go about propagating their religion. The distinction between Chinese and barbarian is most strict, and your Ambassador's request that barbarians shall be given full liberty to disseminate their religion is utterly unreasonable.

It may be, O King, that the above proposals have been wantonly made by your Ambassador on his own responsibility, or peradventure [perhaps] you yourself are ignorant of our dynastic regulations and had no intention of transgressing them when you expressed these wild ideas and hopes. . . . If, after the receipt of this explicit decree, you lightly give ear to the representations of your subordinates and allow your barbarian merchants to

---

[2]A group of islands in the East China Sea at the entrance to Hangzhou Bay.

[3]Island colony west of present-day Hong Kong where Europeans were allowed to carry on trade.
[4]Two Chinese port cities.

proceed to Zhejiang and Tianjin[4] with the object of landing and trading there, the ordinances of my Celestial Empire are strict in the extreme, and the local officials, both civil and military, are bound reverently to obey the law of the land. Should your vessels touch the shore, your merchants will assuredly never be permitted to land or to reside there, but will be subject to instant expulsion. In that event your barbarian merchants will have had a long journey for nothing. Do not say that you were not warned in due time! Tremblingly obey and show no negligence! A special mandate!

Social Change and Intellectual Ferment in Tokugawa Japan

Tokugawa Ieyasu and his immediate successors implemented a four-part plan to stabilize Japan. They tightened control of powerful daimyo families; severed almost all contacts between Japan and the outside world; officially sanctioned and supported Confucianism; and sought to freeze class divisions with military aristocrats (daimyo and samurai) at the top and farmers, artisans, and merchants below them. These policies were remarkably successful. Their subjects, who yearned for order as much as their rulers, experienced internal peace and stable government until the middle of the nineteenth century.

Paradoxically, the problems of the late Tokugawa regime resulted in part from its success. Decades of peace fostered economic expansion accompanied by population growth, urbanization, and social mobility. Japan's population grew from approximately 18 million in 1600 to 30 million by the 1750s, and Edo (present-day Tokyo) grew from a small village into a city of over a million. These changes increased demand for all types of goods, especially rice, and as a result, richer peasants and merchants prospered. Most peasants, however, could not take advantage of the commercialization of agriculture, and many experienced hardship from land shortages and rising rents. In addition, Japan's military aristocrats failed to benefit from the economic boom. Lavish spending and the daimyo's need to maintain residences in both Edo and their own domain led to massive indebtedness.

While economic change was undermining the social basis of the Tokugawa regime, intellectual ferment was eroding its ideological underpinnings. As the memory of earlier civil wars faded, Confucian conservatism lost some of its appeal and foreign ideas seemed less dangerous. In the eighteenth century, two intellectual movements challenged state-sponsored Confucianism. Proponents of National Learning, or *Kokugaku,* rejected Chinese influence, especially Confucianism, and dedicated themselves to the study and glorification of Japan's ancient literature and religion. Other Japanese developed an interest in European medicine, botany, cartography, and gunnery. Their endeavors were known as Dutch Studies because the main sources of information about Europe were the Dutch, who continued to trade on a limited basis with Japan, even after the seclusion policy had been adopted. By the late eighteenth century, those who were dissatisfied with the Tokugawa regime had models for a different future, something that solidly Confucian China lacked.

The National Learning Movement

51 • KAMO MABUCHI, A STUDY OF THE IDEA OF THE NATION

The son of a Shinto priest, Kamo Mabuchi (1697–1769) received training in both ancient Japanese literature and Confucianism. He contributed to the National Learning Movement in two ways. As a poet, he sought to imitate the style of ancient Japanese poetry, and as a scholar, he promoted the study of ancient Japanese verse. Kamo's greatest work is his commentary on the *Collection of Ten Thousand Leaves,* an anthology of Japanese poetry dating from the eighth century. As the following selection illustrates, his intent was to reveal the original simplicity and spontaneity of the Japanese people before their corruption by Chinese influence.

QUESTIONS FOR ANALYSIS

1. What arguments does Kamo make to show the worthlessness of Confucianism?
2. According to Kamo, how was the very nature of the Japanese people affected when Confucianism was introduced?
3. What is Kamo's vision for Japan's future?
4. According to Kamo, what are the drawbacks of Chinese as a written language? What language reforms does he propose for the Japanese?
5. On the basis of your knowledge of Confucianism and Chinese history, in your view, how valid are his criticisms of Chinese thought and the Chinese in general?

Someone remarked to me, "I pay no heed to such petty trifles as Japanese poetry; what interests me is the Chinese Way of governing a nation."

I smiled at this and did not answer. Later, when I met the same man he asked, "You seem to have an opinion on every subject—why did you merely keep smiling when I spoke to you?"

I answered, "You mean when you were talking about the Chinese Confucian teachings or whatever you call them? They are no more than a human invention which reduces the heart of Heaven and Earth to something trivial."

At these words he became enraged, "How dare you call our Great Way trivial?"

I answered, "I would be interested in hearing whether or not the Chinese Confucian learning has actually helped to govern a country successfully." He immediately cited the instances of Yao, Shun, Hsia, Yin, Chou, and so on.[1] I asked if there were no later examples, but he informed me that there were not.

I pursued the matter, asking this time about how far back Chinese traditions went. He answered that thousands of years had passed from Yao's day to the present. I then asked, "Why then did the Way of Yao continue only until the Chou and afterwards cease? I am sure that it is because you restrict yourself to citing events which took

---

Source: From *Sources of Japanese Tradition,* by William Theodore de Bary, pp. 515–518. Copyright © 1966 Columbia University Press. Reprinted with permission of the publisher.

[1]Yao and Shun are mythical enlightened rulers from China's ancient past. Xia, Yin, and Zhou are the names of the first three Chinese dynasties described in historical records. The Yin Dynasty is also known as the Shang.

place thousands of years ago that the Way seems so good. But those are merely ancient legends. It takes more than such specious ideas to run a country!"

When I said this he grew all the more furious, and ranted on about ancient matters. I said, "You are utterly prejudiced."...

Despite the fact that their country has been torn for centuries by disturbances and has never really been well administered, they think that they can explain with their Way of Confucius the principles governing the whole world. Indeed, when one has heard them through, there is nothing to be said: anyone can quickly grasp their doctrines because they consist of mere quibbling. What they value the most and insist on is the establishment and maintenance of good government. Everybody in China would seem to have been in agreement on this point, but belief in it did not in fact lie very deep. It is obvious that many gave superficial assent who did not assent in their hearts. Yet when these principles were introduced to this country it was stated that China had obtained good government through the adoption of them. This was a complete fabrication. I wish it were possible to send to China anyone who clung to such a belief!...

Japan in ancient days was governed in accordance with the natural laws of Heaven and earth. There was never any indulgence in such petty rationalizing as marked China, but when suddenly these teachings were transmitted here from abroad, they quickly spread, for the men of old in their simplicity took them for the truth. In Japan there had been generation after generation, extending back to the remote past, which had known prosperity, but no sooner were these Confucian teachings propagated here than in the time of Temmu[2] a great rebellion occurred.

Later. . . the palace, dress, and ceremonies were [made to look Chinese] and everything took on a superficial elegance; under the surface, however, contentiousness and dishonesty became more prevalent.

Confucianism made men crafty, and led them to worship the ruler to such an excessive degree that the whole country acquired a servant's mentality. . . .

Just as roads are naturally created when people live in uncultivated woodlands or fields, so the Way of the Age of the Gods spontaneously took hold in Japan. Because it was a Way indigenous to the country it caused our emperors to wax increasingly in prosperity. However, the Confucian teachings had not only repeatedly thrown China into disorder, but they now had the same effect in Japan. Yet there are those unwitting of these facts who reverence Confucianism and think that it is the Way to govern the country! This is a deplorable attitude. . . .

When ruling the country a knowledge of Chinese things is of no help in the face of an emergency. In such a situation some man will spontaneously come forth to propose things which are wise and true. In the same way, doctors often study and master Chinese texts, but very seldom do they cure any sickness. On the other hand, medicines which have been transmitted naturally in this country with no reasons or theoretical knowledge behind them, infallibly cure all maladies. It is good when a man spontaneously devotes himself to these things. It is unwise to become obsessed with them. I would like to show people even once what is good in our Way. The fact that the Confucian scholars know very little about government is obvious from the frequent disorders which arise in China whenever the government is left to them. . . .

---

[2]Emperor Temmu (r. 631–686) assumed the throne after raising an army and defeating the forces of his nephew and reigning emperor, Kōbun.

People also tell me, "We had no writing in this country and therefore had to use Chinese characters. From this one fact you can know everything about the relative importance of our countries." I answer, "I need not recite again how troublesome, evil, turbulent a country China is. To mention just one instance—there is the matter of their picture-writing. There are about 38,000 characters in common use, as someone has determined. . . . Every place name and plant name has a separate character for it which has no other use but to designate that particular place or plant. Can any man, even one who devotes himself to the task earnestly, learn all these many characters? Sometimes people miswrite characters, sometimes the characters themselves change from one generation to the next. What a nuisance, a waste of effort, and a bother! In India, on the other hand, fifty letters suffice for the writing of the more than 5,000 volumes of the Buddhist scriptures. . . . In Holland, I understand, they use twenty-five letters. In this country there should be fifty. The appearance of letters used in all countries is in general the same, except for China where they invented their bothersome system.". . . As long as a few teachings were carefully observed and we worked in accordance with the Will of Heaven and earth, the country would be well off without any special instruction. Nevertheless, Chinese doctrines were introduced and corrupted men's hearts. Even though these teachings resembled those of China itself, they were of the kind which heard in the morning are forgotten by evening. Our country in ancient times was not like that. It obeyed the laws of Heaven and earth. The emperor was the sun and moon and the subjects the stars. If the subjects as stars protect the sun and moon, they will not hide it as is now the case. Just as the sun, moon, and stars have always been in Heaven, so our imperial sun and moon, and the stars his vassals, have existed without change from ancient days, and have ruled the world fairly. . . .

Curing Japan's Social Ills

52 • HONDA TOSHIAKI, A SECRET PLAN FOR GOVERNMENT

Honda Toshiaki, a perceptive critic of late Tokugawa society and a prophet of Japan's future, was born in 1721 in northern Japan, where his samurai father had fled after killing a man. Having been provided with a traditional Confucian education, he increasingly was drawn to the study of Western mathematics, science, and geography. As a young man he opened a school in Edo for teaching mathematics, but spent much of his life traveling about Japan to observe and analyze economic and social conditions. He was particularly interested in examining conditions among the poor and learning the reasons for their misery. He concluded that as an island nation, Japan needed to expand commerce and colonize rather than simply focus on agriculture, as a large continental country like China could do. He believed Japan should abandon its seclusion policy and make efforts to learn modern navigation and the techniques for manufacturing modern weaponry. Honda publicized his ideas among his students and correspondents, but his only government service was as advisor to the lord of Kaga, a minor aristocrat. Honda died in Edo in 1821.

Honda's *A Secret Plan for Government,* written in 1798, is his most important work. In it, he outlines an economic and political plan for Japan based on what he calls the "four imperative needs": to learn the effective use of gunpowder; to develop metallurgy; to increase trade; and to colonize the nearby islands of Hokkaido and Sakhalin and the Kamchatka Peninsula. The following excerpt, in which Honda analyzes the roots of Japan's problems, comes at the end of a long discourse on Japanese history.

QUESTIONS FOR ANALYSIS

1. What is Honda's view of the daimyo?
2. How do merchants contribute to Japan's problems, according to Honda?
3. How does Honda justify his assertion that fifteen-sixteenths of all Japanese rice production goes to the merchants? Are his arguments plausible?
4. According to Honda, why is Europe rather than China the better model for Japan's revival?
5. What Confucian influence is evident in Honda's *Plan*? In what ways does Honda reject Confucianism?
6. In your view, what would Kamo Mabuchi (source 51) have thought of Honda's ideas?

Not until Tokugawa Ieyasu[1] used his power to control the strong and give succor to the weak did the warfare that had lasted for three hundred years without a halt suddenly abate. Arrows were left in their quivers and spears in their racks. . . . It must have been because he realized how difficult it would be to preserve the empire for all ages to come if the people were not honest in their hearts that Ieyasu, in his testament, exhorted shoguns who would succeed him to abstain from any irregularities in government, and to rule on a basis of benevolence and honesty. It was his counsel that the shoguns should serve as models to the people, and by their honesty train the people in the ways of humanity and justice. He taught that the shogun should not compel obedience merely by the use of force, but by his acts of benevolence should keep the nation at peace. . . .

He taught the daimyo that the duties of a governor consisted in the careful attempt to guide the people of their domains in such a way as both to bring about the prosperity of the land and to encourage the literary and military arts.

However, in recent days there has been the spectacle of lords confiscating the allocated property of their retainers[2] on the pretext of paying back debts to the merchants. The debts do not then decrease, but usually seem rather to grow larger. One daimyo with an income of 60,000 *koku*[3] so increased his borrowings that he could not make good his debts, and there was a public suit. . . . Even if repayment had been attempted on the basis of his income of 60,000 koku, the debt would not have been completely settled for fifty or sixty years, so long a time that it is difficult to imagine the day would actually come.

Source: Excerpts from Donald Keene, *The Japanese Discovery of Europe, 1720–1830,* revised edition. Copyright © 1952 and 1969 by Donald Keene. Used with the permission of Stanford University Press, www.sup.org.

[1]The founder of the Tokugawa Shogunate, he seized power in 1600, received appointment as shogun in 1603, abdicated from office in 1605, but remained in power until his death in 1616 (see Multiple Voices II, sources 2, 4, and 5).

[2]A reference to the *samurai,* lesser members of the military aristocracy.

[3]A measure of daimyo income, one *koku* is approximately five bushels of rice.

All the daimyo are not in this position, but there is not one who has not borrowed from the merchants. Is this not a sad state of affairs? The merchant, watching this spectacle, must feel like a fisherman who sees a fish swim into his net. Officials of the daimyo harass the farmers for money, which they claim they need to repay the daimyo's debts, but the debts do not diminish. Instead, the daimyo go on contracting new ones year after year. The [daimyo'sj officials are blamed for this situation, and are dismissed as incompetent. New officials then harass and afflict the farmers in much the same way as the old ones, and so it goes on. . . .

No matter how hard the daimyo and their officials rack their brains, they do not seem to be able to reduce the debts. The lords are "sunk in a pool of debts," as it is popularly said, a pool from which their children and grandchildren will be unable to escape. Everything will be as the merchants wish it. The daimyo turn over their domains to the merchants, receiving in return an allowance with which to pay their public and private expenses. . . .

Many fields have turned into wasteland since the famine of 1783, when thousands of farmers starved to death.[4] Wherever one goes . . . , one hears people say, "There used to be a village here. . . . The land over there was once part of such-and-such a county, but now there is no village and no revenue comes from the land." . . . When so many farmers starved, reducing still further their already insufficient numbers, the amount of uncultivated land greatly increased. If the wicked practice of infanticide, now so prevalent, is not stopped, the farming population will dwindle until it tends to die out altogether. Generous protective and relief measures must be put into effect immediately if this evil practice is to be stamped out. . . .

The Confucian scholars of ancient and modern times have talked a great deal about benevolence and compassion, but they possess neither in their

hearts. Officials and authorities talk about benevolent government, but they have no understanding of what that means. Whose fault is it that the farmers are dying of starvation and that good fields are turning into wasteland? The fault lies entirely with the ruler. . . .

> There follows an enthusiastic but often inaccurate account of Europe's accomplishments.

Because astronomy, calendar making, and mathematics are considered the ruler's business, the European kings are well versed in celestial and terrestrial principles, and instruct the common people in them. Thus even among the lower classes one finds men who show great ability in their particular fields. The Europeans as a result have been able to establish industries with which the rest of the world is unfamiliar. It is for this reason that all the treasures of the world are said to be attracted to Europe. There is nowhere the Europeans' ships do not go in order to obtain the different products and treasures of the world. They trade their own rare products, superior implements, and unusual inventions for the precious metals and valuable goods of others, which they bring back to enrich their own countries. Their prosperity makes them strong, and it is because of their strength that they are never invaded or pillaged, whereas for their part they have invaded countless non-European countries. . . .

There is no place in the world to compare with Europe. It may be wondered in what way this supremacy was achieved. In the first place, the European nations have behind them a history of five to six thousand years. In this period they have delved deep into the beauties of the arts, have divined the foundations of government, and have established a system based on a thorough examination of the

---

[4]A reference to the Tenmie famine (1783–1786), one of the three major famines that occurred in eighteenth-century Japan. The famines had various causes, including flooding, drought, typhoons, and insect damage.

factors that naturally make a nation prosperous. Because of their proficiency in mathematics, they have excelled also in astronomy, calendar making, and surveying. They have elaborated laws of navigation such that there is nothing simpler for them than to sail the oceans of the world. . . .

In spite of this example, however, the Japanese do not look elsewhere than to China for good or beautiful things, so tainted are the customs and temperament of Japan by Chinese teachings. . . .

China is a mountainous country that extends as far as Europe and Africa. It is bounded by the ocean to the south, but water communication within the country is not feasible. Since it is impossible to feed the huge population of cities when transport can be effected only by human or animal strength, there are no big cities in China away from the coast. China is therefore a much less favored country than Japan, which is surrounded by water, and this factor shows in the deficiencies and faults of Chinese state policies. China does not merit being used as a model. Since Japan is a maritime nation, shipping and trade should be the chief concerns of the ruler. Ships should be sent to all countries to obtain products needed for national consumption and to bring precious metals to Japan. A maritime nation is equipped with the means to increase her national strength.

By contrast, a nation that attempts to get along on its own resources will grow steadily weaker. . . . To put the matter more bluntly, the policies followed by the various ruling families until now have determined that the lower classes must lead a hand-to-mouth existence. The best part of the harvests of the farmers who live on the domains of the empire is wrenched away from them. The lords spend all they take within the same year, and if they then do not have enough, they oppress the farmers all the more cruelly in an effort to obtain additional funds. This goes on year after year. . . .

Soon all the gold and silver currency will pass into the hands of the merchants, and only merchants will be deserving of the epithets "rich" and "mighty." Their power will thus grow until they stand first among the four classes. When I investigated the incomes of present-day merchants, I discovered that fifteen-sixteenths of the total income of Japan goes to the merchants, with only one-sixteenth left for the samurai. As proof of this statement, I cite the following case. When there are good rice harvests at Yonezawa in Dewa or in Semboku-gun in Akita[5] the price is five or six *mon* for one *sho*.[6] The rice is sold to merchants who ship it to Edo, where the price is about 100 mon, regardless of the original cost. At this rate, if one bought 10,000 ryos[7] worth of rice in Dewa, sent it to Edo, and sold it there, one's capital would be increased to 160,000 ryo. If the 160,000 ryo in turn were used as capital, the return in Edo would be 2,560,000 ryo. With only two exchanges of trade it is possible to make enormous profits.

It may be claimed that of this sum part must go for shipping expenses and pack-horse charges, but the fact remains that one gets back sixteen times what one has paid for the rice. It is thus apparent that fifteen-sixteenths of the nation's income goes to the merchants. In terms of the production of an individual farmer, out of thirty days a month he works twenty-eight for the merchants and two for the samurai; or, out of 360 days in a year, he works 337½ for the merchants and 22½ for the samurai. Clearly, then, unless the samurai store grain it is impossible for them to offer any relief to the farmers in years of famine. This may be why they can do no more than look on when the farmers

---

[5]Dewa and Akita are provinces in northern Honshu.
[6]A *mon* was a copper coin; a *sho* was about 3.2 pints.

[7]Also known as a *koban*, a *ryo* was a Japanese gold coin.

are dying of starvation. And all this because the right system has not been established. It is a most lamentable state of affairs that the farmers have to shoulder the weight of this error and die of starvation as inevitably as "water collecting in a hollow."

By means of the plans outlined in the account of the four imperative needs . . . the present corrupt and jejune society could be restored to its former prosperity and strength. The ancient glories of the warrior-nation of Japan would be revived. Colonization projects would gradually be commenced and would meet with great success. . . . Then, under enlightened government, Japan could certainly be made the richest and strongest country in the world.

A Meeting of Cultures

53 • SHIBA KŌKAN, A MEETING OF JAPAN, CHINA, AND THE WEST

Born into the family of a wealthy Edo hardware merchant, Shiba Kōkan (1747–1818) was trained in Chinese and Japanese painting, but in the 1780s became intrigued by the European prints and paintings circulating in Edo. He experimented with oil-based paints, sought realism in his paintings through shading and perspective, and learned the techniques of copperplate engraving and etching. His visit to Nagasaki, the Dutch commercial center, introduced him to Western science and geography. Beginning in the 1780s, he illustrated and wrote a number of books on these subjects, notable for their laudatory but fanciful descriptions of Europe.

In the 1790s, Kōkan painted *A Meeting of Japan, China, and the West*, a hanging silk scroll just over 40 inches tall and 19 inches wide. At the bottom are three figures, the one on the left a Chinese Confucian scholar, the one in the middle a Japanese samurai, and the one on the right a European. The European is holding a copy of an anatomical treatise opened to show a drawing of the human skeleton. In front of the Chinese scholar is a scroll of his writings, a *ruyi* scepter (a symbol of power and a talisman thought to bring good luck), and what may be a medicinal herb in a Chinese-style vase. The Japanese has one hand on a fan and has a small white snake, perhaps a talisman to ward off disease, wrapped around his wrist.

At the top of the painting, Japanese, Chinese, and Westerners interact in a very different context. While flames engulf a pagoda, the Chinese firefighters on the left are throwing small buckets of water on the flames; the Europeans are using a modern pump and hose; and the Japanese, represented by sumo wrestlers, have large tubs of water available but are making no effort to subdue the fire. Instead, they are using the water to bathe.

QUESTIONS FOR ANALYSIS

1. Consider the postures, seating arrangements, and facial expressions of the three men seated at the table. What do they suggest about the message of the painting?
2. What might be the significance of the following details—the vase with the herb; the Chinese scroll, the printed book, the fan, and the white snake?

3. What is the meaning of the scene depicted at the top of the painting?
4. If Kamo Mabuchi (source 51) and Honda Toshiaki (source 52) had seen this painting, what might they have thought of it?

Shiba Kōkan, A Meeting of Japan, China, and the West

PART THREE

The World in the Age of Western Dominance: 1800–1914

THE experience of Africa is the most striking example of the seismic change in world relationships that occurred in the nineteenth century. In 1800, except for the continent's southernmost tip and a small number of coastal enclaves, Africa was largely untouched by Europeans. By 1914, except for Ethiopia and Liberia, the continent was under the political control of European powers, whose leaders accomplished their takeover without regard for the economic interests and cultural sensitivities of the Africans. In 1884 and 1885, rules for dividing up Africa were laid down at the Berlin West Africa Conference, attended by representatives of twelve European nations, the Ottoman Empire, and the United States. They agreed that each power had to give the others proper notice if it intended to annex African territory and could not do so by simply stamping its name on a map: it had to have real troops or administrators on the scene. Only three decades after the Berlin Conference adjourned, Africa's colonial masters dispatched thousands of Africans to World War I battlefronts in Africa, Europe, and the Middle East, where many died fighting for their European overlords.

The Europeans' land grab in Africa was striking in its speed and magnitude, but it was not unique. Burma, India, Vietnam, Cambodia, Laos, the Malay Peninsula, the East Indies, and hundreds of South Pacific islands also came under direct European or U.S. control in the nineteenth century. Independent states such as Nicaragua, Haiti, the Dominican Republic, the Ottoman Empire, Egypt, Persia, and China were forced to accept varying degrees of Western control of their finances and foreign policy. Australia and New Zealand became European settler colonies. Canada, South Africa, the Philippines, and most of the West Indies remained parts of pre–nineteenth-century empires, although Canada in 1867 and South Africa in 1910 were granted extensive powers of self-government and the Philippines in 1898 changed masters from Spain to the United States. Latin American nations retained full political sovereignty but saw many of their economic assets—banks, railroads, mines, and grazing lands—taken over by Western investors. Only Japan, by adopting the technology, military organization, and industrial economy of the West, avoided subservience to the West and became an imperialist power itself. Never had world economic and political relationships been as one-sided as they were when World War I began in 1914.

The West's expansion resulted in part from the inner dynamics of capitalism, with its drive for new markets, resources, and investment opportunities. It also resulted from nationalist rivalries among the Western powers themselves, most of whose leaders and citizens believed that prestige and prosperity depended on empire-building and overseas investment. It also resulted from the huge disparity between the military and economic strength of Europe and the United States and that of the rest of the world. During the nineteenth century, once-powerful states such as the Ottoman Empire and China faced severe internal problems, and others, such as Mughal India, had already collapsed.

Europe and the United States, however, continued to industrialize, develop new technologies, and build the most powerful armies and navies in history.

Chapter 8

The West in the Age of Industrialization and Imperialism

As FAR-REACHING AS THE TRANSFORMATION of Western civilization since the Renaissance had been, no one in 1800 could have predicted the even greater changes about to occur in the nineteenth century. When Napoleon met defeat at Waterloo in 1815, Europe's population was 200 million, with as many as 25 million people of European descent living in the rest of the world. By 1914, these numbers had increased to 450 million and 150 million, respectively. In 1815, a large majority of Europeans and Americans lived in rural villages and worked the land; by 1914, in highly industrialized nations such as Great Britain, a majority of the population lived in cities and worked in factories or offices. In 1815, despite two decades of revolution, most governments were still aristocratic and monarchical; in 1914, representative government and universal manhood suffrage were the norms in most of Europe, the United States, and the British dominions of Canada, Australia, and New Zealand. In 1815, most governments limited their activities to defense, the preservation of law and order, and some economic regulation; in 1914, governments subsidized education, sponsored scientific research, oversaw public health, monitored industry, provided social welfare programs, and maintained huge military establishments, and, as a result, had grown enormously.

Europe's global role also changed dramatically in these 100 years. In 1815, European political authority around the world appeared to be declining. Great Britain no longer ruled its thirteen American colonies; Portugal and Spain were losing their American holdings; and France recently had lost its prime West Indian colony, Saint Domingue, and had sold 800,000 square miles of North American territory to the

United States through the Louisiana Purchase. Great Britain's decision to outlaw the slave trade in 1807 seemed to be a step toward a diminished European role in Africa, and there was little to suggest that Western nations had the means or inclination to extend their power in the Middle East or East Asia. Only the expansion of Great Britain in India hinted at what the nineteenth century would bring: the Western nations' takeover of Africa and Southeast Asia, their interference in the politics of China and the Middle East, and their dominance of the world's economy.

The most important cause of the West's expansion was the Industrial Revolution—a series of wide-ranging economic changes involving the application of new technologies and energy sources to manufacturing, communication, and transportation. This revolution began in England in the late eighteenth century when a number of inventions transformed the textile industry. By 1914, industrialization had taken root in Europe, Japan, and the United States and was spreading to Canada, Russia, and parts of Latin America. Just as the discovery of agriculture had done many centuries earlier, industrialization profoundly altered the human condition.

Multiple Voices IV

Working Class and Middle Class in Nineteenth-Century Europe

BACKGROUND

"Two nations between whom there is no intercourse and no sympathy; who are ignorant of each other's habits, thoughts and feelings, as if they were dwellers in different zones or inhabitants of different planets; who are formed by different breeding, are fed by different food, are ordered by different manners, and are not governed by the same laws . . . THE RICH AND THE POOR." These words, quoted from *Sybil,* a novel published by Great Britain's future prime minister Benjamin Disraeli in 1845, zero in on a central concern of the author's contemporaries and a subject of ongoing controversy among historians—the issue of poverty in the era of the Industrial Revolution.

Poverty, of course, had always existed in Europe's preindustrial cities, where an unskilled, uneducated, and underemployed underclass was a permanent feature of urban life. It was even more pervasive and devastating in the countryside, where agricultural laborers and small peasants, even the most industrious, were just one crop failure away from financial catastrophe and famine.

Local governments, churches, and individual philanthropists provided support for the poor, but only a few thinkers seriously analyzed its causes or proposed ways to alleviate it. Most agreed that poverty was an unfortunate but inevitable aspect of the human condition—somehow an inscrutable part of God's plan. There are signs that this was beginning to change in the eighteenth century, when rural poverty worsened in many parts of Europe. Numerous English pamphleteers and social critics blamed this on enclosure, the process in which small farmers were denied access to common pasture lands or driven off the land altogether when the open field system, in which villagers were allocated strips of land in various fields, gave way to "enclosed" individual farms. The most famous analysis of poverty was provided by Thomas Malthus, who in his *Essay on the Principle of Population* (1798) argued it was the inevitable result of unbridled population growth, especially among the poor themselves. His solutions were "moral restraint" (delayed marriage and less sex) and less government-sponsored poor relief.

As a result of the Industrial Revolution, poverty increasingly became an urban problem. Industrial cities and mining centers became magnets for countless agricultural workers and small farmers who were squeezed off the land by enclosure, high rents, reduced demand for agricultural labor, and the collapse of rural cottage industry. In the cities, these new arrivals were transformed into a new working class or "proletariat," whose labor generated wealth for the owners of capital and other beneficiaries of the new industrial economy, but whose own lives were marked by low wages, overcrowded housing, poor diet, harsh working conditions, insecure employment, and the inevitable afflictions of old age and sickness. In the views of many, they were industrialization's victims, whose exploitation would continue until governments intervened on their behalf or the workers rose in revolution and abolished capitalism altogether.

The main beneficiaries of urbanization and industrialization were members of the middle class, or bourgeoisie. Comprising merchants, lawyers, bankers, doctors, skilled artisans, and shopkeepers in preindustrial Europe, the middle class in the nineteenth century expanded to include industrialists, managers, government officials, white-collar workers, and skilled professionals in fields such as engineering, architecture, accounting, the sciences, and higher education. The values, interests, and ambitions of these groups increasingly set the tone for nineteenth-century Europe. They were the main supporters of liberal, parliamentary government; set standards of taste in literature, music, and art; and provided the energy and leadership for Europe's economic development. Although members of the middle class actively supported movements on behalf of women's rights, public education, the abolition of slavery, prison reform, and other causes, many of them were unsympathetic to the plight of the working classes, whose poverty they ascribed to moral defects, not victimization. Insights into their views, along with those of workers and their sympathizers, are provided in the sources that follow.

THE SOURCES

Our first source is made up of excerpts from testimony presented in 1832, 1833, and 1842 to three British parliamentary committees charged with gathering information about working conditions in factories and coal mines. The first is an excerpt from the report of the Committee on the Bill to Regulate the Labour of Children in the Mills and Factories, headed by Michael Sadler (1780–1835). Appointed in 1832, Sadler's committee ceased its work and published its findings after it learned that 6 of the 89 workers it had interviewed were fired for giving testimony. Full of vivid descriptions of worker abuse, the report shocked the public but angered opponents of factory legislation, who claimed it was one-sided. The second excerpt is taken from a report prepared in 1833 by another parliamentary committee charged with investigating child labor in factories. Unlike the Sadler committee's report, it contains testimony from factory owners, mine superintendants, teachers, clergy, and other parties drawn from the middle class. The third excerpt presents evidence taken in 1842 by a committee investigating conditions in coal mines.

Our next two sources show that alarm over conditions of the working poor was not limited to England. Source 2 is taken from a work written by a prominent physician, Louis Villermé, under commission from the government-sponsored French Academy of Moral and Political Sciences. Villermé's *Study of the Physical Condition of Cotton, Wool and Silk Workers,* published in 1840, contains information on all of France's major industrial cities, but our excerpt focuses on conditions in Lille, a major city of northern France. The third source is an excerpt from a pamphlet published in 1845 by Alexander Schneer, a minor government official, titled *Living Conditions of the Working Class in Breslau.* It is based on interviews with local physicians and overseers of the poor in Breslau, one of Germany's largest cities until it was incorporated into Poland after World War II.

Our fourth source contains excerpts from two works of Samuel Smiles (1812–1904), a Scottish biographer, journalist, and businessman, who, more than any other writer, expressed the hopes, fears, and values of Europe's middle class. He wrote biographies, histories, and travel books, but gained worldwide fame through his inspirational books on character-building. With an upbeat message that hard work, discipline, and high moral standards guaranteed worldly success, his bestseller *Self Help* (1859) was followed by *Character* (1871), *Thrift* (1875), and *Duty* (1880). Our first excerpt by Smiles, "Self-Help and Individualism," comes from *Self Help*; "Faults of the Poor" is from *Thrift*.

Our fifth selection is an excerpt from *Letters from Berlin* (1891), a description of the lives of Berlin working-class families in the late 1880s based on interviews carried out by the German poet, literary critic, and journalist Otto von Leixner. In his description of the situation of a brass factory worker and his family, von Leixner would seem to lend credence to the arguments of most historians that by the end of the century many workers experienced higher standards of living as a result of higher wages, better housing, sanitation improvements, public education, and government-subsidized systems of national health insurance.

QUESTIONS FOR ANALYSIS

1. Based on the descriptions of working-class life provided by the first three sources, what can be learned or inferred about working conditions in the mills and coal mines?
2. What may be learned or inferred about the domestic lives of working-class families?
3. Based on von Leixner's observations, how does the situation of the late-nineteenth-century Berlin family differ from those of the families described in the parliamentary hearings and in the writings of Villermé and Schneer? What may explain these differences?
4. What insights do these sources provide into nineteenth-century attitudes toward children and the roles of men and women in marriage?
5. Samuel Smiles directly addresses the issue of the causes of working-class poverty and suggests ways it might be alleviated. Several of the individuals who provided testimony in the parliamentary hearings, Villermé, Schneer, and von Leixner also address the issue, although somewhat indirectly. In what ways do they agree and disagree?
6. Several authors oppose government initiatives to regulate working conditions in the mills and mines or to otherwise improve the lot of the poor. What are their reasons for opposing such measures?

▎• Testimony before Parliamentary Committees on Working Conditions in England

> a. Testimony before the Sadler Committee, 1832

Elizabeth Bentley

What age are you?—Twenty-three. . . .

What time did you begin to work at a factory?—When I was six years old. . . .

What kind of mill is it?—Flax-mill. . . .

What were your hours of labour in that mill?—From 5 in the morning till 9 at night, when they were thronged [busy]. . . .

What were your usual hours of labour when you were not so thronged?—From 6 in the morning till 7 at night. . . .

Had you any time to get your breakfast or drinking?—No, we got it as we could.

And when your work was bad, you had hardly any time to eat it at all?—No; we were obliged to leave it or take it home, and when we did not take it, the overlooker took it, and gave it to his pigs . . .

Explain what it is you had to do.—When the frames are full, they have to stop the frames, and take the flyers off, and take the full bobbins off, and carry them to the roller; and then put empty ones on, and set the frames on again.

Does that keep you constantly on your feet?—Yes, there are so many frames and they run so quick.

Your labor is very excessive?—Yes; you have not time for any thing.

Suppose you flagged a little, or were too late, what would they do?—Strap us.

Are they in the habit of strapping those who are last in doffing?—Yes.

Source: "Report from the Committee on the Bill to Regulate the Labour of Children in the Mills and the Factories in the United Kingdom," *British Sessional Papers,* vol. 15 (London, 1832), pp. 195, 196, "Second Report of the Commission of Inquiry into the Employment of Children in Factories,"

British Sessional Papers, vol. 21, pt. D-3 (London, 1833), pp. 26–28, "First Report of the Commission of Inquiry into the Employment of Children in Mines," *British Sessional Papers,* vol. 16 (London, 1842), pp. 149, 230, 258, 263–264.

Constantly?—Yes. . . .

Did you live far from the mill?—Yes, two miles.

Had you a clock?—No, we had not.

Supposing you had not been in time enough in the morning at the mills, what would have been the consequence?—We should have been quartered.

What do you mean by that?—If we were a quarter of an hour too late, they would take off half an hour; we only got a penny an hour, and they would take a halfpenny more. . . .

Were you generally there in time?—Yes, my mother has been up at 4 o'clock in the morning, and at 2 o'clock in the morning; the colliers used to go to their work about 3 or 4 o'clock, and when she heard them stirring she has got up out of her warm bed, and gone out and asked them the time, and I have sometimes been at Hunslet [a neighborhood in Leeds] at 2 o'clock in the morning, when it was streaming down with rain, and we have had to stay till the mill was opened. . . .

> b. *Commission for Inquiry into the Employment of Children in Factories,* Second Report, 1833

John Wright [A Silk Mill Worker in His Mid Thirties]

Are silk-mills clean in general?—They are; they are swept every day, and whitewashed once a year.

What is the temperature of silk-mills?—I don't know exactly the temperature, but it is very agreeable. . . .

Why, then, are those employed in them said to be in such a wretched condition?—In the first place, the great number of hands congregated together, in some rooms forty, in some fifty, in some sixty, and I have known some as many as 100, which must be injurious to both health and growing. In the second place, the privy is in the factory, which frequently emits an unwholesome smell; and it would be worth while to notice in the future erection of mills, that there be betwixt the privy door and the factory wall a kind of a lobby of cage-work. 3dly,

The tediousness and the everlasting sameness in the first process preys much on the spirits, and makes the hands spiritless. 4thly, the extravagant number of hours a child is compelled to labor and confinement, which for one week is seventy-six hours, which makes 3,952 hours for one year, we deduct 208 hours for meals within the factory which makes the net labor for one year 3,744; but the labor and confinement together of a child between ten years of age and twenty is 39,520 hours, enough to fritter away the best constitution. 5thly, About six months in the year we are obliged to use either gas, candles, or lamps, for the longest portion of that time, nearly six hours a day, being obliged to work amid the smoke and soot of the same; and also a large portion of oil and grease is used in the mills.

What are the effects of the present system of labor?—From my earliest recollections, I have found the effects to be awfully detrimental to the well-being of the operative; I have observed frequently children carried to factories, unable to walk, and that entirely owing to excessive labor and confinement. . . .

William Harter [The Owner of Silk Mill in Manchester]

What effect would it have on your manufacture to reduce the hours of labor to ten?—It would instantly much reduce the value of my mill and machinery, and consequently far prejudice my manufacture.

How so?—They are calculated to produce a certain quantity of work in a given time. Every machine is valuable in proportion to the quantity of work which it will turn off in a given time. It is impossible that the machinery could produce as much work in ten hours as in twelve. . . . The produce would vary in about the same ratio as the working time.

What may be said about the sum invested in your mill and machinery?—It is not yet near complete, and the investment is a little short of 20,000 pounds.

Then to what extent do you consider your property would be prejudiced by a bill limiting the working hours to ten?—All other circumstances remaining the same, it is obvious that any property in the mill and machinery would be prejudiced to the extent of one-sixth its value, or upwards of 3,000 pounds.

How would the reduction in the hours of labor affect the cost of your manufactures?—The cost of our manufactures consists in the price of the raw material and of the expense of putting that said material into goods. Now the mere interest of the investment in buildings and machinery, and the expense of keeping the same in repair, forms a large item in the cost of manufacturing. Of course it follows, that the *gross* charge under this head would be the same upon a production of 10,000 pounds and 12,000 pounds, and this portion of the cost of manufacturing would consequently be increased by about 16%.

Do you mean to say, that to produce the same quantity of work which your present mill and machinery is capable of, it requires an additional outlay of upwards of 3,000 pounds?—I say distinctly, that to produce the same quantity of work under a ten-hours bill will require an additional outlay of 3,000 or 4,000 pounds; therefore a ten-hours bill would impose upon me the necessity of this additional outlay in such perishable property as buildings and machinery, or I must be content to relinquish one-sixth portion of my business.

> c. *Testimony before the Committee on the Conditions in Mines, 1842*

Edward Potter

I am a coal viewer, and the manager of the South Hetton colliery. . .

Of the children in the pits we have none under eight, and only three so young. We are constantly beset by parents coming making application to take children under the age, and they are very anxious and very dissatisfied if we do not take the children; and there have been cases in times of brisk trade, when the parents have threatened to leave the colliery, and go elsewhere if we did not comply. . . . In point of fact, we would rather not have boys until nine years of age complete. If younger than that, they are apt to fall asleep and get hurt: some get killed. It is no interest to the company to take any boys under nine. . . .

Hannah Richardson [A Mine Employee]

I've one child that works in the pit; he's going on ten. He is down from 6 to 8. . . . He's not much tired with the work, it's only the confinement that tires him. He likes it pretty well, for he'd rather be in the pit than go to school. There is not much difference in his health since he went into the pit. He was at school before, and can read pretty well, but can't write. I never hear him complain. I've another son in the pit, 17 years old. . . . He went into the pit at eight years old. It's not hurt his health nor his appetite, for he's a good size. It would hurt us if children were prevented from working till 11 or 12 years old, because we've not jobs enough to live now as it is. . . .

Mr. George Armitage [A Local Teacher]

. . . I was a collier at Silkstone until I was 22 years old and worked in the pit above 10 years. . . . I hardly know how to reprobate the practice sufficiently of girls working in pits; nothing can be worse. I have no doubt that debauchery is carried on, for which there is every opportunity; for the girls go constantly, when hurrying,[1] to the men, who work often alone in the bank-faces apart from every one. I think it scarcely possible for girls to remain modest who are in pits, regularly mixing with such company and hearing such language as they do—it is next to

---

[1] Also known as a coal drawer or coal thruster, a hurrier was a child or woman who pulled carts filled with coal from one part of a mine to another.

impossible. I dare venture to say that many of the wives who come from pits know nothing of sewing or any household duty, such as women ought to know—they lose all disposition to learn such things; they are rendered unfit for learning them also by being overworked and not being trained to the habit of it. . . . I think, if girls were trained properly, as girls ought to be, that there would be no more difficulty in finding suitable employment for them than in other places. Many a collier spends in drink what he has shut up a young child the whole week to earn in a dark cold corner as a trapper.[2] . . .

Thomas Wilson [Owner of Three Coal Mines]

I object on general principles to government interference in the conduct of any trade, and I am satisfied that in the mines it would be productive of the greatest injury and injustice. . . . I should also most decidedly object to placing collieries under the present provisions of the Factory Act[3] with respect to the education of children employed therein. First, because, if it is contended that coal-owners, as employers of children, are bound to attend to their education, this obligation extends equally to all other employers, and therefore it is unjust to single out one class only; secondly, because, if the legislature asserts a right to interfere to secure education, it is bound to make that interference general; and thirdly, because the mining population is in this neighborhood so intermixed with other classes, and is in such small bodies in any one place, that it would be impossible to provide separate schools for them.

[2]Trappers were children responsible for opening and closing trap doors that were part of a mine's rudimentary ventilation system.

[3]The Factory Act of 1833, which regulated employment of children and women, in to textile factories.

---

2 • Louis Velermé, Study of the Physical Condition of Cotton, Wool and Silk Workers

The poorest live in the cellars and attics. . . . Commonly the height of the ceiling is six or six and half feet at the highest point, and they are only ten to fourteen or fifteen feet wide. . . .

Their furnishings normally consist, along with the tools of their profession, of a sort of cupboard or a plank on which to deposit food, a stove . . . a few pots, a little table, two or three poor chairs, and a dirty pallet of which the only pieces are a straw mattress and scraps of a blanket. . . .

. . . If a bed exists, it is a few dirty, greasy planks; it is damp and putrescent straw; it is a coarse cloth whose color and fabric are hidden by a layer of grime; it is a blanket that resembles a sieve. . . . The furniture is dislocated, worm-eaten, covered with filth. Utensils are thrown in disorder all over the dwelling. The windows, always closed, are covered by paper and glass, but so black, so smoke-encrusted, that the light is unable to penetrate . . . everywhere are piles of garbage, of ashes, of debris from vegetables picked up from the streets, of rotten straw . . . : thus, the air is unbreathable. One is exhausted, in these hovels, by a stale, nauseating, somewhat piquante odor, odor of filth, odor of garbage. . . .

And the poor themselves, what are they like in the middle of such a slum? Their clothing is in shreds, without substance, consumed, covered, no less than their hair, which knows no comb, with dust from the workshops. And their skin? . . . It is painted, it is hidden if you wish, by indistinguishable deposits of diverse discharges.

Source: From William H. Sewell, *Work and Revolution in France* (Cambridge: Cambridge University Press, 1989), p. 224.

3 · Alexander Schneer, Living Conditions of the Working Class in Breslau

The following replies may provide answers about the nature of the living quarters, the cleanliness, the state of health as well as the state of morals of the classes under discussion.

QUESTION: What is the condition of the living quarters of the class of factory workers, day laborers and journeymen?

REPLY OF THE CITY POOR DOCTOR, DR BLUEMNER: It is in the highest degree miserable. . . .

Many rooms are more like pigsties than quarters for human beings. The apartments in the city are, if possible, even worse than those in the suburbs. . . . The so-called staircase is generally completely in the dark. It is also so decrepit that the whole building shakes with every firm footstep; the rooms themselves are small and so low that it is hardly possible to stand upright, the floor is on a slope, since usually part of the house has to be supported by struts. The windows close badly, the stoves are so bad that they hardly give any heat but plenty of smoke in the room. Water runs down the doors and walls. The ground-floor dwellings are usually half underground. . . .

QUESTION: What is your usual experience regarding the cleanliness of these classes?

DR BLUEMNER: Bad! Mother has to go out to work, and can therefore pay little attention to the domestic economy [housekeeping], and even if she makes an effort, she lacks time and means. A typical woman of this kind has four children, of whom she is still suckling one, she has to look after the whole household, to take food to her husband at work, perhaps a quarter of a mile away . . . she therefore has no time for cleaning and then it is such a small hole inhabited by so many people. The children are left to themselves, crawl about the floor or in the streets, and are always dirty; they lack the necessary clothing to change more often, and there is no time or money to wash these frequently. . . .

QUESTION: What is the state of health among the lower classes?

DR BLUEMNER: Since these classes are much more exposed to diseases, they usually are the first to be attacked by epidemic and sporadic disorders. Chronic rheumatism of the joints is a common illness, since they are constantly subject to colds. In addition, we find hernia with men, diseases of the reproductive organs with women because they have to start work only a few days after childbirth. Children mostly suffer from scrofula, which is almost general.

DR NEUMANN: . . . The very frequent incidence of anemia among girls employed in factories deserves special mention. The hard work, the crowding of many individuals into closed rooms during their period of development, in which much exercise in the fresh air, plenty of sleep and only moderate exertion are most necessary, are sufficient explanation of this disease.

Source: From S. Pollard and C. Holmes, *Documents of European Economic History*, vol. 1, (London: Edward Arnold, 1968), pp. 497–499.

4 • Samuel Smiles, Self Help and Thrift

Self-Help and Individualism

Whatever is done *for* men or classes, to a certain extent takes away the stimulus and necessity of doing for themselves; and where men are subjected to over-guidance and over-government, the inevitable tendency is to render them comparatively helpless.

Even the best institutions can give a man no active help. Perhaps the most they can do is, to leave him free to develop himself and improve his individual condition. But in all times men have been prone to believe that their happiness and well-being were to be secured by means of institutions rather than by their own conduct. . . . Moreover, it is every day becoming more clearly understood, that the function of Government is negative and restrictive, rather than positive and active; being resolvable principally into protection—protection of life, liberty, and property. Laws, wisely administered, will secure men in the enjoyment of the fruits of their labor, whether of mind or body, at a comparatively small personal sacrifice; but no laws, however stringent, can make the idle industrious, the thriftless provident, or the drunken sober. Such reforms can only be effected by means of individual action, economy, and self-denial; by better habits, rather than by greater rights. . . .

What we are accustomed to decry as great social evils, will for the most part be found to be but the outgrowth of man's own perverted life; and though we may endeavor to cut them down and extirpate them by means of Law, they will only spring up again with fresh luxuriance in some other form unless the conditions of personal life and character are radically improved. If this view be correct, then it follows that the highest patriotism and philanthropy consist, not so much in altering laws and modifying institutions as in helping and stimulating men to elevate and improve themselves by their own free and independent individual action.

Faults of the Poor

England is one of the richest countries in the world. Our merchants are enterprizing, our manufacturers are industrious, our labourers are hardworking. There is an accumulation of wealth in the country to which past times can offer no parallel. There never was more food in the empire; there never was more money. There is no end to our manufacturing productions, for the steam-engine never tires. And yet, notwithstanding all this wealth, there is an enormous mass of poverty.

Parliamentary reports have again and again revealed to us the miseries endured by certain portions of our working population. They have described the people employed in factories, workshops, mines, and brickfields, as well as in the pursuits of country life. We have tried to grapple with the evils of their condition by legislation, but it seems to mock us. Those who sink into poverty are fed, but they remain paupers. Those who feed them, feel no compassion; and those who are fed, return no gratitude. . . .

With respect to the poorer classes,—what has become of them in the midst of our so-called civilization? . . .

They work, eat, drink, and sleep: that constitutes their life. They think nothing of providing for tomorrow, or for next week, or for next year. They abandon themselves to their sensual appetites; and make no provision whatever for the future. The thought of adversity, or of coming sorrow, or of the helplessness that comes with years and sickness, never crosses their minds. In these respects, they resemble the savage tribes, who know no better, and do no worse. Like the North American Indians, they debase

Source: Samuel Smiles, *Self Help* (1859) and *Thrift* (1875).

themselves by the vices which accompany civilization, but make no use whatever of its benefits and advantages. . . .

This habitual improvidence—though of course there are many admirable exceptions—is the real cause of the social degradation of the artisan. This too is the prolific source of social misery. But the misery is entirely the result of human ignorance and self-indulgence. For though the Creator has ordained poverty, the poor are not necessarily, nor as a matter of fact, the miserable. Misery is the result of moral causes,—most commonly of individual vice and improvidence. . . .

All this may seem very hopeless; yet it is not entirely so. The large earnings of the working classes is an important point to start with. The gradual diffusion of education will help them to use, and not abuse, their means of comfortable living. The more extended knowledge of the uses of economy, frugality, and thrift, will help them to spend their lives more soberly, virtuously, and religiously. . . . Social improvement is always very slow. . . . It requires the lapse of generations before its effect can be so much as discerned; for a generation is but as a day in the history of civilization. . . .

5 • Otto von Leixner, Letters from Berlin

The first question to be answered is: "Can a Berlin, working class family really live on the wages of the father?" On the basis of my experiences, I can answer that question "Yes." . . .

As is the case with other social classes, there also exists among workers gradations in income from "master" and foreman to the young apprentice; and even among the former are differences according to various branches of industry. But the most fundamental difference is in moral character. If the husband is sober and decent, the wife frugal and hard-working, then a small salary suffices. If these characteristics are lacking, then even a larger salary is inadequate. This is the same for every class. . . .

To prove this, I refer to my visits to families. . . .

The first household belongs to a relatively well-paid worker. He is employed as a molder in a bronze ware workshop, and is a hard-working, respectable man, and a worthy spouse and father. . . . He hardly attends political meetings, the tavern

very rarely. His wife, who previously was a servant girl, is, despite her infirmities, very industrious and thrifty. Their apartment consists of a rather sizable room, with an attached kitchen. Although the husband, wife, and two children live and sleep here, everything is meticulously clean. Colorful calico curtains hang on the two windows, and plants are growing on the window sills. Two beds and a simple sleeping sofa for the children occupy one long wall; the others are taken up by a cupboard, a wardrobe, and a wash-stand. A table and some chairs complete the furnishings.

The average income is 1700 marks.[1] In many years it is larger, but also occasionally smaller. The work is difficult, and when there is much to do at the shop, exhaustion sets in for the father, and he sometimes takes to bed for a week.

259 marks must be paid for rent. The small apartments are expensive, despite their deficiencies, because of high demand. . . .

When the molder is paid on Saturday, he puts aside a part for the rent that must be paid every month. The wife receives 18 marks for household

Source: Otto von Leixner, *Soziale Briefe aus Berlin* (Berlin: F. Pfeilstucker, 1891), trans. by James H. Overfield.

[1]The basic unit of the German currency. One mark equals 100 pfennig.

costs per week, in other words, 2.57 marks per day or 64 pfennig for each person; from this the bill for lighting must be paid. The husband pays for heating, specifically in the following manner: in winter, in other words for five months, 20 small coal briquettes are purchased (6 marks per 100) and a few pieces of kindling wood; they have to make do with this. When needed, they sit by the cookstove in the kitchen. . . .

Their daily food consumption is instructive. The following sketch is an average, and the menu is not always the same. The use of dried peas and lentils, potatoes, flour, bread, and milk is high. Meat products, except for some cheap sausage—spread on bread, not put on in slices—is mostly chopped beef or lungs, in the form of meatballs (*Klops*) or meatloaf (ground meat mixed with bread crumbs or spices and baked in a little fat). To plan ahead for Sunday and holidays, the family cuts back on workdays. . . .

. . . Not even the smallest item is purchased on credit. This is a prime requirement if the small household is to remain on a sound footing. When larger expenses are necessary, then each week a partial amount is put aside, so that the expense can be paid for.

The husband takes coffee with him in the morning in a tin container, and in the evening and at midday he drinks at the most three glasses of beer, with each costing 10 pfennig (he hardly ever drinks anything stronger). On weekdays he smokes two cigars, on Sundays, three, at three pfennig each. He goes to the tavern perhaps once a week, but when he does, he is home by 10:30. . . .

. . . A glance at expenditures shows how much thriftiness is needed not to exceed the amount of income. . . . Amusements which cost money are rare. They consist of excursions to the zoo, where they take a lunch-basket, or to a country park. That is it. Very rarely, once every several years, they go to a cheap vaudeville theater. . . . The husband makes do; he borrows books from the public library and reads them in the evening if he is not too tired; the wife is satisfied with serialized novels and local news in the daily press, or she chats with neighbors after the children have gone to sleep.

So long as things remain on even keel, then a better paid worker, if he lives decently, can get by. . . . But if the husband and wife are frivolous, or irresponsible, then disaster begins. . . .

New Perspectives on Humanity and Society

In 1873, the English naturalist Charles Darwin wrote a letter to the German philosopher and revolutionary Karl Marx in which he stated, "I believe we both earnestly desire the extension of human knowledge; and this in the long run is sure to add to the happiness of mankind." Whether Marx and Darwin added to human happiness is difficult to judge, but there is no doubting their enormous influence. Although nineteenth-century Europe produced more scientists, philosophers, artists, composers, novelists, poets, historians, critics, and social theorists than ever before, and although these intellectuals produced an abundance of provocative new ideas, none matched the wide-ranging influence of these two men.

Darwin (1809–1882) did not invent the theory of evolution. Several Europeans before him had theorized that species were mutable and that all plants and animals, including humans, evolved. Darwin's contributions were the wealth of data he marshaled to support the idea of evolution and his theory that evolution took place as a result of natural selection, not God's plan. Thus, Darwin cast doubt on the biblical creation story, in which God creates time, space, and the universe, including the first humans, in six days and then rests on the seventh. Darwin's theories drew immediate opposition from biblical literalists and others when he published his books, and are still the focus of debates in the early twenty-first century. Darwinism also forced intellectuals to re-examine long-accepted notions about nature, morality, permanence versus change, and, of course, humanity itself. Finally, Darwinism had important political ramifications: imperialists, free traders, nationalists, and fascists all used (or misused) Darwinism to bolster their beliefs.

Just as Darwin was not the first proponent of evolution, Marx was not the first socialist. The first socialists, often referred to as utopian socialists, were early-nineteenth-century visionaries whose dreams of equality and justice lacked philosophical rigor and practical political sense. Marx, an academically trained philosopher knowledgeable in history, economics, and science, sought to establish an intellectual foundation for *scientific socialism* and to describe the mechanism by which socialism would ultimately replace capitalism. Through class conflict, in a process Marx referred to as the *dialectic,* society develops through stages until it reaches the age of industrial capitalism, when the oppressor class, the bourgeoisie, clashes with the factory workers, the proletariat. The proletariat will triumph, argues Marx, because capitalism itself, an intrinsically flawed system, will create the conditions for the proletarian revolution, the end of the dialectic, and a classless society.

Even dedicated disciples of Marx and Darwin concede that much of what they wrote was incomplete, incorrect, or hypothetical. Well before the collapse of most of the world's Marxist governments in the late twentieth century, critics could point to many ways in which Marx misjudged capitalism, workers' attitudes, and the causes of revolution. Opponents of Darwinism contend that its theories are unprovable and that natural selection cannot explain the miraculous complexity of living things. Nonetheless, Darwin and Marx remain a part of that small group of nineteenth-century European thinkers whose work has left an indelible mark on history.

The Marxist Critique of Industrial Capitalism

54 • KARL MARX AND FRIEDRICH ENGELS, THE COMMUNIST MANIFESTO

Karl Marx (1818–1883) was born in Trier, a city in western Germany that had been assigned to the Kingdom of Prussia at the Congress of Vienna in 1815. Marx's parents were Jewish, but in 1817 his father had become a Lutheran so he could continue his career as a lawyer. Young Marx studied law at the University of Bonn before enrolling at the University of Berlin, where he was influenced by the thought of the famous philosopher G. W. F. Hegel (1770–1831), especially his idea of the dialectic—the theory that history unfolds toward a specific goal in a process driven by the clash and resolution of antagonistic forces. After losing his job as a journalist for a Cologne newspaper because of his political views, Marx moved in 1844 to Paris, where he argued about capitalism and revolution with other radicals and continued his studies of economics and history. He also made the acquaintance of another German, Friedrich Engels (1820–1895), an ardent critic of capitalism despite the fortune he amassed from managing a textile mill in Manchester, England. In 1847, Marx and Engels joined the Communist League, a revolutionary society dominated by German political exiles in France and England. In 1848, a year of revolution in Europe, the two men wrote *The Communist Manifesto* to publicize the League's program. It became the most widely read socialist tract in history.

After 1848, Marx and Engels remained friends, with Engels giving Marx enough money to continue his writing and political activities while living in London. Both men continued to write on behalf of socialism, but Marx's works, especially his masterpiece, *Das Kapital* (*Capitalism*), assumed the far greater role in the history of socialism. Furthermore, Marx's views of history, human behavior, and social conflict have influenced not only politics but also philosophy, religion, literature, and all the social sciences.

QUESTIONS FOR ANALYSIS

1. How do Marx and Engels define class, and what do they mean by the "class struggle"?
2. According to Marx and Engels, how does the class struggle in nineteenth-century Europe differ from class struggles in previous eras?
3. According to Marx and Engels, what are the characteristics of the bourgeoisie?
4. Marx and Engels believe that bourgeois society is doomed and that the bourgeoisie will be the cause of their own destruction. Why?
5. The authors dismiss the importance of ideas as a force in human affairs. On what grounds? Ultimately, what is the cause of historical change in their view?
6. What may explain the popularity and influence of *The Communist Manifesto* among workers and those who sympathized with their plight?

I. The Bourgeoisie and Proletariat

The history of all hitherto existing society is the history of class struggles.

Freeman and slave, patrician and plebeian, lord and serf, guild-master and journeyman, in a word, oppressor and oppressed, stood in constant opposition to one another, carried on an uninterrupted, now hidden, now open fight, a fight that each time ended, either in a revolutionary reconstitution of society at large, or in the common ruin of the contending classes. . . .

Our epoch, the epoch of the bourgeoisie, possesses, however, this distinctive feature: It has simplified the class antagonisms. Society as a whole is more and more splitting up into two great hostile camps, into two great classes directly facing each other—bourgeoisie and proletariat.

Source: Karl Marx and Friedrich Engels, *The Manifesto of the Communist Party*, authorized English trans. by Samuel Moore (London: W. Reeves, 1888).

From the serfs of the Middle Ages sprang the chartered burghers of the earliest towns. From these burgesses the first elements of the bourgeoisie were developed.

The discovery of America, the rounding of the Cape, opened up fresh ground for the rising bourgeoisie. The East-Indian and Chinese markets, the colonization of America, trade with the colonies, the increase in the means of exchange and in commodities generally, gave to commerce, to navigation, to industry, an impulse never before known, and thereby, to the revolutionary element in the tottering feudal society, a rapid development.

The feudal system of industry, in which industrial production was monopolized by closed guilds, now no longer sufficed for the growing wants of the new markets. The manufacturing system took its place. The guild-masters were pushed aside by the manufacturing middle class; division of labor between the different corporate guilds vanished in the face of division of labor in each single workshop.

Meantime the markets kept ever growing, the demand ever rising. Even manufacture[1] no longer sufficed. Thereupon, steam and machinery revolutionized industrial production. The place of manufacture was taken by the giant, modern industry, the place of the industrial middle class by industrial millionaires, the leaders of whole industrial armies, the modern bourgeois. . . .

The bourgeoisie, wherever it has got the upper hand, has put an end to all feudal, patriarchal, idyllic relations. It has pitilessly torn asunder the motley feudal ties that bound man to his "natural superiors," and has left no other nexus between man and man than naked self-interest, than callous "cash payment." . . . In one word, for exploitation, veiled by religious and political illusions, it has substituted naked, shameless, direct, brutal exploitation. . . .

We see then: the means of production and of exchange, on whose foundation the bourgeoisie

built itself up, were generated in feudal society. At a certain stage in the development of these means of production and of exchange, the conditions under which feudal society produced and exchanged, the feudal organization of agriculture and manufacturing industry . . . became no longer compatible with the already developed productive forces; they became so many fetters. They had to be burst asunder; they were burst asunder. . . .

A similar movement is going on before our own eyes. Modern bourgeois society with its relations of production, of exchange and of property, a society that has conjured up such gigantic means of production and of exchange, is like the sorcerer who is no longer able to control the powers of the nether world whom he has called up by his spells. . . . It is enough to mention the commercial crises that by their periodical return put the existence of the entire bourgeois society on its trial, each time more threateningly. In these crises a great part not only of the existing products, but also of the previously created productive forces, are periodically destroyed. In these crises there breaks out an epidemic that, in all earlier epochs, would have seemed an absurdity—the epidemic of overproduction.

And how does the bourgeoisie get over these crises? On the one hand, by enforced destruction of a mass of productive forces; on the other, by the conquest of new markets, and by the more thorough exploitation of the old ones. That is to say, by paving the way for more extensive and more destructive crises, and by diminishing the means whereby crises are prevented.

The weapons with which the bourgeoisie felled feudalism to the ground are now turned against the bourgeoisie itself.

But not only has the bourgeoisie forged the weapons that bring death to itself; it has also called into existence the men who are to wield those weapons—the modern working class—the proletarians. . . .

---

[1]"Manufacture" is used here in the sense of making goods by hand rather than machines.

. . . Masses of laborers, crowded into the factory, are organized like soldiers. As privates of the industrial army they are placed under the command of a perfect hierarchy of officers and sergeants. Not only are they slaves of the bourgeois class, and of the bourgeois state; they are daily and hourly enslaved by the machine, by the overseer, and, above all, by the individual bourgeois manufacturer himself. . . .

The lower strata of the middle class—the small tradespeople, shopkeepers, and retired tradesmen generally, the handicraftsmen and peasants—all these sink gradually into the proletariat, partly because their diminutive capital does not suffice for the scale on which modern industry is carried on, . . . partly because their specialized skill is rendered worthless by new methods of production. Thus the proletariat is recruited from all classes of the population.

But with the development of industry the proletariat not only increases in number; it becomes concentrated in greater masses, its strength grows, and it feels that strength more. The various interests and conditions of life within the ranks of the proletariat are more and more equalized, in proportion as machinery obliterates all distinctions of labor, and nearly everywhere reduces wages to the same low level. The growing competition among the bourgeois, and the resulting commercial crises, make the wages of the workers ever more fluctuating. The unceasing improvement of machinery . . . makes their livelihood more and more precarious; the collisions between individual workmen and individual bourgeois take more and more the character of collisions between two classes. Thereupon the workers begin to form combinations (trade unions) against the bourgeois. . . . Here and there the contest breaks out into riots.

Now and then the workers are victorious, but only for a time. The real fruit of their battle lies, not in the immediate result, but in the ever expanding union of the workers. This union is helped on by the improved means of communication that are created by modern industry, and that place the workers of different localities in contact with one another. It was just this contact that was needed to centralize the numerous local struggles, all of the same character, into one national struggle between classes. . . .

Finally, in times when the class struggle nears the decisive hour, the process of dissolution going on within the ruling class, in fact within the whole range of old society, assumes such a violent, glaring character, that a small section of the ruling class cuts itself adrift, and joins the revolutionary class, the class that holds the future in its hands. Just as, therefore, at an earlier period, a section of the nobility went over to the bourgeoisie, so now a portion of the bourgeoisie goes over to the proletariat, and in particular, a portion of the bourgeois ideologists, who have raised themselves to the level of comprehending theoretically the historical movement as a whole.

II. Proletarians and Communists

The distinguishing feature of communism is not the abolition of property generally, but the abolition of bourgeois property. But modern bourgeois private property is the final and most complete expression of the system of producing and appropriating products that is based on class antagonisms, on the exploitation of the many by the few.

In this sense, the theory of the Communists may be summed up in the single sentence: Abolition of private property. . . .

You are horrified at our intending to do away with private property. But in your existing society, private property is already done away with for nine-tenths of its population; its existence for the few is solely due to its nonexistence in the hands of those nine-tenths. . . .

The Communists are further reproached with desiring to abolish countries and nationality.

The working men have no country. We cannot take from them what they have not got. . . .

National differences and antagonism between peoples are daily more and more vanishing, owing to the development of the bourgeoisie, to freedom of commerce, to the world market, to uniformity in the mode of production and in the conditions of life corresponding thereto.

The supremacy of the proletariat will cause them to vanish still faster. United action of the leading civilized countries at least, is one of the first conditions for the emancipation of the proletariat.

. . . In proportion as the antagonism between classes within the nation vanishes, the hostility of one nation to another will come to an end. . . .

We have seen above that the first step in the revolution by the working class is to raise the proletariat to the position of ruling class, to win the battle for democracy.

The proletariat will use its political supremacy to wrest, by degrees, all capital from the bourgeoisie, to centralize all instruments of production in the hands of the State, i.e., of the proletariat organized as the ruling class; and to increase the total of productive forces as rapidly as possible.

Of course, in the beginning, this cannot be effected except by means of despotic inroads on the rights of property, and on the conditions of bourgeois production; by means of measures which . . . are unavoidable as a means of entirely revolutionizing the mode of production.

These measures will of course be different in different countries.

Nevertheless, in the most advanced countries, the following will be pretty generally applicable.

1. Abolition of property in land and application of all rents of land to public purposes.
2. A heavy progressive or graduated income tax.
3. Abolition of all right of inheritance.
4. Confiscation of the property of all emigrants and rebels.[2]
5. Centralization of credit in the hands of the State, by means of a national bank with State capital and an exclusive monopoly.
6. Centralization of the means of communication and transport in the hands of the State.
7. Extension of the number of State factories and instruments of production: the bringing into cultivation of waste lands, and the improvement of the soil generally in accordance with a common plan.
8. Equal obligation of all to work. Establishment of industrial armies, especially for agriculture.
9. Combination of agriculture with manufacturing industries; gradual abolition of the distinction between town and country, by a more equable distribution of the population over the country.
10. Free education for all children in public schools. Abolition of children's factory labor in its present form. . . .

When, in the course of development, class distinctions have disappeared, and all production has been concentrated in the hands of a vast association of the whole nation, the public power will lose its political character. . . . If, by means of a revolution, [the proletariat] makes itself the ruling class, and as such sweeps away by force the old conditions of production, then it will, along with these conditions, have swept away the conditions for the existence of class antagonisms and of classes generally, and will thereby have abolished its own supremacy as a class. . . .

The Communists disdain to conceal their views and aims. They openly declare that their ends can be attained only by the forcible overthrow of all existing social conditions. Let the ruling classes tremble at a Communist revolution. In it the proletarians have nothing to lose but their chains. They have a world to win.

WORKING MEN OF ALL COUNTRIES, UNITE!

---

[2]Presumably individuals who are resisting the new regime or flee during the revolution.

The Principles of Darwinism

55 • CHARLES DARWIN, ON THE ORIGIN OF SPECIES AND THE DESCENT OF MAN

After pursuing his university education at Edinburgh and Cambridge, Charles Darwin (1809–1882) spent five years on the HMS *Beagle* as chief naturalist on a scientific expedition to the South Pacific and the western coast of South America. Darwin observed the bewildering variety of nature and began to speculate on how millions of species of plants and animals had come into existence. On his return to England, he developed his theory of evolution, basing his hypothesis on his own formidable biological knowledge, recent discoveries in geology, work on the selective breeding of plants and animals, and the theories of several authors that competition was the norm for all living things. In 1859, he published *On the Origin of Species*, followed in 1871 by *The Descent of Man*.

QUESTIONS FOR ANALYSIS

1. What does Darwin mean by the terms *struggle for existence* and *natural selection?*
2. How does Darwin defend himself from religiously motivated attacks on his work?
3. What were some implications of Darwin's work for nineteenth-century views of progress? Of nature? Of human nature?
4. Defenders of laissez-faire capitalism sometimes drew upon Darwinian concepts in their arguments against socialism. Which concepts might they have used?
5. Similarly, Darwinian concepts were used to defend militarism and late-nineteenth-century Western imperialism. Which of Darwin's theories might have proved useful in such a defense?

On the Origin of Species

Chapter III Struggle for Existence

It has been seen in the last chapter that amongst organic beings in a state of nature there is some individual variability. . . . But the mere existence of individual variability and of some few well-marked varieties, . . . helps us but little in understanding how species arise in nature. How have all those exquisite adaptations of one part of the organization to another part, and to the conditions of life, and of one organic being to another being, been perfected? . . .

Source: Charles Darwin, "On the Origin of Species," in Charles Darwin, *The Origin of Species* (New York: Appleton and Company, 1896), pp. 75–78, and Charles Darwin, *The Descent of Man* (New York: Appleton and Company, 1896), pp. 62–63, 164–165, 613, 616–617.

Again, . . . how is it that varieties, which I have called incipient species, become ultimately converted into good and distinct species, which in most cases obviously differ from each other far more than do the varieties of the same species? . . . All these results . . . follow from the struggle for life. Owing to this struggle, variations, however slight and from whatever cause proceeding, if they be in any degree profitable to the individuals of a species, in their infinitely complex relations to other organic beings and to their physical conditions of life, will tend to the preservation of such individuals, and will generally be inherited by the offspring. The offspring, also, will thus have a better chance of surviving, for, of the many individuals of any species which are periodically born, but a small number can survive. I have called this principle, by which each slight variation, if useful, is preserved, by the term Natural Selection, in order to mark its relation to man's power of selection. But the expression . . . Survival of the Fittest is more accurate, and is sometimes equally convenient. . . .

I should premise that I use this term in a large and metaphorical sense including . . . not only the life of the individual, but success in leaving progeny. Two canine animals, in a time of dearth, may be truly said to struggle with each other which shall get food and live. But a plant on the edge of a desert is said to struggle for life against the drought. . . . A plant which annually produces a thousand seeds, of which only one of an average comes to maturity, may be more truly said to struggle with the plants of the same and other kinds which already clothe the ground. . . . In these several senses, which pass into each other, I use for convenience's sake the general term of Struggle for Existence.

A struggle for existence inevitably follows from the high rate at which all organic beings tend to increase. Every being, which during its natural lifetime produces several eggs or seeds, must suffer destruction during some period of its life, and during some season or occasional year, otherwise . . . its numbers would quickly become so inordinately great that no country could support the product. Hence, as more individuals are produced than can possibly survive, there must in every case be a struggle for existence, either one individual with another of the same species, or with the individuals of distinct species, or with the physical conditions of life. . . . Although some species may be now increasing, more or less rapidly, in numbers, all cannot do so, for the world would not hold them.

The Descent of Man

Chapter II On the Manner of Development of Man from Some Lower Form

In this chapter we have seen that as man at the present day is liable, like every other animal, to multiform individual differences or slight variations, so no doubt were the early progenitors [ancestors] of man; the variations being formerly induced by the same general causes, and governed by the same general and complex laws as at present. As all animals tend to multiply beyond their means of subsistence, so it must have been with the progenitors of man; and this would inevitably lead to a struggle for existence and to natural selection. . . .

Chapter VI On the Affinities and Genealogy of Man

Now as organisms have become slowly adapted to diversified lines of life by means of natural selection, their parts will have become more and more differentiated and specialized for various functions, from the advantage gained by the division of physiological labor. The same part appears often to have been modified first for one purpose, and then long afterwards for some other and quite distinct purpose; and thus all the parts are rendered more and more complex. But each organism still retains the general type of structure of the progenitor from which it was aboriginally derived. In accordance with this view it seems, if we turn to geological evidence, that organization on the whole has advanced throughout the world by slow and interrupted steps. In the great kingdom of the Vertebrata it has culminated in man. . . .

The most ancient progenitors in the kingdom of the Vertebrata, at which we are able to obtain an obscure glance, apparently consisted of a group of marine animals, resembling the larvae of existing Ascidians.[1] These animals probably gave rise to a group of fishes, as lowly organized as the lancelet;[2] and from these the Ganoids,[3] and other fishes must have developed. From such fish a very small advance would carry us on to the Amphibians. We have seen that birds and reptiles were once intimately connected together; and the Monotremata[4] now connect mammals with reptiles in a slight degree. But no one can at present say by what line of descent the three higher and related classes, namely, mammals, birds, and reptiles, were derived from the two lower vertebrate classes, namely, amphibians and fishes. In the class of mammals the steps are not difficult to conceive which led from the ancient Monotremata to the ancient Marsupials,[5] and from these to the early progenitors of the placental mammals. We may thus ascend to the Lemuridae,[6] and the interval is not very wide from these to the Simiadae.[7] The Simiadae then branched off into two great stems, the New World and Old World monkeys; and from the latter, at a remote period, Man, the wonder and glory of the Universe, proceeded.

Chapter XXI General Summary and Conclusion

I am aware that the conclusions arrived at in this work will be denounced by some as highly irreligious; but he who denounces them is bound to show why it is more irreligious to explain the origin of man as a distinct species by descent from some lower form, through the laws of variation and natural selection, than to explain the birth of the individual through the laws of ordinary reproduction. The birth both of the species and of the individual are equally parts of that grand sequence of events, which our minds refuse to accept as the result of blind chance. The understanding revolts at such a conclusion, whether or not we are able to believe that every slight variation of structure,—the union of each pair in marriage,—the dissemination of each seed,—and other such events, have all been ordained for some special purpose. . . .

Man may be excused for feeling some pride at having risen, though not through his own exertions, to the very summit of the organic scale; and the fact of his having thus risen, instead of having been aboriginally placed there, may give him hope for a still higher destiny in the distant future. But we are not here concerned with hopes or fears, only with the truth as far as our reason permits us to discover it; and I have given the evidence to the best of my ability. We must, however, acknowledge, as it seems to me, that man with all his noble qualities, with sympathy which

---

[1] Marine animals with a rodlike primitive backbone.
[2] Boney fish such as the sturgeon and gar, covered with large armorlike scales.
[3] Any of small translucent marine animals related to vertebrates.
[4] Order of egg-laying mammals such as the platypus.

[5] Mammals, such as the kangaroo, whose females lack placentas and carry their young in an abdominal pouch.
[6] Largely nocturnal tree-dwelling mammals distinct from monkeys.
[7] Apes and monkeys.

feels for the most debased, with benevolence which extends not only to other men but to the humblest living creature, with his god-like intellect which has penetrated into the movements and constitution of the solar system—with all these exalted powers—Man still bears in his bodily frame the indelible stamp of his lowly origin.

Millions on the Move: Nineteenth-Century European Migration

Migration—over land and over seas, by craftsmen and conquerors, hunters and herdsmen, farmers and missionaries—has been a part of human history from its beginning. But in the nineteenth century, more people were on the move over longer distances than ever before. Indians migrated to Southeast Asia, the West Indies, Africa, and South America; Chinese moved to Malaya, Singapore, and the Americas. Most significantly, millions of Europeans migrated to Argentina, Australia, New Zealand, Africa, Canada, and especially the United States.

Although a small number of nineteenth-century migrants left their homes to escape political or religious oppression, most did so to improve their economic condition, or to be more accurate, to escape economic disaster. Throughout Eurasia, decades of population growth had created widespread economic hardship. This demographic surge was especially damaging to peasants and agricultural laborers, who faced land shortages and rising rents. In Europe, their problems were compounded by the mechanization of agriculture, which limited the need for rural labor, and the mechanization of the textile industry, which took away jobs from home-based spinners and weavers.

For millions of Europeans, the open spaces and cheap land of Australia, New Zealand, and the Americas beckoned, as did the prospect of jobs in heavy industry, canal-building, commerce, food processing, manufacturing, and services. Simultaneously, long-distance migration was becoming cheaper, faster, and more reliable with the introduction of railroads and steamships. The average sailing time from Europe to America in the 1860s was 44 days, but by 1900, steamers were making the same voyage in a week or ten days. Travel also became cheaper. Irish immigrants could travel to the United States in the 1880s for $9, which many of them could expect to earn in a week's work.

From the early nineteenth century to 1914, approximately 70 million Europeans emigrated, of whom just over 70 percent went to North America, approximately 20 percent went to South America, and the remainder, primarily British, went to Australia, New Zealand, and British colonies in Africa. It was history's greatest migration, one that brought about profound changes in the lands the migrants left and in those that received them.

The Lures and Pitfalls of Migration

56 • GOTTFRIED MENZEL, THE UNITED STATES OF NORTH AMERICA, WITH SPECIAL REFERENCE TO GERMAN EMIGRATION

The era of mass migration from Europe dates from the 1840s and 1850s, when 4.2 million people left Europe for the United States. Just short of three quarters of these immigrants arrived between 1845 and 1855, the decade that witnessed the largest immigration in proportion to the total population (around 20 million) in U.S. history. The bulk of these immigrants came from Ireland and Germany. The Irish immigrants were overwhelmingly Roman Catholic peasants who left Ireland because of eviction from their lands or the famine following the potato blight of the 1840s and the early 1850s. In contrast, the German immigrants included Lutherans, Catholics, and Jews; by occupation they were a mix of farmers, artisans, professionals, and tradespeople. Most left Germany because of population pressures, land shortages, and guild restrictions, with smaller numbers because of the failure of the liberal/nationalist revolutions of 1848. Growing from 400,000 German immigrants in the 1840s to a peak of more than 1.4 million in the 1890s, immigration from Germany then rapidly declined when German industrialization created a large demand for labor at home.

During the first decade of large-scale German migration, dozens of guides and "advice books" were published for would-be immigrants. Most had a strong bias in favor of migration, and tended to depict the United States positively and unrealistically. A more balanced point of view characterized the guidebook written by the German botanist Gottfried Menzel (1798–1889), who had visited the United States in the early 1840s. His book, *The United States of North America*, appeared in 1853.

QUESTIONS FOR ANALYSIS

1. What can be inferred from Menzel's guidebook about the motives for German emigration?
2. Why, according to Menzel, do many German immigrants have inaccurate notions about their prospects in the United States?
3. What are the main obstacles to a German immigrant's success in the United States, according to Menzel?
4. According to Menzel, what kind of reception can the German immigrant expect from Americans?
5. What is Menzel's overall conclusion about the German migrant and the United States? In his view, was emigration a worthwhile gamble?

In Germany as in most of the European states many people are dissatisfied with the state organization and institutions. They feel themselves hampered by the government, complain of lack of freedom, of too much government, and the like, and direct their gaze to the free states of the great North American Republic, as the land of desired freedom. . . .

Much greater is the number of those who leave their fatherland on account of the poverty of its material resources and in order to better their condition in America. For many people industrial conditions in Germany are such that you cannot blame them for emigrating when they learn that in North America there are far greater productive natural resources and that work has a greater value than in Germany.

He who in Germany has to suffer from want and misery, . . . finds that hope of better fortune overcomes his attachment to the Fatherland. He easily separates himself from his old home and wanders to a distant land believing that he will find life more favorable there.

That it is easier to make a living in America cannot be denied; but it is a matter of regret that those who could better their condition in this way frequently lack the means. Many people who take this risk find only their misfortune or ruin. The numbers of those who return to Germany from America prove that many are not successful there. When an emigrant ship is prepared to sail from the harbor of New York for Hamburg or Bremen, there are usually twenty or more people leaving the land of their disappointed hopes for the old home country after one or two years' bitter experiences. . . . Still others would follow them if they had the means for the trip or if they were not ashamed to return.

Therefore everyone who is thinking of emigrating to America should take care to determine whether or not he is fit for America. He should carefully weigh what he leaves here against what he may find there, lest he should be guilty of too great haste or light-mindedness and make a mistake that he may regret only too soon and bitterly. . . .

A great many books about emigration to America have been written, and every year new ones appear. . . . A book written against emigration, or one advising emigration only for the few, would have little charm and would find few purchasers. But as soon as a book appears which describes the land to which the emigrant would go as a land of paradise, then it is sold and read diligently, and thousands are moved in this way to become emigrants. . . . Through this one-sided presentation of American conditions many are lured to emigrate. It is obvious that the countless speculators who every year gain many millions from emigrants will make a great effort to bring to the attention of the people many books through which the desire for emigration is awakened and increased. They are themselves completely indifferent to the fate of the emigrants, and if emigration turns out to be for their ruin they do not care. . . .

But the descriptions and the letters of the emigrants to their relatives and friends and acquaintances—are they not then true and reliable? This I deny. First, because no one who has emigrated will confess that he was disappointed. . . . He is very right in thinking that few in the old home will have sympathetic pity for him, and many only malicious joy and bitter ridicule. . . .

Secondly, the immigrants wish, for many reasons, to have many of their relatives and countrymen follow them and settle near them. On the one hand, because of the neighborly society and support, the need of which many of them have bitterly experienced. On the other hand, one desires

Source: From Edith Abbott, *Historical Aspects of the Immigration Problem* (Chicago: University of Chicago, 1926), pp. 136–152.

everywhere new arrivals of immigrants because they will buy land, and stock, and so on from those already settled, and its produce increases . . . .

What Does North America Offer That Is Good?

This great country offers its inhabitants noteworthy advantages which may be summarized as follows:

—Although the citizens of the United States are not, as is popularly supposed, free from taxes, yet the taxes on land and cattle which the farmer has to pay are not high, and artisans pay no taxes on their business.

—The citizens are, during a certain age, under obligation to serve in the militia, but except in the case of war this is rarely asked of them except perhaps for suppression of a riot. For regular military service volunteers are always available, since they are well paid. The quartering of soldiers in time of peace is not allowed.

—Complete freedom in the trades and professions, hunting and fishing is allowed to everyone. . . .

—There is no difference in rank. The terms "upper class" and "lower class" have no significance. . . .

—North America, as a country with fertile land still partly unoccupied, a country thinly populated with flourishing trade and general freedom of trade, offers far greater and more abundant means of livelihood than Germany.

—Labor there has a high, and cost of living a lower value; therefore on the whole the people are far less oppressed by want and need. . . .

Against the advantages just enumerated . . . the following disadvantages will not please those who are eager to emigrate.

—The German in America is a complete stranger. Everything is strange, the country, the climate, laws, and customs. One ought to realize what it means to be an alien in a far distant land. More than this, the German in America is despised as alien, and he must often hear the nickname "Dutchman,"[1] at least until he learns to speak English fluently. It is horrible what the German immigrants must endure from the Americans, Irish, and English. . . . The Americans are accustomed to alter their behavior to him [the German immigrant] only after he has become Americanized.

—The educational institutions are, in America, defective and expensive or they are completely lacking. Therefore parents can give their children the necessary education only through great sacrifices or, in case they are poor, the children must be allowed to run wild. . . .

—The majority of the Germans emigrating to America wish to seek their fortunes in agriculture. But the purchase of land has its dangers and difficulties. The price of the land is, in proportion to its productivity, not so low as is generally believed. . . . Where labor is so dear and where agricultural products are so cheap, there no one can exist except the man who is able and willing to do all his own work and does not need to employ outside labor. . . .

I have been approached since my return from North America by a large number of persons for information concerning conditions there and for advice concerning their projected plan of emigration. . . . I found most of them unsuitable for emigration for the following more or less serious reasons:

A weak constitution or shattered health.—The emigrant to America needs a strong and healthy body.

Advanced age.—The man who is already over forty years of age, unless he has some sons who can help him with their labor, cannot count upon success and prosperity in America.

Childlessness with somewhat advanced age.— What will a married couple do when their capacity

---

[1]The term "Dutchman" was derived from the German word for German, *deutsch*, pronounced "doitch."

to labor disappears with the years? They could not earn enough when young to support them in later years. . . .

Lack of experience in the field of Labor on the part of those who expect to establish their fortunes there through hard labor.— . . . Many harbor the delusion that they are already accustomed to the labor required there, or that they will easily learn it if they have worked a little here in this country. But he who has not from his youth up been performing continuously the most severe labor, so much the more will he lack, in America, where work is harder, the necessary strength and ability. . . . Those who spent their youth in schools, offices, or in other sedentary work, play in America a very sad and pitiable role.

A slow easy-going habit of living a life of ease and comfort.—One may find in the great cities of North America all the comforts and conveniences which European cities offer, but in America they are only for the few—for the rich—and to this class German emigrants do not usually belong. Not many persons in America can command even the comforts of the ordinary citizen of Europe. Many people seek compensation in whiskey for their many privations and hardships and this is the way to certain ruin.

Destitution.—If the passage for a single emigrant costs only 50 thaler, at least as much again must be counted for the land journey here and in America. Unfortunately this amount is beyond the reach of those who would have the best chance of improving their condition in America. The artisan, even though he cannot carry on his business there independently but must work in great workshops and factories must often make yet a further land journey in order to find the most suitable place, and he needs, especially if he has a family, a not inconsiderable amount of money. . . . If the means of traveling are not available, he falls into difficulties and distress, is obliged to sell the effects he brought with him for a trifling sum, or considers himself fortunate if he finds a job anywhere at the lowest wage— a wage that will barely keep him and his family from hunger.

"The Gates Should No Longer Be Left Unguarded"

57 • HENRY CABOT LODGE, SPEECH TO THE UNITED STATES SENATE, MARCH 16, 1896

After the Civil War, immigration to the United States reached new heights, with more than 20 million new arrivals between 1870 and 1910. Although these millions included an appreciable number of Japanese and Chinese, close to 98 percent of them came from Europe. Unlike previous European migrants, who had mostly come from England, Germany, and Ireland, these new migrants were mainly from Italy, the Austro-Hungarian Empire, Russia, and Russian Poland. Most were Roman Catholics or, in the case of many Poles and Russians, Jews.

Anti-immigrant sentiment, or nativism, which had flared up in the 1840s and 1850s in response to the influx of Germans and Irish, once again became a powerful force in American life. Workers and small businessmen worried about competition, many Protestants deplored the growing numbers of Catholics and Jews, and Americans in general wondered if the republic could survive after the country was overrun by people unfamiliar with democracy and constitutionalism. Anti-immigrant prejudice was given a "scientific" basis by contemporary theories of race, which ranked the world's races in a hierarchy that placed northern European whites (except the Irish) at the top. Although authors disagreed about where specifically other peoples should be ranked, most agreed that among Europeans, Italians, Slavs, and Jews were near the bottom.

Anti-immigrant groups had some legislative success. In 1870, Congress passed the Naturalization Act, which barred Chinese from citizenship. This was followed in 1882 by the Chinese Exclusion Act, which barred Chinese immigration altogether. In the 1880s and early 1890s, Congress also passed laws authorizing the federal government to bar immigration by convicts, prostitutes, lunatics, and "persons suffering from a loathsome or dangerous contagious disease." Then, in 1894, the Immigration Restriction League (IRL) was founded to push for legislation requiring new immigrants to pass a literacy test that IRL members hoped most potential immigrants would fail. A leader in the fight for immigration restriction was the distinguished Bostonian Henry Cabot Lodge, who served in the House of Representatives from 1887 to 1893 and the Senate from 1893 until his death in 1924. He presented the following remarks to the Senate in support of anti-immigration legislation under consideration in 1896. The bill failed to pass, and millions of immigrants continued to pour into the United States until Congress passed a series of restrictive laws in the 1920s.

QUESTIONS FOR ANALYSIS

1. What, according to Lodge, distinguishes "desirable" and "undesirable" immigrants?
2. What fears does Lodge have about the future of the United States unless immigration is limited?
3. What are Lodge's views of race, and how do they affect his attitude toward immigration? According to Lodge, what are the qualities of the various "races" he discusses?
4. The bill Lodge supported was defeated in the Senate. What arguments against immigration restriction do you think were made by the bill's opponents?
5. In what way might Lodge's views have been influenced by concepts based on Darwin's theories of evolution?

Restricting Immigration

Paupers, diseased persons, convicts, and contract laborers are now excluded [from immigration]. By this bill it is proposed to make a new class of excluded immigrants and add to those which have just been named, the totally ignorant. . . .

Three methods of obtaining this further restriction in late years have been brought to the attention of Congress. The first was the imposition of a capitation tax [head tax] on all immigrants. . . .

The second scheme was to restrict immigration by requiring consular certification of immigrants.[1] . . .

Source: Congressional Record, 54th Congress, First Session, vol. 28 (Washington, D.C.: U.S. Government Printing Office, 1896), pp. 2817–2820.

[1] U.S. consuls in overseas cities would make judgments about immigration eligibility.

The third method was to exclude all immigrants who could neither read nor write, and this is the plan which was adopted by the committee. . . . It is found, in the first place, that the illiteracy test will bear most heavily upon the Italians, Russians, Poles, Hungarians, Greeks, and Asiatics, and very lightly, or not at all, upon English-speaking emigrants or Germans, Scandinavians, and French. In other words, the races most affected by the illiteracy test are those whose emigration to this country has begun within the last twenty years and swelled rapidly to enormous proportions, races with which the English-speaking people have never hitherto assimilated, and who are most alien to the great body of the people of the United States.

On the other hand, immigrants from the United Kingdom and of those races which are most closely related to the English-speaking people, and who with the English-speaking people themselves founded the American colonies and built up the United States, are affected but little by the proposed test. These races would not be prevented by this law from coming to this country in practically undiminished numbers. These kindred races also are those who alone go to the Western and Southern states, where immigrants are desired, and take up our unoccupied lands. The races which would suffer most seriously . . . furnish the immigrants who . . . who remain on the Atlantic seaboard, where immigration is not needed and where their presence is most injurious and undesirable. . . .

Immigration and the Economy

There is no one thing which does so much to bring about a reduction of wages and to injure the American wage earner as the unlimited introduction of cheap foreign labor through unrestricted immigration. Statistics show that the change in the race character of our immigration has been accompanied by a corresponding decline in its quality. The number of skilled mechanics and of persons trained to some occupation or pursuit has fallen off, while the number of those without occupation or training, that is, who are totally unskilled, has risen . . . to enormous proportions. This low, unskilled labor is the most deadly enemy of the American wage earner. . . .

There is no danger . . . to our workingmen from the coming of skilled mechanics or of trained and educated men with a settled occupation or pursuit, for immigrants of this class will never seek to lower the American standard of life and wages. On the contrary, they desire the same standard for themselves. But there is an appalling danger to the American wage earner from the flood of low, unskilled, ignorant, foreign labor . . . which not only takes lower wages but accepts a standard of life and living so low that the American workingman can not compete with it.

Immigration and Citizenship

The English-speaking race . . . has been made slowly during the centuries. Nothing has happened thus far to radically change it here. . . . Analysis shows that the actual mixture of blood in the English-speaking race is very small, and that while the English-speaking people are derived through different channels, no doubt, there is among them nonetheless an overwhelming preponderance of the same race stock, that of the great Germanic tribes who reached from Norway to the Alps. They have been welded together by more than a thousand years of wars, conquests, migrations, and struggles, both at home and abroad, and in so doing they have attained a fixity and definiteness of national character unknown to any other people. . . .

When we speak of a race, then, we do not mean its expressions in art or in language, or its achievements in knowledge. . . . What make a race are their mental and, above all, their moral characteristics, the slow growth and accumulation of centuries of toil and conflict. These are the qualities which determine their social efficiency as a people, which make one race rise and another fall, . . . and which guide us in our short-lived generation as they have guided the race itself across the centuries. . . .

Those qualities are moral far more than intellectual, and it is on the moral qualities of the English-speaking race that our history, our victories, and all our future rest. There is only one way in which you can lower those qualities or weaken those characteristics and that is by breeding them out. If a lower race mixes with a higher in sufficient numbers, history teaches us that the lower race will prevail. The lower race will absorb the higher, not the higher the lower, when the two strains approach equality in numbers. . . . The lowering of a great race means not only its own decline but that of human civilization. . . .

The time has certainly come, if not to stop at least to check, to sift, and to restrict those immigrants. In careless strength, with generous hand, we have kept our gates wide open to all the world. If we do not close them, we should at least place sentinels beside them to challenge those who would pass through. The gates which admit men to the United States and to citizenship in the great republic should no longer be left unguarded.

U.S. Immigration in Political Cartoons

58 • JOSEPH KEPPLER, "WELCOME TO ALL!" AND "LOOKING BACKWARD"; F. VICTOR GILLAM, "THE CAUSE OF IT ALL"; LOUIS DALRYMPLE, "THE UNRESTRICTED DUMPING GROUNDS"

Political cartoons are drawings that use caricature, irony, exaggeration, metaphors, humor, and satire to present a particular point of view about a political issue or an individual politician. They gained popularity in eighteenth-century England and America and flourished briefly in the early stages of the French Revolution, but came into their own as a popular form of political expression in the nineteenth century, when censorship laws were relaxed, new technologies made it possible to print high-quality illustrations in newspapers and magazines, and interest intensified in public affairs and politics. Political cartoons became fixtures on the editorial pages of newspapers and were featured on the covers of magazines. For historians, they provide valuable insights into the past.

We have included four political cartoons, published in the United States between the early 1880s and early 1900s, all of which were part of the nation's ongoing debate over immigration restrictions. The first two cartoons are by Joseph Keppler, who, in 1867 at age 29, migrated from Austria to the United States, where he joined the large German-speaking community in St. Louis. In 1873, he moved to New York City to take a job as chief illustrator for *Frank Leslie's Weekly*, a popular news magazine. In 1876, he founded his own weekly news magazine, *Puck*, named after the mischievous character from Shakespeare's *Midsummer Night's Dream*. Originally published in German, *Puck* began publishing an English version in 1887 and reached a peak of circulation of 85,000 by the late 1880s. Until his death in 1894, Keppler produced close to a thousand political cartoons, many of which opposed restrictions on immigration. His cartoon, "Welcome to All!," shows Uncle Sam welcoming a group of immigrants fleeing the storm clouds of oppression to the "U.S. Ark of Refuge"; it appeared in *Puck* in 1880. Keppler's second cartoon, "Looking Backward," was published in *Puck* in 1893, a time when anti-immigrant sentiment, mainly directed against new arrivals from eastern and Mediterranean Europe, was beginning to peak.

Our third and fourth cartoons both appeared in the magazine *Judge*, which was founded by a group of former *Puck* artists and writers in 1881. Noted for its strong pro-Republican, anti-immigrant stance, it became a successful rival of *Puck*. "The Cause of It All," featured on the front page of *Judge* in 1897, was drawn by the English immigrant F. Victor Gillam, who produced dozens of anti-immigrant cartoons in the 1890s and early 1900s. "The Unrestricted Dumping Ground" was the work of the American-born Louis Dalrymple. It appeared in 1903, two years after President William McKinley, whose apparition is shown in the upper left corner, was assassinated by Leon Czolgosz, the son of Polish immigrants, in Buffalo, New York.

WELCOME TO ALL!

"We may safely say that the present influx of immigration to the United States is something unprecedented in our generation."—*N. Y. Statistical Review.*

"Welcome to All!"

"The Cause of it All"

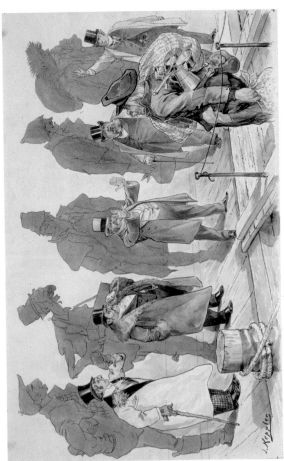

"Looking Backward"

"The Unrestricted Dumping Grounds"

QUESTIONS FOR ANALYSIS

1. What differences do you see in the portrayal of the immigrants in Keppler's "Make Yourself Welcome!" and their portrayal in the two *Judge* cartoons?
2. What is the main message of Keppler's "Looking Backward"?
3. According to the two *Judge* cartoons, what are the consequences of unregulated immigration for the United States?
4. To what extent do the *Judge* cartoons present a view of immigration similar to that of Henry Cabot Lodge in his speech to the Senate?

Women in Society: From "Separate Spheres" to Suffragism

Women's political and legal rights emerged as a subject of public debate during the French Revolution. In October 1789, thousands of women marched from Paris to the palace grounds at Versailles, where their demonstrations forced the royal family and the National Assembly to relocate to Paris, the center of revolutionary agitation. Beginning in 1790, women formed their own political clubs to oppose the laws and customs that were the foundation of France's patriarchal society. In response, legislators passed laws giving women the right to own property, marry without parental consent, initiate divorce, and take legal action against fathers of illegitimate children. In 1793, however, Jacobin revolutionaries outlawed women's political clubs and rejected women's demands for political equality with men. Having women vote, hold public office, and serve in the army would, so they argued, undermine the family and divert women from their calling as wives and mothers. Women experienced more setbacks in the late 1790s, when moderate revolutionaries rescinded most of the laws that had improved women's legal status. Under Napoleon, the Civil Code of 1804 reaffirmed women's legal inferiority to men.

In the conservative atmosphere of the 1820s and 1830s, women's political activism diminished, and prevailing opinion consigned middle- and upper-class women to a domestic role centered on childcare, housekeeping, supervising servants, and providing husbands with a tranquil home. By midcentury, however, women on both sides of the Atlantic, many of whom were active in temperance and antislavery movements, once more began to speak out and organize on behalf of women's rights. A landmark in the history of feminism (a word coined in France in the 1830s) was the women's rights convention held in the upstate New York town of Seneca Falls in 1848, which adopted resolutions demanding for women the vote, divorce and property rights, and equal employment and educational opportunities. Such issues also became the focus of feminists in England in the 1850s and in France and Germany later in the century.

By the late 1800s women had made some gains, especially in the areas of access to higher education and family law. In addition, professions such as nursing and teaching provided new opportunities for many middle-class women, and a few women established careers as doctors and lawyers. Despite the efforts of women's suffrage organizations, however, granting women the vote met stiff resistance. Before World War I only Australia, New Zealand, Finland, Norway, and several U.S. western states had granted women full voting privileges.

Women's Separate Sphere

59 • SARAH STICKNEY ELLIS, THE WIVES OF ENGLAND

Sarah Stickney (1799–1872) was born into a Quaker family in Holderness, England, but at some point renounced Quakerism and converted to Congregationalism before marrying William Ellis (1794–1872) in 1837. By then, her husband, who had served as a missionary in Madagascar and the South Pacific, had taken a position at the home office of the London Missionary Society. In addition to her writing, Ellis was active in the temperance movement and founded a school for girls in London. The author of five novels and a book of poetry, she turned her attention to the "woman question" in 1838, with the publication of her advice book *The Women of England*. Widely read in England and the United States, it was followed by *The Daughters of England, The Mothers of England,* and *The Wives of England* (1843), which is excerpted here. She died in 1872, one week after the death of her husband.

QUESTIONS FOR ANALYSIS

1. According to Ellis, what are the differences between male and female natures?
2. What implications do male and female natures have for the suitability of women's involvement in politics?
3. According to Ellis, what does marriage mean for a wife? What does it mean for a husband?
4. In Ellis's view, why would equality between men and women be a mistake?
5. What implications do Ellis's views have for female education?

Different Natures

As it is the natural characteristic of woman's love in its most refined, . . . to be perpetually doing something for the good or the happiness of the object of her affection, it is but reasonable that man's personal comfort should be studiously attended to; and in this, the complacence and satisfaction which most men evince on finding themselves placed at table before a favourite dish, situated beside a clean hearth, or accommodated with an empty sofa, is of itself a sufficient reward for any sacrifice such indulgence may have cost. In proofs of affection like these, there is something . . . which man can understand without an effort; and he will sit down to eat, or compose himself to rest, with more hearty good-will towards the wife who has been thoughtful about these things, than if she had been all day busily employed in writing a treatise on morals for his especial benefit. . . .

Those who argue for the perfect equality—the oneness of women in their intellectual nature with men, appear to know little of that higher philosophy, by which both, from the very distinctness of their characters, have been made subservient to the purposes of wisdom and of goodness; and after having observed . . . the operation of mind on mind, the powerful and instinctive sympathies which rule our very being, and the associated influence of different natures, all. . . . I own it does appear an ignorant and vulgar contest, to strive to establish the equality of that, which would lose not only its utility, but its perfection, by being assimilated with a different nature. . . .

Separate Spheres

It may be said to be a necessary part of man's nature, and conducive to his support in the position he has to maintain, that he should, in a greater degree than woman, be sufficient unto himself. The nature of his occupations, and the character of his peculiar duties, require this. The contending interests of the community at large, the strife of public affairs, and the competition of business, with the paramount importance of establishing himself as the master of a family, and the head of a household, all require a degree of concentrated effort in favour of self, and a powerful repulsion against others, which woman, happily for her, is seldom or never called upon to maintain. . . .

The love of woman appears to have been created solely to minister; that of man, to be ministered unto. It is true, his avocations lead him daily to some labour, or some effort for the maintenance of his family; and he often conscientiously believes that this labour is for his wife. But the probability is, that he would be just as attentive to his business, and as eager about making money, had he no wife at all. . . .

It is unquestionably the inalienable right of all men, whether ill or well, rich or poor, wise or foolish, to be treated with deference, and made much

Source: From Sarah Stickney Ellis, *The Wives of England* (London, 1843), pp. 70, 76–77, 78, 101–102, 102–105.

of in their own houses. It is true that in the last mentioned case, this duty may be attended with some difficulty in the performance; but as no man becomes a fool, or loses his senses by marriage, the woman who has selected such a companion must abide by the consequences; and even he, whatever may be his degree of folly, is entitled to respect from her, because she has voluntarily placed herself in such a position that she must necessarily be his inferior. . . .

Women and Politics

The excellence of woman as regards her conversation, consists . . . of quick, and delicate, and sometimes playful turns of thought, with a lively and subtle apprehension of the bearings, tendencies, and associations of ideas; so that the whole machinery of conversation . . . may be made, by her good management, to turn off from one subject, and play upon another, as if the direction of some magic influence, which will ever be preserved from detection by the tact of an unobtrusive and sensitive nature.

It is in this manner, and this alone, that women should evince their interest in those great political questions which arise out of the state of the times in which they live. Not that they may be able to attach themselves to a party, still less that they may *make speeches* either in public or in private; but that they may think and converse like rational beings on subjects which occupy the attention of the majority of mankind. . . . If, for instance, a wife would converse with her husband about a candidate for the representation of the place in which they live, she may, if she choose, discuss the merits of the colour which his party wears, and wish it were some other, as being more becoming; she may tell with delight how he bowed especially to her; and she may wish from her heart that the number of votes may be in his favour, because he kissed her child, and called it the prettiest he had ever seen. It is this kind of prattle which may properly be described as *small talk*. . . . Yet this style of talk may be, and sometimes is, applied by women to all sorts of subjects,

not excepting politics, philosophy, and even religion. . . .

Trials of Married Life

With all occasions of domestic derangement, such as washing-days, and other renovations of comfort and order, some men of irritable temperament wage open and determined war. But, may we not ask, in connection with this subject, whether their prejudices against these household movements have not been remotely or immediately excited, by the extreme and unnecessary confusion and disturbance with which they are too frequently accompanied? . . . And if properly managed, so as to interfere as little as possible with his personal comfort, and conducted with general cheerfulness and good humour, such a man might easily be brought to consider them as necessary to the good of his household, as the refreshing shower is to the summer soil.

But we have not yet sufficiently examined that one consideration, which ever remains to be weighed in the balance against the trials of patience arising out of the conduct of men. And here we must first ask—Have you yourself no personal peculiarities exactly opposed to your husband's notions of what is agreeable?—such as habits of disorder, dressing in bad taste, or any other of those minor deviations from delicacy or good breeding which he might not have had an opportunity of observing before marriage? . . .

But if such peculiarities as these are of sufficient importance to cast a shadow over the sunny spots of life, what must we say of some others occasionally observable in the character and conduct of women, to which it is scarcely possible that much charity should be extended? . . .

Have you never made the most of household troubles, spread forth the appurtenances [apparatus] of a wash, allowed the affairs of the kitchen to extend themselves to the parlour, complained unnecessarily of servants and work-people, and appeared altogether in your own person more harassed, exhausted, and forlorn, after your husband's return home, than you did before, on purpose that he might be compelled, not only to pity you, but to bear a portion of your domestic discomfort himself?

When a concatenation [a connected series] of cross occurrences, hinderances, or mistakes, have rendered every moment one of perplexity and haste; have you never, when involved with your husband in such circumstances, added fuel to the fire by your own petulance, or by your still more provoking exclamations of triumph, that you "thought it would come to that?" . . .

Now, it is impossible for any woman of right feelings to hide from her conscience, that if she chooses to marry, she places herself under a moral obligation to make her husband's home as pleasant to him as she can. Instead, therefore, of behaving as if it was the great business of married life to complain, it is her peculiar duty as a wife, and one for which, by her natural constitution, she is especially fitted, to make all her domestic concerns appear before her husband to the very best advantage. She has time for her troubles and turmoils, . . . when her husband is absent, or when she is engaged exclusively in her own department; and if she would make his home what it ought to be to him—"an ever-sunny place," she will studiously shield him, as with the wings of love, from the possibility of feeling that his domestic annoyances give weight and poignancy to those more trying perplexities, which most men, engaged either in business, or in public affairs, find more than sufficient for their peace of mind.

Women's Vote and How to Attain It

60 • EMMELINE PANKHURST, WHY WE ARE MILITANT

Organized efforts by English women to gain the vote began in 1847, when a group of Sheffield women founded the Female Political Association and collected signatures on a prosuffrage petition they submitted to the House of Lords. Four years later, in 1851, Harriet Hardy Mill (1807–1858), the wife of philosopher John Stuart Mill, wrote a widely read pamphlet titled "Enfranchisement of Women." In 1867, nine years after her death, John Stuart Mill, then a member of the House of Commons, proposed an amendment to a voting reform bill that would have given women the vote. It was rejected 194 to 73, a setback that led to the founding of the National Society for Women's Suffrage in 1868. In the following decades, women sought to advance their cause by making resolutions, publicizing their views, and performing symbolic acts such as appearing at polling places and requesting the vote, even though they knew they would be turned away.

In the early 1900s, however, the feminist movement became more militant and confrontational. By 1900, Englishwomen could vote in local elections and stand for election to school boards and municipal offices. This was not enough for Emmeline Pankhurst (1858–1928), who, since the 1870s, had been a strong advocate for women's suffrage and better treatment of working-class and poor women. In 1903, she founded the Women's Social and Political Union (WSPU). Under the leadership of Pankhurst and her daughters, Christabel (1880–1958) and Sylvia (1882–1960), the WSPU tried to advance the cause of women's suffrage by heckling politicians and then by smashing windows, slashing paintings in museums, burning letters in mailboxes, and finally martyrdom, when, in May 1913, a young suffragist threw herself under the hooves of the king's racehorse at Epsom Downs and was killed before thousands of shocked spectators. When arrested, many "suffragettes," as they came to be called, went on hunger strikes. The government responded by approving the forced feeding of prisoners in 1909 and the Prisoners Act of 1913, by which fasting women were released from prison until they had eaten and then rearrested.

In October 1913, Emmeline Pankhurst traveled to New York City to defend the tactics of the WSPU in a speech delivered at Madison Square Garden. It was attended by a disappointing crowd of only 3,000, mainly owing to a last-minute change in scheduling—Mrs. Pankhurst had been held up by immigration authorities for two days after her arrival because of pending legal cases involving her in England.

QUESTIONS FOR ANALYSIS

1. In Pankhurst's view, what was the condition of the women's suffrage movement in the first years of the 1900s?
2. According to Pankhurst, why had "nonmilitant" efforts on behalf of women's suffrage failed?
3. What event sparked the new militancy of the WSPU?
4. According to Pankhurst, why was it so important for women to gain the right to vote in parliamentary elections?
5. How does Pankhurst explain the difficulty women encountered in their efforts to win the vote?

I know that in your minds there are questions like these; you are saying, "Woman Suffrage is sure to come; the emancipation of humanity is an evolutionary process, and how is it that some women, instead of trusting to that evolution, instead of educating the masses of people of their country, instead of educating their own sex to prepare them for citizenship, how is it that these militant women are using violence and upsetting the business arrangements of the country in their undue impatience to attain their end?"

Let me try to explain to you the situation. . . .

The extensions of the franchise to the men of my country have been preceded by very great violence, by something like a revolution, by something like civil war. In 1832,[1] you know we were on the edge of a civil war and on the edge of revolution, and . . . it was after the practice of arson on so large a scale that half the city of Bristol[2] was burned down in a single night, it was because more and greater violence and arson were feared that the Reform Bill of 1832 was allowed to pass into law. In 1867[3] . . . rioting went on all over the country, and as the result of that rioting, . . . as a result of the fear of

Source: Jane Marcus, ed., *Speech, Suffrage and the Pankhursts* (London: Routledge & Kegan Paul, 1987), pp. 153–157, 159–161.

[1]In 1831 and 1832, public excitement over voting reform peaked, as Parliament considered proposals to extend representation to new industrial towns and cities and give voting rights to middle-class men.

[2]On Oct. 31, 1831, a large crowd in Bristol protested against the House of Lords' decision to turn down the

Reform Act by burning down 100 houses, including the Bishop's Palace. The mob looted and burned unpopular citizens' houses and released prisoners from the jails. Soldiers attacked the crowd, and hundreds were killed or severely wounded. Under pressure, Parliament passed the Reform Act of 1832, the first of three major voting laws passed in the 1800s.

[3]The Reform Bill of 1867 extended the right to vote to working-class men.

more rioting and violence the Reform Act of 1867 was put upon the statute books.

In 1884 . . . rioting was threatened and feared, and so the agricultural laborers got the vote.[4]

Meanwhile, during the '80's, women, like men, were asking for the franchise. Appeals, larger and more numerous than for any other reform, were presented in support of Woman's Suffrage. . . . More meetings were held, and larger, for Woman Suffrage than were held for votes for men, and yet the women did not get it. Men got the vote because they were and would be violent. The women did not get it because they were constitutional and law-abiding. . . .

Well, we in Great Britain, on the eve of the General Election of 1905, a mere handful of us . . . set out on the wonderful adventure of forcing the strongest Government of modern times to give the women the vote. . . . The Suffrage movement was almost dead. The women had lost heart. You could not get a Suffrage meeting that was attended by members of the general public. . . .

Two women[5] changed that in a twinkling of an eye at a great Liberal demonstration in Manchester, where a Liberal leader, Sir Edward Grey, was explaining the program to be carried out during the Liberals' next turn of office. The two women put the fateful question, "When are you going to give votes to women?" and refused to sit down until they had been answered. These two women were sent to jail, and from that day to this the women's movement, both militant and constitutional, has never looked back. We had little more than one moribund society for Woman Suffrage in those days. Now we have nearly 50 societies for Woman Suffrage, and they are large in membership, they are rich in money, and their ranks, are swelling

every day that passes. That is how militancy has put back the clock of Woman Suffrage in Great Britain. . . .

We are fighting to get the power to alter bad laws; but some people say to us, "Go to the representatives in the House of Commons, point out to them that these laws are bad, and you will find them quite ready to alter them." Ladies and gentlemen, there are women in my country who have spent long and useful lives trying to get reforms, and because of their voteless condition, they are unable even to get the ear of Members of Parliament, much less are they able to secure those reforms.

Our marriage and divorce laws are a disgrace to civilization. I sometimes wonder, looking back from the serenity of past middle age, at the courage of women. I wonder that women have the courage to take upon themselves the responsibilities of marriage and motherhood when I see how little protection the law of my country affords them. I wonder that a woman will face the ordeal of childbirth with the knowledge that after she has risked her life to bring a child into the world she has absolutely no parental rights over the future of that child. Think what trust women have in men when a woman will marry a man, knowing, if she has knowledge of the law, that if that man is not all she in her love for him thinks him, he may even bring a strange woman into the house, bring his mistress into the house to live with her, and she cannot get legal relief from such a marriage as that. . . .

Take the industrial side of the question: have men's wages for a hard day's work ever been so low and inadequate as are women's wages today? Have men ever had to suffer from the laws, more injustice than women suffer? Is there a single

---

[4]This was the result of the Reform Bill of 1884, which gave the vote to male agricultural workers.

[5]One of these women was Emmeline Pankhurst's elder daughter, Christabel.

reason which men have had for demanding liberty that does not also apply to women?

Why, if you were talking to the *men* of any other nation you would not hesitate to reply in the affirmative. There is not a man in this meeting who has not felt sympathy with the uprising of the men of other lands when suffering from intolerable tyranny, when deprived of all representative rights. You are full of sympathy with men in Russia. You are full of sympathy with nations that rise against the domination of the Turk.[6] You are full of sympathy with all struggling people striving for independence. How is it, then, that some of you have nothing but ridicule and contempt . . . for women who are fighting for exactly the same thing?

All my life I have tried to understand why it is that men who value their citizenship as their dearest possession seem to think citizenship ridiculous when it is to be applied to the women of their race. . . . A thought came to me . . . : that to men women are not human beings like themselves. Some men think we are superhuman; they put us on pedestals; they revere us; they think we are too fine and too delicate to come down into the hurly-burly of life. Other men think us sub-human; they think we are a strange species unfortunately having to exist for the perpetuation of the race. They think that we are fit for drudgery, but that in some strange way our minds are not like theirs, our love for great things is not like theirs, and so we are a sort of sub-human species. We are neither superhuman nor are we sub-human. We are just human beings like yourselves.

Our hearts burn within us when we read the great mottoes which celebrate the liberty of your country; when we go to France and we read the words, liberty, fraternity and equality, don't you think that we appreciate the meaning of those words? And then when we wake to the knowledge that these things are not for us, they are only for our brothers, then there comes a sense of bitterness into the hearts of some women, and they say to themselves, "Will men never understand?" . . .

---

[6]Here Pankhurst refers to the Russian Revolution of 1905 and the struggles of various ethnic groups in the Balkans to throw off rule by the Ottoman Empire.

Images of the Suffrage Campaign in England
61 • ENGLISH POSTERS AND POSTCARDS, 1908–1914

In the opening years of the twentieth century, English politicians debated the rights of striking workers, approved a host of social legislation, introduced inheritance taxes and a progressive income tax, curtailed the powers of the House of Lords, and agonized over the issue of home rule for Ireland. Of all the issues they faced, however, none brought forth as much passion and partisanship as the debate over women's suffrage. The increasing militancy of the Women's Social and Political Union (WSPU), a mass demonstration ("Mud March") of 3,000 prosuffrage women in London in 1907, and the arrest and hunger strike of Mary Wallace Dunlop in 1909 set the stage for the tumultuous events between 1910 and 1914. Parliament, on three occasions, considered but failed to pass women's suffrage bills and prosuffrage militants responded with attacks on Parliament, window-breaking campaigns, arson, and the slashing of paintings in museums.

Against the backdrop of these events, all sides in the debate held rallies, wrote books, published magazines, and sent countless letters to newspaper editors. They also sought to win supporters though art. This was especially true for the suffragists, who founded the Artists' Suffrage League in 1907 and the Suffrage Atelier (workshop) in 1909. Both organizations sought to advance the cause of women's suffrage by producing posters, postcards, banners, and illustrated leaflets. Opponents of women's suffrage could not equal their output in terms of quantity, but they certainly matched their zeal. The following selections provide an opportunity to analyze both sides' work.

The first examples were produced by opponents of suffrage, all in 1912. The first, "No Votes, Thank You," is a poster designed by Harold Bird under the auspices of the National League for Opposing Women's Suffrage (NLOWS), an organization founded in 1910 from a merger of the Women's National Anti-Suffrage League and the Men's League for Opposing Woman's Suffrage. It shows a figure representing womanhood, with a supporter of woman's suffrage brandishing a hammer for breaking windows behind her. Three illustrations from postcards follow. The first, "A Perfect Woman," was designed by John Hassall for the NLOWS. The quotation is from "She Was a Phantom of Delight," a love poem written by William Wordsworth (1770–1850), the English Romantic poet. The two other postcard illustrations (one in the lower right corner below; the other on p. 288) are by anonymous artists. "A Suffragette's Home," the most famous of all the antisuffrage posters, was the work of the prominent commercial illustrator John Hassall (1868–1948). This recruitment poster for the NLOWS shows a husband returning to his home, where his prosuffrage wife has left a note, "Be back in an hour."

The first prosuffrage poster, "Convicts and Lunatics," was designed by Emile Harding Andrews and published in 1908. It reflects the fact that the first women's

The Art Archive / Museum of London

"No Votes, Thank You"

© Mary Evans Picture Library / Alamy

"A Perfect Woman"

Bodleian Library, Oxford, John Johnson Collection: Postcards: Women's Suffrage

"Votes for Women"

Postcard by an anonymous artist, 1912: In personal collection of Rosemary Hards. Cited as such in Lisa Tickner, The Spectacle of Women: Imagery of the Suffrage Campaign (Chicago: University of Chicago Press, 1988), p. 210.

"Hear Some Plain Things"

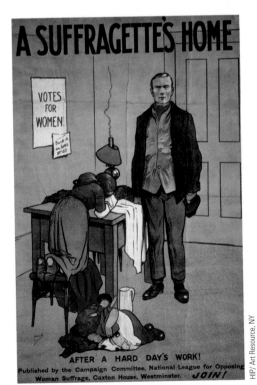

HIP/ Art Resource, NY

"A Suffragette's Home"

colleges were founded at Oxford and Cambridge beginning in the 1860s. The next poster, "The Appeal of Womanhood" by Louise Jacobs, was a direct response to "No Votes, Thank You." With Westminster Abbey and the Palace of Westminster in the background, the female figure representing true womanhood stands up to defend the oppressed women behind her: a laundress, a mother, a prostitute, a widow, and a young girl holding chains in her hand. On the banner, the words "white slavery" refer to the practice of kidnapping young girls and then forcing them into prostitution; "sweated labour" refers to women or girls who work in sweatshops for scant wages.

The last two works are publicity posters for the WSPU and the organization's magazine, *The Suffragette*. The first is the work of Hilda M. Dallas (1878–1958), who uses Joan of Arc as a symbol of the suffragists' struggle. Although the "Maid of Orleans" rallied French resistance against the English in the closing stages of the One Hundred Years War, and indeed was put on trial and executed by the English, she came to represent to suffragists the courage of women standing up for a just cause. The next poster, produced by an anonymous artist in 1914, urges voters to vote against the Liberal party, whose Home Secretary, Reginald McKenna, was responsible for the so-called Cat and Mouse Act of 1913, which allowed for the temporary release of prosuffrage hunger strikers and their rearrest once they had recovered their health.

"Convicts and Lunatics"

"The Appeal of Womanhood"

"The Suffragette"

"The Cat and Mouse Act"

QUESTIONS FOR ANALYSIS

1. How do the antisuffrage posters characterize women who favored the cause of votes for women?
2. What counter-images are presented in the suffragists' posters?
3. What, according to the posters of each side, will be the social implications of giving women the vote?

Nationalism and Imperialism in the Late Nineteenth Century

Nationalism emerged as a powerful force in Europe during the French Revolution, when the French people came to see the wars against Austria, Great Britain, Prussia, and Russia as a patriotic crusade to save their revolution and spread its ideals across the continent. In 1792 and 1793, the fervor of French troops helped save the revolution, and in the early 1800s, it contributed to stunning victories under Napoleon and the extension of French control over much of Europe by 1810. French conquests in turn aroused nationalism among Germans, Italians, Poles, and Russians, who fought to throw off French rule and reassert their independence.

Although successful in defeating France on the battlefield, nationalists had their hopes dashed in 1815 at the Congress of Vienna. Diplomats gave Norway to Sweden, Belgium to the Netherlands, and much of Italy to Austria; divided Poland among Russia, Prussia, and Austria; and kept Germany fragmented. But nationalism could not be eradicated by redrawing maps and diplomatic compromises. Strengthened by romanticism, Darwin-inspired notions of competition and struggle, economic rivalries, and popular journalism, nationalism intensified in the nineteenth century, not only in areas of foreign rule and political fragmentation but also in long-established states such as Great Britain and France. It contributed to some of the nineteenth century's most important political developments, including the revolutions of 1830 and 1848, the unification of Italy in 1870 and of Germany in 1871, runaway militarism among the Great Powers, the emergence of new states in the Balkans, and—what concerns us in this section—late-nineteenth-century imperialism.

Unlike nationalism, which dates from the 1790s, European imperialism goes back to the medieval crusades and sixteenth-century conquests of the Americas. Europe's overseas expansion continued in the late eighteenth and early nineteenth centuries despite the loss of American colonies by France, Great Britain, Portugal, and Spain. The British extended their authority in India; the French subdued Algeria between 1830 and 1847; and the European powers, led by England, forced China to open its ports to foreign trade after the Opium War (1839–1842). Then in the closing decades of the 1800s—the Era of Imperialism—the long history of Western expansion culminated in an unprecedented land grab. Between 1870 and 1914, Great Britain added 4.25 million square miles of territory and 66 million people to its empire; France, 3.5 million square miles of territory and 26 million people; Germany, 1 million square miles and 13 million people; and Belgium, 900,000 square miles and 13 million people. Italy, the United States, and the Netherlands also added colonial territories and subjects.

Anticipated economic gains, missionary fervor, racism, a faith in the West's civilizing mission, and confidence in the superiority of Western technology all contributed to the expansionist fever of the late 1800s. But the most important cause was nationalism. Politicians, journalists, and millions of people from every walk of life were convinced that foreign conquests brought respect, prestige, and a sense of national accomplishment. To have colonies was the mark of a Great Power.

Racism, Militarism, and the New Nationalism

62 • HEINRICH VON TREITSCHKE, EXTRACTS FROM HISTORY OF GERMANY IN THE NINETEENTH CENTURY AND HISTORICAL AND POLITICAL WRITINGS

As nationalism intensified in nineteenth-century Europe, it also changed. In the first half of the century, when nationalists saw conservative monarchies as the main obstacle to national self-determination, nationalism was linked to republicanism and liberalism. Beginning in the 1850s, especially in Germany and Italy, nationalism was championed by pragmatic and moderate leaders who believed that hard-headed politics, not romantic gestures and lofty republican ideals, would bring about national unification and self-rule. By century's end, nationalism was increasingly associated with conservative if not reactionary groups that used it to lure the masses away from socialism and democracy and to justify military spending, imperialism, and aggressive foreign policies.

The German historian Heinrich von Treitschke (1834–1896) represents this link between nationalism and militarism, racism, and authoritarianism. The son of a Prussian general, Treitschke taught history at several universities, including the University of Berlin. He also was a member of the German parliament, the Reichstag, from 1871 to 1884. His best-known work is his seven-volume *History of Germany in the Nineteenth Century*. In this and his numerous other writings, lectures, and speeches, Treitschke advocated militarism, authoritarianism, and war as the paths to national greatness. His views struck a responsive chord among many Germans who feared socialism and democracy and yearned for the day when Germany would be recognized as the world's most powerful nation.

QUESTIONS FOR ANALYSIS

1. According to Treitschke, what is the relationship between the state and the individual?
2. In Treitschke's view, why is monarchy superior to democracy?
3. What qualities of Germans set them apart from other peoples, especially the English and the Jews, according to Treitschke?
4. Early-nineteenth-century nationalists believed that all nations had a contribution to make to human progress. What is Treitschke's view?
5. According to Treitschke, what is the value of war for a nation?

On the German Character

Depth of thought, idealism, cosmopolitan views; a transcendent philosophy which boldly oversteps (or freely looks over) the separating barriers of finite existence, familiarity with every human thought and feeling, the desire to traverse the world-wide realm of ideas in common with the foremost intellects of all nations and all times. All that has at all times been held to be characteristic of the Germans and has always been praised as the essence of German character and breeding.

The simple loyalty of the Germans contrasts remarkably with the lack of chivalry in the English character. This seems to be due to the fact that in England physical culture is sought, not in the exercise of noble arms, but in sports like boxing, swimming, and rowing, sports which undoubtedly have their value, but which obviously tend to encourage a brutal and purely athletic point of view, and the single and superficial ambition of getting a first prize.[1]

Source: From Louis Snyder, *Documents of German History*, pp. 259–262. Copyright © 1958 by Rutgers, the State University. Reprinted by permission of Rutgers University Press.

[1]Treitschke is correct in drawing a distinction between English and German sports. The English prized competitive athletic contests, while the Germans favored group calisthenics and exercises.

On the State

The state is a moral community, which is called upon to educate the human race by positive achievement. Its ultimate object is that a nation should develop in it, a nation distinguished by a real national character. To achieve this state is the highest moral duty for nation and individual alike. All private quarrels must be forgotten when the state is in danger.

At the moment when the state cries out that its very life is at stake, social selfishness must cease and party hatred be hushed. The individual must forget his egoism, and feel that he is a member of the whole body.

The most important possession of a state, its be-all and end-all, is power. He who is not man enough to look this truth in the face should not meddle in politics. The state is not physical power as an end in itself, it is power to protect and promote the higher interests. Power must justify itself by being applied for the greatest good of mankind. It is the highest moral duty of the state to increase its power. . . .

Only the truly great and powerful states ought to exist. Small states are unable to protect their subjects against external enemies; moreover, they are incapable of producing genuine patriotism or national pride and are sometimes incapable of Kultur[2] in great dimensions. Weimar produced a Goethe and a Schiller;[3] still these poets would have been greater had they been citizens of a German national state.

On Monarchy

The will of the state is, in a monarchy, the expression of the will of one man who wears the crown by virtue of the historic right of a certain family; with him the final authority rests. Nothing in a monarchy can be done contrary to the will of the monarch. In a democracy, plurality, the will of the people, expresses the will of the state. A monarchy excels any other form of government, including the democratic, in achieving unity and power in a nation. It is for this reason that monarchy seems so natural, and that it makes such an appeal to the popular understanding. We Germans had an experience of this in the first years of our new empire.[4] How wonderfully the idea of a united Fatherland was embodied for us in the person of the venerable Emperor! How much it meant to us that we could feel once more: "That man is Germany; there is no doubting it!"

On War

The idea of perpetual peace is an illusion supported only by those of weak character. It has always been the weary, spiritless, and exhausted ages which have played with the dream of perpetual peace. A thousand touching portraits testify to the sacred power of the love which a righteous war awakes in noble nations. It is altogether impossible that peace be maintained in a world bristling with arms, and even God will see to it that war always recurs as a drastic medicine for the human race. Among great states the greatest political sin and the most contemptible is feebleness. . . .

War is elevating because the individual disappears before the great conception of the state. The devotion of the members of a community to each other is nowhere so splendidly conspicuous as in war.

Modern wars are not waged for the sake of goods and resources. What is at stake is the sublime moral good of national honor, which has something in the nature of unconditional sanctity, and compels the individual to sacrifice himself for it. . . .

The grandeur of war lies in the utter annihilation of puny man in the great conception of the State, and it brings out the full magnificence of the

---

[2]German for "culture" or "civilization."
[3]Johann Wolfgang von Goethe (1749–1832) and Johann von Schiller (1759–1805) were poets and dramatists who lived before German unification. They both spent much of their adult lives in Weimar, the capital of the Duchy of Saxe-Weimar.
[4]When Germany became a unified state in 1871, the king of Prussia, Wilhelm I, became emperor of Germany.

sacrifice of fellow-countrymen for one another. In war the chaff is winnowed from the wheat. Those who have lived through 1870 cannot fail to understand Niebuhr's[5] description of his feelings in 1813, when he speaks of how no one who has entered into the joy of being bound by a common tie to all his compatriots, gentle and simple alike, can ever forget how he was uplifted by the love, the friendliness, and the strength of that mutual sentiment.

It is war which fosters the political idealism which the materialist rejects. What a disaster for civilization it would be if mankind blotted its heroes from memory. The heroes of a nation are the figures which rejoice and inspire the spirit of its youth, and the writers whose words ring like trumpet blasts become the idols of our boyhood and our early manhood. He who feels no answering thrill is unworthy to bear arms for his country. To appeal from this judgment to Christianity would be sheer perversity, for does not the Bible distinctly say that the ruler shall rule by the sword, and again that greater love hath no man than to lay down his life for his friend? To Aryan[6] races, who are before all things courageous, the foolish preaching of everlasting peace has always been in vain. They have always been man enough to maintain with the sword what they have attained through the spirit. . . .

On the English

The hypocritical Englishman, with the Bible in one hand and a pipe of opium[7] in the other, possesses no redeeming qualities. The nation was an ancient robber-knight, in full armor, lance in hand, on every one of the world's trade routes.

The English possess a commercial spirit, a love of money which has killed every sentiment of honor and every distinction of right and wrong. English cowardice and sensuality are hidden behind unctuous, theological fine talk which is to us free-thinking German heretics among all the sins of English nature the most repugnant. In England all notions of honor and class prejudices vanish before the power of money, whereas the German nobility has remained poor but chivalrous. That last indispensable bulwark against the brutalization of society—the duel—has gone out of fashion in England and soon disappeared, to be supplanted by the riding whip.[8] This was a triumph of vulgarity. The newspapers, in their accounts of aristocratic weddings, record in exact detail how much each wedding guest has contributed in the form of presents or in cash; even the youth of the nation have turned their sports into a business, and contend for valuable prizes, whereas the German students wrought havoc on their countenances for the sake of a real or imaginary honor.[9]

On Jews

The Jews at one time played a necessary role in German history, because of their ability in the management of money. But now that the Aryans

---

[5]Barthold Georg Niebuhr (1776–1831) was a Prussian civil servant and historian best known for his three-volume history of Rome.

[6]Today, the term *Aryan,* or Indo-Iranian, refers to a branch of the Indo-European family of languages, which also includes Baltic, Slavic, Armenian, Greek, Celtic, Latin, and Germanic. Indo-Iranian includes Bengali, Persian, Punjabi, and Hindi. In Treitschke's day *Aryan* was used to refer not only to the prehistoric language from which all these languages derive but also to the racial group that spoke the language and migrated from its base in central Asia to Europe and India in the distant past. In the racial mythology that grew in connection with the term and later was embraced by Hitler and the Nazis, the Aryans provided Europe's original racial stock.

[7]Treitschke is making a point about what he views as the hypocrisy of the British, professed Christians who nonetheless sell opium to the Chinese.

[8]Aristocratic men frequently settled disputes concerning their honor by dueling. To Treitschke, abandoning the duel for less manly pursuits such as hunting and horseback riding was a sign of decadence.

[9]Treitschke is again using examples from sports to underscore the differences between the Germans and the English. English sports such as rugby and football (soccer) were organized into professional leagues; the Germans were still willing to be scarred in duels to defend their honor.

have become accustomed to the idiosyncrasies of finance, the Jews are no longer necessary. The international Jew, hidden in the mask of nationalities, is a disintegrating influence; he can be of no further use to the world. It is necessary to speak openly about the Jews, undisturbed by the fact that the Jewish press befouls what is purely historical truth.

A Defense of French Imperialism

63 • JULES FERRY, SPEECH BEFORE THE FRENCH NATIONAL ASSEMBLY

Jules Ferry (1832–1893), a French politician and ardent imperialist, twice served as premier of France. During his premierships (1880–1881, 1883–1885), France annexed Tunisia and parts of Indochina and directed French explorations in the Congo and of the Niger region of Africa. In debates in the French National Assembly, he frequently defended his policies against socialist and conservative critics who opposed French imperialism. In the following selection from a speech on July 28, 1883, he summarizes his reasons for supporting French expansionism; it also sheds light on his opponents' views.

QUESTIONS FOR ANALYSIS

1. According to Ferry, what recent developments in world trade have made France's need for colonies more urgent?
2. What arguments against imperialism are proposed by Ferry's critics? How does Ferry counter them?
3. Aside from providing markets for French goods, what other economic advantages do colonies offer, according to Ferry?
4. How does Ferry's appeal for colonies reflect nineteenth-century nationalism?

M. JULES FERRY Gentlemen, it embarrasses me to make such a prolonged demand upon the gracious attention of the Chamber, but I believe that the duty I am fulfilling upon this platform is not a useless one: It is as strenuous for me as for you, but I believe that there is some benefit in summarizing and condensing, in the form of arguments, the principles, the motives, and the various interests by which a policy of colonial expansion may be justified; it goes without saying that I will try to remain reasonable, moderate, and never lose sight of the major continental interests which are the primary concern of this country. What I wish to say, to support this proposition, is that in fact, just as in word, the policy of colonial expansion is a political and economic system; I wish to say that one can relate this system to three orders of ideas: economic ideas, ideas of civilization in its highest sense, and ideas of politics and patriotism.

In the area of economics, I will allow myself to place before you, with the support of some figures, the considerations which justify a policy of colonial expansion from the point of view of that need, felt more and more strongly by the industrial populations of Europe and particularly those of our own rich and hard working country:

Source: Ralph Austen, ed., *Modern Imperialism* (Lexington, Massachusetts: D. C. Heath, 1969), pp. 70–73. Copyright © 1969. Used by permission.

the need for export markets. . . . I will formulate only in a general way what each of you, in the different parts of France, is in a position to confirm. Yes, what is lacking for our great industry, drawn irrevocably on to the path of exportation by the (free trade) treaties of 1860,[1] what it lacks more and more is export markets. Why? Because next door to us Germany is surrounded by [tariff] barriers, because beyond the ocean, the United States of America has become protectionist, protectionist in the most extreme sense, because not only have these great markets, I will not say closed but shrunk, and thus become more difficult of access for our industrial products, but also these great states are beginning to pour products not seen heretofore into our own markets. . . . It is not necessary to pursue this demonstration any further. . . .

. . . Gentlemen, there is a second point, a second order of ideas to which I have to give equal attention, but as quickly as possible, believe me; it is the humanitarian and civilizing side of the question. On this point the honorable M. Camille Pelletan[2] has jeered in his own refined and clever manner; he jeers, he condemns, and he says "What is this civilization which you impose with cannon-balls? What is it but another form of barbarism? Don't these populations, these inferior races, have the same rights as you? Aren't they masters of their own houses? Have they called upon you? You come to them against their will, you offer them violence, but not civilization." There, gentlemen, is the thesis; I do not hesitate to say that this is not politics, nor is it history: it is political metaphysics. (*"Ah, Ah" on far left.*)[3]

. . . Gentlemen, I must speak from a higher and more truthful plane. It must be stated openly that, in effect, superior races have rights over inferior races. (*Movement on many benches on the far left.*)

M. Jules Maigne Oh! You dare to say this in the country which has proclaimed the rights of man!

M. de Guilloutet This is a justification of slavery and the slave trade!

M. Jules Ferry If M. Maigne is right, if the declaration of the rights of man was written for the blacks of equatorial Africa, then by what right do you impose regular commerce upon them? They have not called upon you.

M. Raoul Duval We do not want to impose anything upon them. It is you who wish to do so!

M. Jules Maigne To propose and to impose are two different things!

M. Georges Perin[4] In any case, you cannot bring about commerce by force.

M. Jules Ferry I repeat that superior races have a right, because they have a duty. They have the duty to civilize inferior races. . . .

That is what I have to answer M. Pelletan in regard to the second point upon which he touched.

He then touched upon a third, more delicate, more serious point, and upon which I ask your permission to express myself quite frankly. It is the political side of the question. The honorable M. Pelletan, who is a distinguished writer, always comes up with remarkably precise formulations. I will borrow from him the one which he applied the other day to this aspect of colonial policy.

---

[1] Refers to a treaty between Great Britain and France that lowered tariffs between the two nations.
[2] Pelletan (1846–1915) was a radical republican politician noted for his strong patriotism.
[3] Going back to a tradition begun in the legislative assemblies of the French Revolution, democrats and republicans sat on the left, moderates in the center, and conservatives on the right. By the 1880s the "left" also included socialists.
[4] Maigne, Guilloutet, Duval, and Perin were all members of the assembly.

"It is a system," he says, "which consists of seeking out compensations in the Orient with a circumspect and peaceful seclusion which is actually imposed upon us in Europe."

I would like to explain myself in regard to this. I do not like this word "compensation," and, in effect, not here but elsewhere it has often been used in a treacherous way. If what is being said or insinuated is that a republican minister could possibly believe that there are in any part of the world compensations for the disasters which we have experienced,[5] an injury is being inflicted . . . and an injury undeserved by that government. (*Applause at the center and left.*) I will ward off this injury with all the force of my patriotism! (*New applause and bravos from the same benches.*)

Gentlemen, there are certain considerations which merit the attention of all patriots. The conditions of naval warfare have been profoundly altered. ("*Very true! Very true!*")

At this time, as you know, a warship cannot carry more than fourteen days' worth of coal, no matter how perfectly it is organized, and a ship which is out of coal is a derelict on the surface of the sea, abandoned to the first person who comes along. Thence the necessity of having on the oceans provision stations, shelters, ports for defense and revictualling. (*Applause at the center and left. Various interruptions.*) And it is for this

that we needed Tunisia, for this that we needed Saigon and the Mekong Delta, for this that we need Madagascar, that we are at Diego-Suarez and Vohemar[6] and will never leave them! (*Applause from a great number of benches.*) Gentlemen, in Europe as it is today, in this competition of so many rivals which we see growing around us, some by perfecting their military or maritime forces, others by the prodigious development of an ever growing population; in a Europe, or rather in a universe of this sort, a policy of peaceful seclusion or abstention is simply the highway to decadence! Nations are great in our times only by means of the activities which they develop; it is not simply "by the peaceful shining forth of institutions" (*Interruptions on the extreme left and right*) that they are great at this hour. . . .

(The Republican Party) has shown that it is quite aware that one cannot impose upon France a political ideal conforming to that of nations like independent Belgium and the Swiss Republic; that something else is needed for France: that she cannot be merely a free country, that she must also be a great country, exercising all of her rightful influence over the destiny of Europe, that she ought to propagate this influence throughout the world and carry everywhere that she can her language, her customs, her flag, her arms, and her genius. (*Applause at center and left.*)

---

[5]Refers to France's defeat by Prussia and the German states in the Franco-Prussian War of 1870–1871.

[6]Madagascar port cities.

Images of Imperialism in Great Britain

64 • ADVERTISEMENTS AND ILLUSTRATIONS FROM BRITISH BOOKS AND PERIODICALS

Although late-nineteenth-century imperialism had many critics, there is no doubt that in the major imperialist states, it had broad support, not just from investors, missionary groups, and civil servants who had direct interests in Africa and Asia, but also from the general populace. For many of its supporters, imperialism confirmed their faith in progress and their belief in the superiority of white, Christian

Europe over the rest of the world. For nationalists, it was a test and demonstration of the nation's strength and vigor. For those who found their lives in industrial society drab and tedious, it provided vicarious adventure, excitement, and a sense of the exotic.

Late-nineteenth-century popular culture provides ample evidence of the public's enthusiasm for imperialism. Especially in Great Britain, the premier imperialist power, novels, poetry, plays, children's books, advertisements, music hall entertainment, and publications of missionary societies were filled with positive imperialist images, themes, and motifs. Youth organizations such as the Boy Scouts (f. 1908) and Girl Guides (f. 1910) taught the value of service to Britain's imperial cause. The public's exposure to such material reinforced imperialism's appeal and strengthened support for the government's policies.

The following selections are examples of how British popular culture propagated imperial values. The first group of illustrations appeared in *An ABC for Baby Patriots* by Mrs. Earnest Ames. Designed to be read to young children, it was published in 1898 in London and went through several printings. The illustration that accompanies the letter "N" depicts a British naval officer showing off a flotilla of Royal Navy ships on maneuvers off Spithead in the English Channel. The foreigners are a German on the left and a Frenchman on the right.

The second illustration is taken from *The Kipling Reader,* a collection of stories written for young adults by Rudyard Kipling (1865–1936); the book was published in 1908 and illustrated by J. Macfarlane. Kipling, one of the most popular British writers of the era, is best remembered for his support of imperialism and his glorification of the heroism of the British soldier in India and Burma. This illustration depicts Scott, a character in the story "William the Conqueror." Set in India during a famine, the story centers on the romance between Scott and a young woman nicknamed "William," while they toil to save Indians from starvation. Scott has saved hundreds of babies by feeding them milk from a herd of goats he has managed to maintain. In this illustration, he approaches William, who sees "a young man, beautiful as Paris, a god in a halo of gold dust, walking slowly at the head of his flocks, while at his knee ran small naked Cupids."

The third illustration is an advertisement for Lipton Teas that appeared in 1897 in the *Illustrated London News.* The Lipton Company was founded in Glasgow, Scotland, by the son of a poor Irish shopkeeper, Thomas Lipton (1850–1931). He opened a small food shop in Glasgow in 1871 and by 1890 owned 300 food stores throughout Great Britain. In 1890, the multimillionaire decided to cash in on the British taste for tea. Growing tea on plantations he owned in India and Ceylon and marketing it in inexpensive small packets that guaranteed freshness, the Lipton Company soon became synonymous with tea drinking throughout Europe and the United States. Lipton advertisements appeared regularly in the *Illustrated London News* in the 1890s and early 1900s.

The fourth and fifth illustrations are cartoons published in the weekly humor magazine *Punch,* founded in 1841. "On the Swoop" was published in 1894, a time when the European powers were consolidating their territorial claims in Africa. It shows an eagle representing Germany about to pounce on an African village. By then, the German acquisition of Tanganyika had ruined the British imperialists' dream of establishing a string of contiguous colonies stretching from Cairo in Egypt to Cape Town in South Africa. "Britannia and Her Suitors" was published in 1901, when Great Britain was still avoiding entanglements in the diplomatic alliances then taking shape among the continental powers. It shows Britannia dancing with a figure representing its colonies, while in the background, the German emperor Wilhelm II, then allied only with weak Austria-Hungary, looks on unhappily. Farther in the background, Tsar Nicholas II of Russia dances with a figure representing France, with which Russia had been allied since 1894.

QUESTIONS FOR ANALYSIS

1. What views of Africans and Asians are being communicated in each of the illustrations?
2. What message is being communicated about the benefits colonial subjects are accruing from their status?
3. What images are being communicated about the British in their role as imperialists?
4. What concrete examples of nationalism can you see in the various illustrations?
5. How many of the justifications for imperialism presented in Jules Ferry's speech (source 63) can you find represented in the illustrations?
6. Using evidence in the illustrations alone, what conclusions can you draw about the reasons for imperialism's popularity within the general British population?

N n   *N n*

N is the Navy
  We keep at Spithead,
It's a sight that makes foreigners
  Wish they were dead.

N, n.

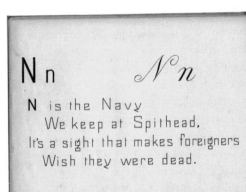

I, i.

I i   *I i*

I is for India,
  Our land in the East
Where everyone goes
  To shoot tigers, and feast.

W w   *W w*

W is the Word
  Of an Englishman True;
When given, it means
  What he says, he will do.

W, w.

From *An ABC for Baby Patriots*

From The Kipling Reader

Advertisement for Lipton Teas, which appeared in the Illustrated London News, a weekly publication

From British Books and Periodicals, "On the Swoop," from Punch, 1894, Punch Cartoon Library & Archive

"On the Swoop," from Punch, 1894

ON THE SWOOP!

PARTNERS.

Britannia. "AFTER ALL, MY DEAR, WE NEEDN'T TROUBLE OURSELVES ABOUT THE OTHERS."
Colonia. "NO; WE CAN ALWAYS DANCE TOGETHER, YOU AND I!"

From Punch, 1901, Punch Cartoon Library & Archive

"Britannia and Her Suitors," from Punch, 1901

Chapter 9

Western Pressures, Nationalism, and Reform in Africa, Southwest Asia, and India in the 1800s

AFRICA, SOUTHWEST ASIA, and India all shared a common experience in the nineteenth century: all three were caught up in a tidal wave of change set off by the political, economic, and cultural onslaught of Europe. In India, the British extended their empire until it encompassed most of the Indian subcontinent, while in Africa the British along with the French, Belgians, Germans, and Italians transformed virtually all of the continent Africa into a giant European colony. In Southwest Asia, Persia experienced growing British and Russian interference in its affairs, culminating in the Anglo-Russian Agreement of 1907, which divided the country into a Russian-dominated north, a British-dominated south, and a nominally independent center. The Ottoman Empire survived, but lost thousands of square miles of territory. In North Africa, which was still part of the Ottoman Empire despite the near independence of its rulers, Algeria and Tunisia became French colonies, and Egypt became a British protectorate. The Ottomans also lost their territory in southeastern Europe, as Greece, Serbia, Romania, Bulgaria, Montenegro, and Albania all gained their independence. In addition, Europeans compromised the sovereignty of the Ottoman state itself. Foreign businessmen, who controlled the empire's banks, railroads, and mines, regulated Ottoman tariff policy and were exempt from many of the empire's laws and taxes. Beginning in 1881,

Europeans supervised the collection and disbursement of state revenues through the Ottoman Public Debt Administration, an agency that existed mainly to guarantee payment of government debts to European creditors.

In all three regions, European penetration threatened ruling elites and traditional political institutions, making some irrelevant, destroying others, and inspiring reform in a few. It also altered these regions' traditional economies. Europeans built railroads and telegraph lines, undertook huge engineering projects such as the Suez Canal, created new demands for raw materials and agricultural goods, and aggressively marketed their own manufactured products. Europeans also introduced unsettling new ideas and values through missionary activity and the promotion of Western education and science. In a century of unparalleled and extraordinary change, the peoples of Africa, southwest Asia, and India were wrenched from their past and forced to face uncertain futures.

The European Assault on Africa

Paradoxically, the century that ended with the nearly complete submission of Africa to European rule began with efforts by some Europeans to end their main business in Africa, the slave trade. Responding to religious, humanitarian, and economic arguments, Denmark outlawed the slave trade in 1792, and Great Britain and the United States did the same in 1807, followed by Sweden, the Netherlands, and France in 1848. Unexpectedly, however, African–European relations underwent a radical transformation in the closing decades of the nineteenth century, and the entire African continent except Liberia and Ethiopia succumbed to European rule.

The European takeover of Africa began in earnest in the 1870s, a decade that saw intensified missionary activity; the discovery of new gold and diamond deposits in southern Africa; heightened commercial competition among European merchants in West Africa and the Niger delta region; and growing interest in Africa on the part of the European public as a result of missionary writings and explorers' tales. In 1878, the Welsh-American explorer Henry M. Stanley (1841–1904), working on behalf of King Leopold II of Belgium, was dispatched to the Congo River basin, where he convinced hundreds of chiefs to sign treaties that led to the founding of the king's huge personal colony, the Congo Free State. In 1880, the Italian-born explorer Pierre Savorgnan de Brazza (1853–1905) signed the first of dozens of treaties with African chieftains that were the basis for the French colonies in equatorial Africa. In 1881, the French established a protectorate over Tunisia, and in 1882, the British occupied Egypt. The Germans annexed Togo in 1883 and Cameroon in 1884. In 1884 and 1885, representatives of twelve European states, the Ottoman Empire, and the United States established guidelines for the further colonization of Africa at the Berlin West Africa Conference. By 1914, the partition of Africa was complete.

A Sampling of Treaties and Agreements

65 • LAGOS TREATY OF CESSION, AUGUST 6, 1861; TREATY BETWEEN THE INTERNATIONAL ASSOCIATION OF THE CONGO AND TONKI, CHIEF OF NGOMBI AND MAMPUYA, SENIOR CHIEF OF MAFELA; AGREEMENT BETWEEN CHARLES D. RUDD, ET AL., AND LOBENGULA, KING OF MATABELELAND; LETTER OF KING LOBENGULA TO QUEEN VICTORIA

During the 1800s, African kings and chiefs signed well over a thousand treaties and agreements with representatives of European states or trading companies, the cumulative effect of which was the near-total subjection of Africa to colonial rule. At the start of the century, such treaties mainly involved British efforts to suppress the slave trade. In midcentury, many agreements were struck to guarantee Europeans access to products such as palm oil, peanuts, indigo, and ivory. By the end of the century, with the scramble for Africa in full swing, such treaties entailed the transfer to European states or trading companies of territory, sweeping political powers, and exclusive access to minerals and other raw materials.

Most of these agreements were hardly treaties in the dictionary sense of an "arrangement or agreement made by negotiation." Vague and frequently misleading discussions of a proposed treaty's content, often accompanied by threats of force, were followed by the drawing up of a brief legalistic document in a European language that few African signees could understand. Not surprisingly, months or years after an African leader affixed his "X" to a treaty, he and his people learned that the document he had signed had provisions he had never discussed and implications he had never imagined. In the selections that follow, we present excerpts from three such treaties along with a letter written in response to one of them by an African king to Queen Victoria of Great Britain.

The first document is a treaty signed in 1861 between Great Britain and King Docemo of Lagos, a city-state on the Niger delta and a center of the slave trade since the fifteenth century. Great Britain had already signed a number of treaties with regional rulers to halt the slave trade, but the results had been deemed unsatisfactory. This treaty went further, in that Britain took possession of actual territory. Such a step, it was hoped, would result in the suppression of slave smuggling out of Lagos, ensure access to the region's raw cotton, and serve as a warning to other rulers on the coast to enforce the ban on slave trading.

The second treaty is one of the several hundred treaties signed in the early 1880s by chiefs in the Congo River basin by which they transferred rights and powers to the International Association of the Congo, a consortium founded in 1878 by King Leopold II of Belgium and his associates. Supposedly a subgroup of the International African Association, a philanthropic organization founded by Leopold in 1876, the International Association of the Congo was meant to enrich the king by giving him personal control over a vast African colony. Leopold did his best to disguise the organization's true purpose by identifying it with the cause of bringing peace and enlightenment to Africa. The task of turning this huge region into a viable colony was given to the Welsh-American journalist/explorer Henry M. Stanley, whose agents used force and trickery to coerce chiefs into signing.

The last agreement, signed in 1888, was between the King Lobengula of Matabeleland and business associates of Cecil Rhodes, the relentless British imperialist who already had enriched himself through his ownership of diamond mines around Kimberly, South Africa, and now was intent on extending his business interests and British authority farther north in present-day Zimbabwe. Lobengula ruled over a kingdom founded by the Ndebele people earlier in the century after they had migrated north to escape political turmoil in southern Africa. After rejecting requests of various Europeans to grant them concessions to mine gold in his territory, in 1888, he accepted the terms offered by Rhodes' group.

Lobengula realized he had been duped after learning he had given Rhodes and his associates the rights to all the minerals in the kingdom, not, as he had thought, the right to dig "one big hole" in his territory with just ten men. In response, he ordered the execution of several of his councilors and sent the following note to Queen Victoria. Some months later, he received a response from one of the queen's advisors, who informed him that after looking into the matter, the queen had concluded that the men who had signed the treaty "may be trusted to carry out the working for gold in the chief's country without molesting his people." The king formally repudiated the treaty, but without effect.

QUESTIONS FOR ANALYSIS

1. What specific powers will the rulers surrender by signing the treaties? What powers, if any, will they maintain?
2. What benefits do the rulers themselves receive as a result of signing the agreements?
3. What benefits will accrue to the European signatories of the treaties?
4. What benefits do the treaties promise for the subjects of the signatories of the treaties?
5. How, according to Lobengula, has he been misled in the agreement he signed?

Lagos Treaty of Cession, August 6, 1861

Article 1. In order that the Queen of England may be the better enabled to assist, defend, and protect the inhabitants of Lagos, and put an end to the slave trade in this and the neighbouring countries, and to prevent the destructive wars so frequently undertaken . . . for the capture of slaves, I, Docemo, do . . . give, transfer, and by these presents grant and confirm unto the Queen of Great Britain, her heirs and successors for ever, the port and Island of Lagos, with all rights, profits, territories, and appurtenances [incidental rights] whatsoever thereunto belonging . . . freely, fully, entirely, and absolutely the inhabitants of the said island

Source: From C. W. Newbury, ed., *British Policy towards West Africa, 1786–1874* (Oxford: Clarendon Press, 1965), pp. 429–430.

and territories, as the Queen's subjects, and under her sovereignty, Crown, jurisdiction, and Government, being still suffered to live there.

Article 2. Docemo will be allowed the use of the title of King in its usual African signification, and will be permitted to decide disputes between natives of Lagos with their consent, subject to appeal to British laws. . . .

In consideration of the cession as before-mentioned of the port and island and territories of Lagos, the representatives of the Queen of Great Britain do promise, subject to the approval of Her Majesty, that Docemo shall receive an annual pension from the Queen of Great Britain. . . .

Additional Article to the Lagos Treaty of Concession, 18 February 1862. King Docemo . . . , perfectly agrees to all the conditions thereof; and with regard to the 3d Article consents to receive as a pension, to be continued during his lifetime, the sum of 1,200 (twelve hundred) bags of cowries[1] per annum, as equal to his net revenue; and I, the undersigned representative of Her Majesty, agree on the part of Her Majesty to guarantee to the said . . . annual pension . . . for his lifetime, unless he, Docemo, should break any of the Articles of the above Treaty, in which case his pension will be forfeited.

---

[1]Cowrie is a term for any number of marine snails that live in the coastal waters of the Indian and Pacific oceans. The snails produce thick polished shells, many of which are brightly colored and speckled. The shells were widely used as currency in West Africa, especially during the era of the transatlantic slave trade. These shells were harvested and processed off the Maldive Islands in the Indian Ocean and sold to Europeans who transported them to Europe as ballast in the holds of their ships. There they were repurchased by slave traders before leaving for Africa. Although costs were involved in purchasing and transporting the shells, they were otherwise worthless to Europeans.

Treaty Between the International Association of the Congo and Tonki, Chief of Ngombi and Mampuya, Senior Chief of Mafela

Art. I.—The chiefs of Ngombi and Mafela recognise that it is highly desirable that the [International Association of the Congo][1] should, for the advancement of civilization and trade, be firmly established in their country. They therefore now, . . . for themselves and their heirs and successors for ever, do give up to the said Association the sovereignty and all sovereign and governing rights to all their territories. They also promise to assist the said Association in its work of governing and civilizing this country, and to use their influence to secure obedience to all laws made by the said . . . Association, and to assist by labour or otherwise, any works, improvements, or expeditions which the said Association shall cause at any time to be carried out in any part of these territories.

Art. II.—The chiefs . . . promise at all times to join their forces with those of the said Association, to resist the forcible intrusion or repulse the attacks of foreigners of any nationality or colour.

Art. III.—The country thus ceded has about the following boundaries, viz., the whole of the Ngombi and Mafela countries, and any others tributary

---

Source: From Henry M. Stanley, *The Congo and the Founding of its Free State. A Story of the Work of Exploration* (New York: Harper & Brothers, 1885), pp. 195–197.

[1]An altered version of this document was published in a book by the explorer Henry Stanley, *The Congo and the Founding of Its Free State* (1885). The original document showed the agreement as being between the African chiefs and the International Association of the Congo (the political and business arm of Leopold's enterprise in the Congo). Before the book went to print, however, the manuscript was edited by King Leopold, who changed the contracting party to the International African Association (the philanthropic society of explorers and geographers founded by Leopold in 1876). This is one example of how Leopold attempted to fool the world about the aims of his project.

to them. . . . All roads and waterways running through this country, the right of collecting tolls on the same, and all game, fishing, mining, and forest rights, are to be the absolute property of the said Association, together with any unoccupied lands as may at any time hereafter be chosen.

Art. IV.—[The International Association of the Congo] agree to pay . . . one piece of cloth per month to each of the undersigned chiefs, besides present of cloth in hand; and the said chiefs hereby acknowledge to accept this bounty and monthly subsidy in full settlement of all their claims on the said Association.

Art. V.—[The International Association of the Congo] promises:—

1. To take from the natives of this ceded country no occupied or cultivated lands, except by mutual agreement.

2. To promote to its utmost the prosperity of the said country.

3. To protect its inhabitants from all oppression or foreign intrusion.

4. It authorizes the chiefs to hoist its flag, to settle all local disputes or palavers [discussions] and to maintain its authority with the natives.

Agreed to, signed and witnessed, this 1st day of April, 1884.

HENRY M. STANLEY.
Tonki, his X mark,
Senior Chief of Ngombi.
Mampuya, his X mark,
Senior Chief of Mafela.

Agreement Between Charles D. Rudd, et al., and Lobengula, King of Matabeleland, 1891

WHEREAS Charles Dunell Rudd of Kimberley, Rochfort Maguire of London, and Francis Robert Thompson of Kimberley hereinafter called the grantees . . . do hereby covenant and agree to pay to me my heirs and successors the sum of One hundred Pounds sterling British Currency on the first day of every lunar month and further to deliver at my Royal Kraal [homestead] one thousand Martini-Henry Breech-loading Rifles[1] together with one hundred thousand rounds of suitable ball cartridge; five hundred of the said Rifles; and fifty thousand of the said cartridge to be ordered from England forthwith and delivered with reasonable despatch . . . so soon as

the said grantees shall have commenced to work mining machinery within my territory and further to deliver on the Zambesi river a Steamboat with guns suitable for defensive purposes upon the said river. . . . I Lobengula King of Matabeleland, Mashonaland and certain adjoining terrotories in . . . do hereby grant and assign unto the said grantees . . . the complete and exclusive charge over all metals and minerals situated and contained in my Kingdoms, Principalities and dominions together with full power to do all things that they may deem necessary to win and procure the same and to hold collect and enjoy the profits and revenue if any derivable from the said metals and minerals . . . , and WHEREAS I have been much molested of late by diverse

Source: Lewis Mitchell, *The Life of the Right Hon. Cecil John Rhodes, 1853–1902*, vol. 2 (London: Edward Arnold, 1910), pp. 244–245.

[1]The Martini-Henry rifle, first produced in 1871, had been standard issue for British troops, but in 1888, the year in which this agreement was signed, it was replaced with the Lee-Metford rifle. Production of the Martini-Henry rifle ended in 1889. After he repudiated the agreement with Rudd, Lobengula refused to accept the first shipment of rifles the English had promised. One can be quite certain that he never received the armed steamboat to patrol the Zambezi.

persons seeking and desiring to obtain grants and concessions of Land and Mining rights in my territories I do hereby authorize the said grantees, . . . to take all necessary and lawful steps to exclude from my Kingdoms, principalities, and dominions all persons seeking land, metals, minerals, or mining rights therein and I do hereby undertake to render them such needful assistance as they may from time to time require for the exclusion of such persons.

This given under my hand this thirtieth day of October in the year of our Lord Eighteen hundred and Eighty-Eight at my Royal Kraal.

his

Lobengula X

mark

Letter of King Lobengula to Queen Victoria

Some time ago a party of men came to my country, the principal one appearing to be a man called Rudd. They asked me for a place to dig for gold, and said they would give me certain things for the right to do so I told them to bring what they could give and I would show them what I would give. A document was written and presented to me for signature. I asked what it contained, and was told that in it were my words and the words of those men. I put my hand to it. About three months afterward I heard from other sources that I had given by that document the right to all the minerals of my country. I called a meeting of my *Indunas* [counsellors], and also of the white men and demanded a copy of the document. It was proved to me that I had signed away the mineral rights of my whole country to Rudd and his friends. I have since had a meeting of my *Indunas* and they will not recognize the paper, as it contains neither my words nor the words of those who got it. . . . I write to you that you may know the truth about this thing.

Source: Quoted in E. D. Morel, *Black Man's Burden* (London: Arnold, 1920), pp. 34–35.

Colonialism at Its Darkest

66 • GEORGE WASHINGTON WILLIAMS, OPEN LETTER TO KING LEOPOLD II OF BELGIUM, 1890

Although George Washington Williams lived only 42 years, summarizing his life in few words is difficult. Born in 1849 into a free black family in Bedford Springs, Pennsylvania, he served in the Union army as a teenager; enlisted in the Mexican army after the Civil War; briefly attended Howard University; earned a divinity degree from Newton Seminary; served as a pastor in Boston and Cincinnati; published a newspaper in Washington, D.C.; studied law; and was elected to the Ohio legislature. Then in 1883, he achieved national prominence with the publication of his *History of the Negro Race in America from 1619 to 1880: Negroes as Slaves, as Soldiers, and as Citizens.*

He became interested in the Congo after President Chester B. Arthur introduced him to Henry Shelton Sanford, a wealthy businessman and diplomat, who, after serving as U.S. minister to Belgium remained in Belgium and became a friend of Leopold. As a result of his lobbying, the United States was the first country to recognize the legal existence of Leopold's colony, the Congo Free State. Sanford sparked Williams' interest in the Congo by describing Leopold's humanitarian goals. After Williams won a newspaper assignment to travel to Europe to do a series of articles on European topics, he interviewed Leopold II in 1889. He reported that Leopold was an impressive figure and had told him that his work in Africa was his "Christian duty to the poor African." Despite attempts by Leopold to discourage him, in 1890 Williams visited the Congo for six months as part of a one-year excursion around Africa. At the end of his visit, the disillusioned American composed an open letter to King Leopold, which later was published as a twelve-page pamphlet and widely distributed in Europe and the United States. This was the first salvo in a two-decade struggle by missionaries, journalists, government officials, and politicians to reveal the false claims and monumental hypocrisy of a colonial enterprise that was the perpetrator of unimaginable cruelties.

QUESTIONS FOR ANALYSIS

1. According to Williams, what is the nature of the administrative structure established by Leopold's officials? What role is played by Belgian officials and soldiers? What role is played by African mercenaries?
2. In what ways are the state's administrators ill-prepared to administer the Congo Free State?
3. In what areas, according to Williams, has Leopold's regime failed to carry through on its promises to the Congolese people?
4. Williams describes the African soldiers in the *Force Publique* as the "greatest curse the country suffers." Why?
5. How has the Congo Free State violated provisions of the acts of the Congress of Berlin in regard to free trade?
6. To what extent does Williams see racism as the root of the problems in the Congo?

Good and Great Friend

It afforded me great pleasure to avail myself of the opportunity afforded me last year, of visiting your State in Africa; and how thoroughly I have been disenchanted, disappointed and disheartened, it is now my painful duty to make known to your Majesty in plain but respectful language.

When I arrived in the Congo, I naturally sought for the results of the brilliant programme:

"fostering care", "benevolent enterprise", an "honest and practical effort" to increase the knowledge of the natives "and secure their welfare". I had never been able to conceive of Europeans, establishing a government in a tropical country, without building a hospital; and yet from the mouth of the Congo River to its head-waters, here at the seventh cataract, a distance of 1,448 miles, there is not a solitary hospital for Europeans, and only three

Source: George Washington Williams, "An Open Letter to His Serene Majesty Leopold II," Stanley Falls, Central Africa, s.d. [Microform copy held by Library of Congress, Washington, D.C.]

sheds for sick Africans in the service of the State, not fit to be occupied by a horse. . . . There is not a single chaplain in the employ of your Majesty's Government to console the sick or bury the dead. Your white men sicken and die in their quarters or on the caravan road, and seldom have Christian burial. . . . The African soldiers[1] and labourers of your Majesty's Government fare worse than the whites . . .

Instead of the natives of the Congo "adopting the fostering care" of your Majesty's Government, they everywhere complain that their land has been taken from them by force; that the Government is cruel and arbitrary, and declare that they neither love nor respect the Government and its flag. Your Majesty's Government has sequestered their land, burned their towns, stolen their property, enslaved their women and children, and committed other crimes too numerous to mention in detail. . . .

There has been, to my absolute knowledge, no "honest and practical effort made to increase their knowledge and secure their welfare." Your Majesty's Government has never spent one franc for educational purposes, nor instituted any practical system of industrialism. Indeed the most unpractical measures have been adopted against the natives in nearly every respect; and in the capital of your Majesty's Government there is not a native . . . employed. The labour system is radically unpractical; the soldiers and labourers of your Majesty's Government are very largely imported from Zanzibar at a cost of £10 per capita, and from Sierra Leone, Liberia, Accra and Lagos at from £1 to £1/10 per capital. These recruits are transported under circumstances more cruel than cattle in European countries. . . .

There are from sixty to seventy officers of the Belgian army in the service of your Majesty's Government in the Congo of whom only about thirty are at their post; the other half are in

Belgium on furlough. . . . But I take the liberty to say that many of these officers are too young and inexperienced to be entrusted with the difficult work of dealing with native races. They are ignorant of native character, lack wisdom, justice, fortitude and patience. They have estranged the natives from your Majesty's Government, have sown the seed of discord between tribes and villages, and some of them have stained the uniform of the Belgian officer with murder, arson and robbery. . . .

From these general observations I wish now to pass to specific charges against your Majesty's Government.

—Your Majesty's Government is deficient in the moral, military and financial strength, necessary to govern a territory of 1,508,000 square miles. . . .

—Your Majesty's Government has established nearly fifty posts, consisting of from two to eight mercenary slave-soldiers from the East Coast. There is no white commissioned officer at these posts; they are in charge of the black Zanzibar soldiers, and the State expects them not only to sustain themselves, but to raid enough to feed the garrisons where the white men are stationed. These piratical, buccaneering posts compel the natives to furnish them with fish, goats, fowls, and vegetables at the mouths of their muskets; and whenever the natives refuse to feed these vampires, they report to the main station and white officers come with an expeditionary force and burn away the homes of the natives. These black soldiers, many of whom are slaves, exercise the power of life and death. They are ignorant and cruel, because they do not comprehend the natives; they are imposed upon them by the State. They make no report as to the number of robberies they commit, or the number of lives they take; they are only

---

[1] A reference to the *Force Publique*, a mercenary army made up largely of Africans and officered by Europeans. By the late 1890s, its number approached 20,000 troops and consumed half the state's budget.

required to subsist upon the natives and thus relieve your Majesty's Government of the cost of feeding them. They are the greatest curse the country suffers now. . . .

—The Courts of your Majesty's Government are abortive, unjust, partial and delinquent. . . . The laws printed and circulated in Europe "for the protection of the blacks" in the Congo, are a dead letter and a fraud. I have heard an officer of the Belgian Army pleading the cause of a white man of low degree who had been guilty of beating and stabbing a black man, and urging race distinctions and prejudices as good and sufficient reasons why his client should be adjudged innocent . . . .

—Your Majesty's Government is excessively cruel to its prisoners, condemning them, for the slightest offences, to the chain gang, the like of which can not be seen in any other Government in the civilized or uncivilized world. Often these ox-chains eat into the necks of the prisoners and produce sores about which the flies circle, aggravating the running wound; . . . These poor creatures are frequently beaten with a dried piece of hippopotamus skin, called a "chicote" [usually spelled "chicotte"], and usually the blood flows at every stroke when well laid on. But the cruelties visited upon soldiers and workmen are not to be compared with the sufferings of the poor natives who, upon the slightest pretext, are thrust into the wretched prisons here in the Upper River . . .

—Women are imported into your Majesty's Government for immoral purposes. . . . The State then hires these woman out to the highest bidder, the officers having the first choice and then the men . . . .

—Your Majesty's Government has violated the General Act of the Conference of Berlin by firing upon native canoes; by confiscating the property of natives; by intimidating native traders, and preventing them from trading with white trading companies; by quartering troops in native villages when there is no war; by permitting the natives to carry on the slave-trade, and by engaging in the wholesale and retail slave-trade itself.

—Your Majesty's Government has been, and is now, guilty of waging unjust and cruel wars against natives, with the hope of securing slaves and women, to minister to the behests of the officers of your Government. In such slave-hunting raids one village is armed by the State against the other, and the force thus secured is incorporated with the regular troops. I have no adequate terms with which to depict to your Majesty the brutal acts of your soldiers upon such raids as these. . . .

—The agents of your Majesty's Government have misrepresented the Congo country and the Congo railway. Mr. H. M. STANLEY, the man who was your chief agent in setting up your authority in this country, has grossly misrepresented the character of the country. Instead of it being fertile and productive it is sterile and unproductive. The natives can scarcely subsist upon the vegetable life produced in some parts of the country. . . . There is no improvement among the natives, because there is an impassable gulf between them and your Majesty's Government, a gulf which can never be bridged. HENRY M. STANLEY'S name produces a shudder among this simple folk when mentioned; they remember his broken promises, his copious profanity, his hot temper, his heavy blows, his severe and rigorous measures, by which they were mulcted of their lands. . . .

All the crimes perpetrated in the Congo have been done in your name, and you must answer at the bar of Public Sentiment for the misgovernment of a people, whose lives and fortunes were entrusted to you. . . .

And all this upon the word of honour of a gentleman, I subscribe myself your Majesty's humble and obedient servant.

GEO. W. WILLIAMS
Stanley Falls, Central Africa,
July 18th, 1890.

"A Noble and Elevated Task"

67 • KING LEOPOLD II, OPEN LETTER TO THE OFFICIALS OF THE CONGO FREE STATE, 1897

George Washington Williams died in 1891 and thus never saw how conditions in the Congo Free State became even more horrific in the 1890s. The cause was world demand for rubber, which was used for tires, hoses, gaskets, and electrical wires and could be produced by tapping the sap of wild rubber vines that grew in profusion in Africa's equatorial forests. Since the gathering of the sap was dangerous and unpleasant, agents of the Congo state and the private firms to which it had offered contracts resorted to force. With their wives and children held as hostages, villagers were sent into the forest knowing that failure to meet quotas would result in the killing of their families, their own execution, whippings, the chopping off of ears and hands, and even castration.

Meanwhile, Leopold II and his supporters did their best to discredit Williams' allegations and keep the system of forced labor a secret. They also sought to perpetuate the myth of the Congo Free State's philanthropic purpose, as shown in the letter Leopold addressed to the state's soldiers and administrators in 1897. It appeared in the periodical *La Colonie Belgique*, published in Brussels between 1895 and 1905 as an instrument for disseminating favorable information about the Congo project. Such efforts failed to stem the tide of revelations by missionaries, journalists, and government officials about the horrors of the Congo. In 1908, the Belgian parliament, after two years of negotiations, took away the Congo Free State from the king and placed it under state control. In return, the parliament agreed to assume responsibility for Leopold's 110 million francs of debt, provide 45.5 million francs for a number of Leopold's building projects (including the royal palace outside Brussels), and pay Leopold 50 million francs "as a mark of gratitude for his great sacrifices made for the Congo."

QUESTIONS FOR ANALYSIS

1. At the beginning of his letter, Leopold would appear to concede that some abuses have occurred in the Congo. What, in his view, has caused such abuses and how can they be expected to end?
2. What are Leopold's views of the general characteristics of African people?
3. According to Leopold, what has the Congo Free State already accomplished on behalf of the Africans and what can it be expected to accomplish in the future?

Brussels, June 16, 1897

Sir,

The task which the State agents have had to accomplish in the Congo is noble and elevated. . . .

Face to face with primitive barbarity, struggling against dreadful customs, thousands of years old, their duty has been to modify gradually those customs. . . .

Source: From Louis Snyder, ed., *The Imperialism Reader* (Princeton: C. Van Nostrand, 1962), pp. 236–238.

The soldiers of the State must be recruited among the natives.[1] They do not easily abandon their sanguinary customs transmitted from generation to generation. The example of white officers and military discipline will make them hate the human trophies of which they are now proud. . . .

The aim of all of us—I desire to repeat it here with you—is to regenerate, materially and morally, races whose degradation and misfortune it is hard to realise. The fearful scourges of which, in the eyes of our humanity, these races seemed the victims, are already lessening, little by little, through our intervention. Each step forward made by our people should mark an improvement in the condition of the natives.

In those vast tracts, mostly uncultivated and many unproductive, where the natives hardly knew how to get their daily food, European experience, knowledge, resource and enterprise, have brought to light unthought-of wealth. If wants are created they are satisfied even more liberally. Exploration of virgin land goes on, communications are established, highways are opened, the soil yields produce in exchange for our varied manufactured articles. Legitimate trade and industry are established. As the economic state is formed, property assumes an intrinsic character, private and public ownership, the basis of all social development, is founded and respected instead of being left to the law of change and of the strongest.

Upon this material prosperity, in which whites and blacks have evidently common interest, will follow a desire on the part of the blacks to elevate themselves. Their primitive nature will not always resist the efforts of Christian culture. Their education, once begun, will no more be interrupted. In its success I see crowning of the task undertaken by our people and so ably seconded by religious missionaries of both sexes. The most urgent part of the programme we wished to realize was to set up direct communication with the natives all over the Congo Basin. And this was done in the course of fifteen years, without the help of any State, if it were not that lent by Belgium. The establishment of a whole, compact series of stations gradually substitutes for savage warfare, carried on incessantly between tribes and villages, a regime of peace.

From a geographical entity, physically determined, the Congo State has become a country with distinct frontiers, occupied and guarded at every point—a result almost without precedent in the history of colonisation, but which is explained by the concentration of our united efforts on a single field of activity. . . .

I thank our agents for their efforts and I reiterate to them the expression of my royal regard.

LEOPOLD

---

[1] A reference to the Africans recruited to be soldiers in the *Force Publique*, the Congo Free State's mercenary army.

Reflections of an African Warrior

68 • NDANSI KUMALO, HIS STORY

Ndansi Kumalo, born in the late 1870s and raised as an Ndebele warrior, was in his mid-teens when his king, Lobengula, signed the agreement that gave Cecil Rhodes and his associates the concession to exploit the mineral wealth of Matabeleland and Mashonaland. He was old enough to fight against the British in Matabele War of 1893–1894, and took up farming after his people's defeat and the establishment of formal British rule under the auspices of Rhodes' South Africa Company. In 1932,

Ndansi Kumalo caught the attention of a British filmmaker who was in Southern Rhodesia to make *Rhodes of Africa,* on the life of Cecil Rhodes. Recruited to play the part of Lobengula, to complete the film he traveled to England, where he related his life story to the English Africanist Margery Perham. The following excerpt comes from her transcription of the interview.

Ndansi Kumalo's narrative begins with a reference to the Ndebele defeat in the Matabele War and goes on to discuss the grievances that led to a revolt against British rule in 1896 and 1897. It concludes with a retrospective look at how British rule changed his life and the lives of his people.

QUESTIONS FOR ANALYSIS

1. According to Ndansi Kumalo, what were the causes of the anti-British revolt of 1896–1897?
2. According to Ndansi Kumalo, why did the situation of the Ndebele rapidly deteriorate after the suppression of the rebellion?
3. Aside from raising revenue, what might the British have hoped to achieve by imposing, and then raising, taxes on the Ndebele?
4. What economic changes did the Ndebele experience as a result of their subjection to the Europeans?
5. Do you agree with Ndansi Kumalo that the arrival of Europeans was a mixed blessing? Why?

. . . So we surrendered to the white people and were told to go back to our homes and live our usual lives and attend to our crops. But the white men sent native police who did abominable things; they were cruel and assaulted a lot of our people and helped themselves to our cattle and goats. These policemen were not our own people; anybody was made a policeman. We were treated like slaves. They came and were overbearing and we were ordered to carry their clothes and bundles. They interfered with our wives and our daughters and molested them. In fact, the treatment we received was intolerable. We thought it best to fight and die rather than bear it. How the rebellion started I do not know; there was no organization, it was like a fire that suddenly flames up. We had been flogged by native police and then they rubbed salt water in the wounds. There was much bitterness because so many of our cattle were branded and taken away from us; we had no property, nothing we could call our own. We said, "It is no good living under such conditions; death would be better—let us fight." . . . We knew that we had very little chance because their weapons were so much superior to ours. But we meant to fight to the last, feeling that even if we could not beat them we might at least kill a few of them and so have some sort of revenge.

I fought in the rebellion. We used to look out for valleys where the white men were likely to approach. We took cover behind rocks and trees and tried to ambush them. We were forced by the nature of our weapons not to expose ourselves. I had a gun, a breech-loader. They—the white men— fought us with big guns and Maxims[1] and rifles.

From Margery Perham, ed., *Ten Africans* (London: Northwestern University Press, 1936), pp. 69–70, 72–75. Copyright © 1936 by Faber & Faber. Reprinted by permission.

[1]Invented by the American-born engineer Hiram S. Maxim, the Maxim gun was an early machine gun.

I remember a fight in the Matoppos when we charged the white men. There were some hundreds of us; the white men also were as many. We charged them at close quarters: we thought we had a good chance to kill them but the Maxims were too much for us. We drove them off at the first charge, but they returned and formed up again. We made a second charge, but they were too strong for us. I cannot say how many white people were killed, but we think it was quite a lot. . . . Many of our people were killed in this fight: I saw four of my cousins shot. One was shot in the jaw and the whole of his face was blown away—like this—and he died. One was hit between the eyes; another here, in the shoulder; another had part of his ear shot off. We made many charges but each time we were beaten off, until at last the white men packed up and retreated. But for the Maxims, it would have been different. . . .

So peace was made. Many of our people had been killed, and now we began to die of starvation; and then came the rinderpest[2] and the cattle that were still left to us perished. We could not help thinking that all these dreadful things were brought by the white people. We struggled, and the Government helped us with grain; and by degrees we managed to get crops and pulled through. Our cattle were practically wiped out, but a few were left and from them we slowly bred up our herds again. We were offered work in the mines and farms to earn money and so were able to buy back some cattle. At first, of course, we were not used to going out to work, but advice was given that the chief should advise the young people to go out to work, and gradually they went. At first we received a good price for our cattle and sheep and goats. Then the tax came. It was 10s.[3] a year. Soon the Government said, "That is too little, you must contribute more; you must pay £1." We did so. Then those who took more than one wife were taxed; 10s. for each additional wife. The tax is heavy, but that is not all. We are also taxed for our dogs; 5s. for a dog. Then we were told we were living on private land; the owners wanted rent in addition to the Government tax; some 10s. some £1, some £2 a year. . . .

Would I like to have the old days back? Well, the white men have brought some good things. For a start, they brought us European implements—plows; we can buy European clothes, which are an advance. The Government has arranged for education and through that, when our children grow up, they may rise in status. We want them to be educated and civilized and make better citizens. . . . But, under the white people, we still have our troubles. Economic conditions are telling on us very severely. We are on land where the rainfall is scanty, and things will not grow well. In our own time we could pick our own country, but now all the best land has been taken by the white people. We get hardly any price for our cattle; we find it hard to meet our money obligations. If we have crops to spare we get very little for them . . . but all the same our taxes do not diminish. We see no prosperous days ahead of us. There is one thing we think an injustice. When we have plenty of grain the prices are very low, but the moment we are short of grain and we have to buy from Europeans at once the price is high. If when we have hard times and find it difficult to meet our obligations some of these burdens were taken off us it would gladden our hearts. As it is, if we do raise anything, it is never our own: all, or most of it, goes back in taxation. We can never save any money. If we could, we could help ourselves: we could build ourselves better houses; we could buy modern means of traveling about, a cart, or donkeys or mules. . . .

---

[2]An acute infectious disease of cattle introduced to Africa in the 1890s.

[3]s = shilling, one-twentieth of a pound.

There are five schools in our district. Quite a number of people are Christians, but I am too old to change my ways. In our religion we believe that when anybody dies the spirit remains and we often make offerings to the spirits to keep them good-tempered. But now the making of offerings is dying out rapidly, for every member of the family should be present, but the children are Christians and refuse to come, so the spirit-worship is dying out. A good many of our children go to the mines in the Union, for the wages are better there. Unfortunately a large number do not come back at all. And some send money to their people—others do not. Some men have even deserted their families, their wives, and children. If they cannot go by train they walk long distances.

Currents of Change in Southwest Asia

The nineteenth century confirmed what had been apparent for at least a century, namely that misgovernment, economic stagnation, and military neglect had enfeebled the once-powerful and culturally sophisticated Persian and Ottoman empires. The Ottoman Empire lost its territories in North Africa and southeastern Europe, and it escaped military defeats by Russia and its onetime province, Egypt, only because Great Britain and France dreaded the consequences of its disintegration and intervened. Persia lost territory on each side of the Caspian Sea to Russia and lands around the Persian Gulf to Great Britain. At times, Russian and British consular officials in Tehran, not the shah, appeared to be in charge of Persian affairs. Economic development occurred, but most of it benefited European businessmen. Ottoman, Persian, and Egyptian governments all welcomed European investors and borrowed heavily from European financiers, who then "rescued" them from their debts in return for monopolies, control of governmental expenditures, and a cut of tax revenues.

Such developments were deeply unsettling to the region's rulers, who feared the collapse and ruin of their states, and humiliating to the region's Muslim majority, for whom victory on the battlefield had always been seen as a sign of Allah's favor. For both groups, the looming question was how to restore Muslim power and the dignity of the Islamic community. One answer had already been provided by Abd al-Wahhab in the late eighteenth century (see source 46). For him and his followers reform meant restoring Islam to its original, pristine form by refocusing on the Quran and Hadith and ridding the faith of all the accretions and innovations that over the ages had corrupted the faith.

This narrowly religious approach to reform garnered continued support in the nineteenth century but had many competitors. In the early 1800s, for Ottoman sultans, Persian shahs, and Egyptian khedives, reform meant strengthening their states by reorganizing the military, ending corruption, improving tax collection, and reforming the judiciary while preserving their authoritarian rule. Reformers in this camp cautiously approved greater intellectual and cultural contacts with the West and accepted the need for European investment. By the 1870s in the Ottoman Empire and in the 1890s in Persia, reformers went further. Islamic modernists advocated plans for economic development, fully accepted Western science, and demanded parliaments, written constitutions, elections, and guarantees of individual freedoms, including freedoms for women.

Reformers of every stripe faced formidable obstacles. Their plans and programs were resisted by powerful families and well-placed officials who benefited from the status quo. They also faced the challenge of convincing Muslims that proposed reforms, many of which were inspired by Western ideas and institutions, were not "un-Islamic." Costs were another problem. The price tag of modern armies, expanded bureaucracies, schools, roads, telegraph lines, bridges, and steamboats outstripped revenues, forcing governments to rely on European loans and investments and accept European control of taxes and expenditures. In other words, the reformers' policies fostered greater economic dependency on the West, one of the things the reformers most wished to avoid.

Despite their achievements, reformers were unable to halt Western intervention or stave off political disaster. Egypt remained a British protectorate. Persia experienced a constitutional revolution in 1905 and 1906, but the result was civil war and the division of the country into a Russian north and a British south, with only the central portion under Persian authority. The Ottoman Empire also experienced political revolution. In 1908, an array of groups coalesced to revive parliamentary government and in 1909 deposed the authoritarian sultan Abdulhamid II. But under its new leaders, the empire lost all but a tiny sliver of its European territories as a result of the Balkan Wars of 1912 and 1913 and lost its Arab provinces during and after World War I. It disappeared altogether when the sultan's government was overthrown by Turkish nationalists in 1920 and replaced by the present-day state of Turkey.

Ottoman Reforms in the Tanzimat Era

69 • SULTAN ABDULMEJID, THE ISLAHAT FERMANI OF 1856

A new era of reform for the Ottoman Empire began on November 3, 1839, when before an assemblage of state officials, dignitaries, religious leaders, and foreign luminaries, Foreign Minister Mustafa Reshid Pasha read, on behalf of the sixteen-year-old Sultan Abdulmejid, a decree that spelled out a program of action to restore the empire to its lost glory after a 150-year descent into "weakness and poverty." With language borrowed from the French Declaration of the Rights of Man and of the Citizen and the American Bill of Rights, the edict promised laws to prohibit bribery, regulate army recruitment and tax collection, and guarantee the security of life and property. Such laws would apply to all Ottoman subjects, with no distinction between Muslims, Christians, and Jews. This edict, known as the "Noble Edict" or the "Rose Chamber Edict," after the palace room in which it was read, launched a three-decade period of *Tanzimat* ("restructuring"), in which reform went beyond revamping the army.

Seventeen years after issuing the Noble Edict, in 1856, Sultan Abdulmejid issued the *Islahat Fermani* (Reform Edict), in which he renewed his government's commitment to reform and proposed a number of new policies. It represents the high point of efforts to reform the Ottoman Empire while maintaining the powers of the sultan and the traditional mix of Muslim, Christian, and Jewish subjects.

QUESTIONS FOR ANALYSIS

1. What benefits were the sultan's non-Muslim subjects to receive as result of this proclamation?
2. What efforts were made to improve the empire's system of justice?
3. What specific economic reforms are proposed? What do they reveal about the state of the empire's economy?
4. To what extent does this document extend meaningful political rights to the sultan's subjects?
5. In what respects does this document reflect European liberal ideas of individual freedom and religious toleration?

Let it be done as herein set forth. . . . It being now my desire to renew and enlarge still more the new Institutions ordained with the view of establishing a state of things conformable with the dignity of my Empire and— . . . by the kind and friendly assistance of the Great Powers, my noble Allies,[1] . . . The guarantees promised on our part by the Hatti-Humaïoun of Gülhané,[2] and in conformity with the Tanzimat, . . . are today confirmed and consolidated, and efficacious measures shall be taken in order that they may have their full and entire effect.

All the privileges and spiritual immunities granted by my ancestors from time immemorial, and at subsequent dates, to all Christian communities or other non-Muslim persuasions established in my empire, under my protection, shall be confirmed and maintained.

Every Christian or other non-Muslim community shall be bound within a fixed period, and with the concurrence of a commission composed . . . of members of its own body, to proceed with my high approbation and under the inspection of my Sublime Porte,[3] to examine into its actual immunities and privileges, and to discuss and submit to my Sublime Porte the reforms required by the progress of civilization and of the age. The powers conceded to the Christian Patriarchs and Bishops[4] by the Sultan Mehmed II[5] and his successors, shall be made to harmonize with the new position which my generous and beneficent intentions ensure to these communities. . . . The ecclesiastical dues, of

Source: E. A. van Dyck, *Report upon the Capitulations of the Ottoman Empire* (Washington D.C.: U.S. Government Printing Office, 1881, 1882), Part I, pp. 106–108.

[1]During the Crimean War (1853–1856), the Ottoman Empire was allied with Great Britain and France against Russia. After the war, both its European allies encouraged the Ottoman government to affirm its commitment to reform.
[2]A reference to the Noble Edict of 1839.
[3]"Sublime Porte," or "High Gate," refers to the gate in Istanbul giving access to the buildings that house the offices of state officials. It came to refer to the sultan's government in much the same way that the term "the White House" refers to the U.S. presidency.
[4]A reference to the heads of the Greek and Armenian Christian churches in the empire.
[5]Mehmed the Great, sultan from 1451 to 1481, authorized autonomous religious communities to give his non-Muslim subjects religious freedom and gain their support.

whatever sort of nature they be, shall be abolished and replaced by fixed revenues of the Patriarchs and heads of communities. . . . In the towns, small boroughs, and villages, where the whole population is of the same religion, no obstacle shall be offered to the repair, according to their original plan, of buildings set apart for religious worship, for schools, for hospitals, and for cemeteries. . . .

Every distinction or designation tending to make any class whatever of the subject of my Empire inferior to another class, on account of their religion, language, or race, shall be forever effaced from Administrative Protocol. The laws shall be put in force against the use of any injurious or offensive term, either among private individuals or on the part of the authorities. . . .

As all forms of religion are and shall be freely professed in my dominions, no subject of my Empire shall be hindered in the exercise of the religion that he professes. . . . No one shall be compelled to change their religion . . . and . . . all the subjects of my Empire, without distinction of nationality, shall be admissible to public employments. . . . All the subjects of my Empire, without distinction, shall be received into the civil and military schools of the government . . . Moreover, every community is authorized to establish public schools of science, art, and industry. . . .

All commercial, correctional, and criminal suits between Muslims and Christian or other non-Muslim subjects, or between Christian or other non-Muslims of different sects, shall be referred to Mixed Tribunals. The proceedings of these Tribunals shall be public; the parties shall be confronted, and shall produce their witnesses, whose testimony shall be received, without distinction, upon an oath taken according to the religious law of each sect. . . .

Penal, correctional, and commercial laws, and rules of procedure for the Mixed Tribunals, shall be drawn up as soon as possible, and formed into a code. . . . Proceedings shall be taken, for the reform of the penitentiary system. . . .

The organization of the police . . . shall be revised in such a manner as to give to all the peaceable subjects of my Empire the strongest guarantees for the safety both of their persons and property. . . . Christian subjects, and those of other non-Muslim sects, . . . shall, as well as Muslims, be subject to the obligations of the Law of Recruitment [for military service]. The principle of obtaining substitutes, or of purchasing exemption, shall be admitted.

Proceedings shall be taken for a reform in the constitution of the Provincial and Communal Councils, in order to ensure fairness in the choice of the deputies of the Muslim, Christian, and other communities, and freedom of voting in the Councils. . . .

As the laws regulating the purchase, sale, and disposal of real property are common to all the subjects of my Empire, it shall be lawful for foreigners to possess landed property in my dominions. . . .

The taxes are to be levied under the same denomination from all the subjects of my Empire, without distinction of class or of religion. The most prompt and energetic means for remedying the abuses in collecting the taxes, and especially the tithes, shall be considered. The system of direct collection shall gradually, and as soon as possible, be substituted for the plan of farming,[6] in all the branches of the revenues of the state.

A special law having been already passed, which declares that the budget of the revenue and the expenditure of the state shall be drawn up and made known every year, the said law shall be most scrupulously observed. . . .

The heads of each community and a delegate, designated by my Sublime Porte, shall be

---

[6]Tax farming, a practice by which the government contracted with private financiers who collected taxes and kept a certain percentage for themselves.

summoned to take part in the deliberations of the Supreme Council of Justice on all occasions which might interest the generality of the subjects of my Empire. . . .

Steps shall be taken for the formation of banks and other similar institutions, so as to effect a reform in the monetary and financial system, as well as to create funds to be employed in augmenting the sources of the material wealth of my empire.

Everything that can impede commerce or agriculture shall be abolished. To accomplish these objects means shall be sought to profit by science, the art, and the funds of Europe, and thus gradually to execute them.

Tanzimat's Failures: An Arab Perspective

70 • ABD AL-RAHMAN AL-KAWAKIBI, MOTHER OF TOWNS

For most of the nineteenth century, the Arabs were the Ottoman sultan's least troublesome non-Turkish subjects. Attached to the Ottoman state through habits of loyalty and their perception that the sultan/caliph was the protector of the world-wide Islamic community, the Arabs, unlike Kurds, Armenians, and Balkan Christians, experienced no surge of nationalism and made no demands for independence or greater autonomy. This began to change, however, in the 1890s, when disillusion-ment with government policies and continued military failure weakened the Arabs' faith in Ottoman rule. The empire, some suggested, was no longer capable of de-fending the interests of Islam; a few went further to suggest that the Islamic com-munity would continue to decline until its founders and natural leaders, the Arabs, regained control.

One of the first spokespersons of Arab nationalism was the Syrian journalist Abd al-Rahman al-Kawakibi, who was born in 1849 into a wealthy family in the Syrian city of Aleppo and died in 1902 in Cairo, perhaps after having been poisoned by Ottoman agents. Kawakibi spent most of his life in Aleppo, where he edited two newspapers, tried his hand as a tobacco merchant, held several administrative posts, and carried on a series of running battles with local Ottoman officials. In 1899, he secretly left Aleppo for Cairo to escape persecution from the Ottoman governor. There, he published two books, *The Characteristics of Tyranny,* a scathing denunciation of Ottoman rule, and *Mother of Towns,* a fictionalized account of an imagined meet-ing in Mecca at which Muslim intellectuals discuss the reasons for Islamic stagnation. In the following excerpt, the character Al-Sayyid al-Furati (probably representing Kawakibi) discusses how the Ottoman government has contributed to the sorry state of Islam.

QUESTIONS FOR ANALYSIS

1. Kawakibi, speaking through the character of Al-Furati, traces "most of the disor-ders" of the Ottoman state back to the beginnings of the Tanzimat Era. Why?
2. How, according to Kawakibi, has the Ottoman drive for administrative centraliza-tion weakened the state?

3. According to Kawakibi, how successfully has the Ottoman state implemented the Tanzimat commitment to the equal treatment of all ethnic and religious groups in the empire?
4. According to Kawakibi, how has Ottoman authoritarianism undermined the empire?
5. How does Kawakibi explain the deplorable state of Turkish–Arab relations? How, in his view, can they be improved?

Then al-Sayyid al-Furati said: ". . . Inasmuch as the disorder that exists in the fundamental administration of Islamic governments has an important role in producing the general stagnation, I therefore add the following causes . . . , enumerating them by means of the headings of the problem only.

"Moreover, the causes that I will mention are the fundamental origins of the disorder in the current policies and administration of the Ottoman empire, this most powerful state whose affairs concern all Muslims. It has experienced most of these disorders in the last 60 years, that is, after it rushed to reorganize its affairs.[1] In doing so, it damaged its ancient foundations . . . , so that its condition deteriorated, especially in the last 20 years, during which time two thirds of the kingdom was lost and the remaining third was destroyed. Among the factors determining the ruin of the state was the loss of men and the squandering of the sultan's power for the sake of preserving his noble self and persisting in his autocratic policies. . . .

"The causes I wish to discuss in summary form are the following.
• Standardization of administrative and penal laws despite differences in the characteristics of the empire's parts and differences in the inhabitants in terms of [their] races and customs. . . .
• Adherence to the principle of centralized administration despite the distance of certain parts from the capital; administrative leadership should reside in those distant parts [so as to know] the situations and the particular features of their inhabitants.
• Administrative confusion resulting from inattention to the integration of morals with procedures among ministers, governors, and commanders. The state must select them from among all the races and nationalities found in the kingdom in order to satisfy them.
• Adhering to [the practice of] racial inconsistencies in the hiring of [government] officials, with the aim of complicating understanding between the officials and the [local] inhabitants and rendering it impractical for them to intermix and secure the administration; this makes agreement upon administrative policy impossible. . . .
• Gross discrimination among various subject races regarding subsidies and penalties.
• Carelessness in the selection of [government] employees and officials, needlessly employing too many of them with the purpose of sustaining cliques, favorites, and habitual flatterers.
• Permissiveness in reward and reproof due to inattention to whether administrative matters are done well or badly, as if the empire had no master. . .
• Loss of sanctity of religious law and the force of [secular] law by not abiding by and executing [them], and insisting on administration being methodical in name but arbitrary in practice.

Source: Translation by Joseph G. Rahme. Printed in Charles Kurzman, ed., *Modernist Islam, 1840–1940* (Oxford: Oxford University Press, 2002), pp. 154–157. Reprinted by permission of Oxford University Press.

[1]A reference to the Tanzimat movement.

- Failure to attend to the customs of the inhabitants, their morale, and their welfare so as to gain their affection, not just outward obedience.
- Obtuseness toward or willful neglect of the needs of the times, the challenge of events, and the progress of the inhabitants, due to a of lack of concern for the future.
- Suppression of awakened thought in an effort to forbid its growth, development, and [to suppress] inquiry into administrative activities, their merits and defects . . .
- Administration of the treasury in a loose manner, without any supervision; purchasing without budgeting; extravagance without reprimand; and damage without any accounting, until the empire became mortgaged to foreigners with heavy debts that are being paid with [the loss of] territory, sovereignty, blood, and rights.
- Administration of important political and civilian interests without consultation of the subjects, and the refusal to discuss them—even though its damage in every act of omission and commission was well known.
- Administration of external affairs through bootlicking, appeasement, the compromise of rights, bribery, capitulations, and money; the administration expends all of that on its neighbors so that they will turn a blind eye to the [country's] destructive, painful sights, and they will put up with the rotten stink of their rule. . . .

Then al-Sayyid al-Furati said: . . .

"There is no disagreement about the fact that one of the most important maxims of governments is to adopt the characters of the subjects, and to unite with them in habits and tastes, even if the habits are not good in themselves. The least a foreign government should do is conform to the subjects' characters, . . . at least until it succeeds in attracting them to its language, then to its morals, then to its nationality. . . . The only exception in this regard was the Turkish Moghuls—that is, the Ottomans, who, on the contrary, take pride in preserving the otherness of their subjects, so that they do not seek their Turkification, nor do they agree to become Arabized; the contemporary ones are becoming Frenchified or Germanified. There is no rational cause for such [behavior] except their intense hatred toward the Arabs, as can be proved by the proverbs about Arabs that flow from their tongues:

—their use of the phrase *'dilenci Arab,'* that is, 'Arab beggar,' for Arabs of the Hijaz [the western part of the Arabian Peninsula].

—their use of the phrase *'kör fellah,'* meaning 'rude peasant,' for Egyptians. . . .

—their use of the term *'Arab'* for slaves and black animals.

—their saying, *'pis Arab,'* that is, 'filthy Arab.'

—*'Arab akh,'* that is, 'Arab mind,' or small; *'Arab tabian,'* that is, 'Arab taste,' or corrupt; *'Arab çenesi,'* that is, 'Arab jawbone,' or excessive babble.

—their saying, *'Bunu yaparsam Arab olayim,'* that is, 'If I do that, may I become an Arab.' . . .

"To all that, the Arabs do not reciprocate, except with two expressions. The first is the Arab saying about them: 'Three were created for oppression and decay: lice, Turks, and the plague.' And the second expression: calling [Turks] 'Byzantines,'[2] an indication of suspicion about their Islamic faith. The cause of this suspicion is that the Turks did not serve Islam, except for the establishment of a few mosques—and if it were not for their rulers wanting to have their names mentioned from the pulpits, even these would not have been established."

---

[2] A reference to the Christian Byzantine Empire, overthrown by the Ottomans in 1453.

The Lure of Concessions

71 • AN AGREEMENT BETWEEN G. F. TALBOT AND THE PERSIAN GOVERNMENT, MARCH 8, 1890

European imperialism did not always involve gunboats, invading armies, and control by colonial administrators; it frequently had more to do with economics than politics. The Ottoman Empire and Persia, for example, remained independent states in the 1800s, but their finances and economies were increasingly controlled and manipulated by European bondholders, bankers, businessmen, and speculators. Their experiences are as much a part of the West's imperialist expansion as those of India, Africa, and Southeast Asia.

For Persia, economic imperialism was epitomized by the numerous government concessions granted to foreign businessmen. These agreements gave Europeans control of a sector of the nation's economy, usually in return for a onetime payment and a percentage of profits. Viewed as a painless way to attract foreign capital, erase deficits, and generate bribes, such arrangements were irresistible to Persian officials. Hundreds of concessions were granted for activities ranging from railroad construction to the administration of a national lottery.

The economic, financial, and legal details of the following document, by which English businessman G. F. Talbot gained a monopoly over the purchase, processing, and marketing of tobacco throughout Persia, was typical of many others. The public's response to the document, however, was exceptional. As the number of concessions mounted in the 1870s and 1880s, many Persians became increasingly frustrated over their inability to dissuade their concession-loving ruler, Shah Nasir al-Din, from selling off the nation's economic future to foreigners. Then, in 1890, they learned of the tobacco concession granted to Talbot. Persians faced the prospect of paying inflated prices for a product they grew, used heavily, and previously had marketed themselves. The country erupted with demonstrations, angry sermons, calls for boycotts, destruction of warehouses, and denunciations of the shah, who, in late 1891, backed down and canceled the concession.

The uproar over the tobacco concession had important ramifications. To pay the indemnities arising from the cancellation agreement, the government contracted a large loan, which opened the door to more borrowing and near bankruptcy in the following decade. More importantly, the events of 1890 and 1891 united merchants, journalists, intellectuals, religious leaders, and everyday Persians in a successful political cause and planted the seeds of the notion that other similar movements might be possible. In this respect, they set the stage for Persia's Constitutional Revolution of 1906 and 1907.

QUESTIONS FOR ANALYSIS

1. What financial benefits accrued to the Persian government as a result of the arrangements spelled out in the agreement?
2. Given that the British anticipated profits of approximately £500,000 per year from the tobacco concession, how equitable were the financial arrangements spelled out in the agreement?
3. In what ways did the agreement limit the powers of the Persian government?

4. It would appear that articles 2 and 6 were meant to protect Persian tobacco farmers and sellers, yet both groups bitterly opposed the agreement. What are some possible explanations for this?

The monopoly of buying, selling, and manufacturing all the tootoon[1] and tobacco . . . in the Kingdom of Persia is granted to Major Talbot by us for fifty years from the date of the signing of this Concession, in accordance with the following stipulations:—

1. The concessionnaires will have to pay £15,000. per annum to the exalted Imperial Treasury whether they benefit or lose by this business . . .

2. In order merely to ascertain the quantities of tootoon and tobacco produced in the protected provinces (of Persia) the concessionnaires will keep a register of the cultivators who wish to work under the conditions of this Concession, and the Persian Government will issue strict orders to the local Governors to compel the cultivators of tobacco and tootoon to furnish such a registration.

Permission for sale, &c., of tootoon, tobacco, cigars, cigarettes, snuff, &c., is the absolute right of the concessionnaires, and no one but the proprietors of this Concession shall have the right to issue the abovementioned permits.

The Guilds of the sellers of tobacco and tootoon who are engaged in this trade will remain permanent in their local trade and transactions, on condition of possessing permits which will be given to them by the concessionnaires.

3. After deducting all the expenses appertaining to this business and paying a dividend of 5 percent on their own capital to the proprietors of this Concession, one quarter of the remaining profit will yearly be paid to the exalted Imperial Treasury, . . .

4. All the materials necessary for this work which the proprietors of this Concession import into the protected provinces (Persia) will be free of all customs duties, taxes, &c.

5. Removal and transfer of tootoon and tobacco in the protected provinces (of Persia) without the permission of the proprietors of this Concession is prohibited. . . .

6. The proprietors of this Concession . . . must purchase all the tobacco, &c., fit for use that is now in hand, and the price that is to be given to the owner or the producer will be settled in a friendly manner . . . , but in case of disagreement between the parties the case will be referred to an Arbitrator accepted by both sides, and the decision of the Arbitrator will be final. . . .

7. The Persian Government engages not to increase the revenues, taxes, and customs that are now levied on tootoon, tobacco, cigars, cigarettes, and snuff for fifty years from the date of the signing of the Concession. . . .

8. Any person or persons who shall attempt to evade (the rules) of these Articles will be severely punished by the Government, and any person or persons found to be secretly in possession of tobacco, tootoon, &c., for sale or trade, will also be fined [and] severely punished by the Government. . . .

14. In case of misunderstanding arising between the Persian Government and the proprietors of this Concession, that misunderstanding shall be referred to an Arbitrator accepted by both sides, and in case of the impossibility of consent to the appointment of an Arbitrator, the matter will be referred to the arbitration of one of the Representatives, resident at Tehran, of the Government of the United States, Germany, or Austria, to appoint an Arbitrator, whose decision shall be final.

Source: Great Britain, *Parliamentary Papers,* 1892, vol. 79, pp. 211–213.

[1]Tootoon, or toutoun, is a type of tobacco grown in northwest Persia that was ground into a coarse yellowish powder and smoked in long wooden pipes with earthenware heads. It was less popular than tobacco, or tombakou, which was smoked in water pipes.

The Beginnings of Islamic Modernism

BACKGROUND

During the nineteenth century, intellectual life in the worldwide Islamic community underwent profound changes. Traditional religious schools—madrasahs—continued to offer their instruction in the Arabic language, interpretation of the Quran and Hadith, logic, and Muslim history. Their graduates continued to enter the ranks of the ulema—religious scholars who served the Islamic community as teachers, judges, mosque leaders, and advisers to the great and powerful. Neither the madrasahs nor the ulema maintained their educational and intellectual monopoly, however. This was the inevitable consequence of a number of factors: the beginning of a flourishing publishing industry; the proliferation of state-sponsored colleges and universities that provided training in Western law, engineering, military science, and medicine; increased opportunities for Muslims to travel, especially to Europe; and a general increase in literacy, in which missionary schools played a small but important part. The result was the emergence of a new type of Islamic intellectual who may have lacked the expertise necessary to interpret traditional religious sources but who could read books in European languages, discuss new developments in engineering and medicine, make arguments based on European law codes, and discuss the history and current affairs in the non-Muslim world.

Islamic intellectual life also was transformed by the new and suddenly urgent need to understand and reverse the Islamic community's descent into a state of political impotence and cultural stagnation, a descent made more painful when compared to the successes of the robust, prosperous, and well-governed societies of Europe. As the nineteenth century unfolded, all but a few intellectuals conceded that the revival of Islamic societies would require some borrowing from the West, although they were acutely aware that many Muslims were deeply troubled by the prospect of a future in which "modernization" would marginalize Islam and undermine longstanding traditions. In response to such concerns, there emerged an important group of Islamic modernists—intellectuals who argued that there was no intrinsic incompatibility between Islam and modern values such as scientific inquiry, rationalism, freedom of religious interpretation, constitutionalism, nationalism, and women's rights. The tensions that did exist resulted from historical accidents or from misreading Islam's true teaching. Such accidents and misreadings could be repaired, and once accomplished, Islam would be renewed and its world prominence restored.

In addition to publicizing their views through traditional lecturing and teaching, Islamic modernizers took advantage of rising literacy rates and the emerging publishing industry by incorporating their ideas into novels, plays, and travel books and contributing news stories and editorials to newspapers, journals, and magazines. As a result, ideas that at first had appealed to a relatively small group of intellectuals came to inspire large numbers of Muslims who sent their sons and daughters to reformed Islamic schools, purchased books, subscribed to modernist journals, and supported constitutional revolutions in Persia in 1906 and the Ottoman Empire in 1908. In the early twenty-first century, despite challenges from many quarters, the goal of reconciling Islam and modern progressive values continues to have broad support.

THE SOURCES

The sources we have chosen are meant to show how Islamic modernists shared a set of common assumptions and values despite the variety of their interests. We begin with two excerpts from works by Sayyid Jamal ad-Din al-Afghani, the best-known and most-traveled Islamic intellectual of the late nineteenth century. The first excerpt is from "Teaching and Learning," a lecture Afghani presented in Kolkata, India, in 1882. This is followed by an excerpt from an essay, "Answer to Renan," written in Paris in 1883 as a response to comments by the French philosopher Ernest Renan (1823–1892) that Arabs are inherently unsuited for science and Islam is hostile to it.

The fact that Afghani wrote one of these works in India and the other in France just a few months later indicates the kind of life he led. He was born in 1838 or early 1839 in Persia, despite later adopting the name Afghani ("the Afghan") to avoid identification with Shia Islam. He was educated at home and at various schools in Persia and the Shia holy city of Najaf, but the decisive experience of his youth took place in Muslim India, which he visited in his late teens and stayed a year or more. Here, he learned to hate Western imperialism but admire Western learning. After leaving India, his life took on a pattern of constant movement and travel to cities that included Kabul, Kolkata, Istanbul, Cairo, Paris, London, Tehran, Munich, Moscow, St. Petersburg, and several cities in Uzbekistan. Wherever he went, he wrote, taught, and lectured about Islamic unity and Muslims' need to adopt Western science and philosophy. He died and was buried in 1897 in Istanbul, where Ottoman Sultan Abdulhamid II, who was attracted to his pan-Islamic ideas, had provided him a small stipend.

Our second excerpt is taken from two works by the Egyptian writer Qasim Amin, *The Liberation of Women* (1899) and *The New Woman* (1900). Qasim Amin was born in 1863 in Alexandria to an Egyptian mother and a Turkish father who had retired to Egypt after serving as governor of Kurdistan. After attending the best Egyptian schools and earning a law degree in Cairo, he pursued further legal studies in France, where he became acquainted with Sayyid Jamal ad-Din al-Afghani and helped produce a journal with the prominent (and temporarily exiled) Egyptian modernist Muhammad Abduh (1849–1905). On his return to Egypt, Amin became a successful lawyer and judge. In 1899, with the publication of his *The Liberation of Women,* he provided a powerful male voice in support of the nascent Egyptian feminist movement that was gaining strength among upper-class Egyptian women in the 1890s. This was followed by *The New Woman,* published in 1900.

The third excerpt is taken from *Government from the Perspective of Islam* by the Persian religious scholar Muhammad Husayn Na'ini (1860–1936). It reveals the attraction of constitutionalism to many modernist Islamic thinkers. Destined for a scholarly career, Na'ini received his original training at the politically conservative Shia seminary in Isfahan, but in the late 1880s, he was converted to the cause of political reform as a result of his studies in Najaf, an important religious center in Ottoman territory. Here, he was tutored by Hasan Shirazi, a cleric who in 1891, had played a key role in the campaign against the British tobacco concession. He also was influenced by Sayyid Jamal ad-Din al-Afghani, who resided for a time in Najaf and was a bitter enemy of the Persian shah. Amin became part of the group of religious scholars who advocated political reform and constitutionalism in the years leading to the Persian revolution of 1906. Returning to Tehran, he threw himself into the chaotic struggle that followed the revolution. His *Government from the Perspective of Islam,* published in 1909, was written to defend constitutionalism and parliamentary government against monarchist counterrevolutionaries. Although he later disavowed some of its arguments, his book remains an important statement of the dangers of monarchical and clerical despotism.

QUESTIONS FOR ANALYSIS

1. What do the authors have to say about the "state of Islam" at the time they are writing? What do they criticize? What hopeful signs do they see for Islam's future?
2. What explanations do the authors provide for the decline of Muslim societies in comparison to the West? On what points do they agree and disagree?
3. How do the authors make use of historical arguments to convince their readers that what they are recommending—science, women's rights, and constitutionalism—are not intrinsically counter to Islam?
4. All three authors realize that their ideas have obstacles to overcome before general acceptance in the Islamic community. What are some of these obstacles?
5. What groups in Islamic societies would find the ideas of authors such as these most attractive? What groups would most likely oppose them?

1 • Sayyid Jamal ad-Din al-Afghani, "Teaching and Learning" and "Answer to Renan"

Teaching and Learning

How difficult it is to speak about science. There is no end or limit to science. The benefits of science are immeasurable; and these finite thoughts cannot encompass what is infinite.

Thus I say: If someone looks deeply into the question, he will see that science rules the world. . . .

The Europeans have now put their hands on every part of the world. The English have reached Afghanistan; the French have seized Tunisia. In

Source: From Sayyid Jamal ad-Din al-Afghani, *An Islamic Response to Imperialism: Political and Religious Writings of Sayyid Jamal ad-Din "al-Afghani,"* translated by Nikki R. Keddie, (Berkeley: University of California Press 1968), pp. 102, 103, 105–107, 182–185. Reprinted by permission of Nikki Keddie.

reality this usurpation, aggression, and conquest have not come from the French or the English. Rather it is science that everywhere manifests its greatness and power. . . . More than this, if we study the riches of the world, we learn that wealth is the result of commerce, industry, and agriculture. Agriculture is achieved only with agricultural science, botanical chemistry, and geometry. Industry is produced only with physics, chemistry, mechanics, geometry, and mathematics; and commerce is based on agriculture and industry.

Thus it is evident that all wealth and riches are the result of science. There are no riches in the world without science, and there is no wealth in the world other than science. . . .

. . . Thus, I say that the Muslims these days do not see any benefit from their education. . . . For long years they expend philosophic thought on grammar to no avail, and after finishing they are unable to speak, write, or understand Arabic.

Rhetoric . . . is the science that enables a man to become a writer, speaker, and poet. However, we see these days that after studying that science they are incapable of correcting their everyday speech.

Logic, which is the balance [scale] for ideas, should make everyone who acquires it capable of distinguishing every truth from falsehood and every right from wrong. However, we see that the minds of our Muslim logicians are full of every superstition and vanity, and no difference exists between their ideas and the ideas of the masses of the bazaar.

Philosophy is the science that deals with the state of external beings, and their causes, reasons, needs, and requisites. It is strange that our 'ulama' [religious scholars] . . . , vaingloriously call themselves sages, and despite this they cannot distinguish their left hand from their right hand, and they do not ask: Who are we and what is right and proper for us? They never ask the causes of electricity, the steamboat, and railroads. . . .

. . . Shame on such a philosopher, and shame on such philosophy. . . .

Hence we can say that reform will never be achieved by the Muslims except if the leaders of our religion first reform themselves and gather the fruits of their science and knowledge.

Answer to Renan

. . . And, since humanity, at its origin, did not know the causes of the events that passed under its eyes and the secrets of things, it was perforce led to follow the advice of its teachers and the orders they gave. This obedience was imposed in the name of the supreme Being to whom the educators attributed all events, without permitting men to discuss its utility or its disadvantages . . .

If it is true that the Muslim religion is an obstacle to the development of sciences, can one affirm that this obstacle will not disappear someday? . . . All religions are intolerant, each one in its way. The Christian religion . . . has emerged from the first period to which I have just alluded; thenceforth free and independent, it seems to advance rapidly on the road of progress and science, whereas Muslim society has not yet freed itself from the tutelage of religion. Realizing, however, that the Christian religion preceded the Muslim religion in the world by many centuries. I cannot keep from hoping that Muhammadan society will succeed someday in breaking its bonds and marching resolutely in the path of civilization after the manner of Western society, for which the Christian faith, despite its rigors and intolerance, was not at all an invincible obstacle. . . .

No one denies that the Arab people, while still in the state of barbarism, rushed into the road of intellectual and scientific progress with a rapidity only equaled by the speed of its conquests, since in the space of a century, it acquired and assimilated almost all the Greek and Persian sciences that had developed slowly during several centuries on their native soil. . . .

Rome and Byzantium were then the seats of theological and philosophical sciences, as well as the shining center and burning hearth of all human knowledge. Having followed for several centuries the path of civilization, the Greeks and Romans walked with assurance over the vast field of science and philosophy. There came, however, a time when their researches were abandoned and their studies interrupted.

The monuments they had built to science collapsed, and their most precious books were relegated to oblivion. The Arabs, ignorant and barbaric as they were in origin took up what had been abandoned by the civilized nations, rekindled the extingushed sciences, developed them and gave them a brilliance they had never had. Is not this the index and proof of their natural love for sciences? It is true that the Arabs took from the Greeks their philosophy . . . ; but these sciences . . . they developed, extended,

clarified, perfected, completed, and coordinated with a perfect taste and a rare precision and exactitude. Besides, the French, the Germans, and the English . . . made no effort in this direction until Arab civilization lit up with its reflections the summits of the Pyrenees and poured its light and riches on the Occident. . . . Is there not in this another proof, no less evident, of the intellectual superiority of the Arabs and of their natural attachment to philosophy? It is true that after the fall of the Arab kingdom . . . , the countries that had become the great centers of science, like Iraq and Andalusia [Muslim Iberia], fell again into ignorance and became the center of religious fanaticism; but one cannot conclude from this sad spectacle that the scientific and philosophic progress of the Middle Ages was not due to the Arab people who ruled at that time.

2 • Qasim Amin, The Liberation of Women and The New Woman

The Liberation of Women

I call on every lover of truth to examine with me the status of women in Egyptian society. I am confident that such individuals will arrive independently at the same conclusion I have, namely the necessity of improving the status of Egyptian women. . . .

Some people will say that today I am publishing heresy. To these people I will respond: Yes, I have come up with a heresy, but the heresy is not against Islam. It is against our traditions and social dealings, which ought to be brought to perfection. Why should a Muslim believe that traditions cannot be changed or replaced by new ones, and that it is his duty to preserve them forever? . . . Is not tradition merely the set of

conventions of a country defining the special customs appropriate to its life and behavior at a specific time and place? . . .

This evidence of history confirms and demonstrates that the status of women is inseparably tied to the status of a nation. When the status of a nation is low, reflecting an uncivilized condition for that nation, the status of women is also low, and when the status of a nation is elevated, reflecting the progress and civilization of that nation, the status of women in that country is also elevated. . . . Prior to Islam, it was acceptable for Arab fathers to kill their daughters, and for men to gratify themselves with women with no legal bonds or numerical limits. This authority still prevails among uncivilized African and American tribes. Some Asians even believe that a woman has no immortal soul, and that she should not live after her husband dies. Other Asians present her to their guests as

Source: From Qasim Amin, *The Liberation of Women and the New Woman: Two Documents in the History of Egyptian* *Feminism* (Cairo, Egypt: American University Press in Cairo, 2000), pp. 3–10, 200.

a sign of hospitality, just as one would present a guest with the best of his possessions. . . .

On the other hand, we find that women in nations with a more advanced civilization have gradually advanced from the low status to which they have been relegated, and have started to overcome the gap that has separated them from men. . . . The American woman is in the forefront, followed by the British, the German, the French, the Austrian, the Italian, and the Russian woman, and so on. Women in all these societies have felt that they deserve their independence, and are searching for the means to achieve it. . . .

Westerners, who like to associate all good things with their religion, believe that the Western woman has advanced because her Christian religion helped her achieve freedom. This belief, however, is inaccurate. Christianity did not set up a system which guarantees the freedom of women; it does not guarantee her rights through either specific or general rules; and it does not prescribe any guiding principles on this topic. . . . If there were a religion which could have had power and influence over local traditions, then the Muslim women today should have been at the forefront of free women on earth.

Islam declared women's freedom and emancipation, and granted women all human rights during a time when women occupied the lowest status in all societies. According to Islamic law, women are considered to possess the same legal capabilities in all civil cases pertaining to buying, donating, trusteeship, and disposal of goods, unhindered by requirements of permission from either their father or their husband. . . .

Within the *shari'a* [the body of Islamic law], the tendency to equate men's and women's rights is obvious even in the context of divorce. Islam has created for women mechanisms worthy of consideration and contrary to what Westerners and some Muslims imagine or believe. . . .

In summary, nothing in the laws of Islam or in its intentions can account for the low status of Muslim women. The existing situation is contrary to the law, because originally women in Islam were granted an equal place in human society.

What a pity! Unacceptable customs, traditions, and superstitions inherited from the countries in which Islam spread have been allowed to permeate this beautiful religion. . . .

The most significant factor that accounts for the perpetuation of these traditions, however, is the succession over us of despotic governments.

A despot spits his spirit into every powerful person, who, whenever possible, dominates a weaker one. This attitude pervades the life of all individuals, regardless of the approval or disapproval of the supreme ruler. These despotic systems have also influenced the relationships between men and women—man in his superiority began to despise woman in her weakness. As a result, corrupt morals became the first sign of a country ruled by a despot. . . .

Despising the woman, a man filled his home with slaves, white or black, or with numerous wives, satisfying himself with any of them whenever his passion and lust drove him. . . .

Despising the woman, a man divorced her without reason.

Despising the woman, a man sat alone at the dining table, while his mother, sisters, and wife gathered after he was done to eat what was left over.

Despising the woman, a man appointed a guardian to protect her chastity. . . .

Despising the woman, a man imprisoned her in the house and boasted about her permanent restriction, which was lifted only when she was to be carried in her coffin to the grave. . . .

Despising the woman, a man secluded her from public life and kept her from involvement in anything except female or personal issues. A woman had no opinions on business, political movements, the arts, public affairs, or doctrinal issues, and she had no patriotic pride or religious feelings.

I do not exaggerate when I say that this has been the status of women in Egypt until the past few years, when we have witnessed a decrease in the power of men. This change is a consequence of the increased intellectual development of men, and the moderation of their rulers.

Yet we cannot claim that this change removes the need for criticism. . . . Among the most important of these are the firmly established tradition of veiling among the majority of the population, and the inadequate socialization of women. Were women's socialization effected in accordance with religious and moral principles, and were the use of the veil terminated at limits familiar in most Islamic schools of belief, then these criticisms would be dropped and our country would benefit from the active participation of all its citizens, men and women alike.

The New Woman

. . . Egyptians . . . must realize that unless their households and families provide a sound environment for educating men with the necessary qualities of success, there will be no hope of acquiring any worthwhile status among the advanced countries of the word. . . Households and families, however, cannot provide a sound environment unless their women are educated, and unless they have shared the idea, hopes, disappointments, and activities of men.

This simple and straightforward truth, which I publicly stated last year [in *The Liberation of Women*], was considered a kind of folly by many and labeled a violation of Islam by the legal scholars. Many [religious] school graduates thought it an excessive imitation of Western life. Some even went so far as to say it was felony against the homeland and religion. Their writings moreover suggested that the emancipation of Eastern women was one of the goals of Christian countries, who intended by to this bring about the destruction of Islam, and that Muslims who supported it were not true Muslims. These claims and other fantasies are not understood by simple souls who listen to them or by those who are ignorant and accept them.

---

3 • Muhammad Husayn Na'ini, Government from the Perspective of Islam

And then, those aware of the history of the world have come to realize that prior to the Crusades, the Christian nations and the Europeans were deprived not only of all the varieties of natural sciences but also of the Sciences of civilization, practical reason, and political axioms. . . . After that fateful event [the Crusades], those nations attributed their defeat to their lack of access to civilizational sciences and their general ignorance. Thus they considered curing this mother of all ailments as the greatest of their goals and pursued knowledge as a lover who seeks after the beloved. So they appropriated the principles of civilization and politics implicit in the Islamic holy books and traditions, and in the edicts of 'Ali[1] and other early leaders of Islam, as they have justly acknowledged . . . Therefore the progress and perseverance of the West in translation, interpretation, and application of these principles on the one hand, and the concomitant regression of the people of Islam and their subjugation at the hands of unbelievers [the Mongol conquerors] resulted in such a state that Muslims gradually forgot the principles of their own historical origins and even supposed that

---

Source: From Joseph G. Rahme, trans. in Charles Kurzman, ed., *Modernist Islam, 1840–1940* (Oxford: Oxford University Press, 2002), 116–119. Reprinted by permission of Oxford University Press.

[1]A reference to Ali, Muhammad's cousin and son-in-law, believed by Shii to be the true successor of Muhammad as head of the Islamic community.

abject subordination is a necessity of Islamic life. Therefore they [Muslims] thought that the commandments of Islam are contrary to civilization, reason, and justice—the fountainhead of progress—and as such, they equated Islam with slavery and savagery.

At this juncture in history [the present], with God's benevolent support, the retrogressive trajectory of the Islamic world has been halted and slavery under the imperious passions of dictatorial rulers has been terminated. The Muslim community has, thanks to the superb guidance and reasoning of its clerical leaders, become aware of the true requirements of its religion and its God-given freedoms.[2]

• • •

The possessive form of government is the case in which a prince considers the nation his personal property to dispose of as his whims and desires dictate. He treats the nation like a stable full of animals meant to satisfy his passions and wishes. He rewards or punishes people insofar as they aid or impede him in realizing his ends. He does not hesitate to imprison, banish, torture, or execute his opponents, tear them to pieces, and feed them to his hounds. Or to encourage his pack of wolves to spill their blood and plunder their property. He can separate any proprietor from his property, and give it to his entourage. He upholds or tramples people's rights as he sees fit. He considers himself the sole possessor of the right to expropriate any holdings, to sell, rent, or give away any part of the nation or its rights, or to exact any taxes for his personal private use. On the slightest suggestion, he sells and mortgages national rights to finance his silly and hedonistic trips abroad.[3] . . . His courtiers help him identity his power of tyranny, domination, passion, and anger with those of the nation. They help him to arrogate to himself god's attribute: "He cannot be questioned about what He does, but they will be questioned." [Qur'an, Sura 21, Verse 23]

The second form of government is that in which rule does not belong to an absolute arbiter. . . . It is a limited form of government, and the ruler's authority is rule-bound and conditional to the same extent. . . .

This form of government is committed to using the nation's resources to meet the nation's needs, not to satiate the passions of the rulers. Therefore, the authority of the government is limited . . . and its interference in its citizens' affairs is conditional upon the necessity of reaching those [national] goals. The citizens are partners with government in the ownership of the nation's powers and resources. Everyone has equal rights, and the administrators are all stewards, not owners. . . . And all citizens share the national right to question the authorities safely, and are safe in doing so. . . . This kind of government is called limited, just, conditional, responsible, and delegated. . . .

The most exalted means of ensuring that a government will not betray the trust of the nation in any way is, of course, having infallible rulers. . . . It is impossible to expect it to happen with frequency in history. Thus in the absence of divine leadership and the exceedingly rare incidents of just kingship, nations may attempt a pale likeness of such a rule only under two conditions:

First, by imposing the aforementioned limits so that government will strictly refrain from interfering in affairs in which it has no right to interfere. Under these conditions, governmental powers are stipulated in degree and kind, and the freedoms and rights of all classes of the people are formally guaranteed, in accordance to the requirements of religion. . . . Since the written document

---

[2]Na'ini is referring to Persia's Constitutional Revolution of 1906 and possibly the Turkish Revolution of 1908.

[3]May refer to Nasir al-Din (r. 1848–1896) or Mozzafar al-Din (r. 1896–1907), Persian shahs who traveled frequently to Europe.

concerning political and civil affairs of the nation . . . sets limits and the penalty for exceeding them, such a document is called the constitutional law or the constitutions. . . .

Second, strengthening the principle of vigilance, accountability, and complete responsibility by appointing a supervisory assembly of the wise, the well-wishers of the nation, and the experts in internal and external affairs, so they can discharge their duties in preventing violation and wrongdoing. The people's representatives are comprised of such individuals and their formal seat is called "the Assembly of National Consultation." True accountability and responsibility will preserve the limits on power and prevent the return of possessive government only if the executive branch is under the supervision of the legislative branch, and the legislative branch is responsible to every individual in the nation. . . .

India Under British Rule

As Great Britain took control of India during the nineteenth century, British administrators, policymakers, and the general public all agreed that this new colony should serve the economic interests of the mother country. It would be a source of raw materials, an area for investment, and a market for British manufactured goods. Many other issues, however, sparked debate. Most of the British realized that at some point, they would leave India and that their colony would become a self-governing, independent state. They had no timetable for leaving, however, and they disagreed about how to prepare their subjects for independence. They would bring some Indians into the colonial administration, but how many and at what levels? They would provide India with schools and colleges, but would they offer Western or traditional Indian learning? They would attempt to "civilize" the Indians, but in doing so, how much traditional Indian culture should be suppressed?

The Indians were even more deeply divided about the meaning and future of British rule. At first, many Indians welcomed the British presence as a way to open the door to Western science, constitutional government, and economic development. Such views persisted into the twentieth century, but by the late 1800s, only a small minority embraced them unequivocally. Many Indians came to resent the British assumption that Western ways were superior to centuries-old Indian beliefs and practices. They also were offended by Britain's one-sided economic policies, which drained India's resources, stifled development, and damaged traditional industries. Finally, they were angered by Great Britain's reluctance to seriously consider Indian self-rule.

As the following documents reveal, an evaluation of the benefits and the harm of British rule in India is no simple matter. Historians continue to debate the issue down to the present day.

The Case for Western Schools

72 • RAMMOHUN ROY, LETTER TO LORD AMHERST

From the 1770s onward, directors of the East India Company, missionaries, and the London government all agreed that Britain had ethical and practical reasons to support schools for their Indian subjects. What they could not agree on was what these schools should teach. At first, the East India Company, in the interest of not disturbing traditional Indian culture and social relationships, sponsored studies in Persian, Arabic, and Sanskrit, the ancient language of India. Such an approach was favored by influential British scholars and intellectuals known as "Orientalists," who greatly admired Indian culture and literature, and most early missionaries, who accommodated their Indian audience by learning Indian dialects and translating the Bible into native languages. By the early 1800s, however, many Indians began to demand schools that taught English and Western curricula to prepare them for employment in the civil service. Their views were supported by a growing number of Englishmen, including some missionaries, who saw little or no value in Indian culture or religions and sought to establish schools that would be agents of Anglicization. The debate between the two sides began in earnest in 1813, when Parliament voted funds "for the revival and promotion of literature and the encouragement of the learned natives of India" and appointed a Committee on Public Instruction to decide how the funds should be spent.

Rammohun Roy, often called the father of modern India, was one of those who strongly supported schools that offered a Western education. Born into a devout high-caste Hindu family in 1772, Roy showed an early genius for languages and a keen interest in religions. He learned Arabic, Persian, Greek, and Sanskrit and as a young man spent five years traveling across India seeking religious enlightenment. After mastering English, he entered the service of the East India Company, ultimately attaining the highest administrative rank possible for an Indian. In 1814, at age 42, he retired to Kolkata, where he founded several newspapers and schools and campaigned to abolish the practice of widow burning, or *sati*. He also established the Society of God, dedicated to combining Christian ethical teaching with certain Hindu beliefs. He wrote the following letter in 1823 to the British governor-general of India, Lord Amherst (1773–1857), to oppose a British plan to sponsor a school in Kolkata to teach Sanskrit and Hindu literature.

In 1835, the debate over Indian education was settled when a committee appointed by the British government decided that the schools it sponsored should provide an English-style education. According to the committee's chair, Thomas Macaulay (1773–1857), the goal was to produce young men "Indian in blood and colour, but English in taste, in opinions, and in intellect."

QUESTIONS FOR ANALYSIS

1. How would you characterize Roy's attitude toward the British? Does he seem comfortable offering the British advice?

2. What does he especially admire about Western learning and literature?
3. What does he view as the weaknesses of traditional Indian learning?
4. According to Roy, what implications would a Hindu-based educational system have for India's political future?

The establishment of a new Sanskrit School in Calcutta evinces the laudable desire of government to improve the natives of India by education—a blessing for which they must ever be grateful, and every well-wisher of the human race must be desirous that the efforts made to promote it should be guided by the most enlightened principles, so that the stream of intelligence may flow in the most useful channels.

When this seminary of learning was proposed, we understood that the government in England had ordered a considerable sum of money to be annually devoted to the instruction of its Indian subjects. We were filled with sanguine hopes that this sum would be laid out in employing European gentlemen of talent and education to instruct the natives of India in mathematics, natural philosophy, chemistry, anatomy, and other useful sciences, which the natives of Europe have carried to a degree of perfection that has raised them above the inhabitants of other parts of the world. . . .

We find that the government are establishing a Sanskrit school under Hindu pandits[1] to impart such knowledge as is already current in India. This seminary (similar in character to those which existed in Europe before the time of Lord Bacon[2] can only be expected to load the minds of youth with grammatical niceties and metaphysical distinctions of little or no practical use to the possessors or to society. The pupils will there acquire what was known two thousand years ago with the addition of vain and empty subtleties since then produced by speculative men such as is already commonly taught in all parts of India.

The Sanskrit language, so difficult that almost a lifetime is necessary for its acquisition, is well known to have been for ages a lamentable check to the diffusion of knowledge, and the learning concealed under this almost impervious veil is far from sufficient to reward the labor of acquiring it. . . .

Neither can much improvement arise from such speculations as the following which are the themes suggested by the Vedanta.[3] In what manner is the soul absorbed in the Deity? What relation does it bear to the Divine Essence? Nor will youths be fitted to be better members of society by the Vedantic doctrines which teach them to believe that all visible things have no real existence, that as father, brother, etc., have no real entity, they consequently deserve no real affection, and therefore the sooner we escape from them and leave the world the better. . . .

If it had been intended to keep the British nation in ignorance of real knowledge, the Baconian philosophy would not have been allowed to displace the system of the schoolmen which was the best calculated to perpetuate ignorance. In the same manner the Sanskrit system of education would be the best calculated to keep this country in darkness, if such had been the policy of the British legislature. But as the improvement of the native population is the object of the

---

Source: Rammohun Roy, *The English Works of Rammohun Roy* (Allahabad, India: Panini Office, 1906), pp. 471–74.

[1]Wise and learned men of Hindu India.

[2]A reference to the English philosopher and prophet of science, Francis Bacon (1561–1626).

[3]A major school of Hindu philosophy based on the study and analysis of three ancient texts, the *Upanishads*, the *Vedanta-sutras*, and the *Bhagavad Gita*.

government, it will consequently promote a more liberal and enlightened system of instruction, embracing mathematics, natural philosophy, chemistry, anatomy, with other useful sciences, which may be accomplished with the sums proposed by employing a few gentlemen of talent and learning educated in Europe and providing a college furnished with necessary books, instruments, and other apparatus.

In presenting this subject to your Lordship, I conceive myself discharging a solemn duty which I owe to my countrymen, and also to that enlightened sovereign and legislature which have extended their benevolent care to this distant land, actuated by a desire to improve the inhabitants, and therefore humbly trust you will excuse the liberty I have taken in thus expressing my sentiments to your Lordship.

A Call to Expel the British

73 • THE AZAMGARH PROCLAMATION

On May 10, 1857, in Meerut in northern India, three Indian infantry regiments that were part of the army maintained by the British East India Company shot their British officers, released all prisoners from jail, and marched on the nearby city of Delhi, which fell on May 11. This sparked similar mutinies across northern India, and with scattered support from peasants, landowners, and a few native princes, rebellion appeared to threaten the very basis of British authority in India. In the following months, however, British forces regrouped, and with the help of loyal Indian troops, crushed the rebels in 1858. Though brief, the Indian Rebellion (also called the Great Rebellion, the Indian Mutiny, the Revolt of 1857, the Uprising of 1857, and the Sepoy Mutiny) was bitterly fought, with atrocities committed by both sides. Two months after it ended, Parliament passed the India Act, which stripped the East India Company of its political authority and placed India directly under the Crown.

The meaning and significance of the Indian Rebellion continue to be widely debated. To some historians, it was the first expression of Indian nationalism; to others it was nothing more than a series of army mutinies that never garnered much support outside the north. There is more agreement about its causes. It was triggered by discontent among the Indian troops (sepoys) in the East India Company's Bengal army, discontent that boiled over into rebellion when the British introduced new cartridges greased with cow fat, which made them obnoxious to Hindu soldiers, and pig fat, which made them obnoxious to Muslims. This was only the spark, however. The rebellion gained support from many groups, some with specific grievances over British rule and others with vague fears about British intentions. Some of these grievances and concerns are revealed in the document that follows.

The document itself, known as the Azamgarh Proclamation, was one of several proclamations that were circulated to win support for the rebellion. This proclamation, supposedly issued in the city of Azamgarh, is thought to be the work of Mirza Mughal, the fifth son of the 82-year-old king of Delhi and Mughal emperor, Bahadur Shah. In some versions, the proclamation is ascribed to the King of Awadh (Oudh), whose territory had been formally annexed by the British in 1856. Whoever the author was, his goal was to bring Hindus and Muslims together to restore Mughal authority once the British had been expelled. To forestall such a dream, the India Act of 1858, by which Parliament stripped the East India Company of its political authority, also abolished the Mughal Empire.

QUESTIONS FOR ANALYSIS

1. What incentives does the author of the proclamation offer to those who would join the rebellion?
2. For each of the groups discussed (zamindars, merchants, artisans) what, according to the proclamation, have been the detrimental effects of British rule?
3. What role does religion play in the proclamation?
4. How do the views of the author of the proclamation differ from those of Rammohun Roy (source 72)?
5. What solutions for India's problems does the proclamation suggest?

It is well known to all that in this age the people of Hindustan,[1] both Hindus and Muslims, are being ruined under the tyranny and oppression of the infidel and treacherous English. It is therefore the bound duty of those who have any sort of connection with any of the Muslim royal families, . . . to stake their lives and property for the well-being of the public . . . and I, who am the grandson of Bahadur Shah Ghazi, emperor of India,[2] having . . . come here to extirpate the infidels residing in the eastern part of the country, and to liberate and protect the poor helpless people now groaning under their iron rule, have, by the aid of the Mujahidins [fighters for Islam against infidels] . . . raised the standard of Mohammad, and persuaded the orthodox Hindus who had been subject to my ancestors, and have been and are still accessories in the destruction of the English, to raise the standard of Mahavir.[3]

Therefore, for the information of the public, the present proclamation, consisting of several sections, is put in circulation, and it is the imperative duty of all to take it into their careful consideration, and abide by it. Parties anxious to participate in the common cause, but having no means to provide for themselves, shall receive their daily subsistence from me; and be it known to all, that the ancient works, both of the Hindus and Muslims, the writings of the miracle-workers, and the calculations of the astrologers, pundits, and fortune-tellers, all agree in asserting that the English will no longer have any footing in India or elsewhere. . . .

Section I.—Regarding Zamindars [landholders].—It is evident that the British government, in making settlements with zamindars, have imposed exorbitant jummas [taxes], and have disgraced and ruined several zamindars by putting up their estates to public auction for arrears of rent, insomuch that on the institution of a suit by a common farmer, a maidservant, or a slave, the respectable zamindars are summoned into court, arrested, put in jail, and disgraced. In litigations regarding zamindars, the immense value of stamps [on official documents], and other unnecessary expenses of the civil courts,

Source: In Charles Ball, *The History of the Indian Mutiny* (London: London Printing and Publishing, 1858–1859), vol. 2, pp. 630–632.
[1]A term that then referred to northern India.

[2]Also the King of Delhi, Bahadur Shah.
[3]"Great Hero." In this context, a name for the Hindu god Vishnu.

which are full of all sorts of crooked dealings, and the practice of allowing a case to hang on for years, are all calculated to impoverish the litigants. Besides this, the coffers of the zamindars are annually taxed with subscriptions for schools, hospitals, roads, etc. Such extortions will have no manner of existence in the royal government; but, on the contrary, the taxes will be light, the dignity and honour of the zamindars safe, and every zamindar will have absolute rule in his own territory.

Section II.—Regarding Merchants.—It is plain that the infidel and treacherous British government has monopolised the trade of all the fine and valuable merchandise, such as indigo, cloth, and other articles of shipping, leaving only the trade of trifles to the people, and even in this they are not without their share of the profits, which they secure by means of customs and stamp fees, etc., so that the people have merely a trade in name. . . . When the royal government is established, all these aforesaid fraudulent practices shall be dispensed with, and the trade of every article, without exception, both by land and water, shall be open to the native merchants of India, who will have the benefit of the government steam-vessels and steam carriages for the conveyance of the merchandise gratis; and merchants having no capital of their own shall be assisted from the public treasury. . . .

Section III.—Regarding Public Servants.—It is not a secret thing, that under the British government, natives employed in the civil and military services, have little respect, low pay, and no manner of influence; and all the posts of dignity and emolument [reward] in both departments, are exclusively bestowed on Englishmen. . . . But under the royal government, . . . the posts . . . which the English enjoy at present . . . will be given to the natives . . . together with landed estates, ceremonial dress, tax-free lands, and

influence. Natives, whether Hindus or Muslims, who fall fighting against the English, are sure to go to heaven; and those killed fighting for the English, will, doubtless, go to hell. Therefore, all the natives in the British service ought to be alive to their religion and interest, and, abjuring their loyalty to the English, side with the royal government. . . .

Section IV.—Regarding Artisans.—It is evident that the Europeans, by the introduction of English articles into India, have thrown the weavers, the cotton-dressers, the carpenters, the blacksmiths, and the shoemakers, &c., out of employ, and have engrossed [taken over] their occupations, so that every description of native artisan has been reduced to beggary. But under the royal government the native artisans will exclusively be employed in the services of the kings, the rajahs, and the rich; and this will no doubt insure their prosperity. Therefore the artisans ought to renounce the English services, and assist the Mujahidins . . . engaged in the war, and thus be entitled both to secular and eternal happiness.

Section V.—Regarding Pundits, Fakirs,[4] and other learned persons.—The pundits and fakirs being the guardians of the Hindu and Muslim religions respectively, and the Europeans being the enemies of both religions, and as at present a war is raging against the English on account of religion, the pundits and fakirs are bound to present themselves to me, and take their share in this holy war, otherwise they will stand condemned. . . .

Lastly, be it known to all, that whoever, out of the above-named classes, shall, after the circulation of this [proclamation], still cling to the British government, all his estates shall be confiscated, and his property plundered, and he himself, with his whole family, shall be imprisoned, and ultimately put to death.

---

[4]The word *pundit* (or *pandit*) referred to learned Hindus who had committed a large number of holy texts to memory. The term *fakir* referred to Islamic and occasionally Hindu mystics renowned for their acts of asceticism and supernatural powers.

The Indian National Congress Debates British Rule

74 • DADABHAI NAOROJI, ADDRESS TO THE INDIAN NATIONAL CONGRESS, 1886; BAL GANGADHAR TILAK, TENETS OF THE NEW PARTY (1907)

A key event in India's political history occurred on December 28, 1885, when 72 delegates gathered in Mumbai to attend the first meeting of the Indian National Congress, an organization that provided much of the leadership for the Indian independence movement of the 1930s and 1940s and became India's most powerful political party after independence. The organization was the brainchild of Allan Octavian Hume (1829–1912), an Englishman who, in 1882, had been dismissed from the Indian Civil Service after more than 30 years of service because of his advocacy for the Indians and well-known tendency to criticize his superiors. He believed that an annual meeting of educated Indians to discuss politics and take stands on political issues would be an effective way to make their views known to the colonial administration.

In its early years, the Congress was dominated by middle- and upper-class Hindus who gathered to hear speeches and pass resolutions on matters of interest to India's educated elite: access to higher positions in the Indian Civil Service and the army, a greater Indian voice in provincial legislative councils, the expansion of educational opportunities, and the lowering of certain taxes. They did not seek Indian independence. This is readily apparent in the speech delivered by the second president of the Congress, Dadabhai Naoroji (1825–1871), at the organization's second meeting in 1886 in Kolkata. Born into a prosperous Mumbai family, Naoroji abandoned a promising career as a mathematician at the age of 30 and moved to London, where he represented an Indian export business while seeking to educate the British public about Indian issues. During one of his many return visits to India, he was instrumental in the founding of the Indian National Congress, and served three terms as its president.

Just twenty years after Naoroji's speech, the Indian National Congress was rocked by a bitter conflict precipitated by a split between the Moderates, who favored cooperation with the British and gradual reform, and the Extremists, who sought immediate independence. Hostility to British rule, fueled by a revival of popular Hinduism and ongoing frustration with British policies, reached a flashpoint in 1905, when the British announced the partition of the province of Bengal, with one part predominantly Hindu and the other mainly Muslim. This was viewed as another example of British high-handedness and an effort to split the Hindu and Muslim communities. The leading spokesman for the Extremists was Bal Gangadhar Tilak (1856–1920), who, as editor of a widely read Marathi-language newspaper, thundered against British rule and defended Hindu traditions. His mottos—"Militancy not Mendicancy" and "Freedom is My Birthright and I Shall Have It"—spread throughout India. Viewing him as a dangerous rabble-rouser, the British imprisoned him in 1897 and 1908. In the following excerpt from a speech delivered in early January 1907, Tilak sets forth his ideas on Indian independence in the wake of the 1906 meeting of the Indian National Congress, at which a schism within the organization had been narrowly avoided.

QUESTIONS FOR ANALYSIS

1. Naoroji begins his speech by claiming that an organization like the Indian National Congress could have come to existence only under British rule, not any previous Indian regime. What are his reasons for this view?
2. What, according to Naoroji, are the "numberless blessings" conferred on India by the British?
3. Overall, how would you characterize Naoroji's views of the British and their goals for India?
4. How do Tilak's views of the British differ from those of Naoroji?
5. According to Tilak, how and why have Indian views of British rule changed over time?
6. Why is Tilak convinced that a boycott will be such an effective weapon against the British?

Dadabhai Naoroji, Speech to the Indian National Congress, 1886

The assemblage of such a Congress is an event of the utmost importance in Indian history. I ask whether in the most glorious days of Hindu rule, you could imagine the possibility of a meeting of this kind, where even Hindus of all different provinces of the kingdom could have collected and spoken as one nation. Coming down to the later empire of our [Muslim] friends, who probably ruled over a larger territory at one time than any Hindu monarch, would it have been possible for a meeting like this to assemble composed of all classes and communities, all speaking one language, and all having uniform and high aspirations of their own? . . .

It is under the civilizing rule of the Queen and people of England that we meet here together, hindered by none, and are freely allowed to speak our minds without the least fear and without the least hesitation. Such a thing is possible under British rule and British rule only. [Loud cheers.] Then I put the *question* plainly: Is this Congress a nursery for sedition and rebellion against the British Government [cries of "no, no"]; or is it another stone in the foundation of the stability of that Government [cries of "yes, yes"]? There could be

but one answer, and that you have already given, because we are thoroughly sensible of the numberless blessings conferred upon us, of which the very existence of this Congress is a proof in a nutshell. [Cheers.] Were it not for these blessings of British rule I could not have come here, as I have done, without the least hesitation and without the least fear that my children might be robbed and killed in my absence; nor could you have come from every corner of the land, having performed, within a few days, journeys which in former days would have occupied as many months. [Cheers] . . . It is to British rule that we owe the education we possess; the people of England were sincere in the declarations made more than half a century ago that India was a sacred charge entrusted to their care by Providence, and that they were bound to administer it for the good of India, to the glory of their own name, and the satisfaction of God. [Prolonged cheering] When we have to acknowledge so many blessings as flowing from English rule . . . is it possible that an assembly like this . . . could meet for the purpose inimical to that rule to which we owe so much? [Cheers.] . . . Let us speak out like men and proclaim that we are loyal to the backbone [cheers]; that we understand

Source: Naoroji speech: *Essays, Speeches, Addresses and Writings (on Indian Politics) of the Hon'ble Dadabhai Naoroji.* Edited by Chundal Lallubhai (Bombay: Caxton Printing Works, 1887), pp. 332–333. Tilak speech: *Bal Gangadhar Tilak, His Writings and Speeches,* 3rd edition (Madras: Ganesh, 1922), pp. 55–57, 61, 63–67.

the benefits English rule has conferred upon us; that we thoroughly appreciate the education that has been given to us, the new light which has been poured upon us, turning us from darkness into light and teaching us the new lesson that kings are made for the people, not people for their kings; and this new lesson we have learned amidst the darkness of Asiatic despotism only by the light of free English civilization. [Loud cheers.]

Bal Gangadhar Tilak, Tenets of the New Party, 1907

. . . One thing is granted, namely, that this government does not suit us. As has been said by an eminent statesman—the government of one country by another can never be a successful, and therefore, a permanent government. . . . One fact is that this alien government has ruined the country. In the beginning all of us were taken by surprise. We were almost dazed. We thought that everything that the rulers did was for our good and that this English government has descended from the clouds to save us not only from foreign invasions but from internecine warfare, or the internal or external invasions, as they call it. We felt happy for a time, but it soon came to light that the peace which was established in this country did this . . . —that we were prevented from going at each other's throats, so that a foreigner might go at the throat of us all. *Pax Britannica* has been established in this country in order that a foreign government may exploit the country. . . . We believed in the benevolent intentions of the government, but in politics there is no benevolence. Benevolence is used to sugarcoat the declarations of self-interest and we were in those days deceived. . . . But soon a change came over us. English education, growing poverty, and better familiarity with our rulers, opened our eyes and our leaders'; especially, the venerable leader Naoroji who was the first to tell us that the drain from the country was ruining it, and if the drain was to continue, there was some great disaster awaiting us. So terribly convinced was he of this that he went

over from here to England and spent twenty-five years of his life in trying to convince the English people of the injustice that is being done to us. He worked very hard. He had conversations and interviews with secretaries of state, with members of Parliament—and with what result?

He has come here at the age of eighty-two to tell us that he is bitterly disappointed. . . .

You can now understand the difference between the old and the new parties. Appeals to the bureaucracy are hopeless. On this point both the new and old parties are agreed. The old party believes in appealing to the British nation and we do not. . . . Your industries are ruined utterly, ruined by foreign rule; your wealth is going out of the country and you are reduced to the lowest level which no human being can occupy. . . . The remedy is not petitioning but boycott. We say prepare your forces, organize your power, and then go to work so that they cannot refuse you what you demand. . . .

I want to have the key of my house, and not merely one stranger turned out of it. Self-government is our goal; we want a control over our administrative machinery. We don't want to become clerks and remain clerks. At present, we are clerks and willing instruments of our own oppression in the hands of an alien government, and that government is ruling over us not by its innate strength but by keeping us in ignorance and blindness to the perception of this fact. . . .

We shall not give them assistance to collect revenue and keep peace. We shall not assist them in fighting beyond the frontiers or outside India with Indian blood and money. We shall not assist them in carrying on the administration of justice. We shall have our own courts, and when time comes we shall not pay taxes. Can you do that by your united efforts? If you can, you are free from tomorrow. . . . This is a lesson of progress, a lesson of helping yourself as much as possible, and if you really perceive the force of it, if you are convinced by these arguments, then and then only is it possible for you to effect your salvation from the alien rule under which you labor at this moment.

Chapter 10

East and Southeast Asia Confront the West

DURING THE NINETEENTH CENTURY, ancient patterns of life in East and Southeast Asia were irrevocably altered by upheavals that felled governments, intensified social conflict, introduced new ideas and technologies, and transformed long-standing relationships among states. These changes were caused in part by social and political forces generated from within these societies themselves, but most resulted from new pressures from the West. Until the nineteenth century, Western involvement in the region had been limited to commerce and modest and generally ineffectual missionary activity. The only exceptions were a few coastal enclaves such as Melaka, which the Dutch took from the Portuguese in 1641, the Philippines, which Spain had ruled since the sixteenth century, and Java, where the Dutch had established indirect and informal control in the eighteenth century. Elsewhere, the region's rulers remained politically independent, and neither they nor their subjects were significantly attracted to or affected by Western culture.

This changed in the nineteenth century. In Southeast Asia, by the time World War I began in 1914, Burma, Laos, Cambodia, Vietnam, Singapore, the states of the Malay Peninsula, and many islands of the East Indies had all joined the Philippines and Java as parts of Western empires. Thailand remained independent but lost territory to France and Great Britain.

China faced severe internal problems and experienced relentless economic and military pressures from Western nations and Japan. Previous Chinese regimes had survived domestic turbulence and foreign threats, but this time, China's problems proved fatal, not just to the Qing Dynasty but also to China's 2,000-year tradition of imperial rule. When the last Qing emperor was overthrown in the Revolution of

1911–1912, no new dynasty was established, and China faced a future without the authority of an emperor, the rule of scholar-officials, and the guidance of official Confucian ideology.

Japan also faced internal conflict and foreign threats, but its experience sharply differed from that of China. Following a period of intense internal debate over Japan's future following the "opening" of Japan by American Commodore Matthew Perry in 1853, a group of patriotic aristocrats overthrew the Tokugawa shogunate in 1867, restored the emperor, and began laying plans for Japan's modernization. By the 1890s, Japan had escaped becoming a victim of imperialism and was well on its way to becoming an imperialist power itself.

Encounters with the West

Signs of changing Western interests and strategies in East and Southeast Asia were first noticeable in the late 1700s, when the British intensified their efforts to convince the Qing government to liberalize its commercial policies. They became more noticeable in the 1810s and 1820s, when the British founded a new colony at Singapore on the southern tip of the Malay Peninsula, the Dutch imposed the harsh Culture System on Java, and the British took two provinces and demanded a huge indemnity from the king of Burma after their victory in the first Anglo-Burmese War. More significant events took place in 1839, when the Opium War between Great Britain and China began; in 1853, when U.S. Commodore Matthew Perry forcibly entered Edo Bay and demanded the opening of Japan to foreign trade; and in 1862, when the Vietnamese emperor Tu Doc ceded control of three provinces to the French after defeat in the first Franco-Vietnamese War. Respectively, these latter three events smashed the myth of Chinese invincibility; precipitated the overthrow of the Japanese shogunate; and led to the near-complete colonization of Southeast Asia.

Opium and Imperialism

75 • LIN ZEXU, LETTER TO QUEEN VICTORIA, 1839

In 1842, only a half century after the Qianlong emperor sent King George III his condescending rejection of the British request for trade concessions (see source 50), the Daoguang emperor (r. 1820–1850) approved the Treaty of Nanjing, which required his government to open five ports to British merchants, cede Hong Kong to the British, lower tariffs, pay Britain an indemnity of $21 million, and free all British prisoners. Acceptance of these humiliating terms was the result of China's defeat in the Opium War (1839–1842), the climax of Chinese efforts to halt the British sale of opium to China.

Although opium derivatives had been used in Chinese medicine for centuries, smoking opium as a narcotic dates only from the seventeenth century. Opium use increased dramatically in the late 1700s, when British merchants with access to the poppy-growing areas of north and northwest India began to sell opium in China. By the early 1800s, millions of Chinese at every social and economic level were addicts, and almost 2 million pounds of opium were being sold in China every year.

Chinese officials viewed the epidemic of opium smoking with alarm, but they disagreed on how to stop it. Some advocated the legalization of opium and the expansion of poppy growing in China to lessen dependence on imports. Others, who favored more drastic measures, won the support of the emperor, who banned opium use in 1838. One year later, he sent one of his officials, Lin Zexu (1785–1850), to Guangzhou to confiscate the foreign merchants' stock of opium and stop the opium trade altogether.

Lin Zexu was a highly respected scholar/administrator who in previous provincial postings in Hubei and Hunan had tried to suppress opium smoking. In Guangzhou, he launched a campaign of moral persuasion and threats to enforce the emperor's ban. Insight into his thinking is provided by a letter he wrote to Great Britain's Queen Victoria in 1839, imploring her to halt her subjects' sale of opium.

Nothing came of his letter, and the noncooperation of British merchants in Guangzhou drove Lin to take more drastic steps. He arrested the leading English opium trader and blockaded the foreign quarter until its merchants agreed to hand over 20,000 chests of opium. In response, the British government dispatched a fleet to Chinese waters and mobilized Indian troops to protect its interests. While the flotilla of almost fifty vessels was en route in late 1839, fighting had already started around Guangzhou. The Opium War had begun.

QUESTIONS FOR ANALYSIS

1. What does Lin's letter reveal about Chinese views of foreign relations and the relationship between the Chinese emperor and other rulers?
2. What differences does Lin see in the motives of Chinese and those of Europeans in regard to trade?
3. What moral arguments does Lin use to persuade the queen to order the end of opium trading? What other arguments does he use?
4. What seems to be Lin's understanding of the powers of the English monarchy?
5. How does Lin view the world outside of China? How do his views differ from and resemble those of the Qianlong emperor (source 50)?

A communication: magnificently our great Emperor soothes and pacifies China and the foreign countries, regarding all with the same kindness. If there is profit, then he shares it with the peoples of the world; if there is harm, then he removes it on behalf of the world. This is because he takes the mind of heaven and earth as his mind.

The kings of your honorable country by a tradition handed down from generation to generation have always been noted for their politeness and

Source: Dun J. Li, *China in Transition, 1517–1911,* 1st edition. © 1969, pp. 64–67.

submissiveness. . . . Privately we are delighted with the way in which the honorable rulers of your country deeply understand the grand principles and are grateful for the Celestial grace. For this reason the Celestial Court in soothing those from afar has redoubled its polite and kind treatment. The profit from trade has been enjoyed by them continuously for two hundred years. This is the source from which your country has become known for its wealth.

But after a long period of commercial intercourse, there appear among the crowd of barbarians both good persons and bad, unevenly. Consequently there are those who smuggle opium to seduce the Chinese people and so cause the spread of the poison to all provinces. Such persons who only care to profit themselves, and disregard their harm to others, are not tolerated by the laws of heaven and are unanimously hated by human beings. . . .

We find that your country is sixty or seventy thousand *li*[1] from China. Yet there are barbarian ships that strive to come here for trade for the purpose of making a great profit. The wealth of China is used to profit the barbarians. That is to say, the great profit made by barbarians is all taken from the rightful share of China. By what right do they then in return use the poisonous drug to injure the Chinese people? Even though the barbarians may not necessarily intend to do us harm, yet in coveting profit to an extreme, they have no regard for injuring others. Let us ask, where is your conscience? I have heard that the smoking of opium is very strictly forbidden by your country; that is because the harm caused by opium is clearly understood. Since it is not permitted to do harm to your own country, then even less should you let it be passed on to the harm of other countries—how much less to China! Of all that China exports to foreign countries, there is not a single thing which

is not beneficial to people: they are of benefit when eaten, or of benefit when used, or of benefit when resold: all are beneficial. Is there a single article from China which has done any harm to foreign countries? Take tea and rhubarb[2] for example; the foreign countries cannot get along for a single day without them. If China cuts off these benefits with no sympathy for those who are to suffer, then what can the barbarians rely upon to keep themselves alive? . . . As for other foodstuffs, beginning with candy, ginger, cinnamon, and so forth, and articles for use, beginning with silk, satin, chinaware, and so on, all the things that must be had by foreign countries are innumerable. On the other hand, articles coming from the outside to China can only be used as toys. We can take them or get along without them. Since they are not needed by China, what difficulty would there be if we closed the frontier and stopped the trade? Nevertheless our Celestial Court lets tea, silk, and other goods be shipped without limit and circulated everywhere without begrudging it in the slightest. . . .

Suppose there were people from another country who carried opium for sale to England and seduced your people into buying and smoking it; certainly your honorable ruler would deeply hate it and be bitterly aroused. We have heard heretofore that your honorable ruler is kind and benevolent. Naturally you would not wish to give unto others what you yourself do not want. . . .

We have further learned that in London, the capital of your honorable rule, and in Scotland, Ireland, and other places, originally no opium has been produced. Only in several places of India under your control . . . has opium been planted from hill to hill, and ponds have been opened for its manufacture. For months and years work is continued in order to accumulate the poison. The obnoxious odor ascends, irritating heaven and frightening the spirits. Indeed you . . . can

---

[1]One *li* equals approximately one-third of a mile.

[2]The roots of Chinese rhubarb (*Da huang*) were used in medicines as a laxative.

eradicate the opium plant in these places, hoe over the fields entirely, and sow in its stead the five grains.[3] Anyone who dares again to plant and manufacture opium should be severely punished. This will really be a great, benevolent government policy that will increase the common weal and get rid of evil. For this, Heaven must support you and the spirits must bring you good fortune, prolonging your old age and extending your descendants. All will depend on this act. . . .

Now we have set up regulations governing the Chinese people. He who sells opium shall receive the death penalty and he who smokes it also the death penalty. Now consider this: if the barbarians do not bring opium, then how can the Chinese people resell it, and how can they smoke it? The fact is that the wicked barbarians beguile the Chinese people into a death trap. How then can we grant life only to these barbarians? He who takes the life of even one person still has to

atone for it with his own life; yet is the harm done by opium limited to the taking of one life only? Therefore in the new regulations, in regard to those barbarians who bring opium to China, the penalty is fixed at decapitation or strangulation. This is what is called getting rid of a harmful thing on behalf of mankind. . . .

Our Celestial Empire towers over all other countries in virtue and possesses power great and awesome enough to carry out its wishes . . . If the merchants of your honorable country wish to enjoy trade with us on a permanent basis they must fearfully obey our law. . . . May you as ruler check [restrain] your wicked and sift [separate out] your vicious people before they come to China, in order to guarantee the peace of your nation, to show further the sincerity of your politeness and submissiveness, and to let the two countries enjoy together the blessings of peace. How fortunate, how fortunate indeed, that we can all enjoy the blessings of peace!

---

[3]Five grains important in ancient China and regarded as sacred. The standard list includes soybeans, rice, wheat, and two kinds of millet.

U.S. Demands on Japan

76 • U.S. PRESIDENT MILLARD FILLMORE, LETTER TO HIS IMPERIAL MAJESTY, THE EMPEROR OF JAPAN

In July 1853, the unannounced arrival in Edo Bay of four American warships under the command of Commodore Matthew C. Perry was for the Japanese the culmination of a series of unsettling interactions with Westerners going back to the late eighteenth century. Since the 1630s, Japan had limited contacts with Europeans to the one Dutch ship allowed to trade each year at Nagasaki. Beginning in the 1790s, however, Japan felt increasing pressures from Russia and Great Britain to abandon its "closed country" policy. When their requests for trading privileges were rebuffed by the shogun's government in 1793 and 1804, Russians attacked trading posts on Sakhalin and the Kuril Islands, which Japan had claimed in 1807. In 1808, a British warship illegally entered Nagasaki harbor in search of Dutch ships (the Netherlands was then under control of Napoleonic France, Britain's enemy) and in 1824, English whaling ships raided two coastal cities. In the 1830s, trade relations with Japan drew the interest of the United States, whose whaling fleet and merchant vessels frequented the waters of the north Pacific. Japan, however, consistently rejected overtures from

U.S. businessmen and government emissaries in the 1830s and 1840s. In 1851, the U.S. government dispatched a fleet of naval vessels to Japan to force negotiations, but the mission was abandoned after its commanding officer was relieved of duty. A second mission under the command of Matthew Perry was undertaken in 1853.

After his flotilla of four warships reached Edo Bay in early July 1853, Perry went ashore to present a list of demands from President Millard Fillmore to the "emperor" (actually the shogun). Impressed by his steam-driven ships and powerful weaponry, the shogun reluctantly signed a treaty of friendship with the United States the following March. Signing the treaty opened Japan to trade and opened a new era in Japanese history.

QUESTIONS FOR ANALYSIS

1. How does the president's letter attempt to dispel Japanese concerns about American intentions?
2. The fact that the president's letter is addressed to the emperor rather than the shogun shows a certain level of misunderstanding about the Japanese government. What other evidence does the letter provide about the state of American knowledge of Japan and its history?
3. How much knowledge of the United States on the part of Japan is presumed by the tone and contents of Fillmore's letter? What characteristics of the United States is Fillmore most eager to describe?
4. Despite efforts by President Fillmore to mitigate Japanese concerns about U.S. intentions, the letter and its demands threw Japan into turmoil. What was there in the letter that may explain this?

GREAT and Good Friend: I have directed Commodore Perry to assure your imperial majesty that I entertain the kindest feelings towards your majesty's person and government, and that I have no other object in sending him to Japan but to propose to your imperial majesty that the United States and Japan should live in friendship and have commercial intercourse with each other. . . .

The Constitution and laws of the United States forbid all interference with the religious or political concerns of other nations. I have particularly charged Commodore Perry to abstain from every act which could possibly disturb the tranquility of your imperial majesty's dominions.

The United States of America reach from ocean to ocean, and our Territory of Oregon and State of California lie directly opposite to the dominions of your imperial majesty. Our steamships can go from California to Japan in eighteen days.

Our great State of California produces about sixty millions of dollars in gold every year, besides silver, quicksilver, precious stones, and many other valuable articles. Japan is also a rich and fertile country, and produces many very valuable articles. Your imperial majesty's subjects are skilled in many of the arts. I am desirous that our two countries should trade with each other, for the benefit both of Japan and the United States.

We know that the ancient laws of your imperial majesty's government do not allow of foreign trade, except with the Chinese and the Dutch; but as the state of the world changes and new

---

Source: United States Senate, 33rd Congress, 2nd Session, Exec. Docs. #34 (1854–1855), vol. 6, pp. 9–11.

governments are formed, it seems to be wise, from time to time, to make new laws. There was a time when the ancient laws of your imperial majesty's government were first made.

About the same time America, which is sometimes called the New World, was first discovered and settled by the Europeans. For a long time there were but a few people, and they were poor. They have now become quite numerous; their commerce is very extensive; and they think that if your imperial majesty were . . . to change the ancient laws as to allow a free trade between the two countries it would be extremely beneficial to both.

If your imperial majesty is not satisfied that it would be safe altogether to abrogate the ancient laws which forbid foreign trade, they might be suspended for five or ten years, so as to try the experiment. If it does not prove as beneficial as was hoped, the ancient laws can be restored. . . .

I have directed Commodore Perry to mention another thing to your imperial majesty. Many of our ships pass every year from California to China; and great numbers of our people pursue the whale fishery near the shores of Japan. It sometimes happens, in stormy weather, that one of our ships is wrecked on your imperial majesty's shores. In all such cases we ask, and expect, that our unfortunate people should be treated with kindness, and

that their property should be protected, till we can send a vessel and bring them away. . . .

Commodore Perry is also directed by me to represent to your imperial majesty that we understand there is a great abundance of coal and provisions in the Empire of Japan. Our steamships, in crossing the great ocean, burn a great deal of coal, and it is not convenient to bring it all the way from America. We wish that our steamships and other vessels should be allowed to stop in Japan and supply themselves with coal, provisions, and water. . . .

These are the only objects for which I have sent Commodore Perry, with a powerful squadron, to pay a visit to your imperial majesty's renowned city of Edo: friendship, commerce, a supply of coal and provisions, and protection for our shipwrecked people.

We have directed Commodore Perry to beg your imperial majesty's acceptance of a few presents.[1] They are of no great value in themselves; but some of them may serve as specimens of the articles manufactured in the United States, and they are intended as tokens of our sincere and respectful friendship.

May the Almighty have your imperial majesty in His great and holy keeping!

Your good friend,
Millard Fillmore.

---

[1]The list of gifts was actually quite extensive. With some gifts designated for the emperor, others for his assistants, and some for general distribution, they included firearms, ammunition, and swords; copious amounts of wine and liquor; agricultural tools; books (including nature books by John James Audubon [1785–1851], the famous painter of birds and other animals); electrical equipment, including a working telegraph system; three stoves; a working miniature locomotive and railroad cars; and eight baskets of potatoes.

The Fall of Vietnam

77 • PHAN THANH GIAN, LETTER TO EMPEROR TU DUC AND LAST MESSAGE TO HIS ADMINISTRATORS

In 1802, decades of civil war ended in Vietnam when Nguyen Anh unified the country under the Nguyen dynasty and as emperor took the name Gia Long. He and his successors sought to govern the country according to the Confucian principles that had played a prominent role in Vietnamese politics and thought for many centuries. The emperors' efforts to turn Vietnam into a model Confucian society led to the persecution of Vietnamese Catholics, who, as a result of mainly French missionary efforts, numbered 300,000 by the nineteenth century. When Catholics were implicated in a rebellion in 1833, Emperor Minh Mang (r. 1820–1841) ordered the imprisonment and execution of a number of converts and European missionaries. Three years later, he closed Vietnamese ports to European shipping. In response, the French sent naval vessels and troops to Vietnam, ostensibly to protect Christianity but also to advance French imperialism. Fighting broke out in earnest in 1858, and although the Vietnamese staunchly resisted, Emperor Tu Duc (r. 1847–1883) accepted a settlement in 1862 by which he ceded to the French three southern provinces around Saigon.

Four years later, an anti-French rebellion broke out west of Saigon, then under the governorship of the prominent Vietnamese statesman Phan Thanh Gian (1796–1867). In response, the French sent in troops and demanded control of the provinces. In 1867, Phan Thanh Gian acquiesced and then committed suicide, but not before he wrote the following two letters, one to Emperor Tu Duc and the other to administrators in his district.

QUESTIONS FOR ANALYSIS

1. What is the basis of Phan Thanh Gian's hope that the emperor can save Vietnam from further humiliation at the hands of the French?
2. What is Phan Thanh Gian's view of the French?
3. What evidence of Phan Thanh Gian's Confucian training do you see in the letter?
4. Why did Phan Thanh Gian decide to acquiesce to the French?

Letter to Emperor Tu Duc

8, July 1867

I, Phan Thanh Gian, make the following report, in expressing frankly, with my head bowed, my humble sentiments, and in soliciting, with my head raised, your discerning scrutiny.

During the period of difficulties and misfortunes that we are presently undergoing, rebellion is rising around the capital, the pernicious [French] influence is expanding on our frontiers. . . .

My duty compels me to die. I would not dare to live thoughtlessly, leaving a heritage of shame to my Sovereign and my Father. Happily, I have confidence in my Emperor, who has extensive knowledge of ancient times and the present and who has studied profoundly the causes of peace and of dissension: . . . In respectfully observing the warnings of Heaven and in having pity on the misery of man . . . in changing the string of the guitar, in modifying the track of the governmental chariot, it is still possible for you to act in accordance with your authority and means.

At the last moment of life, the throat constricted, I do not know what to say, but, in wiping my tears and in raising my eyes toward you affectionately, I can only ardently hope that this wish will be realized.

Source: Letter to Emperor Tu Doc and Last Message to His Administrators, from *We the Vietnamese* by Francois Sully and Donald Kirk. Copyright © 1971 by Praeger Publishers Inc. Reprinted by permission of Henry Holt and Company, LLC.

With respect, I make this report, Tu Duc, twentieth year, sixth moon, seventh day, Phan Thanh Gian.

Last Message to His Administrators

It is written: He who lives in accordance with the will of Heaven lives in virtue; he who does not live according to the will of Heaven lives in evil. To work according to the will of Heaven is to listen to natural reason. . . . Man is an intelligent animal created by Heaven. Every animal lives according to his nature, as water flows to low ground, as fire goes out on dry ground. . . .

The empire of our king is ancient. Our gratitude toward our kings is complete and always ardent; we cannot forget them. Now, the French are come, with their powerful weapons of war to cause dissension among us. We are weak against them; our commanders and our soldiers have been vanquished. Each battle adds to our misery. . . . The French have immense warships, filled with soldiers and armed with huge cannons. No one can resist them. They go where they want, the strongest ramparts fall before them.

I have raised my spirit toward Heaven and I have listened to the voice of reason. And I have said: "It would be as senseless for you to wish to defeat your enemies by force of arms as for a young fawn to attack a tiger. You attract uselessly great misfortunes upon the people whom Heaven has confided to you. I have thus written to all the mandarins and to all the war commanders to break their lances and surrender the forts without fighting.

"But, if I have followed the Will of Heaven by averting great evils from the head of the people, I am a traitor to our king in delivering without resistance the provinces which belong to him. . . . I deserve death. Mandarins and people, you can live under the command of the French, who are only terrible during the battle, but their flag must never fly above a fortress where Phan Thanh Gian still lives."

Multiple Voices VI

Plotting East Asia's Future

BACKGROUND

Events in the 1850s shocked the Japanese and Chinese into an urgent and contentious debate about how best to respond to the demands of Western powers, whose military might and superior technology threatened their autonomy and undermined long-standing convictions about their place in the world. In Japan, the debate was intense, violent, and short-lived. It was resolved by the events of the Meiji Restoration of 1867–1868, in which a faction of aristocrats overthrew the shogun, restored the emperor as head of state, and set Japan on a course of rapid military and economic modernization. In China, serious debate about the nation's future began somewhat later, around 1860, and continued for the next fifty years. As one side or another became ascendant in Beijing, change came in fits and starts until the opening years of the twentieth century, when the imperial government launched an ambitious program to break with its Confucian past.

The debate about Japan's future began with the arrival of Matthew Perry in July 1853 and intensified after the shogun acquiesced to Perry's demands in 1854 and signed a series of treaties that granted full trading rights to the United States and other Western powers between 1855 and 1858. With the isolationist policy abandoned, the debate now shifted to other questions: What steps were needed to provide Japan with the strength to resist further Western encroachments? Was wholesale borrowing from the West required or would rededication to traditional Japanese values suffice? Politically, who was most suited to provide leadership? Such questions were argued about and fought over until decided by the events of 1867 and 1868.

Although the Opium War (1839–1842) revealed glaring deficiencies in the Chinese military and the backwardness of Chinese technology, it took the disastrous events of the 1850s to prod Chinese leaders into thinking about reform. The 1850s saw the outbreak of three major rebellions, massive flooding of the Yellow River, and another defeat by European armies in the Second Opium War (1858–1860). At the close of the war, which included the looting and torching of the emperor's summer palaces and resulted in another humiliating treaty, what came to be known as the Self-Strengthening movement emerged in the writings of officials like Feng Guifen (1809–1874), Zeng Guofan (1811–1872), and Li Honzhang (1823–1901). They and their supporters advocated military and economic modernization, but only as a means of propping up China's traditional Confucian order. Even this essentially conservative approach to reform went too far for traditionalist scholars, who failed to see any reason to borrow from European barbarians. The result was another military defeat in 1895, this time not at the hands of the Europeans, but by the army and navy of their neighbor and former client, Japan.

THE SOURCES

In the sources that follow, we present the views of four writers, two Japanese and two Chinese, on how best to respond to Western pressures in the 1850s and 1860s.

We begin with two memoranda, each addressed to the bakufu (a term for the shogun's administration) in the weeks directly after Commodore Perry's arrival in 1853. Both were prepared in response to a request by Abe Masahiro, the shogun's chief advisor, that major daimyo provide the bakufu with opinions on how best to respond to the American requests. Tokugawa Nariaki (1800–1861), a disciple of the National Learning movement and lord of the Mito domain, argued in a memorandum dated August 14 that Japan had no choice but to fight. Some weeks later, Ii Naosuke (1815–1860), the daimyo of the Hikone domain, made a case for acquiescence, which, as it turned out, was the approach adopted by the shogun the following March when he signed the Kanagawa Convention with the United States.

For the next several years, the two men continued to be on opposite sides in the debate about Japan's future. Both favored strengthening Japan's coastal defenses, but Tokugawa Nariaki's anti-foreignism was much more pronounced. He became identified with those who believed in the revival of the emperor's authority at the expense of the shogunate. Ii Naosuke was a strong supporter of the shogunate, and in 1858, as the shogun's high advisor, signed the Harris Treaty with the United States despite opposition from the emperor. This made him anathema to anti-foreign imperial loyalists, who assassinated him as a symbol of bakufu tyranny and weakness.

With our third source, our attention shifts to China. It was written in 1861 by Feng Guifen (1829–1874), a native of Suzhou who entered government service in 1840 after performing brilliantly on the civil service examinations. Over the next two decades, he prepared policy memoranda for the emperor, organized and led troops against rebel armies, and served as director of scholarly academies in Suzhou and Shanghai. Over time, he became fully aware of the government's failures and military weakness. Nonetheless, when Feng retired from government service in 1859, as a dedicated Confucianist he still believed in China's time-honored governing principles. He was convinced, furthermore, that China could overcome the twin threats of rebellion and foreign encroachment only if it embraced reform. He outlined his thoughts in a collection of essays, *Personal Protests from the Study of Jiaobin*, which he distributed among government officials in 1861. Here, he outlined a policy of "self-strengthening," a traditional Chinese term to describe what a declining dynasty needed to do in order to recover. His essays caught the attention of one of China's leading statesmen, Li Hongzhang (1823–1901), who as prime spokesman for the self-strengthening movement over the next thirty years drew inspiration from Feng's ideas.

Our fourth source is a memorandum written in 1867 by Woren (1804–1871), a dedicated Confucian whose career included tenures as chief judge, grand secretary, and tutor to the child emperor Tongzhi. A passionate opponent of Westernization, he wrote this memorandum as a response to a proposal by Prince Gong, the emperor's uncle and a strong supporter of self-strengthening, to expand the curriculum of the recently founded state-supported foreign language schools by including "astronomy and mathematics" taught by Western educators. Despite vehement opposition by conservatives such as Woren, the curricular changes went forward to include more than astronomy and mathematics: also added were courses on chemistry, physics, geology, metallurgy, economics, and international law. By suggesting in his proposal that the reforms would be limited to only mathematics and astronomy, which the Chinese had studied for centuries, Prince Gong had sought to blunt conservative resistance, which would have been much stronger if his true intent had been known.

QUESTIONS FOR ANALYSIS

1. How do the four authors characterize Westerners? What do the Westerners do well, and what are their deficiencies?
2. According to the authors, why do the actions and ideas of the Westerners threaten East Asian societies?
3. How do the four authors propose to respond to the threat from the West?
4. What do you see as the strengths and weaknesses of their approaches?
5. Despite their differences, what common ground do the four authors share in terms of their ultimate goals?

1 • Tokugawa Nariaki, Memorandum to the Bakufu, August 14, 1853

When we consider the respective advantages and disadvantages of war and peace, we find that if we put our trust in war, the whole country's morale will be increased and even if we sustain an initial defeat we will in the end expel the foreigner; while if we put our trust in peace, even though things may seem tranquil for a time, the morale of the country will be greatly lowered and we will come in the end to complete collapse. This has been amply demonstrated in the history of China. . . .

Although our country's territory is not extensive, foreigners both fear and respect us. That, after all, is because our resoluteness and military prowess have been clearly demonstrated to the world. . . . Despite this, the Americans who arrived recently, though fully aware of *bakufu*'s prohibition, entered Uraga[1] displaying a white flag as a symbol of peace and insisted on presenting their written requests. Moreover they entered Edo Bay, fired heavy guns in salute and even went so far as to conduct surveys without permission. They were arrogant and discourteous, their actions an outrage. Indeed, this was the greatest disgrace we have suffered since the dawn of our history. The saying is that if the enemy dictates terms in one's own capital one's country is disgraced. . . . Should it happen not only that the *bakufu* fails to expel them but also that it concludes an agreement in accordance with their requests, then I fear it would be impossible to maintain our national polity. . . .

The prohibition of Christianity is the first rule of the Tokugawa house. Public notices concerning it are posted everywhere, even to the remotest corner of every province. . . . The *bakufu* can never ignore or overlook the evils of Christianity. Yet if the Americans are allowed to come again this religion will inevitably raise its head once more, however strict the prohibition; and this, I fear, is something we could never justify to the spirits of our ancestors. . . .

To exchange our valuable articles like gold, silver, copper, and iron for useless foreign goods like woolens and satin is to incur great loss while acquiring not the smallest benefit. The best course of all would be for the *bakufu* to put a stop to the trade with Holland. By contrast to open such valueless trade with others besides the Dutch would, I believe, inflict the greatest possible harm on our country. . . .

For some years Russia, England, and others have sought trade with us, but the *bakufu* has not permitted it. Should permission be granted to the Americans, on what ground would it be possible to refuse if Russia and the others request it? . . .

It is widely stated that [apart from trade] the foreigners have no other evil designs and that if only the *bakufu* will permit trade there will be no further difficulty. However, it is their practice first to seek a foothold by means of trade and then to go on to propagate Christianity and make other unreasonable demands. . . .

Though the *Rangakusha* [scholars of Dutch studies][2] group may argue secretly that world conditions are much changed from what they were, Japan alone clinging to ideas of seclusion in isolation amidst the seas, that this is a constant source of danger to us and that our best course would therefore be to communicate with foreign countries and open an extensive trade; yet, to my mind, if the people of Japan stand firmly united, if we

---

Source: W. G. Beasley, *Select Documents on Japanese Foreign Policy, 1853–1868* (Oxford: Oxford University Press, 1955), pp. 102–107. Reprinted by permission of Oxford University Press.

[1] Uraga is a village at the entrance of Edo Bay where Perry anchored his ships in July 1853; when he returned in March 1854, he anchored them closer to Edo, in Edo Bay itself.

[2] "Dutch Studies" refers to the activities of Japanese scholars who beginning in the eighteenth century developed an interest in European thought, which they studied mainly through Dutch translations.

complete our military preparations and return to the state of society that existed before the middle ages [when the emperor ruled the country directly], then we will even be able to go out against foreign countries and spread abroad our fame and prestige. But if we open trade at the demand of the foreigners, for no better reason than that our habits today being those of peace and indolence, men have shown fear merely at the coming of a handful of foreign warships, then it would truly be a vain illusion to think of evolving any long-range plan for going out against foreign countries. . . .

I hear that all, even though they be commoners, who have witnessed the recent actions of the foreigners, think them abominable; and if the *bakufu* does not expel these insolent foreigners root and branch there may be some who will complain in secret. . . . It is inevitable that men should think in this way when they have seen how arrogantly the foreigners acted. . . . That, I believe, is because even the humblest are conscious of the debt they owe their country, and it is indeed a promising sign. Since even ignorant commoners are talking

in this way, I fear that if the *bakufu* does not decide to carry out expulsion, if its handling of the matter shows nothing but excess of leniency and appeasement of the foreigners, then the lower orders may fail to understand its ideas and hence opposition might arise from evil men who have lost their respect for *bakufu* authority. . . .

But if the *bakufu*, now and henceforward, shows itself resolute for expulsion, the immediate effect will be to increase ten-fold the morale of the country and to bring about the completion of military preparations without even the necessity for issuing orders. Hesitant as I am to say so, only by so doing will the *shōgun* be able to fulfill his 'barbarian-expelling' duty and unite the men of every province in carrying out their proper military functions.

But good advice is as hard to accept as good medicine unpleasing to the palate. A temporizing and time-serving policy is the one easiest for men to adopt. It is therefore my belief that in this question . . . it is of the first importance that the *bakufu* pay due heed these matters and that having once reached a decision it should never waiver from it thereafter. . . .

2 • Ii Naosuke, Memorandum to the Bakufu, October 1, 1853

It is impossible in the crisis we now face to ensure the safety and tranquillity of our country merely by an insistence on the seclusion laws as we did in former times. Moreover, time is essential if we are to complete our coast defenses. . . .

There is a saying that when one is besieged in a castle, to raise the drawbridge is to imprison oneself and make it impossible to hold out indefinitely; and again, that when opposing forces face each other across a river, victory is obtained by those who cross the river and attack. . . . Even though the *shōgun*'s ancestors set up seclusion laws, they

left the Dutch and the Chinese to act as a bridge [to the outside world]. Might not this bridge now be of advantage to us in handling foreign affairs, providing us with the means whereby we may for a time avert the outbreak of hostilities and then, after some time has elapsed, gain a complete victory?

I understand that the coal for which the Americans have expressed a desire is to be found in quantity in Kyushu.[1] We should first tell them . . . that we also have need of coal, but that should their need of it arise urgently and unexpectedly during a voyage, they may ask for coal at Nagasaki and if we have any to spare we will provide it. Nor will we grudge them wood and water. As for foodstuffs, the supply varies from province

Source: W. G. Beasley, *Select Documents on Japanese Foreign Policy, 1853–1868* (Oxford: Oxford University Press, 1955), pp. 117–119. Reprinted by permission of Oxford University Press.

[1]Japan's third largest and most southwesterly island. Nagasaki was and is its largest city.

to province, but we can agree to provide food for the shipwrecked and unfortunate. Again, we can tell them, of recent years we have treated kindly those wrecked on our coasts and have sent them all home. There is no need for further discussion of this subject, and all requests concerning it should be made through the Dutch. Then, too, there is the question of trade. Although there is a national prohibition of it, conditions are not the same as they were. The exchange of goods is a universal practice. This we should explain to the spirits of our ancestors. And we should then tell the foreigners that we mean in the future to send trading vessels to the Dutch company's factory at Batavia[2] to engage in trade, that we will allocate some of our trading goods to America, some to Russia, and so on, using the Dutch to trade for us as our agents. . . . By replying in this way we will take the Americans by surprise in offering to treat them generally in the same way as the Dutch. . . .

We must construct new steamships, especially powerful warships, and these we will load with goods not needed in Japan. For a time we will have to employ Dutchmen as masters and mariners, but we will put on board with them Japanese of ability and integrity who must study the use of large guns, the handling of ships, and the rules of navigation. Openly these will be called merchant vessels, but they will in fact have the secret purpose of training a navy. As we increase the number of ships and our mastery of technique, Japanese will be able to sail the oceans freely and gain direct knowledge of conditions abroad without relying on the secret reports of the Dutch. . . . Our defenses thus strengthened, and all being arranged at home, we can act so as to make our courage and prestige resound beyond the seas. . . . Forestalling the foreigners in this way, I believe, is the best method of ensuring that the *bakufu* will at some future time find opportunity to reimpose its ban and forbid foreigners to come to Japan, as was done in the Kansei period [1789–1801]. Moreover, it would make possible the strictest prohibition of Christianity. And since I understand that the Americans and Russians themselves have only recently become skilled in navigation, I do not see how the people of our country, who are clever and quick-witted, should prove inferior to Westerners if we begin training at once. . . .

It is now no easy matter, by means of orders concerning the defense of Edo and the nearby coast, to ensure that all will be fully prepared for any sudden emergency, so not a moment must be wasted. However many firm walls we construct, they will certainly not be as effective as unity of mind if the unforeseen happens. The urgent task of the moment, therefore, is for the *bakufu* to resolve on relieving the nation's anxieties and issue the appropriate orders.

---

[2]Present-day Jakarta, Batavia was the center of Dutch commercial activities in Southeast Asia.

---

3 • Feng Guifen, Personal Protests from the Study of Jiaobin

According to a general geography compiled by an Englishman, the territory of China is eight times that of Russia, ten times that of the United States, one hundred times that of France, and two hundred times that of Great Britain. . . . Yet we are shamefully humiliated by the four nations, not because our climate, soil, or resources are inferior to theirs, but because our people are inferior. . . . Now, our inferiority is not due to our allotment

Source: From Wm. Theodore de Bary and Irene Bloom, *Sources of Chinese Tradition,* 2nd edition, vol. 2 (New York: Columbia University Press, 2000), pp. 235–238.

[i.e., our inherent nature] from Heaven, but is rather due to ourselves. If it were allotted us by Heaven, it would be a shame but not something we could do anything about. Since the inferiority is due to ourselves, it is a still greater shame but something we can do something about. And if we feel ashamed, there is nothing better than self-strengthening. . . .

Why are the Western nations small and yet strong? Why are we large and yet weak? We must search for the means to become their equal, and that depends solely on human effort. With regard to the present situation, several observations may be made: in not wasting human talents, we are inferior to the barbarians; in not wasting natural resources, we are inferior to the barbarians; in allowing no barrier to come between the ruler and the people, we are inferior to the barbarians; and in the matching of words with deeds, we are also inferior to the barbarians. The remedy for these four points is to seek the causes in ourselves. They can be changed at once if only the emperor would set us in the right direction. There is no need to learn from the barbarians in these matters.

We have only one thing to learn from the barbarians, and that is strong ships and effective guns. . . . Funds should be allotted to establish a shipyard and arsenal in each trading port. A few barbarians should be employed, and Chinese who are good in using their minds should be selected to receive instruction so that in turn they may teach many craftsmen. When a piece of work is finished and is as good as that made by the barbarians, the makers should be rewarded with an official *juren* degree[1] and be permitted to participate in the metropolitan examinations on the same basis as other scholars. Those whose products are of superior quality should be rewarded with the *jinshi* degree and be permitted to participate in the palace

examinations like others. The workers should be paid double so that they will not quit their jobs.

Our nation's emphasis on civil service examinations has sunk deep into people's minds for a long time. Intelligent and brilliant scholars have exhausted their time and energy in such useless things as the stereotyped examination essays, examination papers, and formal calligraphy. . . . We should now order one-half of them to apply themselves to the manufacturing of instruments and weapons and to the promotion of physical studies. . . . The intelligence and ingenuity of the Chinese are certainly superior to those of the various barbarians; it is only that hitherto we have not made use of them. . . . There ought to be some people of extraordinary intelligence who can have new ideas and improve on Western methods. At first they may take the foreigners as their teachers and models; then they may come to the same level and be their equals; finally they may move ahead and surpass them. . . .

It may be argued: ". . . Is not what you are proposing contrary to the Way of the sages?" No, it is not. When we speak of repelling the barbarians, we must have the actual means to repel them, and not just empty bravado. If we live in the present day and speak of repelling the barbarians, we should ask with what instruments we are to repel them. . . . [The answer is that] we should use the instruments of the barbarians but not adopt the ways of the barbarians. We should use them so that we can repel them.

Some have asked why we should not just purchase the ships and man them with [foreign] hirelings, but the answer is that this will not do. If we can manufacture, repair, and use them, then they are our weapons. . . . In the end the way to avoid trouble is to manufacture, repair, and use weapons by ourselves. Only thus can we pacify the empire; only thus can we become the leading power in

---

[1] The *juren* degree was awarded to successful candidates in the provincial civil service examinations held every three years in major provincial cities. The *jinshi* degree, China's highest degree, was awarded to successful candidates in the metropolitan examination held every three years in Beijing.

the world; only thus can we restore our original strength, redeem ourselves from former humiliations, and maintain the integrity of our vast territory so as to remain the greatest country on earth.

• • •

Western books on mathematics, mechanics, optics, light, and chemistry contain the best principles of the natural sciences. In the books on geography, the mountains, rivers, strategic points, customs, and native products of the hundred countries are fully listed. Most of this information is beyond the reach of the Chinese people. . . .

If we wish to use Western knowledge, we should establish official translation bureaus in Guangzhou and Shanghai. Brilliant students not over fifteen years of age should be selected from those areas to live and study in these schools on double allowances. Westerners should be appointed to teach them the spoken and written languages of the various nations, and famous Chinese teachers should be engaged to teach them classics, history, and other subjects. At the same time they should learn mathematics. . . . China has many brilliant people. There must be some who can learn from the barbarians and surpass them.

It is from learning that the principles of government are derived. . . . It is my opinion that today we should . . . take the foreign nations as our examples. They live at the same time and in the same world with us; they have attained prosperity and power by their own efforts. Is it not fully clear that they are similar to us and that their methods can easily be put into practice? If we let Chinese ethics and Confucian teachings serve as the foundation, and let them be supplemented by the methods used by the various nations for the attainment of prosperity and power, would it not be the best of all solutions?

4 • Woren, Memorandum on Western Studies

Your Majesty is certainly correct when you say that mathematics, being one of the Six Arts, is a legitimate field of study and should by no means be considered with heretical or unorthodox learning. However, as your humble servant sees it, whatever small advantage can be derived from studying mathematics and astronomy is more than offset by the great harm that would certainly come about when we have to employ Westerners to teach them. . . .

Your humble servant has heard that the foundation of a nation lies in the virtues (such as righteousness and propriety) she possesses rather than in transient advantages she may have or fanciful expedients she can devise. Her true strength is derived from the collective mind of her people rather than some unusual skills she happens to possess.

Now we are asked not only to pursue a small and insignificant skill but also honor foreigners as teachers. Since foreigners are known for their treachery, it is extremely doubtful if they will reveal to us all of their secrets. Even if they did, their contribution would amount to no more than the training of technicians. Throughout history no country has ever become strong by relying on achievement in technology.

Being so large, China has many talented men within her national boundaries. If, say, such subjects as mathematics and astronomy are really important enough to be taught, we can certainly find . . . Chinese experts to reach them. Why do we have to employ foreigners? . . .

Moreover, foreigners have always been our enemies. In [1860], they launched a vicious attack against China without any provocation. They ravaged our capital, thus shaking the nation to its very

Source: Dun J. Li, *China in Transition, 1517–1911* (New York: Van Nostrand Reinhold, 1969), pp. 161–163.

foundation. They not only set fire to the [Winter Palace] and destroyed it but also indiscriminately murdered civilians and officials alike. This humiliation was unprecedented in the 200-year history of our dynasty and has been deeply resented by both scholars and officials. Though the government was then forced to negotiate peace with these foreigners, how can it ever forget the unavenged shame? Since the conclusion of the peace treaty, Christianity has spread far and wide and with great cunning has beguiled and entrapped many innocent but ignorant citizens. In these critical times the only thing the nation can rely on for its survival is the rectitude of its intelligentsia, who, we hope, can continue to maintain people's integrity by pointing out to them the correct path to follow. Now that we are asked to transform our

most talented young men, upon whom the future of our nation relies, into the followers of foreign ways, not only will the best of our tradition suffer regression, but the unorthodox, alien spirit will continue to spread. If this situation continues, I am afraid that in a few years all of us will become foreigners instead of remaining Chinese. . . .

In view of the fact that China has suffered greatly at the hands of foreigners for such a long time, why should we insist on spreading their evil ideas? . . . This is a trap the foreigners have carefully set up: by no means should we fall into it!

It is the hope of your humble servant that Your Majesty . . . will immediately put an end to the proposal in question, so the future of the nation will remain orthodox and safe. This action on your part will bring great benefit to the nation as a whole.

The Emergence of Modern Japan

In the late nineteenth century, Japan accomplished what no other nation had, or has since, been able to do. In only four decades, it set aside the bitter disputes of the 1850s and early 1860s and transformed itself from a secluded, preindustrial society, vulnerable to foreign exploitation, into a powerful, industrialized nation that shocked the world by winning wars against China in 1895 and Russia in 1905. What made this transformation even more remarkable was that it was accompanied by little social upheaval and that, despite its magnitude, the Japanese retained many of their hallowed ideals and beliefs.

Japan's transformation began in 1867, when a faction of aristocrats overthrew the Tokugawa shogunate and then orchestrated the move of the previously secluded and ceremonial emperor from Kyoto to Edo, where he assumed titular authority over a government that they controlled. These events are known as the Meiji Restoration, based on the Japanese word *meiji* ("brilliant rule"), chosen by Emperor Mutsuhito as his reign name.

Patriotic Duty and Business Success

78 • IWASAKI YATARO, LETTER TO MITSUBISHI EMPLOYEES

From the moment the Meiji reformers seized power, they sought to modernize Japan's economy, especially in industries in the manufacturing sector that produced goods for export or for the military. After a rocky start in the 1870s, Japanese industrialization proceeded rapidly, and by 1900, the nation had become an important economic power through a combination of government subsidies and individual entrepreneurship.

The greatest success story in Japan's economic transformation was that of Iwasaki Yataro (1835–1885), the founder of one of the nation's most powerful business conglomerates, Mitsubishi. Born into a farming family, Iwasaki gained a rudimentary education and held several low-level business jobs before he found employment as an official in the service of the aristocratic Tosa clan in the mid-1860s. He was given the task of managing and reducing the Tosa domain's huge debt, which had resulted from purchases of firearms and artillery. His policies, which included paying some debtors with counterfeit money, quickly eliminated the domain's deficit. In 1871, when the domain abandoned its direct ownership of business enterprises, it gave Iwasaki eleven steamships and all the assets connected with its enterprises in the silk, coal, tea, and lumber industries. In return, Iwasaki was expected to pay off additional Tosa debts and provide employment for former samurai. With this to build on, he systematically wiped out foreign and domestic competition and, through a series of shrewd business moves, turned Mitsubishi (a name adopted in 1873) into Japan's second-largest conglomerate, with interests in shipbuilding, mining, banking, insurance, and manufacturing.

Iwasaki wrote the following letter to his employees in 1876 during Mitsubishi's battle with the British Peninsular and Oriental Steam Navigation Company over control of Japanese coastal trade. He had just cut fares in half but had also reduced wages by a third. His appeal to his workers' patriotism and his own sense of mission provide insights into the reasons for Japan's successful modernization.

QUESTIONS FOR ANALYSIS

1. Why does Iwasaki believe that the Japanese must prevent foreigners from becoming involved in the coastal trade?
2. According to Iwasaki, what is at stake in the competition for control of Japan's coastal trade?
3. What advantages and disadvantages does Iwasaki's company have in its rivalry with the Peninsular and Oriental Steam Navigation Company?
4. How does Iwasaki attempt to inspire greater dedication and effort from his workers?

Many people have expressed differing opinions concerning the principles and advantages of engaging foreigners or Japanese in the task of coastal trade. Granted, we may permit a dissenting opinion which suggests that in principle both foreigners and Japanese must be permitted to engage in coastal trade, but once we look into the question of advantages, we know that coastal trade is too important a matter to be given over to the control of foreigners. If we allow the right of coastal navigation to fall into the hands of foreigners in peacetime it means loss of business opportunities and employment for our own people, and in wartime it means yielding the vital right of information to foreigners. In fact, this is not too different from abandoning the rights of our country as an independent nation.

Source: David J Lu, *Japan: A Documentary History* (New York: M.E. Sharpe, 1997), pp. 356–358. Translation © 1997 by David J. Lu. Reprinted with permission of M.E. Sharpe, Inc.

Looking back into the past, in Japan at the time when we abandoned the policy of seclusion and entered into an era of friendly intercourse and commerce with foreign nations, we should have been prepared for this very task. However, due to the fact that our people lack knowledge and wealth, we have yet to assemble a fleet sufficient to engage in coastal navigation. Furthermore, we have neither the necessary skills for navigation nor a plan for developing maritime transportation industry. This condition is the cause of attracting foreign shipping companies to occupy our major maritime transport lines. Yet our people show not a sense of surprise at it. . . .

I now propose to do my utmost, and along with my 35 million compatriots, perform my duty as a citizen of this country. That is to recover the right of coastal trade in our hands, and not to delegate that task to foreigners. Unless we propose to do so, it is useless for our government to revise the unequal treaties[1] or to change our entrenched customs. We need people who can respond, otherwise all the endeavors of the government will come to naught. This is the reason why the government protects our company, and I know that our responsibilities are even greater than the full weight of Mt. Fuji[2] thrust upon our shoulders. There have been many who wish to hinder our progress in fulfilling our obligations. However, we have been able to eliminate one of our worst enemies, the Pacific Mail Company of the United States, from contention by application of appropriate means.[3] Now, another rival has emerged. It is the Peninsular & Oriental Steam Navigation Company of Great Britain which is setting up a new line between Yokohama and Shanghai, and is attempting to claim its right over the ports of Nagasaki, Kobe, and Yokohama. The P & O Company comes to compete for the right of coastal navigation with us. How can we decline the challenge? Heretofore, our company has received

protection from the government, support from the nation, and hard work from its employees through which it has done its duty. However, our company is young and not every phase of its operation is well conducted. In contrast, the P & O Company is backed by its massive capital, its large fleet of ships, and by its experiences of operations in Oriental countries. In competing against this giant, what methods can we employ?

I have thought about this problem very carefully and have come to one conclusion. There is no other alternative but to eliminate unnecessary positions and unnecessary expenditures. This is a time-worn solution and no new wisdom is involved. Even though it is a familiar saying, it is much easier said than done, and this indeed has been the root cause of difficulties in the past and present times. Therefore, starting immediately I propose that we engage in this task. By eliminating unnecessary personnel from the payroll, eliminating unnecessary expenditures, and engaging in hard and arduous work, we shall be able to solidify the foundation of our company. If there is a will there is a way. Through our own effort, we shall be able to repay the government for its protection and answer our nation for its confidence shown in us. Let us work together in discharging our responsibilities and not be ashamed of ourselves. Whether we succeed or fail, whether we can gain profit or sustain loss, we cannot anticipate at this time. Hopefully, all of you will join me in a singleness of heart to attain this cherished goal, forbearing and undaunted by setbacks to restore to our own hands the right to our own coastal trade. If we succeed it will not only be an accomplishment for our company alone but also a glorious event for our Japanese Empire, which shall let its light shine to all four corners of earth. We can succeed or fail, and it depends on your effort or lack of effort. Do your utmost in this endeavor!

---

[1] The commercial treaties with Western powers agreed to by the shogunate after Perry's mission.
[2] The highest mountain in Japan, near Tokyo.

[3] The American firm withdrew from the Japanese market when it was unable to compete with Mitsubishi's low prices, made possible largely by government subsidies.

Images of the West in Late Tokugawa and Meiji Japan

79 • PRINTS AND DRAWINGS, 1853–1891

Following the Europeans' arrival in Japan in 1542, their ideas, dress, weapons, and religion proved attractive to many Japanese. Several hundred thousand Japanese converted to Catholicism, military leaders put European firearms to use, and some Japanese showed an interest in European fashion and cuisine. After the Tokugawa suppressed Christianity and implemented the seclusion policy in the 1600s, however, knowledge of the West was limited to merchants who traded with the Dutch in Nagasaki and a handful of intellectuals interested in European thought. For most Japanese, memory of the South Sea Barbarians disappeared.

Increased interactions with Westerners, culminating in the Perry expedition in 1853 and the opening of Japan to foreign trade in 1854, changed this dramatically. Inspired by a mixture of fear, awe, revulsion, and curiosity, the Japanese developed a deep interest in the West, and a flood of printed material about Europe and the United States appeared in the 1850s and 1860s. After the Meiji Restoration, imitation of the West for a time became a patriotic duty. Employing Western science, technology, military organization, and government practices would make Japan strong and prosperous; adopting Western fashion, etiquette, grooming habits, and architecture would make the Japanese respected and admired. In the late 1880s, however, a reaction against overzealous Westernization set in. Since then, the Japanese have managed to strike a balance between borrowing from the West and preserving the essentials of their traditional culture.

The following six illustrations provide insights into changing Japanese views of the West. The first two are tile prints that appeared soon after the arrival of Commodore Perry. Forerunners of modern newspapers, such prints were produced quickly and anonymously after newsworthy events and sold for a few cents. The first print depicts one of Perry's "black ships," so called because of the dark smoke that belched from their smokestacks. The text provides information on the ship's dimensions and its voyage to Japan. The second print depicts Commander Henry Adams, Perry's second-in-command.

The next two illustrations appeared when the drive to emulate Europeans was under way. The first is part of a series of woodblock prints published in the 1880s entitled *Self-Made Men Worthy of Emulation*. The individual depicted is Fukuchi Genichiro (1841–1909), a journalist who served as editor-in-chief of Tokyo's first daily newspaper. He is shown covering the Satsuma Rebellion of 1877, a failed rebellion by disgruntled samurai against the new Meiji order. The artist is Kobayashi Kiyochika (1847–1911), a self-taught painter whose numerous woodblock prints show the influence of Western painting and perspective. The accompanying text (with an erroneous birth date) reads:

> Fukuchi Genichiro was born in Nagasaki in 1844. An exceptionally bright child, he could recognize characters at the age of five and had begun to read and write at about the age of seven. He resolved to enter the service of the shogunate and, upon coming of age, entered the government, in the service of which he traveled three times to Europe.
>
> He then entered into a successful business career. In 1874 he became president of the Reporters' Association. He personally covered the Satsuma Rebellion in the south. Received by the emperor, he respectfully reported his observations to the throne. His style seemed almost supernatural in its logic, force, and lucidity. He is one of the truly great men of Meiji.

The next illustration (page 365) appeared in a popular book by Kanagaki Robun published in serial form in the 1870s. *Hiking through the West* relates the adventures of two Japanese travelers during a trip to London and back. The illustration depicts, from right to left, an "unenlightened man," dressed as a samurai; a "half-enlightened man"; and an "enlightened man."

Even as Japanese enthusiasm for things Western was peaking, some opposed Japan's rush to Westernize. Government censorship silenced most of these critics, but a few managed to get their ideas into print. Cartoonists Honda Kinkichiro and Kobayashi Kyochika were two such individuals. Honda's cartoons, usually with

One of Commodore Perry's Black Ships

Ryosenji Treasure Museum, Ryosenji Temple

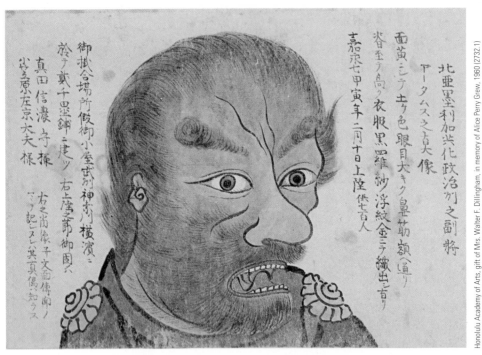

Commodore Perry's Second-in-Command, Commander Henry Adams

Kobayashi Kiyochika, Fukuchi Genichiro

English captions and a Japanese text, appeared in the late 1870s and 1880s in the weekly humor magazine *Marumaru Chinbun.* His "Monkey Show Dressing Room" (page 366) was published in 1879, shortly after Dr. Edward S. Morse introduced Darwin's theory of evolution in a series of lectures at the newly founded Department of Zoology at Tokyo University. The text reads, "Mr. Morse explains that all human beings were monkeys in the beginning. In the beginning—but even now aren't we still monkeys? When it comes to Western things we think the red beards [Westerners] are the most skillful at everything."

Kobayashi, the artist who made the print of Fukuchi Genichiro and who contributed cartoons to *Marumaru Chinbun* in the 1880s, published the cartoon on page 366 in the *Tokyo Daily News* in 1891. It depicts a New Year's dance held in the Rokumeikan, a pavilion built by the government in 1883 to serve as a venue for fancy-dress balls and other entertainments involving Westerners and Japan's elite. Above the dance floor, filled with ill-matched Western and Japanese couples, is a sign that reads, "Hands Dance, Feet Stomp, Call Out Hurrah!"

QUESTIONS FOR ANALYSIS

1. What impression of the West is conveyed by the prints of Perry's ship and his second-in-command, Commander Adams? What specific details help convey this impression?

Kanagaki Robun, Hiking through the West

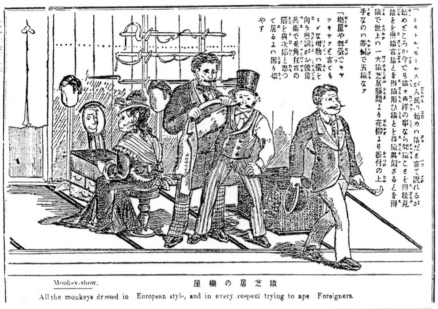

Honda Kinkichiro, "Monkey Show Dressing Room"

Kobayashi Kiyochika, "Hands Dance, Feet Stomp, Call Out Hurrah!"

2. In the illustration on page 365, what are the most significant differences between the three figures? How does the artist convey a sense of the "enlightened man's" superiority?
3. What is there in the drawing of Fukuchi Genichiro and in the accompanying text that makes him "a man worthy of emulation"?
4. Why do you think the artist chose to depict Fukuchi while he was covering the Satsuma Rebellion?
5. What messages are Honda and Kobayashi attempting to convey about Japan's campaign to Westernize?
6. Compare and contrast the depiction of Westerners in "Hands Dance . . ." with the earlier depiction of Commander Adams.

The End of Imperial China

Despite its many achievements, by the early 1900s, the Self-Strengthening movement in China had reached a dead end. For forty years, its supporters, still dedicated to the values of Confucianism and imperial rule, had worked to revive China by selectively and incrementally introducing aspects of Western science, technology, military organization, and jurisprudence. Between 1895 and 1901, a series of events painfully revealed the inadequacy of their approach. China's shocking defeat in the Sino-Japanese War in 1895 and its inability to slow the partition of China by Western imperialists underscored its continued military weakness. The announcement by the Guangzhu emperor of an ambitious reform program in 1898 followed by a *coup d'état* and its suppression after only three months revealed the reformers' powerlessness in the face of conservative opposition. The decision of the government to support the ill-fated antiforeign revolt known as the Boxer Rebellion led to yet another humiliating treaty and general revulsion against the Manchus and their policies.

Following the Boxer debacle, a broad consensus emerged that more was needed than tentative half-measures. Local elites, acting on their own, founded schools, published translations of Western books, and organized police forces modeled on European practice. Families sent their children to study in Europe, Japan, or the United States, and merchants joined boycotts of U.S. goods in response to U.S. anti-Chinese immigration policies. Even the dowager empress Cixi and her conservative entourage, who had scuttled the reform effort in 1898, announced the establishment of a national school system, founded new military academies, set a timetable for the achievement of constitutional government, changed the civil service examination system to include questions on more practical topics, and then abolished the examinations altogether. These ambitious policies, however, failed to win back the support of their ethnic Chinese subjects, many of whom had come to believe that China was being victimized by two forms of foreign oppression, that of the West and that of the Manchus. Nor were Manchu reforms able to weaken the convictions of those who believed China's salvation lay in revolution and a complete break from China's Confucian and imperial past. Long in coming, such a break occurred in 1911.

The Beginnings of Chinese Feminism

80 • QIU JIN, AN ADDRESS TO TWO HUNDRED MILLION FELLOW COUNTRYWOMEN

Inspired by the educational gains of women in Meiji Japan and the example and teachings of Western missionaries, a small but significant feminist movement emerged in late-nineteenth-century and early-twentieth-century China. As was the case in India and the Islamic Middle East, some of the earliest spokespersons for women's liberation were male officials and intellectuals, who viewed the subservience of women as both an embarrassment and an impediment to national progress. In the early 1900s, they were joined by increasing numbers of educated women who founded women's organizations, published women's magazines, and founded schools for girls. A few committed themselves to revolutionary activity.

Among the radical Chinese feminists of the early 1900s, none matched the passion of Qiu Jin (1875–1907). Raised in a moderately wealthy family, she was married by arrangement of her parents at a young age to a merchant's son. Then in 1903 she left her husband and two children and sailed to Japan, where she studied Western politics and philosophy and joined one of the several Tokyo-based Chinese revolutionary organizations. On her return in 1906, she founded a magazine and served as the principal for a girls' school. In 1907, she and her cousin were arrested and beheaded for revolutionary activity.

In the following address, probably written during her stay in Japan, she denounces the oppression of Chinese women, especially the practice of footbinding, the painful and injurious practice in which girls as young as four or five had their feet tightly wrapped and gradually bent until the arch was broken and all toes but the big toe were bent under. When the wrappings were removed seven to ten years later, the teenage girl was a semicripple with feet half their normal size, but she would be ready for matrimony. Girls with "big feet" were considered unmarriageable.

QUESTIONS FOR ANALYSIS

1. According to Qiu, what kind of relationship do most Chinese girls have with their parents?
2. What can be learned from the source about Chinese marriages and the relationship between husbands and wives?
3. What are the motives, according to Qiu, for subjecting women to foot binding and preventing them from learning how to read?
4. According to Qiu, what share of the blame for their oppression must be assumed by women themselves?
5. What are Qiu's solutions for China's problems?

Alas! The greatest injustice in this world must be the injustice suffered by our female population of two hundred million. If a girl is lucky enough to have a good father, then her childhood is at least tolerable. But if by chance her father is an ill-tempered and unreasonable man, he may curse her birth: "What rotten luck: another useless thing." Some men go as far as killing baby girls while most hold the opinion that "girls are eventually someone else's property" and treat them with coldness and disdain. In a few years, without thinking about whether it is right or wrong, he[1] forcibly binds his daughter's soft, white feet with white cloth so that even in her sleep she cannot find comfort and relief until the flesh becomes rotten and the bones broken. What is all this misery for? Is it just so that on the girl's wedding day friends and neighbors will compliment him, saying, "Your daughter's feet are really small"? Is that what the pain is for?

But that is not the worst of it. When the time for marriage comes, a girl's future life is placed in the hands of a couple of shameless matchmakers and a family seeking rich and powerful in-laws. A match can be made without anyone ever inquiring whether the prospective bridegroom is honest, kind, or educated. . . . After her marriage, if the man doesn't do her any harm, she is told that she should thank Heaven for her good fortune. But if the man is bad or he ill-treats her, she is told that her marriage is retribution for some sin committed in her previous existence. If she complains at all or tries to reason with her husband, he may get angry and beat her. When other people find out they will criticize, saying, "That woman is bad; she doesn't know how to behave like a wife.". . . Why is there no justice for women? We constantly hear men say, "The human mind is just

and we must treat people with fairness and equality." Then why do they greet women like black slaves from Africa? How did inequality and injustice reach this state?

Dear sisters, you must know that you'll get nothing if you rely upon others. You must go out and get things for yourselves. In ancient times when decadent scholars came out with such nonsense as "men are exalted, women are lowly," "a virtuous woman is one without talent," and "the husband guides the wife," ambitious and spirited women should have organized and opposed them. . . . Men feared that if women were educated they would become superior to men, so they did not allow us to be educated. Couldn't the women have challenged the men and refused to submit? It seems clear now that it was we women who abandoned our responsibilities to ourselves and felt content to let men do everything for us. As long as we could live in comfort and leisure, we let men make all the decisions for us. When men said we were useless, we became useless; when they said we were incapable, we stopped questioning them even when our entire female sex had reached slave status. . . . When we heard that men liked small feet, we immediately bound them just to please them, just to keep our free meal tickets. As for their forbidding us to read and write, well, that was only too good to be true. . . .

. . . Let us all put aside our former selves and be resurrected as complete human beings. . . . You must know that when a country is near destruction, women cannot rely on the men any more because they aren't even able to protect themselves. If we don't take heart now and shape up, it will be too late when China is destroyed. Sisters, we must follow through on these ideas!

Source: "An Address to Two Hundred Million Fellow Countrywomen" (1906), from Patricia Embrey, *Chinese Civilization: A Sourcebook* (New York The Free Press, a Division of Simón & Schuster).

[1]Although Qiu uses the male pronoun, the actual work of binding feet was performed by female members of the girl's family, usually mothers or grandmothers.

A Call for Revolution

81 • CHINESE REVOLUTIONARY ALLIANCE, REVOLUTIONARY PROCLAMATION, 1907

By the early 1900s, despair over the state of China and disillusionment with Qing rule had given rise to dozens of organizations that sought China's renewal through revolution. With some based in China itself and others in Chinese communities in Japan and elsewhere overseas, these organizations shared a common hatred of Manchu tyranny, but otherwise lacked coordination and any sort of common ideology or long-term program. The founding of the Chinese Revolutionary Alliance (also known as the Chinese Alliance Association and the Chinese United League) in 1905 in Tokyo sought to bring greater unity and direction to the revolutionary movement.

Tokyo was then the home of approximately ten thousand Chinese students and the headquarters of dozens of radical student organizations. It also was the temporary home of Sun Yat-sen (1866–1925), the Western-educated political activist who had founded the revolutionary Revive China Society in 1895 and achieved worldwide notoriety in 1896 when he narrowly escaped being killed after being kidnapped by Manchu agents in London and held for ten days in the Chinese embassy. In 1905, Sun coordinated the merger of a number of Tokyo-based student groups and the Revive China Society to found the Revolutionary Alliance with headquarters in Tokyo and branches in a number of overseas Chinese communities.

In 1907, the Chinese Revolutionary Alliance issued the following proclamation, which in general terms reflects Sun's formulation of the "three people's principles" of nationalism, democracy, and livelihood. Although the organization played no direct role in the revolutionary events of 1911, it provided the nucleus of the Guomindang, or National People's Party, formed by Sun in 1912. The Guomindang battled the Communists for control of China until the communist victory in 1947 and continues to be a major political force in the Taiwan-based Republic of China.

QUESTIONS FOR ANALYSIS

1. What definition of "revolution" is implied in the proclamation? How, according to the proclamation, will the revolution imagined by the Revolutionary Alliance differ from previous revolutions in China?
2. What rationale is provided by the proclamation for ending Manchu rule?
3. What kind of government does the proclamation propose for post-Manchu China?
4. What kinds of social and economic changes will occur as a result of the revolution?
5. What is your overall evaluation of the proclamation as a statement of the Revolutionary Alliance's principles? Does it provide a viable blueprint for China's future?

When China was occasionally occupied by a foreign race, our ancestors could always in the end drive these foreigners out, restore the fatherland, and preserve China for future generations of Chinese. Today when we raise the righteous standard of revolt in order to expel an alien race that has been occupying China, we are doing no more than our ancestors have done or expected us to do. Justice is so much on our side that all Chinese, once familiarizing themselves with our stand, will have no doubt about the righteousness of our cause.

There is a difference, however, between our revolution and the revolutions of our ancestors. The purpose of past revolutions . . . was to restore China to the Chinese, and nothing else. We, on the other hand, strive not only to expel the ruling aliens . . . but also to change basically the political and economic structure of our country. While we cannot describe in detail this new political and economic structure since so much is involved, the basic principle behind it is liberty, equality, and fraternity. The revolutions of yesterday were revolutions by and for the heroes [elites]; our revolution, on the other hand, is a revolution by and for the people. . . .

At this juncture we wish to express candidly and fully how to make our revolution today and how to govern our country tomorrow.

1. *Expulsion of the Manchus from China.* . . . Toward the end of the Ming dynasty they [the Manchus] repeatedly invaded our border areas and caused great difficulties. Then, taking advantage of the chaotic situation in China, they marched southward and forcibly occupied our country. They compelled all Chinese to become their slaves, and those who did not wish to subjugate themselves were slaughtered, numbering millions. . . . Now that the day has finally arrived when the brutal and evil rule by the Manchus must come to an end, we do not expect much resistance when our righteous army begins to move. . . . All the soldiers on the Manchu side, whether they are Manchus or Chinese, will be pardoned despite their past crimes if they express repentance and surrender. If they choose to resist the people's army, they will be killed without mercy. The same can be also said about the Chinese who have collaborated with the Manchu government as traitors.

2. *Restoration of China to the Chinese.* China belongs to the Chinese who have the right to govern themselves. After the Manchus are expelled from China, we will have a national government of our own. . . .

3. *Establishment of a Republic.* . . . In a republic all citizens will have the right to participate in the government, the president of the republic will be elected by the people, and the parliament will have deputies elected by and responsible to their respective constituents. A constitution of the Chinese Republic will then be formulated, to be observed by all Chinese. . . . Anyone who entertains the thought of becoming an emperor will be crushed without mercy.

4. *Equalization of landownership.* The social and economic structure of China must be so reconstructed that the fruits of labor will be shared by all Chinese on an equal basis. . . . The ultimate goal of a responsible society is the guarantee of a satisfactory livelihood for all of its members and everyone, whomever he happens to be, shall have his own means of support, via gainful employment or some other source. Anyone who attempts to monopolize the livelihood of others will be ostracized.

To attain the four goals as outlined above, we propose a procedure of three stages. The first stage

Source: Dun J. Li, *China in Transition, 1517–1911* (New York: Van Nostrand Reinhold, 1969), pp. 137–141. Reprinted by permission of John Wiley & Sons, Inc.

is that of a military rule. In areas that have been recently taken over by the revolutionary army, local governments will be administered by the military command which shall see to it that all the political and social abuses of the past will be eliminated. By political abuses are meant governmental oppression, bureaucratic corruption, extortion by the police, marshals, and other law-enforcement personnel, cruelty in punishment, excessive taxation, and the wearing of pigtails as a symbol of submission to the Manchu government. By social abuses are meant the ownership of domestic slaves, the cruel custom of foot-binding, the smoking of poisonous opium, and the belief in geomancy[1] and other superstitions that are an impediment to modern progress.

The stage of military rule should not last for more than three years. After a district has succeeded in attaining the goals prescribed for the stage of military rule, military rule will come to an end, and the second stage, the stage of provisional constitution, will then begin. . . . The people then govern themselves by electing as their representatives deputies on the district council as well as all the executive officials. . . . Six years after the nation has been pacified, a constitution will be proclaimed to replace the provisional constitution as described above, and the nation then formally enters the third or final stage, the stage of constitutional rule. . . . The President of China will be popularly elected; so will all members of the Parliament. All policies to be pursued by the nation must be in conformity with the letter and spirit of the proclaimed constitution. . . .

This orderly procedure is necessary because our people need time to acquaint themselves with the idea of liberty and equality. Liberty and equality are the basis on which the Republic of China rests.

To the attainment of the four goals and the implementation of the three stages, as outlined above, the Military Government will dedicate itself on behalf of all the people in the nation. It will do so with loyalty, faith, and total determination. . . . The brilliant achievements of China have been known throughout the world, and only recently has she suffered numerous difficulties. We shall overcome these difficulties and march forward. The harder the task is, the harder we shall work.

On this day of restoring China to her own people, we urge everyone to step forward and to do the best he can. As the descendants of Huang-di,[2] we shall regard one another as brothers and sisters and assist each other regardless of the difficulty of the circumstances. . . . We shall do so with one heart and one mind. When our soldiers are willing to sacrifice their lives and when everyone else is sparing no effort for the attainment of our noble goals, the revolution will succeed and the Republic of China will be established. Let each and every one of the 400 million people do his very best.

---

[1]Also known as *Feng shui*, geomancy is an ancient system of Chinese aesthetics believed to use the laws of heaven and earth to improve one's life by receiving positive energy flow, or *qi*; widely used in determining the position of buildings, tombs, and graves.

[2]Huang-di was a legendary Chinese sovereign and cultural hero who in Chinese mythology is considered to be the father of all Han Chinese.

PART FOUR

The Global Community and Its Challenges in the Twentieth and Twenty-First Centuries

W HAT WILL FUTURE HISTORIANS say about the past 100 years of human history? How will they interpret the wars, revolutions, economic transformations, new ideologies, technological breakthroughs, population trends, cultural changes, and countless other events and developments that took place? How will they explain the contradictions between humankind's stupendous achievements and its abysmal failures? From the perspective of the early twenty-first century, no one can answer such questions. Future historians' views of the past century will be shaped by events that have not yet occurred and by values and concerns unique to their own era. What may seem matters of great consequence to us may be insignificant to them, while developments we barely notice may be important parts of their stories.

It would be surprising, however, if future historians did not note the importance of the dramatic shift in world political relationships following World War II. The world of the early 1900s was a Eurocentric world. Europeans and people of European descent living elsewhere were the best-educated and wealthiest people on earth. When one spoke of the Great Powers, they all were European states or European offshoots such as the United States. They ruled Africa and much of Asia, and dominated the global economy. After World War II, Europe's primacy ended. The Europeans' colonial empires disintegrated; their paramount role in international relations was lost; and their economic importance declined in the face of global competition.

Future historians undoubtedly also will highlight the phenomenon of globalization, a word and concept that came into common usage at the end of the twentieth century to describe the unprecedented scale of integration and interaction that had come to dominate world relationships. Human interaction, of course, was nothing new. Long-distance trade, migration, travel, missionary activity, wars of conquest, and the diffusion of new ideas and technologies had been parts of history for thousands of years. Interaction on a global scale increased markedly in the fifteenth and sixteenth centuries, when Europeans opened sea routes to Africa, the Americas, and Asia and launched a new era in commerce, migration, and biological exchange. During the twentieth century, however, breakthroughs in communications and transportation virtually obliterated the limitations of time and space, and the exchange of goods and ideas among the world's peoples reached undreamed-of levels.

Future historians assuredly will note other developments: the ongoing rush of scientific, medical, and technological discoveries; the spectacular expansion of the world's population (from approximately 1.7 billion in 1900 to 6.9 billion in 2010); the relative decline of the world's rural population and the growth of cities; and the emergence of a shared global culture, symbolized by the unlimited possibilities of the Internet and the ubiquity of McDonald's restaurants, Japanese and Korean automobiles, blue jeans, 24-hour cable news networks, and Chinese manufactured goods of every imaginable sort.

What else historians will say about the past 100 years is open to conjecture. They undoubtedly will take note of our recent history's inhumanities and cruelties: its appalling war casualties, its use of torture, and its genocides, not just against Jews in World War II but also against Armenians in World War I; Cambodians in the 1970s; Bosnians, Kosovars, and Tutsi in the 1990s; and the peoples of Darfur in the early 2000s. Will such developments be described as aberrations or the beginning of a new trend toward brutality and callousness in human relationships? Historians surely will discuss the emergence of more than 100 new independent states in Africa and Asia. Will their stories turn out to be celebrations of economic and political achievement or tales of ongoing failure and disillusionment? They will note that the twentieth and early twenty-first centuries were marked by signs of both religious fervor and indifference; environmental disasters and growing environmental consciousness; and the globalization of culture and the continued appeal of national and ethnic identification.

In looking to the future, optimists affirm their faith in progress, holding fast to the dream that reasonable human beings are capable of shaping a future of peace, harmony, and a just sharing of the world's wealth. Pessimists ponder population projections, inevitable energy shortages, worsening pollution, global warming, and the persistence of intractable political conflicts and warn of the coming of a new "dark age." However things develop, recent history has launched humankind on new paths that will determine its future for years to come.

Chapter 11

The Industrialized World in Crisis

N 1922, THE FRENCH INTELLECTUAL Paul Valéry spoke these words in a speech to a university audience in Switzerland:

> The storm has died away, and still we are restless, uneasy, as if the storm is about to break. Almost all the affairs of men remain in terrible uncertainty. We think of what has disappeared, we are almost destroyed by what has been destroyed; we do not know what will be born, and we fear the future, not without reason. We hope vaguely, we dread precisely; . . . we confess that the charm of life is behind us, abundance is behind us, but doubt and disorder are in us and with us. There is no thinking man, however shrewd or learned he may be, who can hope to overcome this anxiety, to escape this darkness, to measure the probable duration of this period when the vital relations of humanity are disturbed profoundly.[1]

How stark a contrast between Valéry's despondency and the optimism that preceded World War I. Before the war, the West's wealth and power reached unimagined heights, and most Americans and Europeans were self-satisfied, proud, and confident. They took for granted their moral and intellectual superiority and were convinced that their world dominance would last indefinitely. The people of Japan, a new entrant into the ranks of industrialized nations, imagined a different future, but like the people of the West, they looked forward to that future with high expectations. Only a few years later, assurance gave way to doubt, hope to despair, and moderation to fanaticism.

The turning point, especially for Europe, was World War I—the four-year exercise in death that resulted in 30 million casualties, billions of squandered dollars, and a disturbing realization that human

---

[1]Paul Valéry, *Variety*, translated from the French by T. Malcolm Crosby (New York: Harcourt Brace, 1927), p. 252.

inventiveness could have dark and devastating consequences. The war and the postwar treaties set the stage for three decades marked by worldwide economic depression, totalitarianism, diplomatic failure, contempt for human rights, and, finally, a second world war with a legacy of 50 to 60 million dead, the attempted annihilation of Europe's Jews, and the dropping of the first atomic bombs.

Interwar intellectuals who shared Paul Valéry's anxiety and gloom prophesied the fall of Western civilization and drew analogies between the decline of the West in the twentieth century and the fatal problems of fifth-century Rome. Post-World War II developments discredited much of their pessimism. The industrialized nations, even devastated Germany and Japan, recovered from the wars, affirmed a commitment to liberal democracy, and rebuilt their economies. What changed was their role in the world. Empires disappeared, and formerly colonial peoples reestablished their political independence. The traumatic events that unfolded between 1914 and 1945 were largely responsible for these changes.

The Trauma of World War I

Why did Europeans find World War I so demoralizing, so unsettling, so devoid of any quality or result that might have justified its appalling costs and casualties? War, after all, was nothing new for Europeans. Dynastic wars, religious wars, commercial wars, colonial wars, civil wars, wars to preserve or destroy the balance of power, wars of every conceivable variety fill the pages of European history books. Some of these wars involved dozens of states, and some, such as the Seven Years' War (1756–1763) and the wars of the French Revolution and Napoleonic Era, were world wars. Yet none of these conflicts prepared Europeans for the war they fought between 1914 and 1918.

The sheer number of battlefield casualties goes far to explain the war's devastating impact. The war's 32 belligerents mobilized approximately 65 million men, of whom just under 10 million were killed and slightly more than 20 million were wounded. To present these statistics in another way, this means that for approximately 1,500 consecutive days, on average 6,000 men were killed every day. Losses were high on both the eastern and western fronts, but those in the west were more appalling. Here, after the Germans almost took Paris in the early weeks of fighting, the war became a stalemate until the armistice on November 11, 1918. Along a 400-mile front stretching from the English Channel through Belgium and France to the Swiss border, defense—a combination of trenches, barbed wire, land mines, poison gas, and machine guns—proved superior to offense—massive artillery barrages followed by charges of troops sent over the top across no man's land to overrun enemy lines. Such attacks produced unbearably long casualty lists but minuscule gains of territory.

Such losses would have been easier to endure if the war had led to a secure and lasting peace. But the hardships and antagonisms of the postwar years rendered such sacrifice meaningless. After the war, winners and losers alike faced inflation, high unemployment, and, after a few years of prosperity in the 1920s, the economic catastrophe known as the Great Depression. Embittered by their defeat and harsh treatment in the Versailles Treaty, Germans abandoned their democratic Weimar Republic for Hitler's Nazi dictatorship in 1933. Japan and Italy, though on the winning side, were disappointed with their territorial gains, and this resentment played into the hands of ultranationalist politicians. The Arabs, who had fought against Germany's ally, the Ottoman Turks, in the hope of achieving nationhood, were embittered when Great Britain and France denied their independence. The United States, disillusioned with war and Great Power wrangling, withdrew into diplomatic isolation, leaving Great Britain and France to enforce the postwar treaties. Britain and France expanded their colonial empires in Africa and the Middle East, but this was scant compensation for their casualties, expenditures, and new responsibilities. There were no true victors in World War I.

The Romance of War

82 • POPULAR ART AND POSTER ART FROM GERMANY, ENGLAND, AND AUSTRALIA

When war came in 1914, crowds cheered, men rushed to enlist, and politicians promised that "the boys would be home by Christmas." Without having experienced a general war since the defeat of Napoleon in 1815, and with little thought to the carnage in the American Civil War or the Franco-Prussian War of 1870–1871, Europeans saw the war as a glorious adventure—an opportunity to fight for the flag or the kaiser or the king; to wear splendid uniforms; and to win glory in battles decided by élan, spirit, and bravery. The war they fought was nothing like the war they imagined, and the disparity between expectations and reality was one of many reasons why World War I brought forth such despair and disillusion.

The four illustrations shown here portray the eagerness and optimism of all belligerents at the war's start as well as their efforts to sustain this enthusiasm as the war dragged on. *The Departure* shows German troops departing for the battlefront in the late summer or fall of 1914. It is the work of the Swedish-born artist Bruno Wennerberg, who moved permanently to Germany in 1898 and died there in 1950. This illustration appeared in the German periodical *Simplicissiumus* in March 1915. Noted before the war for its irreverent satire and criticism of German militarism, *Simplicissimus* lent its full support to the German war effort once the war began.

The second illustration is one of a series of war-related cards included by the Mitchell Tobacco Company in its packs of Golden Dawn Cigarettes in 1914 and early 1915. It shows a sergeant offering smokes to soldiers under his command before battle. Tobacco advertising with military themes reached a saturation point in England during the war years.

The third illustration is an Australian recruitment poster from 1915. Although Australia, like Canada, controlled its internal affairs by the time the war started, its foreign policy was still directed by Great Britain. Hence, when Great Britain

B. Wennerberg, The Departure

B Hennerberg, The Departure, *Simplicissimus*, March 23, 1915, p. 663

Advertisement card from Golden Dawn Cigarettes

Courtesy of Imperial War Museum, London

Australian recruitment poster

Courtesy of Imperial War Museum, London

Septimus Scott, These Women Are Doing Their Bit

The Art Archive/Eileen Tweedy

went to war, so did Australia. The Australian parliament refused to approve conscription, however, so the government had to work hard to encourage volunteers. This particular poster appeared when Australian troops were heavily involved in the Gallipoli campaign (April 1915–January 1916), the allied effort to knock the Ottoman Empire out of the war. Directing its message to young men who were members of sports clubs, the poster promised them an opportunity to enlist in a battalion made up entirely of fellow sportsmen.

The fourth illustration is a poster produced and distributed by the British Ministry of Munitions in early 1917 to encourage women to accept jobs in the munitions industry. It is an example of the effort from 1915 onward to enlist women in the war effort as medical and farm workers, police, porters, drivers, foresters, members of the Women's Auxiliary Army Corps, and, most important, factory laborers. It shows a young and attractive woman offering a jaunty salute to a passing soldier as she arrives for work. It gives no hint of the dangers of munitions work. During the war approximately 300 "munitionettes" were killed in explosions or from chemical-related sicknesses. Women who worked with TNT came to be known as "canaries" because of their yellowish skin. Despite such hazards, almost a million women were working in munitions factories by war's end.

QUESTIONS FOR ANALYSIS

1. What message about the war does each of the four illustrations seek to convey?
2. In what specific ways does each illustration romanticize the life of a soldier or female munitions worker?
3. What impression of battle does the English tobacco card communicate?
4. What does a comparison of Wennerberg's painting and the English poster of the munitions worker suggest about changing views of women's role during the war and in society at large?

Twenty-Four Hours on the Western Front

83 • HENRY S. CLAPHAM, MUD AND KHAKI, MEMOIRS OF AN INCOMPLETE SOLDIER

Until 1914, Henry S. Clapham led a conventional life. Born in 1875 in Hull, he graduated from Queen's College in Taunton, a boarding school for the sons of well-to-do families. After clerking in a law office, he married and began a career as a solicitor in London. He enjoyed playing bridge. In the fall of 1914, however, he answered the call to enlist and by January 1915, he was fighting in northern Belgium. Clapham fought there until October 1915, when a hand wound made him unfit for service. On his return to England, he resumed his career as a lawyer and, like many veterans, turned his diary notes into a book, which appeared in 1917, with the title *Mud and Khaki*. It went through several printings and was republished in 1930.

Clapham's book describes his experiences fighting in and around Ypres, a Belgian city in the low, wet region that abuts the English Channel. It was the site of three major battles, one in the fall of 1914, another in 1915, and the last and bloodiest in 1917.

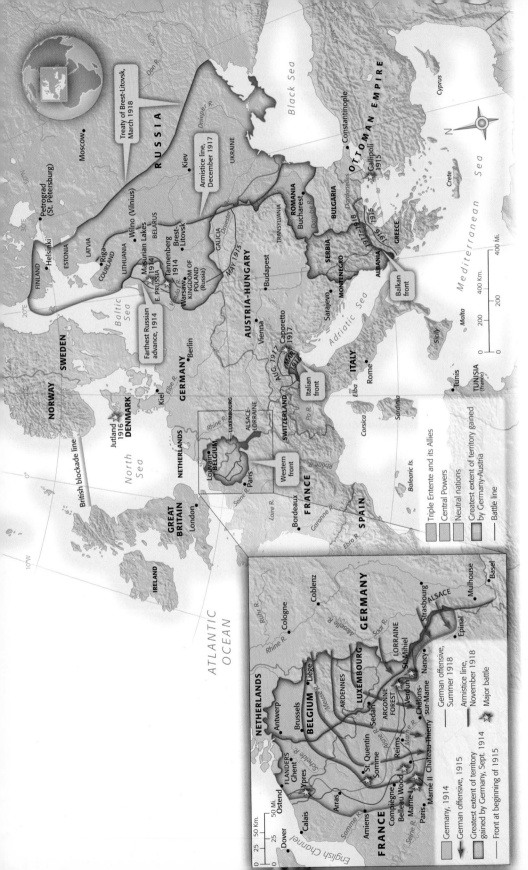

World War I

Clapham fought in the Second Battle of Ypres, which began in April 1915 when the Germans launched an attack on the entrenched English, Canadian, French, and French colonial troops in order to firm up German lines and divert allied troops from an anticipated offensive farther south. After the Germans abandoned their offensive in late May, fighting continued in the region, as Clapham's memoir clearly shows.

The Second Battle of Ypres saw the introduction of poison gas on the western front. Chlorine gas, a product of the German dyestuff industry and developed by the German chemical company IG Farben, could be released from cylinders or delivered by artillery shells. It caused the lungs to produce fluid, causing the victim to drown. Thousands of soldiers around Ypres died as a result of German gas attacks, but the effectiveness of the new weapon diminished when soldiers were supplied with respirators, or gas masks, and learned that holding a wet (often urine-soaked) handkerchief over one's nose and mouth provided some protection. Such countermeasures stimulated both sides to develop other types of poison gas, including phosgene, which causes asphyxiation, and mustard gas, which causes severe blistering.

QUESTIONS FOR ANALYSIS

1. As far as can be determined by Clapham's account, how did the fighting he describes change the battlelines?
2. What aspects of the fighting did Clapham and the other men find most unnerving?
3. Wars inevitably cause immense human suffering, but the suffering in World War I for soldiers and civilians alike was especially traumatic and unbearable. What is there in Clapham's account that may explain this phenomenon?

June 19, 1915

We started again at dusk and passed down the railway cutting, but, instead of turning off into the fields, we went on as far as the Menin Road, at what is known as "Hell Fire Corner." A few hundred yards down the road we found a resting place for the night in some shallow jumping off trenches, a few yards back from the front line. It was very dark, and the trench was small, and sitting in a huddle I got a cramp and felt miserable.

The Huns[1] started by putting over big crumps[2] all around us. They seemed to aim for the relics of a building a hundred yards in the rear, and there

the bricks were flying. . . . Then at 2:50 A.M. our own guns started and kept up a heavy bombardment of the trenches in front until 4:15, by which time it was quite light. . . .

At 4.15 a whistle blew. The men in the front line went over the top, and we scrambled out and took their places in the front trench. In front of us was a small field . . . split diagonally by an old footpath. On the other side of the field was a belt of trees in which lay the Hun trench.

In a few moments flags went up there, to show that it had been captured and that the troops were going on. Another whistle, and we ourselves

Source: H. S. Clapham, *Mud and Khaki: Memoirs of an Incomplete Soldier,* Hutchinson & Co., 1930, pp. 141–153.

[1]A derogatory term for German soldiers. The Huns were a nomadic people of Central Asia whose invasions of the fourth and fifth centuries C.E. contributed to the fall of the Western Roman Empire. The Huns were legendary for their cruelty and ferocity.

[2]A heavy German shell that exploded with a cloud of black smoke.

scrambled over the parapet[3] and sprinted across the field. Personally I was so over weighted that I could only amble. . . . I took the diagonal path, as the line of least resistance, and most of my section did the same.

When I dropped into the Hun trench I found it a great place, only three feet wide, and at least eight deep, and beautifully made of white sandbags, back and front. At that spot there was no sign of any damage by our shells, but a number of dead Huns lay in the bottom. There was a sniper's post just where I fell in, a comfortable little square hole, fitted with seats and shelves, bottles of beer, tinned meats, and a fine helmet hanging on a hook.

Our first duty was to change the [barbed] wire, so . . . I slipped off my pack, and, clambering out again, started to move the wire from what was now the rear, to the new front of the trench. It was rotten stuff, most of it loose coils. . . . What there was movable of it, we got across without much difficulty, and we had just finished when we were ordered to move down the trench, as our diagonal advance had brought us too far to the right.

We moved down along the belt of woodland, which was only a few yards broad, to a spot where one of our companies was already hard at work digging a communication trench[4] back to our old front line. Here there was really no trench at all. One or more of our own big shells had burst in the middle, filling it up for a distance of ten yards and practically destroying both parapet and parados.[5] Some of us started building up the parapet with sandbags, and I saw the twins [two men in Clapham's unit] merrily at work hauling out dead Huns at least twice their own size.

There was a hedge along the back of the trench, so I scrambled through a hole in it, piled my pack, rifle, and other things, including the helmet, on the farther side, and started again on the wire.

Hereabouts it was much better stuff, and it took us some time to get it across and pegged down. We had just got the last knife-rest across, when I saw a man who was placing sandbags on the parapet from the farther side swivel round, throw his legs into the trench, and collapse in a heap in the bottom. Several others were already lying there, and for the first time I realized that a regular hail of machine-gun bullets was sweeping over the trench.

. . . We all started work at a feverish pace, digging out the trench and building up some sort of shelter in front. One chap, a very nice kid, was bowled over almost at once with a bullet in the groin, and lay in the trench, kicking and screaming while we worked. . . .

The attacking battalions had carried several more trenches and we were told that two at least had been held, but our own orders were to consolidate and hold on to the trench we were in at all costs. . . .

I had just filled a sandbag and placed it on the top of the parapet when I happened to glance down, and saw a slight movement in the earth between my feet. I stooped and scraped away the soil with my fingers and found what seemed like palpitating flesh. It proved to be a man's cheek, and a few minutes' work uncovered his head. I poured a little water down his throat, and two or three of us dug out the rest of him. He was undamaged except for his feet and ankles, which were a mass of pulp, and he recovered consciousness as we worked. The first thing he said was in English: "What Corps are you?" He was a big man, and told us he was forty-five and had only been a soldier for a fortnight.

We dragged him out and laid him under the hedge. There was nothing else we could do for him. He had another drink later, but he must have died in the course of the day. I am afraid we forgot all about him . . . The Captain was the next to go. He insisted on standing on the parados, directing

---

[3]A mound built to protect the front of a trench.
[4]A shallow trench built from the front line to a relatively safe area in the rear. Used to supply front-line troops with food and ammunition and to transport killed and wounded soldiers away from the fighting.
[5]A mound built to protect the rear of a trench.

operations, and got a bullet in the lungs. He could walk, and two men were detailed to take him down to the dressing-station. One came back, to be killed later in the day, but the other stopped a bullet *en route,* and followed the Captain.

When we had got our big Hun out, he left a big hole in the ground, and we found a dead arm and hand projecting from the bottom. We dug about, but did not seem to be able to find the body, and when I seized the sleeve and pulled, the arm came out of the ground by itself. We had to dig deeper for our own sake, but there was nothing else left, except messy earth, which seemed to have been driven into the side of the trench. The man helping me turned sick, for it wasn't pretty work. . . .

About 5.30 A.M. the Huns started shelling, and the new communication trench soon became a death-trap. A constant stream of wounded who had come down another trench from the north, passed along the rear. The Huns made a target of the two traverses (unluckily including our own), from which the communication trench opened, and numbers of the wounded were caught just behind us. The trench itself was soon choked with bodies. . . .

The shelling got worse as the day wore on and several more of our men went down. They plastered us with crumps, shrapnel, and whizz-bangs.[6] One of the latter took off a sandbag from the top of the parapet and landed it on my head. It nearly broke my neck and I felt ill for some time after. . . . The worst of it was the inaction. Every minute several shells fell within a few yards and covered us with dust, and the smell of the explosives poisoned my mouth. All I could do was to crouch against the parapet and pant for breath, expecting every moment to be my last. And this went on for hours. I began to long for the shell which would put an end to everything, but in time my nerves became almost numbed, and I lay like a log until roused.

I think it must have been midday when something happened. An alarm was given and we manned the parapet, to see some scores of men retreating at a run from the trench in front. They ran right over us, men of half a dozen battalions, and many dropped on the way. As they passed, something was said of gas, but it appeared that nearly all the officers in the two front trenches had been killed or wounded, someone had raised an alarm of gas, and the men had panicked and run.

A lot of the runaways insisted on gathering by the hedge just behind us, in spite of our warnings not to do so, and I saw at least twenty hit by shrapnel within a few yards of us.

The Brigade-Major arrived, cursing, and called upon some of our own men to advance and re-occupy the trench in front. He led them himself, and they made a very fine dash across. I do not think more than twenty fell, and they reoccupied the trench and, I believe, the third also, before the Huns realized that they were empty. . . .

Soon the runaways began to return. They had been turned back, in some cases, at the point of the revolver, but when their first panic had been overcome, they came back quite willingly, although they must have lost heavily in the process . . .

It was scorchingly hot and no one could eat, although I tried to do so. All day long we were constantly covered with debris from the shell-bursts. Great pieces fell all about us, and, packed like herrings, we crowded in the bottom of the trench. Hardly anything could be done for the wounded. If their wounds were slight, they generally risked a dash to the rear. Every now and then we stood to in expectation of a counterattack, but none developed.

About 6 P.M. the worst moment of the day came. The Huns started to bombard us with a shell which was quite new to us. It sounded like a gigantic firecracker, with two distinct explosions. These shells

---

[6]*Shrapnel* were hollow shells filled with bullets or pieces of metal that scattered on explosion. *Whizz-Bangs* were shells fired by light German field guns.

came over just above the parapet, in a flood, much more quickly than we could count them. After a quarter of an hour of this sort of thing, there was a sudden crash in the trench and ten feet of the parapet, just beyond me, was blown away and everyone around blinded by the dust. With my first glance I saw what looked like half a dozen bodies, mingled with sandbags, and then I smelt gas and realized that these were gas-shells. I had my respirator on in a hurry and most of our own men were as quick. The others were slower and suffered for it. One man was sick all over the sandbags and another was coughing his heart up. We pulled four men out of the debris unharmed. One man was unconscious, and died of gas later. Another was hopelessly smashed up and must have got it full in the chest.

We all thought that this was the end and almost hoped for it, but luckily the gas-shells stopped, and after a quarter of an hour we could take off our respirators. I started in at once to build up the parapet again, for we had been laid open to the world in front, but the gas lingered about the hole for hours, and I had to give up delving in the bottom for a time. As it was it made me feel very sick.

A counter-attack actually commenced as soon as the bombardment ceased, and we had to stand to again. . . . As we leaned over the parapet, I saw the body of a Hun lying twenty yards out in front. It commenced to writhe and finally half-sat up. I suppose the gas had caught him. The man standing next me—a corporal in a county battalion—raised his rifle, and before I could stop him, sent a bullet into the body. It was a rotten thing to see, but I suppose it was really a merciful end for the poor chap, better than his own gas, at any rate.

The men in the front trenches had got it as badly as we had, and if the counter-attack was pressed, it did not seem humanly possible, in the condition we were in, to offer a successful defence. . . . Fortunately, our own guns started and apparently caught the Huns massing. The counter-attack accordingly crumpled up.

In the midst of it all, someone realized that the big gap in the parapet could not be manned, and four of us, including myself, were ordered to lie down behind what was left of the parados and cover the gap with our rifles. It was uncomfortable work, as . . . the place was a jumble of dead bodies. We could not stand up to clear them away, and in order to get a place at all, I had to lie across the body of a gigantic Hun. . . .

We managed to get some sort of parapet erected in the end. It was more or less bulletproof, at any rate. At dusk some scores of men came back from the front line, wounded or gassed. They had to cross the open at a run or a shamble, but I did not see any hit. Then the Brigade-Major appeared, and cheered us by promising a relief that night. It still rained shells, although not so hard as before dusk, and we did not feel capable of standing much more of it.

The Reality of the War in Art

84 • PAUL NASH, THE MENIN ROAD; C. R. W. NEVINSON, THE HARVEST OF BATTLE; OTTO DIX, SHOCK TROOPS ADVANCING UNDER A GAS ATTACK

Many artists fought in World War I or were sent to the front to serve as official painters. What they could draw and paint was carefully monitored by their governments. In England, for example, it was forbidden to display a painting that portrayed dead English soldiers. Thus, most of the artistic works that expressed disillusionment with the war appeared only after the hostilities ended. Such was the case with all three works shown here.

Paul Nash, The Menin Road

C. R. W. Nevinson, The Harvest of Battle

Otto Dix, Shock Troops Advancing Under a Gas Attack

Bildarchiv Preussischer Kulturbesitz/Art Resource, NY

The first painting, *The Menin Road,* is the work of the English artist Paul Nash (1889–1946). The son of a lawyer, Nash was just beginning to attract attention as a landscape painter when war broke out. He joined the Artists' Rifles, a volunteer corps formed in 1859 and originally composed of professional painters, musicians, actors, architects, and others involved in creative endeavors. He served on the western Front, and when injured and invalided to London, his wartime sketches attracted the attention of officials of the War Propaganda Bureau, who offered him a position as an official war artist. On his return to the front in the fall of 1917, he observed the Battle of Menin Road, a five-day engagement in late September that was part of the Third Battle of Ypres. In the battle, which was preceded by a huge artillery barrage, British and Australian troops advanced about a mile and a half against German positions. The devastation of this much-fought-over part of Belgium made a lasting impression on Nash, who painted *The Menin Road* shortly after the armistice.

The second painting, *The Harvest of Battle,* is also the work of an English painter, C. R. W. Nevinson. Born in 1889, Nevinson was an art student in France when the war started. He served on the front line in the medical corps, but because of poor health saw no combat. His experience of treating wounded soldiers made a deep impression on him. After the war, he expressed his feelings about the war's human cost in several paintings. The *Harvest of Battle* was completed in 1919.

Otto Dix (1891–1969), who created the etching *Shock Troops Advancing Under a Gas Attack,* is one of Germany's most important twentieth-century artists. In the war, he served as a machine-gunner, artillery man, and aerial observer on the western and eastern fronts. Deeply disillusioned with postwar society and its failure to recognize the sacrifices of its veterans, he became a pacifist whose powerful antiwar drawings and paintings led to his arrest and brief imprisonment by the Nazis. Only in the desperate closing days of World War II was he drafted to serve in the German army. *Shock Troops Advancing Under a Gas Attack* is one of fifty etchings Dix produced in 1923 and 1924 collectively titled *War.*

QUESTIONS FOR ANALYSIS

1. What broad statements about the costs of World War I is each artist attempting to make? What do you find more significant, the differences or similarities in their messages?
2. What specific details in each work help the artist put across his message?

The Russian Revolution and the Foundation of the Soviet State

One of the most important results of World War I was the downfall of Russia's tsarist regime and its replacement by a Bolshevik dictatorship inspired by the doctrines of Karl Marx. Tsar Nicholas II, facing battlefield defeat, army defections, and rioting in St. Petersburg, abdicated in March 1917. Tsarist rule was replaced by a liberal provisional government charged with presiding over Russia until a constituent assembly could meet and write a new constitution. Seven months later, the Bolsheviks wrested power from the provisional government and after a four-year civil war they established the world's first communist state.

Nicholas II's Russia was full of discontent. Its millions of peasants no longer were serfs, but they still lived in abysmal poverty. Some moved to Moscow or St. Petersburg to work in factories, but without political power or labor unions, most exchanged the squalor of the rural village for the squalor of the urban slum. Meanwhile, many intellectuals, mostly from Russia's small middle class, became more deeply alienated from the tsar's regime and threw their support to political causes ranging from anarchism to constitutional monarchy. With the fervor of religious zealots, for decades they argued, organized parties, hatched plots, planned revolution, assassinated government officials (including Tsar Alexander II in 1881), published pamphlets by the thousands, and tried, not always successfully, to stay one step ahead of the secret police.

Nicholas II raised his subjects' hopes in 1905, when after rioting in St. Petersburg he promised constitutional reforms and a parliament. Russians soon realized, however, that he had no intention of surrendering control of such crucial areas as finance, defense, and ministerial appointments. Meanwhile, workers and peasants cursed their government, and revolutionaries continued to plot. World War I provided the final push to a regime teetering on the brink of collapse.

The Marxist faction that orchestrated the downfall of the provisional government and then took control of the post-revolutionary Russian state was the Bolsheviks, which under the leadership of Vladimir Lenin (1870–1924) emerged in 1903 after a splintering of the Russian Social Democratic Labor party at its meeting in Brussels and London. Lenin developed a distinctive Marxist philosophy that affirmed Marx's idea that capitalism's demise and socialism's triumph could be achieved only through revolution. Lenin, however, broke with Marx in several respects. Unlike Marx, who believed that the revolution would result from a spontaneous uprising of the urban proletariat in mature industrialized societies, Lenin was confident that revolution was possible in societies like Russia with little industrialization and a small working class. The revolution would result from planning and organization by a small cadre of professional revolutionaries who would make all tactical and ideological decisions.

Living in exile in Zurich, Switzerland, when the tsar's government fell, Lenin reentered Russia with the help of the German government, which anticipated his presence would destabilize Russia and undermine its war effort. This is exactly what happened in October 1917 (in early November by the Gregorian calendar used in the West), when under Lenin's direction, a Bolshevik *coup d'état* resulted in the formation of the world's first Marxist state.

Forging the Soviet State

85 • COMMUNIST DECREES AND LEGISLATION, 1917–1918

On October 25, 1917, with the Bolsheviks in control of public buildings and other key points in Petrograd, Lenin confidently opened the Second Congress of Soviets with the words, "We shall now proceed to construct the Socialist order." As Lenin soon found out, building that new socialist order proved difficult. For one thing, while the Bolsheviks had a broad set of revolutionary aspirations for Russia, they had no blueprint for how to govern the country or how to restructure Russian society. Furthermore, the Bolsheviks were a minority party, as shown by the results of the elections for the Constituent Assembly in November 1917: the Bolsheviks received only 29 percent of the vote, as opposed to 58 percent for the Socialist-Revolutionaries, a party that garnered much of its support from the peasantry. Finally, they faced formidable problems—a ruined economy, continuing involvement in World War I until March 1918, and civil war from 1918 to 1921.

Despite these challenges, the Bolsheviks had no choice but to plunge ahead. In their first year in power, they issued hundreds of decrees that touched every aspect of Russian life and government. Some of these programs and policies lasted until the Soviet Union's demise in 1991.

What follows is a sample of the decrees issued by the Bolsheviks in 1917 and 1918. The Decree on Land, issued on October 26 by the Second Congress of Soviets only hours after the Bolsheviks seized power, recognized land seizures that peasants had already carried out.

The Decree on Suppression of Hostile Newspapers and the Decree Dissolving the Constituent Assembly both were steps toward one-party dictatorship. The Bolsheviks, both before and after seizing power, had supported convening a popularly elected Constituent Assembly, but the election of November 1917 resulted in only 168 Bolshevik deputies out of 703 and a clear Socialist-Revolutionary majority. The Assembly convened on January 5, 1918, only to be dissolved by the Bolsheviks on January 7. It was the Soviet Union's last democratically elected parliament until 1989.

The Edict on Child Welfare, issued in January 1918, was the brainchild of Alexandra Kollontai (1873–1952), a leading Social Democrat who fled Russia in 1908 to escape arrest and, like Lenin, returned to Petrograd after the fall of the tsar's government. She became a member of the executive committee of the Petrograd Soviet and played a leading role in the events leading up to the Bolshevik coup. As commissioner of social welfare under the Bolsheviks, she was responsible for laws that legalized abortion, liberalized marriage and divorce, and granted women equal standing with men.

The Decree on Nationalization of Large-Scale Industries was issued in June 1918 after the beginning of the civil war. Until then, industry had remained under private ownership, supposedly subject to "workers' control." Now it was nationalized without compensation to the owners.

QUESTIONS FOR ANALYSIS

1. What rationale is provided in these documents for the "undemocratic" steps taken by the Bolsheviks to dissolve the Constituent Assembly and close down hostile newspapers?
2. What are the economic ramifications of the decrees on land use and the nationalization of industry? Who benefits, and who is hurt?
3. How will these decrees change essential features of Russian society and social relationships?
4. To what extent do the steps taken by the Bolsheviks as reflected in these decrees reflect Marx and Engels's views in *The Communist Manifesto* (source 54), especially in the section in which they discuss the first steps to be taken by the proletariat after its seizure of power (p. 265)?
5. In what specific ways do these decrees increase the role of the state? What implications might this have for the Soviet Union's future?

Decree on Land, October 26, 1917

1. *Private ownership of land shall be abolished forever* . . .

   All land . . . *shall be alienated without compensation* and become the property of the whole people, and pass into the use of all those who cultivate it. . . .

2. All mineral wealth, e.g., ore, oil, coal, salt, etc., as well as all forests and waters of state importance, shall pass into the exclusive use of the state. All the small streams, lakes, woods, etc., shall pass into the use of the communities, to be administered by the local self-government bodies.

3. Lands on which *high-level scientific* farming is practised, e.g., orchards, plantations, seed plots, nurseries, hot-houses, etc. *shall not be divided up, but shall be converted into model farms,* to be turned over for exclusive use *to the state or to the communities,* depending on the size and importance of such lands. . . .

6. The right to use the land shall be accorded to all citizens of the Russian state (without distinction of sex) desiring to cultivate it by their own labor, with the help of their families, or in partnership, but only as long as they are able to cultivate it. . . .

Decree on Suppression of Hostile Newspapers, October 27, 1917

Everyone knows that the bourgeois press is one of the most powerful weapons of the bourgeoisie. Especially in this critical moment when the new authority, that of the workers and peasants, is in process of consolidation, it was impossible to leave this weapon in the hands of the enemy at a time when it is not less dangerous than bombs and machine guns. This is why temporary and extraordinary measures have been adopted for the purpose of cutting off the stream of mire and calumny in which the . . . press would be glad to drown the young victory of the people.

As soon as the new order will be consolidated, all administrative measures against the press will be suspended; full liberty will be given it within the limits of responsibility before the laws, in accordance with the broadest and most progressive regulations in this respect. . . .

Decree Dissolving the Constituent Assembly, January 7, 1918

The October Revolution, by giving the power to the Soviets, and through the Soviets to the toiling and exploited classes, aroused the desperate resistance of the exploiters, and in the crushing of this resistance it fully revealed itself as the beginning of the socialist revolution. The toiling classes learnt by experience that the old bourgeois parliamentarism had outlived its purpose and was absolutely incompatible with the aim of achieving Socialism, and that not national institutions, but only class institutions (such as the Soviets), were capable of overcoming the resistance of the propertied classes and of laying the foundations of a socialist society. To relinquish the sovereign power of the Soviets, to relinquish the Soviet republic won by the people, for the sake of bourgeois parliamentarism and the Constituent Assembly, would now

Source: Decree on land: V. I. Lenin, *Selected Works,* (Moscow, Foreign Languages Publishing House, 1950–1952), Vol. II, book I, pp. 339–341. Suppression of Hostile Newspapers: English translation in *Bolshevik Propaganda:* Hearings before a Subcommittee of the Committee on the Judiciary, U.S. Senate, 56th Congress, 3rd Session, p. 1243. Dissolution of Constituent Assembly: V. I. Lenin, Draft Decree on the Dissolution of the Constituent Assembly, *Selected Work* (Moscow: Foreign Languages Publishing House, 1950–1952), Vol. II, book I, 382–384. Edict on Child Welfare: From Alexandra Kollontai, *Selected Writings,* Alix Holt, ed. and trans. (Westport, CT: Lawrence Hill and Company, 1977), pp. 140–141. Decree of Nationalization of Large-Scale Industries: in James Bunyan, *Intervention, Civil War, and Communism in Russia, April–December 1918; Documents and Materials* (Baltimore: The Johns Hopkins Press, 1936), pp. 397–399.

be a retrograde step and cause the collapse of the October workers' and peasants' revolution. . . .

The Right Socialist Revolutionary and Menshevik[1] parties are in fact waging outside the walls of the Constituent Assembly a most desperate struggle against the Soviet power, calling openly in their press for its overthrow and characterizing as arbitrary and unlawful the crushing by force of the resistance of the exploiters by the toiling classes, which is essential in the interests of emancipation from exploitation. They are defending the saboteurs, the servitors of capital, and are going to the length of undisguised calls to terrorism, which certain "unidentified groups" have already begun to practice. It is obvious that under such circumstances the remaining part of the Constituent Assembly could only serve as a screen for the struggle of the counterrevolutionaries to overthrow the Soviet power.

Accordingly, the Central Executive Committee resolves: The Constituent Assembly is hereby dissolved.

Edict on Child Welfare, January 1918

After a search that has lasted centuries, human thought has at last discovered the radiant epoch where the working class, with its own hands, can freely construct that form of maternity protection which will preserve the child for the mother and the mother for the child. . . .

The new Soviet Russia calls all you working women, you working mothers with your sensitive hearts, you bold builders of a new social life, you teachers of the new attitudes, you children's doctors and midwives, to devote your minds and emotions to building the great edifice that will provide social protection for future generations. From the date of publication of this decree, all large and small institutions under

the commissariat of social welfare that serve the child, from the children's home in the capital to the modest village creche [a day nursery], shall be merged into one government organization and placed under the department for the protection of maternity and childhood. As an integral part of the total number of institutions connected with pregnancy and maternity, they shall continue to fulfill the single common task of creating citizens who are strong both mentally and physically. . . . For the rapid elaboration and introduction of the reforms necessary for the protection of childhood in Russia, commissions are being organized under the auspices of the departments of maternity and childhood. . . . The commissions must base their work on the following main principles:

1. The preservation of the mother for the child: milk from the mother's breast is invaluable for the child.
2. The child must be brought up in the enlightened and understanding atmosphere provided by the socialist family.
3. Conditions must be created which permit the development of the child's physical and mental powers and the child's keen comprehension of life.

Decree on Nationalization of Large-Scale Industries, June 28, 1918

For the purpose of combating decisively the economic disorganization and the breakdown of the food supply, and of establishing more firmly the dictatorship of the working class and the village poor, the Soviet of People's Commissars has resolved:

1. To declare all of the following industrial and commercial enterprises which are located in the Soviet Republic, with all their capital and

---

[1]The Mensheviks split from the Bolsheviks at a meeting of the Social-Democratic Labor Party in 1903, mainly over

Lenin's insistence that the party should be directed by a small group of dedicated professional revolutionaries.

property, whatever they may consist of, the property of the Russian Socialist Federated Soviet Republic. [A long list of mines, mills, and factories follows.]

2. The administration of the nationalized industries shall be organized . . . by the different departments of the Supreme Council of National Economy. . . .

4. Beginning with the promulgation of this decree, the members of the administration, the directors, and other responsible officers of the nationalized industries will be held responsible to the Soviet Republic both for the intactness and upkeep of the business and for its proper functioning. . . .

5. The entire personnel of every enterprise—technicians, workers, members of the board of directors, and foremen—shall be considered employees of the Russian Socialist Federated Soviet Republic; their wages shall be fixed in accordance with the scales existing at the time of nationalization and shall be paid out of the funds of the respective enterprises. . . .

6. All private capital belonging to members of the boards of directors, stockholders, and owners of the nationalized enterprises will be attached [taken by state authority] pending the determination of the relation of such capital to the turnover capital and resources of the enterprises in question. . . .

The Soviet Path to Industrialization

86 • JOSEPH STALIN, THE TASKS OF BUSINESS EXECUTIVES

Joseph Stalin (1879–1953), the son of a shoemaker from the province of Georgia, was a candidate for the priesthood before he abandoned Christianity for Marxism and became a follower of Lenin in 1903. By 1917, he was secretary of the Bolshevik party, an office he retained after the revolution. Following Lenin's death in 1924, Stalin used his position in the party to defeat his rival, Leon Trotsky (1879–1940), the leader of the Red Army during the civil war and Lenin's heir apparent. Shortly after taking power in 1928, Stalin launched a bold restructuring of the Soviet economy.

In 1928, the New Economic Policy (NEP), which Lenin had implemented in 1921, still guided Soviet economic life. Through the NEP, Lenin had sought to restore agriculture and industry after seven years of war, revolution, and civil conflict. Although the state maintained control of banks, foreign trade, and heavy industry, peasants could sell their goods on the open market, and owners of small businesses could hire labor, operate small factories, and keep their profits. The NEP saved the Union of Soviet Socialist Republics (USSR) from economic collapse, but the NEP's concessions to capitalism troubled Marxist purists, and it did little to foster industrialization. Thus, in 1928, Stalin abandoned the NEP and replaced it with the first Five-Year Plan, which established a centralized planned economy in which Moscow bureaucrats regulated agriculture, manufacturing, finance, and transportation. In agriculture, the plan abolished individual peasant holdings and combined them into large collective and state farms. In manufacturing, it emphasized heavy industry and the production of goods such as tractors, trucks, and machinery. Stalin launched second and third Five-Year Plans in 1933 and 1938.

In a speech delivered in 1931 to a conference of industrial managers, or "business executives," Stalin described his motives for instituting the Five-Year Plan.

QUESTIONS FOR ANALYSIS

1. What factors convince Stalin that the Soviet Union has the capacity to reach its industrial goals in 1931?
2. Why does Stalin believe that the Soviet system is superior to capitalism?
3. How does Stalin try to inspire the industrial managers to work for industrialization?
4. What does Stalin mean when he refers to the Soviet Union's responsibility to the "world proletariat"?
5. How do Stalin's views of the weaknesses of capitalism resemble those of Marx and Engels in the *Communist Manifesto*? (See source 54.)
6. How do Stalin's views of economic development resemble and differ from those of the Japanese businessman Iwasaki Yataro (source 78)?

Comrades! The deliberations of your conference are drawing to a close. You are now about to adopt resolutions. I have no doubt that they will be adopted unanimously. In these resolutions—I know something about them—you approve the control figures of industry for 1931 and pledge yourselves to fulfil them.

A Bolshevik's word is his bond. Bolsheviks are in the habit of fulfilling their pledges. But what does the pledge to fulfil the control figures for 1931 mean? It means ensuring a general increase of industrial output by 45 percent. And this is a very big task. More than that. Such a pledge means that you not only promise to fulfil our Five-Year Plan in four years—that is decided, and no more resolutions are needed on that score—*it means that you promise to fulfil it in three years in all the basic, decisive branches of industry.*

It is good that the conference gives a promise to fulfil the plan for 1931, to fulfil the Five-Year Plan in three years. But we have been taught by "bitter experience." We know that promises are not always kept. In the beginning of 1930, also, a promise was given to fulfil the plan for the year. At that time it was necessary to increase the output of our industries by 31 to 32 percent. But that promise was not kept to the full. Actually, the increase in industrial output in 1930 amounted to 25 percent. We must ask ourselves: will not the same thing occur again this year? The directors and managers of our industries now promise to increase the industrial output in 1931 by 45 percent. But what guarantee have we that this promise will be kept? . . .

In the history of states and countries, in the history of armies, there have been cases when every opportunity for success and for victory was on hand, but these opportunities were wasted because the leaders did not see them, did not know how to make use of them, and the armies suffered defeat.

Have we all the possibilities that are needed to fulfil the control figures for 1931?

Yes, we have these possibilities.

What are these possibilities? What are the necessary factors that make these possibilities real?

First of all, adequate *natural resources* in the country: iron ore, coal, oil, grain, cotton. Have we these resources? Yes, we have. We have them in larger quantities than any other country. . . .

What else is needed?

Source: In *Problems in Leninism* (Moscow: Foreign Languages Publishing House, 1947), pp. 359–360, 365–366.

A *government* capable and willing to utilize these immense natural resources for the benefit of the people. Have we such a government? We have. . . .

What else is needed?

That this government should enjoy the *support* of the vast masses of workers and peasants. Does our government enjoy such support? Yes, it does. You will find no other government in the world that enjoys such support from the workers and peasants as does the Soviet government. . . .

What else is needed to fulfil and over fulfil the control figures for 1931?

A *system* which is free of the incurable diseases of capitalism and which is greatly superior to capitalism. Crises, unemployment, waste, poverty among the masses—such are the incurable diseases of capitalism. Our system does not suffer from these diseases because power is in our hands, in the hands of the working class; because we are conducting a planned economy, systematically accumulating resources and properly distributing them among the different branches of national economy. . . .

The capitalists are cutting the ground from under their own feet. And instead of emerging from the crisis they aggravate it; new conditions accumulate which lead to a new, and even more severe crisis: The superiority of our system lies in that we have no crises of over-production, we have not and never will have millions of unemployed, we have no anarchy in production; for we are conducting a planned economy. . . .

It is sometimes asked whether it is not possible to slow down the tempo a bit, to put a check on the movement. No, comrades, it is not possible!

The tempo must not be reduced! On the contrary, we must increase it as much as is within our powers and possibilities. This is dictated to us by our obligations to the workers and peasants of the U.S.S.R. This is dictated to us by our obligations to the working class of the whole world.

To slacken the tempo would mean falling behind. And those who fall behind get beaten. But we do not want to be beaten. No, we refuse to be beaten! One feature of the history of old Russia was the continual beatings she suffered for falling behind, for her backwardness. She was beaten by the Mongol Khans. She was beaten by the Turkish beys. She was beaten by the the Swedish feudal lords. She was beaten by the Polish and Lithuanian gentry. She was beaten by the British and French capitalists. She was beaten by the Japanese barons. All beat her—for her backwardness: for military backwardness, for cultural backwardness, for political backwardness, for industrial backwardness, for agricultural backwardness. She was beaten because to do so was profitable and could be done with impunity. . . . They beat her, saying: "You are abundant," so one can enrich oneself at your expense. They beat her, saying: "You are poor and impotent," so you can be beaten and plundered with impunity. Such is the law of the exploiters—to beat the backward and the weak. It is the jungle law of capitalism. You are backward, you are weak—therefore you are wrong; hence, you can be beaten and enslaved. You are mighty—therefore you are right; hence, we must be wary of you.

That is why we must no longer lag behind.

Liberalism and Democracy Under Siege

On April 2, 1917, U.S. President Woodrow Wilson went before a joint session of Congress to seek a declaration of war against Germany so the world could "be made safe for democracy." As late as 1921, it appeared that such a goal had been realized, at least in Europe. Except for Bolshevik Russia, all 27 European states, including the six new states created by postwar treaties, were working democracies with parliamentary governments, constitutions, and guarantees of basic freedoms. In 1922, however, when Benito Mussolini became dictator of Italy, this was the beginning of an authoritarian tide that swept across Europe, leaving only ten parliamentary democracies when World War II started in 1939. They included the four Scandinavian states of Finland, Sweden, Norway, and Denmark; Czechoslovakia in eastern Europe; three small states, Belgium, the Netherlands, and Switzerland; and only two major powers, Britain and France.

No single cause can explain the broad failure of liberal democracy across much of Europe. General factors include the shallowness or absence of a parliamentary tradition; inexperienced leadership; fears of communism; low levels of education and literacy; the continued hostility to democracy on the part of powerful elites; ethnic conflict; and the difficulty of reintegrating millions of veterans into civilian life. The single most important factor, however, was the devastating human cost of the Great Depression, which in the 1930s resulted in business failures, shuttered factories, crumbling agricultural prices, and unemployment levels reaching 30 percent or higher. In the face of this calamity, dispirited Europeans *en masse* turned to antidemocratic leaders and movements that offered simple explanations and miraculous solutions for their nations' problems. There is no better example of the Great Depression's political effect than the meteoric rise of the German Nazi party, which received a scant 2.6 percent of the vote in the pre-Depression national election in May 1928 but attracted 37.8 percent of the vote in the election held in July 1932.

Most of the new authoritarian regimes were conservative in that they represented the interests of large landowners, wealthy businessmen, the army, and certain elements within organized churches—whose opposition to democracy predated World War I. Such governments shut down parliaments, abolished opposing political parties, ended free speech, and promised order, if necessary through violence. But they offered no new ideologies, no blueprints for social change, and no grandiose plans for territorial expansion. In contrast stood the antidemocratic movement known as fascism, which takes its name from the *Fasci italiani di Combattimento* (Italian League of Combat), the political party led by Italy's dictator, Mussolini. Applied mainly to Mussolini's Italy and Hitler's Germany, but also to its sympathizers in other European states, fascism rejected liberalism, socialism, and democracy. It also glorified violence and war, saw life in terms of struggle, promoted service to the nation as the supreme calling, and required absolute obedience to a single infallible ruler. Fascist regimes turned schools, theaters, newspapers, churches, museums, and radio broadcasts into instruments of propaganda. They also brought catastrophe to the people they ruled, the groups they hated, and the nations they attacked.

The State as a Spiritual and Moral Fact

87 • BENITO MUSSOLINI, THE POLITICAL AND SOCIAL DOCTRINE OF FASCISM

Benito Mussolini (1883–1945), Europe's first fascist dictator, was the son of a blacksmith and a schoolteacher who as a youth participated in socialist and revolutionary political movements. He discarded radicalism for nationalism during World War I, when, as a journalist, he called for Italy's entry into the war and served as a soldier until he was wounded in 1917. After the war, he founded his own private army of some 40 unemployed army veterans, which he called the *Fasci italiani di Combattimento*. The ultranationalist fascists portrayed themselves as Italy's only protection from socialists, communists, labor unions, and anarchists, whom they battled in the streets. Many Italians, dismayed by inflation, high taxes, widespread unemployment, strikes, rural violence, corruption, and ineffectual leadership, looked to the Fascists for Italy's salvation. In 1921, Mussolini was elected to the Italian Chamber of Deputies as leader of the newly formed Italian Fascist Party (*Partito Nazionale Fascista*), which then had 300,000 members. In 1922, even though the Fascists and their supporters controlled less than 10 percent of the seats in the Italian parliament, Mussolini demanded that King Victor Emmanuel III name him premier. When the king hesitated, Mussolini organized a March on Rome, in which thousands of Fascists converged on the capital, prompting the resignation of the cabinet and causing the king to name Mussolini premier. He and his supporters quickly suppressed opposition and undermined the Italian parliamentary system. By 1924, Italy's fascist dictatorship under *Il Duce*, "The Leader," was secure.

Claiming that fascism was based on "action," not ideology, Mussolini at first declined to explain fascist doctrine. In 1932, however, he wrote (or had written for him) the following statement in *Enciclopedia Italiana*.

QUESTIONS FOR ANALYSIS

1. What is Mussolini's rationale for opposing pacifism and glorifying war?
2. To Mussolini, what are the flaws of Marxism?
3. What is the rationale for the fascist rejection of democracy?
4. What is the relationship between the individual and the state, according to Mussolini?
5. What does Mussolini mean when he says, "the State is a spiritual and moral fact"?
6. Most of what Mussolini wrote describes what fascism opposes. Are there positive features in its ideology?

Fascism, the more it considers and observes the future and the development of humanity quite apart from political considerations of the moment, believes neither in the possibility nor the utility of perpetual peace. It thus repudiates the doctrine of Pacifism—born of a renunciation of the struggle and an act of cowardice in the face of sacrifice. War alone brings up to its highest tension all human energy and puts the stamp of nobility upon the peoples who have the courage to meet it. All other trials are substitutes, which never really put men into the position where they have to make the great decision—the alternative of life or death. Thus a doctrine which is founded upon this harmful postulate of peace is hostile to Fascism. And thus hostile to the spirit of Fascism, though accepted for what use they can be in dealing with particular political situations, are all the international leagues and societies which, as history will show, can be scattered to the winds when once strong national feeling is aroused by any motive—sentimental, ideal, or practical. This anti-pacifist spirit is carried by Fascism even into the life of the individual; the proud motto of the Squadrista,[1] *"Me ne frego"* (I don't give a damn), written on the bandage of the wound, is an act of philosophy not only . . . it is the education to combat, the acceptance of the risks which combat implies, and a new way of life for Italy. . . .

Such a conception of life makes Fascism the complete opposite of that doctrine, the base of the so-called scientific and Marxian Socialism, the materialist conception of history; according to which the history of human civilization can be explained simply through the conflict of interests among the various social groups and by the change and development in the means and instruments of production. That the changes in the economic field—new discoveries of raw materials, new methods of working them, and the inventions

of science—have their importance no one can deny; but that these factors are sufficient to explain the history of humanity excluding all others is an absurd delusion. Fascism, now and always, believes in holiness and in heroism; that is to say, in actions influenced by no economic motive, direct or indirect. . . . And above all Fascism denies that class war can be the preponderant force in the transformation of society. These two fundamental concepts of Socialism being thus refuted, nothing is left of it but the sentimental aspiration—as old as humanity itself—towards a social convention in which the sorrows and sufferings of the humblest shall be alleviated. But here again Fascism repudiates the conception of "economic" happiness, to be realized by Socialism and, as it were, at a given moment in economic evolution to assure to everyone the maximum of well-being. Fascism denies the materialist conception of happiness as a possibility, and abandons it to its inventors, the economists of the first half of the nineteenth century: that is to say, Fascism denies the validity of the equation, well-being = happiness, which would reduce men to the level of animals, caring for one thing only—to be fat and well-fed—and would thus degrade humanity to a purely physical existence.

After Socialism, Fascism combats the whole complex system of democratic ideology, and repudiates it. . . . Fascism denies that the majority, by the simple fact that it is a majority, can direct human society; it denies that numbers alone can govern by means of a periodic consultation, and it affirms the immutable, beneficial, and fruitful inequality of mankind, which can never be permanently leveled through the mere operation of a mechanical process such as universal suffrage. . . . Democracy is a regime nominally without a king, but it is ruled by many kings—more absolute, tyrannical, and ruinous than one sole king, even though a tyrant. . . .

Source: Carnegie Endowment for International Peace, *International Conciliation,* No. 306 (Jan, 1935), pp. 13–17.

[1]Party members who did much of the street fighting against socialists and communists during the early struggle for power.

The foundation of Fascism is the conception of the State, its character, its duty, and its aim. Fascism conceives of the State as an absolute, in comparison with which all individuals or groups are relative, only to be conceived of in their relation to the State. . . . In 1929, at the first five-yearly assembly of the Fascist regime, I said:

"For us Fascists, the State is not merely a guardian, preoccupied solely with the duty of assuring the personal safety of the citizens; nor is it an organization with purely material aims, such as to guarantee a certain level of well-being and peaceful conditions of life; for a mere council of administration would be sufficient to realize such objects. . . . The State, as conceived of and as created by Fascism, is a spiritual and moral fact in itself . . . and such an organization must be in its origins and development a manifestation of the spirit. The State is the guarantor of security both internal and external, but it is also the custodian and transmitter of the spirit of the people, as it has grown up through the centuries in language, in customs, and in faith. And the State is not only a living reality of the present, it is also linked with the past and above all with the future, and thus transcending the brief limits of individual life, it represents the immanent spirit of the nation. . . . The individual in the Fascist State is not annulled but rather multiplied, just in the same way that a soldier in a regiment is not diminished but rather increased by the number of his comrades.

The Fascist State organizes the nation, but leaves a sufficient margin of liberty to the individual; the latter is deprived of all useless and possibly harmful freedoms, but retains what is essential; the deciding power in this question cannot be the individual, but the State alone." . . .

Fascism is the doctrine best adapted to represent the tendencies and the aspirations of a people, like the people of Italy, who are rising again after many centuries of abasement and foreign servitude. But empire demands discipline, the co-ordination of all forces and a deeply felt sense of duty and sacrifice: this fact explains many aspects of the practical working of the regime, the character of many forces in the State, and the necessarily severe measures which must be taken against those who would oppose this spontaneous and inevitable movement of Italy in the twentieth century, and would oppose it by recalling the outworn ideology of the nineteenth century—repudiated wheresoever there has been the courage to undertake great experiments of social and political transformation: for never before has the nation stood more in need of authority, of direction, and of order. If every age has its own characteristic doctrine, there are a thousand signs which point to Fascism as the characteristic doctrine of our time. For if a doctrine must be a living thing, this is proved by the fact that Fascism has created a living faith; and that this faith is very powerful in the minds of men, is demonstrated by those who have suffered and died for it.

The Dreams of the Führer

88 • ADOLF HITLER, MEIN KAMPF

Born to an Austrian customs official and his German wife in 1889, Adolf Hitler moved to Vienna at the age of 19 to seek a career as an artist or architect. His efforts failed, however, and he lived at the bottom of Viennese society, drifting from one low-paying job to another. In 1912, he moved to Munich, where his life fell into the same purposeless pattern. Enlistment in the German army in World War I rescued Hitler, giving him comradeship and a sense of direction he had lacked. After the war, a shattered Hitler returned to Munich, where in 1919, he joined the small German Workers' Party, which in 1920 changed its name to the National Socialist German Workers' Party, or Nazis.

After becoming leader of the National Socialists, Hitler staged an abortive *coup d'état* against the government of the German state of Bavaria in 1923. For this, he was sentenced to a five-year prison term (serving only nine months), during which time he wrote the first volume of *Mein Kampf (My Struggle)*. To a remarkable degree, this work, which he completed in 1925, provided the ideas that inspired his millions of followers and guided the National Socialists until their destruction in 1945.

QUESTIONS FOR ANALYSIS

1. What broad purpose does Hitler see in human existence?
2. How, in Hitler's view, are the Aryans and Jews dissimilar?
3. What is Hitler's view of political leadership?
4. What role do parliaments play in a "folkish" state, according to Hitler?
5. How does Hitler plan to reorient German foreign policy? What goals does he set for Germany, and how are they to be achieved?
6. Based on these excerpts, what can you infer about his objections to the ideologies of democracy, liberalism, and socialism?
7. How do Hitler's views of race compare to those of von Treitschke (source 62)?

Nation and Race

There are some truths that are so plain and obvious that for this very reason the everyday world does not see them or at least does not apprehend them. . . .

So humans invariably wander about the garden of nature, convinced that they know and understand everything, yet with few exceptions are blind to one of the fundamental principles Nature uses in her work: the intrinsic segregation of the species of every living thing on the earth. . . . Each beast mates with only one of its own species: the titmouse with titmouse, finch with finch, stork with stork, field mouse with field mouse, house mouse with house mouse, wolf with wolf. . . . This is only natural.

Any cross-breeding between two not completely equal beings will result in a product that is in between the level of the two parents. That means that the offspring will be superior to the parent who is at a biologically lower level of being but inferior to the parent at a higher level. This

means the offspring will be overcome in the struggle for existence against those at the higher level. Such matings go against the will of Nature for the higher breeding of life.

A precondition for this lies not in the blending of beings of a higher and lower order, but rather the absolute victory of the stronger. The stronger must dominate and must not blend with the weaker orders and sacrifice their powers. Only born weaklings can find this cruel, but after all, they are only weaker and more narrow-minded types of men; unless this law dominated, then any conceivable higher evolution of living organisms would be unthinkable. . . .

Nature looks on this calmly and approvingly. The struggle for daily bread allows all those who are weak, sick, and indecisive to be defeated, while the struggle of the males for females gives to the strongest alone the right or at least the possibility to reproduce. Always this struggle is a means of advancing the health and power of resistance of the species, and thus a means to its higher evolution.

Source: Adolf Hitler, *Mein Kampf* (Munich: F. Eher Nachfolger, 1927), trans. by J. Overfield.

As little as nature approves the mating of higher and lower individuals, she approves even less the blending of higher races with lower ones; for indeed otherwise her previous work toward higher development perhaps over hundreds of thousands of years might be rendered useless with one blow. If this were not the case, progressive development would stop and even deterioration might set in. . . .

All the great civilizations of the past died out because contamination of their blood caused them to become decadent. . . . In other words, in order to protect a certain culture, the type of human who created the culture must be preserved. But such preservation is tied to the inalterable law of the necessity and the right of victory of the best and the strongest.

Whoever would live must fight. Whoever will not fight in this world of endless competition does not deserve to live. . . . He interferes with the victory path of the best race and with it, the precondition for all human progress. . . .

It is an idle undertaking to argue about which race or races were the original standard-bearers of human culture and were therefore the true founders of everything we conceive by the word humanity. It is much simpler to deal with the question as it pertains to the present, and here the answer is simple and clear. What we see before us today as human culture, all the yields of art, science, and technology, are almost exclusively the creative product of the Aryans.[1] Indeed this fact alone leads to the not unfounded conclusion that the Aryan alone is the founder of the higher type of humanity, and further that he represents the prototype of

what we understand by the word: MAN. He is the Prometheus[2] from whose brow the bright spark of genius has forever burst forth, time and again rekindling the fire, which as knowledge has illuminated the night full of silent mysteries, and has permitted humans to ascend the path of mastery over the other beings of the earth. Eliminate him—and deep darkness will again descend on the earth after a few thousand years; human civilization will die out and the earth will become a desert. . . .

The Jew provides the greatest contrast to the Aryan. With no other people of the world has the instinct for self-preservation been so developed as by the so-called chosen race.[3] The best proof of this statement rests in the fact that this race still exists. Where can another people be found in the past 2,000 years that has undergone so few changes in its inner qualities, character, etc. as the Jews? What people has undergone upheavals as great as this one—and nonetheless has emerged unchanged from the greatest catastrophes of humanity? What an infinitely tenacious will to live and to preserve one's kind is revealed in this fact. . . .

Since the Jew . . . never had a civilization of his own, others have always provided the foundations of his intellectual labors. His intellect has always developed by the use of those cultural achievements he has found ready at hand around him. Never has it happened the other way around.

For though their drive for self-preservation is not smaller, but larger than that of other people, and though their mental capabilities may easily give the impression that their intellectual powers are equal to those of other races, the Jews lack

---

[1]*Aryan,* strictly speaking, is a linguistic term referring to a branch of the Indo-European family of languages known as Indo-Iranian. It also is used to refer to a people who as early as 4000 B.C.E. began to migrate from their homeland in the steppes of western Asia to Iran, India, Mesopotamia, Asia Minor, and Europe. In the nineteenth century, *Aryan* was used to refer to the racial group that spoke Indo-European languages. According to Hitler and the Nazis, the Aryans provided Europe's original racial stock and stood in contrast to other peoples such as the Jews, who spoke Semitic languages.

[2]In Greek mythology, Prometheus was the titan (titans were offspring of Uranus [Heaven] and Gaea [Earth]) who stole fire from the gods and gave it to humans, along with all other arts and civilization.

[3]A reference to the Jewish belief that God had chosen the Jews to enter into a special covenantal relationship in which God promised to be the God of the Hebrews and favor them in return for true worship and obedience.

the most basic characteristic of a truly cultured people, namely an idealistic spirit.

It is a remarkable fact that the herd instinct brings people together for mutual protection only so long as there is a common danger that makes mutual assistance necessary or unavoidable. The same pack of wolves that an instant ago combined to overcome their prey will soon after satisfying their hunger again become individual beasts. . . . It goes the same way with the Jews. His sense of self sacrifice is only apparent. It lasts only so long as it is strictly necessary. . . . Jews act together only when a common danger threatens them or a common prey attracts them. When these two things are lacking, then their characteristic of the crassest egoism returns as a force, and out of this once unified people emerges in a flash a swarm of rats fighting bloodily against one another. . . .

That is why the Jewish state—which should be the living organism for the maintenance and improvement of the race—has absolutely no borders. For the territorial definition of a state always demands a certain idealism of spirit on the part of the race which forms the state and especially an acceptance of the idea of work. . . . If this attitude is lacking then the prerequisite for civilization is lacking.

> Hitler describes the process by which Jews in concert with communists have come close to subverting and controlling the peoples and nations of Europe.

Here he stops at nothing, and his vileness becomes so monstrous that no one should be surprised if among our people the hateful figure of the Jew is taken as the personification of the devil and the symbol of evil. . . .

How close they see their approaching victory can be seen in the frightful way that their dealings with members of other races develop.

The black-haired Jewish youth, with satanic joy on his face, lurks in wait for hours for the innocent girls he plans to defile with his blood, and steal the young girl from her people. With every means at hand he seeks to undermine the racial foundations of the people they would subjugate. . . .

Around those nations which have offered sturdy resistance to their internal attacks, they surround them with a web of enemies; thanks to their international influence, they incite them to war, and when necessary, will plant the flag of revolution, even on the battlefield.

In economics he shakes the foundations of the state long enough so that unprofitable business enterprises are shut down and come under his financial control. In politics he denies the state its means of self-preservation, destroys its means of self-maintenance and defense, annihilates faith in state leadership, insults its history and traditions, and drags everything that is truly great into the gutter.

Culturally, he pollutes art, literature and theater, makes a mockery of natural sensibilities, destroys every concept of beauty and nobility, the worthy and the good, and instead drags other men down to the sphere of its own lowly type of existence.

Religion is made an object of mockery, morality and ethics are described as old-fashioned, until finally the last props of a people for maintaining their existence in this world are destroyed.

Personality and the Ideal of the Folkish[4] State

. . . The folkish state must care for the well-being of its citizens by recognizing in everything the worth of the person, and by doing so direct it to the highest level of its productive capability,

---

[4]The word Hitler uses, *völkisch,* is an adjective derived from *Volk,* meaning "people" or "nation," which Hitler defined in a racial sense; thus a "folkish" state is one that expresses the characteristics of and furthers the interests of a particular race, in this case the Aryans.

thus guaranteeing for each the highest level of participation.

Accordingly, the folkish state must free the entire leadership, especially those in political leadership, from the parliamentary principle of majority rule by the multitude, so that the right of personality is guaranteed without any limitation. From this is derived the following realization. *The best state constitution and form is that which with unquestioned certainty raises the best minds from the national community to positions of leading authority and influence. . . .*

There are no majority decisions, rather only responsible individuals, and the word "advice" will once again have its original meaning. Each man will have advisers at his side, *but the decision will be made by one man.*

The principle that made the Prussian army in its time the most splendid instrument of the German people will have to become someday the foundation for the construction of our completed state: *authority of every leader downward and responsibility upward. . . .*

This principle of binding absolute responsibility with absolute authority will gradually bring forth an elite group of leaders which today in an era of irresponsible parliamentarianism is hardly thinkable.

The Direction and Politics of Eastern Europe

The foreign policy of the folkish state has as its purpose to guarantee the existence on this planet of the race that it gathers within its borders. With this in mind it must create a natural and healthy ratio between the number and growth of the population and the extent and quality of the land and soil. . . . Only a sufficiently large space on the earth can assure the independent existence of a people. . . .

The National Socialist movement must seek to eliminate the disproportion between our people's population and our territory—viewing this as a source of food as well as a basis for national power—and between our historical past and our present hopeless impotence. While doing so it must remain conscious of the fact that we as protectors of the highest humanity on earth are bound also by the highest duty that will be fulfilled only if we inspire the German people with the racial ideal, so that they will occupy themselves not just with the breeding of good dogs, horses, and cats but also show concern about the purity of *their own* blood. . . .

State boundaries are made by man and can be changed by man.

. . . And only in force lies the right of possession. If today the German people are imprisoned within an impossible territorial area and for that reason are face to face with a miserable future, this is not the commandment of fate, any more than a revolt against such a situation would be a violation of the laws of fate; . . . the soil on which we now live was not bestowed upon our ancestors by Heaven; rather, they had to conquer it by risking their lives. So with us, in the future we will win soil and with it the means of existence of the people . . . only through the power of the triumphant sword.

But we National Socialists must go further: *The right to land and soil will become an obligation if without further territorial expansion a great people is threatened with its destruction.* And that is particularly true when the people in question is not some little nigger people, but the German mother of life, which has given cultural shape to the modern world. *Germany will either become a world power or will no longer exist. . . .*

And so we National Socialists consciously draw a line below the direction of our foreign policy before the war. We take up where we broke off six hundred years ago. We put a stop to the eternal pull of the Germans toward the south and western Europe and turn our gaze to the lands of the east. We put an end to the colonial and commercial policy of the prewar period and shift to the land-oriented policy of the future.

When today we speak of new territory and soil in Europe, we think primarily of *Russia* and her subservient border states.

The Nazi Message: 1932

89 • SIX POLITICAL POSTERS

By 1932, Germany's democratic Weimar Republic was in deep crisis. Controlled by a center-left coalition dominated by the moderate socialist Social Democratic Party, the republic had survived threats of a communist revolution; a host of economic problems, including the hyperinflation of 1923; and the implacable opposition from communists on the left and a host of right-wing parties that opposed any form of democracy. But as the German economy unraveled and unemployment soared after the onset of the Great Depression in 1929, public support for the Weimar government dissolved as Chancellor Heinrich Brüning's austerity policies and tax increases only worsened the economic pain. Ominously, in the Reichstag elections of 1930, extremist parties on the far left (the Communists) and the far right (the National Socialists) both made substantial gains.

Germany's political crisis peaked in 1932, when between March and November, Germans went to the polls in no less than four national elections: an election for president in March and a run-off for the same office in April in which Hitler challenged the aging incumbent and war hero Paul von Hindenburg; and two elections for the Reichstag, one on July 31 and the other on November 6. The Nazis were the big winners. Although Hitler lost to von Hindenburg in both presidential votes (by a margin of 53 percent to 37 percent in the runoff, with the remainder going to the Communist candidate), the elections increased Hitler's national exposure and popularity. In the July Reichstag vote, the Nazis increased their representation from 100 to 233, giving them an almost 100-seat advantage over their nearest rival, the Social Democrats. The Nazis lost support in the November Reichstag vote, but they easily kept their majority. Three more months of crisis-driven bargaining and failed deal-making ended in January 1933, when President Hindenburg saw no choice but to name Hitler chancellor, knowing full well that this was a death sentence for the Weimar Republic.

The rise of the Nazis from an obscure regional right-wing party to the dominant political power in Germany is a monument to their effective use of propaganda. Hitler was convinced that Germany had lost the propaganda battle to the Allies in World War I and vowed not to repeat its mistakes. Propaganda, he believed, was the only way to reach the masses, who lacked the interest, intellect, and attention span to grasp complex issues.

Hitler himself directed Nazi propaganda efforts until 1928, when Joseph Goebbels assumed greater responsibilities. Later, as Hitler's Minister of Propaganda, Goebbels made ample use of radio and cinema, but in the heated days from 1930 to 1933, he and other Nazi propagandists relied on the Nazis' stock-in-trade—parades, mass rallies and meetings, speech-making, slogans, and posters. The political poster, widely used during the campaign for women's suffrage in the early 1900s and by all belligerents during World War I, was elevated to a high art by the Nazis. They specialized in large, brightly colored posters that were hung on walls or the side panels of trucks. Their pictures, accompanied by brief mottoes or slogans, communicated simple messages deigned to appeal to different audiences—farmers, workers, veterans, women, and young people.

The six selections we have chosen are a small sampling of the many dozens of posters produced in 1932. The first three were produced for the presidential elections in March and April. The first shows Hitler staring back at the viewer from a stark black background. The second shows a down-and-out German family with the following message, "Husbands! Wives! Millions of men without work! Millions of children without a future! Save the German family! Elect Adolf Hitler!" The third poster reads "Country People in Need. Who helps? Adolf Hitler!"

The next two posters were produced in connection with the first Reichstag vote in July, with both directed against the Nazis' main rival, the Social Democrats (SPD). The first depicts a representative of the SPD as a "guardian angel" for a rich capitalist, who is given features typically connected with Jews in Nazi caricatures. It carries the message, "Marxism is the Guardian Angel for Capitalism." It draws attention to the fact that the Social Democrats had received contributions from businessmen whose fear of Hitler was greater than their misgivings about socialism. The second poster features a worker under the motto "We build things up!" He is leaning on "our building stones": "Work, Freedom, Bread." He peers down at two figures, one a caricature of Heinrich Brüning, the German chancellor from 1930 to May 31, 1932. His "Building Plan" includes "Promises, Government Cuts, Unemployment, and Emergency Decrees, Article 48." Article 48 refers to the provision of the Weimar constitution that gave the president powers to pass laws and issue decrees without the consent of the Reichstag. Brüning had convinced Hindenburg to invoke such powers on numerous occasions, most recently to ban activities of the Nazi SA (*Sturmabteilung*), which had been responsible for much of the street violence in Germany's major cities. The other figure represents a Social Democrat, whose sign reads, "Cuts in social services, Corruption, Terror, Agitation, Lies." The last poster is more straightforward. It shows masses of Germans flocking into the openings in a giant swastika with the words "The People Vote Slate 1, National Socialists." The swastika was adopted by Hitler as a Nazi symbol in 1920, and was associated with the party's racial beliefs in the superiority of the "Aryan race" and anti-Semitism.

QUESTIONS FOR ANALYSIS

1. What message was the poster "Hitler" meant to convey?
2. On the basis of the content of the posters, what might one conclude about the problems confronting German society in the early 1930s?
3. According to the message of the posters, what solutions to Germany's problems do the Nazis propose?
4. How are everyday Germans portrayed in the posters? What do these portrayals reveal about the appeal of Nazism?

Hitler

Husbands! Wives!

Country People in Need

Marxism Is the Guardian Angel for Capitalism

We Build Things Up

The People Vote Slate I

5. How are Jews and Social Democrats portrayed in the posters? Why might the SPD figure in poster #4 have been depicted as wearing only a loincloth?
6. With exception of "Marxismus Is the Guardian Angel for Capitalism," none of the posters has a blatant anti-Semitic message. This was true for almost all the posters produced in 1932. Why might the Nazis have decided to blunt this part of their message?

The Legacy of World War II

In the two decades after World War I, weapons became more destructive, nationalism more fanatical, and leaders' ambitions more fantastic. As a result, the war that began in Asia in 1937 and in Europe in 1939—World War II—became the most devastating and destructive war in history. Modern communication and transportation systems enabled generals to plan and execute massive campaigns such as the German invasion of the Soviet Union in 1941 and the Allies' Normandy invasion in 1944. The airplane became an instrument of mass destruction, making possible the German assault on English cities in 1940, the Japanese attack on Pearl Harbor in 1941, the around-the-clock bombing of Germany by Britain and the United States from 1943 to 1945, and the American fire-bombing of Tokyo in 1945.

Only the closing months of the war, however, fully revealed the destructive possibilities of modern technology and large bureaucratic states. As Allied armies liberated Europe in the winter and spring of 1945, they found in the Third Reich's concentration and extermination camps the horrifying results of the Nazi assault on political enemies, religious dissidents, prisoners of war, Gypsies, Slavs, and especially Jews. Then on August 6, the United States dropped an atomic bomb on Hiroshima, Japan. It killed nearly 80,000 people, seriously injured twice that number, and obliterated three-fifths of the city. On August 9, the United States dropped a second atomic bomb on Nagasaki, intending to demolish the Mitsubishi shipyards. It missed its target but destroyed half the city and killed 75,000 people.

A half-century later, the names Hiroshima and Nagasaki still evoke nightmares in a world where thousands of nuclear warheads exist and many nations have the capacity to manufacture nuclear weapons. Similarly, the Nazi campaign to exterminate Europe's Jews continues to haunt the imagination. Racism and ethnic hatreds are universally condemned, but they flourish in many parts of the world.

Was the Holocaust an aberration resulting from the unique prejudices of the Germans and the perverse views of a handful of their leaders? Or was something much more basic in human nature involved? These are just two of the many disturbing questions raised by the Nazi-perpetuated Holocaust.

"Führer, You Order We Obey"
90 • RUDOLF HÖSS, MEMOIRS

On gaining power, the Nazis began to implement the anti-Jewish policies Hitler and the Nazis had promised in *Mein Kampf* and thousands of books, pamphlets, and speeches. Jewish shops were plundered while police looked the other way, Jewish physicians were excluded from hospitals, Jewish judges lost their posts, Jewish students were denied admission to universities, and Jewish veterans were stripped of their benefits. In 1935, the Nazis promulgated the Nuremberg Laws, which deprived Jews of citizenship and outlawed marriage between Jews and non-Jews. In November 1938, the regime organized nationwide violence against Jewish synagogues and shops in what came to be known as *Kristallnacht,* or "night of the broken glass."

After the war began in late 1939, conquests in Eastern Europe gave the Nazis new opportunities to address the "Jewish problem." In early 1941, they began to deport Jews from Germany and conquered territories to Poland and Czechoslovakia, where their victims were employed as slave laborers or placed in concentration camps. In June 1941, special units known as *Einsatzgruppen* ("special action forces") were organized to exterminate Jews in territories conquered on the eastern front. In 18 months, they gunned down more than 1 million Jews and smaller numbers of Gypsies and Slavs. Then in January 1942, at the Wannsee Conference outside Berlin, Nazi leaders approved the Final Solution to the so-called Jewish problem. Their goal was the extermination of European Jewry, and to reach it, they constructed special camps where their murderous work could be done efficiently and quickly. When World War II ended, the Nazis had not reached their goal of annihilating Europe's 11 million Jews. They did, however, slaughter close to 6 million, thus earning themselves a permanent place in the long history of man's inhumanity to man.

The following excerpt comes from the memoirs of Rudolf Höss (1900–1947), the commandant of the Auschwitz concentration camp in Poland from 1940 to 1943. After serving in World War I, Höss abandoned plans to become a priest and became involved in a number of right-wing political movements, including the Nazi Party, which he joined in the early 1920s. After serving a jail sentence for participating in the murder of a teacher suspected of "treason," Höss became a farmer and then, in 1934, a member of the Nazi SS, or *Schutzstaffel* (Guard Detachment). The SS, under its leader Heinrich Himmler, grew from a small security force to guard Hitler and other high-ranking Nazis into a powerful party organization involved in police work, state security, intelligence gathering, administration of conquered territories, and management of the concentration camps. After postings at the Dachau and Sachsenhausen camps, Höss was appointed commandant of Auschwitz, a huge, sprawling complex where more than a million Jews were gassed or shot and tens of thousands of prisoners served as slave laborers in nearby factories. In 1943, Höss became overseer of all the Third Reich's concentration camps, but he returned to Auschwitz in 1944 to administer the murder of 400,000 Hungarian Jews. After his capture in 1946, he was tried and convicted for crimes against humanity by the international military tribunal at Nuremberg. He was hanged on April 16, 1947. While awaiting trial, Höss was encouraged to compose a memoir to sharpen his recollection of his experiences. In the following passage, he discusses his views of the Jews and his reaction to the mass killings he planned and witnessed.

QUESTIONS FOR ANALYSIS

1. What does Höss claim his attitude was toward the Jews?
2. How do his statements about the Jews accord with his assertion that he was a fanatic National Socialist?
3. Does Höss make any distinction between the Russians and the Jews that he had exterminated?
4. What was Höss's attitude toward the Final Solution? How does Höss characterize his role in the mass extermination of the Jews?
5. How did his involvement in the Holocaust affect him personally? How, according to Höss, did it affect other German participants?
6. What would you describe as the key components of Höss's personality? To what extent was his personality shaped by the Nazi philosophy to which he was dedicated?
7. What insight does this excerpt provide about the issue of how much the German people knew of and participated in the Holocaust?

Since I was a fanatic National Socialist, I was firmly convinced that our idea would take hold in all countries, modified by the various local customs, and would gradually become dominant. This would then break the dominance of international Jewry. Anti-Semitism was nothing new throughout the whole world. It always made its strongest appearance when the Jews had pushed themselves into positions of power and when their evil actions became known to the general public. . . . I believed that because our ideas were better and stronger, we would prevail in the long run. . . .

I want to emphasize here that I personally never hated the Jews. I considered them to be the enemy of our nation. However, that was precisely the reason to treat them the same way as the other prisoners. I never made a distinction concerning this. Besides, the feeling of hatred is not in me, but I know what hate is, and how it manifests itself. I have seen it and I have felt it.

The original order . . . to annihilate all the Jews stated, "All Jews without exception are to be destroyed." It was later changed by Himmler so that those able to work were to be used in the arms factories. This made Auschwitz the assembly point for the Jews to a degree never before known. . . .

When he gave me the order personally . . . to prepare a place for mass killings and then carry it out, I could never have imagined the scale, or what the consequences would be. Of course, this order was something extraordinary, something monstrous. However, the reasoning behind the order of this mass annihilation seemed correct to me. At the time I wasted no thoughts about it. I had received an order; I had to carry it out. I could not allow myself to form an opinion as to whether

this mass extermination of the Jews was necessary or not. At the time it was beyond my frame of mind. Since the Führer himself had ordered "The Final Solution of the Jewish Question," there was no second guessing for an old National Socialist, much less an SS officer. "Führer, you order. We obey" was not just a phrase or a slogan. It was meant to be taken seriously.[1]

Since my arrest I have been told repeatedly that I could have refused to obey this order, and even that I could have shot Himmler dead. I do not believe that among the thousands of SS officers there was even one who would have had even a glimmer of such a thought. . . . Of course, many SS officers moaned and groaned about the many harsh orders. Even then, they carried out every order. . . . As leader of the SS, Himmler's person was sacred. His fundamental orders in the name of the Führer were holy. There was no reflection, no interpretation, no explanation about these orders. They were carried out ruthlessly, regardless of the final consequences, even if it meant giving your life for them. Quite a few did that during the war.

It was not in vain that the leadership training of the SS officers held up the Japanese as shining examples of those willing to sacrifice their lives for the state and for the emperor, who was also their god. SS education was not just a series of useless high school lectures. It went far deeper, and Himmler knew very well what he could demand of his SS. . . .

Whatever the Führer and Himmler ordered was always right. Even democratic England has its saying, "My country, right or wrong," and every patriotic Englishman follows it.

Before the mass destruction of the Jews began, all the Russian politruks[2] and political commissars

Source: From Rudolf Höss, *Death Dealer: The Memoirs of the SS Kommandant at Auschwitz* by Rudolf Hoss, edited by Stephen Paskuly, translated by Andrew Pollinger (Amherst, NY: Prometheus Books, 1992), pp. 141–142, 153–159, 161–162, 164. Copyright © 1992 by Steven Paskuly. Reprinted with permission of the publisher.

[1]All SS members swore the following oath: "I swear to you Adolf Hitler, as Führer and Chancellor of the Reich, loyalty and bravery. I vow to you and to the authorities appointed by you obedience unto death, so help me God."
[2]Communist Party members.

were killed in almost every camp during 1941 and 1942. According to the secret order given by Hitler, the Einsatzgruppen searched for and picked up the Russian politruks and commissars from all the POW camps. They transferred all they found to the nearest concentration camp for liquidation. . . . The first small transports were shot by firing squads of SS soldiers.

While I was on an official trip, my second in command, Camp Commander Fritzsch, experimented with gas for killings. He used a gas called Cyclon B, prussic acid,[3] which was often used as an insecticide in the camp to exterminate lice and vermin. There was always a supply on hand. When I returned Fritzsch reported to me about how he had used the gas. We used it again to kill the next transport.

The gassing was carried out in the basement of Block 11. I viewed the killings wearing a gas mask for protection. Death occurred in the crammed-full cells immediately after the gas was thrown in. Only a brief choking outcry and it was all over. . . .

At the time I really didn't waste any thoughts about the killing of the Russian POWs. It was ordered; I had to carry it out. But I must admit openly that the gassings had a calming effect on me, since in the near future the mass annihilation of the Jews was to begin. Up to this point it was not clear to me . . . how the killing of the expected masses was to be done. Perhaps by gas? But how, and what kind of gas? Now we had discovered the gas and the procedure. I was always horrified of death by firing squads, especially when I thought of the huge numbers of women and children who would have to be killed. Now I was at ease. We were all saved from these bloodbaths, and the

victims would be spared until the last moment. That is what I worried about the most when I thought of Eichmann's[4] accounts of the mowing down of the Jews with machine guns and pistols by the Einsatzgruppen. Horrible scenes were supposed to have occurred: people running away even after being shot, the killing of those who were only wounded, especially the women and children. Another thing on my mind was the many suicides among the ranks of the SS Special Action Squads who could no longer mentally endure wading in the bloodbath. Some of them went mad. Most of the members of the Special Action Squads drank a great deal to help get through this horrible work. According to [Captain] Hoffle's accounts, the men of Globocnik's[5] extermination section drank tremendous quantities of alcohol.

In the spring of 1942 the first transports of Jews arrived from Upper Silesia. All of them were to be exterminated. They were led from the ramp across the meadow, later named section B-II of Birkenau,[6] to the farmhouse called Bunker I. Aumeier, Palitzsch, and a few other block leaders led them and spoke to them as one would in casual conversation, asking them about their occupations and their schooling in order to fool them. After arriving at the farmhouse they were told to undress. At first they went very quietly into the rooms where they were supposed to be disinfected. At that point some of them became suspicious and started talking about suffocation and extermination. Immediately a panic started. Those still standing outside were quickly driven into the chambers, and the doors were bolted shut. In the next transport those who were nervous or upset were identified and watched closely at all

---

[3]Cyclon (or Zyklon) B is a blue crystalline substance; its active ingredient, hydrocyanic acid, sublimates into a gas upon contact with air. It causes death by combining with the red blood cells and preventing them from carrying oxygen.
[4]Adolf Eichmann (1906–1962) was a bureaucrat originally in charge of Jewish emigration. After the Wannsee Conference, he was given the responsibility for organizing the deportation of Jews to the death camps. He fled to Argentina

in 1946 but was captured by Israeli agents, who took him to Israel, where he was tried and executed in 1962.
[5]Odiho Globocnik was the officer responsible for organizing and training SS units in Eastern Europe.
[6]Birkenau was the German name for the town where a large addition to the Auschwitz complex was built in late 1941 and early 1942.

times. As soon as unrest was noticed these trouble-makers were inconspicuously led behind the farmhouse and killed with a small-caliber pistol, which could not be heard by the others. . . .

I also watched how some women who suspected or knew what was happening, even with the fear of death all over their faces, still managed enough strength to play with their children and to talk to them lovingly. Once a woman with four children, all holding each other by the hand to help the smallest ones over the rough ground, passed by me very slowly. She stepped very close to me and whispered, pointing to her four children, "How can you murder these beautiful, darling children? Don't you have any heart?"

Another time an old man hissed while passing me, "Germany will pay a bitter penance for the mass murder of the Jews." His eyes glowed with hatred as he spoke. In spite of this he went bravely into the gas chamber without worrying about the others. . . .

Occasionally some women would suddenly start screaming in a terrible way while undressing. They pulled out their hair and acted as if they had gone crazy. Quickly they were led behind the farmhouse and killed by a bullet in the back of the neck from a small-caliber pistol. . . . As the doors were being shut, I saw a woman trying to shove her children out the chamber, crying out, "Why don't you at least let my precious children live?" There were many heartbreaking scenes like this which affected all who were present.

In the spring of 1942 hundreds of people in the full bloom of life walked beneath the budding fruit trees of the farm into the gas chamber to their death, most of them without a hint of what was going to happen to them. To this day I can still see these pictures of the arrivals, the selections, and the procession to their death. . . .

. . . Many of the men often approached me during my inspection trips through the killing areas and poured out their depression and anxieties to me, hoping that I could give them some reassurance. During these conversations the question arose again and again, "Is what we have to do here necessary? Is it necessary that hundreds of thousands of women and children have to be annihilated?" And I, who countless times deep inside myself had asked the same question, had to put them off by reminding them that it was Hitler's order. I had to tell them that it was necessary to destroy all the Jews in order to forever free Germany and the future generations from our toughest enemy.

. . . However, secret doubts tormented all of us. Under no circumstances could I reveal my secret doubts to anyone. I had to convince myself to be like a rock when faced with the necessity of carrying out this horribly severe order, and I had to show this in every way, in order to force all those under me to hang on mentally and emotionally. . . .

Hour upon hour I had to witness all that happened. I had to watch day and night, whether it was the dragging and burning of the bodies, the teeth being ripped out, the cutting of the hair,[7] I had to watch all this horror. For hours I had to stand in the horrible, haunting stench while the mass graves were dug open, and the bodies were dragged out and burned. I also had to watch the procession of death itself through the peephole of the gas chamber because the doctors called my attention to it. I had to do all of this because I was the one to whom everyone looked, and because I had to show everybody that I was not only the one who gave the orders and issued the directives, but that I was also willing to be present at whatever task I ordered my men to perform. . . .

And yet, everyone in Auschwitz believed the Kommandant really had a good life. Yes, my family had it good in Auschwitz, every wish that my wife or my children had was fulfilled. The children could live free and easy. My wife had her

---

[7]Teeth extracted from the corpses were soaked in muriatic acid to remove muscle and bone before the gold fillings were extracted. Some of the gold was distributed to dentists, who used it in fillings for SS men and their families; the rest was deposited in the Reichsbank. Hair was used to make felt and thread.

flower paradise. The prisoners tried to give my wife every consideration and tried to do something nice for the children. By the same token no former prisoner can say that he was treated poorly in any way in our house. My wife would have loved to give a present to every prisoner who performed a service for us. The children constantly begged me for cigarettes for the prisoners. The children especially loved the gardeners. In our entire family there was a deep love for farming and especially for animals. Every Sunday I had to drive with them across all the fields, walk them through the stables, and we could never skip visiting the dog kennels. Their greatest love was for our two horses and our colt. The prisoners who worked in the household were always dragging in some animal the children kept in the garden. Turtles, martens, cats, or lizards; there was always something new and interesting in the garden. The children splashed around in the summertime in the small pool in the garden or the Sola River. Their greatest pleasure was when daddy went into the water with them. But he had only a little time to share all the joys of childhood.

Today I deeply regret that I didn't spend more time with my family. I always believed that I had to be constantly on duty. Through this exaggerated sense of duty I always had made my life more difficult than it actually was. My wife often urged me, "Don't always think of your duty, think of your family too." But what did my wife know about the things that depressed me? She never found out.[8]

---

[8]In an interview with a court-appointed psychiatrist during the Nuremberg trials in 1946, Höss stated that his wife actually did learn of his participation in the mass executions at the camp, and that afterward they became estranged and ceased having sexual relations.

August 6, 1945

91 • IWAO NAKAMURA AND ATSUKO TSUJIOKA, RECOLLECTIONS

In 1951, Dr. Arata Osada, a professor of education at the University of Hiroshima, sponsored a project in which young Japanese from primary grades through the university level were asked to write down their memories of the August 6 bombing and its aftermath. Moved by their recollections, he arranged to have published a sample of their compositions in 1951. His stated purpose was to reveal the horrors of nuclear war and thereby encourage nuclear disarmament. An English translation appeared in 1980.

QUESTIONS FOR ANALYSIS

Readers are encouraged to formulate their own questions about the events and experiences described in these memoirs.

Iwao Nakamura

11th Grade Boy (5th Grade at the Time)

Today, as I begin to write an account of my experiences after five years and several months have passed, the wretched scenes of that time float up before my eyes like phantoms. And as these phantoms appear, I can actually hear the pathetic groans, the screams.

Source: Iwao Nakamura and Atsuko Tsujioka, "Recollections from Arata Osada," in *Children of Hiroshima* (London: Taylor and Francis, 1981), pp. 173–175, 265–269. Reprinted by permission of Taylor & Francis Group.

In an instant it became dark as night, Hiroshima on that day. Flames shooting up from wrecked houses as if to illuminate this darkness. Amidst this, children aimlessly wandering about, groaning with pain, their burned faces twitching and bloated like balloons. An old man, skin flaking off like the skin of a potato, was trying to get away on weak, unsteady legs, praying as he went. A man frantically calling out the names of his wife and children, both hands to his forehead from which blood trickled down. Just the memory of it makes my blood run cold. This is the real face of war. . . .

I, who cannot forget, was in the fifth year of primary school when it happened. To escape the frequent air raids, I and my sisters had been evacuated to the home of our relatives in the country, but on August 2, I returned to my home at Naka Kakomachi (near the former Prefectural Office) during the summer vacation, to recover from the effects of a summer illness that had left me very weak. . . .

It was after eight on August 6 and the midsummer sun was beginning to scorch down on Hiroshima. An all-clear signal had sounded and with relief we sat down for breakfast a little later than usual. Usually by this time, my father had left the house for the office and I would be at the hospital for treatment.

I was just starting on my second bowl of rice. At that moment, a bluish-white ray of light like a magnesium flare hit me in the face, a terrific roar tore at my eardrums and it became so dark I could not see anything. I stood up, dropping my rice bowl and chopsticks. I do not know what happened next or how long I was unconscious. When I came to, I found myself trapped under what seemed like a heavy rock, but my head was free. It was still dark but I finally discovered that I was under a collapsed wall. It was all so sudden that I kept wondering if I was dreaming. I tried very hard to crawl free, but the heavy wall would not budge. A suffocating stench flooded the area and began to choke me. My breathing became short, my ears began to ring, and my heart was pounding

as if it were about to burst. "I can't last much longer," I said to myself, and then a draft of cold air flowed past me and some light appeared. The taste of that fresh air is something I shall never forget. I breathed it in with all my might. This fresh air and the brighter surroundings gave me renewed vigor and I somehow managed to struggle out from under the wall. . . .

Nothing was left of the Hiroshima of a few minutes ago. The houses and buildings had been destroyed and the streets transformed into a black desert, with only the flames from burning buildings giving a lurid illumination to the dark sky over Hiroshima. Flames were already shooting out of the wreckage of the house next door. We couldn't see my two brothers. My mother was in tears as she called their names. My father went frantic as he dug among the collapsed walls and scattered tiles. It must have been by the mercy of God that we were able to rescue my brothers from under the wreckage before the flames reached them. They were not hurt, either. The five of us left our burning home and hurried toward Koi. Around us was a sea of flames. The street was filled with flames and smoke from the burning wreckage of houses and burning power poles which had toppled down blocked our way time after time, almost sending us into the depths of despair. It seems that everyone in the area had already made their escape, for we saw no one but sometimes we heard moans, a sound like a wild beast. . . . As we passed Nakajima Primary School area and approached Sumiyoshi Bridge, I saw a damaged water tank in which a number of people had their heads down, drinking. I was so thirsty and attracted by the sight of people that I left my parents' side without thinking, and approached the tank. But when I got near and was able to see into the tank, I gave an involuntary cry and backed away. What I saw reflected in the blood-stained water were the faces of monsters. They had leaned over the side of the tank and died in that position. From the burned shreds of their sailor uniforms, I knew they were schoolgirls, but they had no hair left and their burned faces were crimson with blood; they no longer appeared human. After we came out on the main road and crossed Sumiyoshi Bridge, we finally came across some living human beings—but maybe it would be more correct to say that we met some people from Hell. They were naked and their skin, burned and bloody, was like red rust and their bodies were bloated up like balloons. . . . The houses on both sides of this street, which was several dozen yards wide, were in flames so that we could only move along a strip in the center about three or four yards wide. This narrow passage was covered with seriously burned and injured people, unable to walk, and with dead bodies, leaving hardly any space for us to get through. At places, we were forced to step over them callously, but we apologized in our hearts as we did this. Among them were old people pleading for water, tiny children seeking help, students unconsciously calling for their parents, brothers, and sisters, and there was a mother prostrate on the ground, moaning with pain but with one arm still tightly embracing her dead baby. But how could we help them when we ourselves did not know our own fate?

When we reached the Koi First Aid Station, we learned that we were among the last to escape from the Sumiyoshi Bridge area. After my father had received some medical treatment, we hurried over Koi Hill to our relatives at Tomo Village in Asa County. When we were crossing the hill late that evening, we could see Hiroshima lying far below, now a mere smoldering desert. After offering a silent prayer for the victims, we descended the hill toward Tomo.

Atsuko Tsujioka

Student, Hiroshima Women's Junior College

It happened instantaneously. I felt as if my back had been struck with a big hammer, and then as if I had been thrown into boiling oil. I was unconscious for a while. When I regained my senses, the whole area was covered with black smoke. . . . I lay on the ground with my arms pressed against my chest, and called for help, again and again: "Mother! Mother! Father!"

But, of course, neither Mother nor Father answered me. . . . I could hear the other girls shouting for their mothers in the hellish darkness, and I sensed that they were getting away. I got up and just ran after them desperately. Near Tsurumi Bridge, a red hot electric wire got wrapped around my ankles. I pulled free of it somehow, without thinking, and ran to the foot of the Tsurumi Bridge. By that time, there was white smoke everywhere. I had been working in a place called Tanaka-cho, about 600 yards from the blast center. I seemed to have been blown quite a bit north and had to take a completely different route to the bridge, which would have been straight ahead of me if I was where I should have been.

There was a large cistern at the foot of the bridge. In the tank were some mothers, one holding her naked, burned baby above her head, and another crying and trying to give her baby milk from her burned breast. Also in the tank were schoolchildren, with only their heads, and their hands clasped in prayer, above the surface of the water. They were sobbing for their parents, but everyone had been hurt, so there was no one to help them. People's hair was white with dust, and scorched; they did not look human. "Surely not me," I thought, and I looked down at my own hands. They were bloody and what looked like rags hung from my arms, and inside was fresh-looking flesh, all red, white and black. I was shocked and reached for the handkerchief I carried in the pocket of my trousers, but there was no handkerchief or pocket. The lower part of the trousers had been burned away. I could feel my face swelling up, but there was nothing I could do about it. I and some friends decided to try to get back to our houses in the suburbs. Houses were blazing on both sides of the street as we walked along, and my back started hurting worse.

We heard people calling for help inside wrecked buildings, and then saw the same buildings go up in flames. A boy of about six, covered in blood, was jumping up and down in front of one of the burning houses, holding a cooking pot in his hands and yelling something we could not understand. . . . I wonder what happened to those people? And the ones trapped in the buildings. In our rush to get home quickly, the four of us were proceeding toward the center of the atomic explosion, in the opposite direction from everyone else. However, when we reached Inari-machi, we could not go any further because the bridge had been destroyed, so we headed for Futaba Hill, instead. My legs gave out near Futaba, and I almost crawled the last part of the way to the foot of the hill, saying, "Wait for me! Please wait for me!"

Luckily for us, we met some kind soldiers in white coats there, who took us to a place we could lie down and rest, and treated our wounds. They dug around and told me that they had removed pieces of tile from the back of my head. They bandaged my head for me and tried to console us by saying, "Rest here now. Your teacher is bound to come and get you soon." . . .

That first night ended. There were cries for water from early morning. I was terribly thirsty. There was a puddle in the middle of the barracks. I realized that the water was filthy, but I scooped up some of it with my shoe and drank it. It looked like coffee with milk. . . . I found out that there was a river just behind the barracks and went out with my shoes and drank to my heart's content. After that, I went back and forth many times to get water for those lying near me, and for the injured soldiers. . . . Mercurochrome had been painted on my burns once, and they got black and sticky. I tried to dry them out in the sun. My friends and the other people were no longer able to move. The skin had peeled off of their burned arms, legs, and backs. I wanted to move them, but there was no place on their bodies that I could touch. Some people came around noon on the second day and gave us some rice balls. Our faces were burned and swollen so badly that we could hardly open our mouths, so we got very little of the rice into them. My eyes had swollen up by the third day, and I could not move

around. I lay down in the barracks with my friends. I remember being in a kind of dream world, talking on and on with my delirious friends. . . .

Another time, I must have been dreaming: I thought that my father and sister were coming up the hill to get me. I was so glad that I forced my eyes open with my fingers to see, but it was dark and I could not see anything. People who came to the barracks would call out the names and addresses of the people they were looking for. My father and four or five of our neighbors had been searching for me since the bombing. They found me in a corner of the barracks at the foot of Futaba Hill, on the evening of the third day. They were able to find me because the wooden name tag my father had written for me was on my chest. The writing on the tag had been burned all the way through it, as if it had been etched.

"Atsuko! This is your father!"

I was so happy I couldn't speak. I only nodded my head. My eyes were swollen closed. I could not see my father, but I was saved.

I still have the scars from that day; on my head, face, arms, legs, and chest. There are reddish black scars on my arms and the face that I see in the mirror does not look as if it belongs to me. It always saddens me to think that I will never look the way I used to. I lost all hope at first. I was obsessed with the idea that I had become a freak and did not want to be seen by anyone. I cried constantly for my good friends and kind teachers who had died in such a terrible way.

My way of thinking became warped and pessimistic. Even my beautiful voice, that my friends had envied, had turned weak and hoarse. When I think of the way it was then, I feel as if I were being strangled. But I have been able to take comfort in the thought that physical beauty is not everything, that a beautiful spirit can do away with physical ugliness. This has given me new hope for the future. I am going to study hard and develop my mind and body, to become someone with culture and inner beauty.

The Decision to Drop the Atomic Bomb

BACKGROUND

The chain of events and decisions that led to the dropping of atomic bombs on Hiroshima and Nagasaki began with a letter sent to President Franklin D. Roosevelt in 1939 by Albert Einstein, the world-famous physicist who had fled Nazi Germany in 1932 to escape the scourge of Nazi anti-Semitism. Although signed by Einstein, it was largely written by the less-well-known Hungarian physicist Leó Szilárd. The letter warned that German scientists were pursuing research on nuclear chain reactions with the goal of producing weapons of enormous power; it recommended that the U.S. government fund and coordinate similar research. In response, Roosevelt appointed a committee of scientists to investigate the possibility of uranium chain reactions. Only in 1941, however, after hearing the results of promising nuclear research in England, did he order an all-out effort to produce an atomic weapon. A year later, the project was placed under the control of the army and code-named the Manhattan Project.

Under the direction of Brigadier General Leslie Groves, the Manhattan Project became a huge, desperate enterprise, employing more than 100,000 persons, who worked under the direction of the country's leading nuclear physicists and engineers at 37 installations and a dozen university laboratories. Success was achieved on July 16, 1945, when the first atomic bomb, equal in force to 20,000 tons of TNT and 20,000 times more powerful than the largest conventional bomb, was exploded in the New Mexico desert. In less than a month, atomic bombs reduced Hiroshima and Nagasaki to ashes, and World War II was over.

President Truman, unaware of the Manhattan Project as a senator from Missouri and as Roosevelt's vice president, first learned of the new weapon at his first cabinet meeting on April 13, a day after Roosevelt's death, and received a full briefing from Secretary of War Henry R. Stimson on April 25. In response, Truman appointed a small committee, known as the Interim Committee, to advise him on the use of atomic weapons during and after the war. Chaired by Stimson, it consisted of seven other members: George Harrison, Stimson's special assistant; James Byrnes, a presidential advisor; Ralph Bard, undersecretary of the navy; William Clayton, undersecretary of state; and Vannevar Bush, Karl Compton, and James Conant, three prominent academic scientists who during the war worked for the National Defense Research Council, an agency created by President Roosevelt to oversee and fund scientific research for military purposes. Throughout the late spring and summer, the committee met to discuss and make recommendations on a wide range of issues, including if and how atomic bombs should be used. Their recommendations were communicated to the president by Stimson. In its deliberations, the committee was advised by high-ranking military officers, business leaders, and a small committee of scientists, known as the Scientific Panel.

The events and decisions that occurred in the late spring and summer of 1945 are described in connection with the discussion of the sources that follows.

THE SOURCES

The first source is an excerpt from a summary of comments made by General George Marshall during a meeting with Secretary of War Henry Stimson on May 29, 1945. Marshall was sworn in as army chief of staff by President Roosevelt on September 1, 1939, the day Germany invaded Poland, and still was serving in the closing weeks of the war. With Germany having surrendered on May 8, at the May 29 meeting, the two men discussed the final campaign against Japan.

The second source is an excerpt from a memoir written by Arthur Compton, a member of the Scientific Panel. A Nobel Prize winner for his work on x-rays, Compton was director of the Metallurgical Laboratory at the University of Chicago, where the world's first nuclear chain reaction was produced in December 1942. Here Compton describes a meeting of the Interim Committee on May 31, 1945.

The third and fourth sources were written by scientists who had participated in the Manhattan Project. The Franck Report, submitted to the Interim Committee on June 11, was prepared by the Committee on the Social and Political Implications of Atomic Energy, a group of scientists from the University of Chicago Metallurgical Laboratory who had reservations about the military use of atomic weapons. Its chairperson was James Franck, a German-born chemist and Nobel laureate (1925) for his work on the bombardment of atoms by electrons. A notable feature of the report is its consideration of the ramifications of using the atomic bomb for the postwar world. The next source is excerpted from a petition circulated by Leó Szilárd, a Hungarian-born physicist, and signed by 69 other scientists. Szilárd, who, with Enrico Fermi, designed the first successful nuclear reactor, was deeply moved by the wartime destruction he had seen as a young man in Hungary during World War I. Although he had urged Einstein to write President Roosevelt about the need for research on the military uses of atomic energy in 1939, and had made major contributions to the Manhattan Project, he became increasingly dismayed as scientists lost control of the research to the military. In May and June of 1945, he sought to discourage the U.S. government from using the bomb. Szilárd was one of the signatories of the Franck Report and was the inspiration for the petition sent to President Truman on June 17.

The Interim Committee dismissed the key recommendations of the Franck Report, and in all likelihood, President Truman never read Szilárd's petition. On July 16, while attending the Potsdam Conference in Germany, Truman learned of the successful test of the atomic bomb in New Mexico and received a full report on July 21. On July 25, he ordered the U.S. military to prepare for an atomic attack on Japan sometime after August 1. On July 26, the United States, China, and Great Britain issued the Potsdam Declaration, which urged Japan to surrender unconditionally or face "the prompt and complete destruction of the Japanese armed forces and just as inevitably the utter devastation of the Japanese homeland." No mention was made of a new and terrible weapon. Although some Japanese civilian leaders continued to work for an agreement that would end the war, in the end, Japan refused the terms of the Potsdam Declaration, and attacks on Hiroshima and Nagasaki followed.

The last sources were written by the two men who were most responsible for the decision to use atomic weapons, President Truman and Secretary of War Stimson. The first document is a brief letter dated August 11 from President Truman to Samuel Cavert, general secretary of the Federal Council of Churches, an ecumenical organization representing some 30 major Protestant and Orthodox denominations in the United States. On August 9, Cavert had sent a telegram to President Truman stating, "Many Christians are deeply disturbed over use of atomic bombs against Japanese cities because of their necessarily indiscriminate destructive effects and because their use sets extremely dangerous precedent for future of mankind." The last source is an excerpt from an article Stimson wrote for *Harper's Magazine* in 1947 after his retirement from public service. In it, he describes the work of the Interim Committee and his reasons for advising the president to use the bomb.

QUESTIONS FOR ANALYSIS

1. How many different ideas for using the atomic bomb as a means for ending the war can you find in the sources?
2. What were the arguments made by individuals who cautioned against the use of the atomic bomb or who thought it should be "demonstrated" rather than used against the enemy?
3. What points were made against such arguments?
4. What were the main arguments of those who believed that the bomb should be used against Japanese targets without prior warning?
5. Inevitably, the question must be asked: What would you have decided if you had been president?

1 • Memorandum of Conversation with General Marshall

The Secretary [Stimson] referred to the burning of Tokyo and the possible ways and means of employing the larger bombs. . . .

General Marshall said he thought these weapons might first be used against straight military objectives such as a large naval installation and then if no complete result was derived from the effect of that, he thought we ought to designate a number of large manufacturing areas from which the people would be warned to leave—telling the Japanese that we intended to destroy such centers. There would be no individual designations so that the Japs would not know exactly where we were to hit—a number should be named and the hit should follow shortly after. Every effort should

Source: Memorandum of Conversation with General Marshall, May 29, 1945, National Archives.

be made to keep our record of warning clear. We must offset by such warning methods the opprobrium which might follow from an ill considered employment of such force.

The General then spoke of his stimulation of the new weapons and operations people to the development of new weapons and tactics to cope with the care and last ditch defense tactics of the suicidal Japanese. He sought to avoid the attrition we were now suffering from such fanatical but hopeless defense methods—it requires new tactics. He also spoke of gas and the possibility of using it in a limited degree, say on the outlying islands where

operations were now going on or were about to take place. . . . It did not need to be our newest and most potent—just drench them and sicken them so that the fight would be taken out of them—saturate an area, possibly with mustard [gas], and just stand off. . . . There would be the matter of public opinion which we had to consider, but that was something which might also be dealt with. The character of the weapon was no less humane than phosporous and flame throwers and need not be used against dense populations or civilians—merely against these last pockets of resistance which had to be wiped out but had no other military significance. . . .

2 • Arthur Compton, Recollection of Interim Committee Meeting

Throughout the morning's discussions it seemed to be a foregone conclusion that the bomb would be used. It was regarding only the details of strategy and tactics that differing views were expressed. At the luncheon following the morning meeting, I was seated at Mr. Stimson's left. In the course of the conversation I asked the Secretary whether it might not be possible to arrange a nonmilitary demonstration of the bomb in such a manner that the Japanese would be so impressed that they would see the uselessness of continuing the war. The Secretary opened this question for general discussion by those at the table. Various possibilities were brought forward. One after the other it seemed necessary that they should be discarded.

It was evident that everyone would suspect trickery. If a bomb were exploded in Japan with previous notice, the Japanese air power was still adequate to give serious interference. An atomic bomb was an intricate device, still in the developmental stage. Its operation would be far from routine. If during the final adjustments of the bomb

the Japanese defenders should attack, a faulty move might easily result in some kind of failure. Such an end to an advertised demonstration of power would be much worse than if the attempt had not been made. It was now evident that when the time came for the bombs to be used we should have only one of them available, followed afterwards by others at all-too-long intervals. We could not afford the chance that one of them might be a dud. If the test were made on some neutral territory, it was hard to believe that Japan's determined and fanatical military men would be impressed. If such an open test were made first and failed to bring surrender, the chance would be gone to give the shock of surprise that proved so effective. On the contrary, it would make the Japanese ready to interfere with an atomic attack if they could. Though the possibility of a demonstration that would not destroy human lives was attractive, no one could suggest a way in which it could be made so convincing that it would be likely to stop the war.

Ten days later, at Oppenheimer's invitation, Lawrence, Fermi, and I spent a long week end at Los Alamos. . . . We were determined to find, if

Source: From Arthur Compton, *Atomic Quest* (New York: Oxford University Press, 1956), pp. 238–241. Reprinted with permission of Oxford University Press.

we could, some effective way of demonstrating the power of an atomic bomb without loss of life that would impress Japan's warlords. If only this could be done!

Ernest Lawrence was the last one of our group to give up hope for finding such a solution. The difficulties of making a purely technical demonstration that would carry its impact effectively into Japan's controlling councils were indeed great. We had to count on every possible effort to distort even obvious facts. Experience with the determination of Japan's fight[ing] men made it evident that the war would not be stopped unless these men themselves were convinced of its futility.

---

3 • The Franck Report

Certain and perhaps important tactical results undoubtedly can be achieved, but we nevertheless think that the question of the use of the very first available atomic bombs in the Japanese war should be weighed very carefully, not only by military authority, but by the highest political leadership of this country. If we consider international agreement on total prevention of nuclear warfare as the paramount objective, and believe that it can be achieved, this kind of introduction of atomic weapons to the world may easily destroy all our chances of success. Russia, and even allied countries which bear less mistrust of our ways and intentions, as well as neutral countries, will be deeply shocked. It will be very difficult to persuade the world that a nation which was capable of secretly preparing and suddenly releasing a weapon, as indiscriminate as the rocket bomb and a thousand times more destructive, is to be trusted in its proclaimed desire of having such weapons abolished by international agreement. We have large accumulations of poison gas, but do not use them, and recent polls have shown that public opinion in this country would disapprove of such a use even if it would accelerate the winning of the Far Eastern war. It is true, that some irrational element in mass psychology makes gas poisoning more revolting than blasting by explosive, even though gas warfare is in no way more "inhuman" than the war of bombs and bullets. Nevertheless, it is not at all certain that the American public opinion, if it could be enlightened as to the effect of atomic explosives, would support the first introduction by our own country of such an indiscriminate method of wholesale destruction of civilian life.

Thus, from the "optimistic" point of view—looking forward to an international agreement on prevention of nuclear warfare—the military advantages and the saving of American lives, achieved by the sudden use of atomic bombs against Japan, may be outweighed by the ensuing loss of confidence and wave of horror and repulsion, sweeping over the rest of the world, and perhaps dividing even the public opinion at home.

From this point of view a demonstration of the new weapon may best be made before the eyes of representatives of all United Nations, on the desert or a barren island. The best possible atmosphere for the achievement of an international agreement could be achieved if America would be able to say to the world, "You see what weapon we had but did not use. We are ready to renounce its use in the future and to join other nations in working out adequate supervision of the use of this nuclear weapon."

This may sound fantastic, but then in nuclear weapons we have something entirely new in the order of magnitude of destructive power, and if we want to capitalize fully on the advantage which its possession gives us, we must use new and

---

Source: The Franck Report (June 11, 1945), from U.S. National Archives, Washington, D.C.: Record Group 77, Manhattan Engineer District Records, Harrison-Bundy File, folder #76.

imaginative methods. After such a demonstration the weapon could be used against Japan if a sanction of the United Nations (and of the public opinion at home) could be obtained, perhaps after a preliminary ultimatum to Japan to surrender or at least to evacuate a certain region as an alternative to the total destruction of this target. . . .

4 • The Szilárd Petition

. . . We, the undersigned scientists, have been working in the field of atomic power. Until recently, we have had to fear that the United States might be attacked by atomic bombs during this war and that her only defense might lie in a counterattack by the same means. Today, with the defeat of Germany, this danger is averted and we feel impelled to say what follows:

The war has to be brought speedily to a successful conclusion and attacks by atomic bombs may very well be an effective method of warfare. We feel, however, that such attacks on Japan could not be justified, at least not unless the terms which will be imposed after the war on Japan were made public in detail and Japan were given an opportunity to surrender.

If such public announcement gave assurance to the Japanese that they could look forward to a life devoted to peaceful pursuits in their homeland and if Japan still refused to surrender our nation might then, in certain circumstances, find itself forced to resort to the use of atomic bombs. Such a step, however, ought not to be made at any time without seriously considering the moral responsibilities which are involved.

The development of atomic power will provide the nations with new means of destruction. The atomic bombs at our disposal represent only the first step in this direction, and there is almost no limit to the destructive power which will become available in the course of their future development. Thus a nation which sets the precedent of using these newly liberated forces of nature for purposes of destruction may have to bear the responsibility of opening the door to an era of devastation on an unimaginable scale. . . .

Source: A Petition to the President of the United States, July 17, 1945, from U.S. National Archives, Record Group #77, Records of the Chief of Engineers, Manhattan Engineer District, Harrison-Bundy File, folder #76.

5 • President Harry Truman, Letter to Samuel Cavert

August 11, 1945

My dear Mr. Cavert,

I appreciated very much your telegram of August 9. Nobody is more disturbed over the use of Atomic bombs than I am but I was greatly disturbed by the unwarranted attack by the Japanese on Pearl Harbor and their murder of our prisoners of war. The only language they seem to understand is the one we have been using to bombard them.

When you have to deal with a beast you have to treat him as a beast. It is regrettable but nevertheless true.

Sincerely yours,
Harry S. Truman

Source: President Harry Truman, Letter to Samuel Cavert, August 11, 1945, from Harry S. Truman Presidential Library and Museum.

424 • The Global Community and Its Challenges

6 • Henry Stimson, The Decision to Use the Atomic Bomb

In the middle of July 1945, the intelligence section of the War Department General Staff estimated Japanese military strength as follows: in the home islands, slightly under 2,000,000; in Korea, Manchuria, China proper, and Formosa, slightly over 2,000,000; in French Indo-China, Thailand, and Burma, over 200,000; in the East Indies area, including the Philippines, over 500,000; in the by-passed Pacific islands, over 100,000. The total strength of the Japanese Army was estimated at about 5,000,000 men. . . . As we understood it in July, there was a very strong possibility that the Japanese government might determine upon resistance to the end, in all the areas of the Far East under its control. In such an event the Allies would be faced with the enormous task of destroying an armed force of five million men and five thousand suicide aircraft, belonging to a race which had already amply demonstrated its ability to fight literally to the death.

The strategic plans of our armed forces for the defeat of Japan, as they stood in July, had been prepared without reliance upon the atomic bomb, which had not yet been tested in New Mexico. We were planning an intensified sea and air blockade, and greatly intensified strategic air bombing, through the summer and early fall, to be followed on November 1 by an invasion of the southern island of Kyushu. This would be followed in turn by an invasion of the main island of Honshu in the spring of 1946. The total U.S. military and naval force involved in this grand design was of the order of 5,000,000 men; if all those indirectly concerned are included, it was larger still.

We estimated that if we should be forced to carry this plan to its conclusion, the major fighting would not end until the latter part of 1946, at the earliest. I was informed that such operations might be expected to cost over a million casualties to American forces alone. Additional large losses might be expected among our allies, and, of course, if our campaign were successful and if we could judge by previous experience, enemy casualties would be much larger than our own.

It was already clear in July that even before the invasion we should be able to inflict enormously severe damage on the Japanese homeland by the combined application of "conventional" sea and air power. The critical question was whether this kind of action would induce surrender. It therefore became necessary to consider very carefully the probable state of mind of the enemy, and to assess with accuracy the line of conduct which might end his will to resist.

The face of war is the face of death; death is an inevitable part of every order that a wartime leader gives. The decision to use the atomic bomb was a decision that brought death to over a hundred thousand Japanese. . . . But this deliberate, premeditated destruction was our least abhorrent choice. The destruction of Hiroshima and Nagasaki put an end to the Japanese war. It stopped the fire raids and the strangling blockade; it ended the ghastly specter of a clash of great land armies. . . .

Source: From Harry L. Stimson, "The Decision to Use the Atomic Bomb," *Harper's Weekly*, February 1947 by Harper's Magazine. Copyright © 1947 by *Harper's Magazine*.

Chapter 12

Anticolonialism, Nationalism, and Revolution in Africa, Asia, and Latin America

DURING THE NINETEENTH CENTURY, the industrialized nations of Europe and the United States—"the West"—achieved unprecedented global dominance. For India and most of Africa and Southeast Asia, this meant colonial status and outright political control by Western nations. For China, Persia, the Ottoman Empire, and many states in Latin America, it meant the subordination of their economic interests to those of the West and erosion of their political sovereignty. Most Europeans and Americans viewed these developments as just and inevitable. Their preponderance confirmed their intellectual and moral superiority to black-, yellow-, and brown-skinned people, whom the English writer Rudyard Kipling had depicted in his poem "The White Man's Burden" as "half devil and half child."

In the first half of the twentieth century, however, Africans, Asians, and Latin Americans challenged the West's ascendancy. In areas of formal empire, mounting anticolonialism gave rise to organized parties and movements whose supporters demanded more political power and, ultimately, independence. Such movements were strongest in India, where opposition to British rule escalated from polite requests by educated Indians for greater political responsibility to nationwide boycotts and mass demonstrations for independence. Despite French, British, and Dutch repression in Southeast Asia, dozens of political parties and underground organizations worked for the peaceful end or violent overthrow of colonial regimes. In Africa—although colonized only in the late 1800s and despite its ethnic and linguistic diversity—articulate and forceful proponents of pan-Africanism, anticolonialism, and nationalism also emerged. In the Arab Middle East, where nationalist aspirations after World War I were dashed by the mandate system and the continuation of the British protectorate in Egypt, opponents of Anglo-French political control sought independence for Egypt, Iraq, Lebanon, and Syria.

While nationalism in colonial areas was directed against foreign rule, in those parts of Asia and Latin America where states were independent but nonetheless subservient in many respects to U.S. and European interests, it focused on overcoming economic dependency and political weakness. In Turkey, this meant a sharp break from its past and implementation of a program of secularization and modernization under Mustafa Kemal Atatürk. In China, nationalism resulted in a struggle to rebuild the country and end foreign interference in the face of warlordism, civil war, and Japanese invasions of Manchuria in 1931 and China itself in 1937. In Latin America, nationalism inspired new plans for economic development after the Great Depression of the 1930s ruined the worldwide market for the region's minerals and agricultural products. In several Latin American countries, such efforts intensified conflict between entrenched elites and populist leaders who promised the masses social reforms.

When World War II ended in 1945, many Western leaders thought they could return to the world they had dominated before the war. In the immediate postwar years, the Dutch, French, and British all used force to maintain their empires but soon realized the futility of their efforts. Based on developments in the first half of the twentieth century, Asian and African demands for independence proved irresistible.

African Society and Identity Under Colonial Rule

Compared with the experience of India, the unfolding of colonialism in Africa resembles watching a film shown at high speed. The European "scramble for Africa" began in the early 1880s, and after overcoming resistance and deciding among themselves who controlled what, Africa's new masters gave serious thought to what policies would determine the future of their new acquisitions. Not long after these issues had been resolved, World War II was fought, and independence movements swept through Africa. In 1957, the Gold Coast, a British colony, became the independent nation of Ghana, sparking a chain of events that resulted in the establishment of dozens of new independent states within the next decade and a half.

So brief was Africa's colonial experience, and so rapid was the Europeans' exit, that nationalism in Africa never became the broad popular movement that emerged in India during the long struggle against British rule. In addition, nationalist movements in Africa were hampered by other factors: the indifference of many chiefs, farmers, and petty traders who benefited from European rule; the paucity of Africans with formal education and political experience; the gap between educated city-dwellers and the rural masses; and rivalries among ethnic groups. Nevertheless, Africans in the interwar years found ways to express their opposition to colonial rule. They demonstrated against labor conscription, new taxes, and government-mandated land confiscations. They organized political associations, published journals, wrote books and editorials, joined independent African Christian churches, attended international meetings, and sent representatives to European capitals to state their grievances. A new generation of African nationalist leaders emerged, and a growing audience listened to what they had to say.

Eagles into Chickens

92 • JAMES AGGREY, PARABLE OF THE EAGLE

James Aggrey, an educator and clergyman who was among the most prominent Africans of his day, was born in 1875 in the Gold Coast, a British colony. He was educated in a Protestant mission school, became a convert to Christianity, and at age 23 traveled to the United States to study for the ministry. He remained in the United States for 20 years, studying economics and agriculture, speaking out against racial prejudice, and working among poor blacks of South Carolina. He returned to Africa in 1918 and died in 1927. "Parable of the Eagle" was written in the early 1920s.

QUESTIONS FOR ANALYSIS

1. According to the lesson of Aggrey's parable, what psychological and emotional damage results from colonialism?
2. If the lessons of Aggrey's parable had been translated into actual policy by colonial administrators, what aspects of colonial rule would have been affected?

A certain man went through a forest seeking any bird of interest he might find. He caught a young eagle, brought it home and put it among his fowls and ducks and turkeys, and gave it chickens' food to eat even though it was an eagle, the king of birds.

Source: James Aggrey, "Parable of the Eagle," in Edwin Smith, *Aggrey of Africa* (London: Student Christian Movement, 1929).

Five years later a naturalist came to see him and, after passing through his garden, said: "That bird is an eagle, not a chicken."

"Yes," said its owner, "but I have trained it to be a chicken. It is no longer an eagle, it is a chicken, even though it measures fifteen feet from tip to tip of its wings."

"No," said the naturalist, "it is an eagle still: it has the heart of an eagle, and I will make it soar high up to the heavens."

"No," said the owner, "it is a chicken, and it will never fly."

They agreed to test it. The naturalist picked up the eagle, held it up, and said with great intensity: "Eagle, thou art an eagle; thou dost belong to the sky and not to this earth; stretch forth thy wings and fly."

The eagle turned this way and that, and then, looking down, saw the chickens eating their food, and down he jumped.

The owner said: "I told you it was a chicken."

"No," said the naturalist, "it is an eagle. Give it another chance tomorrow."

So the next day he took it to the top of the house and said: "Eagle, thou art an eagle; stretch forth thy wings and fly." But again the eagle, seeing the chickens feeding, jumped down and fed with them.

Then the owner said: "I told you it was a chicken."

"No," asserted the naturalist, "it is an eagle, and it still has the heart of an eagle; only give it one more chance, and I will make it fly tomorrow."

The next morning he rose early and took the eagle outside the city, away from the houses, to the foot of a high mountain. The sun was just rising, gilding the top of the mountain with gold, and every crag was glistening in the joy of that beautiful morning.

He picked up the eagle and said to it: "Eagle, thou art an eagle; thou dost belong to the sky and not to this earth; stretch forth thy wings and fly!"

The eagle looked around and trembled as if new life were coming to it; but it did not fly. The naturalist then made it look straight at the sun. Suddenly it stretched out its wings and, with the screech of an eagle, it mounted higher and higher and never returned. It was an eagle, though it had been kept and tamed as a chicken! My people of Africa, we were created in the image of God, but men have made us think that we are chickens, and we still think we are; but we are eagles. Stretch forth your wings and fly! Don't be content with the food of chickens!

The Value of African Tradition

93 • KABAKA DAUDI CHWA, EDUCATION, CIVILIZATION, AND "FOREIGNIZATION" IN BUGANDA

The Great Lakes region of east-central Africa, dominated by the kingdom of Buganda, was an area of extensive European missionary activity in the nineteenth century. British Protestant missionaries arrived in 1877 and were followed by French Catholic missionaries in 1879. With the hold of traditional religion already weakened by conversions to Islam, the missionaries made numerous converts, especially among young courtiers in the entourage of Buganda's hereditary ruler, known as the *kabaka*. In the 1880s, Protestant–Catholic rivalries among the chiefs led to civil war, the weakening of the kabaka's power, and the establishment in 1894 of the British protectorate of Uganda, of which Buganda was the largest part.

Daudi Chwa (1897–1939), as a 2-year-old, was named kabaka of Buganda after his father had been deposed and exiled for leading a campaign against the British. A convert to Christianity, he was a figurehead, since the British gave his major chiefs a free hand to administer the colony. He did play an active and successful role in opposing the plan to consolidate Uganda, Kenya, and Tanganyika into one colony in the 1930s. Toward the end of his life, Daudi Chwa developed reservations about the effects of colonial rule, especially in the cultural and religious spheres. In 1935, four years before his death, he expressed his views in a pamphlet, "Education, Civilization, and 'Foreignization' in Buganda."

QUESTIONS FOR ANALYSIS

1. How would you characterize the traditional system of justice of the Baganda? By what means did this system deter behavior that was counter to the people's rules and customs?
2. According to the kabaka, in what ways do traditional Baganda moral values resemble those of Christianity?
3. According to the kabaka, what have the people of Buganda (the Baganda) gained and lost as a result of European colonization?
4. What sort of thinking about the "backwardness" of the Baganda does the kabaka try to counter in his letter?
5. In the kabaka's view, what should be the proper balance between traditional and European beliefs and practices?

Everyone knows that education and civilization were started simultaneously in this country in their respective rudimentary forms by the kind efforts of the members of the various Missionary Societies and have now been enhanced largely due to the assistance rendered by the Protectorate Government.

Naturally, Education and Civilization gained tremendous favour among the Baganda,[1] and as a consequence there are numerous Schools in remote villages in Buganda Kingdom for the Education of the young generations. . . .

Now my fears are that instead of the Baganda acquiring proper and legitimate education and

civilization there is possible danger that they may be drifting to "foreignization.". . . To be more explicit, what I mean by the word "foreignization" is that instead of the Baganda acquiring proper education at the various Schools and of availing themselves of the legitimate amenities of civilization, I am very much afraid the young generation of this country is merely drifting wholesale towards "foreignization" of their natural instincts and is discarding its native and traditional customs, habits and good breeding. . . .

I am well aware that it has been said more than once that the Baganda have neither morals nor public opinion. . . . I do not wish . . . to uphold

Source: Donald A. Low, *The Mind of Buganda* (Berkeley: University of California Press, 1971), pp. 134–138. Reprinted by permission of the University of California Press.

[1]The Baganda are the people of the kingdom of Buganda.

the Baganda as a Nation of Angels—But what I do maintain is that prior to the advent of the Europeans the Baganda had a very strict moral code of their own which was always enforced by a constant and genuine fear of some evil or incurable or even fatal disease being suffered invariably by the breaker of this moral code. In fact I maintain the Baganda observed most strictly the doctrine of the Ten Commandments in spite of the fact that Christianity and the so-called Christian morals were absolutely unknown to the Baganda. . . .

(a) Theft was always punished very severely, invariably by the loss of the right hand of the offender, so as to render him incapable of committing the same offense again.

(b) Adultery was almost unknown among the Baganda and any man found guilty of such offense was always ostracized from Society.

(c) Murder was invariably followed by a very severe vendetta between the members of the family or clan of the victim and those of the offender.

(d) Filial obedience was most honored among the Baganda and disobedience or disrespect of one's parents was always supposed to be punished by some higher power by the infliction of some horrible or incurable disease upon the offender.

(e) False evidence was looked upon with contempt. The person who bore false evidence and the person against whom it was given were both subjected to a very severe test by forcing them to drink a certain kind of strong drug known as "Madudu," which was supposed to result in making one of the parties who was in the wrong unconscious.

In this connection I should like to point out that although polygamy was universally recognized among the Baganda and was never considered as immoral yet prostitution was absolutely unheard of. Civilization, education and freedom are the direct causes of the appalling state of affairs as regards prostitution and promiscuous relationships between the Baganda men and women. . . .

As an illustration of the strictness of the old moral code of the Baganda I should like to point out here one of the most important native customs of looking after the daughters in a Muganda's[2] home. It was one of the worst filial offenses for a daughter to become pregnant while living with her parents. As soon as she was discovered in that condition she was at once expelled from her parents' house, and was absolutely cut off from them. She could not eat with them nor would her parents touch her until the child was born and some rites had been gone through which necessitated a great deal of hardship and shame on the part of the girl and her seducer. This custom was intended to stimulate morality among the Baganda girls, since any girl who went astray before she was given in marriage suffered this indignity and was always looked upon with contempt by all her relatives and friends. Furthermore any girl who was given in marriage and was found not to be a virgin merited unspeakable disfavor in the eyes of her parents, relations and friends. All this, however, is of course, no longer the case. The present so-called education and civilization prevailing in this country has completely destroyed this moral code by removing the constant fear just referred to above from the minds of the young generation of the Baganda by the freedom and liberty which are the natural consequences of the present World civilization. . . .

I am strongly of opinion that most of the traditional customs and etiquette of the Baganda . . . were quite consistent with the principles of Christianity. In support of this argument it is only necessary to mention a few customs of the Baganda to show that they unconsciously possessed a sense of the modern Christian morality:

(a) It was one of the most important behaviors among the Baganda for one's neighbor to be considered as his own relative and to share with him in his happiness or unhappiness. . . .

---

[2]Muganda is the word for an individual Bagandan.

(b) It was the recognized etiquette for a Muganda to salute every one that he met on the road, whether he knew him or not.

(c) When a Muganda was taking his meal and any one passed by, it was always the custom to invite him to share it with him.

(d) It was always the duty of everyone who hears an alarm at any time of day or night or a cry for help to go at once and render assistance to the party in distress or danger. . . .

(e) It was the duty of every Muganda, when requested, to assist any traveller in directing him to his destination, or to give him food or water, and even to give him shelter from rain or for the night. . . .

My intention therefore in this article is to emphasize the fact that while boasting of having acquired Western education and civilization in an amazingly short period, we have entirely and completely ignored our native traditional customs. In other words we have "foreignized" our native existence by acquiring the worst foreign habits and customs of the Western people. I am only too well aware that this is inevitable in all countries where Western civilization has reached, so I have considered it my duty in this article to warn very strongly all members of the young generation of the Baganda that while they are legitimately entitled to strive to acquire education and civilization they should also take a very great care that acquisition of Western Education and Civilization does not automatically destroy their best inherent traditions and customs which, in my own opinion, are quite as good as those found among the Western Civilized countries but which only require developing and remodelling where necessary on the lines and ideas of western civilization.

New Leaders and New Sources of Conflict in the Middle East

The immediate aftermath of World War I brought political disaster to the Middle East. The Turks, who had fought on Germany's side, were forced in 1920 to accept the humiliating Treaty of Sèvres, which stripped Turkey of its Arab territories; limited the Turkish army to 50,000 men; gave France, Britain, and Italy control of its finances; and proposed to cede parts of Turkey itself to Italy, Greece, and the new states of Kurdistan and Armenia. The sultan, overwhelmed by problems of lawlessness, army desertions, and inflation, not only accepted the treaty but failed to offer resistance when the Greeks landed troops in western Anatolia in May 1919.

The Turks' former subjects, the Arabs, also experienced bitter disappointment. Promised self-rule for joining the Anglo-French alliance and fighting against their Ottoman overlords, they learned in 1919 that the British and French had agreed in 1916 to divide Arab lands between them and that this, rather than the promises of Arab independence, would determine the postwar settlement. In 1920, Iraq, Syria, Palestine, Lebanon, and Jordan all became British or French mandates, a status that differed little from old-style colonialism. Arabs also were incensed by the continuation of the British protectorate in Egypt and by the British intention of honoring their wartime promises to support the establishment of a national homeland in

Palestine for the Jewish people. Farther east, another major Islamic state, Persia, under the decrepit rule of the Qajar Dynasty, also seemed on the verge of becoming a British protectorate.

Efforts to reverse the postwar settlements succeeded in Turkey and Persia. Under Mustafa Kemal, the Turks rallied to drive out the Greeks and smash the nascent Armenian state between 1919 and 1922. In 1922, they abolished the sultanate, and in 1923, the European powers agreed to replace the Treaty of Sèvres with the Treaty of Lausanne, which recognized the integrity and independence of the new Turkish republic. Assuming near-dictatorial powers, Mustafa Kemal now had an opportunity to transform Turkey into a modern secular state. In Persia, which barely avoided becoming a British protectorate in 1919, Colonel Reza Khan (1878–1944) was named shah in 1925 and, like his hero Kemal, sought to build up his country (which officially adopted the name Iran in 1935) through economic development, educational reform, and secularization.

Arab efforts to achieve independence and prevent Jewish immigration to Palestine were less successful. Of the 20 Arab states that stretched from Morocco in the west to Iraq in the east, only Saudi Arabia and parts of Yemen were truly independent in the interwar years. Egypt and Iraq attained limited self-rule, but the presence of British troops and continuing British influence over foreign and military affairs were sources of resentment in both countries. The drive for independence was even more frustrating in French-controlled Lebanon and Syria. In the 1930s, the French reneged on promises to relinquish their authority, and Lebanon remained a mandate until 1943 and Syria until 1946. Arabs throughout the Middle East also were angered by growing Jewish migration to Palestine, especially in the wake of the Nazi takeover of Germany.

While confronting these postwar political problems, the people and leaders of the region faced other difficult issues. What could be done to end poverty and illiteracy? How could the teachings and expectations of Islam be reconciled with the realities and demands of modernization? Was modernization itself desirable, and, if so, how was it to be achieved? Was the goal of Arab nationalism the expulsion of the British and French and the stifling of Zionism, or was it the attainment of a single united Arab state? In the face of the changes that swept across the region in the first half of the twentieth century, finding answers to questions such as these became more urgent and more difficult.

Secularism and Nationalism in Republican Turkey

94 • MUSTAFA KEMAL, SPEECH TO THE CONGRESS OF THE PEOPLE'S REPUBLICAN PARTY

The arch-symbol of secularism and nationalism in the Muslim world in the interwar years was Mustafa Kemal (1881–1938), a military hero during World War I who went on to serve as the first president of the Turkish republic. Disgusted by the Ottoman sultan's acquiescence to the Greek occupation of the Turkish port of Smyrna (Izmir) in 1919, Kemal assumed leadership of a resistance movement that by 1923 had overthrown the sultan, defeated the Greeks, and won the annulment of the punitive Treaty of Sèvres. Exercising broad powers as president of Turkey, until his death in 1938 Kemal sought to transform Turkey into a modern secular nation-state. To accomplish this, he broke the power of Islam over education and the legal system, encouraged industrialization, accorded women full legal rights, mandated the use of a new Turkish alphabet, and ordered Turks to adopt Western-style dress. Directing all Turks to adopt hereditary family names, he took for himself the name Atatürk, or "Great Turk."

Having consolidated his authority, Kemal decided in 1927 to review his accomplishments and impress upon his subjects the need for continued support. He chose as the occasion the meeting of Turkey's only legal political party, the People's Republican Party, which he had founded. He delivered an extraordinary speech. Three months in preparation, it lasted six days.

In these excerpts he discusses Turkey's past and future; explains his reasons for abolishing the caliphate, the ancient office by virtue of which Ottoman sultans had been the theoretical rulers of all Muslims; and justifies his suppression of the Progressive Republican Party, which despite its name was a party of conservatives who opposed Turkey's modernization.

QUESTIONS FOR ANALYSIS

1. According to Kemal, what were the "erroneous ideas" that had guided the Ottoman state in the past?
2. Why does Kemal argue that nation-states, not empires, are the most desirable form of political organization?
3. What is Kemal's view of the West?
4. What are his views of Islam?
5. What arguments does Kemal offer against the continuation of the caliphate?
6. How does Kemal justify his suppression of the Progressive Republicans? What, in his view, were the positive results of this step?

[Nationalism and Empire]

. . . Among the Ottoman rulers there were some who endeavored to form a gigantic empire by seizing Germany and Western Europe. One of these rulers hoped to unite the whole Islamic world in one body, to lead it and govern it. For this purpose he obtained control of Syria and Egypt and assumed the title of Caliph.[1] Another Sultan pursued the twofold aim, on the one hand of gaining the mastery over Europe, and on the other of subjecting the Islamic world to his authority and government. The continuous counterattacks from

---

Source: Mustafa Kemal, *A Speech Delivered by Ghazi Mustapha Kemal* (Leipzig: F. F. Koehler, 1929), pp. 376–379, 589–594, 717, 721–722.

[1]A reference to Selim I, who conquered Egypt and Syria in 1515–1516; it is doubtful that he actually considered himself caliph—that is, leader and protector of all Muslims.

the West, the discontent and insurrections in the Muslim world, as well as the dissensions between the various elements which this policy had artificially brought together within certain limits, had the ultimate result of burying the Ottoman Empire, in the same way as many others, under the pall of history. . . .

To unite different nations under one common name, to give these different elements equal rights, subject them to the same conditions and thus to found a mighty State is a brilliant and attractive political ideal; but it is a misleading one. It is an unrealizable aim to attempt to unite in one tribe the various races existing on the earth, thereby abolishing all boundaries. Herein lies a truth which the centuries that have gone by and the men who have lived during these centuries have clearly shown in dark and sanguinary events.

There is nothing in history to show how the policy of Panislamism[2] could have succeeded or how it could have found a basis for its realization on this earth. As regards the result of the ambition to organize a State which should be governed by the idea of world-supremacy and include the whole of humanity without distinction of race, history does not afford examples of this. For us, there can be no question of the lust of conquest. . . .

In order that our nation should be able to live a happy, strenuous, and permanent life, it is necessary that the State should pursue an exclusively national policy and that this policy should be in perfect agreement with our internal organization and be based on it. When I speak of national policy, I mean it in this sense: To work within our national boundaries for the real happiness and welfare of the nation and the country by, above all, relying on our own strength in order to retain our existence. But not to lead the people to follow fictitious aims, of whatever nature, which could only bring them misfortune, and expect from the civilized world civilized human treatment, friendship based on mutuality. . . .

[The Issue of the Caliphate]

I must call attention to the fact that Hodja Shukri, as well as the politicians who pushed forward his person and signature, had intended to substitute the sovereign bearing the title of Sultan or Padishah by a monarch with the title of Caliph.[3] The only difference was that, instead of speaking of a monarch of this or that country or nation, they now spoke of a monarch whose authority extended over a population of three hundred million souls belonging to manifold nations and dwelling in different continents of the world. Into the hands of this great monarch, whose authority was to extend over the whole of Islam, they placed as the only power that of the Turkish people, that is to say, only from 10 to 15 millions of these three hundred million subjects. The monarch designated under the title of Caliph was to guide the affairs of these Muslim peoples and to secure the execution of the religious prescriptions which would best correspond to their worldly interests. He was to defend the rights of all Muslims and concentrate all the affairs of the Muslim world in his hands with effective authority. . . .

If the Caliph and Caliphate, as they maintained, were to be invested with a dignity embracing the whole of Islam, ought they not to have realized

---

[2]The program of uniting all Muslims under one government or ruler.

[3]These events took place in January 1923. After Sultan Mehmed V was deposed on November 1, 1922, his cousin was designated caliph. Because of their long rule and vast territories, Ottoman sultans by the nineteenth century were viewed by many Muslims as caliphs—that is, successors of the prophet Muhammad, with jurisdiction over all of Islam. Shukri was a *hodja* (or *hojjd*), a Turkish religious leader; he hoped that the new Turkish state would continue to support the caliphate even after the sultanate was abolished. In 1924, however, Kemal abolished the caliphate.

in all justice that a crushing burden would be imposed on Turkey, on her existence; her entire resources and all her forces would be placed at the disposal of the Caliph? . . .

I made statements everywhere, that were necessary to dispel the uncertainty and anxiety of the people concerning this question of the Caliphate. . . . I gave the people to understand that neither Turkey nor the handful of men she possesses could be placed at the disposal of the Caliph so that he might fulfill the mission attributed to him, namely, to found a State comprising the whole of Islam. The Turkish nation is incapable of undertaking such an irrational mission.

For centuries our nation was guided under the influence of these erroneous ideas. But what has been the result of it? Everywhere they have lost millions of men. "Do you know," I asked, "how many sons of Anatolia have perished in the scorching deserts of the Yemen? Do you know the losses we have suffered in holding Syria and Iraq and Egypt and in maintaining our position in Africa? And do you see what has come out of it? Do you know? . . .

"New Turkey, the people of New Turkey, have no reason to think of anything else but their own existence and their own welfare. She has nothing more to give away to others." . . .

[The Suppression of the Progressive Republicans]

As you know, it was at the time that the members of the opposition had founded a party under the name of "Republican Progressive Party" and published its program. . . .

Under the mask of respect for religious ideas and dogmas the new Party addressed itself to the people in the following words:

"We want the re-establishment of the Caliphate; we do not want new laws; we are satisfied with the religious law; we shall protect the Medressas, the Tekkes, the pious institutions, the Softahs, the Sheikhs[4] and their disciples. Be on our side; the party of Mustafa Kemal, having abolished the Caliphate, is breaking Islam into ruins; they will make you into unbelievers. . . ."

Read these sentences, Gentlemen, from a letter written by one of the adherents of this program: . . . "They are attacking the very principles which perpetuate the existence of the Muslim world. . . . The assimilation with the Occident means the destruction of our history, our civilization. . . ." Gentlemen, facts and events have proved that the program of the Republican Progressive Party has been the work emanating from the brain of traitors. This Party became the refuge and the point of support for reactionary and rebellious elements. . . .

The Government and the Committee found themselves forced to take extraordinary measures. They caused the law regarding the restoration of order to be proclaimed, and the Independence Courts to take action. For a considerable time they kept eight or nine divisions of the army at war strength for the suppression of disorders, and put an end to the injurious organization which bore the name "Republican Progressive Party."

The result was, of course, the success of the Republic. . . .

Gentlemen, it was necessary to abolish the fez,[5] which sat on our heads as a sign of ignorance, of fanaticism, of hatred to progress and civilization,

---

[4]A *medressa* (also madrasah or madrassa) is an advanced school of Islamic learning; a *tekke* is a small teaching mosque usually built over the tomb of a saint; a *softah* is a student in an Islamic school; a *sheikh*, or *shaykh*, is a master of a religious order of Sufis, who adopted a mystical approach to Islam.

[5]The fez was a brimless hat popular among Turkish men during the nineteenth century; its lack of a brim allowed the wearer to touch his forehead to the ground while kneeling during prayer without removing the hat.

and to adopt in its place the hat, the customary headdress of the whole civilized world, thus showing, among other things, that no difference existed in the manner of thought between the Turkish nation and the whole family of civilized mankind. We did that while the law for the Restoration of Order was still in force. If it had not been in force we should have done so all the same; but one can say with complete truth that the existence of this law made the thing much easier for us. As a matter of fact the application of the law for the Restoration of Order prevented the morale of the nation being poisoned to a great extent by reactionaries.

Gentlemen, while the law regarding the Restoration of Order was in force there took place also the closing of the Tekkes, of the convents, and of the mausoleums, as well as the abolition of all sects[6] and all kinds of titles such as Sheikh, Dervish, . . . Occultist, Magician, Mausoleum Guard, etc.[7]

One will be able to imagine how necessary the carrying through of these measures was, in order to prove that our nation as a whole was no primitive nation, filled with superstitions and prejudices.

Could a civilized nation tolerate a mass of people who let themselves be led by the nose by a herd of Sheikhs, Dedes, Seids, . . . Babas and Emirs,[8] who entrusted their destiny and their lives to chiromancers,[9] magicians, dice-throwers and amulet sellers? Ought one to conserve in the Turkish State, in the Turkish Republic, elements and institutions such as those which had for centuries given the nation the appearance of being other than it really was? Would one not therewith have committed the greatest, most irreparable error to the cause of progress and reawakening?

If we made use of the law for the Restoration of Order in this manner, it was in order to avoid such a historic error; to show the nation's brow pure and luminous, as it is; to prove that our people think neither in a fanatical nor a reactionary manner.

Gentlemen, at the same time the new laws were worked out and decreed which promise the most fruitful results for the nation on the social and economic plane, and in general in all the forms of the expression of human activity . . . the Citizens' Legal Code, which ensures the liberty of women and stabilizes the existence of the family.

Accordingly we made use of all circumstances only from one point of view, which consisted therein: to raise the nation on to that step on which it is justified in standing in the civilized world, to stabilize the Turkish Republic more and more on steadfast foundations . . . and in addition to destroy the spirit of despotism for ever.

---

[6]Islamic religious orders.

[7]A *dervish*, or *darvish*, was a member of an Islamic sect famous for its whirling dances that symbolized the movement of the heavenly spheres. An *occultist* was a Sufi who achieved a state of withdrawal from the world. A *mausoleum guard* guarded the tomb of a saint or holy person.

[8]A *dede* was head of a Sufi order. *Seids*, or *sayyids*, were descendents of the prophet Muhammed through his daughter Fatima. *Baba* was a popular surname among Sufi preachers. In this context *emir* is an honorary Turkish title.

[9]People who told the future by reading palms.

Impasse in Palestine

95 • REPORT OF THE PALESTINE ROYAL COMMISSION (THE PEEL COMMISSION), JULY 1937

Despite six wars, dozens of minor conflicts, continual negotiations, and countless proposals, the Arab–Israeli conflict remains a source of ongoing tension in the Middle East and beyond. The immediate cause was the founding of the state of Israel in 1947 and the displacement of approximately 750,000 Palestinian Arabs during and after the 1948 Arab-Israeli War, but the roots of conflict go much deeper.

Its origins go back to 70 C.E., when the Jews were exiled from Palestine by the Romans, forcing them into a long period in which they resettled in other parts of the Middle East, North Africa, Europe, and years later the Americas. In their years of exile, Jews maintained a strong attachment to the "Land of Canaan," which according to Hebrew scriptures, God had given them as their promised land after becoming His chosen people. Only in the nineteenth century, however, in response to growing anti-Semitism and fears over the loss of Jewish identity, did a number of intellectuals and religious leaders conclude that Jews could escape persecution and preserve their traditions only by returning to their former homeland in Palestine, the region between the Mediterranean Sea and the Jordan River. This movement came to be known as Zionism, derived from Mount Zion, one of the two major hills overlooking Jerusalem, the ancient Jewish capital and religious center.

The first advocates of Jewish resettlement in Palestine were Russian Jews reacting to the anti-Jewish pogroms of the 1880s and 1890s. Political Zionism, which advocates the foundation of a Jewish state (not just resettlement), dates from the late 1890s, when the Vienna-based journalist Theodor Herzl published *Der Judenstaat* (*The Jewish State*) in 1896 and one year later convened the first international Zionist conference in Basel, Switzerland. On the eve of World War I, approximately 60,000 Jews, about half of whom were recent immigrants, lived in Palestine compared to 620,000 Muslims and 70,000 Christians.

The situation in Palestine became more volatile in the 1920s and 1930s. The Palestinian Arabs, who had come to identify themselves politically with Syria, were bitterly disappointed when Great Britain and France reneged on their wartime promises to support the creation of an independent Arab state and instead turned the former Arab provinces of the Ottoman Empire into mandates. They were embittered further when the British, who held the Palestinian mandate, made good on the wartime pledge of their foreign minister Arthur Balfour to facilitate Jewish immigration to Palestine and make it a "national home" for the Jewish people. Between 1919 and 1939, the number of Jews in Palestine's population grew from slightly under 10 percent to 30 percent. These Jews purchased land, established industries, founded Jewish schools and universities, and with support from the Zionist Organization laid the groundwork for the foundation of a Jewish state. Meanwhile, Arabs pressured British authorities to halt Jewish immigration, limit land sales to Jews, and grant immediate independence to Syria. With Arab frustration growing, in 1936 sporadic violence escalated into Arab general strikes, tax boycotts, bombings, and property destruction directed against Jews and British officials.

In response, the British government sent the former Secretary of State for India, Lord William Peel, to Palestine to head a commission charged with the task of investigating the causes of the violence and recommending solutions. After gathering information and interviewing well over 100 people, the commission published its report in mid-1937. Concluding that compromise and cooperation were impossible, it recommended the partition of Palestine into three parts: Jewish territory in the northwest; Arab territory in the east and south; and continued British control of Nazareth, Jerusalem, and a corridor between Jerusalem and the coast (see map on page 441). Although the proposals were endorsed by the British government, they bitterly divided the Jews and were rejected totally by the Arabs. The political future of Palestine was not settled until 1947, when the independent state of Israel was born. But the discord continued.

QUESTIONS FOR ANALYSIS

1. What do the Arab and Jewish lists of grievances reveal about the economic and social status of the two communities?
2. Given the two sides' lists of grievances, what reasonable chance did the British have of satisfying each side?
3. Why, according to the report's authors, are the Arab and Jewish communities inherently and permanently incompatible?
4. On what basis do the report's authors predict that the Arab–Jewish conflict will worsen?
5. Why, according to the report, does the use of force provide no long-term solution to the problems of the region?
6. How, according to the report, will continuation of the status quo damage Great Britain's standing in the world?
7. Overall, does the tone and content of the report seem more sympathetic to the Arabs or Jews?
8. Arabs resolutely rejected the commission's plan for partition. Among Jews, the plan had supporters and opponents. What arguments might these groups have offered to defend their point of view? Consult the map in addition to the report itself for possible answers to these questions.

Conclusions and Recommendations

Arab Grievances

(1) The failure to develop self-governing institutions.
(2) The acquisition of land by the Jews.
(3) Jewish immigration.
(4) The use of Hebrew and English as official languages.
(5) The employment of British and Jewish officers, and exclusion of Arabs from the higher posts.
(6) The creation of a large class of landless Arabs, and the refusal of Jews to employ Arab labourers.
(7) Inadequate funds for Arab education.

Whilst we believe that these grievances are sincerely felt, we are of opinion that most of them cannot be regarded as legitimate under the terms of the Mandate and we are therefore not called upon to make recommendations on them. It is only in regard to the last that we are able to suggest any remedy. We would welcome increased expenditure on Arab education, especially in the direction of village agricultural schools.

Jewish Grievances

(1) Obstruction in the establishment of the National Home owing to dilatory action in dealing with proposals demanding executive action.
(2) The display of "pro-Arab" proclivities by officials and their failure to carry out the Mandate. . . .
(3) Great delay in the decision of civil suits; inefficiency in criminal procedure, as instanced by the fact that 80 Jews were murdered during 1936, and no capital sentence was carried out.

Source: Report of the Palestine Royal Commission, June 22, 1937. Reprinted by permission of Her Majesty's Copyright Office. Reproduced under the terms of the Click-Use license.

(4) Toleration by the Government of subversive activities, more especially those of the Mufti of Jerusalem.[1]

(5) As regards the land, failure to introduce a land system appropriate to the needs of the country, the continuance of the system of *Masha'a*;[2] no arrangement for the consolidation of holdings, great delay in the ascertainment of rights during land settlement, difficulty in obtaining a satisfactory title to land when purchased; . . . insufficient encouragement of irrigation and drainage schemes.

(6) Reluctance really to facilitate [Jewish] immigration, . . . and uncontrolled illegal Arab immigration.

(7) Trans-Jordan should be opened to Jewish immigration.[3]

(8) The necessary steps have not been taken to secure the removal or alleviation of restrictions on the importation of Palestine citrus fruits into foreign countries.

(9) Progressive Jewish Municipalities are unduly restricted by Government rules and regulations.

(10) Failure to ensure public security.

> While the authors of the report rejected most Arab grievances as "illegitimate" under terms of the mandate, they proposed numerous administrative and policy changes in response to the grievances of the Jewish community. They concluded the section as follows.

These are the recommendations which we submit . . . They are the best palliatives we can devise for the disease from which Palestine is suffering, but they are only palliatives. They might reduce the inflammation and bring down the temperature, but they cannot cure the trouble. The disease is so deep-rooted that, in our firm conviction, the only hope of a cure lies in a surgical operation.

The Force of Circumstances

Before submitting the proposals we have to offer for its drastic treatment we will briefly restate the problem of Palestine. . . .

An irrepressible conflict has arisen between two national communities within the narrow bounds of one small country. About 1,000,000 Arabs are in strife, open or latent, with some 400,000 Jews. There is no common ground between them. The Arab community is predominantly Asiatic in character, the Jewish community predominantly European. They differ in religion and in language. Their cultural and social life, their ways of thought and conduct, are as incompatible as their national aspirations. . . . The War and its sequel have inspired all Arabs with the hope of reviving in a free and united Arab world the traditions of the Arab golden age. The Jews similarly are inspired by their historic past. They mean to show what the Jewish nation can achieve when restored to the land of its birth. National assimilation between Arabs and Jews is thus ruled out. . . . Neither Arab nor Jew has any sense of service to a single State.

---

[1] A reference to Hajj Amin al-Husayni (1895[?]–1974), who as Mufti of Jerusalem (the Sunni cleric who oversaw Islamic holy places in Jerusalem) helped organize attacks on Jews and British officials in 1937–1938. He also helped found the Arab Higher Committee, which called for nonpayment of taxes, organized a general strike of Arab workers and businesses, and demanded an end to Jewish immigration. The committee was banned by the mandate administration in September 1937. Amin al-Husayn fled to Lebanon and then Iraq to escape arrest by the British. During World War II, he lived in Rome and Berlin and made pro-Axis radio broadcasts for Arab audiences. The degree of his knowledge of and support for the Holocaust is the subject of ongoing debate among historians.

[2] The collective ownership of land by a village community.

[3] The emirate of Transjordan, to the east of the Jordan River, was created in 1921 to provide a kingdom for Abdullah bin al-Hussein, who had led the Arab revolt against the Ottomans in World War I. The original mandate exempted Britain from the responsibility of encouraging Jewish immigration to Transjordan, so this grievance was rejected by the Peel Commission.

The conflict has grown steadily more bitter. It has been marked by a series of five Arab outbreaks, culminating in the rebellion of last year. . . .

This intensification of the conflict will continue. . . . The educational systems, Arab and Jewish, are schools of nationalism, and they have only existed for a short time. Their full effect on the rising generation has yet to be felt. And patriotic "youth-movements", so familiar a feature of present-day politics in other countries of Europe or Asia, are afoot in Palestine. As each community grows, moreover, the rivalry between them deepens. The more numerous and prosperous and better-educated the Arabs become, the more insistent will be their demand for national independence and the more bitter their hatred of the obstacle that bars the way to it. As the Jewish National Home grows older and more firmly rooted, so will grow its self-confidence and political ambition. . . .

Meantime the "external factors" will continue to play the part they have played with steadily increasing force from the beginning. On the one hand, Saudi Arabia, the Yemen, Iraq and Egypt are already recognized as sovereign states, and Trans-Jordan as an "independent government." In less than three years' time Syria and the Lebanon will attain their national sovereignty.[4] The claim of the Palestinian Arabs to share in the freedom of all Asiatic Arabia will thus be reinforced. . . . That they are as well qualified for self-government as the Arabs of neighbouring countries has been admitted.

On the other hand, the hardships and anxieties of the Jews in Europe are not likely to grow less in the near future. . . . The appeal to the good faith and humanity of the British people will lose none of its force. The Mandatory [Great Britain] will be urged unceasingly to admit as many Jews into Palestine as the National Home can provide with a livelihood and to protect them when admitted from Arab attacks. . . .

In these circumstances, we are convinced that peace, order and good government can only be maintained in Palestine for any length of time by a rigorous system of repression. . . . If "disturbances", moreover, should recur on a similar scale to that of last year's rebellion, the cost of military operations must soon exhaust the revenues of Palestine and ultimately involve the British Treasury to an incalculable extent. The moral objections to maintaining a system of government by constant repression are self-evident. Nor is there any need to emphasize the undesirable reactions of such a course of policy on opinion outside Palestine.

And the worst of it is that such a policy leads nowhere. However vigorously and consistently maintained, it will not solve the problem. It will not allay, it will exacerbate the quarrel between the Arabs and the Jews. The establishment of a single self-governing Palestine will remain just as impracticable as it is now. It is not easy to pursue the dark path of repression without seeing daylight at the end of it. . . .

In these last considerations lies a final argument for seeking a way out, at almost any cost, from the existing deadlock in Palestine. For a continuance or rather an aggravation—for that is what continuance will be—of the present situation cannot be contemplated without the gravest misgivings. It will mean constant unrest and disturbance in peace and potential danger in the event of war. It will mean a steady decline in our prestige. It will mean the gradual alienation of two peoples who are traditionally our friends: for already the Arabs of Palestine have been antagonized and the patience of their kinsmen throughout the Arab world is being strained; and already the Jews, particularly,

[4]Saudi Arabia was recognized as an independent state in 1927; Iraq became independent in 1932, although Britain maintained military bases and continued to exercise influence over Iraqi foreign policy. The report exaggerates the progress toward independence in Egypt, Yemen, Syria, and Lebanon.

Peel Commission proposal for partition of Palestine

we understand, in the United States, are questioning the sincerity with which we are fulfilling the promises we made and suggesting that negligence or weakness on our part is the real cause of all the trouble. . . .

Manifestly the problem cannot be solved by giving either the Arabs or the Jews all they want. . . . But, while neither race can justly rule all Palestine, we see no reason why, if it were practicable, each race should not rule part of it.

No doubt the idea of Partition as a solution of the problem has often occurred to students of it, only to be discarded. There are many who would have felt an instinctive dislike to cutting up the Holy Land. . . . Others may have felt that Partition would be a confession of failure. . . . Others, again, if they thought of Partition, dismissed it, no doubt, as impossible. The practical difficulties seemed too great. And great they unquestionably are. . . . We do not underestimate them. They cannot be brushed aside. Nevertheless . . . , those difficulties do not seem so insuperable as the difficulties inherent in the continuance of the Mandate or in any other alternative arrangement which has been proposed to us or which we ourselves could devise. Partition seems to offer at least a chance of ultimate peace. We can see none in any other plan.

Anticolonialism in India and Southeast Asia

By the late nineteenth century, when Indians were already in a full-scale debate about their relationship with Great Britain and some were demanding independence, many Southeast Asians were experiencing direct European political control for the first time. Nonetheless, in the first half of the twentieth century, developments in both areas showed some marked similarities. Nationalism swept through the Indian population, and despite their many differences in religion, education, and caste status, millions of Indians came to agree that Great Britain should "quit India" and allow Indian self-rule. Nationalism also intensified in Southeast Asia, especially in Vietnam and the Dutch East Indies, where force was needed to suppress anticolonial movements in both areas in the 1920s and 1930s.

The reasons for this upsurge of anti-European sentiment included revivals of Hinduism in India, Buddhism in Burma, and Islam in Southeast Asia, all of which heightened people's awareness of their differences from the West; the emergence of Japan, which demonstrated that an Asian nation could become a great power; the carnage of World War I, which raised doubts about the Europeans' "superiority"; and the spread of Western education and political ideologies. Most telling, however, was anger over the disparity between the Europeans' stated good intentions about their colonies' futures and their actual record of economic exploitation, racial prejudice, and authoritarian rule.

To these factors were added the influence of charismatic leaders such as Mohandas Gandhi, who drew the Indian masses into the nationalist movement; Jawaharlal Nehru, who guided the Indian Congress Party after 1941; Ho Chi Minh, who built a strong nationalist coalition in Vietnam; and Achmed Sukarno, who rallied Indonesian nationalists despite opposition from the Dutch.

World War II was the catalyst for the creation of independent nations throughout the region in the late 1940s and the 1950s, but events and leaders of the first half of the twentieth century set the stage.

Gandhi's Vision for India

96 • MOHANDAS GANDHI, INDIAN HOME RULE

Mohandas Gandhi, the outstanding figure in modern Indian history, was born in 1869 in a village north of Mumbai on the Arabian Sea. His father was a government official who presided over an extended family with strict Hindu practices. Gandhi studied law in England, and after failing to establish a legal practice in Mumbai moved to South Africa in 1893 to serve the country's large Indian population.

In South Africa, he became incensed over discriminatory laws against Indians, many of whom were indentured servants employed by whites or petty merchants. During his struggle to improve the lot of South Africa's Indian population, Gandhi developed his philosophy of *satyagraha,* usually translated into English as "soul force." Satyagraha sought justice not through violence but through love, a willingness to suffer, and conversion of the oppressor. Central to Gandhi's strategy was nonviolent resistance: his followers disobeyed unjust laws and accepted the consequences—even beatings and imprisonment—to reach the hearts of the British and change their thinking.

Gandhi first wrote about his theories of satyagraha in 1908 after meeting with a group of Indians in England who favored force to oust the British. In response, he composed a pamphlet, "Hind Swaraj," or "Indian Home Rule," in which he explains his theory of nonviolent resistance and his doubts about the benefits of modern civilization. Written as a dialogue between a "reader" and an "editor" (Gandhi), "Indian Home Rule" was printed in hundreds of editions and still serves as the best summary of Gandhi's philosophy.

QUESTIONS FOR ANALYSIS

1. What does Gandhi see as the major deficiency of modern civilization?
2. According to Gandhi, how has civilization specifically affected women?
3. Why does Gandhi have faith that Hindus and Muslims will be able to live in peace in India?
4. What, according to Gandhi, is true civilization, and what is India's role in preserving it?
5. What leads Gandhi to his conviction that love is stronger than force?
6. Why did Gandhi's attack on civilization gain him support among the Indian masses?

Chapter VI

Civilization

Reader: Now you will have to explain what you mean by civilization. . . .

Editor: Let us first consider what state of things is described by the word "civilization." Its true test lies in the fact that people living in it make bodily welfare the object of life. We will take some examples: The people of Europe today live in better-built houses than they did a hundred years ago. This is considered an emblem of civilization, and this is also a matter to promote bodily happiness. Formerly, they wore skins, and used as their weapons spears. Now, they wear long trousers, and for embellishing their bodies they wear a variety of clothing, and, instead of spears,

Source: Mohandas Gandhi, *Indian Home Rule* (Madras, India: Ganesh & Co., 1922), pp. 30–35, 47–50, 63, 64, 85, 68, 90, 91.

they carry with them revolvers containing five or more chambers. If people of a certain country, who have hitherto not been in the habit of wearing much clothing, boots, etc., adopt European clothing, they are supposed to have become civilized out of savagery. Formerly, in Europe, people plowed their lands mainly by manual labor. Now, one man can plow a vast tract by means of steam-engines, and can thus amass great wealth. This is called a sign of civilization. Formerly, the fewest men wrote books, that were most valuable. Now, anybody writes and prints anything he likes and poisons people's minds. Formerly, men traveled in wagons; now they fly through the air, in trains at the rate of four hundred and more miles per day. This is considered the height of civilization. It has been stated that, as men progress, they shall be able to travel in airships and reach any part of the world in a few hours. Men will not need the use of their hands and feet. They will press a button, and they will have their clothing by their side. They will press another button, and they will have their newspaper. A third, and a motor-car will be in waiting for them. They will have a variety of delicately dished up food. Everything will be done by machinery. Formerly, when people wanted to fight with one another, they measured between them their bodily strength; now it is possible to take away thousands of lives by one man working behind a gun from a hill. This is civilization. Formerly, men worked in the open air only so much as they liked. Now, thousands of workmen meet together and for the sake of maintenance work in factories or mines. Their condition is worse than that of beasts. They are obliged to work, at the risk of their lives, at most dangerous occupations, for the sake of millionaires. Formerly, men were made slaves under physical compulsion, now they are enslaved by temptation of money and of the luxuries that money can buy. There are now diseases of which people never dreamed before, and an army of doctors is engaged in finding out their

cures, and so hospitals have increased. This is a test of civilization. Formerly, special messengers were required and much expense was incurred in order to send letters; today, anyone can abuse his fellow by means of a letter for one penny. True, at the same cost, one can send one's thanks also. Formerly, people had two or three meals consisting of homemade bread and vegetables; now, they require something to eat every two hours, so that they have hardly leisure for anything else. What more need I say? All this you can ascertain from several authoritative books. These are all true tests of civilization. And, if any one speaks to the contrary, know that he is ignorant. This civilization takes note neither of morality nor of religion. . . .

This civilization is irreligion, and it has taken such a hold on the people in Europe that those who are in it appear to be half mad. They lack real physical strength or courage. They keep up their energy by intoxication. They can hardly be happy in solitude. Women, who should be the queens of households, wander in the streets, or they slave away in factories. For the sake of a pittance, half a million women in England alone are laboring under trying circumstances in factories or similar institutions. This awful fact is one of the causes of the daily growing suffragette movement.

This civilization is such that one has only to be patient and it will be self-destroyed.

Chapter X

The Hindus and the Muslims

READER: But I am impatient to hear your answer to my question. Has the introduction of Islam not unmade the nation?

EDITOR: India cannot cease to be one nation because people belonging to different religions live in it. The introduction of foreigners does not necessarily destroy the nation, they merge in it.

A country is one nation only when such a condition obtains in it. That country must have a faculty for assimilation. India has ever been such a country. In reality, there are as many religions as there are individuals, but those who are conscious of the spirit of nationality do not interfere with one another's religion. If they do, they are not fit to be considered a nation. If the Hindus believe that India should be peopled only by Hindus, they are living in dreamland. The Hindus, the Muslims, the Parsees[1] and the Christians who have made India their country are fellow-countrymen, and they will have to live in unity if only for their own interest. In no part of the world are one nationality and one religion synonymous terms; nor has it ever been so in India.

READER: But what about the inborn enmity between Hindus and Muslims?

EDITOR: That phrase has been invented by our mutual enemy.[2] When the Hindus and Muslims fought against one another, they certainly spoke in that strain. They have long since ceased to fight. How, then, can there be any inborn enmity? Pray remember this too, that we did not cease to fight only after British occupation. The Hindus flourished under Muslim sovereigns and Muslims under the Hindu. Each party recognized that mutual fighting was suicidal, and that neither party would abandon its religion by force of arms. Both parties, therefore, decided to live in peace. With the English advent the quarrels recommenced. . . .

Hindus and Muslims own the same ancestors, and the same blood runs through their veins. Do people become enemies because they change their religion? Is the God of the Muslim different from the God of the Hindu? Religions are different

roads converging to the same point. What does it matter that we take different roads, so long as we reach the same goal? Wherein is the cause for quarreling?

Chapter XIII

What Is True Civilization?

READER: You have denounced railways, lawyers and doctors. I can see that you will discard all machinery. What, then, is civilization?

EDITOR: The answer to that question is not difficult. I believe that the civilization India has evolved is not to be beaten in the world. Nothing can equal the seeds sown by our ancestors. Rome went, Greece shared the same fate, the might of the Pharaohs was broken, Japan has become westernized, of China nothing can be said, but India is still, somehow or other, sound at the foundation. The people of Europe learn their lessons from the writings of the men of Greece or Rome, which exist no longer in their former glory. In trying to learn from them, the Europeans imagine that they will avoid the mistakes of Greece and Rome. Such is their pitiable condition. In the midst of all this, India remains immovable, and that is her glory. It is a charge against India that her people are so uncivilized, ignorant, and stolid, that it is not possible to induce them to adopt any changes. It is a charge really against our merit. What we have tested and found true on the anvil of experience, we dare not change. Many thrust their advice upon India, and she remains steady. This is her beauty; it is the sheet-anchor of our hope.

Civilization is that mode of conduct which points out to man the path of duty. Performance of duty and observance of morality are convertible

---

[1]Followers of the Zoroastrian religion who fled India when Islamic armies conquered Persia in the seventh century C.E.

[2]The British.

terms. To observe morality is to attain mastery over our mind and our passions. So doing, we know ourselves. The Gujarati[3] equivalent for civilization means "good conduct." If this definition be correct, then India, as so many writers have shown, has nothing to learn from anybody else, and this is as it should be.

Chapter XVII

Passive Resistance

READER: Is there any historical evidence as to the success of what you have called soul-force or truth-force? No instance seems to have happened of any nation having risen through soul-force. I still think that the evil-doers will not cease doing evil without physical punishment.

EDITOR: . . . The force of love is the same as the force of the soul or truth. We have evidence of its working at every step. The universe would disappear without the existence of that force. But you ask for historical evidence. It is, therefore, necessary to know what history means. . . .

The fact that there are so many men still alive in the world shows that it is based not on the force of arms but on the force of truth or love. Therefore the greatest and most unimpeachable evidence of the success of this force is to be found in the fact that, in spite of the wars of the world, it still lives on.

Thousands, indeed, tens of thousands, depend for their existence on a very active working of this force. Little quarrels of millions of families in their daily lives disappear before the exercise of this force. Hundreds of nations live in peace. History does not and cannot take note of this fact. History is really a record of every interruption of the even working of the force of love or of the soul. . . . Soul-force, being natural, is not noted in history.

READER: According to what you say, it is plain that instances of the kind of passive resistance are not to be found in history. It is necessary to understand this passive resistance more fully. It will be better, therefore, if you enlarge upon it.

EDITOR: Passive resistance is a method of securing rights by personal suffering; it is the reverse of resistance by arms. When I refuse to do a thing that is repugnant to my conscience, I use soul-force. For instance, the government of the day has passed a law which is applicable to me: I do not like it; if, by using violence, I force the government to repeal the law, I am employing what may be termed body-force. If I do not obey the law and accept the penalty for its breach, I use soul-force. It involves sacrifice of self.

Everybody admits that sacrifice of self is infinitely superior to sacrifice of others. Moreover, if this kind of force is used in a cause that is unjust, only the person using it suffers. He does not make others suffer for his mistakes. Men have before now done many things which were subsequently found to have been wrong. No man can claim to be absolutely in the right, or that a particular thing is wrong, because he thinks so, but it is wrong for him so long as that is his deliberate judgment. It is, therefore, meet [proper] that he should not do that which he knows to be wrong, and suffer the consequence whatever it may be. This is the key to the use of soul-force. . . .

READER: From what you say, I deduce that passive resistance is a splendid weapon of the weak but that, when they are strong, they may take up arms.

EDITOR: This is gross ignorance. Passive resistance, that is, soul-force, is matchless. It is superior to the force of arms. How, then, can it be considered only a weapon of the weak? Physical-force men are strangers to the courage that is requisite in a passive resister. Do you believe that a coward

---

[3]An Indian dialect spoken in Gujarat, in northwest India.

can ever disobey a law that he dislikes? Extremists are considered to be advocates of brute-force. Why do they, then, talk about obeying laws? I do not blame them. They can say nothing else. When they succeed in driving out the English, and they themselves become governors, they will want you and me to obey their laws. And that is a fitting thing for their constitution. But a passive resister will say he will not obey a law that is against his conscience, even though he may be blown to pieces at the mouth of a cannon.

What do you think? Wherein is courage required—in blowing others to pieces from behind a cannon or with a smiling face to approach a cannon and to be blown to pieces? Who is the true warrior—he who keeps death always as a bosom-friend or he who controls the death of others? Believe me that a man devoid of courage and manhood can never be a passive resister.

This, however, I will admit: that even a man, weak in body, is capable of offering this resistance. One man can offer it just as well as millions. Both men and women can indulge in it. It does not require the training of an army; it needs no Jiu-jitsu. Control over the mind is alone necessary, and, when that is attained, man is free like the king of the forest, and his very glance withers the enemy.

Passive resistance is an all-sided sword; it can be used anyhow; it blesses him who uses it and him against whom it is used. Without drawing a drop of blood, it produces far-reaching results.

A Vietnamese Condemnation of French Rule

97 • NGUYEN THAI HOC, LETTER TO THE FRENCH CHAMBER OF DEPUTIES

Having taken control of Vietnam's southern region, known as Cochin China, in the 1860s, the French extended their authority over Tongking (northern Vietnam) and Annam (central Vietnam) in the mid-1880s. Convinced of their civilizing mission, the French sought to undermine Vietnam's Confucian culture by creating a French-trained Vietnamese elite willing to cooperate with the colonial regime. Although some members of Vietnam's upper class resisted French rule (including the young emperor Duy Tân, whose plot to overthrow the French was uncovered in 1916), most at first sought some sort of compromise between Western culture and Confucianism.

Revolutionary nationalistic movements gained adherents in the 1920s, however, as Vietnamese anger grew over continued exploitation and repression, even though 90,000 Vietnamese troops and laborers had helped the French during World War I. The leading nationalist organization was the Viet Nam Quoc Dan Dang (Vietnamese Nationalist Party, or VNQDD), founded in 1927 by Nguyen Thai Hoc, a teacher from Hanoi. As a young man, he sought to improve conditions in Vietnam through moderate reforms but became disillusioned with the French and turned to revolution. In 1929, with VNQDD membership at about 1,500, its leaders plotted an anti-French insurrection. The uprising, known as the Yen Bai Revolt, was crushed in 1930, and the VNQDD leaders were arrested and executed.

While awaiting his execution, Nguyen Thai Hoc wrote the following letter to France's parliament, the Chamber of Deputies. A defense of his actions and a denunciation of French colonialism, the letter was also released to the Vietnamese public.

QUESTIONS FOR ANALYSIS

1. In Nguyen Thai Hoc's view, what are French intentions in Vietnam, and what has been the effect of French occupation?
2. How did Nguyen Thai Hoc evolve from a moderate reformer to a revolutionary?
3. If implemented, how would his suggestions to Governor General Varenne have improved the lot of the Vietnamese people?
4. What does the French response to the Yen Bai uprising reveal about the nature of French colonial rule?
5. What do you suppose Nguyen Thai Hoc hoped to accomplish by writing this letter?

Gentlemen:

I, the undersigned, Nguyen Thai Hoc, a Vietnamese citizen, twenty-six years old, chairman and founder of the Vietnamese Nationalist Party, at present arrested and imprisoned at the jail of Yen Bai, Tongking, Indochina, have the great honor to inform you of the following facts:

According to the tenets of justice, everyone has the right to defend his own country when it is invaded by foreigners, and according to the principles of humanity, everyone has the duty to save his compatriots when they are in difficulty or in danger. As for myself, I have assessed the fact that my country has been annexed by you French for more than sixty years. I realize that under your dictatorial yoke, my compatriots have experienced a very hard life, and my people will without doubt be completely annihilated, by the naked principle of natural selection. Therefore, my right and my duty have compelled me to seek every way to defend my country which has been invaded and occupied, and to save my people who are in great danger.

At the beginning, I had thought to cooperate with the French in Indochina in order to serve my compatriots, my country and my people, particularly in the areas of cultural and economic development. As regards economic development, in 1925 I sent a memorandum to Governor General Varenne,[1] describing to him all our aspirations concerning the protection of local industry and commerce in Indochina. I urged strongly in the same letter the creation of a Superior School of Industrial Development in Tongking. In 1926 I again addressed another letter to the then Governor General of Indochina in which I included some explicit suggestions to relieve the hardships of our poor people. In 1927, for a third time, I sent a letter to the Resident Superieur[2] in Tongking, requesting permission to publish a weekly magazine with the aim of safeguarding and encouraging local industry and commerce. With regard to the cultural domain, I sent a letter to the Governor General in 1927, requesting (1) the privilege of opening tuition-free schools for the children of the lower classes, particularly children of workers and peasants; (2) freedom to open popular publishing houses and libraries in industrial centers.

It is absolutely ridiculous that every suggestion has been rejected. My letters were without answer; my plans have not been considered; my requests have been ignored; even the articles that I sent to

---

Source: Harry Benda and John Larkin, *The World of Southeast Asia* (New York: Harper & Row, 1967), pp. 182–185. Copyright © 1967 by Harper & Row, Publishers. Reprinted by permission of the authors.

[1]Alexandre Varenne was governor general of Indochina from 1925 to 1929.
[2]The *résident supérieur* of Tongking was the chief French administrator for northern Vietnam.

newspapers have been censored and rejected. From the experience of these rejections, I have come to the conclusion that the French have no sincere intention of helping my country or my people. I also concluded that we have to expel France. For this reason, in 1927, I began to organize a revolutionary party, which I named the Vietnamese Nationalist Party, with the aim of overthrowing the dictatorial and oppressive administration in our country. We aspire to create a Republic of Vietnam, composed of persons sincerely concerned with the happiness of the people. My party is a clandestine organization, and in February 1929, it was uncovered by the security police. Among the members of my party, a great number have been arrested. Fifty-two persons have been condemned to forced labor ranging from two to twenty years. Although many have been detained and many others unjustly condemned, my party has not ceased its activity. Under my guidance, the Party continues to operate and progress towards its aim.

During the Yen Bai uprising someone succeeded in killing some French officers. The authorities accused my party of having organized and perpetrated this revolt. They have accused me of having given the orders for the massacre. In truth, I have never given such orders, and I have presented before the Penal Court of Yen Bai all the evidence showing the inanity of this accusation. Even so, some of the members of my party completely ignorant of that event have been accused of participating in it. The French Indochinese government burned and destroyed their houses. They sent French troops to occupy their villages and stole their rice to divide it among the soldiers. Not just members of my party have been suffering from this injustice—we should rather call this cruelty than injustice—but also many simple peasants, interested only in their daily work in the rice fields, living miserable lives like buffaloes and horses, have been compromised in this reprisal. At the present time, in various areas there are tens of thousands of men, women, and children, persons of all ages, who have been massacred.[3] They died either of hunger or exposure because the French Indochinese government burned their homes. I therefore beseech you in tears to redress this injustice which otherwise will annihilate my people, which will stain French honor, and which will belittle all human values.

I have the honor to inform you that I am responsible for all events happening in my country under the leadership of my party from 1927 until the present. You only need to execute me. I beg your indulgence for all the others who at the present time are imprisoned in various jails.

---

[3]Many civilian deaths resulted from French actions following the revolt, but Nguyen Thai Hoc's estimate of 10,000 or more deaths is an exaggeration.

Latin America in an Era of Economic Challenge and Political Change

A popular slogan among Latin America's politicians, business leaders, and landowners in the late nineteenth century was "order and progress," and to an extent exceptional in the region's history, they achieved both. Around 1870, Latin America's economy entered a period of export-driven expansion that lasted until the 1920s. The region became a major supplier of wheat, beef, mutton, coffee, raw rubber, nitrates, copper, tin, bananas, and a host of other primary products to Europe and the United States and a major market for European and U.S. manufactured goods. Land prices soared, and English and U.S. capital flowed into Latin America as investments and loans.

Latin America's boom took place in a climate of relative political stability. In Argentina, Chile, and Brazil, this meant republican governments controlled by an oligarchy of landowning families, sometimes in alliance with wealthy businessmen; in Mexico, Peru, Ecuador, and Venezuela, it meant rule by a dictator (*caudillo*), who also usually represented the interests of landowners and businessmen. Oligarchs and dictators alike sought economic growth by maintaining law and order, approving land confiscations from the Church and peasantry, and keeping foreign business interests happy by maintaining low taxes and tariffs.

Latin America in these years is often viewed as an example of *neocolonialism*. Although nations in the region all had achieved political independence in the early 1800s, economic relationships reminiscent of the colonial era persisted. Latin America still depended on the export of primary products to industrialized Europe and the United States, and depended on those same regions for manufactured goods and capital. The beneficiaries of the system were the landowning elite, European and U.S. bondholders, and foreign businesses with investments in construction, railroads, shipping, and mining. Dependency on foreign markets, capital, and manufactured goods made Latin American governments vulnerable to diplomatic arm-twisting by their powerful economic "partners," and in some instances, military intervention.

By the 1930s, the neocolonial economy and the political order it supported both were in shambles as a result of the Great Depression. Demand for Latin America's agricultural products and raw materials plummeted, driving millions into unemployment and depriving the region of the foreign exchange needed to buy manufactured goods from abroad. Foreign loans and investments dried up after the international banking system and stock markets collapsed. Governments faced insolvency, and capital shortages crippled plans to end the economic slump through industrialization. Latin Americans increasingly resented European and especially U.S. ownership of mines, oil fields, railroads, banks, processing plants, and prime agricultural land. Once welcomed as a means of attracting capital and encouraging growth, foreign ownership now was condemned as imperialist plunder.

Economic Dependency and Its Dangers

98 • FRANCISCO GARCÍA CALDERÓN, LATIN AMERICA: ITS RISE AND PROGRESS

For most of the nineteenth century, the United States had relatively little involvement in Latin America. U.S. interests in the region focused almost exclusively on Mexico, whose territories in the American west and southwest became part of the United States after the Mexican War of 1846–1848. Other U.S. schemes to annex Cuba, Nicaragua, and the Mexican provinces of Yucatan and Lower California proved impractical or failed to generate support.

U.S.–Latin American relations changed beginning in the 1880s, however. As the United States industrialized, it gradually replaced Great Britain as the region's main purchaser of exports and supplier of manufactured goods. By 1910, U.S. investments had increased to $1.6 billion, almost all of it "new money" invested since the end of the Civil War in 1865. As U.S. businesses expanded their operations in Latin America, successive administrations in Washington pledged to protect their interests. In 1905, President Theodore Roosevelt announced that the United States reserved the right to intervene in the internal affairs of any state in the Western Hemisphere that was guilty of "chronic wrongdoing," a euphemism for failure to pay its debts or maintain law and order. Roosevelt's successor, William Howard Taft, was even more explicit. He stated that his foreign policy would include "active intervention to secure our merchandise and our capitalists' opportunity for profitable investment." These were not idle words. Between 1898 and 1934, the United States annexed Puerto Rico and intervened militarily in Cuba, Mexico, Guatemala, Honduras, Nicaragua, Panama, Colombia, and the Dominican Republic.

Condemnation of Latin America's economic dependence on foreigners and denunciations of "Yankee imperialism" became commonplace with the onset of the Great Depression, but such criticisms began earlier. One of the first such critics was the Peruvian diplomat and author Francisco García Calderón. Born into a wealthy and politically prominent family in Lima in 1883, García Calderón entered the Peruvian foreign service soon after graduating from the University of San Marcos. A career diplomat with postings to London and Paris and ambassadorships to Belgium and Portugal, he wrote numerous essays and books on Latin America. His most widely read book was *Latin America: Its Rise and Progress,* which ranged over the region's history and discussed a number of contemporary issues, including immigration, the state of the economy, and Latin America's foreign relations. First published in 1912, it attracted a wide readership only in the 1920s, when it went through numerous editions in several languages.

QUESTIONS FOR ANALYSIS

1. According to García Calderón, how has U.S. foreign policy toward Latin America evolved since the time of the Monroe Doctrine?
2. How does he explain these changes?
3. According to García Calderón, what benefits have accrued to Latin America as a result of foreign investments? How has Latin America been hurt by such investments?
4. How does García Calderón characterize Latin Americans, and how do they differ from the "Anglo-Saxons" of the United States?
5. How have the Latin American states contributed to their own economic problems?
6. If one accepts the premises of García Calderón's arguments, what would the Latin American states have had to do to overcome the problems connected with foreign economic dependency?

The nation [the United States] which was peopled by nine millions of men in 1820 now numbers eighty millions—an immense demographic power; in the space of ten years, from 1890 to 1900, this population increased by one-fifth. By virtue of its iron, wheat, oil, and cotton, and its victorious industrialism, the democracy aspires to a world-wide significance. . . . Yankee pride increases with the endless multiplication of wealth and population, and the patriotic sentiment has reached such intensity that it has become transformed into imperialism. . . .

Interventions have become more frequent with the expansion of frontiers. The United States have recently intervened in the territory of Acre [in western Brazil], there to found a republic of rubber gatherers; at Panama, there to develop a province and construct a canal; in Cuba, to maintain order in the interior; in San Domingo, to support the civilizing revolution and overthrow the tyrants; in Venezuela, and in Central America, to enforce upon these nations. . . , the political and financial tutelage of imperial democracy. In Guatemala and Honduras the loans concluded with the monarchs of North American finance have reduced the people to a new slavery. Supervision of the customs and the dispatch of pacificatory [peace-keeping] squadrons to defend the interests of the Anglo-Saxon[1] have enforced peace and tranquility: such are the means employed. . . . Mr. Pierpont Morgan[2] proposes to encompass the finances of Latin America by a vast network of Yankee banks. Chicago merchants and Wall Street financiers created the Meat Trust in the Argentine. . . . It has even been announced . . . that a North American syndicate wished to buy enormous belts of land in Guatemala. . . . The fortification of the Panama Canal and the possible acquisition of the Galapagos Islands in the Pacific, are fresh manifestations of imperialistic progress.

. . .

Unexploited wealth abounds in [Latin] America. Forests of rubber . . . , mines of gold and diamonds, rivers which flow over beds of auriferous [gold-bearing] sand, . . . coffee, cocoa, and wheat, whose abundance is such that these products are enough to glut the markets of the world. But there is no national capital [for investment]. This contrast between the wealth of the soil and the poverty of the States gives rise to serious economic problems. . . .

Since the very beginnings of independence the Latin democracies, lacking financial reserves, have had need of European gold. . . . The necessities of the war [of independence] with Spain and the always difficult task of building up a new society demanded the assistance of foreign gold; loans accumulated. . . . The lamentable history of these bankrupt democracies dates from this period.

For geographical reasons, and on account of its very inferiority, South America cannot dispense with the influence of the Anglo-Saxon North, with its exuberant wealth and its industries. South America has need of capital, of enterprising men, of bold explorers, and these the United States supply in abundance. The defence of the South should consist in avoiding the establishment of privileges or monopolies, whether in favor of North Americans or Europeans.

• • •

The descendants of the Spanish conquerors, who knew nothing of labor or thrift, have incessantly resorted to fresh loans in order to fill the gaps in their budgets. Politicians knew of only one

---

Source: From Francisco Garcia Calderon, *Latin America: Its Rise and Progress*, Bernard Miall, trans. (Charles Scribner's Sons and T. Fisher Unwin, Ltd., 1913), pp. 298, 301–303, 306, 311, 378–382.

[1]A loosely used term, Anglo-Saxon usually refers to people of English descent.
[2]John Pierpont Morgan (1837–1913), founder of the investment bank J. P. Morgan and Company, was one of the wealthiest and most powerful financiers in the United States.

solution of the economic disorder—to borrow, so that little by little the Latin-American countries became actually the financial colonies of Europe.

Economic dependence has a necessary corollary—political servitude. French intervention in Mexico[3] was originally caused by the mass of unsatisfied financial claims; foreigners, the creditors of the State, were in favor of intervention. England and France, who began by seeking to ensure the recovery of certain debts, finally forced a monarch upon the debtor nation. The United States entertained the ambition of becoming the sole creditor of the [Latin] American peoples: this remarkable privilege would have assured them of an incontestable hegemony over the whole continent.

The budgets of various States complicate still further an already difficult situation. They increase beyond all measure, without the slightest relation to the progress made by the nation. They are based upon taxes which are one of the causes of the national impoverishment, or upon a protectionist tariff which adds greatly to the cost of life. The politicians, thinking chiefly of appearances, neglect the development of the national resources for the immediate augmentation of the fiscal revenues; thanks to fresh taxes, the budgets increase. These resources are not employed in furthering profitable undertakings, such as building railroads or highways, or increasing the navigability of the rivers. The bureaucracy is increased in a like proportion, and the budgets, swelled in order to dupe the outside world, serve only to support a nest of parasites. In the economic life of these countries the State is a kind of beneficent providence which . . . increases the common poverty by taxation, display, useless enterprises, the upkeep of military and civil officials, and the waste of money borrowed abroad. . . .

To sum up, the new continent, politically free, is economically a vassal. This dependence is inevitable; without European capital there would have been no railways, no ports, and no stable government in [Latin] America. But the disorder which prevails in the finances of the country changes into a real servitude what might otherwise have been a beneficial relation.

---

[3]In 1861, Spain, Great Britain, and France sent troops to Mexico to force the government to pay its debts. After gaining assurances of future payments, Spain and Great Britain withdrew their troops, but Emperor Napoleon III of France went forward with a plan to establish a new Mexican government under French protection. The French-sponsored candidate for emperor of Mexico was Archduke Ferdinand Maximilian of Hapsburg, brother of Austrian emperor Franz Josef. Maximilian served as emperor from 1863 to 1865, when the threat of U.S. intervention convinced Napoleon III to abandon his Mexican project.

Mexican Muralists and Their Vision

99 • JOSÉ CLEMENTE OROZCO, HISPANO-AMERICA—THE REBEL SOCIETY AND HIS INTERNATIONAL ENEMIES, AND DIEGO RIVERA, IMPERIALISM

In 1921, Mexico's newly appointed secretary of public education, José Vasconselos, as part of his program to promote Mexican national pride, encouraged Mexico's composers, choreographers, writers, and artists to explore Mexico's past, including its Indian past, in their works. In the 1920s many muralists took advantage of his offer to make available the walls of public buildings for their work. Among them were José Clemente Orozco and Diego Rivera, whose paintings of the historical experiences of Mexicans and other Latin American people brought them international fame.

José Clemente Orozco (1883–1949) hoped to become an architect, but at age 26 began training as a painter in the Mexican Academy of Fine Arts. As a Marxist and supporter of the Mexican Revolution, he rejected the style of the officially approved European masters and introduced themes and topics dealing with the struggles of Mexico's Indian and mestizo populations. After completing murals at the National Preparatory School and several other buildings in Mexico City and other cities, he accepted a number of commissions in the United States, including one for Dartmouth College in New Hampshire. For Dartmouth, he chose as his theme the history of the Americas from preconquest to the modern age. The section shown below, given the name *Hispano-America—The Rebel and His International Enemies,* shows an armed peasant—standing amidst images of crumbling churches, an abandoned factory, politicians, soldiers, and capitalists. It is thought that the military figure on the right is General John J. Pershing, who in the so-called Punitive Expedition of 1916–1917 led U.S. forces into Mexico against the paramilitary forces of Francisco "Pancho" Villa, who had attacked the town of Columbus, New Mexico, early in 1916. The masked figure behind him is thought to be President Woodrow Wilson, who ordered the attack.

José Clemente Orozco, Hispano-America—The Rebel and His International Enemies

Diego Rivera, Imperialism

Diego Rivera, "Portrait of America, Imperialism," Peter A. Juley & Son Collection, Smithsonian American Art Museum (contract J2010.15)

Another great Mexican muralist, Diego Rivera (1886–1957), also achieved fame from his paintings in Mexico City in the 1920s and then traveled to the United States, where he was commissioned to paint murals for the San Francisco Stock Exchange, the Detroit Institute of Art, and Rockefeller Center in New York City. The latter work was destroyed after it was discovered that Rivera, a dedicated Marxist, had included in it a portrait of the Russian revolutionary, Vladimir Lenin.

After the Rockefeller Center controversy, Rivera completed a series of 21 paintings depicting U.S. history collectively known as *Portrait of America*.

Accepting no fee, Rivera painted these murals for an old, ramshackle building rented by the Communist Party Opposition, an anti-Stalinist organization founded in 1929. Used as a lecture hall and study center, the space was known as the New Workers' School. The thirteenth painting, *Imperialism,* shown on page 455, is dominated by the guns of U.S. tanks and warships protruding from the portal of the New York Stock Exchange. In the forefront is a mass of Latin American rebels, in whose midst are seen a murdered Caribbean black and a Cuban revolutionary. In the upper right appears the figure of Augusto Sandino, the leader of a rebellion against the U.S. military presence in Nicaragua, who had just been assassinated on orders of the Nicaraguan government. He looks down on the operations of Standard Oil and United Fruit, two U.S. organizations heavily involved in Latin America.

Only black-and-white photographs of *Imperialism* remain. When the school closed, the murals (which had been painted on larger moveable wooden panels) were given to the New York chapter of the International Ladies Garment Workers' Union, which stored them in its recreation center in Forest Park, Pennsylvania. A fire in 1969 destroyed all the paintings but three, which are now in private collections.

QUESTIONS FOR ANALYSIS

1. In Orozco's painting, what message is the painter communicating about the crumbling churches, the abandoned factories, the business owners, and the army officers?
2. What message does Orozco convey about the character and qualities of the central figure, the peasant?
3. What does Rivera's painting imply about the character, motives, and impact of U.S. imperialism?
4. In what specific ways do the paintings reveal the Marxist sympathies of the two Mexican painters?
5. What is the overall message of the two paintings? Is it optimistic about Latin America's prospects?

Economic Nationalism in Mexico
100 • LÁZARO CÁRDENAS, SPEECH TO THE NATION

Following the overthrow of dictator Porfirio Diáz in 1911, in 1917 Mexican revolutionaries overcame their rivalries and drafted a new constitution that confirmed the principles of free speech, religious toleration, universal suffrage, the separation of powers, and the protection of private property. It also committed the government to social reform and greater control over foreign corporations. In the face of continuing conflict, however, these latter provisions remained a dead letter until the presidency of Lázaro Cárdenas, from 1934 to 1940. In a series of bold steps, he confiscated millions of acres of land from large estates for redistribution to peasants, introduced free and compulsory elementary education, and sponsored legislation to provide medical and unemployment insurance. His most audacious step, however, was the nationalization of Mexico's oil industry. In 1936, a dispute between Mexican labor unions and U.S. and British oil companies erupted into a strike, and in the ensuing legal battle, 17 oil companies refused to accept the pro-union ruling of an arbitration board appointed by Cárdenas, even after the Mexican Supreme Court upheld the decision. In response, Cárdenas ordered government seizure of the oil companies' property. Cárdenas announced his decision on March 18, 1938, in a radio speech to the nation. In the following excerpt, Cárdenas comments on the role of the oil companies in Mexico's economic and social development.

QUESTIONS FOR ANALYSIS

1. In the account of Cárdenas, which actions by the foreign oil companies forced him to nationalize the oil industry?
2. According to Cárdenas, what truth is there in the oil companies' claims that they have benefited Mexico?
3. According to Cárdenas, who is ultimately responsible for the actions of the oil companies?
4. Which political activities of the oil companies does Cárdenas condemn?
5. What hardships does Cárdenas anticipate for the Mexican people as a result of his decision?
6. In what ways is Cárdenas's speech an appeal to Mexican nationalism?

In each and every one of the various attempts of the Executive to arrive at a final solution of the conflict within conciliatory limits . . . the intransigence of the [oil] companies was clearly demonstrated. Their attitude was therefore premeditated and their position deliberately taken, so that the Government, in defense of its own dignity, had to resort to application of the Expropriation Act, as there were no means less drastic or decision less severe that might bring about a solution of the problem. . . .

It has been repeated *ad nauseam* that the oil industry has brought additional capital for the development and progress of the country. This assertion is an exaggeration. For many years throughout the major period of their existence, oil companies have enjoyed great privileges for development and expansion, including customs and tax exemptions and innumerable prerogatives; it is these factors of special privilege, together with the prodigious productivity of the oil deposits granted them by the Nation often against public will and law, that represent almost the total amount of this so-called capital.

Potential wealth of the Nation; miserably underpaid native labor; tax exemptions; economic privileges; governmental tolerance—these are the factors of the boom of the Mexican oil industry.

Let us now examine the social contributions of the companies. In how many of the villages

Source: Benjamin Keen, ed. and trans. *Readings in Latin American Civilization* (Boston: Houghton Mifflin, 1955), pp. 362–364.

bordering on the oil fields is there a hospital, or school or social center, or a sanitary water supply, or an athletic field, or even an electric plant fed by the millions of cubic meters of natural gas allowed to go to waste?

What center of oil production, on the other hand, does not have its company police force for the protection of private, selfish, and often illegal interests? These organizations . . . are charged with innumerable outrages, abuses, and murders, always on behalf of the companies that employ them.

Who is not aware of the irritating discrimination governing construction of the company camps? Comfort for the foreign personnel; misery, drabness, and insalubrity for the Mexicans. Refrigeration and protection against tropical insects for the former; indifference and neglect, medical service and supplies always grudgingly provided, for the latter; lower wages and harder, more exhausting labor for our people.

The tolerance which the companies have abused was born, it is true, in the shadow of the ignorance, betrayals, and weakness of the country's rulers; but the mechanism was set in motion by investors lacking in the necessary moral resources to give something in exchange for the wealth they have been exploiting.

Another inevitable consequence of the presence of the oil companies . . . has been their persistent and improper intervention in national affairs. The oil companies' support to strong rebel factions against the constituted government . . . during the years 1917 to 1920 is no longer a matter for discussion by anyone. Nor is anyone ignorant of the fact that in later periods and even at the present time, the oil companies have almost openly encouraged the ambitions of elements discontented with the country's government, every time their interests were affected either by taxation or by the modification of their privileges or the withdrawal

of the customary tolerance. They have had money, arms, and munitions for rebellion, money for the anti-patriotic press which defends them, money with which to enrich their unconditional defenders. But for the progress of the country, for establishing an economic equilibrium with their workers through a just compensation of labor, for maintaining hygienic conditions in the districts where they themselves operate, or for conserving the vast riches of the natural petroleum gases from destruction, they have neither money, nor financial capabilities, nor the desire to subtract the necessary funds from the volume of their profits.

Nor is there money with which to meet a responsibility imposed upon them by judicial verdict, for they rely on their pride and their economic power to shield them from the dignity and sovereignty of a Nation which has generously placed in their hands its vast natural resources and now finds itself unable to obtain the satisfaction of the most elementary obligations by ordinary legal means.

As a logical consequence of this brief analysis, it was therefore necessary to adopt a definite and legal measure to end this permanent state of affairs in which the country sees its industrial progress held back by those who hold in their hands the power to erect obstacles as well as the motive power of all activity and who . . . abuse their economic strength to the point of jeopardizing the very life of a Nation endeavoring to bring about the elevation of its people through its own laws, its own resources, and the free management of its own destinies.

With the only solution to this problem thus placed before it, I ask the entire Nation for moral and material support sufficient to carry out so justified, important, and indispensable a decision. . . .

And, finally, as the fear may arise among the interests now in bitter conflict in the field of international affairs[1] that a deviation of raw materials fundamentally necessary to the struggle in which

---

[1]World War II in Europe was still more than a year away, but the Japanese invasion of China was in full swing, Spain was in the midst of its civil war, and Hitler had just annexed Austria.

the most powerful nations are engaged might result from the consummation of this act of national sovereignty and dignity, we wish to state that our petroleum operations will not depart a single inch from the moral solidarity maintained by Mexico with the democratic nations, whom we wish to assure that the expropriation now decreed has as its only purpose the elimination of obstacles erected by groups who do not understand the evolutionary needs of all peoples and who would themselves have no compunction in selling Mexican oil to the highest bidder. . . .

China in an Era of Political Disintegration and Revolution

The overthrow of the Qing Dynasty in the revolution of 1911 failed to produce China's long-awaited national revival. In the aftermath of the revolution, Sun Yat-sen and his dreams of democracy were pushed aside by General Yuan Shikai, who ruled the Chinese "republic" as a dictator between 1912 and 1916 and was planning to have himself declared emperor when he died in 1916. After his death, China was carved up by dozens of generally unscrupulous and irresponsible warlords—military strongmen whose local authority was based on their control of private armies and whose grip on China was not completely broken until after the Communists took power in 1949. With a weak national government, the Chinese endured continued Western domination of their coastal cities and were able to offer only feeble resistance when the Japanese conquered Manchuria in 1931 and invaded China itself in 1937. Massive flooding of the Yellow River and widespread famine in north China in the 1920s deepened the people's misery.

With Confucian certainties shattered and China disintegrating, intellectuals intensely debated China's predicament. The 1920s were years of intellectual experiment and inquiry, in which members of study groups, journalists, poets, fiction writers, academics, and students scrutinized what it meant to be Chinese and debated the country's future. Most of these intellectuals rejected traditional Chinese values, customs, and education, arguing that only a sharp break from the past would enable China to stand up to Japan and the West. Most of them believed that China needed to model itself on the West, although what specific Western values and institutions should be borrowed was a matter of debate.

In politics, two revolutionary parties—the Nationalist Party, or Guomindang, and the Chinese Communist Party—competed for support. The Guomindang, led by Sun Yat-sen until his death in 1925, was theoretically dedicated to Sun's "three principles of the people": democracy, nationalism, and livelihood. The party came to be identified with the educated, Western-oriented bourgeoisie of China's coastal cities and in practice, under General Chiang Kai-shek (1887–1975), concentrated less on social reform and democracy than on fighting warlords and Communists. The Chinese Communist Party, founded in 1921, was dedicated to Marxism-Leninism, with its leadership provided by intellectuals and its major support eventually coming from China's rural masses.

Aided by agents of the Soviet Union, the Guomindang and the Communists formed a coalition in 1923 to destroy the warlords. Their combined forces launched the Northern Expedition against the warlords in 1926, but the alliance disintegrated in 1927 when Chiang Kai-shek, buoyed by his early victories and generous financial support from Chinese businessmen, purged the Communists from the army and ordered Guomindang troops in Shanghai to kill Communist leaders who had gathered there. Communist troops and their leaders fled to the countryside, where, under the leadership of Mao Zedong (1893–1976), they rebuilt the party into a formidable military and political force. After a long struggle against the Guomindang and the Japanese, the Communists gained control of China in 1949.

Chinese Nationalism and the May 4th Movement

101 • DENG YINGCHAO, THE SPIRIT OF THE MAY 4TH MOVEMENT

On May 4, 1919, word reached Beijing that the diplomats at the Paris Peace Conference had rejected Chinese demands that the prewar German concessions in Shandong province be returned to Chinese control; instead, they were to be retained by Japan. Incensed by this rebuff from the Western powers, which had welcomed China as an ally in World War I, and resentful of Japan for taking one more piece of Chinese territory, university students in Beijing erupted in anger. Three thousand of them descended on Tiananmen Square, where they shouted slogans, waved banners, attacked a pro-Japanese official, and burned the house of a cabinet minister. The movement spread to universities, and with support from journalists, merchants, and well-known politicians such as Sun Yat-sen, students organized a national boycott of Japanese goods. After the Beijing warlord government attempted to crack down by arresting some 1,500 students in Beijing, the movement gained even more support, with whole factories going on strike and students refusing to attend classes. In response, the arrested Beijing students were released, the cabinet fell, and China refused to sign the Versailles Treaty.

This was more than a one-time victory for China's students. The "May 4th incident" became a national movement, one that made nationalism a part of China's political landscape.

Deng Yingchao was a 16-year-old student at a women's teachers' college in Tianjin when the May 4th demonstrations in Beijing spread to her university. The experience changed her life. Not only did she become a political activist, but she also met her future husband, Zhou Enlai, who served as China's premier and foreign minister after the Communist revolution. She joined the Communist Party in 1924 and was one of the few women who was part of the Long March, the 6,000-mile trek of

Mao Zedong's followers from Jiangxi province to Shaanxi in 1934–1935. After the Communist victory in 1949, she was revered as the nation's "elder sister" and became a member of the party's Central Committee. She weathered numerous political storms and died in Beijing at age 88.

The following excerpt is from an article written by Deng in 1949 in commemoration of the events of May 4, 1919. It captures the hopeful enthusiasm of the young participants in the May 4th movement and conveys the broad significance of the events.

QUESTIONS FOR ANALYSIS

1. What does Deng Yingchao's article reveal about the level of enthusiasm among the student protesters? What does it tell us about the students' goals?
2. Aside from the immediate impact of the demonstrations in Beijing, what were the deeper causes of the student protests, according to Deng?
3. What can be gathered from Deng's article about the level of public support for the student protesters in Tianjin?
4. According to Deng, what was the long-term significance of the May 4th movement?
5. Writing from the perspective of 1949, Deng suggests that the Communist movement in China can be traced back to the May 4th movement. To what degree does her recounting of events affirm such an interpretation?

On May 4, 1919, students in Beijing held a demonstration asking the government to refuse to sign the Versailles Peace Treaty and to punish the traitors at home. . . . The following day, when the news reached Tainjin, it aroused the indignation of students there who staged their own demonstrations of May 7th. They then started organizing such patriotic societies as the Tianjin Students Union, the Tianjin Women's Patriotic Society, and the Tianjin Association of National Salvation. We had no political theory to guide us at that time, only our strong patriotic enthusiasm. In addition to the Beijing students' demands, we demanded "Abolish the Twenty-one Demands!"[1] "Boycott Japanese Goods!" "Buy Chinese-Made Goods!" Furthermore, we emphatically refused to become slaves to foreign powers!

Despite the fact that it was a patriotic students' demonstration, the Northern Warlord government resorted to force to quell the protest. The police dispersed the march with rifles fixed with bayonets and sprayed us with hoses; and later resorted to rifle butts and even arrests. However, our political awareness awakened a new spirit in us in our new struggle with the government. New European ideas and culture poured into China after World War I. Also the success of the 1917 October Revolution in Russia brought progressive Marxism-Leninism to China. . . .

What we did know intuitively was that alone, we students did not have enough strength to save China from foreign powers. Therefore, we knew that we "must awaken all our compatriots."

Source: Deng Yingchao, "The Spirit of the May 4 Movement," in *Women of China,* May 1989, pp. 40–42.

[1]The Twenty-One Demands, presented to China by Japan in 1915, required China to confirm Japan's claim to the former German concessions in Shandong and various economic concessions in Manchuria and Mongolia. They also demanded extensive Japanese rights in China itself, including the appointment of Japanese advisors to the Chinese government.

We therefore organized many speakers' committees to spread propaganda among the people. I became the head of the speakers' group in the Tianjin Women's Patriotic Society and in the Tianjin Students Union. Frequently we gave speeches outside the campus. At first, we women dared not to give speeches on the street due to the feudalistic tradition that existed in China then. So the female students went instead to the places where people gathered either for an exhibition or to see a show, while the male students gave speeches in the street to passersby. There were always a lot of listeners. We told them why we should be united to save our country; that traitors in the government must be punished; and that people should have the right to freedom of assembly and association. We talked about the suffering of the Korean people after their country was conquered; and we publicly lodged our protests against the Northern Warlord government that persecutes progressive students. Usually tears streamed down our cheeks when we gave our speeches and our listeners were often visibly moved.

In addition to making speeches we also made home visits to out-of-the-way places or to slum areas. We went door-to-door to give our pleas, and some families gave us a warm welcome, but others just slammed the door on us. However, nothing could discourage us.

We delivered handbills and published newspapers to spread our patriotic enthusiasm even further. *The Paper of the Students Union,* for example, was run by the Tianjin Students Union and each issue sold more than 20,000 copies—a considerable number at that time! It was originally published every three days; however, later it was expanded into a daily newspaper. . . .

The Women's Patriotic Society also published a weekly. Both papers reported foreign and national current events, students' movements across the country, student editorials, progressive articles, and cultural and art news.

The reactionary Northern Warlord government, however, turned a deaf ear to us. They ultimately bowed to Japanese powers, shielded the traitors, and tried to suppress the students' movement. At that time people were denied expressing their patriotic views. So what we then struggled most urgently for was freedom of assembly and association; the right to express one's political views; and for freedom of the press. United under this common goal, we struggled bravely.

> After describing the numerous clashes between students and university and governmental authorities in 1919 and 1920, Deng comments on the broad significance of the May 4th movement.

The women's liberation movement was greatly enhanced by the May 4th Movement; this became an important part of the movement. And slogans such as "sexual equality," "freedom of marriage," "co-educational universities," "social contacts for women," and "job opportunity for women," were put forward.

In Tianjin we merged the men's students union with the women's. Fearing ridicule and that public opinion would be against it, some of the women were hesitant at first. However, the male and female activists among us took the lead and we worked together bravely to overcome all obstacles. In our work, we were equal and we respected each other. . . . Women students, particularly the more progressive ones, worked especially hard for we knew we were pioneers among Chinese women to show that women are not inferior to men. Inspired by the new ideals, among the progressive students men broke with the tradition of sexual discrimination and treated us with respect. . . .

At this time cultural movements were developing rapidly and students were receptive to publications which promoted new ideas. In Beijing, for example, there were *New Youth, Young China,* and *New Tide* magazines. In Tianjin, the Students Union every week would invite a progressive professor . . . to give us an academic lecture on new literary ideas such as how to write in vernacular Chinese rather than in classical stereotyped writings.

Today these things are commonplace, but then it was very new and important.

As more scientific subjects and new ideas poured into China, we felt an urgency to learn, discuss, study, and understand them. Thus by the end of that summer, a smaller and well-organized group—the Awakening Society—was established by 20 of the more progressive activists among us students. . . .

At that time we didn't have a definite political conviction, nor did we know much about Communism. We just had a vague idea that the principle of distribution in the most advantageous society was "from each according to his ability, to each according to his needs." We knew only that a revolution led by Lenin in Russia had been successful; and that the aim of that revolution was to emancipate the majority of the people who were oppressed, and to established a classless society.

How we did long for such a society! But at that time we could not learn about such a society because we could scarcely find any copy of Lenin's ideas or information about the October Revolution.

The Maoist Version of Marxism

102 • MAO ZEDONG, REPORT ON AN INVESTIGATION OF THE PEASANT MOVEMENT IN HUNAN AND STRATEGIC PROBLEMS OF CHINA'S REVOLUTIONARY WAR

Mao Zedong, born into a well-to-do peasant family in Hunan province in 1893, was a university student when he participated in the anti-Qing revolution of 1911. During the next several years, while serving as a library assistant at Beijing University, he embraced Marxism and helped organize the Chinese Communist Party, which was officially founded in 1921. During the 1920s he developed his unique Chinese variant of Marxism, which was based on the premise that peasants, not the urban proletariat, would lead China to socialism.

After the break from the Guomindang in 1927, the Communists took their small army to the remote and hilly region on the Hunan–Jiangxi border, where in 1931 they proclaimed the Chinese Soviet Republic. In 1934, Chiang Kai-shek's troops surrounded the Communists' forces, but as they moved in for the kill, more than 100,000 Communist troops and officials broke their encirclement and embarked on the Long March. This legendary trek lasted more than a year and covered 6,000 miles before a remnant found safety in the remote mountains around Yan'an in northern Shaanxi province. It was here that Mao, now the party's leader, rebuilt his army and readied himself and his followers for what would be 14 more years of struggle against the Japanese and the Guomindang.

The following excerpts are drawn from two of Mao's most important writings. The first, his "Report on an Investigation of the Peasant Movement in Hunan," was written in 1927 after he visited Hunan province to study the activities and accomplishments of peasant associations, groups of peasants who, with the help of Communist organizers, had seized land, humiliated or killed landlords, and taken control of their communities. In it, Mao seeks to convince other party members that the peasants are the main source of revolution in China. The second excerpt, from his "Strategic Problems of China's Revolutionary War," is based on a series of lectures delivered at the Red Army College in late 1936. In it, Mao assesses China's military situation and outlines his strategy for victory over the Guomindang through guerrilla warfare.

QUESTIONS FOR ANALYSIS

1. What specific developments in Hunan province reinforced Mao's convictions about the peasantry as a revolutionary force?
2. What criticisms have been made of the Hunan peasant movement, and how does Mao attempt to counter these criticisms?
3. What can be learned from these two writings about Mao's views of the role of the Communist Party in China's revolutionary struggle?
4. According to Mao, what have been the sources of oppression of the Chinese people? Once these sources of oppression are removed, what will China look like?
5. According to Mao, what are the four unique characteristics of China's revolutionary war, and how do they affect Mao's military strategy?
6. What are the characteristics of Mao's "active defense" as opposed to "passive defense"?
7. How do Mao's ideas about revolution resemble and differ from those of Marx?

Report on an Investigation of the Peasant Movement in Hunan [1927]

. . . All the wrong measures taken by the revolutionary authorities concerning the peasant movement must be speedily changed. Only thus can the future of the revolution be benefited. For the present upsurge of the peasant movement is a colossal event. In a very short time, in China's central, southern and northern provinces, several hundred million peasants will rise like a mighty storm, like a hurricane, a force so swift and violent that no power, however great, will be able to hold it back. They will smash all the trammels that bind them and rush forward along the road to liberation. They will sweep all the imperialists, warlords, corrupt officials, local tyrants and evil gentry into

their graves. Every revolutionary party and every revolutionary comrade will be put to the test, to be accepted or rejected as they decide. There are three alternatives. To march at their head and lead them? To trail behind them, gesticulating and criticizing? Or to stand in their way and oppose them? Every Chinese is free to choose, but events will force you to make the choice quickly. . . .

"Yes, peasant associations are necessary, but they are going rather too far." This is the opinion of the middle-of-the-roaders. But what is the actual situation? True, the peasants are in a sense "unruly" in the countryside. Supreme in authority, the peasant association allows the landlord no say and sweeps away his prestige. This amounts to striking the landlord down to the dust and keeping him

Source: Mao Zedong, *Selected Works* (New York: International Publishers, 1954). Reprinted by permission.

there. . . . People swarm into the houses of local tyrants and evil gentry who are against the peasant association, slaughter their pigs and consume their grain. They even loll for a minute or two on the ivory-inlaid beds belonging to the young ladies in the households of the local tyrants and evil gentry. At the slightest provocation they make arrests, crown the arrested with tall paper-hats, and parade them through the villages, saying, "You dirty landlords, now you know who we are!" . . . This is what some people call "going too far," or "exceeding the proper limits in righting a wrong," or "really too much." Such talk may seem plausible, but in fact it is wrong. First, the local tyrants, evil gentry and lawless landlords have themselves driven the peasants to this. For ages they have used their power to tyrannize over the peasants and trample them underfoot; that is why the peasants have reacted so strongly. . . . Secondly, a revolution is not a dinner party, or writing an essay, or painting a picture, or doing embroidery; it cannot be so refined, so leisurely and gentle, so temperate, kind, courteous, restrained and magnanimous. A revolution is an insurrection, an act of violence by which one class overthrows another. A rural revolution is a revolution by which the peasantry overthrows the power of the feudal landlord class. Without using the greatest force, the peasants cannot possibly overthrow the deep-rooted authority of the landlords which has lasted for thousands of years. . . . To put it bluntly, it is necessary to create terror for a while in every rural area. . . .

A man in China is usually subjected to the domination of three systems of authority: (1) the state system, . . . ranging from the national, provincial and county government down to that of the township; (2) the clan system, . . . ranging from the central ancestral temple and its branch temples down to the head of the household; and (3) the supernatural system (religious authority), ranging from the King of Hell down to the town and village gods belonging to the nether world, and from the Emperor of Heaven down to all the various gods and spirits belonging to the celestial world. As for women, in addition to being dominated by these three systems of authority, they are also dominated by the men (the authority of the husband). These four authorities—political, clan, religious and masculine—are the embodiment of the whole feudal-patriarchal system and ideology, and are the four thick ropes binding the Chinese people, particularly the peasants. . . .

The political authority of the landlords is the backbone of all the other systems of authority. With that overturned, the clan authority, the religious authority and the authority of the husband all begin to totter. . . . In many places the peasant associations have taken over the temples of the gods as their offices. Everywhere they advocate the appropriation of temple property in order to start peasant schools and to defray the expenses of the associations, calling it "public revenue from superstition." In Liling County, prohibiting superstitious practices and smashing idols have become quite the vogue. . . .

In places where the power of the peasants is predominant, only the older peasants and the women still believe in the gods, the younger peasants no longer doing so. Since the latter control the associations, the overthrow of religious authority and the eradication of superstition are going on everywhere. As to the authority of the husband, this has always been weaker among the poor peasants because, out of economic necessity, their womenfolk have to do more manual labor than the women of the richer classes and therefore have more say and greater power of decision in family matters. . . . With the rise of the peasant movement, the women in many places have now begun to organize rural women's associations; the opportunity has come for them to lift up their heads, and the authority of the husband is getting shakier every day. In a word, the whole feudal-patriarchal system and ideology is tottering with the growth of the peasants' power.

Strategic Problems of China's Revolutionary War [1936]

What then are the characteristics of China's revolutionary war?

I think there are four.

The first is that China is a vast semi-colonial country which is unevenly developed both politically and economically. . . .

The unevenness of political and economic development in China—the coexistence of a frail capitalist economy and a preponderant semi-feudal economy; the coexistence of a few modern industrial and commercial cities and the boundless expanses of stagnant rural districts; the coexistence of several millions of industrial workers on the one hand and, on the other, hundreds of millions of peasants and handicraftsmen under the old regime; the coexistence of big warlords controlling the Central government and small warlords controlling the provinces; . . . and the coexistence of a few railway and steamship lines and motor roads on the one hand and, on the other, the vast number of wheel-barrow paths and trails for pedestrians only, many of which are even difficult for them to negotiate. . . .

The second characteristic is the great strength of the enemy.

What is the situation of the Guomindang, the enemy of the Red Army? It is a party that has seized political power and has relatively stabilized it. It has gained the support of the principal counter-revolutionary countries in the world. It has remodeled its army, which has thus become different from any other army in Chinese history and on the whole similar to the armies of the modern states in the world; its army is supplied much more abundantly with arms and other equipment than the Red Army, and is greater in numerical strength than any army in Chinese history. . . .

The third characteristic is that the Red Army is weak and small. . . .

Our political power is dispersed and isolated in mountainous or remote regions, and is deprived of any outside help. In economic and cultural conditions the revolutionary base areas are more backward than the Guomindang areas. The revolutionary bases embrace only rural districts and small towns. . . .

The fourth characteristic is the Communist Party's leadership and the agrarian revolution.

This characteristic is the inevitable result of the first one. It gives rise to the following two features. On the one hand, China's revolutionary war, though taking place in a period of reaction in China and throughout the capitalist world, can yet be victorious because it is led by the Communist Party and supported by the peasantry. Because we have secured the support of the peasantry, our base areas, though small, possess great political power and stand firmly opposed to the political power of the Guomindang which encompasses a vast area; in a military sense this creates colossal difficulties for the attacking Guomindang troops. The Red Army, though small, has great fighting capacity, because its men under the leadership of the Communist Party have sprung from the agrarian revolution and are fighting for their own interests, and because officers and men are politically united.

On the other hand, our situation contrasts sharply with that of the Guomindang. Opposed to the agrarian revolution, the Guomindang is deprived of the support of the peasantry. Despite the great size of its army it cannot arouse the bulk of the soldiers or many of the lower-rank officers. . . . Officers and men are politically disunited and this reduces its fighting capacity. . . .

Military experts of new and rapidly developing imperialist countries like Germany and Japan positively boast of the advantages of strategic offensive and condemn strategic defensive. Such an idea is fundamentally unsuitable for China's revolutionary war. Such military experts point out that the great shortcoming of defense lies in the fact that, instead of gingering up [enlivening] the people, it demoralizes them. . . . Our case is different. Under the slogan of safeguarding the revolutionary base areas and safeguarding China, we can rally the greatest majority of the people to fight single-mindedly, because we are the victims of oppression and aggression. . . .

In military terms, our warfare consists in the alternate adoption of the defensive and the offensive. . . . It remains a defensive until a campaign of "encirclement and annihilation" is smashed, and then it immediately begins as an offensive; they are but two phases of the same thing, as one campaign of "encirclement and annihilation" of the enemy is closely followed by another. Of the two phases, the defensive phase is more complicated and more important than the offensive phase. It involves numerous problems of how to smash the campaign of "encirclement and annihilation." . . .

In the civil war, when the Red Army surpasses the enemy in strength, there will no longer be any use for strategic defensive in general. Then our only directive will be strategic offensive. Such a change depends on an overall change in the relative strength of the enemy and ourselves. The only defensive measures that remain will be of a partial character.

Chapter 13

The Global Community Since 1945

WRITING THE HISTORY of the recent past presents unique challenges for early twenty-first-century historians. Their basic task—getting the facts right and determining "what happened"—is relatively easy. Although the inability of historians to examine certain sealed documents in government archives is an obstacle, this is offset by many advantages. Historians of the recent past have lived through many of the events they are describing, can interview eyewitnesses and participants, and have access to not only information contained in books, newspapers, and government documents but also in films, video recordings, and photographs. Many important documents have been digitized, making it possible to do historical research in front of one's computer screen rather than in distant archives and libraries.

Writing history, however, requires more than factual accuracy and telling "what happened." It also entails making interpretations, judging what's important and what's trivial, and determining how events fit into patterns and trends. To do these tasks well, historians need a perspective that includes knowledge of what preceded and what followed the events they are discussing. Historians of the recent past, not knowing the future, will always lack this perspective and thus can make only educated guesses about the meaning of recent events.

Consider, for example, the sudden disintegration of the Soviet Union in the late 1980s and early 1990s. Politicians, journalists, and historians—indeed, everyone who had anything to say about it—agreed at the time that a historic turning point had occurred. The demise of the Soviet Union, they argued, not only ended the Cold War and diminished the threat of nuclear holocaust, it also revealed fatal flaws in communism, confirmed the triumph of capitalism, and opened up new possibilities for world peace and cooperation. The U.S. political scientist Francis Fukuyama went even further in his book, *The End of History and the Last Man* (1992). To him, the disintegration of the Soviet Union and the democratization of its eastern European satellites meant the "end of history." Liberal democracy and capitalism had proved their superiority to all other ideologies, paving the way for their general acceptance around the globe.

From the perspective of the early twenty-first century, it is unclear how many of these judgments will prove correct. In post-Soviet Russia, democracy has hardly flourished. Under the presidency of Vladimir Putin, who took power in 2000, the government took control of much of the media, stifled unfriendly journalists, and harassed and prosecuted critics. Putin had strong public support and was re-elected with 71 percent of the vote in 2004. Public opinion polls have suggested that Russians have few reservations about his policies and those of his hand-picked successor, Dmitry Medvedev, who was elected in 2008 and promptly named Putin as prime minister. Meanwhile, relations between Russia and the United States and, to a lesser degree, between Russia and the states of Western Europe have not been without tension. Russian leaders have resented Western carping about Russia's democratic failings. They also strongly opposed the expansion of the North Atlantic Treaty Organization to include many former communist states in eastern Europe and the plan announced by President George W. Bush in 2007 to build a missile-defense system in Central Europe. For their part, U.S. leaders have been aggravated by Russia's meddling in its neighbors' politics, its tepid support for their Middle East policies, and its willingness to use its vast gas and oil reserves as a political weapon. In 2008 the world press proclaimed that the harsh U.S. reaction to the Russian invasion of Georgia brought tensions to a "Cold War level."

Will the Cold War return? Will Russia remain an authoritarian state? Will some future leader tap the wellsprings of Russian nationalism to launch post-Soviet Russia on a path of conquest and expansion? Or are steps taken by President Obama (the decision to scrap the proposed missile defense system in Central Europe in 2009 and the agreement with President Medvedev to reduce nuclear weapons in 2010) harbingers of improved relations? Until questions such as these are answered, no historian will be able to gauge the true significance of what happened to the Soviet Union in 1991.

What is true of the fall of the Soviet Union also applies to many other recent events and developments. Is the emergence of radical Islam a prelude to a "battle of civilizations" between the West and Islam or a passing phase in Islam's history? What are we to make of the bursting of the dot.com bubble between 2000 and 2002 and the worldwide economic collapse following the crash of the U.S. housing market in 2008? Are they signs of capitalism's fatal flaws or simply unfortunate bumps in the road toward ever greater prosperity? The stunning reemergence of China as an economic powerhouse raises many questions, the most basic of which is whether its distinctive form of authoritarian capitalism provides a viable alternative to the democratic capitalism of the West.

Many other unanswered questions exist. Are the recent gains of Western women in education, job opportunities, and legal status the first stage toward greater gender equality worldwide or will they remain a uniquely Western phenomenon? Will the environmental movement be hailed as a triumph of human foresight or mourned as something that came too late and accomplished too little? Will Africa lift itself from the curse of economic underdevelopment? No one will be able to answer these and countless other questions for another 50 years or more, and until then it is well to keep in mind the response of Chinese foreign minister Zhou Enlai to a question posed to him about the long-term significance of the French Revolution of 1789 during an interview with U.S. national security advisor Henry Kissinger in the early 1970s: "It's too soon to tell."

The 1950s and 1960s: Cold War Origins and Decolonization

Despite the enormous costs and casualties of World War I, international political relations in the 1920s and 1930s remained essentially what they had been before 1914. Not only did European powers retain their African and Asian colonies, but they also extended their authority into new regions such as the Middle East, where Syria and Lebanon came under control of the French and Palestine, Transjordan, and Iraq came under control of the British as a result of the mandate system established at the Paris Peace Conference. With the United States withdrawing into isolationism and the new communist regime in the Soviet Union shunned as a pariah, international affairs continued to be dominated by Great Britain, France, and later Germany. Japan was the only non-European state that could boast of great power status.

The aftermath of World War II was far different. With ruined economies and exhausted populations, European states relinquished their dominance of world affairs to the United States and the Soviet Union, the two states whose size, industrial might, and military strength largely had been responsible for defeating the Axis powers. The unlikely alliance between the democratic, capitalist United States and the totalitarian, communist Soviet Union began to break down, however, in the closing stages of the war and disintegrated completely after the war ended. The establishment of Soviet-dominated regimes in Eastern and Central Europe and the Soviet Union's annexation of Latvia, Estonia, Lithuania, and parts of Poland confirmed the West's fears about communist designs for world domination. Simultaneously, staunch Western opposition to Soviet expansion reinforced Soviet leaders' conviction that capitalist nations were determined to destroy communism. Out of these mutual fears began the Cold War, the conflict between the Soviet Union and the United States that dominated world diplomacy until the late 1980s.

Another symptom of Europe's diminished international role after Word War II was the disintegration of its colonial empires. Decolonization had many causes, including the military and financial exhaustion of postwar Britain and France, the expansion and subsequent collapse of Japan's Asian empire, Soviet and U.S. opposition to colonialism, the upsurge of nationalism in the colonies, and the leadership of such men as Mohandas Gandhi and Jawaharlal Nehru in India, Sukarno in Indonesia, Kwame Nkrumah in Ghana, Ho Chi Minh in Vietnam, Jomo Kenyatta in Kenya, and many others. By the mid-1960s, just short of 90 former European colonies, most of them in Asia and Africa, had become independent.

European states continued to play an important though secondary role in world affairs in the second half of the twentieth century. After their impressive postwar economic recovery, the people of Europe, especially Western Europe, enjoyed high incomes, excellent health care, and exceptional educational opportunities. But the age of European domination had come to an end.

U.S. Perceptions and Cold War Strategies

103 • NATIONAL SECURITY COUNCIL, UNITED STATES OBJECTIVES AND PROGRAMS FOR NATIONAL SECURITY (NSC PAPER NUMBER 68)

Of the thousands of papers, memoranda, reports, and policy statements produced by U.S. officials in the opening stages of the Cold War, two stand out as particularly important. The first, the so-called "Long Telegram," was written in 1946 by career diplomat George Kennan while serving in the U.S. embassy in Moscow. In a telegram to the State Department, Kennan argued that Soviet expansionism and hostility to the outside world were rooted less in Marxism than in a deep sense of Russian inferiority and insecurity. He argued further that the USSR's influence had to be "contained" in areas of vital strategic importance to the United States.

Of equal importance was a report entitled "United States Objectives and Programs for National Security," which was submitted to President Truman in April 1950. It was prepared by the National Security Council, an advisory body to the president that in 1950 consisted of the president himself; the vice-president; the secretaries of state, defense, and the treasury; and the chairman of the National Security Resources Board. Its function was to advise the president on the integration of domestic, foreign, and military policies relating to national security.

In early 1950, when the report was being prepared, many of the key events in the Cold War had already occurred. Winston Churchill had warned of the dangers of Soviet expansionism in his famous Iron Curtain speech in March 1946. The Truman Doctrine of 1947 pledged military aid to Greece and Turkey and any other country resisting a communist takeover; the Marshall Plan (1947) sought to blunt the appeal of communism by allocating millions of dollars to rebuild the economies of Western Europe; and the North Atlantic Treaty Organization (NATO) was established in 1949 to counter Soviet military strength in Eastern Europe. Although no European countries became communist after Czechoslovakia in 1947, American fears of international communism deepened in 1949, when China became communist and the Soviets detonated their first atomic bomb. Against this background, President Truman approved the formation of an *ad hoc* committee to prepare a position paper on a suitable U.S. response to the perceived communist threat. Under the chairmanship of Paul Nitze, the Director of Policy Planning for the State Department, the committee produced a blueprint for U.S. Cold War strategy in April 1950, two months before the onset of the Korean War.

QUESTIONS FOR ANALYSIS

1. According to this document, how did World War II fundamentally alter diplomatic relationships?
2. What view of the Soviet Union does this document present?
3. According to the report, what is the Soviet strategy for subverting the free world?
4. What does "containment" mean?
5. What must be done to ensure containment's effectiveness?

Within the past thirty-five years the world has experienced two global wars of tremendous violence. . . . During the span of one generation, the international distribution of power has been fundamentally altered. For several centuries it had proved impossible for any one nation to gain such preponderant strength that a coalition of other nations could not in time face it with greater strength. The international scene was marked by recurring periods of violence and war, but a system of sovereign and independent states was maintained, over which no state was able to achieve hegemony.

Two complex sets of factors have now basically altered this historical distribution of power. First,

the defeat of Germany and Japan and the decline of the British and French Empires have interacted with the development of the United States and the Soviet Union in such a way that power has increasingly gravitated to these two centers. Second, the Soviet Union, unlike previous aspirants to hegemony, is animated by a new fanatic faith, antithetical to our own, and seeks to impose its absolute authority over the rest of the world. Conflict has, therefore, become endemic and is waged, on the part of the Soviet Union, by violent or non-violent methods in accordance with the dictates of expediency. . . .

On the one hand, the people of the world yearn for relief from the anxiety arising from the risk of

Source: NSC-68, U.S. Department of State, *Foreign Relations of the United States* 1950, vol. 1.

atomic war. On the other hand, any substantial further extension of the area under the domination of the Kremlin would raise the possibility that no coalition adequate to confront the Kremlin with greater strength could be assembled. It is in this context that this Republic and its citizens in the ascendancy of their strength stand in their deepest peril.

The issues that face us are momentous, involving the fulfillment or destruction not only of this Republic but of civilization itself. They are issues which will not await our deliberations. With conscience and resolution this Government and the people it represents must now take new and fateful decisions. . . .

Our overall policy at the present time may be described as one designed to foster a world environment in which the American system can survive and flourish. It therefore rejects the concept of isolation and affirms the necessity of our positive participation in the world community.

This broad intention embraces two subsidiary policies. One is a policy which we would probably pursue even if there were no Soviet threat. It is a policy of attempting to develop a healthy international community. The other is the policy of "containing" the Soviet system. . . .

As for the policy of "containment," it is one which seeks by all means short of war to (1) block further expansion of Soviet power, (2) expose the falsities of Soviet pretensions, (3) induce a retraction of the Kremlin's control and influence and (4) in general, so foster the seeds of destruction within the Soviet system that the Kremlin is brought at least to the point of modifying its behavior to conform to generally accepted international standards.

It was and continues to be cardinal in this policy that we possess superior overall power in ourselves or in dependable combination with other like-minded nations. One of the most important ingredients of power is military strength. In the concept of "containment,"

the maintenance of a strong military posture is deemed to be essential for two reasons: (1) as an ultimate guarantee of our national security and (2) as an indispensable backdrop to the conduct of the policy of "containment." . . .

At the same time, it is essential to the successful conduct of a policy of "containment" that we always leave open the possibility of negotiation with the U.S.S.R. A diplomatic freeze—and we are in one now—tends to defeat the very purposes of "containment" because it raises tensions at the same time that it makes Soviet retractions and adjustments in the direction of moderated behavior more difficult. It also tends to inhibit our initiative and deprives us of opportunities for maintaining a moral ascendancy in our struggle with the Soviet system. . . .

It is quite clear from Soviet theory and practice that the Kremlin seeks to bring the free world under its dominion by the methods of the cold war. The preferred technique is to subvert by infiltration and intimidation. Every institution of our society is an instrument which it is sought to stultify and turn against our purposes. Those that touch most closely our material and moral strength are obviously the prime targets, labor unions, civil enterprises, schools, churches, and all media for influencing opinion. The effort is not so much to make them serve obvious Soviet ends as to prevent them from serving our ends, and thus to make them sources of confusion in our economy, our culture, and our body politic. The doubts and diversities that in terms of our values are part of the merit of a free system, the weaknesses and the problems that are peculiar to it, the rights and privileges that free men enjoy, and the disorganization and destruction left in the wake of the last attack on our freedoms, all are but opportunities for the Kremlin to do its evil work. Every advantage is taken of the fact that our means of prevention and retaliation are limited by those principles and scruples which are precisely the ones that give our freedom and democracy its meaning for us. None of our scruples deter those whose only code is, "morality is that which serves the revolution."

At the same time the Soviet Union is seeking to create overwhelming military force, in order to back up infiltration with intimidation. In the only terms in which it understands strength, it is seeking to demonstrate to the free world that force and the will to use it are on the side of the Kremlin, that those who lack it are decadent and doomed. In local incidents it threatens and encroaches both for the sake of local gains and to increase anxiety and defeatism in all the free world.

The possession of atomic weapons at each of the opposite poles of power, and the inability (for different reasons) of either side to place any trust in the other, puts a premium on a surprise attack against us. It equally puts a premium on a more violent and ruthless prosecution of its design by cold war, especially if the Kremlin is sufficiently objective to realize the improbability of our prosecuting a preventive war. It also puts a premium on piecemeal aggression against others, counting on our unwillingness to engage in atomic war unless we are directly attacked. We run all these risks and the added risk of being confused and immobilized by our inability to weigh and choose, and pursue a firm course based on a rational assessment of each. . . .

Our position as the center of power in the free world places a heavy responsibility upon the United States for leadership. We must organize and enlist the energies and resources of the free world in a positive program for peace which will frustrate the Kremlin design for world domination by creating a situation in the free world to which the Kremlin will be compelled to adjust. Without such a cooperative effort, led by the United States, we will have to make gradual withdrawals under pressure until we discover one day that we have sacrificed positions of vital interest. . . .

In summary, we must, by means of a rapid and sustained build-up of the political, economic, and military strength of the free world, and by means of an affirmative program intended to wrest the initiative from the Soviet Union, confront it with convincing evidence of the determination and ability of the free world to frustrate the Kremlin design of a world dominated by its will. Such evidence is the only means short of war which eventually may force the Kremlin to abandon its present course of action and to negotiate acceptable agreements on issues of major importance.

The whole success of the proposed program hangs ultimately on recognition by this Government, the American people, and all free peoples, that the cold war is in fact a real war in which the survival of the free world is at stake. Essential prerequisites to success are consultations with Congressional leaders designed to make the program the object of nonpartisan legislative support, and a presentation to the public of a full explanation of the facts and implications of the present international situation. The prosecution of the program will require of us all the ingenuity, sacrifice, and unity demanded by the vital importance of the issue and the tenacity to persevere until our national objectives have been attained.

Soviet Goals and Strategies in the 1950s

104 • NIKITA KHRUSHCHEV, SPEECH AT RECEPTION FOR MILITARY ACADEMY GRADUATES, NOVEMBER 1958

Under Joseph Stalin, postwar Soviet foreign policy was characterized by unbending opposition to the West, relentless propaganda, and willingness to risk military confrontation. After Stalin's death in 1953 and a brief period of collective leadership,

Soviet policy took a new turn in 1955 when Nikita Khrushchev assumed control of the party and government.

Born in 1894, Khrushchev became a Bolshevik in 1918 and fought in the Red Army during the civil war. He attended a technical school and moved up the party ladder through positions in Moscow and Ukraine; and after World War II he became a member of the Politburo, the decision-making committee at the top of the Communist hierarchy. On becoming party secretary and premier in the mid-1950s, Khrushchev softened some of the harshest aspects of Stalin's dictatorship at home and pursued peaceful coexistence in foreign affairs. The doctrine of peaceful coexistence maintained that socialism's triumph over capitalism would result from economic, technological, and scientific competition, not warfare. Although Khrushchev did not hesitate to use military force against the anticommunist revolt in Hungary in 1956, he sought to improve East–West relations by meeting with Western leaders, visiting Europe and the United States, and publicly supporting disarmament. After several years of bad agricultural harvests and his humiliating withdrawal of missiles from Cuba in 1962, he fell from power in 1964 and retired to his villa outside Moscow, where he died in 1971.

The following excerpt is taken from a speech Khrushchev delivered in November 1958 at a reception for graduates of the Soviet Union's military academies. It shows that even while supporting peaceful coexistence, he harbored deep hostility toward the Soviet Union's Cold War rivals.

QUESTIONS FOR ANALYSIS

1. According to Khrushchev, what are the aims of Soviet foreign policy?
2. Why, according to Khrushchev, is it necessary for the Soviet Union to maintain a large military establishment?
3. What, according to Khrushchev, is the overall goal of the capitalist nations?
4. How does Khrushchev interpret the West's policy toward the newly independent nations of Africa and Asia?
5. Why is Khrushchev convinced that the Soviet Union and communism will triumph over the United States and capitalism?
6. How does the image of the Soviet Union portrayed by Khrushchev differ from the image described in NSC-68 (source 103)?

Comrades,

The Communist Party and the Soviet Government, all our people, are doing everything to maintain the Armed Forces of the Soviet Union at the necessary standard and to equip them with the latest weapons. But we are not doing it to prepare our Army for any wars of conquest, as the imperialists try to insinuate. By attributing aggressive aims to the Soviet Union, our enemies betray their own ambition of organizing military campaigns against peaceful countries and gaining predatory imperialist domination over the world.

Source: From Nikita Khrushchev, *For Victory in Peaceful Competition with Capitalism* (New York: E. P. Dutton, 1960), 749–757.

We have no aggressive aims whatsoever. The Soviet people have been brought up on the grand ideas of Marxism-Leninism, in the spirit of respect for the freedom and independence of all countries, the spirit of international friendship. We proceed from the fact that there are no unpopulated countries, and that for this reason conquering a country or territory is tantamount to enslaving its people and exploiting them and their wealth. This goes entirely against our ideology, the great teaching of Marxism-Leninism. . . .

We know our strength very well. The socialist camp is now strong and powerful as never before. Yet we cannot disregard the strength of the imperialist camp. The ruling circles in the imperialist countries see what formidable economic and cultural progress has been made in the Soviet Union, the Chinese People's Republic, and all the socialist countries.

The imperialists would like to halt the development of the socialist countries by means of war. They would like thereby to check or completely destroy the socialist trend in social development, so as to preserve their domination, to preserve the capitalist system.

Not to be caught by surprise, to keep the aggressive forces at arm's length from the Soviet Union and all the socialist countries, to discourage the imperialists from using war as a means of settling the ideological controversy between socialism and capitalism, we must see to it that our Armed Forces are always ready to repel the aggressor, and to rout him. *(Prolonged applause.)*. . .

Comrades, we live at the wonderful time when the scientific foresight of our great teachers, Marx and Lenin, about the triumph of socialism over moribund capitalism is coming true and the disgraceful colonial system is in the act of collapsing. The peoples in the colonial countries are emerging from centuries of colonial oppression and fighting stubbornly to become masters of their destiny, their national wealth.

The imperialists are going to all lengths to preserve their domination and keep the colonial countries in a state of dependence. They are looking for new forms of keeping the peoples of economically underdeveloped countries dependent upon them. They are building up aggressive pacts and alliances, such as NATO, the Baghdad Pact, SEATO,[1] and others. With this object U.S. and British imperialists conclude diverse bilateral treaties and military agreements with a number of countries.

But all these pacts, blocs, and agreements are nothing but an artfully camouflaged form of the same old imperialist policy of keeping these countries in complete subjection to the principal imperialist Powers under the pretext of defending them from the "communist threat," and paralyzing the struggle of their peoples for liberation from colonialists, from these dyed-in-the-wool imperialist exploiters.

The imperialists stop at nothing to appropriate the resources of the peoples of colonial and dependent countries. Aided by venal men occupying high government posts in some of the dependent countries, the imperialists try to drag these countries into their own camp so they should themselves help the imperialists in shoring up rotten and corrupt regimes and keep the peoples in the dependencies in colonial slavery. . . .

At present the rulers of some capitalist countries agree to unequal treaties with the United States. But to conceal this in some way, they claim that these treaties are allegedly defensive and a safeguard against the Soviet threat, although it is common knowledge that the Soviet Union has never threatened anyone, and does not threaten anyone now. Our enemies harp on some Soviet "threat,"

---

[1]All of these were regional collective security organizations designed to halt Soviet aggression. An attack on one member was to be construed as an attack on all. NATO (North Atlantic Treaty Organization) was founded in 1949; SEATO (Southeast Asia Treaty Organization) was founded in 1954; the Baghdad Pact (Middle Eastern Treaty Organization) was signed 1955.

while the kings and rulers of certain states have something else in mind. What they fear is their own peoples, and they want the United States to back them, to protect them from the righteous wrath of the people. . . .

In hammering together their military blocs, the imperialists do not conceal their aggressive designs. Generals in countries that are party to these aggressive blocs often make provocative statements against the peaceful nations. Recently, Field Marshal Montgomery[2] known for his inflammatory statements and attacks upon the Soviet Union, retired from the post of Deputy Supreme Commander of NATO Armed Forces in Europe. Now he has been replaced by another Englishman, General Gale.[3] No sooner had he assumed his duties than he adopted the methods of his predecessor. . . . He bragged brazenly about the possibilities of military adventures against the Soviet Union and other peaceful countries. Among other things, he extolled in every way the modern means of communication and the air power of the NATO countries. In the past, Gale declared, it took eight hours to connect Paris and Oslo, whereas now it takes just a few seconds. In the past the Western armed forces had just so many airfields, he said, whereas now they have so and so many bases. . . .

We have said repeatedly that it is best to cease these inflammatory speeches, which cause alarm and fear in people. It would be far more sensible to work for a settlement of controversial issues by negotiation, barring threats, let alone the use of weapons, so that people could live peacefully and enjoy the fruits of their labor.

But statesmen of the more aggressive imperialist groups carry on their notorious policy "from positions of strength." Recently Mr. Dulles[4] declared

again in a speech that the Western Powers were prepared to use armed force to retain control of West Berlin. . . .

Mr. Dulles likes to refer to God in his speeches. If he is really a pious man, we should recommend under the circumstances that he go to church and pray that God give him, a man in a high post, the patience and intelligence to get his proper bearings in the international situation and not to abuse his standing, not to frighten people, but to strive for a sensible settlement of controversial issues without resort to threats of war. *(Applause.)*

High-ranking statesmen such as Mr. Dulles must not liken themselves to a duellist who reaches instantly for his sword or pistol in an argument. They would do well to bear in mind that the partner whom they want to attack, apparently has the same, and perhaps an even more powerful and dangerous weapon. *(Prolonged applause.)* . . .

While encircling the Soviet Union with their military bases, the American imperialists like to use the language of chess players. They often say that they want to check us, that is, to put us in a difficult position. But it must be borne in mind that if one side wants to check, the other side might, for its part, also declare check, and even checkmate. *(Stormy applause.)* . . .

Our seven-year plan[5] has set grand tasks. The time is not far distant when we shall catch up to the United States in per capita production of key industrial items. Our country will achieve the highest living standard and have the world's shortest working day.

To use a figure of speech, we are putting everything projected in our seven-year plan on the scales. Let the capitalists give the working people all that has been, and soon will be, achieved in the socialist countries. But the capitalist system

---

[2]Bernard Law Montgomery (1887–1976) was a British general in World War II and served as deputy supreme allied commander of NATO from 1953 to 1958.
[3]Sir Richard N. Gale (1896–1982) was a British career officer who served in both world wars. He was deputy to the NATO supreme Allied commander in Europe from 1958 to 1967.

[4]John Foster Dulles (1888–1959) was secretary of state under Eisenhower. A staunch anticommunist, he was architect of anti-Soviet alliances and stated he would "go to the brink" of war to halt communist aggression.
[5]The Soviet Union's recently adopted economic plan.

cannot give the working people, the whole nation, what the socialist system can give.

We want the people to choose for themselves what suits them best, what system accords with the fundamental interests of the toilers and what system gives some the opportunity of enriching themselves by exploiting and plundering others. We are sure that the peoples will make the right choice. All peoples will choose the path charted by Marxism-Leninism. *(Stormy applause.)*

The future is with us, with socialism, with communism! We have created all the conditions we need to advance with giant strides along the road shown us by Marx and Lenin—the road to communism. And no hostile forces will stop our advance! *(Stormy, prolonged applause. All rise.)*

Great Britain Lets Go of India

105 • DEBATE IN THE HOUSE OF COMMONS, MARCH 4 AND 5, 1947

A turning point in the dismantling of Europe's empires took place in August 1947 when the Indian people gained independence from Great Britain and the new states of India and Pakistan were created. After the greatest imperial power released its hold on the "jewel in the crown" of its empire, nationalist leaders throughout Asia and Africa demanded equal treatment, and European politicians found it more difficult to justify continued colonial rule elsewhere.

British and Indian leaders had debated the timing and framework of Indian independence for decades, but World War II brought the issue to a head. Many Indians, still embittered by the meager benefits they had received for their sacrifices in World War I, showed little enthusiasm for the British cause in World War II. In 1942, after Japan's conquest of Southeast Asia, the British government sent Sir Stafford Cripps to Delhi to offer India dominion status after the war if the leaders of the independence movement, Gandhi and Jinnah, would support the war against Japan. Negotiations broke down, however, leading Gandhi to launch the "Quit India" movement, his last nationwide passive resistance campaign against British rule. Anti-British feeling intensified in 1943 when a disastrous famine took between 1 million and 3 million lives and the pro-Japanese Indian National Army, organized by Subhas Bose, declared war on Great Britain.

A shift in postwar British politics also affected India's future. The 1945 elections initiated six years of rule by the Labour Party, which had less enthusiasm for the idea of empire than the Conservatives. In the face of mounting restiveness in India, Prime Minister Clement Attlee dispatched a three-person mission to India in early 1946 charged with preserving Indian unity in the face of growing Hindu–Muslim antagonism and arranging for India's independence as soon as possible. Although Hindus and Muslims could not reconcile their differences, on February 20, 1947, the Labour government announced its plan to end British rule in India no later than June 1948.

This led to an emotional two-day debate in Parliament in which Conservatives and some Liberals argued that independence should be delayed. Labour had a strong majority, however, and in March 1947, Parliament approved its plan. At midnight on

August 14–15, 1947, predominantly Hindu India and predominantly Muslim Pakistan became independent states.

The following excerpts are from the parliamentary debates of March 4 and 5, 1947. All the speakers are opposing a proposal by Sir John Anderson, a Liberal representing the Scottish universities, that Great Britain should promise independence by June 1948 but withdraw the offer and require further negotiations if a suitable Hindu–Muslim agreement could not be achieved.

QUESTIONS FOR ANALYSIS

1. What were the points of disagreement among members of Parliament about the benefits and harm of British colonial rule in India?
2. Some speakers who believed that British colonialism had benefited India still supported independence. Why?
3. The critics of British rule in India supported immediate independence. What was their line of argument?
4. According to the speakers, what military and economic realities make it impractical to continue British rule in India?
5. How do the speakers view developments in India as part of broader historical trends?
6. Most of the speakers were members of the Labour Party and thus sympathetic to socialism. What examples of socialist perspectives can you find in their speeches?

Mr. Clement Davies[1] (Montgomery) It is an old adage now, that "the old order changeth, yielding place to new," but there has been a more rapid change from the old to the new in our time than ever before. We have witnessed great changes in each one of the five Continents, and for many of those changes this country and its people have been directly or indirectly responsible. . . . In all the lands where the British flag flies, we have taught the peoples the rule of law and the value of justice impartially administered. We have extended knowledge, and tried to inculcate understanding and toleration.

Our declared objects were twofold—first, the betterment of the conditions of the people and the improvement of their standard of life; and, second, to teach them the ways of good administration and gradually train them to undertake responsibility so that one day we could hand over to them the full burden of their own self-government. Our teachings and our methods have had widespread effect, and we should rejoice that so many peoples in the world today are awake, and aware of their own individualities, and have a desire to express their own personalities and their traditions, and to live their own mode of life. . . . Our association with India during two centuries has been, on the whole—with mistakes, as we will admit—an honorable one. So far as we were able we brought peace to this great sub-continent; we have introduced not only a system of law and order, but also a system of administration of justice, fair and impartial, which has won their respect. . . . We have tried to inculcate into them the feeling that

---

Source: Parliamentary Debates, 5th ser., vol. 434 (London: His Majesty's Printing Office, 1947).

[1]A London lawyer (1884–1962). A Liberal Member of Parliament (MP) from 1929 until the time of his death.

although they are composed of different races, with different languages, customs, and religions, they are really part of one great people of India.

The standard of life, pathetically low as it is, has improved so that during the last 30 years there has been an increase in the population of 100 million and they now number 400 million people. We have brought to them schools, universities, and teachers, and we have not only introduced the Indians into the Civil Service but have gradually handed over to them, in the Provinces and even in the Central Government, the administration and government of their own land and their own people. . . . Then in 1946, there was the offer of complete independence, with the right again, if they so chose, of contracting in and coming back within the British Commonwealth of Nations.[2]

I agree that these offers were made subject to the condition that the Indian peoples themselves would co-operate to form a Central Government and draw up not only their own Constitution, but the method of framing it. Unfortunately, the leaders of the two main parties in India have failed to agree upon the formation of even a Constituent Assembly, and have failed, therefore, to agree upon a form of Constitution. . . .

What are the possible courses that could be pursued? . . . The first of the courses would be to restore power into our own hands so that we might not only have the responsibility but the full means of exercising that responsibility. I believe that that is not only impossible but unthinkable at this present stage. . . . Secondly, can we continue, as we do at present, to wait until an agreement is reached for the formation of a Central Government with a full Constitution, capable of acting on behalf

of the whole of India? The present state of affairs there and the deterioration which has already set in—and which has worsened—have shown us that we cannot long continue on that course.

The third course is the step taken by His Majesty's Government—the declaration made by the Government that we cannot and do not intend in the slightest degree to go back upon our word, that we do not intend to damp the hopes of the Indian peoples but rather to raise them, and that we cannot possibly go on indefinitely as we have been going on during these past months; that not only shall they have the power they now really possess but after June 1948, the full responsibility for government of their own peoples in India. . . .

Mr. Sorensen[3] (Leyton, West) I have considerable sympathy with the hon. and gallant Member for Ayr Burghs (Sir T. Moore),[4] because, politically, he has been dead for some time and does not know it. His ideas were extraordinarily reminiscent of 50 years ago, and I do not propose, therefore, to deal with so unpleasant and decadent a subject. When he drew attention to the service we have rendered to India—and we have undoubtedly rendered service—he overlooked the fact that India has had an existence extending for some thousands of years before the British occupation, and that during that period she managed to run schools, establish a chain of rest houses, preserve an economy, and reach a high level of civilization, when the inhabitants of these islands were in a condition of barbarism and savagery. One has only to discuss such matters with a few representative Indians to realize that they can draw up a fairly powerful indictment of the evil we have taken to India as well as the good. . . .

---

[2]The British Commonwealth of Nations was founded by Parliament in 1931 through the Statute of Westminster. It is a free association of nations comprising Great Britain and a number of its former dependencies that have chosen to maintain ties of friendship and practical cooperation. Members acknowledge the British monarch as the symbolic head of their association. Since 1946 it has been known as the Commonwealth of Nations.

[3]A clergyman (1884–1971). A Labour MP from 1929 to 1931 and from 1939 to 1954.

[4]A Conservative MP (1929–1962) who had just spoken against the government's plan for Indian independence.

Whatever may have been the origin of the various problems in India, or the degree of culpability which may be attached to this or that party or person, a situation now confronts us which demands decision. . . . That is why, in my estimation, the Government are perfectly right to fix a date for the transference of power. . . . Responsibility is ultimately an Indian matter. Acute problems have existed in India for centuries, and they have not been solved under our domination. Untouchability, the appalling subjugation of women, the division of the castes, the incipient or actual conflict between Muslim and Hindu—all those and many others exist.

I do not forget what is to me the most terrible of all India's problems, the appalling poverty. It has not been solved by us, although we have had our opportunity. On the contrary, in some respects we have increased that problem, because, despite the contributions that we have made to India's welfare, we have taken a great deal of wealth from India in order that we ourselves might enjoy a relatively higher standard of life. Can it be denied that we have benefited in the past substantially by the ignorant, sweated labor of the Indian people? We have not solved those social problems. The Indians may not solve them either. There are many problems that the Western world cannot solve, but at least, those problems are India's responsibility. Indians are more likely, because they are intimate with their own problems, to know how to find their way through those labyrinths than we, who are, to the Indian but aliens and foreigners.

Here I submit a point which surely will receive the endorsement of most hon. Members of this House. It is that even a benevolent autocracy can be no substitute for democracy and liberty. . . .

I would therefore put two points to the House tonight. Are we really asked by hon. Members

on the other side to engage in a gamble, first by continuing as we are and trying to control India indefinitely, with the probability that we should not succeed and that all over India there would be rebellion, chaos, and breakdown? Secondly, are we to try to reconquer India and in doing so, to impose upon ourselves an economic burden which we could not possibly afford? How many men would be required to keep India quiet if the great majority of the Indians were determined to defy our power? I guarantee that the number would not be fewer than a million men, with all the necessary resources and munitions of war.

Are we to do this at a time when we are crying out for manpower in this country, when in the mines, the textile industry, and elsewhere we want every man we can possibly secure? There are already 1,500,000 men under arms. To talk about facing the possibility of governing and policing India and keeping India under proper supervision out of our own resources is not only nonsense, but would provide the last straw that breaks the camel's back. . . .

FLIGHT-LIEUTENANT CRAWLEY[5] (BUCKINGHAM) Right hon. and hon. Members opposite, who envisage our staying in India, must have some idea of what type of rule we should maintain. A fact about the Indian services which they seem to ignore is that they are largely Indianized. Can they really expect the Services, Indianized to the extent of 80 or 90 percent, to carry out their policy any longer? Is it not true that in any situation that is likely to arise in India now, if the British remain without a definite date being given for withdrawal, every single Indian member of the Services, will, in the mind of all politically conscious Indians become a political collaborator? We have seen that in Palestine where Arab hates Arab and Jew hates Jew if they think they are collaborating with the British.[6] How could we get

---

[5]An educator and journalist (1908–1992) who served in the Royal Air Force during World War II. A Labour MP from 1945 to 1951.

the Indianized part of the Services to carry out a policy which, in the view of all political Indians, is anti-Indian? The only conceivable way in which we could stay even for seven years in India would be by instituting a type of rule which we in this country abhor more than any other—a purely dictatorial rule based upon all the things we detest most, such as an informative police, not for an emergency measure, but for a long period and imprisonment without trial. . . .

MR. HAROLD DAVIES[7] (LEEK) . . . I believe that India is the pivot of the Pacific Ocean area. All the peoples of Asia are on the move. Can we in this House, by wishful thinking, sweep aside this natural desire for independence, freedom, and nationalism that has grown in Asia from Karachi to Peking,[8] from Karachi to Indonesia and Indo-China? That is all part of that movement, and we must recognize it. I am not a Utopian. I know that the changeover will not be easy. But there is no hon. Member opposite who has given any concrete, practical alternative to the decision, which has been made by my right hon. friends. What alternative can we give?

This little old country is tottering and wounded as a result of the wars inherent in the capitalist system. Can we, today, carry out vast commitments from one end of the world to another? Is it not time that we said to those for whom we have spoken so long, "The time has come when you shall have your independence. That time has come; the moment is here"?

---

[6]The British were attempting to extricate themselves from Palestine, which they had received as a mandate after World War I and was the scene of bitter Arab–Jewish rivalry (see source 95).

[7]An author and educator (1904–1984). A Labour MP from 1959 to 1964.
[8]Karachi, a port city on the Arabian Sea, was soon to become Pakistan's first capital city.

Problems and Prospects of Postcolonial Asia and Africa, 1960s–1980s

As one colony after another achieved independence in the 1950s and 1960s, euphoria swept across Africa and Asia. All the indignities of colonialism and all the ways it had branded colonized peoples with the mark of inferiority could now be forgotten. With a unity of purpose forged in the struggle against colonial rule, leaders and common people alike were ready to show the world they could govern themselves effectively. Their economic outlook was no less optimistic: with the heavy hand of the colonial master lifted from their economies, they anticipated rapid economic development and the alleviation of poverty.

Many of these states have achieved their dreams. But in the first three decades of independence, most experienced more difficulties and disappointments than anyone could have imagined at the time of independence. Many were nations in name only, with boundaries drawn by European administrators during the colonial era without regard for cultural affinities, ethnic groupings, religious traditions, and economic viability. Throughout much of Asia and Africa, shallow national loyalties were undermined by regionalism and ethnic conflict, and soon civil wars and military coups took their toll on democratic governments. With some notable exceptions, such as India, the norm became one-party dictatorships, which at best were controlled by nationalist leaders with the interests of their countrymen at heart, but at their worst were dominated by venal, short-sighted, even genocidal leaders who enriched themselves and their henchmen while their nations' economies crumbled. In some parts of Africa lawlessness, random violence, and warlordism overwhelmed even the dictators, and effective government essentially disappeared.

Economic development in the early stages of independence also came slowly. In the 1960s and 1970s, South Korea and Taiwan, former colonies of Japan, and Singapore and Hong Kong, former colonies of Great Britain, became major industrial and financial powers, but the spectacular success of these four "Asian Tigers" was unique. Elsewhere, oil-rich states in the Persian Gulf, Middle East, and Nigeria generated huge revenues in oil sales but failed to develop the balanced economies needed to improve their people's standard of living or provide a foundation for lasting economic growth. In India, agricultural and industrial growth occurred but not fast enough to keep pace with its rising population, while in Africa, low rates of literacy, lack of infrastructure, and political instability doomed most of the continent to minimal economic growth and deepening poverty.

In their efforts to provide economic growth and political order for their citizens, the approximately 100 new independent nations that emerged from the 1940s through the late 1970 faced different obstacles, undertook different strategies, and achieved varying results. The sources that follow in this section provide insights into some of their experiences.

The Colonial Legacy: Ethnic Tensions in Nigeria

106 • C. ODUMEGWU OJUKWU, SPEECHES AND WRITINGS

Political challenges for the newly independent states of sub-Saharan Africa were daunting: poor communications, low literacy levels, peasant resistance to taxation by distant governments, underdeveloped economies, arbitrary national boundaries, and unrealistically high expectations. Overshadowing everything else, however, was the persistence of strong local and ethnic loyalties that led people to judge national policies by the narrow standard of how they benefited one's region or tribe. In the Republic of Congo (soon to be renamed the Democratic Republic of Congo and later Zaire), rebellion and civil war broke out in January 1960, literally within hours of the formal end of Belgian rule. Newly independent Nigeria held together longer, but it too fell victim to civil war in 1967, when the eastern province of Biafra declared its independence.

When Nigeria became independent in 1960, its constitution was the product of protracted deliberations involving British administrators and representatives of the colony's major ethnic groups, the Hausa-Fulani, the Yoruba, and the Igbo. It established a central government with a prime minister and legislature and three provinces with extensive powers: the Northern Region, which was dominated by the Hausa-Fulani and was overwhelmingly Muslim; the Western Region, which was dominated by the Yoruba and was Protestant; and the Eastern Region, which was dominated by the Igbo and was mainly Roman Catholic. Denouncing corruption and the government's failure to address mounting economic problems, army officers, mostly Igbo, led a *coup d'état* in 1966 and then created a strong centralized national government at the expense of Nigeria's provinces. This angered the Hausa-Fulani and the Yoruba, who feared that the more highly educated and economically sophisticated Igbo would dominate the new regime. The result was another coup, led by Yakuba Gowon, an army officer from the Northern Region, and massacres of Igbo living outside the Eastern Region. The Eastern Region refused to recognize the new government and declared itself the independent Republic of Biafra in May 1967.

The leader of the Biafran independence movement was Chukwuemeka Odumegwu Ojukwu, who was born into a wealthy Igbo family and educated in England, where he received a master's degree in history from Oxford. He rose through the ranks of the Nigerian army and in 1967 became head of state and army commander-in-chief of newly independent Biafra. Immediately attacked by Nigerian forces, Biafra held out until 1970, when Ojukwu capitulated and fled to Guinea. Yakuba Gowon now ruled a reunited Nigeria, which he divided into 12 provinces rather than 3 to defuse ethnic conflict. For the next two decades, except between 1979 and 1983, Nigeria was ruled by military dictators.

The following excerpts are from General Ojukwu's speeches and writings from 1966 to 1969. They reveal his views of Nigeria's history and politics and his thoughts on the meaning of Biafran independence.

QUESTIONS FOR ANALYSIS

1. In Ojukwu's opinion, how did the British and the Northern Nigerians contribute to the problems of the Nigerian state?
2. What characteristics define the people of Eastern Nigeria, in Ojukwu's view?
3. According to Ojukwu, what have been the major flaws of the Nigerian government since independence? How will the new state of Biafra avoid these shortcomings?
4. What specific reasons does Ojukwu provide for the decision of Eastern Nigerians to secede?
5. What does Ojukwu see as the broader significance of the Biafran independence movement?

The Background of a Crisis

The constitutional arrangements of Nigeria, as imposed upon the people by the erstwhile British rulers, were nothing but an implicit acceptance of the fact that there was no basis for Nigerian unity.

It was Britain, first, that amalgamated the country in 1914, unwilling as the people of the North were.[1] It was Britain that forced a federation of Nigeria, even when the people of the North objected to it very strongly. It was Britain, while keeping Nigeria together, that made it impossible for the people to know themselves and get close to each other, by maintaining an apartheid policy in Northern Nigeria which herded all Southerners into little reserves, barring them from Northern Nigerian schools, and maintaining different systems of justice in a country they claimed to be one.[2]

It was Britain, for her economic interest, that put the various nations in Nigeria side by side and called it a federation, so as to have a large market. . . .

On October 1, 1960, independence was granted to the people of Nigeria in a form of "federation," based on artificially made units. The Nigerian Constitution installed the North in perpetual dominance over Nigeria. . . . Thus were sown, by design or by default, the seeds of factionalism and hate, of struggle for power at the center, and of the worst types of political chicanery and abuse of power. One of two situations was bound to result from that arrangement: either perpetual domination of the rest of the country by the North . . . or a dissolution of the federation bond. . . .

Nigeria in the end came to be run by compromises made and broken between the Northerners and consenting Southern politicians. This led to interminable violent crises, to corruption and nepotism, and to the arbitrary use of power. . . .

Key projects in the National Development Plan were not pursued with necessary vigor. Instead of these, palaces were constructed for the indulgence of ministers and other holders of public offices—men supposed to serve the interest of the common man. Expensive fleets of flamboyant and luxurious cars were purchased. Taxpayers' money was wasted on unnecessary foreign travel by ministers, each competing with the other only in their unbridled excesses.

. . . Internal squabbles for parochial and clannish patronage took the place of purposeful coordinated service of the people. Land, the basic heritage of the people, was converted into the private estates of rapacious individuals who, thus trampling on the rights of the people, violated their sacred trust under this system. . . . Nepotism became rife. Tribalism became the order of the day. In appointments and promotions mere lip service was paid to honesty and hard work.

Grievances of the Eastern Nigerians

In the old Federation some of you here will remember quite vividly what the contribution of the people from this area, now known as Biafra, was to the betterment of the areas in which we chose to reside and believed was our country. Socially we gave our best in Nigeria. Politically, we led the struggle for independence and sustained it. Economically, the hope of Nigeria was embedded deeply in this area and we contributed everything for the common good of Nigeria.

Source: Chukwuemeka Odumegwu Ojukwu, *Biafra; Selected Speeches and Random Thoughts of C. Odumegwu Ojukwu, with Diaries of Events* (New York: Harper & Row, 1969). Copyright © 1969, renewed 1997 by Chukwuemeka Odumegwu Ojukwu. Reprinted by permission of Harper-Collins Publisher.

[1]The provinces of Northern and Southern Nigeria were brought under a common administration by Sir Frederick Lugard, governor-general of Nigeria between 1912 and 1919.

[2]Many Eastern Nigerians had moved to other parts of the country, mainly to pursue business opportunities. Many believed they were treated as second-class citizens, especially in the Muslim north.

Our people moved from this area to all parts of the old Federation, and particularly to Northern Nigeria. Where there was darkness we gave them light! In Northern Nigeria, where they had no shelter we gave them houses. Where they were sick, as indeed most Northerners are, we brought them health. Where there was backwardness we brought progress. And where there was ignorance we brought them education. As a result of all this, we became people marked out in the various communities in which we lived.

Initially we were marked out as people who were progressive. Next, as people who were successful. Finally as people who should be the object of jealousy—people who were to be hated, and this hatred arose as a result of our success. . . . We were relegated to the position of second-class citizens and later to slavery—yes, slavery—because as we worked, our masters enjoyed the fruits of our labor.

We reached a stage where the people from this part were fast losing their identity. They hid away the fact that they came from this area. . . .

The Northern attitude is the attitude of horse and rider. . . . We were carrying the North physically, economically, and in every other way. For all that we received no thanks. They only got furious if we did not travel fast enough. Then they would kick. But, for every mule there comes a time when it bucks and says, "No, I will carry no more." We have bucked. We will carry Northern Nigeria no more!

The New Biafran Society

Born out of the gruesome murders and vandalism of yesterday, Biafra has come to stay as a historical reality. We believe that the future we face and our battle for survival cannot be won by bullets alone, but by brainpower, modern skills, and the determination to live and succeed. . . .

Nepotism and tribalism are twin evils. I believe that these can be avoided if we set about making sure that every appointment in our society is based on one and only one criterion—merit. We should ensure that this term "merit" is no mumbo-jumbo. It should be something that is obvious for everyone to see: that is, when you have given somebody a job, the reason for giving that job to that person in preference to others must be generally clear. . . .

Tribalism is, perhaps, more deeply rooted. . . . When I first came to this area as the military governor, one of the first things I did was to erase tribe from all public documents. We are all Biafrans. "Where do you come from?" you are asked, and the answer is simple: "I come from Biafra." The government must not emphasize tribal origin if it is trying to stamp out tribalism. . . .

Every effort should be made by future governments to educate our people away from tribalism. I would like to see movement of people across tribal frontiers. The government should encourage people to move from their own areas to be educated elsewhere. Yes, I would even go further to support government measures to encourage intertribal marriages. . . . It is only a gesture, but if the government really believes that tribalism could be wiped out, something like a bounty should be given to that young man who marries across tribe, to show that the government appreciates what he has done. . . .

I see a new breed of men and women, with new moral and spiritual values, building a new society—a renascent and strong Biafra.

I see the realization of all our cherished dreams and aspirations in a revolution which will not only guarantee our basic freedoms but usher in an era of equal opportunity and prosperity for all.

I see the evolution of a new democracy in Biafra as we advance as partners in our country's onward march to her destiny.

When I look into the future, I see Biafra transformed into a fully industrialized nation, wastelands and slums giving way to throbbing industrial centers and cities. . . .

I see agriculture mechanized by science and technology. . . .

I see a Republic knit with arteries of roads and highways; a nation of free men and women dedicated to the noble attributes of justice and liberty for which our youth have shed their blood; a people with an art and literature rich and unrivaled.

I am sure all Biafrans share these hopes for our country's future and destiny. . . . We are building a society which will destroy the myth that the black man cannot organize his own society.

. . . We are taking our rightful place in the world as human beings. . . . The black man cannot progress until he can point at a progressive black society. Until a society, a virile society entirely black, is established, the black man, whether he is in America, whether he is in Africa, will never be able to take his place side by side with the white man. We have the unique opportunity today of breaking our chains.

. . . We owe it, therefore, to Africa not to fail. Africa needs a Biafra. Biafra is the breaking of the chains. . . .

The Challenge of Religious Rivalries: Two Competing Visions of India

107 • JAWAHARLAL NEHRU, "A SECULAR STATE" AND GIRILAL JAIN, EDITORIALS FROM THE INDIAN *SUNDAY TIMES*

Religious tension between India's majority Hindus and smaller communities of Muslims and Sikhs divided India's political leaders in the 1930s and early 1940s; set off communal rioting that caused the deaths of tens of thousands in 1946; and ultimately led to the founding of two separate states, predominantly Muslim Pakistan and predominantly Hindu India, after the end of British rule in August 1947. In the year following independence, as many as 14 million Muslims, Hindus, and Sikhs crossed borders to escape entrapment in a state that was hostile to their faith. Newly formed governments were unable to deal with migrations of such staggering magnitude, and massive violence and slaughter occurred on both sides of the border. As many as 500,000 deaths may have occurred.

Despite partition and the mass migrations of 1947 and 1948, independent India remained religiously divided among Hindus (approximately 82 percent of the population), Muslims (approximately 13 percent), and smaller communities of Christians, Sikhs, Parsis, Jains, and Buddhists. In 1949, under the leadership of the Congress Party, a constituent assembly that also served as India's first parliament approved a constitution that declared India to be a secular state committed to religious freedom and partiality to no single religious group.

None of India's religious groups has been completely satisfied with the results of India's commitment to secularism. Many Hindus remain convinced that the government has bent over backward to protect Muslims and Sikhs; Muslims and Sikhs, conversely, continue to believe that the government has pandered to Hindus. Religious tensions intensified in the 1980s, as Muslims began to make converts among low-caste Hindus in the south, Sikhs agitated for an independent Punjab, and Hindus in 1982 organized their own political party, the Bharatiya Janata (Indian People's Party), or BJP, whose goal was the "Hinduization" of India.

The ongoing tensions between secularism and Hindu nationalism are represented by excerpts from the works of two authors, written 30 years apart. "A Secular

State" is a brief essay written by Jawaharlal Nehru (1889–1964) in 1961. As leader of the Congress Party and India's prime minister from 1947 to 1964, the upper-class, English-educated Nehru shaped India's early economic and political development more than any other individual did. The other excerpts are from editorials by Girilal Jain, a prominent journalist who served as editor-in-chief of the New Delhi *Times of India* between 1978 and 1988. Born into a poor rural family in 1922 and educated at Delhi University, Jain was drawn to Hindu nationalism and the BJP in the 1980s. He wrote the following editorials in 1990, when Hindu–Muslim tensions were peaking over the Babri mosque, built in the city of Ayodhya in the sixteenth century on a site believed by Hindus to be the birthplace of one of the most revered Hindu gods, Lord Rama. Hindus demanded the destruction of the mosque, which was no longer used, so that a temple in honor of Rama could be built. In 1989, Hindu nationalists began laying the foundations for a Hindu temple near the mosque, and in 1990, the year in which Jain wrote his editorials "The Harbinger of a New Order" and "Limits of the Hindu Rashtra [Polity]" for the *Sunday Mail,* they attacked and damaged the mosque. In December 1992, 150,000 Hindus stormed the mosque and destroyed it, precipitating a government crisis and causing violence that took 2,000 lives.

QUESTIONS FOR ANALYSIS

1. According to Nehru, what is the meaning of the term "secularism" in the context of Indian society?
2. According to Nehru, how will the abandonment of secularism affect India and its future?
3. What does Jain mean when he says that the issues that concern the BJP have to do with "civilization," not religion?
4. How does Jain define the West? How does he view the West's role in Indian history?
5. Why, according to Jain, is the controversy over the Ayodhya mosque so significant for India's future?
6. In Jain's view, why have the Muslims been satisfied to go along with the secularist policies of the Indian state?
7. What is Jain's vision of India's future? How does it differ from the future imagined by Nehru?

Nehru, "A Secular State"

It is perhaps not very easy even to find a good word in Hindi for 'secular'. Some people think that it means something opposed to religion. That obviously is not correct. What it means is that it is a state which honours all faiths equally and gives them equal opportunities; that, as a state, it does not allow itself to be attached to one faith or religion, which then becomes the state religion. . . .

Source: Printed in Jawaharlal Nehru, *Nehru An Anthology,* Sarvepalli Gopal, ed. (Delhi/Oxford: Oxford University Press, 1980), pp. 330–331. Reprinted by permission of Oxford University Press India.

The word secular . . . [also] conveys . . . the idea of social and political equality. Thus a caste-ridden society is not properly secular. I have no desire to interfere with any person's belief, but when those beliefs become petrified in caste divisions, they affect the social structure of the state. They prevent us from realizing the idea of equality which we claim to place before ourselves. . . .

In a sense, this is a more or less modern conception. India has a long history of religious tolerance. That is one aspect of a secular state, but it is not the whole of it. In a country like India, which has many faiths and religions, no real nationalism can be built up except on the basis of secularity. Any narrower approach must necessarily exclude a section of the population, and then nationalism itself will have a much more restricted meaning than it should possess. In India we would have then to consider Hindu nationalism, Muslim nationalism, Sikh nationalism or Christian nationalism and not Indian nationalism.

As a matter of fact, these narrow religious nationalisms are relics of a past age and are no longer relevant today. They represent a backward and out-of-date society. In the measure we have even today so-called communal troubles, we display our backwardness as social groups. . . .

In a country like England, the state is, under the constitution, allied to one particular religion, the Church of England, which is a sect of Christianity. Nevertheless, the state and the people there largely function in a secular way. Society, therefore, in England is more advanced in this respect than in India, even though our constitution may be, in this matter, more advanced.

We have not only to live up to the ideals proclaimed in our constitution, but make them a part of our thinking and living and thus build up a really integrated nation. That, I repeat, does not mean absence of religion, but putting religion on a different plane from that of normal political and social life. Any other approach in India would mean the breaking up of India. . . .

Jain, "The Harbinger of a New Order"

A specter haunts dominant sections of India's political and intellectual elites—the specter of a growing Hindu self-awareness and self-assertion. Till recently these elites had used the bogey of Hindu "communalism" and revivalism as a convenient device to keep themselves in power and to "legitimize" their slavish imitation of the West. Unfortunately for them, the ghost has now materialized.

Millions of Hindus have stood up. It will not be easy to trick them back into acquiescing in an order which has been characterized not so much by its "appeasement of Muslims" as by its alienness, rootlessness and contempt for the land's unique cultural past. Secularism, a euphemism for irreligion and repudiation of the Hindu ethos, and socialism, a euphemism for denigration and humiliation of the business community to the benefit of ever expanding rapacious bureaucracy, . . . have been major planks of this order. Both have lost much of their old glitter and, therefore, capacity to dazzle and mislead. . . .

The Hindu fight is not at all with Muslims; the fight is between Hindus . . . and the state, Indian in name and not in spirit and the political and intellectual class trapped in the debris the British managed to bury us under before they left. The proponents of the Western ideology are using Muslims as auxiliaries and it is a pity Muslim "leaders" are allowing themselves to be so used. . . .

Source: Giralal Jain, "The Harbinger of a New Order" and "Limits of the Hindu Rashtra" from Koenrad Elst, *Ayodhya and After* (New Delhi: Crescent Printing Works, 1991), pp. 364–367, 369–371, 373–375. Reprinted by permission of the author.

Jain, "Limits of the Hindu Rashtra"

The first part of this story begins, in my view, with the mass conversion of Harijans to Islam in Meenakshipuram in Tamil Nadu in 1981[1] and travels via the rise of Pakistan-backed armed secessionist movements in Punjab and Jammu and Kashmir,[2] and the second part with the spectacular success of the Bharatiya Janata Party (BJP) in the last polls. . . .

India . . . has been a battleground between two civilizations (Hindu and Islamic) for well over a thousand years, and three (Hindu, Muslim and Western) for over two hundred years. None of them has ever won a decisive enough and durable enough victory to oblige the other two to assimilate themselves fully into it. So the battle continues. This stalemate lies at the root of the crisis of identity the intelligentsia has faced since the beginning of the freedom movement in the last quarter of the nineteenth century. . . .

The more resilient and upwardly mobile section of the intelligentsia must, by definition, seek to come to terms with the ruling power and its mores, and the less successful part of it to look for its roots and seek comfort in its cultural past. . . . Thus in the medieval period of our history there grew up a class of Hindus in and around centers of Muslim power who took to the Persian-Arabic culture and ways of the rulers; similarly under the more securely founded and far better organized and managed [British] Raj there arose a vast number of Hindus who took to the English language, Western ideas, ideals, dress and eating habits; . . . they, their progeny and other recruits to their class have continued to dominate independent India.

They are the self-proclaimed secularists who have sought, and continue to seek, to remake India in the Western image. . . . Behind them has stood, and continues to stand, the awesome intellectual might of the West, which may or may not be anti-India, depending on the exigencies of its interests, but which has to be antipathetic to Hinduism. . . .

Some secularists may be genuinely pro-Muslim. . . . But, by and large, that is not the motivating force in their lives. They are driven, above all, by the fear of what they call regression into their own past which they hate and dread. Most of the exponents of this viewpoint have come and continue to come understandably from the Left, understandably because no other group of Indians can possibly be so alienated from the country's cultural past as the followers of Lenin, Stalin and Mao, who have spared little effort to turn their own countries into cultural wastelands.

The state in independent India has, it is true, sought, broadly speaking, to be neutral in the matter of religion. But this is a surface view of the reality. The Indian state has been far from neutral in civilizational terms. It has been an agency, and a powerful agency, for the spread of Western values and mores. It has willfully sought to replicate Western institutions, the Soviet Union too being essentially part of Western civilization. It could not be otherwise in view of the orientation and aspirations of the dominant elite of which Nehru remains the guiding spirit . . . Muslims have found such a state acceptable principally on three counts. First, it has agreed to leave them alone in respect of their personal law. . . . Secondly, it has allowed them to expand their traditional . . . educational system in madrasahs[3] attached to mosques. Above all, it has helped them avoid the necessity to come to terms with Hindu civilization

---

[1]Hindus were incensed when large numbers of low-caste Hindus, or Harijans, were converted to Islam in 1981. It was believed that the missionary campaign was financed by Saudi Arabians.

[2]The province of Punjab and the province of Jammu and Kashmir were created at the time of independence. With mixed populations of Hindus, Muslims, and Sikhs, they have been plagued by religious conflict.

[3]Madrasahs are advanced schools of learning, or colleges, devoted to Islamic studies.

in a predominantly Hindu India. This last count is the crux of the matter. . . .

In the past up to the sixteenth century, great temples have been built in our country by rulers to mark the rise of a new dynasty or to mark a triumph. . . . In the present case, the proposal to build the Rama temple has also helped produce an "army" which can in the first instance achieve the victory the construction can proclaim.

The raising of such an "army" in our democracy, however flawed, involves not only a body of disciplined cadres, which is available in the shape of the RSS,[4] a political organization, which too is available in the Bharatiya Janata Party, but

also an aroused citizenry. . . . The Vishwa Hindu Parishad[5] and its allies have fulfilled this need in a manner which is truly spectacular.

The BJP-VHP-RSS leaders have rendered the country another great service. They have brought Hindu interests, if not the Hindu ethos, into the public domain where they legitimately belong. But it would appear that they have not fully grasped the implications of their action. Their talk of pseudo-secularism gives me that feeling. The fight is not against what they call pseudosecularism; it is against secularism in its proper definition whereby man as animal usurps the place of man as spirit. . . .

---

[4]RSS stands for the Rashtriya Swayamsevak Sangh, a militant Hindu organization founded in 1925 dedicated to the strengthening of Hindu culture.

[5]The Vishwa Hindu Parishad (VHP), or World Hindu Society, was founded in 1964. It is dedicated to demolishing mosques built on Hindu holy sites.

New Nations and the Cold War: The Experience of Vietnam

108 • LAO DONG PARTY DIRECTIVE FOR THE SOUTH: "SITUATION AND TASKS FOR 1959"

For many states in Africa and Asia, the achievement of independence from Great Britain, France, Japan, or some other colonial power led directly to interference in their affairs by one or both of the world's two new superpowers, the United States and the Soviet Union. These Cold War rivals, for a host of ideological, diplomatic, economic, and strategic reasons, intervened by providing arms to opposing sides in civil wars, working to destabilize unfriendly regimes, helping organize coups, and propping up sympathetic rulers through foreign aid. Such interference prolonged civil wars in Africa, enabled kleptocratic dictators to stay in power, and led to a shooting war in Korea from 1950 to 1953.

Nowhere, however, did the Cold War cause as much conflict and suffering as in the three former French colonies of Laos, Cambodia, and Vietnam. Recognized as independent nations in 1954, they became the locus of the Second Indochina War, caused mainly by U.S. efforts to stop the spread of communism in Southeast Asia. The United States committed 3.4 million military personnel to the war, 60,000 of whom were killed or became missing in action. The South and North Vietnamese, however, suffered 1,200,000 military deaths and almost an equal number of civilian deaths. An unknown number of Cambodians and Laotians also died when the

United States subjected both countries to bombing attacks to halt the movement of military supplies and personnel from North Vietnam to South Vietnam through their territories. When the fighting stopped in 1975, Vietnam, Laos, and Cambodia all had communist rulers. In Cambodia's case, the ruler was Pol Pot, whose policies resulted in the deaths of anywhere from 1.2 million to 3 million of his countrymen before he was overthrown in 1979.

The roots of the conflict go back to September 1945, when Ho Chi Minh (1890–1969), the communist leader of the Viet Minh (the Vietnam Independence League), declared Vietnamese independence and went on to lead his supporters in the First Indochina War, in which France, with U.S. aid, fought to reestablish its colonial authority. The war ended in 1954, when the Geneva Accord temporarily divided Vietnam into a communist north and non-communist south, with the question of reunification to be decided by a nationwide referendum in 1956. Such an election never occurred, due mainly to the establishment of a permanent state in the south under the government of Ngo Dinh Diem. Supported by the United States, the Republic of Vietnam developed into an authoritarian state in which Diem imposed censorship, ordered the arrest of opponents on vague charges of treason, alienated the country's Buddhist majority by his pro-Catholic policies, and manipulated plans for land reform to benefit his family and supporters. Opposition to Diem came from Buddhists, disgruntled peasants, frustrated nationalists, and some five to ten thousand Viet Minh cadres (professional revolutionaries), who had stayed in the south after the division of the country in 1954.

Against this background, in late 1958 or early 1959, the leaders of North Vietnam's ruling political party, the Lao Dong (Workers' Party), reconsidered their strategy on how to reunite the country now that elections no longer were a possibility. In the midst of an ambitious program of industrialization and land reform and cautioned against provoking another war in Southeast Asia by the Soviet Union, it issued a directive for its "southern strategy." It promised its supporters in the south financial support and guidance but ordered them to avoid assassinations and direct attacks against the South Vietnamese army. They should focus on tightening their organization and using propaganda to pressure and discredit the Diem government but resort to force only to protect themselves from government informers, security officials, and corrupt landlords. This cautious policy would soon be abandoned, but not the underlying sense of purpose, conviction, confidence, and singlemindedness that would guide the North Vietnamese until April 30, 1975, when their troops took Saigon, the capital of South Vietnam, and brought an end to this long and costly struggle.

QUESTIONS FOR ANALYSIS

1. According to the authors of the document, how is the conflict in Vietnam part of broader movements taking place in other parts of the world?
2. How do the authors of the document interpret U.S. motives in South Vietnam?

3. According to the party's statement, what are the short- and long-term goals of the party for Vietnam?
4. According to the authors, how has rule by "U.S.-Diem" affected the lives of the people in South Vietnam? What will be its future effect, and how does this affect the party's strategy for achieving its goals?
5. Based on their analysis of the situation, what strategies should the parties' allies in South Vietnam pursue for 1959?

World Situation

1) The forces of the socialist camp in every area—economic, political, military and scientific grows unceasingly stronger. . . .

The continuous defeats of the imperialist camp: in the Middle East, the Far East, Africa, Latin America, etc., have weakened imperialism. The movement of peace, democracy and national independence in the world, developing strongly by relying on the strength of the socialist camp. Not only as the potential to check and smash a war provoked by imperialism, but to push it back from one place to another. It is clear that our camp led by the Soviet Union is the mainstay in defending world peace.

2) The movement of national liberation and nationalism . . . is increasingly on the rise in Africa, Asia, Latin America. The colonial system of imperialism has entered the phase of disintegration and collapse. . . .

3) The imperialist economy, especially that of U.S. imperialism, has fallen into serious crisis, influencing those countries dependent on the U.S., and pushing the people of those countries to step up more and more their struggle to escape from their slavery to the U.S. economy: Western Europe, Asia, and Africa.

4) Weakened, defeated and expelled everywhere, imperialism in general and the U.S. in particular, show extreme stubbornness; sickeningly, cynically, they stick to the positions they have seized and provoke wars to dominate peoples. . . .

• • •

The South

1) The American imperialists more and more actively intervene in the South, turning it into a new type colony and military base, aiming at sabotaging peace and reunification of our country. The U.S. has become the number one enemy of the Southern people and the people of the whole country.

The Diem[1] ruling clique, is really only the lackey carrying out every scheme and policy of their American masters.

2) From 1957 to now, the activities of the U.S.-Diem [regime] exhibit them to be determined to poisonously carry out their country-stealing and country-selling scheme.

Their activities have the following notable points:

—Using anti-Communist and denunciation of Communist labels to make every effort to terrorize and repress. . . . They do not carry out all democratic rights, stubbornly opposing peace, unification and rejecting every proposal for peace, unification from the North. They carry out brazenly fascist policies with regard to politics.

—Striving to build, strengthen and increase military forces in order to repress and provoke war. Widening strategic military lines of communications (highways) and new military bases. Striving to recruit

---

Source: From Gareth Porter, ed. and trans., *Vietnam: The Definitive Documentation of Human Decisions* (Stanfordville, NY: Earl M. Coleman Enterprises, 1979), vol. 2, 36–41. Reprinted by permission of the author.

[1]Ngo Dinh Diem (1901–1963), an implacable anticommunist, served as president of South Vietnam until he was overthrown and assassinated in 1963 in a military coup tacitly supported by the United States.

troops by force, to gather troops, to gather people, to expel villagers, to coerce people's labor, and to do everything possible to destroy old resistance bases.

—Increasing sweeps to mercilessly plunder the human, material and financial means of the people. Aim at impoverishing the peasants by every cruel trick: stealing the land of the peasants, confusing land ownership, increasing rent, increasing old taxes, instituting new taxes, lotteries, collections, fines, gambling and especially under the farce they call community development.

—Sowing the seeds of a degenerate, lavish, cowboy, U.S.-style culture, developing gambling, prostitution in every form in order to deprave the people's spirit, hoping to put them to sleep and make them worthless. . . .

—Because the economy is more and more dependent on American aid, more and more in decline, everyday, because of the policy of long-term division of the country and preparing to provoke war, because of the policy of increasing terrorism and repression, merciless exploitation and plunder, the life of the Southern people, especially workers, peasants and poor strata in the cities is more and more miserable; hunger and famine have appeared in scattered places in the countryside and the cities. Agriculture is declining, industry and commerce are stagnating, peasants are going bankrupt, and many suicides because of poverty and indigence have occurred under the U.S.-Diem regime are very pitiful.

—Because of their miserable, dark real life experience, popular strata from the countryside to the cities are gradually understanding that it is caused by the policies of U.S.-Diem. Aspirations for national independence, peaceful unification of the country, demands for improvement of daily life, demands for democratic freedom among popular strata, peasants and urban workers are clearer and deeper everyday, and the neutralist tendencies are growing among bourgeois people. . . .

The peoples movement against U.S.-Diem during the past period has developed continually and unceasingly.

—The characteristic of the movement is that it has gone deep into the interests of the masses, mobilizing classes, religions, and the people to participate and to form a broader front from the countryside to the cities. . . .

—Looking generally at the movement there are many advances, struggle slogans are very realistic. The Struggle front is broad. Forms of struggle are abundant, the level of struggle sometimes is fierce and decisive. We have won definite victories, caused very many difficulties and obstacles for the enemy. They must exhaust themselves with every step in carrying out their cruel policies. . . .

Tasks for 1959 (Three immediate tasks)

. . . Based on the above situation between the enemy and ourselves now and the changes about to take place, we can see that the three immediate tasks of the Party put forward by the District conference from 1957 to now are fundamentally still appropriate. The tasks have not changed, but the forms and the level of the struggle movement in the near future must be broader, stronger and more decisive.

1) Continue to do everything possible to stay the dictatorial, fascist hands of U.S.-Vietnam, politically, and economically, demanding freedom, food and clothing, to protect the living rights and democratic rights for the people.

2) Stop the U.S.-Diem warmongering scheme to sabotage peace. Demand peaceful unification of the fatherland, and immediately demand establishment of relations between the two zones.

Because the U.S. imperialist intervention in every aspect, economic, political, military and cultural is the origin of all the southern people's suffering . . . , we must especially pay attention to raising slogans opposing the U.S. and demanding national independence in the South.

Only if we educate the people to raise still higher their consciousness and spirit of opposing U.S. imperialism and colonialism in the struggle for the real daily rights, can we build and develop strongly the anti-U.S. forces to demand national independence and divide and isolate further the feudalist and reactionary forces in the South. . . .

3) Build real specialized strength, that is to push strongly the building and strengthening of the Party section, in order to raise the influence and role of the Party. Strengthen the peasant worker alliance, broaden the popular front, go deep to create specialized bases in the U.S.-Diem army and government.

Utopian Dreams in Mao's China

109 • TAN MANNI, LUSHAN'S PIG-IRON SPUTNIK

On October 1, 1949, with the Guomindang armies of Chiang Kai-shek in full retreat, Mao Zedong, the leader of the Chinese Communist Party, stood above the Gate of Heavenly Peace in Beijing and proclaimed the People's Republic of China. China's civil war had ended, and the fate of 540 million Chinese lay in the hands of Mao Zedong and a small number of his followers who for 25 years had struggled to unify China under communist rule.

Mao and the communists had ambitious plans. They envisioned a strong, independent China, no longer vulnerable to imperialism and its attendant humiliations. They envisioned a China in which poverty would be eradicated through agricultural modernization, industrialization, and a program of road-building, railroad construction, and energy development. They envisioned a China in which ancient inequalities—between men and women, landlords and peasants, the learned and the illiterate, bureaucrats and subjects—would no longer exist. But was it possible to achieve rapid economic development in a truly egalitarian society? Finding an answer to this question became Mao's greatest challenge.

Between 1949 and 1953, large-scale businesses were nationalized, and land seized from rich landowners was redistributed to peasants. In 1953, in imitation of Stalin's Soviet Union, China instituted its first Five Year Plan. Its key components were centralized economic planning, the collectivization of agriculture, and rapid industrialization, with emphasis on steel, industrial equipment, chemicals, and electric power.

Despite annual growth rates of 18 percent, Mao was unhappy with such an approach. Central planning meant larger and more powerful bureaucracies, while rapid industrialization brought disproportionate wealth and status to elite managers and engineers. Thus by late 1957, Mao was prepared to take China into a new stage of its socialist development—the Great Leap Forward.

The Great Leap Forward shifted the focus of China's economic development from cities to the countryside, where millions of peasants, in the selfless pursuit of socialism, would dedicate themselves not just to farming but also to road construction, stock-raising, iron-making, and other enterprises to transform China into a modern socialist society. By the end of 1958, 120 million households had joined 26,000 large communes, which party officials ran according to strict egalitarian principles: private plots were abolished; commune members all received the same pay and food ration irrespective of their work; families were organized collectively, with meals and child care provided by the commune. They joined militias; built and operated backyard iron foundries and other factories; worked on construction projects; and in some cases prospected for uranium. Those with talent were encouraged to write inspirational poetry and songs.

The Great Leap Forward was a disaster. People were worked to exhaustion; the backyard iron foundries produced millions of iron pots and tools, but most were unusable; worst of all, farm output failed to reach unrealistically high production targets, and as the communes' grain, vegetables, and meat were handed over to the state to feed city-dwellers, famine swept through rural China and claimed 20 million lives between 1959 and 1962.

Why did the Great Leap Forward fail? Some answers are provided by the following article, which appeared in the journal *China Reconstructs* in 1959. It author, Tan Manni, describes how a commune in Lushan County, a region in Jiangxi Province, reached a "sputnik" in iron production. Sputnik was the name of the first man-made satellite sent into orbit by the USSR in 1957. The term was used during the Great Leap Forward for high production goals in agriculture and manufacturing.

QUESTIONS FOR ANALYSIS

1. What does the selection reveal about the level of economic and technological development in Lushan County at the time of the Great Leap Forward?
2. According to the author, how do the workers view their labors? What methods have been used to motivate them?
3. What does the article reveal about the reasons for the poor quality of pig iron produced in the Lushan County foundries?
4. What does the article reveal about the reasons for the fall in agricultural production during the Great Leap Forward?
5. What changes in social and family relationships accompanied the Great Leap Forward? Why were they necessary?

Furnace fields are everywhere . . . plots of hundreds of small earthen furnaces were "growing," in late autumn when I was there, alongside fields of sweet potatoes and tobacco. . . .

Small red flags fly overhead indicating the sections belonging to the various companies and squads of farmer-steelworkers, who are organized like militia units. . . .

At one of the ten-foot-high furnaces, a man climbs a wooden ladder to dump coke and firewood through the top. After a few minutes beside the 1,000-degree heat, he descends and another worker goes up to tamp the fuel down with his rake. A third man follows to pull the hot rake away from the blast of the fire. Beside the furnace another crew is pushing the handle of the huge homemade wooden bellows. With all his might one of them pulls the handle, half as tall as himself, and pushes it back with the weight of his body. Three other men standing by to take their turns jokingly cheer him on. . . .

Source: "Lushan's Pig Iron Sputnik," *China Reconstructs* (now *China Today*), vol. VIII, no. 1 (January 1959), pp. 6–9.

The river a few miles away from the county town is another scene of activity. Undaunted by cold north wind, 25,000 students, women, and local government workers are ankle-deep in the water, washing for the iron-bearing sand that has been carried down from the nearby mountains. On the banks, groups of students off their working shift hold classes, and a crew of older women minds the children for the mothers beside the temporary living quarters made for workers from distant parts of the county. . . .

The office of the county Communist Party committee where I stayed in the county town of Lushan is like the headquarters of an army, for the party had undertaken direct leadership of the iron campaign. Any time of the day or night, one can hear someone shouting into the telephone, "Long distance . . . urgent . . . coal . . . tons."

This is the verve which enabled Lushan, the small mountainous county which six months ago possessed neither a blast furnace nor an engineer, or even an automobile, to startle the entire country by proving it could turn out 1,000 tons of iron a day. That record on last August 28 opened a new page in the nation-wide campaign for iron and steel, for it did away with the belief that smelting by local methods does not add up to much.

Lushan's achievement was called a "sputnik," and within the next month it inspired seventy-three more counties to reach that level. Now the record has been surpassed hundreds of times, but the county's 430,000 people are still seized by the iron and steel fever. Each day 100,000 of them work directly in its production, and many thousands more "at the rear" help transport ore after a day's work in the fields.

The people of Lushan began making small amounts of iron early in the summer, in line with the country's policy of developing small local industry as well as large plants, and to meet their own needs in making labor-saving farm machinery. . . . In Lushan, local materials and simple homemade tools were used to cut down initial investment and half of the funds were contributed by the people themselves. A dozen blacksmiths who at the beginning did not know how to smelt ore, led by the party vice-secretary, studied and experimented until they found a suitable process, and then passed the technique on to 600 other farmer-steelworkers. . . .

. . . The farming had to be done with as few people as possible so as to free as many workers as possible to build and operate more furnaces, and mine and transport ore and coal. . . .

As the work could not go ahead without full mass support and understanding, the meetings to discuss the proposal [to set higher production goals] became hot debates—a struggle of ideas. It was through this that the farmers came to realize their real power to produce. Party leaders put the need for iron in terms of the country's own needs—it could bring hydroelectric power stations on every one of the 600 reservoirs the people had built in the spring, better farm tools and machines, multi-storied buildings. They also pointed out that more iron for national construction would mean more tractors, rail lines and other improvements for all.

The way [to proceed], most people agreed, was large-scale organization. Lushan's mountains had ore but few people to do the mining. On the plains, on the other hand, there was manpower to spare. So their coops[1] decided that only by merging could they better deploy the working force. This later formed the basis for the people's commune which now embraces all of Lushan county.

Suggestions for nurseries and canteens to release more women were also adopted. In one large village alone, these measures freed 2,100 women for productive work. . . .

When the time came to sign up for iron work, 95 percent of the county's able-bodied persons applied, and 65,000 were soon actually making

---

[1]Cooperative farms.

iron. Shock teams were organized to man the furnaces, mine the ore, mold crucibles, and repair roads to facilitate transport. They built 500 new furnaces, and methods were developed to make the older ones yield twenty times as much iron per heat.

In the fortnight which preceded the target date of August 28, few people got a full night's sleep. It was just in those weeks that news came of the aggressive military build-up by the United States in the Taiwan Straits area and of provocations against the mainland.[2] Determination became even greater. On August 27, just as the furnaces

were being lit, word arrived about the nation-wide call to raise the 1958 national production of steel to 10.7 million tons, twice as much as the year before. On August 28, Lushan's furnaces yielded 1,068 tons of pig iron. The "sputnik" had succeeded and Lushan had set a new standard for local iron production.

Soon the daily average was far surpassing this one-time figure. In the autumn, 40,000 more workers came from neighboring counties. By early November 150,000 tons were being produced in one day—as much as had been planned for the whole year.

---

[2]In August 1958, China demanded the withdrawal of U.S. forces from Taiwan after the Chinese air force began bombing raids against Quemoy, an offshore island near the port of Amoy controlled by the Nationalist government of Taiwan.

A standoff ensued. China continued the bombardment until December but made no attacks on the supply ships sent to Quemoy under U.S. Navy escort.

Women Between Tradition and Change, 1960s–1970s

During the twentieth century, political leaders of industrialized nations, revolutionaries such as Lenin and Mao, and nationalist heroes as different as Atatürk and Gandhi all supported the ideal of women's equality with men. The United Nations Charter of 1945 committed the organization to the same ideal, and the UN Universal Declaration of Human Rights of 1948 reaffirmed the goal of ending all forms of gender-based discrimination. Beginning in the 1960s, powerful feminist movements with agendas ranging from equal educational access to legalized abortion took root in the Western industrialized nations and to a lesser degree in Asia, Latin America, and Africa.

Despite this broad support for gender equality, progress for women worldwide was uneven in the 1970s and 1980s. In developed industrial societies, women undoubtedly made great strides. Large numbers of women entered professions such as law, medicine, and university teaching; contraception and abortions were legalized in some nations; laws forbidding gender-based discrimination were passed. Nonetheless, even in developed countries with strong feminist movements women still earned less than men for doing the same job, were underrepresented in managerial positions, and played less significant roles in politics than did men. Furthermore, movements for gender equality met strong opposition from individuals and groups who were convinced that they threatened the family, undermined morality, and left women unhappy and unfulfilled.

In less economically developed parts of the world, efforts to improve the status of women faced even more obstacles. Movements to improve women's legal status were hindered by the small pool of educated women and by the gap between middle-class, urban women and the millions of women in urban slums or rural villages who struggled against poverty. Religious fundamentalists in the Islamic world and elsewhere also sought to keep women in traditional roles. Even in China and India, both of which adopted strong antidiscrimination laws, it proved difficult to modify, let alone eradicate, centuries-old educational patterns, work stereotypes, marriage customs, and attitudes. More so than in almost any other area of modern life, tradition held its own against movements and ideologies seeking to liberate African, Asian, and Latin American women from the burdens of patriarchy and inequality.

Liberal Feminism and Women's Liberation in the United States

110 • NATIONAL ORGANIZATION FOR WOMEN, 1966 STATEMENT OF PURPOSE AND NEW YORK RADICAL WOMEN, "NO MORE MISS AMERICA!" SEPTEMBER, 1968

After having won the right to vote in most Western democracies by the 1920s, the powerful feminist movements of the nineteenth and early twentieth centuries lost momentum. In the 1930s and 1940s, women diverted their energies to surviving the Great Depression and contributing to their nations' efforts in World War II. After 1945, as prosperity returned to the United States and Europe, women were generally content to accept the domestic roles prescribed for them by the family-oriented ethos of the postwar era.

Beginning in the 1960s, feminism reemerged as a powerful force, with much of its impetus and energy derived from movements originating in the United States. The revival of feminism gathered strength in the early 1960s with the appointment by President John F. Kennedy of the Presidential Commission on the Status of Women in 1961, the publication of Betty Friedan's *The Feminine Mystique* in 1963, and the inclusion of gender as one of the categories protected by the Civil Right Act of 1964. The National Organization for Women (NOW), which concentrated on redressing gender-based vocational and educational inequalities, seemed ready after its founding in 1966 to assume leadership of a moderate and liberal women's movement.

Within only a few years, however, calls for legal equality gave way to demands for women's liberation, as the feminist movement became increasingly radical and militant. Radical feminists of the late 1960s were young, and like black militants, were angered by the disparity between American rhetoric about equality and the reality of their lives. In 1967 and 1968, the first radical feminist groups were formed in Chicago, New York, and San Francisco. In 1968, the New York Radical Women pioneered the technique of consciousness-raising, in which women met to participate in open-ended discussions of how societal oppression personally affected them.

The two following excerpts provide insights into the concerns and priorities of moderate and radical U.S. feminists in the 1960 and early 1970s. The first excerpt is from the Statement of Purpose adopted by the National Organization for Women in 1966 (and does not necessarily represent current language or priorities of the organization). It was written by the organization's first president, Betty Friedan, who in 1963 had published the best-selling *The Feminine Mystique,* an indictment of the 1950s cult of domesticity. The second excerpt is from the manifesto "No More Miss America!" distributed by the New York Radical Women in September 1968 at the Miss America Pageant in Atlantic City, New Jersey. Convinced that the pageant encouraged sex-based stereotyping, the women picketed, crowned a sheep as "Miss America," tossed symbols of female "torture" (high heels, dish detergent, bras, and girdles) into a trash can, and interrupted the closing ceremonies. They also handed out the manifesto that is excerpted below. The events at Atlantic City captured headlines around the world and made "women's liberation" a household phrase.

QUESTIONS FOR ANALYSIS

1. According to the NOW Statement of Principles, why are the mid-1960s the right time to advance the "unfinished revolution" of women's equality?
2. According to the NOW statement, what factors have kept women from full equality with men?
3. What evidence does the NOW statement provide to show that women's status and prospects declined in the 1950 and 1960s?
4. According to the "No More Miss America!," what qualities are rewarded at the Miss America Pageant? How is this a disservice to women in general?
5. To what extent do the NOW Statement of Purpose and "No More Miss America!" share common values and goals? Where do the two documents disagree?

NOW Statement of Purpose

Enormous changes taking place in our society make it both possible and urgently necessary to advance the unfinished revolution of women toward true equality, now. With a life span lengthened to nearly 75 years it is no longer either necessary or possible for women to devote the greater part of their lives to child-rearing; yet childbearing and rearing which continues to be a most important part of most women's lives—still is used to justify barring women from equal professional and economic participation and advance.

Today's technology has reduced most of the productive chores which women once performed in the home and in mass-production industries based upon routine unskilled labor.

Source: NOW 1966 Statement of Purpose. Reprinted by permission of National Organization for Women. This is a historical document (1966) and may not reflect the current language or priorities of the organization. New York

Radical Women, "No More Miss America!" reprinted in *The Times Were a Changin': The Sixties Reader,* ed. Irwin Unger and Debi Unger (New York: Three Rivers Press, 1998), pp. 213.

This same technology has virtually eliminated the quality of muscular strength as a criterion for filling most jobs, while intensifying American industry's need for creative intelligence. In view of this new industrial revolution created by automation in the mid-twentieth century, women can and must participate in old and new fields of society in full equality—or become permanent outsiders.

Despite all the talk about the status of American women in recent years, the actual position of women in the United States has declined, and is declining, to an alarming degree throughout the 1950's and 60's. Although 46.4% of all American women between the ages of 18 and 65 now work outside the home, the overwhelming majority—75%—are in routine clerical, sales, or factory jobs, or they are household workers, cleaning women, hospital attendants. About two-thirds of Negro women workers are in the lowest paid service occupations. Working women are becoming increasingly—not less—concentrated on the bottom of the job ladder. . . . In 1964, of all women with a yearly income, 89% earned under $5,000 a year; half of all full-time year round women workers earned less than $3,690; only 1.4% of full-time year round women workers had an annual income of $10,000 or more.

Further, . . . too few women are entering and finishing college or going on to graduate or professional school. Today, women earn only one in three of the B.A.'s and M.A.'s granted, and one in ten of the Ph.D.'s.

In all the professions considered of importance to society, and in the executive ranks of industry and government, women are losing ground. Where they are present it is only a token handful. Women comprise less than 1% of federal judges; less than 4% of all lawyers; 7% of doctors. . . . And, increasingly, men are replacing women in the top positions in secondary and elementary schools, in social work, and in libraries—once thought to be women's fields.

Official pronouncements of the advance in the status of women hide not only the reality of this dangerous decline, but the fact that nothing is being done to stop it. . . . Until now, too few women's organizations and official spokesmen have been willing to speak out against these dangers facing women. Too many women have been restrained by the fear of being called "feminist." There is no civil rights movement to speak for women, as there has been for Negroes and other victims of discrimination. The National Organization for Women must therefore begin to speak. . . .

WE DO NOT ACCEPT the token appointment of a few women to high-level positions in government and industry as a substitute for serious continuing effort to recruit and advance women according to their individual abilities. To this end, we urge American government and industry to mobilize the same resources of ingenuity and command with which they have solved problems of far greater difficulty than those now impeding the progress of women.

WE BELIEVE that this nation has a capacity at least as great as other nations, to innovate new social institutions which will enable women to enjoy the true equality of opportunity and responsibility in society, without conflict with their responsibilities as mothers and homemakers. . . . We question the present expectation that all normal women will retire from job or profession for 10 or 15 years, to devote their full time to raising children, only to reenter the job market at a relatively minor level. . . . Above all, we reject the assumption that these problems are the unique responsibility of each individual woman, rather than a basic social dilemma which society must solve. True equality of opportunity and freedom of choice for women requires such practical, and possible innovations as a nationwide network of child-care centers, which will make it unnecessary for women to retire completely from society until their children are grown, and national programs to provide retraining for women who have chosen to care for their children full-time.

WE BELIEVE that it is as essential for every girl to be educated to her full potential of human ability as it is for every boy—with the knowledge that such education is the key to effective participation in today's economy and that, for a girl as for a boy, education can only be serious where there is expectation that it will be used in society. . . . Moreover, we consider the decline in the proportion of women receiving higher and professional education to be evidence of discrimination. This discrimination may take the form of quotas against the admission of women to colleges, and professional schools; lack of encouragement by parents, counselors and educators; denial of loans or fellowships; or the traditional or arbitrary procedures in graduate and professional training geared in terms of men, which inadvertently discriminate against women. . . .

WE REJECT the current assumptions that a man must carry the sole burden of supporting himself, his wife, and family, and that a woman is automatically entitled to lifelong support by a man upon her marriage, or that marriage, home and family are primarily woman's world and responsibility. . . . We believe that a true partnership between the sexes demands a different concept of marriage, an equitable sharing of the responsibilities of home and children and of the economic burdens of their support. We believe that proper recognition should be given to the economic and social value of homemaking and child-care. To these ends, we will seek to open a reexamination of laws and mores governing marriage and divorce, for we believe that the current state of "half-equity" between the sexes discriminates against both men and women, and is the cause of much unnecessary hostility between the sexes.

WE BELIEVE that women must now exercise their political rights and responsibilities as American citizens. They must refuse to be segregated on the basis of sex into separate-and-not-equal ladies' auxiliaries in the political parties, and they must demand representation according to their numbers in the regularly constituted party committees . . . participating fully in the selection of candidates and political decision-making, and running for office themselves:

IN THE INTERESTS OF THE HUMAN DIGNITY OF WOMEN, we will protest, and endeavor to change, the false image of women now prevalent in the mass media, and in the texts, ceremonies, laws, and practices of our major social institutions. Such images perpetuate contempt for women by society and by women for themselves. We are similarly opposed to all policies and practices—in church, state, college, factory, or office—which, in the guise of protectiveness, not only deny opportunities but also foster in women self-denigration, dependence, and evasion of responsibility, undermine their confidence in their own abilities and foster contempt for women. . . .

WE BELIEVE THAT women will do most to create a new image of women by acting now, and by speaking out in behalf of their own equality, freedom, and human dignity—not in pleas for special privilege, nor in enmity toward men, who are also victims of the current, half-equality between the sexes—but in an active, self-respecting partnership with men. By so doing, women will develop confidence in their own ability to determine actively, in partnership with men, the conditions of their life, their choices, their future and their society.

"No More Miss America!"

We Protest:

The *Degrading Mindless-Boob-Girlie Symbol.* . . . The parade down the runway blares the metaphor of the 4-H Club county fair, where the nervous animals are judged for teeth, fleece, etc., and where the best "specimen" gets the blue ribbon. So are women in our society forced daily to compete for male approval, enslaved by ludicrous "beauty" standards we ourselves are conditioned to take seriously.

Racism with Roses. Since its inception in 1921, the Pageant has not had one Black finalist, and this has not been for a lack of test-case contestants. . . . Nor has there ever been a *true* Miss America—an American Indian.

Miss America as Military Death Mascot. The highlight of her reign each year is a cheerleader-tour of American troops abroad—last year she went to Vietnam to pep-talk our husbands, fathers, sons and boyfriends into dying and killing with a better spirit. . . . We refuse to be used as Mascots for Murder. . . .

Competition Rigged and Unrigged. We deplore the encouragement of an American myth that oppresses men as well as women: the win-or-you're-worthless competitive disease. The "beauty contest" creates only one winner to be "used" and forty-nine losers who are "useless."

The Woman As Pop Culture Obsolescent Theme. . . . What is so ignored as last year's Miss America? This only reflects the gospel of our society, according to Saint Male: women must be young, juicy, malleable—hence age discrimination and the cult of youth. And we women are brain-washed into believing this ourselves! . . .

The Irrelevant Crown on the Throne of Mediocrity. Miss America represents what women are supposed to be: unoffensive, bland, apolitical. If you are tall, short, over or under what weight the Man prescribes you should be, forget it. Personality, articulateness, intelligence, commitment—unwise. Conformity is the key to the crown—and, by extension, to success in our society.

Miss America as Dream Equivalent To—? In this reputedly democratic society, where every little boy supposedly can grow up to be President, what can every little girl hope to grow up to be? Miss America. That's where it's at. Real power to control our own lives is restricted to men, while women get patronizing pseudopower, an ermine cloak and a bunch of flowers . . .

Miss America as Big Sister Watching You. The Pageant exercises Thought Control . . . to further make women oppressed and men oppressors; to enslave us all the more in high-heeled, low-status roles; to inculate false values in young girls; to use women as beasts of buying; to seduce us to prostitute ourselves before our own oppression.

Women and Religious Fundamentalism: The Example of Iran

111 • ZAND DOKHT, "THE REVOLUTION THAT FAILED WOMEN"

Although the Pahlavi rulers of Iran, Reza Shah (1925–1941) and Muhammad Reza Shah (1941–1979), gave women political rights, allowed them to abandon the veil for Western-style dress, and encouraged female literacy and higher education, in the 1970s, millions of Iranian women shared the growing disgust with their government's autocracy, corruption, and secularism. Women played a prominent role in the massive demonstrations that preceded Reza Shah's downfall in 1979 and led to his replacement by an Islamic fundamentalist regime under Ayatollah Ruhulla Khomeini (1902–1989). True to its Islamic principles, Khomeini's government revoked Palhavi legislation on women and the family and reinstated strict Islamic practices.

Iranian women who had taken advantage of educational opportunities and had benefited professionally during the Pahlavi years opposed the Islamic republic's effort to turn back the clock. In 1979, representatives from various women's organizations founded the Women's Solidarity Committee, dedicated to the protection of women's rights in Iran. Although later banned in Iran itself, a branch of the organization was maintained in London by Iranian women living in England. Known as the Iranian Women's Solidarity Group, in the 1980s it published pamphlets and newsletters on issues pertaining to women in Iran. The following selection, written by a Solidarity Committee member, Zand Dokht, appeared in one of their publications in 1981.

QUESTIONS FOR ANALYSIS

1. In what specific ways did the Islamic Revolution in Iran affect women?
2. According to the author, how do Iran's new leaders envision a woman's role in society?
3. How does the author explain the fact that so many Iranian women supported the revolution that toppled the shah?
4. Why in the author's view did Pahlavi-era reforms fail to satisfy large numbers of Iranian women?

When Khomeini created his Islamic Republic in 1979, he relied on the institution of the family, on support from the women, the merchants, and the private system of landownership. The new Islamic constitution declared women's primary position as mothers. The black veil, symbol of the position of women under Islam, was made compulsory. Guards were posted outside government offices to enforce it, and women were sacked from their jobs without compensation for refusing to wear the veil. . . .

Schools were segregated, which meant that women were barred from some technical schools, even from some religious schools, and young girls' education in the villages was halted. Lowering the marriage age for girls to 13, reinstating polygamy and *Sigben* [temporary wives] . . . meant that women did not need education and jobs, they only needed to find husbands.

The Ayatollahs[1] in their numerous public prayers, which grew to be the only possible national activity, continuously gave sermons on the advantages of marriage, family, and children being brought up on their mother's lap. They preached that society would be pure, trouble free, criminalless (look at the youth problem in the West) if everybody married young, and if men married as many times as possible (to save the unprotected women who might otherwise become prostitutes). . . . Another *masterpiece* of the revolutionary Islamic government was to create a system of arranged marriages in prisons, between men and women prisoners, to "protect" women after they leave prison.

Because abortion and contraception are now unobtainable, marriage means frequent pregnancy. If you are 13 when you get married, it is likely that you will have six children by the time you are 20. This, in a country where half the total population are already under 16, is a tragedy for future generations.

Religious morality demands that all pleasures and entertainments be banned. Wine, music, dancing, chess, women's parts in theater, cinema,

---

Source: From Miranda Davies, ed., *Third World, Second Sex* (London: Zed Press, 1983), 152–155. Reprinted by permission of Zed Books.

[1]Ayatollah is a title of respect for high Shiite Muslim religious leaders.

and television—you name it. Khomeini banned it. He even segregated the mountains and the seas, for male and female climbers and swimmers. . . .

Perhaps nowhere else in the world have women been murdered for walking in the street open-faced. The question of the veil is the most important issue of women's liberation in Muslim countries. The veil, a long engulfing black robe, is the extension of the four walls of the home, where women belong. The veil is the historical symbol of woman's oppression, seclusion, denial of her social participation and equal rights with men. It is a cover which defaces and objectifies women. To wear or not to wear the veil, for Muslim women is "the right to choose." . . .

Why do women, workers, and unemployed, support this regime which has done everything in its power to attack their rights and interests? The power of Islam in our culture and tradition has been seriously underestimated . . . and it was through this ideology that Khomeini directed his revolutionary government. The clergy dealt with everyday problems and spoke out on human relationships, sexuality, security, and protection of the family and the spiritual needs of human beings. It was easy for people to identify with these issues and support the clergy, although nobody knew what they were later to do.

Women's attraction to Khomeini's ideas was not based simply on his Islamic politics, but also on the way he criticized the treatment of women—as secretaries and media sex objects—under the Shah's regime. Women were genuinely unsatisfied and looking for change. Some educated Iranian women went back to Iran from America and Europe to aid the clergy with the same messages, and became the government's spokeswomen. They put on the veil willingly, defended Islamic virtues and spiritual values while drawing from their own experiences in the West. They said it was cold and lonely. Western women were only in pursuit of careers and self-sufficiency, and that their polygamous sexual relationships had not brought them liberation, but confusion and exploitation. These women joined ranks with an already growing force of Muslim women, to retrieve the tradition of true/happy Muslim women—in defense of patriarchy.

The mosque is not just a place of prayer, it is also a social club for women. It provides a warm, safe room for women to meet, chat, or listen to a sermon, and there are traditional women-only parties and picnics in gardens or holy places. Take away these traditional and religious customs from women as the Shah—with his capitalist and imperialist reforms, irrelevant to women's needs—tried to do and a huge vacuum is left. Khomeini stepped in to fill that vacuum. The reason why Khomeini won was that the Shah's social-economic program for women was dictatorial, bureaucratic, inadequate (especially in terms of health education) and therefore irrelevant to women's needs. . . .

African Tradition and Western Values: The Issue of Female Genital Mutilation

112 • ASSOCIATION OF AFRICAN WOMEN FOR RESEARCH AND DEVELOPMENT, A STATEMENT ON GENITAL MUTILATION

Female genital mutilation, also referred to as genital cutting or female circumcision, refers to any ritual procedure that involves the partial or complete removal of the external female genitals. The operation, which in different societies may take place anytime from shortly after birth to the onset of puberty, is usually performed by midwives or village women without benefit of anesthesia or antibiotics. No accurate statistics on the prevalence of the practice exist. It is most common in sub-Saharan Africa, especially in the Sudan region, but it is also practiced in many other parts of the world. Presumably instituted to encourage chastity by dulling a woman's sexual desire, the practice has come under harsh criticism both from within the societies in which it exists and from outsiders, especially from the West. Efforts to suppress the practice have had, however, little effect among peoples who consider the custom part of their ethnic and religious heritage and a necessary rite of passage into womanhood.

Western-inspired campaigns to end genital mutilation have frequently backfired, especially in Africa, where the custom is most deeply rooted. The following statement, issued in 1980 by the Association of African Women for Research and Development (AAWORD), which was founded in 1977 in Dakar, Senegal, reveals that even Africans who oppose the practice resent Western interference.

QUESTIONS FOR ANALYSIS

1. What is the basis of the authors' assertion that critics of female circumcision are guilty of "latent racism"?
2. How have Western criticisms of female circumcision hindered the efforts of African critics to limit the practice?
3. In the view of the authors, what would be an appropriate Western approach to the issue of female circumcision?
4. How might an ardent Western critic of female circumcision in Africa counter the arguments contained in the AAWORD statement?

In the last few years, Western public opinion has been shocked to find out that in the middle of the 20th century thousands of women and children have been "savagely mutilated" because of "barbarous customs from another age.". . . There have been press conferences, documentary films, headlines in the newspapers, information days, open letters, action groups—all this to mobilize public opinion and put pressure on governments of the countries where genital mutilation is still practiced. . . .

. . . In trying to reach their own public, the new crusaders have fallen back on sensationalism, and have become insensitive to the dignity of the very women they want to "save." They are totally unconscious of the latent racism which such a campaign evokes in countries where ethnocentric prejudice is so deep-rooted. And in their conviction that this is a "just cause," they have forgotten that these women from a different race and a different culture are also *human beings,* and that solidarity can only exist alongside self-affirmation and mutual respect. . . .

AAWORD, whose aim is to carry out research which leads to the liberation of African women in particular, *firmly condemns* genital mutilation and all other practices—traditional or modern—which oppress women and justify exploiting them

Source: Association of African Women for Research and Development, A Statement on Genital Mutilation.

economically or socially, as a serious violation of the fundamental rights of women. . . .

However, as far as AAWORD is concerned, the fight against genital mutilation, although necessary, should not take on such proportions that the wood cannot be seen for the trees. Young girls and women who are mutilated in Africa are usually among those who cannot even satisfy their basic needs and who have to struggle daily for survival. This is due to the exploitation of developing countries, manifested especially through the impoverishment of the poorest social classes. In the context of the present world economic crisis, tradition, with all of its constraints, becomes more than ever a form of security for the peoples of the Third World, and especially for the "wretched of the earth." For these people, the modern world, which is primarily Western and bourgeois, can only represent aggression at all levels—political, economic, social and cultural. It is unable to propose viable alternatives for them.

Moreover, to fight against genital mutilation without placing it in the context of ignorance, obscurantism, exploitation, poverty, etc., without questioning the structures and social relations which perpetuate this situation, is like "refusing to see the sun in the middle of the day." This, however, is precisely the approach taken by many Westerners, and is highly suspect, especially since Westerners necessarily profit from the exploitation of the peoples and women of Africa, whether directly or indirectly.

Feminists from developed countries—at least those who are sincerely concerned about this situation rather than those who use it only for their personal prestige—should understand this other aspect of the problem. They must accept that it is a problem for *African women,* and that no change is possible without the conscious participation of African women. They must avoid ill-timed interference, maternalism, ethnocentrism and misuse of power. These are attitudes which can only widen the gap between the Western feminist movement and that of the Third World. . . .

On the question of such traditional practices as genital mutilation, African women must no longer equivocate or react only to Western interference. They must speak out in favour of the total eradication of all these practices, and they must lead information and education campaigns to this end within their own countries and on a continental level.

Tradition Trumps Legislation: The Case of the Indian Dowry System

113 • EDITORIAL AGAINST DOWRY FROM MANUSHI

Although some improvement in the status of Indian women took place under British rule, major legislation to advance gender equality took place only after Indian independence in 1947. Women received the right to vote, hold political office, own property, and divorce their husbands; in addition, child marriage and polygamy were outlawed, and restrictions against intercaste marriages were eased. In 1961, the government also outlawed dowries, the gifts of property a new bride's family was expected to make to the husband or the husband's family. The intent of the legislation was to lessen the financial burdens of families with daughters and encourage men from higher castes to marry women from lower castes.

As the following editorial shows, however, the practice of dowries continued, often with tragic results for young married women. This anonymous editorial was originally published in 1979 in *Manushi,* an Indian magazine for women.

QUESTIONS FOR ANALYSIS

1. According to the author of this editorial, is the giving and taking of dowries the result of recent developments or of long-standing Indian traditions?
2. According to the author, why have efforts to end the practice of dowries failed?
3. What does the author see as the solution to the problem?
4. According to the author, to what degree do dowry murders fit into a general pattern of mistreatment of women in Indian society?

Most people are not even aware that the giving and taking of dowry is a legal offense. Since the Prohibition of Dowry Act was passed in 1961, the custom has flowered and flourished, invading castes and communities among whom it was hitherto unknown—sprouting new forms and varieties. It is percolating downwards and becoming so widespread even among the working classes that it is no longer possible to consider it a problem of the middle class alone. . . .

Marriages are made and broken for such items as cars, scooters, TVs, refrigerators and washing machines, wedding receptions in five-star hotels or an air ticket plus the promise of a job for the son-in-law in a foreign country.

In India, we have a glorious heritage of systematic violence on women in the family itself, sati[1] and female infanticide being the two better-known forms. Today, we do not kill girl-babies at birth. We let them die through systematic neglect—the mortality rate among female children is 30–60% higher than among male children. Today, we do not wait till a woman is widowed before we burn her to death. We burn her in the lifetime of her husband so that he can get a new bride with a fatter dowry.

"Woman burnt to death. A case of suicide has been registered. The police are enquiring into the matter." For years, such three-line news items have appeared almost every day in the newspapers and gone unnoticed. It is only lately that dowry deaths are being given detailed coverage. It is not by accident that fuller reporting of such cases has coincided with a spurt of protest demonstrations.

We, as women, have too long been silent spectators, often willing participants in the degrading drama of matrimony—when girls are advertised, displayed, bargained over, and disposed of with the pious injunction: "Daughter, we are sending you to your husband's home. . . . You are not to leave it till your corpse emerges from its doors." Death may be slow in coming—a long process of killing the girl's spirit by harassment, taunts, torture. It may be only too quick—fiery and sudden. Dousing the woman with kerosene and setting her on fire seems to have become the most popular way of murdering a daughter-in-law because with police connivance it is the easiest to make out as a case of suicide or accident.

Source: from Madhu Kishwar and Ruth Vanita, *In Search of Answers: Voices from Manushi* (London: Zed Books, 1984), 246–248. Reprinted by permission of Zed Books.

[1]Sati is the custom in which a Hindu widow is willingly cremated on the funeral pyre of her dead husband as a sign of devotion to him.

And for every one reported murder, hundreds go unreported, especially in rural areas where it is almost impossible to get redress unless one is rich and influential. . . .

Why is it that gifts have to be given with the daughter? Hindu scriptures proclaim that the girl herself is the most precious of gifts "presented" by her father to her husband. Thus the money transaction between families is bound up with the marriage transaction whereby the girl becomes a piece of transferrable property. So little is a woman worth that a man has literally to be paid to take her off her father's hands. The dramatic increase in dowry-giving in the post-independence period reflects the declining value of women in our society. Their only worth is as reproducers who provide "legitimate" heirs for their husbands' property. . . .

. . . We appeal, therefore, to all the women's organizations to undertake a broad-based united action on this issue and launch an intensive, concerted campaign instead of the isolated, sporadic protests which . . . can have only a short-term, limited impact.

Perhaps even more urgent is the need to begin the movement from our own homes. Are we sure that none of us who participated so vociferously in these demonstrations will take dowry from our parents or give it to our daughters in however veiled a form? That we will rather say "No" to marriage than live a life of humiliations and compromises? Do we have the courage to boycott marriages where dowry is given? . . . Will we socially ostracize such people, no matter how close they are to us? All the protest demonstrations will be only so much hot air unless we are prepared to create pressures against dowry beginning from our own homes.

Communism's Retreat

The Cold War era was a time of moral and ideological absolutes. On one side was the communist world, characterized by authoritarian, one-party governments, centralized economic planning, and a commitment to the worldwide victory of Marxism over capitalism. On the other side was the "free world," a bloc of nations led by the United States, with the goal of defending capitalism and spreading liberal democracy. For more than 40 years, these two blocs formed formidable military alliances, built up huge nuclear arsenals, supported giant intelligence establishments, and competed for support among nonaligned nations. For both sides, the dualisms of the Cold War—communism versus capitalism, the United States versus the Soviet Union, NATO versus the Warsaw Pact—gave direction and meaning to international politics.

In reality, the Cold War was never completely about ideology. From its start, the United States and its allies propped up dictators when it served their purposes. Furthermore, cracks and fissures appeared in both coalitions as early as the 1950s. Anti-Soviet revolts took place in Eastern Europe in 1956 and 1968, and relations between China and the Soviet Union cooled in the mid-1960s. Also in the 1960s, the prospering, stable democracies of Western Europe, inspired by the independent diplomatic course of France's leader, Charles de Gaulle, no longer unquestioningly accepted U.S. policies concerning military deployment in Europe and U.S. involvement in Vietnam.

There were times when the Cold War seemed about to end, but on each occasion, old tensions returned. Peaceful coexistence in the late 1950s gave way to renewed acrimony after the downing of a U.S. spy plane over Soviet territory in 1960, the building of the Berlin Wall in 1961, and the Cuban missile crisis of 1962. U.S.–Soviet relations improved in the 1970s, but again deteriorated after the Soviet invasion of Afghanistan in 1979. In the early 1980s, President Ronald Reagan branded the Soviet Union an "evil empire," and Soviet suspicions of the United States deepened. No one expected anything other than continuing U.S.–Soviet conflict.

By 1991, however, the Cold War was over. In one state after another, communist regimes in Eastern Europe either collapsed or were voted out of power and replaced by democracies. Within the Soviet Union, Premier Mikhail Gorbachev in 1985 initiated policies of *glasnost* (openness) and *perestroika* (restructuring) to rejuvenate Soviet society. But his efforts to save communism by democratization and economic liberalization had unexpected results: by the end of 1991, communist rule and the Soviet Union itself had ceased to exist.

Profound changes also took place in China. After the death of Mao Zedong in 1976, China's new leader, Deng Xiaoping, deemphasized ideology and egalitarianism in favor of pragmatism and economic development. He ordered the opening of small private businesses, fostered a market economy in agriculture, sought foreign investment, supported scientific and technological education, and encouraged Chinese exports of manufactured goods. The result was economic growth rates of 12 percent annually in the early 1990s. China remained officially communist, but with its commitment to "market socialism," it was far different from the isolated, ideology-driven China of previous decades.

China's New Course

114 • DENG XIAOPING, SPEECHES AND WRITINGS

Of all the events of the late twentieth century, China's full entry into the global economy and its decision to commit itself to economic development may prove to be the most significant. For centuries, China was the world's most successful state in terms of size, wealth, technological sophistication, and strength of its political institutions. This was easy to forget in the nineteenth and twentieth centuries, when China became a pawn of the Western powers and a victim of political breakdown, military defeat, and deepening poverty. In the 1980s, however, China's leaders set a new course that seems destined to restore China to its preeminence in Asia, if not its primacy among the world's powers.

The man who launched China on its new path was Deng Xiaoping. Born into the family of a well-off landowner in 1904, Deng studied in China and then in post–World War I France, where he supported himself as a kitchen helper and a laborer. He also embraced Marxism, which he studied further in Moscow in 1925–1926. On his return to China in 1927, he joined the Communist Party and became one of Mao's most loyal followers.

After the communists took control of China in 1949, Deng became a Politburo member and party secretary general, with responsibility for overseeing economic development in southwest China. He supported the strategy of developing China's economy by following the Stalinist model of agricultural collectivization, centralized planning, and investment in heavy industry. This was scrapped in 1958 when Mao instituted the Great Leap Forward. As we have seen (source 109), the Great Leap Forward was a spectacular failure, and in its wake, Deng and other moderates dismantled the communes and reintroduced centralized planning.

This made Deng a prime candidate for vilification after Mao launched the Great Cultural Revolution in 1966. Designed to revive revolutionary fervor and rescue China from materialism and Soviet-style bureaucratization, the revolution unleashed the energies of millions of young people who were urged to rise up and smash "bourgeois" elements throughout society. Deng fell from power, was paraded through the streets in a dunce cap, and was put to work in a mess hall and a tractor repair shop. As the Cultural Revolution faded, Deng was reinstated as a party official, and after Mao's death in 1976, he led the moderates in their struggle with the radical faction led by Mao's widow, Jiang Qing. Deng's faction won, and in December 1978, the Central Committee of the Chinese Communist Party officially abandoned Mao's emphasis on ideology and class struggle in favor of a moderate, pragmatic policy designed to achieve the Four Modernizations in agriculture, industry, science and technology, and the military.

To encourage economic growth, the government fostered free markets, competition, and private incentives. Although Deng claimed that China had entered its "second revolution," it was an economic revolution only. When millions of Chinese demonstrated for democracy in the spring of 1989, the government crushed the demonstration in Beijing with soldiers and tanks, thus ensuring the continuation of the party dictatorship. After 1989, Deng withdrew from public life, and he died in early 1997. The following excerpts are from speeches and interviews given by Deng between 1983 and 1986.

QUESTIONS FOR ANALYSIS

1. According to Deng, what had been the shortcomings of China's economic development planning under Mao Zedong?
2. According to Deng, how is China's new economic policy truly Marxist and truly socialist?
3. How does Deng view China's role in the world? What implications will China's new economic priorities have for its foreign policy?
4. What is Deng's rationale for opposing democracy in China?

Maoism's Flaws

Comrade Mao Zedong was a great leader. . . . But he made the grave mistake of neglecting the development of the productive forces. I do not mean he didn't want to develop them. The point is, not all of the methods he used were correct. For instance, the people's communes were established in defiance of the laws governing socio-economic development. The most important lesson we have learned, among a great many others, is that we must be clear about what socialism is and how to build it. . . .

The goal for Marxists is to realize communism, which must be built on the basis of highly developed productive forces. What is a communist society? It is a society in which there is vast material wealth and in which the principle of from each according to his ability, to each according to his needs is applied. . . .

Our experience in the 20 years from 1958 to 1978 teaches us that poverty is not socialism, that socialism means eliminating poverty. Unless you are developing the productive forces and raising people's living standards, you cannot say that you are building socialism.

After the Third Plenary Session[1] we proceeded to explore ways of building socialism in China. . . . The first goal we set was to achieve comparative prosperity by the end of the century. . . . So taking population increase into consideration, we planned to quadruple our GNP [Gross National Product], which meant that per capita GNP would grow from $250 to $800 or $1,000. We shall lead a much better life when we reach this level, although it is still much lower than that of the developed countries. That is why we call it comparative prosperity. When we attain that level, China's GNP will have reached $1,000 billion,

representing increased national strength. And the most populous nation in the world will have shaken off poverty and be able to make a greater contribution to mankind. With a GNP of $1,000 billion as a springboard, within 30 or 50 more years—50, to be more accurate—China may reach its second goal, to approach the level of the developed countries. How are we to go about achieving these goals? . . . We began our reform in the countryside. The main point of the rural reform has been to bring the peasants' initiative into full play by introducing the responsibility system and discarding the system whereby everybody ate from the same big pot. Why did we start in the countryside? Because that is where 80 per cent of China's population lives. If we didn't raise living standards in the countryside, the society would be unstable. Industry, commerce and other sectors of the economy cannot develop on the basis of the poverty of 80 per cent of the population. After three years of practice the rural reform has proved successful. . . . The countryside has assumed a new look. The living standards of 90 per cent of the rural population have been raised. . . .

Urban reform is more complicated and risky. This is especially true in China, because we have no experience in this regard. Also, China has traditionally been a very closed society, so that people lack information about what's going on elsewhere. . . .

It is our hope that businessmen and economists in other countries will appreciate that to help China develop will benefit the world. China's foreign trade volume makes up a very small portion of the world's total. If we succeed in quadrupling the GNP, the volume of our foreign trade will increase considerably, promoting China's economic relations with other countries and

Source: Deng Xiaoping, *Fundamental Issues in Present-Day China* (Beijing: Foreign Languages Press, 1987), pp. 42–44, 69–72, 101–102, 105–109, 162–163. Reprinted by permission.

[1]The Third Plenary Session of Eleventh Central Committee of the Chinese Communist Party, held in December 1978, approved the Four Modernizations Program favored by Deng.

expanding its market. Therefore, judged from the perspective of world politics and economics, China's development will benefit world peace and the world economy. . . .

True Socialism

Our modernization programme is a socialist programme, not anything else. All our policies for carrying out reform, opening to the outside world and invigorating the domestic economy are designed to develop the socialist economy. We allow the development of individual economy, of joint ventures with both Chinese and foreign investment and of enterprises wholly owned by foreign businessmen, but socialist public ownership will always remain predominant. The aim of socialism is to make all our people prosperous, not to create polarization. If our policies led to polarization, it would mean that we had failed; if a new bourgeoisie emerged, it would mean that we had strayed from the right path. In encouraging some regions to become prosperous first, we intend that they should help the economically backward ones to develop. Similarly, in encouraging some people to become prosperous first, we intend that they should help others who are still in poverty to become better off, so that there will be common prosperity rather than polarization. A limit should be placed on the wealth of people who become prosperous first, through the income tax, for example. In addition, we should encourage them to contribute money to run schools and build roads. . . . We should encourage these people to make donations, but it's better not to give such donations too much publicity.

In short, predominance of public ownership and common prosperity are the two fundamental socialist principles that we must adhere to. We shall firmly put them into practice. And ultimately we shall move on to communism.

Special Economic Zones

In establishing special economic zones[2] and implementing an open policy, we must make it clear that our guideline is just that—to open and not to close.

I was impressed by the prosperity of the Shenzhen[3] Special Economic Zone during my stay there. The pace of construction in Shenzhen is rapid. It is particularly fast in Shekou, because the authorities there are permitted to make their own spending decisions up to a limit of U.S. $5 million. Their slogan is "time is money, efficiency is life." In Shenzhen, it doesn't take long to erect a tall building; the workers complete a storey in a couple of days. . . . Their high efficiency is due to the "contracted responsibility system," under which they are paid according to their performance, and to a fair system of rewards and penalties.

A special economic zone is a medium for introducing technology, management and knowledge. It is also a window for our foreign policy. Through the special economic zone we can import foreign technology, obtain knowledge and learn management, which is also a kind of knowledge. . . . Public order in Shenzhen is reportedly better than before, and people who slipped off to Hong Kong have begun to return. One reason is that there are more job opportunities and people's incomes and living standards are rising, all of which proves that cultural and ideological progress is based on material progress.

China's Foreign Relations

Reviewing our history, we have concluded that one of the most important reasons for China's long years of stagnation and backwardness was its policy of closing the country to outside contact. Our experience shows that China cannot rebuild itself with its doors closed to the outside and

---

[2]Special Economic Zones were restricted areas where foreign firms could set up businesses and house foreign personnel.

[3]A district in southern China's Guangdong province, situated just north of Hong Kong. The area was one of the first Special Economic Zones.

that it cannot develop in isolation from the rest of the world. It goes without saying that a large country like China cannot depend on others for its development; it must depend mainly on itself, on its own efforts. Nevertheless, while holding to self-reliance, we should open our country to the outside world to obtain such aid as foreign investment capital and technology. . . .

China's Political Future

The recent student unrest[4] is not going to lead to any major disturbances. But because of its nature it must be taken very seriously. Firm measures must be taken against any student who creates trouble at Tiananmen Square. . . . In the beginning, we mainly used persuasion, which is as it should be in dealing with student demonstrators. But if any of them disturb public order or violate the law, they must be dealt with unhesitatingly. Persuasion includes application of the law. When a disturbance breaks out in a place, it's because the leaders there didn't take a firm, clear-cut stand. This is not a problem that has arisen in just one or two places or in just the last couple of years; it is the result of failure over the past several years to take a firm, clear-cut stand against bourgeois liberalization. It is essential to adhere firmly to the Four Cardinal Principles;[5] otherwise bourgeois liberalization will spread unchecked— and that has been the root cause of the problem. . . .

In developing our democracy, we cannot simply copy bourgeois democracy, or introduce the system of a balance of three powers. I have often criticized people in power in the United States, saying that actually they have three governments. Of course, the American bourgeoisie uses this system in dealing with other countries, but when it comes to internal affairs, the three branches often pull in different directions, and that makes trouble. We cannot adopt such a system. . . .

Without leadership by the Communist Party and without socialism, there is no future for China. This truth has been demonstrated in the past, and it will be demonstrated again in future. When we succeed in raising China's per capita GNP to $4,000 and everyone is prosperous, that will better demonstrate the superiority of socialism over capitalism, it will point the way for three quarters of the world's population and it will provide further proof of the correctness of Marxism. Therefore, we must confidently keep to the socialist road and uphold the Four Cardinal Principles.

We cannot do without dictatorship. We must not only affirm the need for it but exercise it when necessary. Of course, we must be cautious about resorting to dictatorial means and make as few arrests as possible. But if some people attempt to provoke bloodshed, what are we going to do about it? We should first expose their plot and then do our best to avoid shedding blood, even if that means some of our own people get hurt. However, ringleaders who have violated the law must be sentenced according to law. Unless we are prepared to do that, it will be impossible to put an end to disturbances. If we take no action and back down, we shall only have more trouble down the road.

The struggle against bourgeois liberalization is also indispensable. We should not be afraid that it will damage our reputation abroad. China must take its own road and build socialism with Chinese characteristics—that is the only way China can have a future. We must show foreigners that China's political situation is stable. If our country were plunged into disorder and our nation reduced to a heap of loose sand, how could we ever prosper? The reason the imperialists were able to bully us in the past was precisely that we were a heap of loose sand.

---

[4]Deng made these remarks in December 1986, when student demonstrations and speechmaking on behalf of the pro-democracy movement had been going on in Tiananmen Square in Beijing for several years.

[5]Issued by Deng in 1979, the Four Cardinal Principles were (1) the socialist path, (2) the dictatorship of the proletariat, (3) party leadership, and (4) Marxism/Leninism/Mao Zedong thought.

A Plan to Save Communism in the Soviet Union

115 • MIKHAIL GORBACHEV, PERESTROIKA

In the 1970s and early 1980s, the Soviet Union was viewed as one of the world's two superpowers, with an enormous army, a huge industrial establishment, a record of impressive technological achievement, and a seemingly unshakable authoritarian government. In reality, industrial output and agricultural production were stagnating, the people's morale was plummeting, and the fossilized bureaucracy was mired in old policies and theories that no longer worked. Against this background Mikhail Gorbachev became general secretary of the Communist Party in March 1985 and began the task of rejuvenating Soviet communism by introducing policies based on *glasnost*, or openness, and *perestroika*, or restructuring.

Gorbachev, who was 54 years old when he took power, was born of peasant parents and had studied law and agricultural economics. After filling a variety of positions in the Communist Party, he became a member of the politburo in 1979. In 1987, he published a book, *Perestroika,* from which the following excerpt is taken. In it, he describes his goals for Soviet communism. He fell from power in 1991, with his reforms having led not to communism's reform but to its demise and not to the Soviet Union's revival but to its collapse.

QUESTIONS FOR ANALYSIS

1. What developments in the Soviet Union led Gorbachev to the conclusion that Soviet society and government were in need of reform?
2. In Gorbachev's analysis, what caused Soviet society to "lose its momentum"?
3. In Gorbachev's view, how will the "individual" in Soviet society be affected by his reforms?
4. To what extent is perestroika democratic?
5. What similarities and differences do you see between Gorbachev's statements about perestroika and Deng's comments about the needs of China (source 114)?

Russia, where a great Revolution took place seventy years ago, is an ancient country with a unique history filled with searchings, accomplishments, and tragic events. It has given the world many discoveries and outstanding personalities.

However, the Soviet Union is a young state without analogues in history or in the modern world. Over the past seven decades—a short span in the history of human civilization—our country has traveled a path equal to centuries. One of the mightiest powers in the world rose up to replace

Source: From *Perestroika* by Mikhail Gorbachev, pp. 18–19, 21–25, 30–36. Copyright © 1987 by Mikhail Gorbachev. Reprinted by permission of HarperCollins Publishers.

the backward semi-colonial and semi-feudal Russian Empire. . . .

At some stage—this became particularly clear in the latter half of the seventies—something happened that was at first sight inexplicable. The country began to lose momentum. Economic failures became more frequent. Difficulties began to accumulate and deteriorate, and unresolved problems to multiply. Elements of what we call stagnation and other phenomena alien to socialism began to appear in the life of society. A kind of "braking mechanism" affecting social and economic development formed. And all this happened at a time when scientific and technological revolution opened up new prospects for economic and social progress. . . .

Analyzing the situation, we first discovered a slowing economic growth. In the last fifteen years the national income growth rates had declined by more than a half and by the beginning of the eighties had fallen to a level close to economic stagnation. A country that was once quickly closing on the world's advanced nations began to lose one position after another. . . .

. . . We spent, in fact we are still spending, far more on raw materials, energy, and other resources per unit of output than other developed nations. Our country's wealth in terms of natural and manpower resources has spoilt, one may even say corrupted, us. . . .

The presentation of a "problem-free" reality backfired: a breach had formed between word and deed, which bred public passivity and disbelief in the slogans being proclaimed. It was only natural that this situation resulted in a credibility gap: everything that was proclaimed from the rostrums and printed in newspapers and textbooks was put in question. Decay began in public morals; the great feeling of solidarity with each other that was forged during the heroic times of the Revolution, the first five-year plans, the Great Patriotic War,[1]

and postwar rehabilitation was weakening; alcoholism, drug addiction, and crime were growing; and the penetration of the stereotypes of mass culture alien to us, which bred vulgarity and low tastes and brought about ideological barrenness, increased.

. . . [M]ass distribution of awards, titles, and bonuses often replaced genuine concern for the people, for their living and working conditions, for a favorable social atmosphere. An atmosphere emerged of "everything goes," and fewer and fewer demands were made on discipline and responsibility. Attempts were made to cover it all up with pompous campaigns and undertakings and celebrations of numerous anniversaries centrally and locally. The world of day-to-day realities and the world of feigned prosperity were diverging more and more. . . .

By saying all this I want to make the reader understand that the energy for revolutionary change has been accumulating amid our people and in the Party for some time. And the ideas of perestroika have been prompted not just by pragmatic interests and considerations but also by our troubled conscience, by the indomitable commitment to ideals which we inherited from the Revolution and as a result of a theoretical quest which gave us a better knowledge of society and reinforced our determination to go ahead.

Today our main job is to lift the individual spiritually, respecting his inner world and giving him moral strength. We are seeking to make the whole intellectual potential of society and all the potentialities of culture work to mold a socially active person, spiritually rich, just, and conscientious. An individual must know and feel that his contribution is needed, that his dignity is not being infringed upon, that he is being treated with trust and respect. When an individual sees all this, he is capable of accomplishing much.

---

[1]World War II.

Of course, perestroika somehow affects everybody; it jolts many out of their customary state of calm and satisfaction at the existing way of life. Here I think it is appropriate to draw your attention to one specific feature of socialism. I have in mind the high degree of social protection in our society. On the one hand, it is, doubtless, a benefit and a major achievement of ours. On the other, it makes some people spongers.

There is virtually no unemployment. The state has assumed concern for ensuring employment. Even a person dismissed for laziness or a breach of labor discipline must be given another job. Also, wage-leveling has become a regular feature of our everyday life: even if a person is a bad worker, he gets enough to live fairly comfortably. The children of an outright parasite will not be left to the mercy of fate. We have enormous sums of money concentrated in the social funds from which people receive financial assistance. The same funds provide subsidies for the upkeep of kindergartens, orphanages, Young Pioneer[2] houses, and other institutions related to children's creativity and sport. Health care is free, and so is education. People are protected from the vicissitudes of life, and we are proud of this.

But we also see that dishonest people try to exploit these advantages of socialism; they know only their rights, but they do not want to know their duties: they work poorly, shirk, and drink hard. There are quite a few people who have adapted the existing laws and practices to their own selfish interests. They give little to society, but nevertheless managed to get from it all that is possible. . . .

The policy of restructuring puts everything in its place. We are fully restoring the principle of socialism. "From each according to his ability, to each according to his work," and we seek to affirm social justice for all, equal rights for all, one law

for all, one kind of discipline for all, and high responsibilities for each. Perestroika raises the level of social responsibility and expectation. . . .

It is essential to learn to adjust policy in keeping with the way it is received by the masses, and to ensure feedback, absorbing the ideas, opinions, and advice coming from the people. The masses suggest a lot of useful and interesting things which are not always clearly perceived "from the top.". . .

The Plenary Meeting encouraged extensive efforts to strengthen the democratic basis of Soviet society, to develop self-government and extend glasnost, that is openness, in the entire management network. We see now how stimulating that impulse was for the nation. Democratic changes have been taking place at every work collective, at every state and public organization, and within the Party. More glasnost, genuine control from "below," and greater initiative and enterprise at work are now part and parcel of our life. . . .

Perestroika means overcoming the stagnation process, breaking down the braking mechanism, creating a dependable and effective mechanism for the acceleration of social and economic progress and giving it greater dynamism.

Perestroika means mass initiative. It is the comprehensive development of democracy, socialist self-government, encouragement of initiative and creative endeavor, improved order and discipline, more glasnost, criticism, and self-criticism in all spheres of our society. It is utmost respect for the individual and consideration for personal dignity.

Perestroika is the all-round intensification of the Soviet economy, the revival and development of the principles of democratic centralism in running the national economy, the universal introduction of economic methods, the renunciation of management by injunction and by administrative methods, and the overall encouragement of innovation and socialist enterprise.

---

[2]A youth organization sponsored by the Soviet regime.

Perestroika means a resolute shift to scientific methods, an ability to provide a solid scientific basis for every new initiative. It means the combination of the achievements of the scientific and technological revolution with a planned economy.

Perestroika means priority development of the social sphere aimed at ever better satisfaction of the Soviet people's requirements for good living and working conditions, for good rest and recreation, education, and health care. It means unceasing concern for cultural and spiritual wealth, for the culture of every individual and society as a whole.

Perestroika means the elimination from society of the distortions of socialist ethics, the consistent implementation of the principles of social justice. It means the unity of words and deeds, rights and duties. It is the elevation of honest, highly-qualified labor, the overcoming of leveling tendencies in pay and consumerism.

I stress once again: perestroika is not some kind of illumination or revelation. To restructure our life means to understand the objective necessity for renovation and acceleration. And that necessity emerged in the heart of our society. The essence of perestroika lies in the fact that it *unites socialism with democracy* and revives the Leninist concept of socialist construction both in theory and in practice. Such is the essence of perestroika, which accounts for its genuine revolutionary spirit and its all-embracing scope.

The goal is worth the effort. And we are sure that our effort will be a worthy contribution to humanity's social progress.

Terrorism in a Global Age

On the morning of September 11, 2001, four U.S. commercial airliners—two from Logan Airport in Boston, one from Dulles International Airport in Washington, D.C., and one from Newark International Airport in New Jersey—were hijacked shortly after departure by members of al-Qaeda, a terrorist organization founded in the 1980s by Osama bin Laden. One of the four jets was commandeered by passengers and crashed in a field in southwestern Pennsylvania with no survivors, but the other three found their targets. One was flown to Washington, D.C., where it crashed into the Pentagon, the symbol of U.S. military might; the other two were flown to New York City, where they smashed into the twin towers of the World Trade Center, a symbol of U.S. capitalism. The twin towers were destroyed, more than 3,000 people were killed, and fighting terrorism became the priority of governments around the world.

Terrorism as a political weapon has a long history. Many histories of the subject begin with the first century C.E., when Roman authorities financed dissidents and malcontents to murder enemies in subject territories or neighboring states, and members of a small Jewish sect assassinated officials and prominent individuals in and around Jerusalem to bring about the end of Roman rule in Palestine. Terrorism's history includes the Persian religious sect, the Assassins, who used murder to end the rule of the Seljuk Turks in Southwest Asia; Catholics who sought to undermine England's Protestant government by plotting to blow up the houses of

Parliament in 1605; and European anarchists and radical socialists who assassinated some 50 prominent politicians and heads of state from the late 1800s through the early 1900s. The assassination of Austro-Hungarian Archduke Franz-Ferdinand in July 1914 by a member of the Serbian sect called "Union or Death" led directly to the outbreak of World War I one month later.

After subsiding during and after World War I, terrorism revived after World War II. Beginning in the late 1940s, terrorist acts have taken place in every part of the world and have been carried out by groups espousing many different causes: radical Zionists in post–World War II Palestine; anticolonialists in Africa and Asia; left-wing radicals in Europe; Arabs bent on the destruction of Israel; abortion foes in the United States; religious extremists in India, Northern Ireland, Indonesia, and Africa; enemies of apartheid in South Africa; and Chechen separatists in Russia, to name but a few. They also include obscure religious sects such as Aum Shinrikyo, whose members killed 12 and injured thousands when they released sarin gas in the Tokyo subway system in 1995; alienated individuals such as Theodore Kaczynski, the American opponent of technology whose letter bombs killed 3 and injured 23 before his arrest in 1997; and self-proclaimed patriots like Timothy McVeigh, who sought to strike a blow against the "tyranny" of the U.S. government in 1995, when his truck bomb destroyed the federal building in Oklahoma City and killed 168.

In recent decades, terrorism has been identified especially with the Middle East, whose peoples are both victims of terrorism and a major source of recruitment, organizational effort, and financing for terrorist activities around the world. Terrorist bombings, hijackings, kidnappings, and assassinations related to political and religious conflict in the region took more than 1,000 lives from the 1970s through the 1990s, but it was the attacks on the World Trade Center and the Pentagon on September 11, 2001, that caused a seismic shift in world politics and made the prevention of terrorism the twenty-first century's first great challenge. The two sources in this section seek to provide insight into the beliefs and values of those who were responsible for that attack.

The Worldview of Osama bin Laden

116 • OSAMA BIN LADEN, DECLARATION OF JIHAD AGAINST AMERICANS OCCUPYING THE LAND OF THE TWO HOLY MOSQUES

Osama bin Laden, the founder of al-Qaeda, was born in 1957 in Saudi Arabia, the son of a billionaire owner of a construction company and a cultured Syrian woman who was his tenth or eleventh wife. Young bin Laden led a privileged existence of private schooling, Scandinavian vacations, and English lessons in Oxford. At 17, he enrolled as a civil engineering student at King Abdul Aziz University in Jidda, Saudi Arabia, where he became interested in Islamic theology and forged friendships with Islamic radicals. In 1980, he went to the Pakistani–Afghan border to aid Afghan holy warriors, or mujahedeen, who were fighting Soviet troops who had invaded Afghanistan in late 1979 to prop up the pro-Soviet regime. Using his inheritance (perhaps as much as $300 million), he organized an office to provide support and weapons for the thousands of Muslim volunteers; from the mid-1980s onward, he joined the fighting. Out of these contacts and activities, al-Qaeda (meaning "the base" in Arabic) took shape under bin Laden's guidance.

On his return to Saudi Arabia, bin Laden became an outspoken critic of the Saudi regime for its corruption, secularism, and acceptance of the U.S. military presence during and after the first Persian Gulf War. In 1991, he fled to Sudan, where he extended and expanded al-Qaeda to include as many as several thousand agents who worked in cells ranging from the Philippines to the United States. Between 1992 and 1995, al-Qaeda was linked to attacks on U.S. troops in Yemen and Somalia, the bombing of an American-operated Saudi National Guard training center in Riyadh, and unsuccessful plots to assassinate Pope John Paul II, U.S. president Clinton, and Egyptian president Hosni Mubarak. Under U.S. pressure, Sudan expelled bin Laden in 1996, forcing al-Qaeda to relocate its base to Afghanistan, which was coming under the control of the radical Islamic group known as the Taliban. Between 1996 and 2000, al-Qaeda was responsible for more acts of terrorism, including the car bombing of an apartment building in Dhahran, Saudi Arabia, that killed 19 U.S. soldiers; the simultaneous bombings of U.S. embassies in Tanzania and Kenya that killed 234 and injured several thousand; and the attack on the USS *Cole* in Aden, Yemen, that killed 17 U.S. sailors and wounded 39. After the attacks of September 11, 2001, the United States invaded Afghanistan, ended Taliban rule, and smashed al-Qaeda headquarters and training camps. Bin Laden eluded capture, however, presumably moving to the mountainous region straddling the Pakistani–Afghan border.

Bin Laden has published little and as leader of a secret terrorist organization has given few interviews or public speeches. One exception is the speech he delivered to his followers in Afghanistan in August 1996 in which he "declared war" on the United States. Printed in Arabic-language newspapers and audiotaped for world-wide distribution, bin Laden's speech describes his motives and priorities.

QUESTIONS FOR ANALYSIS

1. How does bin Laden perceive the Muslims' place in the world? Who are their main enemies?
2. Why does bin Laden oppose the existing government of Saudi Arabia?
3. What are the goals of the "Zionist-Crusaders alliance," according to bin Laden?
4. What lessons can be learned, according to bin Laden, by the U.S. response to terrorist attacks and military setbacks in Beirut, Aden, and Somalia?
5. Why is bin Laden convinced that Muslims will triumph in their struggle with the United States?
6. What do you perceive as bin Laden's ultimate political and religious goals?

It should not be hidden from you that the community of Islam has suffered from aggression, iniquity and injustice imposed on them by the Zionist-Crusaders alliance and their collaborators. . . . Their blood was spilled in Palestine and Iraq. The horrifying pictures of the massacre of Qana[1] in Lebanon are still fresh in our memory. Massacres in Tajikistan, Burma, Kashmir, Assam, the Philippines, Fatani, Oga-din, Somalia, Eritrea, Chechnya and in Bosnia-Herzegovina[2] took place, massacres that send shivers in the body and shake the conscience. All of this and the world watched and listened, and not only didn't respond to these atrocities, but also with a conspiracy between the USA and its allies and under the cover of the iniquitous United Nations the dispossessed people were even prevented from obtaining arms to defend themselves.

The people of Islam awakened and realized that they are the main target for the aggression of the Zionist-Crusaders alliance. All false claims and propaganda about "Human Rights" were hammered down and exposed by the massacres that took place against the Muslims in every part of the world. . . .

Today we work to lift the iniquity that had been imposed on the Umma [the Muslim community] by the Zionist-Crusaders alliance, particularly after they have occupied the blessed land of Jerusalem . . . and the land of the two Holy Places.[3] . . . We wish to study the means by which we could return the situation [in Saudi Arabia] to its normal path and to return to the people their own rights, particularly after the large damages and the great aggression on the life and the religion of the people. . . .

Injustice [in Saudi Arabia] had affected the people in industry and agriculture. It affected the people of the rural and urban areas. And almost everybody complains about something. The situation at the land of the two Holy Places became like a huge volcano at the verge of eruption that would destroy the Kuffar [non-believers] and the corruption and its sources. . . . People are fully concerned about their everyday living; everybody talks about the deterioration of the economy, inflation, ever increasing debts and jails full of prisoners.

Through its course of actions the regime has torn off its legitimacy:

(1) Suspension of the Islamic Sharia law and exchanging it with man-made civil law. . . .

(2) The inability of the regime to protect the country and allowing the enemy of the Umma, the American crusader forces, to occupy the land for the longest of years. . . . As a result of the policy imposed on the country, especially in the oil industry where production is restricted or expanded and prices are fixed to suit the American economy, ignoring the economy of the country. Expensive deals were imposed on the country to purchase arms. People are asking what then is the justification for the very existence of the regime?

But to our deepest regret the regime refused to listen to the people. . . .

Source: "Declaration of Jihad Against Americans Occupying the Land of the Two Holy Mosques," from http//azzam. com/html/articlesdeclaration htm.

[1]In April 1996, the Israelis launched a two-week bombardment of territory in southern Lebanon against the terrorist group Hezbollah. On April 18, 100 civilians were killed when the Israelis shelled the battalion headquarters of a UN peacekeeping force where some 800 Lebanese had taken refuge. The Israelis blamed "technical and procedural errors," an explanation questioned by an official UN report.

[2]This is a rather wide-ranging list. The massacres in Assam, a province of northeastern India, were carried out by an Assam separatist group in 1990 and claimed several dozen victims, not all of whom were Muslims. Attacks on Burmese (Myanmar) Muslims in the early 1990s were carried out by Buddhists.

[3]Mecca, the birthplace of Muhammad and the site of the Kabah, Islam's holiest shrine, and Medina, the city to which Muhammad and his followers fled in 622 C.E. Both are in Saudi Arabia.

The regime is fully responsible for what has been incurred by the country and the nation; however, the occupying American enemy is the principal and the main cause of the situation. Therefore efforts should be concentrated on destroying, fighting and killing the enemy until, by the Grace of Allah, it is completely defeated. . . .

* * *

It is incredible that our country is the world's largest buyer of arms from the USA and the area's biggest commercial partner of the Americans who are assisting their Zionist brothers in occupying Palestine and in evicting and killing the Muslims there, by providing arms, men and financial support. To deny these occupiers . . . the enormous revenues from their trade with our country is a very important help for our Jihad against them. . . .

We expect the women of the land of the two Holy Places and other countries to carry out their role in boycotting the American goods. If economic boycott is intertwined with the military operations of the Mujahedeen [holy warriors], then defeating the enemy will be even nearer, by the Permission of Allah. . . .

* * *

A few days ago the news agencies had reported that the Defense Secretary[4] of the Crusading Americans had said that "the explosions at Riyadh and Al Khobar[5] had taught him one lesson: that is, not to withdraw when attacked by coward terrorists."

We say to the Defense Secretary that his talk can induce a grieving mother to laughter! . . .

Where was this false courage of yours when the explosion in Beirut took place in 1983? You were turned into scattered bits and pieces at that time; 241 marine soldiers were killed.[6] And where was this courage of yours when two explosions made you leave Aden in less than twenty-four hours![7] But your most disgraceful case was in Somalia;[8] where you moved an international force, including twenty-eight thousand American soldiers. . . . However, when tens of your soldiers were killed in minor battles and one American pilot was dragged in the streets of Mogadishu you left the area carrying disappointment, humiliation, defeat and your dead with you. Clinton appeared in front of the whole world threatening and promising revenge, but these threats were merely a preparation for withdrawal. You have been disgraced by Allah and you withdrew; the extent of your impotence and weaknesses became very clear. . . .

Since the sons of the land of the two Holy Places feel and strongly believe that fighting against the nonbelievers in every part of the world is absolutely essential; then they would be even more enthusiastic, more powerful and larger in number upon fighting on their own land, the place of their births . . . They know that the Muslims of the world will assist and help them to victory. I say to you William [Perry] that these youths love death as you love life. They inherit dignity, pride, courage, generosity, truthfulness and sacrifice from father to father. They are most . . . steadfast at war. They inherit these values from their ancestors. . . .

---

[4]William Perry, secretary of defense between 1994 and 1997.

[5]In November 1995, a car bomb at a Saudi National Guard training center in Riyadh killed 5 Americans; the bombing of Khobar Towers, a U.S. Air Force housing complex in Dhahran, Saudi Arabia, killed 19 Americans.

[6]President Reagan ordered the withdrawal of Marine peacekeepers after a bomb killed 241 Marines and Navy seamen in October 1983 in Beirut.

[7]The Pentagon withdrew 100 army personnel after the U.S. embassy in Aden was bombed in 1993.

[8]President Clinton ordered the withdrawal of U.S. peacekeepers from Somalia by March 1994 after a clash with Somali warlords in Mogadishu in October 1993 resulted in the deaths of 18 Army Rangers.

These youths believe in what has been told by Allah and His messenger about the greatness of the reward for the Mujahedeen martyrs. . . .

Those youths know that their reward in fighting you, the USA, is double their reward in fighting someone else. They have no intention except to enter paradise by killing you. . . .

In the heat of battle they do not care, and cure the insanity of the enemy by their "insane" courage. Terrorizing you, while you are carrying arms on our land, is a legitimate and morally required duty. It is a legitimate right well known to all humans and other creatures. Your example and our example is like a snake which entered into a house of a man and got killed by him. The coward is the man who lets you walk, while carrying arms, freely on his land and provides you with peace and security.

Those youths are different from your soldiers. Your problem will be how to convince your troops to fight, while our problem will be how to restrain our youths to wait for their turn in fighting. . . .

The youths hold you responsible for all of the killings and evictions of the Muslims and the violation of the sanctities, carried out by your Zionist brothers in Lebanon; you openly supplied them with arms and finance. More than 600,000 Iraqi children have died due to lack of food and medicine and as a result of the unjustifiable aggression imposed on Iraq and its nation.[9]

The children of Iraq are our children. You, the USA, together with the Saudi regime are responsible for the shedding of the blood of these innocent children. . . .

It is a duty now on every tribe on the Arab Peninsula to fight in the cause of Allah and to cleanse the land from those occupiers. Allah knows that their blood is permitted to be spilled and their wealth is a booty to those who kill them. . . . Our youths know that the humiliation suffered by the Muslims as a result of the occupation of their Holy Places cannot be removed except by explosions and Jihad.

---

[9]The alleged victims of economic sanctions imposed on Iraq after the first Persian Gulf War (1991).

The Final Step Toward Martyrdom

117 • MOHAMMED ATTA, THE LAST NIGHT

Mohammed Atta was born in a Cairo suburb on September 1, 1968, and died on September 11, 2001, when he flew a hijacked American Airlines passenger jet into one of the towers of the World Trade Center in lower Manhattan. The son of a lawyer, Atta graduated with a degree in architecture from Cairo University. He then moved to Hamburg, Germany, where he was a student at the Technical University. Devoted to Islam, he made a pilgrimage to Mecca in 1995, and on his return to Hamburg began an Islamic prayer group. At some point, he was recruited by al-Qaeda, and by the late 1990s, his Hamburg apartment was a meeting place for the Hamburg cell. Late in 1999, it is likely that he met Osama bin Laden at al-Qaeda's base in Afghanistan. In June 2000, Atta entered the United States and attended a flight school in Venice, Florida. In 2001, he briefly visited Germany and Spain and then returned to Florida, where he took additional flying lessons. On the morning of September 11, he and another conspirator drove from their motel in South Portland, Maine, to Portland International Airport, flew to Boston, and boarded American Airlines Flight 11.

It was later discovered that Atta had left behind a bag containing airline uniforms, flight manuals, and a four-page document in Arabic, copies of which were also found in the effects of two of the other terrorists. The document is a list of instructions for the terrorists to review on the night of September 10. Excerpts from these instructions follow.

QUESTIONS FOR ANALYSIS

1. According to Atta, how should the participants prepare themselves for what lies ahead of them?
2. Is Atta totally confident about the success of the mission? What might go wrong, and what can be done to prevent failure?
3. What rewards can the participants expect from their anticipated martyrdom?
4. What feelings does Atta express about the victims of their actions?
5. On the basis of this document, what conclusions can be drawn about Atta's and, by extension, the other participants' motives?

---

1. Make an oath to die and renew your intentions. Shave excess hair from the body and wear cologne. Shower.[1]

2. Make sure you know all aspects of the plan well, and expect the response, or a reaction, from the enemy.

3. Read al-Tawba and Anfal[2] and reflect on their meanings and remember all of the things that God has promised for the martyrs.

4. Remind your soul to listen and obey and remember that you will face decisive situations that might prevent you from 100 percent obedience, so tame your soul, purify it, convince it, make it understand, and incite it.

5. Pray during the night and be persistent in asking God to give you victory, control and conquest, and that he may make your task easier and not expose us.

6. Remember God frequently, and the best way to do it is to read the Holy Quran. . . .

7. Purify your soul from all unclean things. Completely forget something called "this world."

The time for play is over and the serious time is upon us. How much time have we wasted in our lives? Shouldn't we take advantage of these last hours to offer good deeds and obedience?

8. You should feel complete tranquility, because the time between you and your marriage [in heaven] is very short [soon to come]. Afterward begins the happy life, where God is satisfied with you, and eternal bliss "in the company of the prophets, the companions, the martyrs and the good people, who are all good company.". . .

9. Keep in mind that, if you fall into hardship, how will you act and how will you remain steadfast and remember that you will return to God and remember that anything that happens to you could never be avoided, and what did not happen to you could never have happened to you. . . .

10. Remember the words of Almighty God [lines from the Quran]: . . . "How many small groups beat big groups by the will of God." And his words: "If God gives you victory, no one can beat you. And if he betrays you, who can give you

---

Source: The original letter was translated by Capital Communications Group, Inc., Washington, D.C. Reprinted with permission.

[1] These are ritual acts of self-purification to prepare oneself for martyrdom and salvation.

[2] The ninth and eighth chapters (surahs) of the Quran, sometimes referred to as the "war chapters," they describe the need for holy war against Islam's persecutors.

victory without Him? So the faithful put their trust in God."...

12. Bless your body with some verses of the Quran [done by reading verses into one's hands and then rubbing the hands over whatever is to be blessed], the luggage, clothes, the knife, your personal effects, your ID, your passport, and all of your papers.

13. Check your weapon before you leave and long before you leave. (You must make your knife sharp and you must not discomfort your animal during the slaughter.)...

The Second Step

When the taxi takes you to (M) [this initial probably stands for *matar,* airport in Arabic] remember God constantly while in the car....

When you have reached (M) and have left the taxi, say a supplication of place ["O Lord, I ask you for the best of this place, and ask you to protect me from its evils"], and everywhere you go ... smile and be calm, for God is with the believers. And the angels protect you without you feeling anything. Say this supplication: "God is more dear than all of his creation." And say: "O Lord, protect me from them as you wish." And say: "O Lord, take your anger out on them [the enemy] and we ask you to protect us from their evils." And say: "O Lord, block their vision from in front of them, so that they may not see." And say: "God is all we need, he is the best to rely upon."...

All of their equipment and gates and technology will not prevent, nor harm, except by God's will. The believers do not fear such things. The only ones that fear it are the allies of Satan, who are the brothers of the devil ... [and who] who are fascinated with Western civilization, and have drunk the love [of the West] like they drink water....

Whoever says, "There is no God but God," with all his heart, goes to heaven. The prophet, peace be upon him, said: "If you put all the worlds and universes on one side of the balance, and 'No God but God' on the other, 'No God but God' will weigh more heavily." You can repeat these words confidently, and this is just one of the strengths of these words....

Also, do not seem confused or show signs of nervous tension. Be happy, optimistic, calm because you are heading for a deed that God loves and will accept [as a good deed]. It will be the day, God willing, you spend with the women of paradise....

The Third Phase

When you ride the (T) [this initial probably stands for *tayyara,* airplane in Arabic], before your foot steps in it, and before you enter it, you make a prayer and supplications. Remember that this is a battle for the sake of God.... When the (T) moves, even slightly, toward (Q) [unknown reference], say the supplication of travel....

And then it takes off.... Pray for yourself and all of your brothers that they may be victorious and hit their targets and [unclear] and ask God to grant you martyrdom facing the enemy, not running away from it, and for him to grant you patience and the feeling that anything that happens to you is for him....

When the confrontation begins, strike like champions who do not want to go back to this world. Shout, "Allahu Akbar" ["God is great"], because this strikes fear in the hearts of the non-believers.... Know that the gardens of paradise are waiting for you in all their beauty, and the women of paradise are waiting, calling out, "Come hither, friend of God." They have dressed in their most beautiful clothing.

If God decrees that any of you are to slaughter, you should dedicate the slaughter to your fathers ... because you have obligations toward them.... If you slaughter, do not cause the discomfort of those you are killing, because this is one of the practices of the prophet, peace be upon him....

Then implement the way of the prophet in taking prisoners. Take prisoners and kill them. As Almighty God said: "No prophet should have prisoners until he has soaked the land with blood. You want the bounties of this world [in exchange for prisoners] and God wants the other world [for you], and God is all-powerful, all-wise." . . .

. . . When the hour of reality approaches, the zero hour . . . wholeheartedly welcome death for the sake of God. Always be remembering God. Either end your life while praying, seconds before the target, or make your last words: "There is no God but God, Muhammad is his messenger."

Afterward, we will all meet in the highest heaven, God willing. . . .

And may the peace of the God be upon the prophet.

The Wealth and Poverty of Nations

One of the greatest challenges for historians of the recent past is making sense of the combination of recent economic, political, technological, and cultural changes described by *globalization*, a word with several layers of meaning. It refers, first of all, to a world of free trade, open markets, and capitalist competition in which goods, services, and capital flow across seamless international borders. It also refers to a world in which a remarkable series of technological breakthroughs—computers, communications satellites, fiberoptic cable, and especially the Internet—have destroyed the barriers of time and space. It refers, finally, to a world of increasing cultural homogeneity in which tastes in music, art, architecture, personal dress, and countless other areas of life have become increasingly standardized and, for better or worse, westernized.

Historians agree that globalization represents an acceleration and intensification of trends that have been a part of world history for thousands of years. Where it will take us is impossible to predict. Its supporters see universal benefits from worldwide economic growth, strengthened democracies through better-informed citizenry, increased capacity to deal with global environmental problems, and even a heightened sense of human community. Its detractors, of which there are many, see a widening divide between haves and have-nots, dangerous political transitions, the triumph of an ethos of corporate greed, and a bland uniformity in world culture. Whichever side is correct, understanding the roots and meaning of globalization will be a primary challenge for future historians.

Economic and Social Development in a New Era of Globalization

118 • WORLD BANK, WORLD DEVELOPMENT INDICATORS

The statistics in the following tables enable us to draw some conclusions about short-term economic and social developments during the recent era of intensified globalization. The data were compiled by the World Bank, one of many international organizations concerned with alleviating world poverty by encouraging economic development. Founded at the Bretton Woods Conference in New Hampshire in 1944, the World Bank uses funds subscribed by member nations (today numbering 186) to make loans to governments and private businesses for projects that further economic development. Although most loans at first were allocated for post–World War II reconstruction projects, since the 1950s the bank has supported projects mainly in developing nations.

Since 2000, the World Bank has sought to contribute to achieving the so-called Millennium Development Goals adopted by 189 member states of the United Nations in September 2000. Designed to "free all men, women, and children from the abject and dehumanizing conditions of extreme poverty," the eight goals to be achieved by 2015 are eradicating extreme poverty and hunger; achieving universal primary education; promoting gender equality and empowering women; reducing child mortality; improving maternal health; combating HIV/AIDS, malaria, and other diseases; ensuring environmental sustainability; and developing a global partnership for economic development.

Since 1978, the World Bank has published annually its *World Development Report,* which contains commentary on development strategies and statistics on economic, demographic, fiscal, and educational trends. Since 2001, most of the statistical data have been published separately as *World Development Indicators.* The World Bank draws on a wide range of sources for the information in its annual reports, including reports from governments, U.N. agencies, and nongovernmental organizations. Inevitably, in any given year, some data may be missing due to a nation's refusal to cooperate or its inability to do so because of conflict or natural disaster. In the accompanying tables, the use of a dash (–) shows that no data are available. Furthermore, many factors affect the reliability of the data, including weak statistical methods used by some governments, differences in coverage, and disagreements over key definitions. Despite such difficulties, the data allow us to make broad comparisons over time.

Of the more than 100 nations covered in the World Bank reports, 29 have been included in the following tables. They represent all the world's regions and range from some of the world's poorest states to the some of the richest. The tables provide data on eight topics:

1. Population
2. Per capita Gross National Income (GNI), a number calculated by dividing the country's population into the Gross Domestic Income, which is calculated by adding a country's Gross Domestic Product (the value of all goods and services produced within a country in a given time) and net receipts of primary income (compensation of employees and property income) from non-resident sources. In other words, income produced by a U.S.-owned company in Mexico counts toward the U.S. GNI, but not income produced by a Japanese-owned company in the U.S. Such information gives a broad idea of a country's standard of living but is not necessarily an accurate gauge of the prevalence of poverty. For this, further information about wealth distribution would be needed.
3. Life expectancy

4. Infant mortality. This measures the number of infants per one thousand who die before their first birthday.
5. Literacy of adults aged 15 years or older. Literacy is defined as the ability to read and write simple sentences about one's daily life experiences.
6. Per capita energy consumption, a number calculated by converting a country's total energy consumption into the equivalent of the energy produced by 1 kilogram of oil, and then dividing it by the country's population.
7. Percentage of population with access to improved sanitation facilities, defined as those capable of preventing human, animal, and insect contact with human waste. They may range from simple, protected pit latrines to flush toilets with connection to a sewer system.

QUESTIONS FOR ANALYSIS

1. What population trends are revealed in the tables?
2. To what extent do the tables reveal uneven development among the world's major regions?
3. Does the information in the tables suggest that the gap between rich and poor nations is getting larger or smaller?
4. For those nations that have not achieved significant economic progress, what insights do the tables provide into reasons for their lack of success?
5. What information do the tables provide on the relationship between economic growth and environmental quality?
6. On the basis of the information in the tables, would it appear that things are getting better or worse for humankind?

World Bank Statistics

	Population (millions)			GNI per Capita (U.S. dollars)			Life Expectancy at Birth			
									Male	Female
	1976	1990	2008	1976	1990	2008	1960	1977	2008	2008
Zimbabwe	6.5	9.8	12	550	640	115	45	52	44	45
Congo, Democratic Republic	25.4	37.3	64	140	220	150	40	46	46	49
Ethiopia	28.7	51.2	81	100	120	208	36	39	54	57
Sierra Leone	3.1	4.1	6	200	240	320	37	46	46	49
Uganda	11.9	16.3	32	240	220	420	44	53	52	54
Haiti	4.7	6.5	10	150	370	450(2005)	42	51	59	63
Mali	5.8	8.5	13	100	270	580	37	42	48	49
Ghana	10.1	14.9	23	580	390	630	40	48	56	58
India	620.4	849.5	1140	150	350	1,040	43	51	62	65
Nigeria	77.1	115.5	151	380	290	1,170	39	48	47	48
Egypt	38.1	52.1	82	280	600	1,800	46	54	68	72
Indonesia	135.2	178.2	227	240	570	1,880	41	48	69	73
Syria	7.7	12.4	21	780	980	2,160	48	57	72	76
China	835.8	1,337.7	1325	410	370	2,542	53	64	71	75
Guatemala	6.5	9.2	14	630	900	2,680	47	57	67	74
Thailand	43	55.8	67	380	1,420	3,670	51	61	66	72
South Africa	26	35.9	49	1,340	2,560	5,820	53	60	50	53
Brazil	110	150.4	192	1,140	2,680	7,300	57	62	69	76
Chile	10.5	13.2	17	1,050	1,770	9,270	57	67	76	82
Mexico	62	86.2	106	1,090	2,010	9,990	58	65	73	78
Poland	34.3	38.2	38	2,860	1,790	11,730	66	71	71	80
Korea, Rep.	36	42.8	49	670	5,400	21,530	54	63	77	83
Israel	3.6	3.9	7	3,920	9,700	24,720	69	72	79	83
Italy	56.2	57.7	60	3,050	18,520	35,460	69	73	79	85
Japan	112.8	123.5	128	4,910	26,930	38,130	68	76	79	86
Canada	23.2	26.5	33	7,510	20,440	43,460	71	74	79	83
United Kingdom	56.1	57.4	61	4,020	16,190	46,040	70	73	78	82
United States	215.1	250	304	7,890	22,240	47,930	70	73	76	81
Switzerland	6.4	6.7	8	8,850	33,160	55,510	71	74	80	85

(Continued)

World Bank Statistics (continued)

	Adult Literacy Rate (% over 15 years old)				Infant Mortality Rate per 1,000 Live Births		
		Male		Females			
	1974	1990	2008	2008	1970	1990	2008
Zimbabwe	–	63	94	89	96	51	62
Congo, Democratic Republic.	15	61	–	–	141	126	126
Ethiopia	–	–	–	–	158	124	69
Sierra Leone	15	21	52	29	197	163	123
Uganda	25	48	86	82	109	114	85
Haiti	20	53	–	–	141	105	54
Mali	10	32	35	18	204	139	103
Ghana	25	60	66	50	111	58	51
India	36	48	75	51	137	83	52
Nigeria	–	51	–	–	139	120	96
Egypt	40	48	75	58	158	66	20
Indonesia	62	77	95	89	118	56	31
Syria	53	64	90	77	96	30	14
China	–	73	97	91	69	37	18
Guatemala	47	55	80	69	100	58	29
Thailand	82	93	96	92	27	26	13
South Africa	–	–	90	88	79	45	48
Brazil	64	81	90	90	95	56	22
Chile	90	93	99	99	78	18	7
Mexico	76	87	95	91	72	36	15
Poland	98	–	100	99	33	15	6
Korea, Rep.	92	96	*	*	51	8	5
Israel	84	–	*	*	20	10	4
Italy	98	95+	99	99	30	9	3
Japan	99	95+	*	*	13	5	3
Canada	98	95+	*	*	19	7	6
United Kingdom	98	*	*	*	19	8	5
United States	99	*	98	99	20	9	7
Switzerland	99	95+	*	*	15	7	4

* = Literacy rates above 95%

(Continued)

530